ECONOMICS TODAY

THE MICRO VIEW

ECONOMICS TODAY

Third Canadian Edition

THE MICRO VIEW

Roger LeRoy Miller
Institute for University Studies
Arlington, Texas

Brenda Abbott
Northern Alberta Institute of Technology

Sam Fefferman
Northern Alberta Institute of Technology

Ronald K. Kessler
British Columbia Institute of Technology

Terrence Sulyma
Northern Alberta Institute of Technology

Toronto

Library and Archives Canada Cataloguing in Publication

Economics today : the micro view / Roger LeRoy Miller ... [et al.]. — 3rd Canadian ed.

First ed. written by Roger LeRoy Miller, Nancy W. Clegg.
Includes index.
ISBN 0-321-25352-3

1. Microeconomics. I. Miller, Roger LeRoy. II. Miller, Roger LeRoy. Economics today.

HB172.E43 2005 338.5 C2004-904474-5

0-321-25352-3

Vice President, Editorial Director: Michael J. Young
Senior Acquisitions Editor: Gary Bennett
Marketing Manager: Jeff Clarke
Developmental Editor: Angela Kurmey
Production Editor: Jen Handel
Copy Editor: Rohini Herbert
Proofreader: Laurel Sparrow
Production Coordinator: Patricia Ciardullo
Permissions and Photo Research: Sandy Cooke
Page Layout: Nelson Gonzalez
Art Director: Mary Opper
Interior and Cover Design: Lisa LaPointe
Cover Image: Windsor & Wiehahn/Gettyimages

5 09 08 07

Printed and bound in the United States of America.

Statistics Canada information is used with the permission of the Minister of Industry, as Minister responsible for Statistics Canada. Information on the availability of the wide range of data from Statistics Canada can be obtained from Statistics Canada's Regional Offices, its World Wide Web site at http://www.statcan.ca, and its toll-free access number 1-800-263-1136. The Statistics Canada CANSIM II database can be accessed at http://cansim2.statcan.ca/cgi-win/CNSMCGI.EXE.

Photo Credits
Pages 1and 16, CP Photo/Chris Wattie; pages 28 and 48, CP Photo/*Peterborough Examiner*/Clifford Skarstedt; pages 60 and 85, Ian Barrett; pages 91 and 107, © Steve Mason/Getty Images; pages 110 and 129, Ryan Remiorz/Canadian Press; pages 135 and 145, The Slide Farm/Al Harvey; pages 158 and 175, © Stephen Ferry/Gamma Liaison; pages 178 and 196, Lucas Oleniuk/Toronto Star; pages 199 and 223, Dick Hemingway; pages 229 and 252, Superstock; pages 262 and 286, photo courtesy of Moosehead; pages 292 and 308, CP Photo/Tom Hanson; pages 312 and 328, *The Toronto Star*; pages 332 and 347, CP Photo/Frank Gunn; pages 350 and 365, Jon Murray/The Province; pages 368 and 380, CP Photo/*Toronto Star*/Dick Loek; pages 383 and 403, © H&R Tax Services.

This one's for you, Mom and Dad. Thanks for always being there when I needed you.

—B.A.

I would like to thank my loving family—Brenda, Amy, Tara, Michael, and Shane—for all their patience and support.

—S.F.

For my wife, Lynne, who has helped me to create liminal spaces.

—R.K.K.

To John and Mary Sulyma for instilling in me a thirst for knowledge and a love of learning. To Andrea, Drew, and Vanya for their love and support.

—T.S.

BRIEF CONTENTS

Part 1 *Introduction* 1

Chapter 1 The Nature of Economics 1

APPENDIX A **Reading and Working with Graphs** 20

Chapter 2 Production Possibilities and Economic Systems 28

APPENDIX B **The Production Possibilities Curve and Comparative Advantage** 54

Chapter 3 Demand and Supply 60

Part 2 *Dimensions of Microeconomics* 91

Chapter 4 Elasticity 91

Chapter 5 Extensions of Demand, Supply, and Elasticity 110

Chapter 6 Consumer Choice 135

APPENDIX C **More Advanced Consumer Choice Theory** 148

Chapter 7 Rents, Profits, and the Financial Environment of Business 158

Chapter 8 The Firm: Cost and Output Determination 178

Part 3 *Market Structure, Resource Allocation, and Regulation* 199

Chapter 9 Perfect Competition 199

Chapter 10 Monopoly 229

APPENDIX D **The Deadweight Loss Due to Monopoly** 257

Chapter 11 Monopolistic Competition and Oligopoly 262

Chapter 12 Regulation and Competition Policy 292

Part 4 *Productive Factors, Poverty, the Environment, and the Public Sector* 312

Chapter 13 Labour Demand and Supply 312

Chapter 14 Unions and Labour Market Monopoly Power 332

Chapter 15 Income and Poverty 350

Chapter 16 Environmental Economics 368

Chapter 17 The Public Sector 383

ANSWERS TO ODD-NUMBERED PROBLEMS 407

ANSWERS TO "FOR CRITICAL ANALYSIS" QUESTIONS 420

GLOSSARY 433

INDEX 441

CONTENTS

Preface xv
Acknowledgments xix

Part 1 *Introduction* 1

Chapter 1 The Nature of Economics 1

1.1 Scarcity 2
1.2 Defining Economics 3
EXAMPLE 1-1 **The Economics of Web Page Design** 4
1.3 Rational Decision Making 5
EXAMPLE 1-2 **The Opportunity Cost of Finding a Mate—Lower on the Internet?** 7
EXAMPLE 1-3 **What Does a Year at College Really Cost?** 8
POLICY EXAMPLE 1-1 **Chinese Smuggling** 9
EXAMPLE 1-4 **Giving Charity to Oneself?** 10
1.4 The Scientific Method 10
EXAMPLE 1-5 **Incentives Work for Pigeons and Rats, Too** 12
1.5 Positive versus Normative Economics 14
1.6 Economic Policy and Socioeconomic Goals 14
ISSUES AND APPLICATIONS: **Decriminalizing Marijuana, An Economics Perspective** 16
APPENDIX A **Reading and Working with Graphs** 20
Direct and Inverse Relationships 20
Constructing a Graph 20
The Slope of a Line (A Linear Curve) 24

Chapter 2 Production Possibilities and Economic Systems 28

2.1 The Production Possibilities Curve 29
2.2 Applications of the Production Possibilities Curve 30
EXAMPLE 2-1 **Skipping Class without Skipping Lectures** 31
POLICY EXAMPLE 2-1 **The Multibillion Dollar Park** 33
EXAMPLE 2-2 **Making Death Illegal—At Least, Inside City Limits** 34
2.3 Consumption Goods versus Capital Goods 36
EXAMPLE 2-3 **Canadian Postsecondary Education Pays Off Big Time!** 38
2.4 Specialization and Greater Productivity 39
EXAMPLE 2-4 **Why Men Marry: Is It for Love or the Marriage Premium?** 41
2.5 Economic Systems 43
2.6 Capitalism in More Depth 44
POLICY EXAMPLE 2-2 **The Edmonton Revolution in Public Education** 46
ISSUES AND APPLICATIONS: **Private or Public Auto Insurance: What Is Best for Canada?** 48
APPENDIX B **The Production Possibilities Curve and Comparative Advantage** 54
Before Specialization and Trade 54

After Specialization and Before Trade 55
After Specialization and After Trade 56

Chapter 3 Demand and Supply 60

3.1 The Law of Demand 61
POLICY EXAMPLE 3-1 Price per Constant-Quality Unit and Teen Marijuana Use 62
3.2 Shifts in Demand 65
EXAMPLE 3-1 Is Dental Care Becoming an Inferior Good? 66
EXAMPLE 3-2 Getting Your Degree via the Internet 67
EXAMPLE 3-3 Garth Brooks, Used CDs, and the Law of Demand 69
3.3 The Law of Supply 70
3.4 Shifts in Supply 73
EXAMPLE 3-4 Falling Costs of Fighting the War on Terror 75
3.5 Putting Demand and Supply Together 76
3.6 Changes in Equilibrium 79
POLICY EXAMPLE 3-2 Assisted Human Reproduction Not for Sale in Canada? 81
EXAMPLE 3-5 Air Canada Losses Are Flying High 83
ISSUES AND APPLICATIONS: Is Canada the Prescription for Lower Drug Prices in the United States? 85

Part 2 Dimensions of Microeconomics 91

Chapter 4 Elasticity 91

4.1 Price Elasticity 92
EXAMPLE 4-1 "If They Doubled the Price, We'd Still Drink Coffee" 93
EXAMPLE 4-2 The Price Elasticity of Demand for World's Fair Tickets 94
4.2 Price Elasticity Ranges 95
POLICY EXAMPLE 4-1 To Cut Drug Abuse, Make the Price of a "High" Higher 95
EXAMPLE 4-3 A Pricing Decision at Disneyland Paris 99
4.3 Determinants of the Price Elasticity of Demand 99
EXAMPLE 4-4 What Do Real-World Price Elasticities of Demand Look Like? 101
4.4 Cross-Elasticity of Demand 102
POLICY EXAMPLE 4-2 Should Public Libraries Be Shut Down? 103
EXAMPLE 4-5 Frequent Flyer Miles as Income 104
4.5 Elasticity of Supply 105
ISSUES AND APPLICATIONS: To Combat Cigarette Consumption, Should the Government Raise Taxes on Beer? 107

Chapter 5 Extensions of Demand, Supply, and Elasticity 110

5.1 The Price System 111
EXAMPLE 5-1 Technology and the Death of Intermediaries 112
EXAMPLE 5-2 Should Shortages in the Ticket Market Be Solved by Scalpers? 114
5.2 Price Ceilings and Price Floors 115
POLICY EXAMPLE 5-1 Rent Controls in Manitoba 117

5.3	Price Supports: Offer to Purchase and Marketing Boards	120
	POLICY EXAMPLE 5-2 Wheat Farmers and the Canadian Wheat Board	122
5.4	Quantity Restrictions	123
	POLICY EXAMPLE 5-3 Should the Legal Quantity of Cigarettes Supplied Be Set at Zero?	123
5.5	Elasticity and Excise Taxes	124
	POLICY EXAMPLE 5-4 An Excise Tax on Music Piracy?	128
	ISSUES AND APPLICATIONS: For-Profit Health Care in Canada?	129
Chapter 6	**Consumer Choice**	135
6.1	Utility Theory	136
6.2	Diminishing Marginal Utility	139
	EXAMPLE 6-1 Newspaper Vending Machines versus Candy Vending Machines	140
	EXAMPLE 6-2 The World of Water in Saudi Arabia	144
	ISSUES AND APPLICATIONS: Contingent Valuation: Pricing the "Priceless"	145
	APPENDIX C More Advanced Consumer Choice Theory	148
	On Being Indifferent	148
	Properties of Indifference Curves	149
	The Marginal Rate of Substitution	150
	The Indifference Map	151
	The Budget Constraint	152
	Consumer Optimum Revisited	153
	Effects of Changes in Income	154
	The Price-Consumption Curve	154
	Deriving the Demand Curve	155
Chapter 7	**Rents, Profits, and the Financial Environment of Business**	158
7.1	Economic Rent	159
	EXAMPLE 7-1 Do Entertainment Superstars Make Super Economic Rents?	161
7.2	The Legal Organization of Firms	162
7.3	The Profits of a Firm	165
	POLICY EXAMPLE 7-1 Nonprofit Firms Join in the Quest for Profits	166
7.4	Interest	168
7.5	Corporate Financing Methods	171
	EXAMPLE 7-2 How to Read the Financial Press: Share Prices	173
	ISSUES AND APPLICATIONS: Can Investors Profit from Publicly Available Stock Tips?	175
Chapter 8	**The Firm: Cost and Output Determination**	178
8.1	Short Run versus Long Run	179
	EXAMPLE 8-1 Europeans Use More Capital	180
8.2	Short-Run Costs to the Firm	184
	EXAMPLE 8-2 The Cost of Driving a Car	188
8.3	Why the Long-Run Average Cost Curve Is U-Shaped	193

EXAMPLE 8-3 Economies of Scale at Dell Computer Corporation 194
ISSUES AND APPLICATIONS: Technology and Costs 196

Part 3 Market Structure, Resource Allocation, and Regulation 199

Chapter 9 Perfect Competition 199

9.1 The Characteristics of Perfect Competition 200
EXAMPLE 9-1 The Global Coal Market 201
9.2 Determining Output and Profit in the Short Run 203
POLICY EXAMPLE 9-1 Quelling Fears of "Mad Cow Disease" in Asia 206
EXAMPLE 9-2 High Sunk Costs Can Mean Deep Discounts 209
9.3 Short-Run Supply and Equilibrium 211
9.4 Long-Run Equilibrium 216
EXAMPLE 9-3 How the Dot-Com Boom Went Bust 217
9.5 Long-Run Industry Supply Curves 218
9.6 Social Evaluation of Perfect Competition 220
ISSUES AND APPLICATIONS: Does Your Local Video Store Have a Future? 223

Chapter 10 Monopoly 229

10.1 The Characteristics of Monopoly 230
EXAMPLE 10-1 Microsoft's Abuse of Monopoly 232
POLICY EXAMPLE 10-1 Should Canada Post Remain a Monopoly— Or Does it Matter? 236
10.2 Determining Output, Price, and Profit in Monopoly 236
POLICY EXAMPLE 10-2 In Germany, Watch Out— Your Price May Be Too Low 239
10.3 On Making Higher Profits: Price Discrimination 241
EXAMPLE 10-2 Fuji Film Price Discrimination 244
10.4 Social Evaluation of Monopoly 245
POLICY EXAMPLE 10-3 Swapping Songs on the Internet: Is It Really Free? 248
10.5 The Regulation of a Natural Monopoly 249
ISSUES AND APPLICATIONS: Should a Company Be Allowed to Monopolize Genetic Information? 252
APPENDIX D The Deadweight Loss Due to Monopoly 257
Consumer Surplus 257
Producer Surplus 258
Allocative Efficiency and Perfect Competition 259
Allocative Inefficiency and Monopoly 259

Chapter 11 Monopolistic Competition and Oligopoly 262

11.1 The Characteristics of Monopolistic Competition 263
EXAMPLE 11-1 The Makeover of Bluenotes 265
11.2 Short-Run Price, Output, and Profit in Monopolistic Competition 266
11.3 Long-Run Equilibrium in Monopolistic Competition 267
11.4 The Characteristics of Oligopoly 269
11.5 Price Behaviour in Oligopoly 272

EXAMPLE 11-2 The Prisoners' Dilemma 272
POLICY EXAMPLE 11-1 Taxpayers Get Snowed in Quebec 275
EXAMPLE 11-3 OPEC Continues to Rule the World Oil Market 276
EXAMPLE 11-4 DeBeers Diamond Cartel: A Thing from the Past? 278
POLICY EXAMPLE 11-2 Turbulence in the Canadian Airline Industry 279
EXAMPLE 11-5 High Switching Costs in the Credit World 280
EXAMPLE 11-6 Do Pet Products Have Nine Lives? 282
11.6 Nonprice Forms of Competition in Oligopoly 283
11.7 Social Evaluation of Oligopoly 285
EXAMPLE 11-7 Can Advertising Lead to Efficiency? 285
ISSUES AND APPLICATIONS: Game Theory: Opening Up the Brewing Industry 286

Chapter 12 Regulation and Competition Policy 292

12.1 Types of Government Regulation 293
POLICY EXAMPLE 12-1 Can the CRTC Effectively Regulate Cable TV? 296
EXAMPLE 12-1 The Effectiveness of Auto Safety Regulation 297
12.2 Explaining Regulators' Behaviour 298
12.3 Short-Run versus Long-Run Effects of Deregulation 299
POLICY EXAMPLE 12-2 Ontario's Feeble Attempt at Energy Deregulation 300
EXAMPLE 12-2 Cutting Through the "Red Tape" 301
12.4 How Competition Policy Benefits the Consumer 302
EXAMPLE 12-3 HMV Boycotts Rolling Stones Products 305
EXAMPLE 12-4 Suzy Shier Pays $1 Million to Settle Misleading Advertising Dispute 307
ISSUES AND APPLICATIONS: Media Concentration in Canada: A Public Concern? 308

Part 4 Productive Factors, Poverty, the Environment, and the Public Sector 312

Chapter 13 Labour Demand and Supply 312

13.1 Demand for Labour 313
13.2 Shifts in the Demand for and Supply of Labour 319
POLICY EXAMPLE 13-1 Should the Minimum Wage Be Raised to Help Young People? 321
EXAMPLE 13-1 Does It Pay to Study? 322
13.3 The Impact of Other Factors of Production 323
EXAMPLE 13-2 Cost Minimization and the Substitution of Software for Labour 327
ISSUES AND APPLICATIONS: Are Immigrants Pushing Down Canadian Wages? 328

Chapter 14 Unions and Labour Market Monopoly Power 332

14.1 The Canadian Labour Movement 333

	EXAMPLE 14-1 Europe's Management-Labour Councils	334
14.2	Union Goals and Labour Unions	335
	EXAMPLE 14-2 Strike Activity in Canada	336
14.3	Pricing and Employment in Various Market Conditions	341
	EXAMPLE 14-3 Monopsony in College Sports	341
	ISSUES AND APPLICATIONS: Pro Sports Means Big Bucks	347
Chapter 15	**Income and Poverty**	350
15.1	The Distribution of Wealth and Income	351
	EXAMPLE 15-1 Increasing Income Inequality and Working Spouses	353
	EXAMPLE 15-2 Relative Income Inequality throughout the Richest Countries	354
	EXAMPLE 15-3 Are We Running to Stay in Place?	355
15.2	Determinants of Income Differences	356
	EXAMPLE 15-4 Economics, Aging, and Productivity	358
15.3	Poverty and Federal Income Support Programs	361
	EXAMPLE 15-5 Poverty Rates in the European Union	361
	ISSUES AND APPLICATIONS: Eradicating Child Poverty	365
Chapter 16	**Environmental Economics**	368
16.1	Private versus Social Costs	369
	EXAMPLE 16-1 The Black Sea Becomes the Dead Sea: The Results of Externalities	371
16.2	Pollution	372
16.3	Common Property	374
	EXAMPLE 16-2 Wind as a Renewable Resource	374
	EXAMPLE 16-3 Privatizing the Right to Pollute	376
	EXAMPLE 16-4 Preventing Overfishing by Trading Quotas	377
16.4	Recycling	378
	EXAMPLE 16-5 Reducing Waste by Recycling	378
	EXAMPLE 16-6 We Are Running Out of Everything!	379
	ISSUES AND APPLICATIONS: Climate Change Impacts All Nations	380
Chapter 17	**The Public Sector**	383
17.1	Externalities and Other Economic Functions of Government	384
	POLICY EXAMPLE 17-1 Who Should Pay the High Cost of a Legal System?	387
	EXAMPLE 17-1 Are Lighthouses a Public Good?	389
17.2	The Political Functions of Government	390
	POLICY EXAMPLE 17-2 Do Government-Funded Sports Stadiums Have a Net Positive Effect on Local Economies?	390
	EXAMPLE 17-2 Education Transfer Payments	391
17.3	Tax Rates and the Canadian Tax System	395
	POLICY EXAMPLE 17-3 Average and Marginal Tax Rates Around the World	397
	EXAMPLE 17-3 Employment Insurance	399
	ISSUES AND APPLICATIONS: Should We Switch to a Flat Tax?	403

Answers to Odd-Numbered Problems 407

Answers to "For Critical Analysis" Questions 420

Glossary 433

Index 441

PREFACE

From the Authors

In creating *Economics Today: The Micro View*, Third Canadian Edition, substantial revisions to the previous edition were made, based on the helpful suggestions and comments provided by adopters and reviewers. We were careful to ensure that any changes we made to the second edition would maintain the straightforward and approachable style that has made this book so popular in post-secondary institutions across Canada.

As instructors with extensive teaching experience in both college and university settings, we want to continue to present a text that students can relate to based on their personal, social, and career interests. We also hope that this book will encourage students to broaden their interests to include local, national, and global economic issues. Many of our students will not take subsequent economics courses; in that case, we want them to be ready for the world, and not just for intermediate economics courses.

The approach used in *Economics Today: The Micro View*, Third Canadian Edition, is based on the belief that students learn more when they are involved and engaged in the material they are studying. The presentation of issues and applications in a Canadian setting is a major strength of this text. Each chapter begins with an issue that introduces certain economic principles; those principles are presented throughout the chapter, and at the end of the chapter an Issues and Applications section explains how those principles can be applied to that issue. This section ends with For Critical Analysis questions, which help reinforce the theory at hand and encourage the students to reflect on economics in the "real" world—their world.

In addition, each chapter contains numerous short Examples and Policy Examples that further illustrate the points being made in the text. Each of these examples is accompanied by For Critical Analysis questions, which encourage students to actively apply the economic principles presented in the chapter. Mindful of the importance of global events to Canada's economic well-being, we have used many examples and issues that connect Canada with the rest of the world. Suggested solutions to all of the For Critical Analysis questions are provided at the end of the text.

Over the years, we have found that more of our students are heading for degrees in business rather than economics. In recognition of this trend, the accompanying Study Guide includes a Business Section in most chapters, providing business applications that apply economic theory to accounting, marketing, finance, management, and small business. In the text, business students will find additional examples that apply economic theory to business situations.

In the end, we believe that *Economics Today: The Micro View* and the Study Guide will provide students with a relevant and interesting resource—one that will present students with a "window of the world" that will help them in their personal lives as citizens and professionals. We hope that you will enjoy this book and begin to appreciate the many ways in which economics can be a part of your day-to-day activities.

What's New in the Third Canadian Edition?

This edition includes changes in the sequencing of various chapters; reorganization and consolidation of material within and between chapters; changes in chapter content; numerous updated issues, applications, and examples boxes; and significant pedagogical revisions.

Compared to the last edition, the changes related to sequencing, reorganizing, and consolidating, can be summarized as follows:

1. The material relating to scarcity, resources, and opportunity cost has been moved from Chapter 2 in the second Canadian edition to Chapter 1, The Nature of Economics, in this edition.
2. Chapter 3, Economies in Transition, in the second Canadian edition has been deleted in this edition. The content related to the three basic economic questions, economic systems, pure capitalism, and mixed economies, has been incorporated into Chapter 2, Production Possibilities and Economic Systems, in the third Canadian edition.
3. The chapter on Extensions of Demand, Supply, and Elasticity (Chapter 8 in the second Canadian edition) has been moved to Chapter 4 in this edition, so as to directly follow the chapters that cover Demand and Supply (Chapter 3) and Elasticity (Chapter 4).
4. Chapter 9, The Financial Environment of Business, and Chapter 17, Rent, Interest, and Profits, from the second Canadian edition have been merged in this edition to form a new Chapter 7, Rents, Profits, and the Financial Environment of Business. The material on profits from Chapter 10 of the second Canadian edition has also been moved into this chapter.
5. The economic theory related to the regulation of a natural monopoly has been moved from the Regulation and Competition Policy chapter in the previous edition to Chapter 10 Monopoly, in the third Canadian edition.

6. The chapter on Oligopoly (Chapter 11 in the third Canadian edition) has been reorganized to ensure that all the topics related to Game Theory are covered in the same section of the chapter.
7. The chapter covering the Public Sector (Chapter 6 in the second Canadian edition) now appears as the last chapter in this edition.

Changes in content include the following:

- In Chapter 1, The Nature of Economics, the coverage of topics related to the economic way of thinking and rational decision making at the margin has been expanded.
- In Chapter 2, Production Possibilities and Economic Systems, the principle of comparative advantage is more thoroughly presented. The production possibilities curve is used to illustrate the gains from specialization and trade.
- In Chapter 3, Demand and Supply, simultaneous shifts in demand and supply is more thoroughly explained, with the aid of graphs.
- Chapter 5, Extensions of Demand, Supply, and Elasticity, now contains a graphic illustration of how elasticity governs the effects that a per-unit tax has on tax incidence and resource allocation.
- In Chapter 9, Perfect Competition, topics related to short-run and long-run industry equilibrium, long-run adjustments to changes in demand and technology, and the efficiency of competitive markets are more thoroughly explained.
- A new appendix, Appendix D, The Deadweight Loss Due to Monopoly, directly follows Chapter 10, Monopoly. Using the concepts of consumer and producer surplus, Appendix D contrasts perfect competition and monopoly in terms of allocative efficiency.
- Chapter 12, Regulation and Competition Policy provides an expanded discussion of the specific business practices that are prohibited under Canada's current Competition Act. As well, the latest amendments to the Competition Act are reviewed.

In completing the third Canadian edition, many applications and example boxes have been changed or updated to reflect current events and issues. What follows is just a sample of some of the new issues discussed:

- Decriminalizing Marijuana, An Economics Perspective (Issues and Applications, Chapter 1)
- Skipping Class without Skipping Lectures (Example, Chapter 2)
- Assisted Human Reproduction Not for Sale in Canada? (Policy Example, Chapter 3)
- Swapping Songs on the Internet: Is It Really Free? (Policy Example, Chapter 10)
- The Makeover of Bluenotes (Example, Chapter 11)
- Climate Change Impacts All Nations (Issues and Applications, Chapter 16)

Many enhancements have been made to the pedagogical elements for this edition. They include the following:

- Each chapter's opening Issues and Applications and Did You Know That...? is more closely integrated with discussions that subsequently take place within the chapter.
- Each chapter is organized around a set of Learning Objectives, which replace the Preview Questions and Chapter Outline in the previous edition. The Learning Objectives will motivate student learning by providing more precise information in terms of the essential knowledge that should be gleaned from each chapter.
- The Concepts in Brief boxes found throughout each chapter and the Summary Discussion of Learning Objectives presented at the end of each chapter are organized around the chapter's Learning Objectives. These pedagogical elements will sharpen students' focus and reinforce their understanding of the key principles and ideas presented in the chapter.
- The end-of-chapter Problems are linked to the chapter's Learning Objectives. This feature ensures that the end-of-chapter problems test students' understanding of the chapter material in a comprehensive manner. As well, this pedagogical element encourages students to take a more active role in learning and applying the theory covered as they progress through each chapter. Students now have the opportunity to work on problems as soon as they have covered the relevant learning objectives. If students encounter some difficulty in answering a problem, they can easily refer back to the relevant material in the chapter.
- Suggested solutions to the For Critical Analysis questions for *all* of the chapter Examples, Policy Examples, and Issues and Applications, are provided at the end of the text. This feature should enhance students' understanding and appreciation of how the example or issue relates to the concepts and principles presented in the chapter.
- Additional questions relating to the chapter examples and issues appear in the end-of-chapter problems section and the testbank that accompanies this text. This approach reinforces the view that students can expect to be tested on material covered in the chapter's Examples, Policy Examples, and Issues and Applications.
- A comprehensive Glossary appears at the end of this text. This pedagogical element provides a convenient way to quickly look up the meaning of a key term encountered in the text or in the supplements that accompany the text.
- Supplements that accompany this text will be linked to the chapter Learning Objectives. This ensures that these supplements are integrated very closely to this text.

Economic Principles in Practice

CHAPTER OPENING ISSUES. Each opening issue motivates student interest in the key chapter concepts. The issue presented is revisited in the Issues and Applications section at the culmination of the chapter.

2

Production Possibilities and Economic Systems

High and soaring Canadian car insurance rates created havoc for politicians and consumers alike in 2003. The issue of skyrocketing auto insurance almost toppled the once very popular New Brunswick Conservative government during the summer 2003 provincial election. In October 2003, in his first speech as Ontario's new premier, Dalton McGuinty announced a freeze on Ontario auto insurance rates. Within days, the free-enterprise Alberta Conservative government followed suit with its own 18-month rate freeze.

The concepts presented in this chapter will help you understand the economic issues that have fuelled the public's outrage over auto insurance rates in Canada.

LEARNING OBJECTIVES

After reading this chapter, you should be able to:

2.1 Define the production possibilities curve and identify its assumptions.
2.2 Use the production possibilities curve to illustrate the concepts of scarcity, trade-offs, unemployment, productive efficiency, allocative efficiency, increasing opportunity cost, and economic growth.
2.3 Use the production possibilities curve to explain the trade-off between consumption goods and capital goods.
2.4 Distinguish between absolute advantage and comparative advantage and use these concepts to explain how specialization and trade can increase production and consumption.

ISSUES AND APPLICATIONS. The Issues and Applications feature is designed to encourage students not just to apply economic concepts, but also to think critically about them. Each begins with the concepts being applied in this instance, and is followed by For Critical Analysis questions that could be used to prompt in-class discussions. Suggested answers to these questions are given at the back of the text, as well as in the Instructor's Manual at the end of the appropriate chapter.

CHAPTER 3: DEMAND AND SUPPLY 85

ISSUES AND APPLICATIONS

Is Canada the Prescription for Lower Drug Prices in the United States?

Concepts Applied: Changes in Demand and Supply, Changes in Equilibrium Price and Quantity

ROLL BACK DRUG PRICES

Americans show their demands while joining the RX Express, a group travelling by train from Miami to Toronto to buy medicine at prices 30 to 60 percent cheaper than in the United States.

The Dramatic Growth in the Canadian Internet Drug Export Industry

The Canadian prescription export industry started to attract international attention when busloads of American seniors travelled to drugstores, located just north of the American border, to purchase drugs in 1999. It was estimated that 10 million American consumers would spend $1 billion on prescription drugs sold through Canadian Internet pharmacies in 2003.

This rapidly growing Canadian export industry is based on the fact that many popular brand name prescription drugs sell for significantly lower prices in Canada than in the United States.

Why are brand name prescription drugs so much cheaper in Canada than in the United States? A number of factors help explain this difference.

In Canada, brand name prescription drugs are regulated by the Patent Medicine Prices Review Board to prevent excessive price gouging of the Canadian consumer. A new drug brought into the Canadian market, while protected by a 20-year patent, cannot cost more than the most expensive existing drug in its therapeutic class. If no similar drugs are sold in Canada, the board will ensure that the new drug's price will not exceed the average price charged in other countries

POLICY EXAMPLES. Many of the economic debates reported in the media involve important policy issues. Here, students are presented with various key policy questions on both the domestic and international fronts. Each Policy Example is followed by a For Critical Analysis question that encourages students to consider exactly what is involved in the discussion and what the further ramifications might be. Suggested solutions to these questions are provided at the back of the text and in the Instructor's Manual.

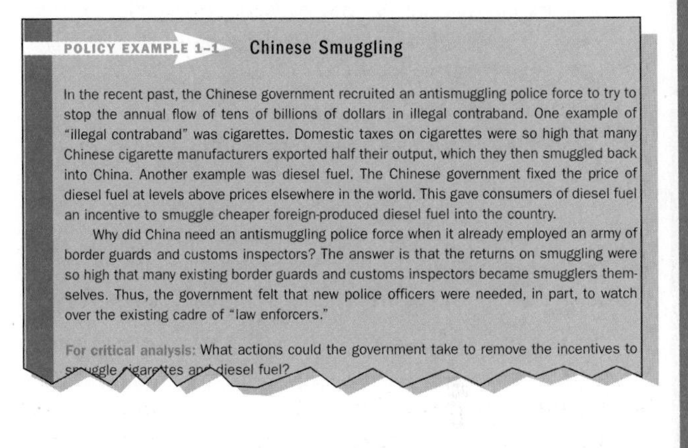

POLICY EXAMPLE 1-1 Chinese Smuggling

In the recent past, the Chinese government recruited an antismuggling police force to try to stop the annual flow of tens of billions of dollars in illegal contraband. One example of "illegal contraband" was cigarettes. Domestic taxes on cigarettes were so high that many Chinese cigarette manufacturers exported half their output, which they then smuggled back into China. Another example was diesel fuel. The Chinese government fixed the price of diesel fuel at levels above prices elsewhere in the world. This gave consumers of diesel fuel an incentive to smuggle cheaper foreign-produced diesel fuel into the country.

Why did China need an antismuggling police force when it already employed an army of border guards and customs inspectors? The answer is that the returns on smuggling were so high that many existing border guards and customs inspectors became smugglers themselves. Thus, the government felt that new police officers were needed, in part, to watch over the existing cadre of "law enforcers."

For critical analysis: What actions could the government take to remove the incentives to smuggle cigarettes and diesel fuel?

EXAMPLES. Many thought-provoking and relevant examples highlight Canadian, as well as international, events and demonstrate economic principles. The For Critical Analysis questions that follow encourage students to apply the knowledge and information gained from the example. Possible answers to the questions are provided at the back of the text and in the Instructor's Manual.

EXAMPLE 1-2 The Opportunity Cost of Finding a Mate—Lower on the Internet?

For many single people looking for a companion, the biggest difficulty is not necessarily a lack of potential mates. The problem is that the time spent dating in search of "Ms. Right" or "Mr. Right" could otherwise be devoted to alternative activities, the highest-valued of which is the opportunity cost of time spent on each date.

This provides a fundamental rationale for the existence of such Internet-based companies as Match.com. For about $25 per month, a person looking for "that special someone" with desired characteristics, similar interests, and so on can enter personal information into a database and be matched, by computer, with someone else. According to the company's "director of flirting and dating," its business is all "about numbers, and it's also about time." In short, it is about the high opportunity cost of finding a compatible partner. For the really picky who face especially high opportunity costs of screening candidate mates for very specific characteristics, there are special Internet services available, albeit at higher prices. Goodgenes.com is open to graduates of Ivy League universities and a select group of other top-notch colleges and universities. For Jewish men and women, there is JDate.com, and Matrimony.org helps link Islamic singles. There is even Singleswithscruples.com, which provides assistance to those who face the high opportunity cost of finding currently unattached individuals who are not morally or ethically challenged.

For critical analysis: Why do the prices charged by websites specializing in people who

Pedagogy With a Purpose: The Micro View

This third Canadian edition of *Economics Today: The Micro View* is loaded with the same highly regarded pedagogy of the previous edition. It helps students apply what they learn.

FOR CRITICAL ANALYSIS. At the end of each Example and Policy Example, students are asked to reflect on real-world problems by answering For Critical Analysis questions. The answers to the questions are found at the end of the student text and in the Instructor's Manual.

DID YOU KNOW THAT . . . ? Each chapter starts with a provocative question to engage students' interest and lead them into the content of the chapter.

LEARNING OBJECTIVES. On the first page of each chapter, several learning objectives are presented, giving purpose and focus to the chapter. These are then fully reviewed at the end of the chapter.

GRAPHS. Articulate and precise, the four-colour graphs illustrate key concepts.

KEY TERMS. Key terms are printed in bold type, and are defined in the margin of the text the first time they appear. These terms are also reproduced alphabetically in the Glossary at the end of the text.

CONCEPTS IN BRIEF. At the end of each major section in each chapter, Concepts in Brief summarizes the main points, thus reinforcing students' knowledge as well as testing their learning. The Concepts in Brief are organized around the chapter's learning objectives.

SUMMARY DISCUSSION OF LEARNING OBJECTIVES. Every chapter ends with a concise but thorough summary of how the chapter addresses each learning objective.

PROBLEMS. A variety of problems support each chapter, with each problem linked to the appropriate learning objective in the chapter. Answers for all odd-numbered problems are provided at the back of the textbook. The complete set of problem answers (both even- and odd-numbered) appears in the Instructor's Manual.

Teaching/Learning Package

Instructor's Resource CD-ROM

This resource provides all of the following supplements in one convenient package.

- **Instructor's Manual.** The Instructor's Manual has been adapted for this third Canadian edition of *Economics Today*. This extensive manual includes chapter overviews, objectives, and outlines; points to emphasize, including more theoretical issues for those who wish to stress theory; suggested questions for further class discussion; answers to the For Critical Analysis questions and end-of-chapter problems from the text; and selected references.
- **Pearson Education Canada TestGen.** This software enables instructors to view and edit the existing test-bank questions, add new questions, and generate custom tests. It includes a minimum of 100 multiple-choice questions, 10 short-answer questions, and 5 essay questions per chapter.
- **PowerPoint Presentations.** PowerPoint Presentations are available for each chapter of the text to highlight and illustrate important ideas.
- **CBC/Pearson Education Canada Video Library.** This collection of video cases includes segments from CBC's *Venture* and *Marketplace* that apply the subject of economics to real-life situations. Written cases and questions to accompany the segments can be found in the Instructor's Manual and on our password-protected Video Central website.

Companion Website

This website, created specifically for *Economics Today*, contains resources for students and instructors, including chapter objectives, self-test questions, weblinks, and an online glossary. Access the Companion Website at **www.pearsoned.ca/millermicro**.

Study Guide

Available in Micro and Macro versions, the Study Guides have been adapted by the text authors. Each chapter includes:

- Putting the chapter into perspective
- Learning objectives
- Chapter outline
- Key terms and concepts
- Completion questions
- True-or-false questions
- Multiple-choice questions
- Matching questions
- Working with graphs
- Problems
- A Business Section, giving applications and problems that relate to economic theory in business

ACKNOWLEDGMENTS

We could not have completed the third Canadian edition without the help of a terrific team of professionals at Pearson Education Canada. Thanks to Gary Bennett, our Senior Acquisitions Editor, for giving us this opportunity! Our Developmental Editor, Angela Kurmey, was a constant source of timely advice and encouragement. Jennifer Handel, Production Editor, guided the book through the final stages with a calm and sure hand. Our Copy Editor, Rohini Herbert, juggled four authors and four different writing styles with great dexterity.

We would also like to thank the following professors who helped with the development of this text by offering us their insightful comments and constructive criticisms:

Bogdan Buduru, Concordia University
Shernaz Choksi, Vanier College
David Desjardins, John Abbott College
Bruno Fullone, George Brown College
Pierre-Pascal Gendron, Humber College Institute of Technology and Advanced Learning
Ross Gowan, Fanshawe College
Carl Graham, Assiniboine Community College
Susan Kamp, University of Alberta
Joan McEachern, Kwantlen University College
John Pirrie, St. Lawrence College
Stephen Rakoczy, Humber College Institute of Technology and Advanced Learning
James Seldon, University College of the Cariboo
Angela Trimarchi, University of Waterloo

In completing this work, we sincerely appreciate the support and patience we have received from each of our families.

Finally, we would like to thank our colleagues and students at Northern Alberta Institute of Technology and British Columbia Institute of Technology for their valuable advice and support during the writing of this book.

In keeping with the cyber-age, and because we would appreciate suggestions about what to do in future editions, you and your students can contact us via email. Visit the *Economics Today* Companion Website at **www.pearsoned.ca/millermicro** to contact us. We look forward to hearing from you!

Brenda Abbott
Sam Fefferman
Ronald K. Kessler
Terrence Sulyma

PEARSON Education Canada The Pearson Education Canada **COMPANION WEBSITE**

A Great Way to Learn and Instruct Online

The Pearson Education Canada Companion Website is easy to navigate and is organized to correspond to the chapters in this textbook. Whether you are a student in the classroom or a distance learner you will discover helpful resources for in-depth study and research that empower you in your quest for greater knowledge and maximize your potential for success in the course.

[www.pearsoned.ca/millermicro]

Enter

PEARSON Addison Wesley

Jump to... http://www.pearsoned.ca/millermicro

Home Search Help Profile

Companion Website

Home >

AW Companion Website

Economics Today: The Micro View, Third Canadian Edition, by Miller, Abbott, Fefferman, Kessler, and Sulyma

Student Resources

The modules in this section provide students with tools for learning course material. These modules include:

- Chapter Objectives
- Quizzes
- Animated Figures
- Internet Exercises
- Glossary Flashcards

In the quiz modules students can send answers to the grader and receive instant feedback on their progress through the Results Reporter. Coaching comments and references to the textbook may be available to ensure that students take advantage of all available resources to enhance their learning experience.

Instructor Resources

A link to this book on the Pearson Education Canada online catalogue (vig.pearsoned.ca) provides instructors with additional teaching tools. Downloadable PowerPoint Presentations and an Instructor's Manual are just some of the materials that may be available. The catalogue is password protected. To get a password, simply contact your Pearson Education Canada Representative or call Faculty Sales and Services at 1-800-850-5813.

PART 1
INTRODUCTION

CHAPTER 1

The Nature of Economics

On May 27, 2003, the Canadian government introduced a new act in parliament that proposes to decriminalize the possession of small amounts of marijuana. The government claims that this new act, if passed, would (1) reduce the level of substance abuse in Canada, and (2) effectively use the limited resources of our justice system. Critics of this proposal argue that it will increase the level of marijuana use in Canada and at the same time reward those who engage in criminal activity. The economic concepts that you will learn in this chapter will help you critically assess both sides of this issue.

LEARNING OBJECTIVES

After reading this chapter, you should be able to:

1.1 Explain the meaning of scarcity.

1.2 Define economics and distinguish between microeconomics and macroeconomics.

1.3 Describe how resource use decisions are affected by the rationality assumption, costs and benefits at the margin, and incentives.

1.4 Explain the three key processes involved in the scientific method.

1.5 Distinguish between positive and normative economics.

1.6 Describe the relationship among theories, policies, and socioeconomic goals.

DID YOU KNOW THAT...

In 2002, more than two-thirds of all Canadian households owned a computer, with over 50 percent owning more than one. Seventy-five percent of all Canadians had access to the Internet, and approximately 65 percent of Canadian adults accessed the Internet from home. Over 60 percent of Canadian households preferred communicating via e-mail to other methods.

While the average family spent more than 32 hours online per week, 59 percent of Canadians with Internet access had yet to make an online purchase.

The world around us continues to change rapidly, and much of that change stems from the significant decline in cost and increase in convenience associated with information technology. Since 1961, the average cost of computer processing equipment has fallen at a rate of 19 percent per year. Your own decisions about what type of computer to buy, how to access the Internet, and how much time you spend online each week involve an untold number of variables. But, as you will see, there are economic underpinnings for nearly all the decisions you make.

SOURCE: "THE CANADIAN INTERNET FACT PAGE." PUBLISHED BY IPSOS-REID. ACCESSED SEPT 17, 2003. http://www.angusreid.com/ca/data/dsp_little_cdn_fact_book.cfm#

1.1 Scarcity

You can't have it all! You were probably first exposed to this very important economics lesson when, as a toddler, your parents denied your request to buy you a new toy at the supermarket. You undoubtedly experienced this same lesson many times over by the time you enrolled in this course. After you graduate, you may face such choices as buying a brand new car, putting a down payment on a condo, travelling to faraway places, or getting married and starting a family. As a senior member of your community, you may have to choose between spending tax dollars on building a new hospital and improving the education system for the next generation.

Whenever individuals or communities cannot obtain everything they desire, choices occur. Choices occur because of the fundamental economic problem of *scarcity*. Scarcity is the most basic concept in all of economics.

Scarcity The condition that arises because wants always exceed what can be produced with limited resources.

Scarcity refers to the condition that arises because wants always exceed what can be produced with limited resources.

As a result of scarcity, we do not and cannot have enough income and wealth to satisfy our every desire.

Scarcity is not the same thing as poverty. Scarcity occurs among the rich as well as the poor. Even the richest person faces scarcity because available time is limited. Low income levels do not create more scarcity. High income levels do not create less scarcity.

Scarcity and Wants

Goods The physical items that consumers are willing to pay for.

Services The tasks performed by others that consumers are willing to pay for.

Wants refer to the goods and services that we wish to consume as well as the goals that we seek to achieve. **Goods** are physical items that we as consumers are willing to pay for, such as meat, jeans, DVDs, and cars. **Services** are the tasks performed by others that we as consumers are willing to pay for, such as haircuts, education, and medical, dental, and legal services. The goals that we seek to achieve can be individual or social in nature. The important thing to note is that we are referring to goods, services, and goals that require the use of our limited resources.

Scarcity and Resources

Production Any activity that results in the conversion of resources into goods and services.

The scarcity concept arises from the fact that resources are insufficient to satisfy our every desire. Resources are the inputs used in the production of the things that we want. **Production** can be defined as virtually any activity that results in the conversion of resources into goods and services. Production includes delivering things from one part of the country to another. It includes taking ice from an ice tray to put in your soft-drink glass. The resources used in production are called *factors of production,* and some economists use the terms *resources* and *factors of production* interchangeably. The total quantity of all resources that an economy has at any one time determines what that economy can produce.

Factors of production can be classified in many ways. Here is one such classification:

Land Nonhuman gifts of nature.

Labour Productive contributions made by individuals who work.

Physical capital Factories and equipment used in production.

Human capital The education and training of workers.

Entrepreneurship Human resources that perform the functions of risk taking, organizing, managing, and assembling other factors of production to make business ventures.

1. **Land** encompasses all the nonhuman gifts of nature, including timber, water, fish, minerals, and the original fertility of the land. It is often called the *natural resource.*
2. **Labour** is the human resource, which includes all productive contributions made by individuals who work, such as steelworkers, ballet dancers, and professional baseball players.
3. **Physical capital** consists of the factories and equipment used in production. It also includes improvements to natural resources, such as irrigation ditches.
4. **Human capital** is the economic characterization of the education and training of workers. How much the nation produces depends not only on how many hours people work but also on how productive they are, and that, in turn, depends in part on education and training. To become more educated, individuals have to devote time and resources, just as a business has to devote resources if it wants to increase its physical capital. Whenever a worker's skills increase, human capital has been improved.
5. **Entrepreneurship** is actually a subdivision of labour and involves human resources that perform the functions of risk taking, organizing, managing, and assembling the other factors of production to make business ventures. Entrepreneurship also encompasses taking risks that involve the possibility of losing large sums of wealth on new ventures. It includes new methods of doing common things, and generally experimenting with any type of new thinking that could lead to making more money income. Without entrepreneurship, virtually no business organization could operate.

Rent Income earned by land.

Wages Income earned by labour.

Interest Income earned by capital.

Profit Income earned by the entrepreneur.

When resources are used to produce goods and services, they earn income. The incomes earned by land, labour, capital, and entrepreneurship are referred to as **rent**, **wages**, **interest**, and **profit**, respectively.

1.2 Defining Economics

What is economics exactly? *Economics* is one of the social sciences and, as such, seeks explanations of real events. All social sciences analyze human behaviour. The physical sciences, on the other hand, generally analyze the behaviour of electrons, atoms, and other nonhuman phenomena.

Economics A social science that studies how people allocate their limited resources to satisfy their wants.

Economics is a social science that studies how people allocate their limited resources to satisfy their wants. That is, economics is concerned with how individuals, groups, and societies respond to the economic problem of scarcity.

Resources are limited relative to wants. Consumers, managers, business owners, citizens, and politicians must continually make choices among alternative courses of action. For example, as a consumer, you choose how to spend your limited income on a vast array of goods and services. If you own a business or manage a government department, you will have to decide what resources to hire in order to best promote the goals of your organization, while working within a limited budget. As a citizen and potential politician, you make decisions that affect how limited tax dollars are used for the betterment of society. Economics helps us study how such choices can be made.

As Example 1–1 suggests, even a web page designer, who prefers to engage in artistic endeavours, must practise economics on a regular basis.

EXAMPLE 1–1 **The Economics of Web Page Design**

Canadians with Internet access at work spend 1.6 billion hours per year surfing the Net for personal reasons. In addition, over 15 million Canadian adults access the Internet from home. While at home, each Canadian family spends more than 1600 hours online per year, on average.

Companies that want to sell their products realize that these Internet use statistics suggest that advertisements posted on the Net can potentially reach very large audiences, not only in Canada but worldwide as well. These companies also know that when individuals access the Internet, the home pages of the individuals are typically those of their Internet service provider, a popular search engine, such as Yahoo!, or their favourite media website. Consequently, many companies advertise on these web pages. That is why each time you access the Net, you see advertising banners, buttons, animations, keywords, hot links, and other promotions. In 2003, Canadian Internet advertising revenues exceeded $150 million, which amounted to a 30 percent increase in revenue compared with the year before.

The owner of any web page that carries advertising faces the economic problem of scarcity. For example, advertisers widely consider the home page of Yahoo! search engine as "prime real estate" because so many people see it each day. But there is relatively little space on the computer screen to view Yahoo!'s opening page, without having to scroll further down the screen. Thus, when Yahoo! allocates space to promote its own services and products, it gives up space that it could sell to advertisers. On the other hand, if Yahoo! fills up too much of its prime screen space with ads, some users will switch to a less cluttered search engine. Web designers try to minimize the placement of ads on valuable prime screen space by using animations that can feature a number of different ads on the same space on a web page. However, Net surfers are only willing to spend a limited amount of time to view such animations. All of these considerations make web design a crucial economic concern.

For critical analysis: What are the"unlimited wants" and "limited resources" that face a person in charge of designing a frequently visited web page?

SOURCE: "ONLINE ADVERTISING RESEARCH STUDY" http://www.iabcanada.com/iab_resources/quick_facts.shtml; "THE CANADIAN INTERNET FACT PAGE." IPSOS REID. http://www.ipsos-reid.com/ca/data/dsp_little_cdn_fact_book.cfm.

Microeconomics versus Macroeconomics

Microeconomics The study of decision making undertaken by individuals and by firms in specific parts of the economy.

Macroeconomics The study of the behaviour of the economy as a whole.

Aggregates Economy-wide measures.

Economics is typically divided into two fields of study: *microeconomics* and *macroeconomics*.

Microeconomics studies decision making undertaken by individuals and by firms in specific parts of the economy. It is like looking through a microscope to focus on individual households, firms, industries, and occupations.

Macroeconomics studies the behaviour of the economy as a whole. It deals with economy-wide phenomena, such as changes in unemployment, the general price level, and national income.

Microeconomic analysis, for example, is concerned with the effects of changes in the price of gasoline relative to that of other energy sources. It examines the effects of new taxes on a specific product or industry. If price controls were to be reinstituted in Canada, how individual firms and consumers would react to them would be in the realm of microeconomics. The raising of wages by an effective union strike would also be analyzed using the tools of microeconomics.

By contrast, such issues as the rate of inflation, the amount of economy-wide unemployment, and the yearly growth in the output of goods and services in the nation all fall into the domain of macroeconomic analysis. In other words, macroeconomics deals with **aggregates**, or economy-wide measures, such as total output in an economy.

The Power of Economic Analysis

Knowing that an economic problem of scarcity exists every time you make a decision is not enough. As you study economics, you will be encouraged to develop a framework of analysis that will allow you to effectively analyze possible solutions to each economic problem—whether you are a student trying to decide how much studying time you should devote to a course, a consumer making the choice between renting and owning your next home, a business owner interested in setting the most profitable price for your product, or a government leader searching for the policy that would most effectively create jobs in your province. The remainder of this chapter is concerned with introducing you to a powerful framework of analysis that includes the *economic way of thinking*, the *scientific approach*, and *policy analysis* based on valued economic goals.

Indeed, just as taking an art or literature appreciation class increases the pleasure you receive when you view paintings or read novels, taking an economics course will increase your understanding when viewing news clips on the Internet, watching the news on TV, listening to newscasts on the radio, or reading newspapers.

CONCEPTS IN BRIEF

Learning Objective 1.1: Explain the meaning of scarcity.

- Scarcity refers to the condition that arises because wants always exceed what can be produced with the available limited resources. Scarcity is ever present in both rich and poor nations.
- Limited resources include such items as land, labour, physical capital, human capital, and entrepreneurship. Wants refer to the goods and services that we wish to consume as well as the goals that we seek to achieve.

Learning Objective 1.2: Define economics and distinguish between microeconomics and macroeconomics.

- Economics is a social science that studies how people allocate limited resources to satisfy unlimited wants.
- The field of economics can be further subdivided into microeconomics and macroeconomics.
- Microeconomics focuses on the specific parts of the economy, such as the individual household, firm, industry, or occupation.
- Macroeconomics focuses on the behaviour of the economy as a whole and seeks to explain economy-wide phenomena, such as changes in unemployment, the general price level, and national income.
- Economics offers a useful framework of analysis that includes the economic way of thinking, the scientific approach, and policy analysis.

1.3 Rational Decision Making

Economic way of thinking
Assumes that the typical response to an economic problem of scarcity is rational behaviour.

The **economic way of thinking** assumes that the typical response to an economic problem of scarcity is rational behaviour. That is, individuals behave as if they compare the costs and benefits of different possible choices when they make resource use decisions. They behave in this manner in order to further their own self-interest.

Economists presume that individuals act *as if* motivated by self-interest and respond predictably to opportunities for gain. This central insight of economics was first clearly articulated by Adam Smith in 1776. Smith wrote in his most famous book, *An Inquiry into the Nature and Causes of the Wealth of Nations*, that "it is not from the benevolence of the butcher, the brewer, or the baker that we expect our dinner, but from their regard to their own interest." Otherwise stated, the *typical* person about whom economists make behavioural predictions is assumed to look out for his or her own self-interest in a rational manner. The word *typical* is very important. Economists know that not all people respond in the same way when faced with the same circumstances. If offered a free trip to Hawaii for participating in a marketing experiment, for example, most people will take part. There inevitably will be some who do not want to go to Hawaii, perhaps because they do not like travelling, and so they will not participate in the study. But, *on average*, the promised trip to Hawaii will be sufficient to attract participants because people behave in a predictably self-interested way.

The Rationality Assumption

Rationality assumption An individual makes decisions based on maximizing his or her own self-interest.

The **rationality assumption** of economics, simply stated, is as follows:

> An individual makes decisions based on maximizing his or her own self-interest.

The distinction here is between what people may think—the realm of psychology and psychiatry and perhaps sociology—and what they do. Economics does *not* involve itself in analyzing individual or group thought processes. Economics looks at what people actually do in life with their limited resources. It does little good to criticize the rationality assumption by stating, "Nobody thinks that way" or "I never think that way" or "How unrealistic! That's as irrational as anyone can get!"

Take the example of driving. When you consider passing another car on a two-lane highway with oncoming traffic, you have to make very quick decisions: You must estimate the speed of the car you are going to pass, the speed of the oncoming cars, the distance between your car and the oncoming cars, and your car's potential rate of acceleration. If we were to apply a model to your behaviour, we would use the laws of calculus. In actual fact, you and most other drivers in such a situation do not actually think of using the laws of calculus, but we could predict your behaviour *as if* you understood the laws of calculus.

In practical terms, the rationality assumption implies that an individual will adopt a course of action if the action's relevant benefits exceed its relevant costs. Let us proceed to examine what we mean by *relevant* costs and benefits.

Opportunity Cost

The natural fact of scarcity implies that we must make choices. One of the most important results of this fact is that every choice made (or not made, for that matter) means that some opportunity had to be sacrificed. Every choice involves giving up another opportunity to do or use something else.

Consider a practical example. Every choice you make to study one more hour of economics requires that you give up the opportunity to do any of the following activities: study more of another subject, listen to music, sleep, browse at a local store, read a novel, or work out at the gym. Many more opportunities are forgone if you choose to study economics for an additional hour.

Because there were so many alternatives from which to choose, how could you determine the value of what you gave up to engage in that extra hour of studying economics? First of all, no one else can tell you the answer because only you can *subjectively* put a value on each alternative. Only you know the value of another hour of sleep or of an hour looking for the latest CDs. That means that only you can determine the highest-valued alternative that you had to sacrifice in order to study economics one more hour. It is you who must come up with the *subjective* estimate of the expected value of the best alternative.

Opportunity cost The value of the best alternative that must be given up because a choice was made.

The value of the best alternative that must be sacrificed to satisfy a want is called *opportunity cost*. The **opportunity cost** of any action is the value of what is given up—the highest-ranked alternative—because a choice was made. When you study one more hour, there may be many alternatives available for the use of that hour, but assume that you can do only one thing in that hour—your highest-ranked alternative. What is important is the choice that you would have made if you had not studied one more hour. Your opportunity cost is the *highest-ranked* alternative, not *all* alternatives.

> In economics, cost is a forgone opportunity.

In this chapter's Issues and Applications, we use the concept of *opportunity cost* to help explain why some individuals support decriminalizing marijuana in Canada. Our justice system has its own economic problem—that of allocating its limited resources, such as lawyers, prosecutors, judges, courtrooms, court employees, police staff, and witnesses, in a manner that provides maximum justice in what society would consider the most important or serious criminal cases. The *opportunity cost* of the current policy of using our limited justice system resources to convict individuals who possess very small amounts of marijuana is the forgone opportunity to prosecute those who have committed much more serious crimes.

In Example 1–2 we will examine how the relatively high opportunity cost of searching for a compatible romantic partner has helped create an industry based in cyberspace.

EXAMPLE 1–2

The Opportunity Cost of Finding a Mate—Lower on the Internet?

For many single people looking for a companion, the biggest difficulty is not necessarily a lack of potential mates. The problem is that the time spent dating in search of "Ms. Right" or "Mr. Right" could otherwise be devoted to alternative activities, the highest-valued of which is the opportunity cost of time spent on each date.

This provides a fundamental rationale for the existence of such Internet-based companies as Match.com. For about $25 per month, a person looking for "that special someone" with desired characteristics, similar interests, and so on can enter personal information into a database and be matched, by computer, with someone else. According to the company's "director of flirting and dating," its business is all "about numbers, and it's also about time." In short, it is about the high opportunity cost of finding a compatible partner. For the really picky who face especially high opportunity costs of screening candidate mates for very specific characteristics, there are special Internet services available, albeit at higher prices. Goodgenes.com is open to graduates of Ivy League universities and a select group of other top-notch colleges and universities. For Jewish men and women, there is JDate.com, and Matrimony.org helps link Islamic singles. There is even Singleswithscruples.com, which provides assistance to those who face the high opportunity cost of finding currently unattached individuals who are not morally or ethically challenged.

For critical analysis: Why do the prices charged by websites specializing in people who share very specific characteristics tend to be higher than the prices charged by general dating services, such as Match.com?

Making Decisions at the Margin

As you progress through this text, you will be reminded frequently that in order to rationally evaluate a possible course of action, you must compare the action's *marginal benefit* with its *marginal cost*. **Marginal benefit** refers to all the *extra* benefits that one receives in pursuing a course of action, while **marginal cost** refers to all the *extra* costs or sacrifices incurred. In order to ensure that you properly identify the marginal cost relevant to your decision at hand, you must be careful not to include *sunk costs*. **Sunk costs** refer to irreversible costs incurred prior to your decision.

Marginal benefit All the *extra* benefits that one receives in pursuing a course of action.

Marginal cost All the *extra* costs or sacrifices incurred.

Sunk costs Irreversible costs incurred prior to your decision.

As an example, suppose you are in the process of estimating the extra (marginal) transportation costs associated with a Nova Scotia vacation that you are planning to take. You own your car and you have paid the annual insurance and car licence fee long before contemplating this vacation. If you decide to use your own car for this trip, the annual licence fee and insurance are sunk costs that are not relevant to the decision of travelling to Nova Scotia. As such, you should not include these two costs in your estimate of the extra (marginal) transportation costs. To better understand the notion of marginal and sunk costs, we refer you to Example 1–3: "What Does a Year at College Really Cost?"

Making decisions at the margin will often reveal that there can be too much of a good thing! As an example, suppose that at a time when marijuana use is at an all-time low, one of the contenders for prime minister, in a federal election campaign, proposes a policy for eliminating all marijuana use in Canada. While this type of zero tolerance policy proposal can win votes, if implemented, it can result in the transfer of a massive amount of policing resources away from the prevention of serious violent crimes in order to achieve a very small reduction in marijuana use. In other words, the marginal cost of the zero tolerance policy far exceeds the marginal benefit!

EXAMPLE 1–3 **What Does a Year at College Really Cost?**

Jane Sanders is currently earning $1600 per month working full time in Hamilton, Ontario. She lives in a one-bedroom apartment and pays $500 per month in rent. Her monthly food, personal care, and entertainment expenses are $400 per month. Since she does not own a vehicle, she pays $65 per month for a bus pass.

Jane is in the process of estimating the extra cost related to the decision to enroll full time in the first year of a business program at a college in the Hamilton area. If she enrolls, she will give up her full-time job for the eight-month period of the first-year program. If Jane goes to college, she plans to continue to live in her one-bedroom apartment, take the bus to the college campus, and maintain her current lifestyle. Jane estimates that her decision to enroll in college for the first year (eight-month period) will cost $10 777, estimated as follows:

TABLE 1–1

Rent	$500 × 8 =	$ 4000
Food, Personal Care, Entertainment	$400 × 8 =	$ 3200
Public Transportation	$ 65 × 8 =	$ 520
Tuition, Books, College Fees		$ 3057
Total Cost		**$10 777**

For critical analysis: Did Jane correctly determine the extra cost related to the decision to enroll in college full time for eight months? What else must Jane try to estimate in order to make a rational decision? Explain.

Responding to Incentives

Incentive Inducement to take a particular action.

If it is reasonable to assume that individuals make decisions by comparing marginal costs and benefits, then we are in a position to better understand and predict how people respond to incentives. We define an **incentive** as an inducement to take a particular action. The inducement can be a reward, or a "carrot," which would take the form of an increase in benefit or a decrease in cost. Alternatively, the inducement can be a punishment or a "stick," in the form of an increase in cost or a decrease in benefit. To the extent that a change in incentives implies a change in the relation between the marginal costs and benefits associated with various choices, individual decisions will change.

Indeed, much of human behaviour can be explained in terms of how individuals respond to changing incentives over time. School students are motivated to do better by a variety of incentive systems, ranging from gold stars and certificates of achievement when they are young to better grades with accompanying promises of a "better life" as they get older. The rapid growth in Internet use noted in this chapter's *Did You Know That* section can be explained in terms of increased incentives due to the decline in cost and increase in convenience associated with information technology. Even the slow growth in the number of Canadians shopping online can be explained by the negative incentive related to their heightened concerns about the security of giving out credit card numbers and other private information over the web.

In the Policy Example 1–1: Chinese Smuggling you are asked to help the Chinese government reduce the incentives to smuggle cigarettes and diesel fuel by identifying actions that either increase the marginal cost or decrease the marginal benefit of this type of illegal activity.

POLICY EXAMPLE 1–1 **Chinese Smuggling**

In the recent past, the Chinese government recruited an antismuggling police force to try to stop the annual flow of tens of billions of dollars in illegal contraband. One example of "illegal contraband" was cigarettes. Domestic taxes on cigarettes were so high that many Chinese cigarette manufacturers exported half their output, which they then smuggled back into China. Another example was diesel fuel. The Chinese government fixed the price of diesel fuel at levels above prices elsewhere in the world. This gave consumers of diesel fuel an incentive to smuggle cheaper foreign-produced diesel fuel into the country.

Why did China need an antismuggling police force when it already employed an army of border guards and customs inspectors? The answer is that the returns on smuggling were so high that many existing border guards and customs inspectors became smugglers themselves. Thus, the government felt that new police officers were needed, in part, to watch over the existing cadre of "law enforcers."

FOR CRITICAL ANALYSIS: What actions could the government take to remove the incentives to smuggle cigarettes and diesel fuel?

Defining Self-Interest

Self-interest does not always mean increasing one's wealth as measured in dollars and cents. We assume that individuals seek many goals, not just increased monetary wealth. Thus, the self-interest part of our economic-person assumption includes goals relating to prestige, friendship, love, power, helping others, creating works of art, and many other matters. The giving of gifts can be considered a form of charity that is, nonetheless, in the self-interest of the giver. As Example 1–4 explains, donors may even expect to get some of their giving back.

CONCEPTS IN BRIEF

Learning Objective 1.3: Describe how resource use decisions are affected by the rationality assumption, costs and benefits at the margin, and incentives.

- The economic way of thinking assumes that the typical response to an economic problem is rational behaviour.
- The rationality assumption suggests that an individual makes decisions based on maximizing his or her own self-interest.
- In order to maximize self-interest, an individual will use his or her resources in satisfying those wants where the marginal (extra) benefit exceeds the marginal (extra) cost. Marginal cost is measured in terms of opportunity cost, which is the highest-valued alternative that must be sacrificed to satisfy a want.
- A change in marginal cost or marginal benefit will change the incentives that an individual faces and will lead to a change in resource use decisions.

EXAMPLE 1–4 **Giving Charity to Oneself?**

Economists have long recognized that charitable giving is in the self-interest of the donors. It makes them feel that they are contributing to society, helping the less fortunate and, more pragmatically, saving on the income tax they pay. But perhaps there are other reasons as well. Let us look at some of the evidence from the year 2000, the most recent year for which these data are available.

FIGURE 1–1 *Percentage of Household Income Spent on Donations by Level of Household Income, Canadians Aged 15 and Older, 1997 and 2000*

SOURCE: ADAPTED FROM THE STATISTICS CANADA PUBLICATION *CARING CANADIANS, INVOLVED CANADIANS: HIGHLIGHTS FROM THE 2000 NATIONAL SURVEY OF GIVING, VOLUNTEERING AND PARTICIPATING*, 2000, CATALOGUE 71-542, AUGUST 17, 2001, PAGE 21.

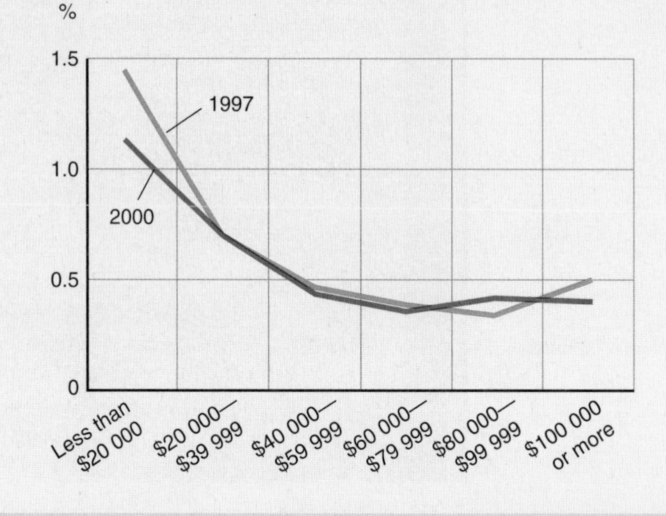

Although donors with higher household incomes made larger dollar donations, they tend to give a smaller *percentage* of their overall pretax income to charity. As the accompanying figure shows, those households earning less than $20 000 per year contributed over 1 percent of their pretax income to charity in 2000 compared with less than 0.5 percent of pretax income from those earning in excess of $100 000 per year.

One explanation that would make this giving pattern *rational* is that the poorer households are those most likely to have used charity in the past or need it in the future. Perhaps these households, unable to build large savings accounts to help them through periods of economic misfortune, look to public charity as a kind of insurance and to their donations as the premiums they pay for it.

For critical analysis: Can you devise an explanation for this pattern of giving charity among the lower-income households, using the notions of costs and benefits?

1.4 The Scientific Method

Models or theories Simplified representations of the real world used to understand and predict economic phenomena.

Economics is a social science that makes use of the same kinds of methods used in other sciences, such as biology, physics, and chemistry. Similar to these other sciences economics engages in key processes that include making assumptions, forming models or theories, and testing these models with real-world facts. Economic **models** or **theories** are simplified representations of the real world that we use to help us understand and predict economic phenomena in the real world. There are, of course, differences among the sciences. The social sciences, especially economics, make little use of laboratory methods in which changes in variables can be explained under controlled conditions. Rather, social scientists, and especially economists, usually have to examine what has already happened in the real world to test their models.

Models and Realism

At the outset, it must be emphasized that no model in *any* science, and therefore no economic model, is complete in the sense that it captures *every* detail or interrelationship that exists. Indeed, a model, by definition, is an abstraction from reality. It is conceptually impossible to construct a perfectly complete realistic model. For example, in physics, we cannot account for every molecule and its position, nor every atom and subparticle. Not only would such a model be prohibitively expensive to build but also working with it would be impossibly complex.

The nature of scientific model building is such that the model should capture only the essential relationships that are sufficient to analyze the particular problem or answer the particular question with which we are concerned. *An economic model cannot be faulted as unrealistic simply because it does not represent every detail of the real world.* A map of a city that shows only major streets is not necessarily unrealistic if, in fact, all you need to know is how to navigate through the city using major streets. As long as a model is realistic in terms of shedding light on the *central* issue at hand or forces at work, it may be useful.

A map is a basic model. It is always a simplified representation, always unrealistic. But it is also useful in making (refutable) predictions about the world. If the model—the map—predicts that when you take Campus Avenue to the north, you always reach the campus, that is a (refutable) prediction. If our goal is to explain observed behaviour, the simplicity or complexity of the model we use is irrelevant. If a simple model can explain observed behaviour in repeated settings just as well as a complex one, the simple model has some value and is probably easier to use.

Assumptions

Every model, or theory, is based on a set of assumptions. Assumptions define the conditions under which a model is meant to apply. By eliminating detail that is not considered to be essential to the economic phenomena under investigation, assumptions help simplify a model.

In the theory of the firm, we assume that, typically, firms attempt to maximize profits when deciding how much of a product to produce in an industry. This assumption leads to an economic model of the firm that provides numerous predictions about how the firm will react to various events and incentives. As an example, one prediction would be that if a firm can sell its product at a higher price, it will tend to produce more of this product. Another prediction would be that if a major cost of producing this product increases, such as energy costs, the firm will likely reduce the level of production of this product. Finally, this model would predict that if the government lowered the taxes imposed on the firms in this industry, this would entice firms to increase their supply of this product.

While the owners of the firms in the industry under investigation may well have a variety of other motives for producing the product, the profit-maximizing assumption model is valid to the extent that it consistently provides accurate predictions of real-world behaviour.

THE *CETERIS PARIBUS* ASSUMPTION: ALL OTHER THINGS BEING EQUAL. Constructing a model typically involves making generalizations of how variables in our environment relate to each other. It would be impossible to isolate the effects of changes in one variable on another variable if we always had to worry about the many additional variables that might also enter the analysis. As in other sciences, economics uses the ***ceteris paribus* assumption**, which is the assumption that nothing changes except the factor or factors being studied. *Ceteris paribus* means "other things constant" or "other things being equal."

***Ceteris paribus* [KAY-ter-us PEAR-uh-bus] assumption** The assumption that nothing changes except the factor or factors being studied; "other things constant," or "other things equal."

Consider an example taken from economics. One of the most important determinants of how much of a particular product a family buys is the price of that product relative to other products. We know that in addition to relative prices, other factors influence decisions about making purchases. Some of them have to do with income, others with tastes, and yet others with custom and religious beliefs. Whatever these other factors are, we hold them constant when we look at the relationship between changes in prices and changes in how much of a given product people will purchase. Researchers at an American university used the *ceteris paribus* assumption in their experiment in the animal world, as explained in Example 1–5.

EXAMPLE 1–5 **Incentives Work for Pigeons and Rats, Too**

Researchers at Texas A&M University in Houston, Texas, did a series of experiments with pigeons and rats. They allowed them to "purchase" food and drink by pushing various levers. The "price" was the number of times a lever had to be pushed. A piece of cheese required 10 pushes, a drop of root beer only one. The "incomes" that the animals were given equalled a certain number of total pushes per day. Once the income was used up, the levers did not work.

The researchers discovered that holding income constant, when the price of cheese went down, the animals purchased more cheese. Similarly, they found that when the price of root beer was increased, the animals purchased less root beer. These are exactly the predictions we make about human behaviour.

For critical analysis: What were the animals doing when they changed their "purchasing" behaviour?

Testing Models

We generally do not attempt to determine the usefulness, or "goodness," of a model merely by evaluating how realistic its assumptions are. Rather, we consider a model good if it yields usable predictions and implications for the real world. In other words, can we use the model to predict what will happen in the world around us?

Once we have determined that the model does predict real-world phenomena, the scientific approach to the analysis of the world around us requires that we consider evidence. Evidence is used to test the usefulness of a model. This is why we call economics an *empirical* science, **empirical** meaning using real-world data to test the usefulness of a model. Economists are often engaged in empirically testing their models.

Empirical Using real-world data to test the usefulness of a model.

Consider two competing models for the way students act when doing complicated probability problems to choose the best gambles. One model predicts that, on the basis of the assumption of rational self-interest, students who are paid more for better performance will, in fact, perform better on average during the experiment. A competing model might be that students whose last names start with the letters A through L will do better than students with last names starting with M through Z, irrespective of how much they are paid. The model that consistently predicts more accurately is the model that we would normally choose. In this example, the "alphabet" model did not work well: The first letter of the last name of the students who actually did the experiment was irrelevant in predicting how well they would perform the mathematical calculations necessary to choose the correct gambles. The model based on rational self-interest predicted well, in contrast.

Models of Behaviour, Not Thought Processes

Take special note of the fact that economists' models do not relate to the way people *think*; they relate to the way people *act*, to what they do in life with their limited resources. Models tend to generalize human behaviour. Normally, the economist does not attempt to predict how people will think about a particular topic, such as a higher price of oil products, accelerated inflation, or higher taxes. Rather, the task at hand is to predict how people will act, which may be quite different from what they say they will do (much to the consternation of poll takers and market researchers). The people involved in examining thought processes are psychologists and psychiatrists, who are not usually economists.

An Economic Model: The Circular Flow of Income

A simple model economists use to explain the workings of the economy is the Circular Flow of Income. Figure 1–2 shows the basic form of the Circular Flow model.

When using the Circular Flow model, we make two main assumptions. The first is that households—people like you and me—produce nothing, but *own* everything in the economy. This makes sense when you think that we own our own labour, and we also own all the firms—whether as shareholders or as entrepreneurs. Firms own nothing, since the shareholders own it all, but they *produce* everything in the economy. As soon as someone produces a good or a service to be sold in the economy, we call that producer a firm.

A good place to start thinking about this model is with the firms. The firms go to the labour market and hire workers to produce their output. In exchange, the firms pay the workers a wage, and income flows *from* the firms *to* the households. Households need food, shelter, and clothing, and so they go to the product (or output) market to purchase goods and services. In exchange for the goods and services, the households give the firms a part of their incomes, and income flows *from* the households *to* the firms. So, the flow of income in the economy is circular; it flows from firms to households and back to firms again.

We can complicate our model to make it a little more realistic. Most households wish to save part of their income. That part therefore does not flow through the product market but, instead, flows to the financial market—to savings accounts with banks, credit unions, and trust companies. These financial institutions hold the households' savings, which they lend to firms that need funds for investment. Thus, the income paid out by firms to workers still returns to them via the product market and the financial market.

Whether this is a useful model depends on how well it predicts real-world events. For example, what would happen to the economy if the government decided to put a tax (or an additional tax) on household incomes? Households would have less money to spend and/or save. The Circular Flow model predicts that households would purchase less and save less, and the flows to the firms would diminish. If the flows to the firms diminished, the firms would produce less, and hire fewer workers—thus compounding the problem of shrinking incomes. We could test this prediction by looking at Canada's and other similar countries' experiences when taxes have risen. We would almost certainly find a slowing in the growth of the economy; our model would represent this as a slowing of the flows between the households and the firms.

If we ask what would happen to our economy if the Americans asked Canadian firms to produce twice as many automobile parts for them than in the past, what will our model predict? We have not included the foreign sector in our simple model, but we could look

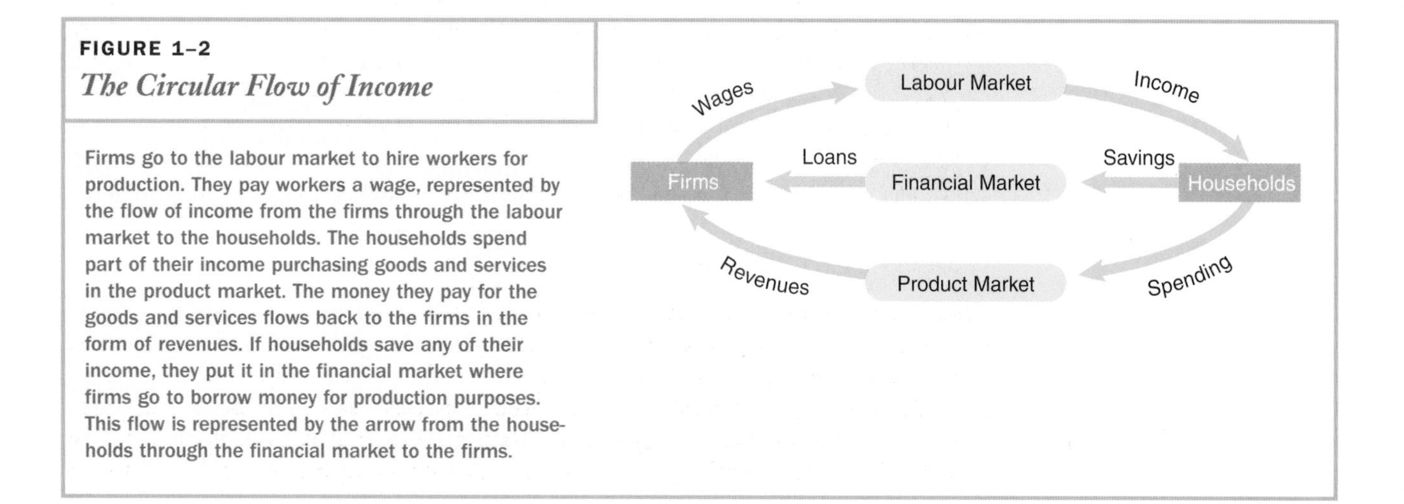

FIGURE 1–2
The Circular Flow of Income

Firms go to the labour market to hire workers for production. They pay workers a wage, represented by the flow of income from the firms through the labour market to the households. The households spend part of their income purchasing goods and services in the product market. The money they pay for the goods and services flows back to the firms in the form of revenues. If households save any of their income, they put it in the financial market where firms go to borrow money for production purposes. This flow is represented by the arrow from the households through the financial market to the firms.

at the opportunity to increase our sales to the United States as a large injection of income into the firms. The firms would go to the labour market and hire more workers to produce the extra output. Increased income would flow from the firms to the households and, *ceteris paribus*, back to the firms again. The economy would grow with the increased economic activity.

1.5 Positive versus Normative Economics

Economic theory uses *positive analysis*, a value-free approach to inquiry. No subjective or moral judgments enter into the analysis. Positive analysis relates to such statements as "If *A*, then *B*." For example, "If the price of gasoline goes up relative to all other prices, then the amount of it that people will buy will fall." That is a positive economic statement. It is a statement of *what is,* and its validity can be tested by observing the facts. It is not a statement of anyone's value judgment or subjective feelings. For many problems analyzed in the hard sciences, such as physics and chemistry, the analyses are considered to be virtually value-free. After all, how can someone's values enter into a theory of molecular behaviour? But economists face a different problem. They deal with the behaviour of individuals, not molecules. That makes it more difficult to stick to what we consider to be value-free or *positive economics* without reference to our feelings. **Positive economics** refers to analysis that can be tested by observing the facts.

Positive economics refers to analysis that can be tested by observing the facts.

Normative economics refers to analysis based on value judgments made about what ought to be.

When our values are interjected into the analysis, we enter the realm of *normative economics*, involving *normative analysis*. **Normative economics** refers to analysis based on value judgments made about what ought to be. A positive economic statement is: "If the price of gas rises, people will buy less." If we add to that analysis the statement "so we should not allow the price to go up," we have entered the realm of normative economics—we have expressed a value judgment. In fact, any time you see the word *should*, you will know that values are entering into the discussion. Just remember that positive statements are concerned with *what is*, whereas normative statements are concerned with *what ought to be*.

In the last section of this chapter, we will introduce the important social and economic goals that governments try to achieve when they design economic policy. Normative analysis is often encountered when you examine the various goals that form the basis of policy. As an example, in this chapter's Issues and Applications, you will see that the proposal to decriminalize marijuana is, in part, based on certain goals, such as "the punishment should fit the crime," which are normative in nature.

A Warning: Recognize Normative Analysis

It is easy to define positive economics. It is quite another matter to catch all unlabelled normative statements in a textbook such as this one (or any other), even though the authors go over the manuscript many times before it is printed. Therefore, do not get the impression that a textbook's authors will be able to keep all personal values out of the book. They will slip through. In fact, the very choice of which topics to include in an introductory textbook involves normative economics. There is no value-free, or objective, way to decide which topics to include in a textbook. The authors' values ultimately make a difference when choices have to be made. But from your own standpoint, you might want to be able to recognize when you are engaging in normative, as opposed to positive, economic analysis. Reading this text will help equip you for that task.

1.6 Economic Policy and Socioeconomic Goals

As we noted above, economic models will enhance your ability to understand and predict behaviour. In the chapters to come, we will illustrate how these models prove useful in formulating, assessing, and reacting to government policies that affect you as a consumer, an employee, an investor, a business owner, and a concerned citizen.

Policies Action plans designed to achieve goals.

Most government economic **policies** are action plans designed to achieve commonly accepted socioeconomic goals. The goals that are most frequently considered, when forming and evaluating economic policies, are described below.

1. Full Employment: an economy in which people looking for work find jobs reasonably quickly.
2. Efficiency: an economy in which resources are allocated to the production of goods and services in a way that achieves maximum benefit for society.
3. Economic Growth: an economy with the ability to increase its rate of production over time to enhance society's well being.
4. Price Stability: an economy in which prices remain relatively stable over time.
5. Equity: an economy that moves closer toward some social consensus of fairness. An example often used as a basis of economic policy is the goal of a *more equitable distribution of income*, which aims to reduce the level of poverty in the economy.

Theory and Policy

Economic theory plays a useful role in helping us understand how existing and proposed policies relate to major socioeconomic goals. As you progress through this text, you will be surprised at the frequency with which a proposed policy is shown to conflict with the very goals it is meant to promote, once you employ the relevant economic model.

For example, a local politician may propose a rent control policy aimed at reducing apartment rents in order to make housing more affordable to the poor. That is, the rent control policy is aimed at promoting a more equitable distribution of income. However, once you become familiar with the demand-and-supply model presented in Chapter 4, you will see that this policy will more likely conflict with the goal of an equitable distribution of income because of the resulting shortages in livable accommodation. Moreover, this same policy will also conflict with the goal of full employment to the extent that construction workers are laid off as fewer new apartments are being built.

We hope that you will enjoy the challenge of using economic models to formulate superior alternative policies. A superior policy refers to a plan of action that promotes as many socioeconomic goals as possible with minimal goal conflict. In the rent control example, you may find that relevant economic theory suggests that a policy of increasing competition in the apartment construction and rental industries may prove to be the superior policy. By increasing the supply of affordable, quality housing units, the goals of full employment and equitable distribution can both be promoted!

CONCEPTS IN BRIEF

Learning Objective 1.4: Explain the three key processes involved in the scientific method.

- In using the scientific method one makes assumptions, constructs models or theories, and tests these models with the facts.
- Assumptions define the conditions under which a model is meant to apply. A model is a simplification of reality. We consider a model as useful if it does a good job of predicting real-world phenomena.

Learning Objective 1.5: Distinguish between positive and normative economics.

- Positive economics is value-free and relates to statements that can be tested by such facts as "If A, then B." Normative economics involves value judgments, and normative statements typically contain such words as "should" or "ought to." Positive statements are prevalent in economic theories, whereas normative statements are often encountered in the goals used to evaluate policy.

Learning Objective 1.6: Describe the relationship among theories, policies, and socioeconomic goals.

- Policies refer to action plans aimed at promoting various important socioeconomic goals.
- Models or theories are used to identify how specific policies affect goals.
- Key socioeconomic goals include full employment, efficiency, economic growth, price stability, and equity.

ISSUES AND APPLICATIONS

Decriminalizing Marijuana, An Economics Perspective

Concepts Applied: Scarcity, Microeconomics versus Macroeconomics, Opportunity Cost, Economic Way of Thinking, Incentives, Scientific Model, Positive versus Normative, Policy Analysis

Under Bill C-38, marijuana use in small amounts would still be an illegal act, subject to economic penalties.

On May 27, 2003, the Canadian government announced the Renewal of Canada's Drug Strategy. As part of this strategy, the Canadian government introduced to parliament *Bill C-38, An Act to Amend the Contraventions Act and the Controlled Drugs and Substances Act.*

Renewal of Canada's Drug Strategy: The Proposals of *Bill C-38*

Under the proposed *Bill C-38*, cannabis (marijuana and hashish) possession and production will remain illegal in Canada, but the approach to enforcement will change. This cannabis reform bill includes measures that:

- replace the current criminal court process and resulting criminal penalties for possession of 15 grams or less of marijuana or one gram or less of hashish with a ticket bearing a specified fine.
- provide law enforcement officers with the discretion to give a ticket or issue a summons to appear in criminal court in cases where possession is between 15 grams and 30 grams of marijuana.
- provide for greater alternative penalties when aggravating factors are present, including possession while operating a vehicle or while on or near school grounds.
- create new offences providing tougher penalties for illegal growers. For the larger growers, there would be a doubling of the maximum penalty from the current seven years to a proposed 14 years of imprisonment.

Renewal of Canada's Drug Strategy: The Policy's Goals

In addition to *Bill C-38*, the government proposed to spend $245 million to support the goals of the Renewal of Canada's Drug Strategy, which can be summarized as follows.

1. The strategy will help avoid the complications and expense of using the criminal process for minor offences, resulting in more effective use of limited justice system resources.
2. The strategy will decrease the number of people who abuse and experiment with illegal drugs. This, in turn, will decrease the avoidable health, social, and economic costs that accompany substance abuse.
3. The strategy will modify the penalties for marijuana possession to offer a range that helps ensure that the punishment assessed is appropriate to the seriousness of the crime.

Renewal of Canada's Drug Strategy: Will the Policy Achieve Its Goals?

The concepts studied in this chapter of the text can help us analyze Canada's proposed drug policy in terms of its stated goals. Our previous discussion of *scarcity* should make us appreciate that the justice system has its own economic problem—that of allocating its limited resources, such as lawyers, prosecutors, judges, courtrooms, court employees, police staff, and witnesses, in a manner that provides maximum justice in what society would consider the most important or serious criminal cases. The *opportunity cost* of using our limited justice system resources to attempt to convict individuals who possess very small amounts of marijuana is the forgone opportunity to fairly judge those who are charged with much more serious crimes. As a result, there is the danger that individuals who are truly guilty of committing very serious crimes will be set free while others who are innocent may be given very severe sentences.

The *economic way of thinking* can help us assess whether the proposed drug policy will achieve the second goal stated above, which is to decrease the number of people who abuse and experiment with illegal drugs. In deciding to produce more or less illegal drugs, such as marijuana, the growers, like any other rational business, will compare the marginal benefit with the marginal cost of its production decision. The government, by increasing the penalty assessed for those who are caught growing marijuana, is increasing the marginal cost of producing marijuana. In this way, the government is taking the "stick" approach in terms of creating an incentive to reduce the amount of marijuana that will be available to potential users.

If we apply the economic way of thinking to those individuals or consumers making decisions to use illegal drugs, such as marijuana, the effect of the new drug policy is not as clear. On the one hand, decriminalizing the use of small amounts of marijuana has the effect of reducing the marginal cost of consuming marijuana and serves as a "carrot" type of incentive to increase the use of marijuana. This, in turn, will result in potentially greater monetary gains for those who supply marijuana, thus increasing the marginal benefit associated with producing additional cannabis. It is possible that, lured by the increased demand to use marijuana, growers will decide to produce more marijuana under the new drug policy, despite the risk of larger penalties.

The Canadian government argues that its proposed drug policy will result in individual consumers reducing their use of marijuana for the following reasons: First, some of the $245 million that is part of the new drug policy will be spent on public education campaigns that focus on the serious nature of illegal drug use. Second, under the current law, where possession of small amounts of marijuana is a criminal act, in about half of all incidents in which law enforcement officers encounter individuals in possession of cannabis, no charge is laid, and so no penalty is assessed. Under the new policy, those caught possessing marijuana would be issued tickets assessing fines for possession of the illegal substance. The government is suggesting that the proposed drug policy will actually result in higher rates of enforcement of cannabis offences and therefore will discourage the use of this illegal substance.

In terms of the third goal of the proposed drug policy, listed above, many recent polls suggest that Canadians feel that the possession of small amounts of marijuana does not warrant a criminal charge. In these instances, the punishment far outweighs the nature of the crime. Being prosecuted and convicted in a criminal court bears a stigma that can have far-reaching consequences in an individual's life in such areas as job choices, travel, and education. Participating in the criminal court process can also involve personal upheaval. An alternative policy of issuing tickets bearing fines for possession of small amounts of marijuana would seem to be more in line with the belief that "the level of punishment should fit the nature of the crime."

For critical analysis:

1. This issue and application focuses on the production and consumption related to one industry in Canada, the cannabis industry. Is this a microeconomic or macroeconomic focus? Explain.
2. Classify each of the three goals of the new drug strategy as primarily positive or normative in nature. Explain your answer.
3. A scientific model contains assumptions, is a simplification of reality, and does a good job of predicting real-world phenomena. Describe how the economic way of thinking serves as a scientific model that explains criminal behaviour relating to the production of marijuana.
4. Explain the specific ways in which the new drug policy can operate to increase the marginal cost related to the individual consumer's decision to use marijuana.
5. How does this issue and application illustrate the process of policy analysis?

SOURCE: "Cannabis Reform Bill" Health Canada Online, May 2003. http://www.hc-sc.gc.ca/english/media/releases/2003/2003_34bk2.htm. Accessed Sept. 13, 2003.

SUMMARY DISCUSSION OF LEARNING OBJECTIVES

1.1 **Scarcity**. Scarcity refers to the condition that arises because human wants in terms of goods, services, and goals always exceed what can be produced with the available limited resources—land, labour, entrepreneurship, and physical and human capital.

1.2 **Defining Economics**. Economics is a social science that studies how people allocate limited resources to satisfy unlimited wants. Economics is usually divided into microeconomics, which is the study of individual decision making by households and firms in specific parts of the economy, and macroeconomics, which is the study of economy-wide phenomena, such as inflation, unemployment, and national income.

1.3 **Rational Decision Making**. Under the rationality assumption, the individual will employ resources in uses where the marginal benefit exceeds the marginal cost so as to maximize his or her own self-interest. Marginal cost is measured in terms of opportunity cost, which is the highest valued alternative that must be sacrificed to satisfy a want. A change in marginal cost or marginal benefit will change the incentives that an individual faces and will lead to a change in resource use decisions.

1.4 **The Scientific Method**. In using the scientific method, one makes assumptions, constructs models or theories, and tests these models with the facts. Models are simplified representations of the real world that make predictions that can be tested by the facts.

1.5 **Positive versus Normative Economics**. Positive economics deals with *what is*, whereas normative economics deals with *what ought to be*. Positive statements are of the "if... then" nature and are testable by facts. By contrast, normative statements are based on subjective value judgments.

1.6 **Economic Policy and Socioeconomic Goals**. Theories can help us identify how various policies affect socioeconomic goals, such as full employment, efficiency, economic growth, price stability, and equity.

PROBLEMS

(Answers to the odd-numbered problems appear at the back of the book.)

LO 1.1 Explain the meaning of scarcity.

1. Identify the factor of production that best relates to each of the following:
   a. a degree in engineering
   b. underground oil reserves
   c. the factor that earns profit
   d. a newly constructed pulp and paper mill
   e. the factor that earns wages

LO 1.2 Define economics and distinguish between microeconomics and macroeconomics.

2. According to Example 1–1, "The Economics of Web Page Design," what aspects of web design make it an "economic concern"?
3. Categorize the following issues as either a microeconomic issue or a macroeconomic issue.
   a. The national unemployment rate increases.
   b. The wage increases of nurses do not keep up with the wage increases of doctors.
   c. The price of cigarettes increases due to a tax imposed on cigarette manufacturers.
   d. The Canadian annual inflation rate exceeds the average annual increase in Canadian wages.
   e. The nation's total annual rate of production declines.
   f. In response to strong competition, a Canadian retail corporation files for bankruptcy.

LO 1.3 Describe how resource use decisions are affected by the rationality assumption, costs and benefits at the margin, and incentives.

4. In order to spend a winter in Victoria, B.C., Paul Dafoe rents out his Montreal condo, as well as his car, to a married couple attending university. Paul estimates that the total cost associated with his decision to winter in Victoria for the eight-month period is \$15 000. He calculates this total cost by adding the following costs: round trip airfare; eight months' rental fees for a Victoria condo; estimated total grocery, personal care, and entertainment expenses while staying in Victoria; and total rental car expenses incurred in Victoria. Is \$15 000 the correct marginal cost associated with Paul's decision to winter in Victoria? Explain.
5. Your bank advertises that cash withdrawals from your bank machine are "free" if you always keep a minimum monthly balance of \$5000 in your chequing account. In this case, are your cash withdrawals truly "free"? Explain.
6. According to Example 1–2, "The Opportunity Cost of Finding a Mate—Lower on the Internet?", what economic concept helps explain the popularity of online dating websites? Explain.

7. The mayor of a Canadian city justifies the construction of a beautiful new city hall on the basis of there being sufficient tax dollars available to pay for this project. Is the mayor's decision to construct the city hall a rational one? Explain.
8. Since health care is an essential service, all health-care services should be provided free of charge. Moreover, the government should continue to increase the resources to health care until all hospital waitlists across the nation disappear. Is this view consistent with making decisions at the margin? Explain.

LO 1.4 Explain the three key processes involved in the scientific method.

9. Give a refutable implication (one that can be tested by evidence from the real world) for each of the following models:
   a. The accident rate of drivers is inversely related to their age.
   b. The rate of inflation is directly related to the rate of change in the nation's money supply.
   c. The wages of professional basketball players are directly related to their high-school grade-point averages.
   d. The rate at which bank employees are promoted is inversely related to their frequency of absenteeism.
10. Consider the following statements on the basis of positive economic analysis that assumes *ceteris paribus*. List one other thing that might change and thus alter the outcome stated.
    a. Increased demand for laptop computers will drive up their price.
    b. Falling gasoline prices will result in additional vacation travel.
    c. A reduction in corporate income tax rates will result in more people working.

LO 1.5 Distinguish between positive and normative economics.

11. Identify which of the following statements use positive economic analysis and which use normative analysis.
    a. Increasing the minimum wage will reduce employment opportunities for young people.
    b. A teacher should earn a higher salary than a hockey player, as the teacher's job is far more valuable to society.
    c. Everyone should enjoy free access to dental care.
    d. If the price of admission to each NHL hockey game is reduced, there will be an increase in ticket sales for each NHL game.

LO 1.6 Describe the relationship among theories, policies, and socioeconomic goals.

12. Identify which socioeconomic goal(s) may be promoted and which goal(s) may be conflicted with, for each policy listed below.
    a. Policy: In order to provide free public-health services, the government severely taxes Canadian corporation profits.
    b. Policy: The government raises the rate of income tax on all employees. The extra tax dollars raised are used to compensate upper-income investors who were swindled by fraud schemes.
    c. Policy: The government increases the monthly benefits (payments) to those collecting welfare. These people immediately spend the extra income on new goods and services.
    d. Policy: The government levies a special tax on all luxury goods. The taxes collected are used to keep college and university tuition fees relatively low.

APPENDIX A

READING AND WORKING WITH GRAPHS

Independent variable A variable whose value is determined independently of, or outside, the equation under study.

Dependent variable A variable whose value changes according to changes in the value of one or more independent variables.

A graph is a visual representation of the relationship between variables. In this appendix, we will stick to just two variables: an **independent variable**, which can change freely in value, and a **dependent variable**, which changes only as a result of changes in the value of the independent variable. For example, if nothing else is changing in your life, your weight depends on the amount of food you eat. Food is the independent variable and weight the dependent variable.

A table is a list of numerical values showing the relationship between two (or more) variables. Any table can be converted into a graph, which is a visual representation of that list. Once you understand how a table can be converted to a graph, you will understand what graphs are and how to construct and use them.

Consider a practical example. A conservationist may try to convince you that driving at lower highway speeds will help you conserve gas. Table A–1 shows the relationship between speed—the independent variable—and the distance you can go on a litre of gas at that speed—the dependent variable. This table does show a pattern of sorts. As the data in the first column get larger in value, the data in the second column get smaller.

TABLE A–1

Gas Consumption as a Function of Driving Speed

Kilometres per Hour	Kilometres per Litre
70	11
80	10
90	9
100	8
110	7
120	6
130	5

Now, let us take a look at the different ways in which variables can be related.

Direct and Inverse Relationships

Direct relationship A relationship between two variables that is positive, meaning that an increase in one variable is associated with an increase in the other, and a decrease in one variable is associated with a decrease in the other.

Inverse relationship A relationship between two variables that is negative, meaning that an increase in one variable is associated with a decrease in the other, and a decrease in one variable is associated with an increase in the other.

Two variables can be related in different ways, some simple, others more complex. For example, a person's weight and height are often related. If we measured the height and weight of thousands of people, we would surely find that taller people tend to weigh more than shorter people. That is, we would discover that there is a **direct relationship** between height and weight. By this, we simply mean that an increase in one variable is usually associated with an increase in the related variable. This can easily be seen in part (a) of Figure A–1.

Let us look at another simple way in which two variables can be related. Much evidence indicates that as the price of a specific commodity rises, the amount purchased decreases—there is an **inverse relationship** between the variable's price per unit and quantity purchased. A table listing the data for this relationship would indicate that for higher and higher prices, smaller and smaller quantities would be purchased. We see this relationship in part (b) of Figure A–1.

Constructing a Graph

Let us now examine how to construct a graph to illustrate a relationship between two variables.

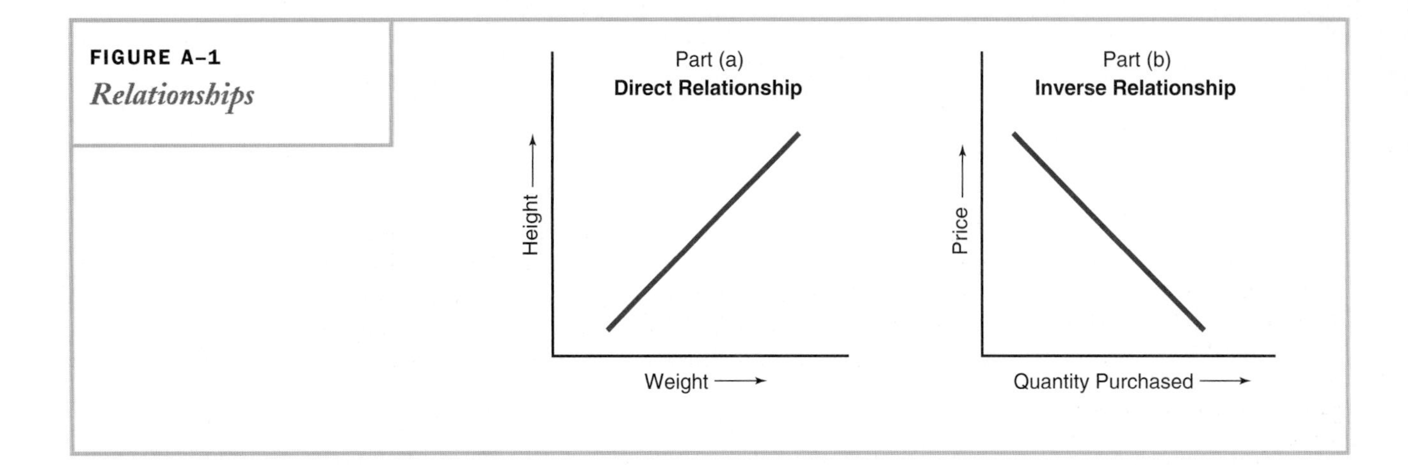

FIGURE A–1
Relationships

A Number Line

Number line A line that can be divided into segments of equal length, each associated with a number.

The first step is to become familiar with what is called a **number line.** One is shown in Figure A–2. There are two things that you should know about it.

1. The points on the line divide the line into equal segments.
2. The numbers associated with the points on the line increase in value from left to right; saying it the other way around, the numbers decrease in value from right to left. However you say it, what we are describing is formally called an *ordered set of points.*

On the number line, we have shown the line segments—that is, the distance from 0 to 10 or the distance between 30 and 40. They all appear to be equal and, indeed, are equal to 13 mm. When we use a distance to represent a quantity, such as barrels of oil, graphically, we are scaling the number line. In the example shown, the distance between 0 and 10 might represent 10 barrels of oil, or the distance from 0 to 40 might represent 40 barrels. Of course, the scale may differ on different number lines. For example, a distance of 1 cm could represent 10 units on one number line but 5000 units on another. Note that on our number line, points to the left of 0 correspond to negative numbers and points to the right of 0 correspond to positive numbers.

Of course, we can also construct a vertical number line. Consider the one in Figure A–3. As we move up this vertical number line, the numbers increase in value; conversely, as we descend, they decrease in value. Below 0 the numbers are negative, and above 0 the numbers are positive. And as on the horizontal number line, all the line segments are equal. This line is divided into segments such that the distance between −2 and −1 is the same as the distance between 0 and 1.

Combining Vertical and Horizontal Number Lines

By drawing the horizontal and vertical lines on the same sheet of paper, we are able to express the relationships between variables graphically. We do this in Figure A–4.

We draw them (1) so that they intersect at each other's 0 point, and (2) so that they are perpendicular to each other. The result is a set of coordinate axes, where each line is called an axis. When we have two axes, they span a plane.

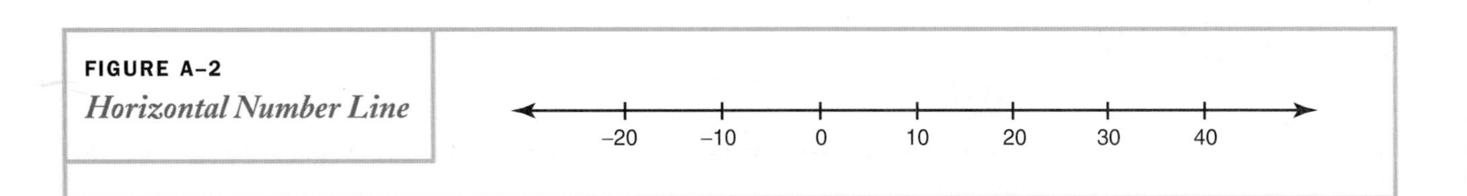

FIGURE A–2
Horizontal Number Line

FIGURE A–3
Vertical Number Line

FIGURE A–4
A Set of Coordinate Axes

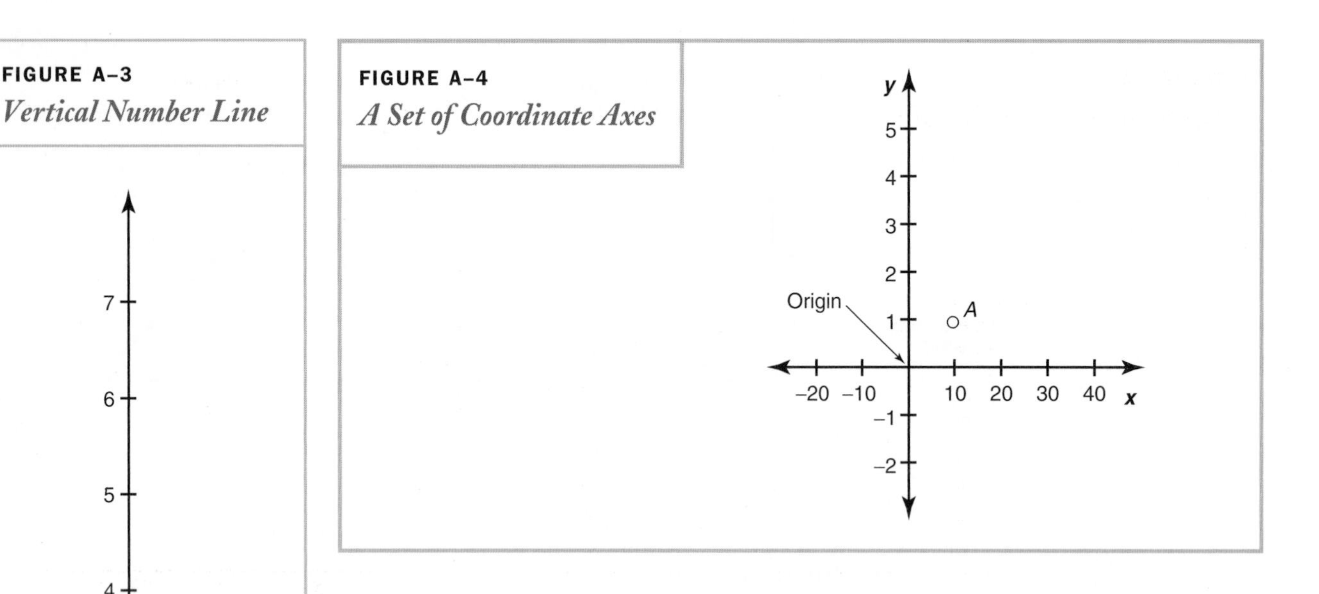

y-axis The vertical axis in a graph.

x-axis The horizontal axis in a graph.

Origin The intersection of the *y* axis and the *x* axis in a graph.

For one number line, you need only one number to specify any point on the line; equivalently, when you see a point on the line, you know that it represents one number or one value. With a coordinate value system, you need two numbers to specify a single point in the plane; when you see a single point on a graph, you know that it represents two numbers or two values.

The basic things that you should know about a coordinate number system are that the vertical number line is referred to as the ***y*-axis**, the horizontal number line is referred to as the ***x*-axis**, and the point of intersection of the two lines is referred to as the **origin.**

Any point such as *A* in Figure A–4 represents two numbers—a value of *x* and a value of *y*. But we know more than that; we also know that point *A* represents a positive value of *y* because it is above the *x*-axis, and we know that it represents a positive value of *x* because it is to the right of the *y*-axis.

Point *A* represents a "paired observation" of the variables *x* and *y*; in particular, in Figure A–4, *A* represents an observation of the pair of values $x = 10$ and $y = 1$. Every point in the coordinate system corresponds to a paired observation of *x* and *y*, which can be simply written (x, y)—the *x*-value is always specified first, then the *y*-value. When we give the values associated with the position of point *A* in the coordinate number system, we are, in effect, giving the coordinates of that point. *A*'s coordinates are $x = 10$, $y = 1$, or (10, 1).

Graphing Numbers in a Table

Consider Table A–2. Column 1 shows different prices for T-shirts, and column 2 gives the number of T-shirts purchased per week at these prices. Note the pattern of these numbers. As the price of a T-shirt falls, the number of T-shirts purchased per week increases. Therefore, an inverse relationship exists between these two variables, and as soon as we represent it on a graph, you will be able to see the relationship. We can graph this relationship using a coordinate number system—a vertical and a horizontal number line for each of these two variables. Such a graph is shown in part (b) of Figure A–5.

TABLE A–2
T-Shirts Purchased

(1) Price of a T-Shirt	(2) Number of T-Shirts Purchased per Week
$10	20
9	30
8	40
7	50
6	60
5	70

FIGURE A–5
Graphing the Relationship between T-Shirts Purchased and Price

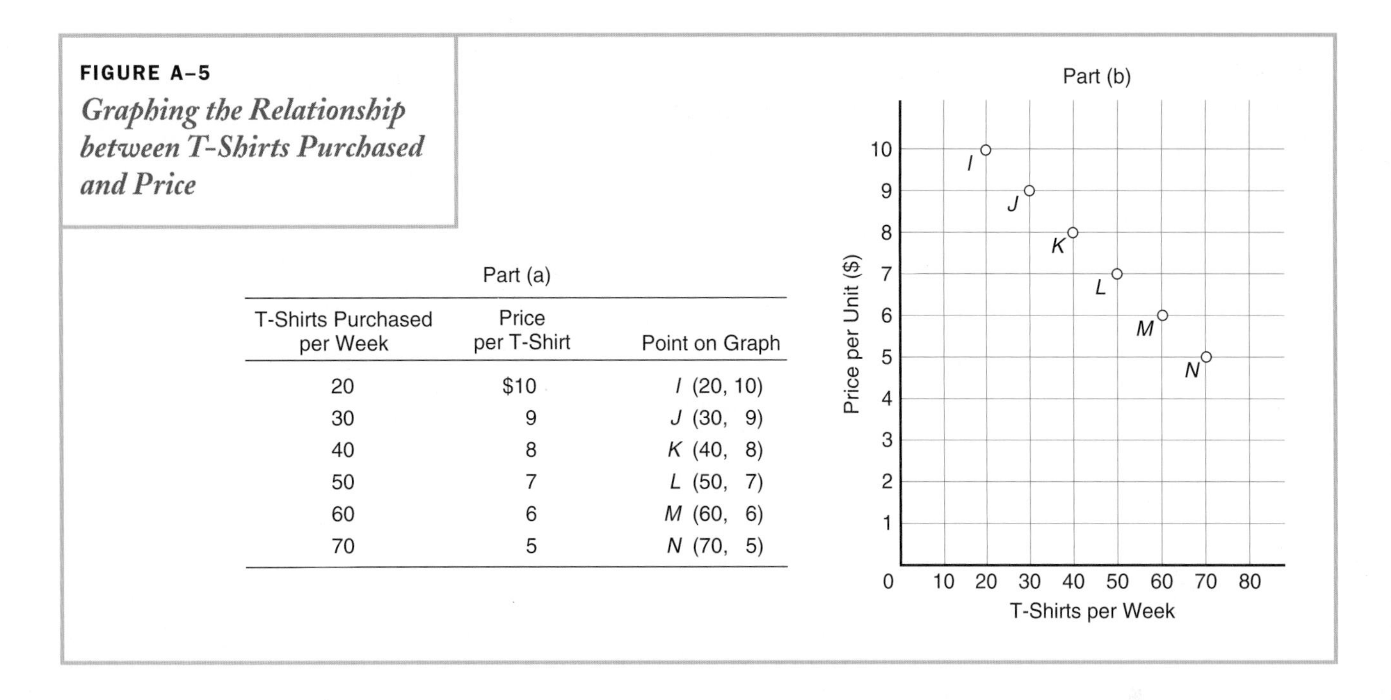

Part (a)

T-Shirts Purchased per Week	Price per T-Shirt	Point on Graph
20	$10	*I* (20, 10)
30	9	*J* (30, 9)
40	8	*K* (40, 8)
50	7	*L* (50, 7)
60	6	*M* (60, 6)
70	5	*N* (70, 5)

In economics, it is conventional to put dollar values on the *y*-axis. We therefore construct a vertical number line for price and a horizontal number line, the *x*-axis, for quantity of T-shirts purchased per week. The resulting coordinate system allows the plotting of each of the paired observation points; in part (a), we repeat Table A–2, with a column added expressing these points in paired-data (x, y) form. For example, point *J* is the paired observation (30, 9). It indicates that when the price of a T-shirt is \$9, 30 will be purchased per week.

If it were possible to sell parts of a T-shirt ($\frac{1}{2}$ or $\frac{1}{20}$ shirt), we would have observations at every possible price. That is, we would be able to connect our paired observations, represented as lettered points. Let us assume that we can make T-shirts perfectly divisible. We would then have a line that connects these points, as shown in the graph in Figure A–6.

FIGURE A–6
Connecting the Observation Points

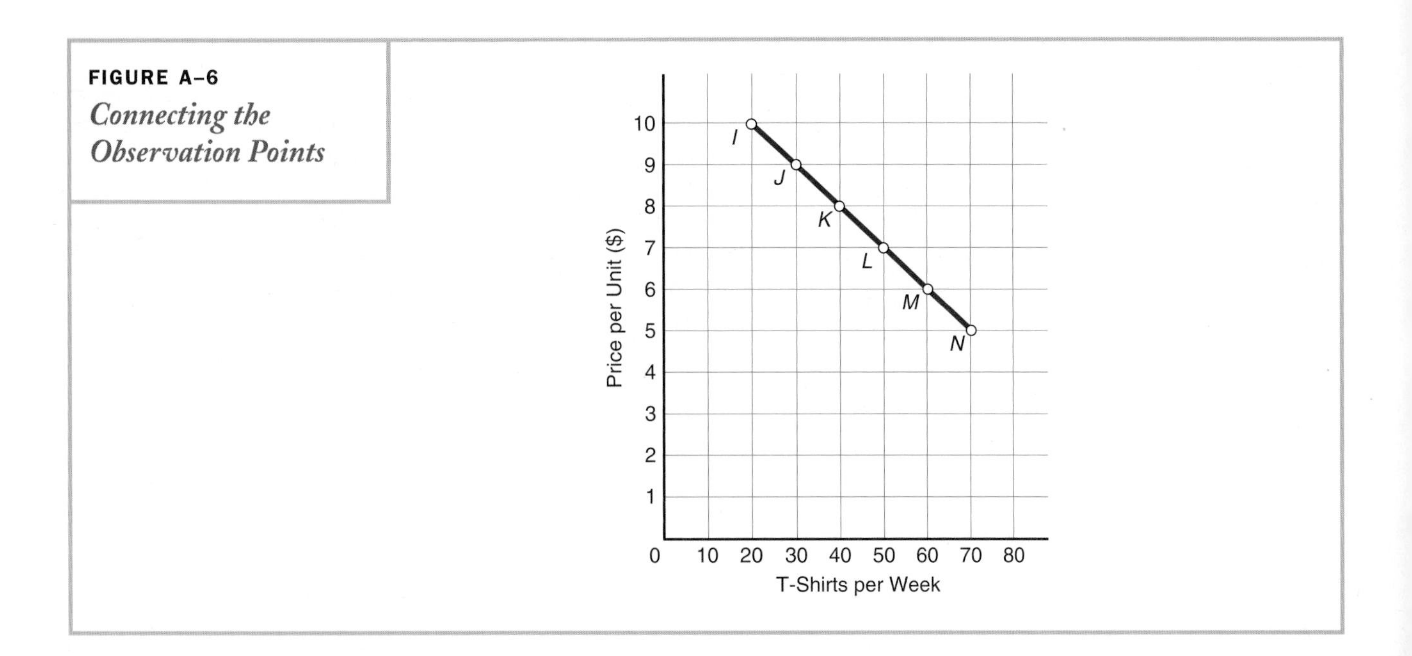

In short, we have now represented the data from the table in the form of a graph. Note that an inverse relationship between two variables shows up on a graph as a line or curve that slopes downward from left to right. (You might as well get used to the idea that economists call a straight line a "curve," even though it may not curve at all. Much of economists' data turn out to be curves, and so they refer to everything represented graphically, even straight lines, as curves.)

The Slope of a Line (A Linear Curve)

An important property of a curve represented on a graph is its *slope*. Consider Figure A–7, which represents the quantities of shoes per week that a seller is willing to offer at different prices. Note that in part (a) of Figure A–7, as in Figure A–5, we have expressed the coordinates of the points in parentheses in paired-data form.

The *slope* of a line is defined as the change in the y-values divided by the corresponding change in the x-values as we move along the line. Let us move from point E to point D in part (b) of Figure A–7. As we move, we note that the change in the y-values, which is the change in price, is +\$20 because we have moved from a price of \$20 to a price of \$40 per pair. As we move from E to D, the change in the x-values is +80; the number of pairs of shoes willingly offered per week rises from 80 to 160 pairs. The slope calculated as a change in the y-values divided by the change in the x-values is, therefore,

$$\frac{20}{80} = \frac{1}{4}$$

It may be helpful for you to think of slope as a "rise" (movement in the vertical direction) over a "run" (movement in the horizontal direction). We show this abstractly in Figure A–8. The slope is measured by the amount of rise divided by the amount of run. In the example in Figure A–8, and of course in Figure A–7, the amount of rise is positive and so is the amount of run. That is because it is a direct relationship. We show an inverse relationship in Figure A–9. The slope is still equal to the rise divided by the run, but in this case, the rise and the run have opposite signs because the curve slopes downward. That means that the slope will have to be negative and that we are dealing with an inverse relationship.

FIGURE A–7
A Positively Sloped Curve

Part (a)

Pairs of Shoes Offered per Week	Price per Pair	Point on Graph
400	\$100	A (400,100)
320	80	B (320, 80)
240	60	C (240, 60)
160	40	D (160, 40)
80	20	E (80, 20)

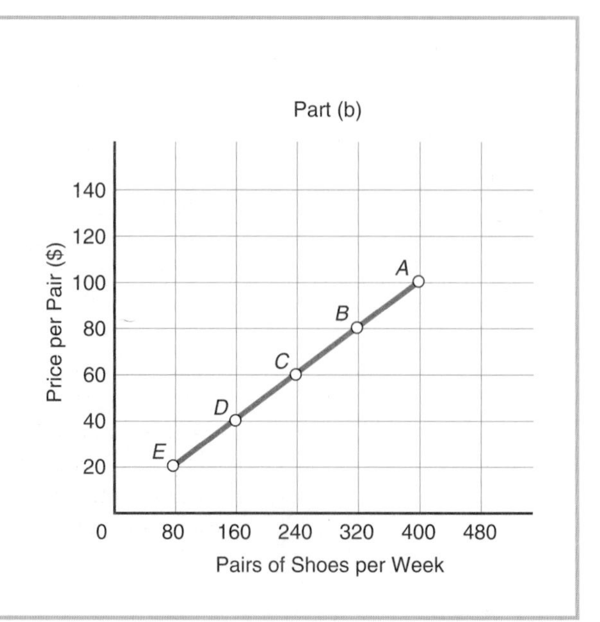

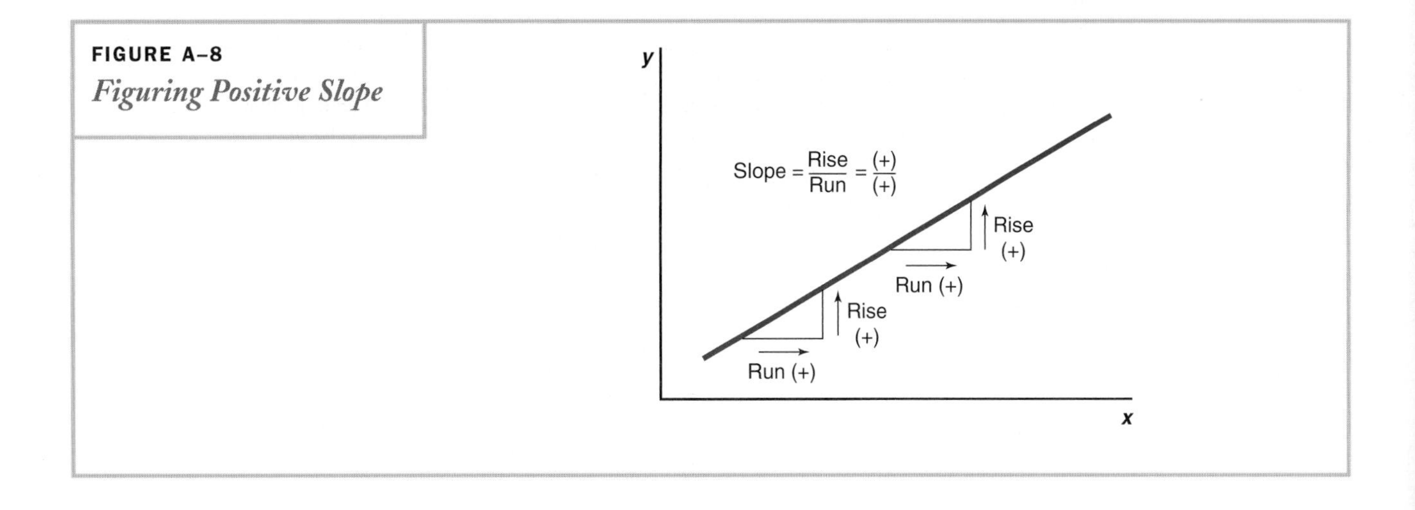

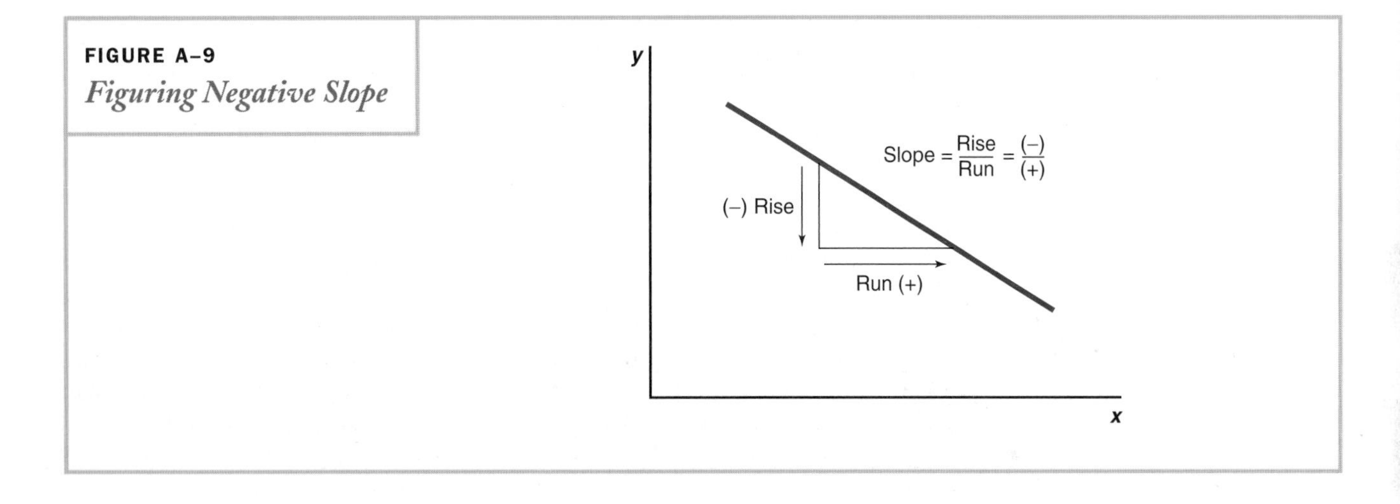

Now, let us calculate the slope for a different part of the curve in part (b) of Figure A–7. We will find the slope as we move from point *B* to point *A*. Again, we note that the slope, or rise over run, from *B* to *A* equals

$$\frac{20}{80} = \frac{1}{4}$$

A specific property of a straight line is that its slope is the same between any two points; in other words, the slope is constant at all points on a straight line in a graph.

We conclude that for our example in Figure A–7, the relationship between the price of a pair of shoes and the number of pairs of shoes willingly offered per week is linear, which simply means "in a straight line," and our calculations indicate a constant slope. Moreover, we calculate a direct relationship between these two variables, which turns out to be an upward-sloping (from left to right) curve. Upward-sloping curves have positive slopes—in this case, it is +1/4.

We know that an inverse relationship between two variables shows up as a downward-sloping curve—rise over run will be a negative slope because the rise and run have opposite signs as shown in Figure A–9. When we see a negative slope, we know that increases in one variable are associated with decreases in the other. Therefore, we say that downward-sloping curves have negative slopes. Can you verify that the slope of the graph representing the relationship between T-shirt prices and the quantity of T-shirts purchased per week in Figure A–6 is −1/10?

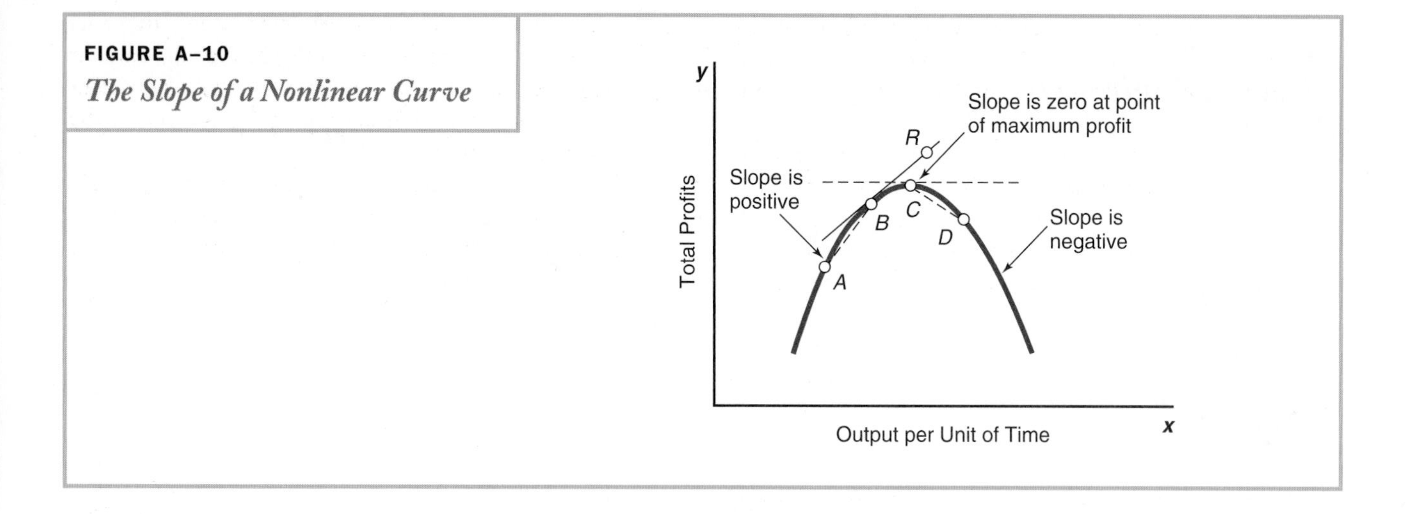

FIGURE A–10
The Slope of a Nonlinear Curve

Slopes of Nonlinear Curves

The graph presented in Figure A–10 indicates a *nonlinear* relationship between two variables—total profits and output per unit of time. Inspection of this graph indicates that at first, increases in output lead to increases in total profits; that is, total profits rise as output increases. But beyond some output level, further increases in output cause decreases in total profits.

Can you see how this curve rises at first, reaches a peak at point *C*, and then falls? This curve relating total profits to output levels appears mountain-shaped.

Considering that this curve is nonlinear (it is obviously not a straight line), should we expect a constant slope when we compute changes in *y* divided by corresponding changes in *x* in moving from one point to another? A quick inspection, even without specific numbers, should lead us to conclude that the slopes of lines joining different points in this curve, such as between *A* and *B*, *B* and *C*, or *C* and *D*, will *not* be the same. The curve slopes upward (in a positive direction) for some values and downward (in a negative direction) for other values. In fact, the slope of the line between any two points on this curve will be different from the slope of the line between any two other points. Each slope will be different as we move along the curve.

Instead of using a line between two points to discuss slope, mathematicians and economists prefer to discuss the slope *at a particular point*. The slope at a point on the curve, such as point *B* in the graph in Figure A–10, is the slope of a line *tangent* to that point. A tangent line is a straight line that touches a curve at only one point. For example, it might be helpful to think of the tangent at *B* as the straight line that just "kisses" the curve at point *B*.

To calculate the slope of a tangent line, you need to have some additional information besides the two values of the point of tangency. For example, in Figure A–10, if we knew that the point *R* also lay on the tangent line and we knew the two values of that point, we could calculate the slope of the tangent line. We could calculate rise over run between points *B* and *R*, and the result would be the slope of the line tangent to the one point *B* on the curve.

APPENDIX SUMMARY

1. Direct relationships involve a dependent variable changing in the same direction as the change in the independent variable.
2. Inverse relationships involve the dependent variable changing in the opposite direction of the change in the independent variable.

3. When we draw a graph showing the relationship between two economic variables, we are holding all other things constant (the Latin term for which is *ceteris paribus*).
4. We obtain a set of coordinates by putting vertical and horizontal number lines together. The vertical line is called the y-axis; the horizontal line, the x-axis.
5. The slope of any linear (straight-line) curve is the change in the y-values divided by the corresponding change in the x-values as we move along the line. Otherwise stated, the slope is calculated as the amount of rise over the amount of run, where rise is movement in the vertical direction and run is movement in the horizontal direction.
6. The slope of a nonlinear curve changes; it is positive when the curve is rising and negative when the curve is falling. At a maximum or minimum point, the slope of the nonlinear curve is zero.

APPENDIX PROBLEMS

(Answers to the odd-numbered problems appear at the back of the book.)

A-1. Explain which is the independent variable and which is the dependent variable in the following examples.

a. Once you determine the price of a notebook at your college bookstore, you will decide how many notebooks to buy.
b. You will decide how many credit hours to register for this semester once the university tells you how many work-study hours you will be assigned.
c. You are anxious to receive your Economics exam grade because you studied many hours in the weeks preceding the exam.

A-2. For the following items, state whether a direct or an indirect relationship exists.

a. The number of hours you study for an exam and your exam mark.
b. The price of pizza and the quantity purchased.
c. The number of games your college basketball team won last year and the number of season tickets sold this year.

A-3. Complete the schedule and plot the following function:

$y = 3x$

x	y
4	
3	
2	
1	
0	
−1	
−2	
−3	
−4	

A-4. Review Figure A–4, and then state whether the following paired observations are on, above, or below the x-axis and on, to the left of, or to the right of the y-axis.

a. (−10, 4)
b. (20, −2)
c. (10, 0)

A-5. Calculate the slope for the function you graphed in Problem A-3.

A-6. Complete the schedule and plot the following function:

$y = x^2$

x	y
4	
3	
2	
1	
0	
−1	
−2	
−3	
−4	

A-7. Indicate at each ordered pair whether the slope of the curve you plotted in Problem A-6 is positive, negative, or zero.

A-8. State whether the following functions imply a positive or negative relationship between x and y.

a. $y = 5x$
b. $y = 3 + x$
c. $y = -3x$

CHAPTER 2

Production Possibilities and Economic Systems

High and soaring Canadian car insurance rates created havoc for politicians and consumers alike in 2003. The issue of skyrocketing auto insurance almost toppled the once very popular New Brunswick Conservative government during the summer 2003 provincial election. In October 2003, in his first speech as Ontario's new premier, Dalton McGuinty announced a freeze on Ontario auto insurance rates. Within days, the free-enterprise Alberta Conservative government followed suit with its own 18-month rate freeze.

The concepts presented in this chapter will help you understand the economic issues that have fuelled the public's outrage over auto insurance rates in Canada.

LEARNING OBJECTIVES

After reading this chapter, you should be able to:

2.1 Define the production possibilities curve and identify its assumptions.

2.2 Use the production possibilities curve to illustrate the concepts of scarcity, trade-offs, unemployment, productive efficiency, allocative efficiency, increasing opportunity cost, and economic growth.

2.3 Use the production possibilities curve to explain the trade-off between consumption goods and capital goods.

2.4 Distinguish between absolute advantage and comparative advantage and use these concepts to explain how specialization and trade can increase production and consumption.

2.5 Explain the differences between the pure capitalist, pure command, and mixed economic systems.

2.6 Describe the features of pure capitalism and explain how capitalism answers the three basic economic questions.

DID YOU KNOW THAT...

Identity theft is the fastest growing fraud in both Canada and the United States. Between 2000 and 2003, the annual identity theft complaints increased five-fold in North America. In the first nine months of 2003, the PhoneBusters National Call Centre received 8178 identity theft complaints by Canadian consumers reporting total losses of more than $14.1 million. This amounts to an annual increase of 113 percent over the losses reported in 2002 in Canada.

One hard drive stolen from a computer at a Regina data management company contained names, addresses, dates of birth, social insurance numbers, pension statements, personal records for workers' compensation, and personal applications for provincial government rebates for over 300 000 Canadian individuals. Thieves use this stolen information to gain unlawful access to personal bank accounts and credit cards and to fraudulently apply for loans. In economics, identity theft can be viewed as a form of capital investment undertaken by dishonest individuals, as explained in this chapter.

SOURCE: "PUBLIC ADVISORY: SPECIAL REPORT FOR CONSUMERS ON IDENTITY THEFT." MAY 21, 2003. THE DEPARTMENT OF THE SOLICITOR GENERAL OF CANADA. ACCESSED NOVEMBER 29, 2003. http://www.sgc.gc.ca/publications/policing/Identity_Theft_Consumers_e.asp; "STATISTICS ON IDENTITY THEFT." SEPTEMBER 2003. PHONE BUSTERS. ACCESSED NOVEMBER 29, 2003. http://www.phonebusters.com/Eng/Statistics/idtheft_canada_stats_2003.html; "IDENTITY THEFT IN CANADA." EXPOSITOR STAFF. BRANTFORD, ONTARIO. CANADIAN CREDIT CENTRE. FEB 1, 2003. ACCESSED NOVEMBER 29, 2003. ARTICLE CREDIT: COPYRIGHT 2003. THE LEADER-POST (REGINA) COPYRIGHT 2003, CANWEST GLOBAL COMMUNICATIONS CORP.

2.1 The Production Possibilities Curve

We begin this chapter by introducing an economic model called the production possibilities curve. We will use this model to sharpen your understanding of concepts discussed in Chapter 1, such as scarcity, choice, opportunity cost, efficiency, full employment, and economic growth. As well, we will illustrate how production possibilities can be expanded through specialization and trade. Finally, we will complete this chapter by examining the different economic systems that nations and industries can use to determine production possibilities.

Production possibilities curve (PPC) A curve that represents all possible production combinations of two goods that can be produced.

The **production possibilities curve (PPC)** is a curve representing all possible production combinations of two goods that can be produced under the following assumptions:

1. The nation's resources—land, labour, capital, and entrepreneurship—are fully and efficiently employed producing just these two goods (or services).
2. The production is measured over a specific period time—for example, one year.
3. The quantity and quality of resources used to produce these two goods are fixed over this period of time.
4. The technology is fixed over this period of time.

Technology Society's pool of applied knowledge concerning how goods and services can be produced.

Technology is defined as society's pool of applied knowledge concerning how goods and services can be produced by managers, workers, engineers, scientists, and craftspeople, using land and capital. You can think of technology as the formula (or recipe) used to combine factors of production. When better formulas are developed, more production can be obtained from the same amount of resources. The level of technology sets the limit on the amount and types of goods and services that we can derive from any given amount of resources. The production possibilities curve is drawn under the assumption that we use the best technology that we currently have available and that this technology does not change over the time period under study.

Production Possibilities Curve: An Example

Figure 2–1 describes a production possibilities curve for Canada for the two goods automobiles and newsprint for 2004 (the data in Figure 2–1 are hypothetical). We assume for the moment that automobiles and newsprint are the only two goods that can be produced in Canada.

FIGURE 2–1

The Society's Trade-Off between Automobiles and Newsprint

The production of automobiles is measured in millions of units per year, while the production of newsprint is measured in millions of tonnes per year. The various combinations are given in part (a) and plotted in part (b). Connecting the points *A–G* with a relatively smooth line gives the production possibilities curve for automobiles and newsprint. Point *R* lies outside the production possibilities curve and is therefore unattainable at the point in time for which the graph is drawn. Point S lies inside the production possibilities curve and therefore represents an inefficient use of available resources or unemployment.

Part (a)

Combination	Newsprint (millions of tonnes per year)	Automobiles (millions of units per year)
A	0	3.0
B	1	2.9
C	2	2.7
D	3	2.4
E	4	2.0
F	5	1.4
G	6	0

Part (b)

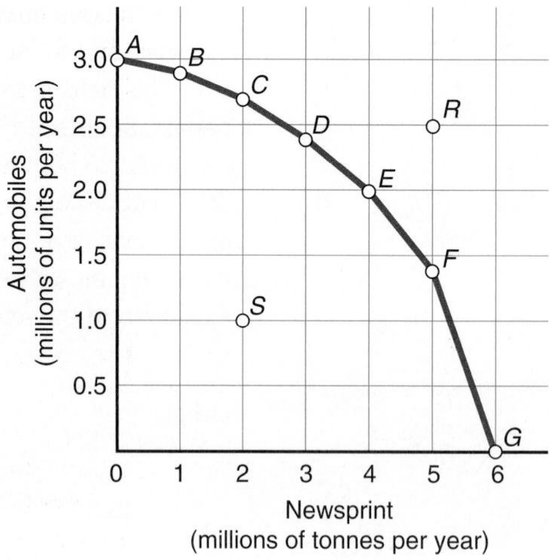

Part (a) of Figure 2–1 gives the various production combinations of automobiles and newsprint, assuming full and efficient employment of resources and a fixed level of resources and technology. If all resources are devoted to automobile production (point *A*), 3 million autos can be produced per year. Instead, if Canada decides to devote all her resources to newsprint production (point *G*), 6 million tonnes of newsprint per year can be produced. In between are other alternative possible production combinations. All of these production combinations are plotted as points *A, B, C, D, E, F,* and *G* in part (b) of Figure 2–1. Once these points are connected with a smooth curve, Canada's production possibilities curve is constructed.

Note that this production possibilities curve indicates the *maximum* quantity of one good that can be produced in 2004, given some quantity of the other good that is to be produced. Therefore, if we are given that 2 million autos are to be produced in 2004, then the maximum amount of newsprint that can be produced in 2004 is 4 million tonnes at point *E* on the curve.

2.2 Applications of the Production Possibilities Curve

We now turn to examine how we can apply the production possibilities curve model to better understand concepts introduced in Chapter 1.

The Production Possibilities Curve, Scarcity, and Trade-Offs

Recall from the previous chapter that *scarcity* refers to the condition that arises because wants always exceed what can be produced with limited resources. The production possibilities curve in Figure 2–1 can be viewed as a boundary that separates the attainable production combinations, on or inside the curve, from the unattainable points outside of the curve (such as point *R* in Figure 2–1). That is, even though we are assuming that the resources are being fully and efficiently employed using the most up-to-date technology, Canada faces a *limit*, in terms of what it can produce, as portrayed by the production possibilities curve. The existence of this boundary, in the face of unlimited wants, gives us a vision of the economic problem of scarcity.

The fact that the production possibilities curve slopes downward to the right suggests that due to scarcity, society is forced to make choices that involve trade-offs. In Figure 2–1 you can clearly see that if Canada is currently at point *E* in the current year, and chooses to move to point *F*, next year, when it can produce additional tonnes of newsprint, Canada has to trade off some automobile production. Note that trade-offs will occur anywhere *on* the production possibilities curve.

As a student, you face the scarcity problem of using a limited amount of time to achieve both your academic and personal goals. Every time you attend a class or a study group session you trade off the opportunity to spend that time learning in a different manner or engaging in a work- or leisure-related activity. As Example 2–1 illustrates, new technologies are changing the nature of the trade-offs students face when they consider whether they will attend their next class or choose the best alternative use of their time.

EXAMPLE 2-1 **Skipping Class without Skipping Lectures**

At Harvard University, there is a department called the Instructional Computing Group. Employees videotape about 30 courses per semester and place them on the university's internal website for students to review if they missed class.

Every student, naturally, has his or her own subjective estimate of the expected value of the next-best alternative to attending class. For each student, the value of an hour spent in class depends in part on what time of the day the class meets. Harvard's online lecture-review system permits students to reallocate the uses of their time. If a student would rather be in a rowboat on the Charles River at 1:00 on a spring afternoon instead of attending her Harvard economics class, she can miss the class. Then she can view the class lecture, say, at 5:00, when she rates the value of that study activity to be higher than her next-highest-valued activity for that hour of the day.

Of course, there is still an opportunity cost associated with skipping the actual class meeting. The student misses out on the opportunity to ask questions of her professor during the lecture and to interact with other class members. Nevertheless, there is evidence that many Harvard students prefer to reallocate their daily schedule in favour of virtual class attendance—professors in some of the courses with videotaped lectures have been increasingly concerned about noticeable drops in physical attendance in class meetings.

For critical analysis:

1. What opportunity costs (sacrifices) might you incur when you skip your classes?
2. In classes where group discussion or group work is an essential feature of the learning process, who bears some of the additional costs of higher absenteeism rates resulting from posting lectures on the Web?

The Production Possibilities Curve and Unemployment

Recall that full employment is one of the important socioeconomic goals identified in Chapter 1. Our simple production possibilities model helps us better understand the importance of this goal. Suppose in Figure 2–1 Canada failed to achieve the goal of full employment, where, roughly speaking, would Canada's production combination be located—inside, on, or outside of the production possibilities curve? The answer would be somewhere *inside* the production possibilities curve, such as point *S* in Figure 2–1. When Canada is inside her production possibilities curve, this clearly shows that a major cost of unemployment is that society forgoes some production of goods and services. That is, unemployment leads to a lower standard of living for society as a whole. If Canada were to eliminate this unemployment and move from point *S* to point *E*, would this involve a trade-off? The answer is no, as the extra production would be derived from putting unemployed workers back to work, allowing more of both goods to be produced.

The Production Possibilities Curve and Efficiency

The production possibilities curve can be used to define the notion of efficiency. Whenever the economy is operating on the PPC at such points as *A*, *B*, *C*, or *D*, we say that its production is efficient. Such points as *S* in Figure 2–1, which lie beneath the production possibilities curve, are said to represent production situations that are not efficient.

Productive efficiency Occurs when an economy is producing the maximum output with given technology and resources.

PRODUCTIVE EFFICIENCY. Efficiency can mean many things to many people. Even within economics, there are different types of efficiency. Here, we are discussing efficiency in production, or **productive efficiency**, which occurs when an economy is producing the maximum output with given technology and resources.

A simple commonsense definition of productive efficiency is getting the most out of what we have as an economy. Clearly, we are not getting the most out of what we have if we are at point *S* in part (b) of Figure 2–1. We can move from point *S* to, say, point *C*, thereby increasing the total quantity of automobiles produced without any decrease in the total quantity of newsprint produced. We can move from point *S* to point *E*, for example, and have both more automobilies and more newsprint. Point *S* is called a **productively inefficient point**, which is defined as any point below the production possibilities curve, assuming resources are fully employed.

Productively inefficient point Any point below the production possibilities curve, assuming resources are fully employed.

Allocative efficiency Producing the mix of goods and services most valued by consumers.

ALLOCATIVE EFFICIENCY. The concept of **allocative efficiency** is concerned with producing the mix of goods and services most valued by consumers. While all of the points along the production possibilities curve in Figure 2–1 are productively efficient, only one production combination on this curve will be allocatively efficient. Suppose that point *E* in Figure 2–1 part (b) is the most highly valued combination. If Canada ends up producing this combination, it is being allocatively efficient.

Stated in terms of the concepts learned in Chapter 1, if society were to move away from point *E,* in either direction, the marginal benefit derived from this move would be less than the marginal cost associated with this move. In other words, the extra value derived from producing a different combination of cars and newsprint would be less than the value given up by departing from point *E*. If the firms that produce these goods make decisions on the basis of society's marginal benefits and marginal costs, rational behaviour has the potential to lead us to this allocatively efficient production combination.

In this chapter's Issues and Applications, the merits of providing auto insurance via privately owned companies is compared with the merits of having the government administer auto insurance in Canada. One of the advantages of private auto insurance is that each injured individual can take the necessary legal action to ensure that the dollar value of the compensation resulting from an accident claim (marginal benefit) is sufficient to cover the full marginal cost related to the individual's injuries and losses sustained from the accident. In this way, private auto insurance promotes allocative efficiency. In contrast, under public auto insurance, the government dictates the maximum insurance payouts to injured parties for claims, such as those relating to the pain and suffering incurred in an accident. Since these maximum payouts are often set in a manner that attempts to reduce the total cost of these claims, the public insurance system may tend to underallocate resources in the payment of claims to injured individuals.

Policy Example 2–1 describes recent policy decisions made by the government of British Columbia that affect the production combination of two highly valued types of goods—natural wilderness area-related goods and oil- and gas-related goods. This example encourages you to use the goal of allocative efficiency to evaluate policies that affect the way in which our resources are used.

POLICY EXAMPLE 2–1 **The Multibillion Dollar Park**

In October 1997, the British Columbia NDP government established the Muskwa Kechika land-use area, a wilderness area larger than Switzerland, located in the northeast part of the province. In 2000, more land was added, bringing the total Muskwa Kechika Management Area (M-KMA) to 6.3 million hectares, which made it the largest land-use decision of its kind in North America. Rich in untouched beauty, natural resources, and abundant animal life, the M-KMA remains one of North America's last true wilderness spots south of the 60th parallel.

The management intent for the M-KMA is to maintain in perpetuity the wilderness quality, the diversity and abundance of wildlife, and the ecosystems on which the wildlife depends. One of the primary challenges is to be able to prevent corporate interests from exploiting the region's natural resources by engaging in logging, oil and gas drilling, and mining practices that would jeopardize the area's natural beauty and wildlife. Indeed, natural resource exploration and production have already been prohibited on 1.1 million hectares of M-KMA designated parkland.

On June 25, 2003, the British Columbia Liberal government announced that it would allow exploration of extensive natural gas deposits, with a potential development value of $16 billion, in parts of the M-KMA.

For critical analysis: Explain the trade-off that is illustrated in this example. Using the concepts of marginal cost and benefit, discuss whether the policy decision to open up parts of the M-KMA to oil and gas exploration promotes allocative efficiency.

SOURCES: " PRE-TENURE PLANS OPEN MUSKWA-KECHIKA TO GAS EXPLORATION." NEWS RELEASES, MINISTRY OF SUSTAINABLE RESOURCE MANAGEMENT, GOVERNMENT OF BRITISH COLUMBIA. JUNE 25, 2003. ACCESSED NOVEMBER 9, 2003. http://www2.news.gov.bc.ca/nrm_news_releases/2003SRM0011-000604.htm; "MUSKWA-KECHIKA MANAGEMENT AREA." RESOURCE MANAGEMENT DIVISION, MINISTRY OF SUSTAINABLE RESOURCE MANAGEMENT, GOVERNMENT OF BRITISH COLUMBIA. JULY 23, 2003. ACCESSED NOVEMBER 9, 2003. http://srmwww.gov.bc.ca/rmd/lrmp/mk/; "CORPORATE SPECIAL INTERESTS TO DOMINATE MANAGEMENT OF LARGEST PROTECTED AREA IN NORTH AMERICA." CREATIVE RESISTANCE. APRIL 11, 2002. ACCESSED NOVEMBER 9, 2003. http://www.creativeresistance.ca/awareness/april11-2002-muskwa-kechika-management-area.htm.

The Production Possibilities Curve and Opportunity Cost

We have re-created the curve in Figure 2–1 as Figure 2–2. Each combination, *A* through *G*, of automobiles and newsprint is represented on the production possibilities curve. Starting with the production of zero newsprint, Canada could produce 3 million automobiles with its available resources and technology. When we increase production of newsprint from zero to 1 million tonnes per year, we have to give up the automobile production represented by that first vertical arrow, *Aa*. From part (a) of Figure 2–1 you can see that this is 0.1 million autos a year (3.0 million − 2.9 million). Again, if we increase production of newsprint by 1 million tonnes per year, we go from *B* to *C*. In order to do so, we have to give up the vertical distance *Bb*, or 0.2 million automobiles a year. By the time we go from 5 million to 6 million tonnes of newsprint, to obtain that 1 million tonne increase we have to forgo the vertical distance *Ff*, or 1.4 million automobiles. In other words, the opportunity cost of the last 1 million tonnes of newsprint is 1.4 million autos, compared with 0.1 million autos, the opportunity cost for the first million tonnes of newsprint (starting at zero production).

Consider equal increments of newsprint production, as measured on the horizontal axis. All of the horizontal arrows—*aB*, *bC*, and so on—are of equal length (1 million tonnes). The opportunity cost of going from 5 million tonnes of newsprint per year to

FIGURE 2-2
The Law of Increasing Relative Cost

Consider equal increments of newsprint production, as measured on the horizontal axis. All of the horizontal arrows—*aB*, *bC*, and so on—are of equal length (1 million tonnes). The opportunity cost of going from 5 million tonnes of newsprint per year to 6 million *(Ff)* is much greater than going from zero tonnes to 1 million tonnes *(Aa)*. The opportunity cost of each additional equal increase in newsprint production rises.

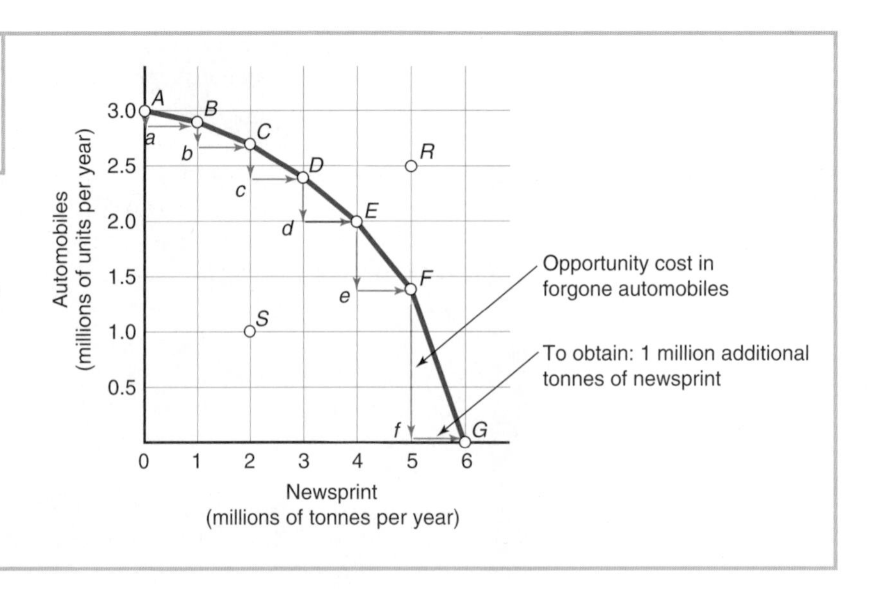

6 million (*Ff*) is much greater than going from zero tonnes to 1 million tonnes (*Aa*). The opportunity cost of each additional equal increase in newsprint production rises.

Law of increasing relative cost When society takes more resources and applies them to the production of any specific good, the opportunity cost increases for each additional unit produced.

LAW OF INCREASING RELATIVE COST. What we are observing is called the **law of increasing relative cost**: When society takes more resources and applies them to the production of any specific good, the opportunity cost increases for each additional unit produced. The reason that, as a country, we face the law of increasing relative cost (which causes the production possibilities curve to bow outward) is that certain resources are better suited for producing some goods than they are for others. Resources are generally not *perfectly* adaptable for alternative uses. When increasing the output of a particular good, producers must use less adaptable resources than those already used in order to produce the additional output. Hence the cost of producing the additional units increases. In our hypothetical example here, at first, the mechanical technicians in the automobile industry would shift over to producing newsprint. After a while, though, upholstery specialists and windshield installers would also be asked to help. Clearly, they would be less effective in making newsprint.

As a rule of thumb, the more *specialized the resources, the more bowed the production possibilities curve*. At the other extreme, if all resources are equally suitable for newsprint production or automobile production, the curves in Figures 2–1 and 2–2 would approach a straight line representing a constant opportunity cost situation.

As Example 2–2 explains, the land available to a town with established borders can be an example of a fixed resource that is fully employed and used with available technology along a production possibilities curve. As the example illustrates, deciding how to allocate a fixed amount of land recently posed a "grave" problem for a town in France.

EXAMPLE 2–2 **Making Death Illegal—At Least, Inside City Limits**

Le Lavandou, France, a Riviera community known for breathtaking views of a rocky coastline along a clear-blue section of the Mediterranean Sea, recently drew international ridicule when it passed a law that appeared aimed at regulating death. Specifically, the law stated, "It is forbidden without a cemetery plot to die on the territory of the commune."

continued

Of course, it is not possible for a law to prevent someone from dying inside a town. The purpose of the law was to indicate a permissible choice along a production possibilities curve. Land is a scarce resource with many alternative uses, and so trade-offs involving different productive uses of land arise everywhere on the planet where people establish communities. Le Lavandou is no exception. The town's cemetery had filled up, and the townspeople had to decide whether to allocate more land to cemetery plots, providing a service for deceased individuals and for their family and friends, or to continue allocating remaining land resources to the production of other goods and services. The point of the legal requirement was to emphasize that the town had decided not to incur an opportunity cost by allocating more space to cemetery plots.

Nonetheless, it was still true that someone who happened to die in Le Lavandou without first buying an existing cemetery plot was technically breaking the law.

For critical analysis: What is likely to happen to the opportunity cost of cemetery services as the world's population continues to increase and spread over available land resources?

The Production Possibilities Curve and Economic Growth

Over any particular time period, a society cannot be outside the production possibilities curve. Over time, however, it is possible to have more of everything. This occurs through economic growth. Figure 2–3 shows the production possibilities curve for automobiles and newsprint shifting outward. The two additional curves represent new choices open to an economy that has experienced economic growth. Such economic growth occurs because of many things, including increases in the quantity of resources available, increases in the productivity of existing resources, and changes in technology.

Scarcity still exists, however, no matter how much economic growth there is. At any point in time, we will always be on some production possibilities curve; thus, we will always face trade-offs. The more we want of one thing, the less we can have of others.

If a country experiences economic growth, the production possibilities curve between automobiles and newsprint will move outward, as is shown in Figure 2–3. This takes time and does not occur automatically. One reason it will occur involves the choice about how much to consume today.

FIGURE 2–3

Economic Growth Allows for More of Everything

If the country experiences economic growth, the production possibilities curve between automobiles and newsprint will shift out, as shown. This takes time, however, and it does not occur automatically. This means, therefore, that we can have more automobiles and more newsprint only after a period of time during which we have experienced economic growth.

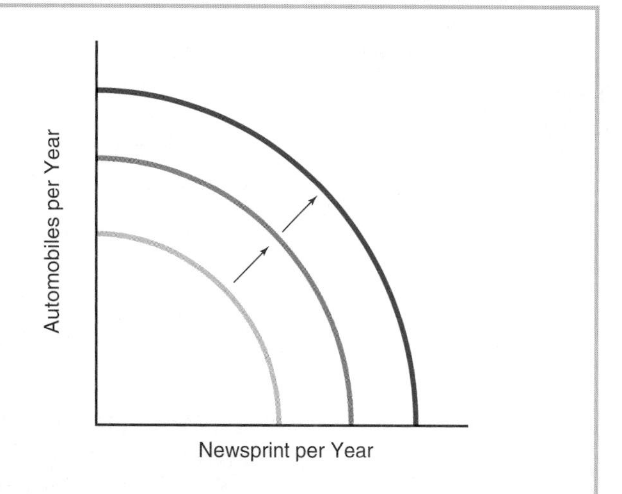

2.3 Consumption Goods versus Capital Goods

Consumption The use of goods and services for direct personal satisfaction.

The production possibilities curve and economic growth can be used to examine the trade-off between present consumption and future consumption. **Consumption** is the use of goods and services for direct personal satisfaction. These goods and services are what we call consumption or consumer goods—food, clothes, and entertainment, for example. And we have already defined physical capital as the manufactured goods, such as machines and factories, used to make other goods and services.

Why We Make Capital Goods

Why would we be willing to use productive resources to make things—capital goods—that we cannot consume directly? For one thing, capital goods enable us to produce larger quantities of consumer goods or to produce them less expensively than we otherwise could. Before fish are "produced" for the market, such equipment as fishing boats, nets, and poles are produced first. Imagine how expensive it would be to obtain fish for the market without using these capital goods. Catching fish with one's hands is not an easy task. The price per fish would be very high if capital goods were not used.

Forgoing Current Consumption

Whenever we use productive resources to make capital goods, we are implicitly forgoing current consumption. We are waiting until some time in the future to consume the fruits that will be reaped from the use of capital goods. In effect, when we forgo current consumption to invest in capital goods, we are engaging in an economic activity that is forward looking—we do not get instant utility or satisfaction from our activity.

At the start of this chapter, in the *Did You Know That* section, we noted the rapid growth of identity theft in Canada. Even an individual contemplating a theft faces a choice between increased current consumption versus increased capital accumulation. That is, instead of breaking into a home to steal a consumer item, such as a TV or stereo, the identity thief uses sophisticated electronic devices to steal the identity of others. While securing the identity of others does not, in itself, provide immediate self-gratification in terms of current consumption, it does allow the sophisticated thief the ability to enhance his or her future consumption through the fraudulent use of credit cards and debit cards. Just as a new machine can reduce the costs of a legitimate business, identity theft lowers the cost of engaging in illegal activity by reducing the probability of being "caught in the act." That is, identity thieves often acquire the personal data of others, without ever having any direct contact with the victims. Indeed, identity theft can be viewed as a form of capital investment undertaken by dishonest individuals.

The Trade-Off between Consumption Goods and Capital Goods

To have more consumer goods in the future, we must accept fewer consumer goods today. In other words, an opportunity cost is involved here. Every time we make a choice for more goods today, we incur an opportunity cost of fewer goods tomorrow, and every time we make a choice of more goods in the future, we incur an opportunity cost of fewer goods today. With the resources that we do not use to produce consumer goods for today, we invest in capital goods that will produce more consumer goods for us later. The trade-off is shown in Figure 2–4. On the left in part (a), you can see this trade-off depicted as a production possibilities curve between capital goods and consumption goods.

Assume that we are willing to give up $1 billion worth of consumption today. We will be at point *A* in the left-hand diagram of part (a). This will allow the economy to grow. We will have more future consumption because we invested in more capital goods today. In the right-hand diagram of part (a), we see two goods represented, food and recreation. The production possibilities curve will move outward if we collectively decide to restrict consumption each year and invest in capital goods.

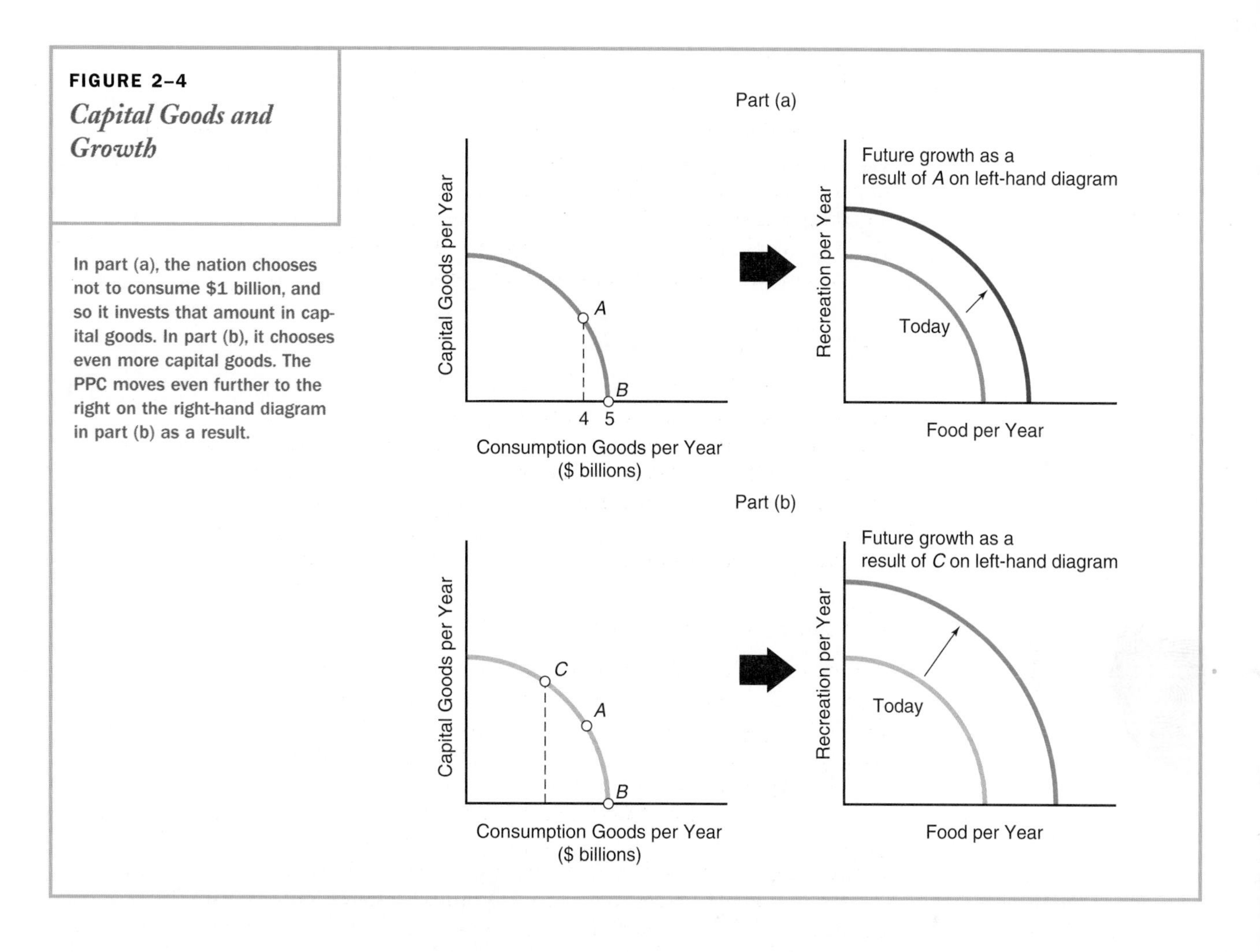

FIGURE 2–4
Capital Goods and Growth

In part (a), the nation chooses not to consume $1 billion, and so it invests that amount in capital goods. In part (b), it chooses even more capital goods. The PPC moves even further to the right on the right-hand diagram in part (b) as a result.

In part (b), we show the results of our willingness to forgo more current consumption. We move to point *C*, where we have much fewer consumer goods today, but produce a lot more capital goods. This leads to more future growth in this simplified model, and thus, the production possibilities curve in the right-hand side of part (b) shifts outward more than it did in the right-hand side of part (a).

In other words, the more we give up today, the more we can have tomorrow, provided, of course, that the capital goods are productive in future periods and that society desires the consumer goods produced by this additional capital.

At the individual consumer's level, one's decision to enroll in a postsecondary educational institution, on a full-time basis, entails a trade-off between additional capital goods and additional consumer goods. As we noted in Chapter 1, the decision to enroll in a college or university on a full-time basis entails the extra costs of lost employment income for eight months per year, as well as additional out-of-pocket costs, such as tuition, fees, and textbooks. These additional educational costs mean that the individual full-time student sacrifices some current consumption goods when enrolled in a postsecondary institution.

So, what does an individual gain when he or she purchases additional years of postsecondary education? Since postsecondary education is a form of human capital, the student should be more productive upon graduation and therefore should earn a higher level of income in future years. This means that the college or university graduate will be able to consume a greater quantity of consumer goods in the future. Example 2–3 examines whether the facts support the view that Canadian postsecondary education is a productive form of human capital.

EXAMPLE 2-3 Canadian Postsecondary Education Pays Off Big Time!

The table that accompanies this example indicates that Canadian college and university students can, indeed, look forward to a higher level of consumption upon graduation, and the future prospects continually improve as one accumulates even greater levels of postsecondary education.

In 2002, in Canada, an individual with a college diploma earned an annual average income of $33 130, which was $5922 in excess of the $27 208 annual average income earned by a high school graduate. An individual with a university bachelor's degree earned an annual average income of $41 501, which was $8371 in excess of the $33 130 annual average income earned by a college graduate. Finally, an individual with a university master's or doctoral degree earned an annual average income of $50 642, which was $9141 in excess of the $41 501 annual average income earned by a bachelor's degree graduate.

The accompanying table also presents annualized percentage rates of return for each of the three postsecondary education achievement levels for Canada for 2002. These rates of return are computed by utilizing a sophisticated compound interest formula to compare the extra annual income gained (marginal benefit) with the extra annual costs (marginal cost), including the extra forgone income, tuition, fees, and textbook costs, associated with each of the three levels of postsecondary education. The rate of return calculations in the table assume that a typical student enrolls in a postsecondary educational institution at 19 years of age and, upon graduation, works till he or she is 60 years of age.

As you can see from the accompanying table, the annual percentage rates of return are 12 percent, 14 percent, and 13 percent for a diploma, bachelor's degree, and master's/doctoral degree, respectively. The fact that each rate of return is positive implies that for each level of postsecondary education, the marginal benefit exceeds the marginal cost, making the investment a productive one. What is perhaps even more impressive is that each rate of return compares very favourably with other alternative investments available. In November 2003, a two-year term deposit of between $5000 and $100 000 at a typical Canadian chartered bank earned a mere 2 percent a year, while a 10-year term deposit for the same dollar investment earned just 3.375 percent per year. Clearly, an investment in postsecondary education in Canada pays off big time!

TABLE 2-1

Highest Level of Education Achieved	Canadian Annual Average	Annual Rate of Return in Percent
High School Graduate Salary	$27 208	
College Graduate Salary	$33 130	12%
Bachelor Degree Graduate Salary	$41 501	14%
Masters/Doctorate Degree Graduate Salary	$50 642	13%

SOURCE: "POST-SECONDARY EDUCATION PAYS OFF BIG—ESPECIALLY FOR ALBERTANS." MINISTRY OF LEARNING, GOVERNMENT OF ALBERTA, SEPTEMBER 8, 2003. ACCESSED NOVEMBER 8, 2003. http://www.learning.gov.ab.ca/news/2003/September/nr-PostSecPays.asp.

For Critical Analysis: Sketch two identical production possibilities curves for 2005 for the two goods—postsecondary education and current consumption goods. On the first production possibilities curve, show point *A*, which describes the production combination chosen by a 2005 high-school graduate who decides not to enroll in postsecondary education. On the second production possibilities curve, show point *B*, which describes the production combination chosen by a 2005 high-school graduate who decides to seek and obtain a bachelor's degree. For each of the two production possibilities curves, roughly sketch the appropriate 2020 production possibilities curve.

CONCEPTS IN BRIEF

Learning Objective 2.1: Define the production possibilities curve and identify its assumptions.

- The production possibilities curve describes all possible combinations of two goods that can be produced assuming (1) full and efficient employment of resources, (2) a fixed time period, (3) fixed quantity and quality of resources, and (4) fixed technology.

Learning Objective 2.2: Use the production possibilities curve to illustrate the concepts of scarcity, trade-offs, unemployment, productive efficiency, allocative efficiency, increasing opportunity cost, and economic growth.

- The production possibilities curve emphasizes that there is a limit to what can be produced, despite the fact that human wants are unlimited. This illustrates the scarcity problem.
- The downward-sloping nature of the production possibilities curve implies that more of one good results in less of the other desirable good, which illustrates a trade-off situation.
- An increasing opportunity cost situation is depicted by a "bowed-out" production possibilities curve. This occurs when resources are not equally productive when used to produce different goods.
- Unemployment is reflected in a production combination inside the production possibilities curve. This illustrates that unemployment results in lost production.
- Each production combination on the production possibilities curve is productively efficient in that each combination represents the maximum level of output that can be produced with a fixed amount of resources. Allocative efficiency is achieved when the nation produces the production combination, on the production possibilities curve, that society values the most.
- Economic growth is illustrated by an outward shift, over time, in the production possibilities curve.

Learning Objective 2.3: Use the production possibilities curve to explain the trade-off between consumption goods and capital goods.

- A production possibilities curve that involves capital goods and consumption goods illustrates that when we use more of our resources to produce capital goods and promote economic growth, we must forgo present consumption goods.

2.4 Specialization and Greater Productivity

Individuals and societies have sought to increase their production possibilities through specialization. **Specialization** involves working at a relatively well-defined, limited endeavour, such as accounting or teaching. Individuals, regions, and nations produce a narrow range of products. Most people, in fact, do specialize. For example, you could probably change the oil in your car if you wanted to. Typically, though, you would take your car to a garage and let the mechanic do it. You benefit by letting the garage mechanic specialize in changing the oil and in completing other repairs on your car. The specialist has all the proper equipment to do the work and will likely get the job finished sooner than you could. Specialization usually leads to greater productivity, not only for each individual but also for the country.

Specialization Involves working at a relatively well-defined, limited endeavour; individuals, regions, and nations produce a narrow range of products.

Absolute Advantage

Specialization occurs because different individuals and different nations have different skills. Sometimes, it seems that some individuals are better at doing everything than anyone else and are said to have an **absolute advantage**, the ability to perform a task using the fewest number of labour hours. A president of a large company might be able to type better than any of the typists, file better than any of the file clerks, and wash windows

Absolute advantage The ability to perform a task using the fewest number of labour hours.

better than any of the window washers. The president has an absolute advantage in all of these endeavours— by using fewer labour hours for each task than anyone else in the company. The president does not, however, spend time doing those other activities. Why not? Because a president is paid the most for undertaking managerial duties and specializes in that one particular task despite having an absolute advantage in all tasks. Indeed, absolute advantage is irrelevant in predicting how the president's time is spent; only *comparative advantage* matters.

Comparative Advantage

Comparative advantage The ability to perform an activity at the lowest opportunity cost.

Comparative advantage is the ability to perform an activity at the lowest opportunity cost. You have a comparative advantage in one activity whenever you have the lowest opportunity cost of performing that activity. Take the example of a lawyer and her secretary who can both review law cases and type legal opinions. Suppose the lawyer can review two law cases or type one legal opinion in one hour. At the same time, her secretary can review one law case or type one legal opinion in one hour. Here, the lawyer has an absolute advantage in reviewing law cases and seemingly is just as good as her secretary at typing legal opinions. Is there any reason for the lawyer and her secretary to "trade"? The answer is yes, because such trading will lead to higher output.

Consider the scenario of no trading. Assume that during each eight-hour day, the lawyer and her secretary devote half of their day to reviewing law cases and half to typing legal opinions. The lawyer would review eight law cases (4 hours $\times$ 2 per hour) and type four legal opinions (4×1). During that same period, the secretary would review four law cases (4×1) and type four legal opinions (4×1). Each day the combined output for the lawyer and her secretary would be 12 reviewed law cases and eight typed legal opinions.

If the lawyer specialized only in reviewing law cases and her secretary specialized only in typing legal opinions, their combined output would rise to 16 reviewed law cases (8×2) and eight typed legal opinions (8×1). Overall, production would increase by four law cases per day.

The lawyer has a comparative advantage in reviewing cases. In the time it takes her to review one case ($\frac{1}{2}$ hour) she could have typed one-half of a legal opinion. Her opportunity cost of reviewing the law case is therefore one-half of a legal opinion. The secretary, however, gives up typing an entire legal opinion each time she reviews a case. Since the lawyer's opportunity cost of reviewing law cases is less than her secretary's, she has the comparative advantage in reviewing law cases. See if you can work out why the secretary has a comparative advantage in typing legal opinions.

You may be convinced that everybody can do everything better than you. In this extreme situation, do you still have a comparative advantage? The answer is yes. To discover your comparative advantage, you need to find a job in which your *disadvantage* relative to others is the smallest. You do not have to be a mathematical genius to figure this out. The market tells you very clearly by offering you the highest income for the job for which you have the smallest disadvantage compared with others. Stated differently, to find your comparative advantage, no matter how much better everybody else can do the jobs that you want to do, you simply find which job maximizes your income.

The coaches of sports teams are constantly faced with determining each player's comparative advantage. Former Blue Jay Dave Winfield was originally one of the best pitchers in college baseball, winning the most valuable player award for pitching for the University of Minnesota Golden Bears in the 1973 College World Series. After he was drafted by the San Diego Padres, the coach decided to make him an outfielder, even though he was one of the best pitchers on the roster. The coach wanted Winfield to concentrate on his hitting. Good pitchers do not bring in as many fans as home-run kings. Dave Winfield's comparative advantage was clearly in hitting homers, rather than practising and developing his pitching game.

Scarcity, Self-Interest, and Specialization

In Chapter 1, you learned about the assumption of rational self-interest. It says that for the purposes of our analyses, we assume that individuals are rational in that they will do what is in their own self-interest. They will not consciously carry out actions that will make them worse off. In this chapter, you learned that scarcity requires people to make choices. We assume that they make choices based on their self-interest and attempt to maximize benefits net of opportunity cost. In so doing, individuals recognize their comparative advantage and end up specializing. Ultimately, when people specialize, they increase the money they make and become richer, as illustrated by Example 2–4.

EXAMPLE 2–4 **Why Men Marry: Is It for Love or the Marriage Premium?**

Earnings of married men are typically 10 to 20 percent higher than those of unmarried men. This wage differential between married and unmarried men is known as the "marriage premium."

It is likely that the efforts of these men's wives account for the marriage premium. If a wife devotes most of her time to managing the household, the husband has more time to devote to his job, which helps boost his earnings. The estimates displayed provide support for this idea. The figure shows that the marriage premium for husbands with stay-at-home wives is about 10 times as large as for husbands with wives who have jobs outside the home. If the trend toward more women with jobs outside the home continues, more men will have to devote their time to household activities, and the average marriage premium for men is likely to decline.

FIGURE 2–5 *Estimates of the Marriage Premium*

Married men with stay-at-home wives earn about 31 percent more than men who have never been married. Married men with wives who work outside the home full time earn only about 3 percent more.

SOURCE: HYUNBAE CHUN AND INJAE LEE, "WHY DO MARRIED MEN EARN MORE: PRODUCTIVITY OR MARRIAGE SELECTION?" *ECONOMIC INQUIRY* 39 (APRIL 2001), PP. 307–319.

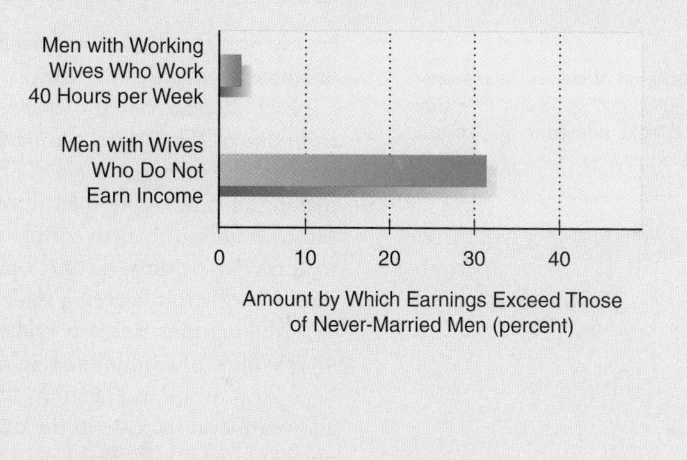

For critical analysis: How might you use the concept of specialization to explain the marriage premium? Explain.

Comparative Advantage and Trade Among Nations

Though most of our analysis of absolute advantage, comparative advantage, and specialization has dealt with individuals or firms, it is equally applicable to countries. First, consider Canada. The Prairie provinces have a comparative advantage in the production of grains and other agricultural goods. Ontario and Quebec in Central Canada tend to specialize in industrialized production, such as automobiles and newsprint. Not surprisingly, grains are shipped from the Prairies to Central Canada, and automobiles are shipped in the reverse direction. Such specialization and trade allow for higher incomes and standards of living. If both the Prairies and Central Canada were politically defined as separate countries, the same analysis would still hold, but we would call it international trade. Indeed, Europe is smaller than Canada in area, but instead of one nation, Europe has 15. What we call *interprovincial trade* in Canada is called *international trade* in Europe. There is no difference, however, in the economic results—both yield greater economic efficiency and higher average incomes.

Political problems that do not normally arise within a particular nation often do between nations. For example, if Nova Scotia crab fishers develop a cheaper method of harvesting crabs than fishers in British Columbia, British Columbia fishers will lose out. They cannot do much about the situation, except try to lower their own costs of production. If crab fishers in Alaska, however, develop a cheaper method, both Nova Scotia and British Columbia fishers can (and likely will) try to raise political barriers to prevent Alaskan fishers from freely selling their product in Canada. Canadian crab fishers will use such arguments as "unfair" competition and loss of Canadian jobs. In so doing, they are only partly right: Crab-fishing jobs may decline in Canada, but jobs will not necessarily decline overall. If the argument of Canadian crab fishers had any validity, every time a region in Canada developed a better way to produce a product manufactured somewhere else in the country, employment in Canada would decline. That has never happened and never will.

When countries specialize where they have a comparative advantage and then trade with the rest of the world, the average standard of living in the world rises. In effect, international trade allows the world to move from inside the global production possibilities curve toward the curve itself, thereby improving worldwide economic efficiency.

The Division of Labour

Division of labour Occurs when individuals specialize in a subset of tasks related to a specific product.

In any firm that includes specialized human and nonhuman resources, there is a division of labour among those resources. **Division of labour** occurs when individuals specialize in a subset of tasks related to a specific product. The best-known example of all time comes from one of the earliest and perhaps most famous economists, Adam Smith, who, in his book *The Wealth of Nations* (1776), illustrated the benefits of a division of labour in the making of pins: "One man draws out the wire, another straightens it, a third cuts it, a fourth points it, a fifth grinds it at the top for receiving the head; to make the head requires two or three distinct operations; to put it on is a peculiar business, to whiten the pins is another; it is even a trade by itself to put them into the paper."

Making pins this way allowed 10 workers without very much skill to make almost 48 000 pins "of a middling size" in a day. One worker, toiling alone, could have made perhaps 20 pins a day; therefore, 10 workers could have produced 200. Division of labour allowed for an increase in the daily output of the pin factory from 200 to 48 000! (Smith did not attribute all of the gain to the division of labour according to talent but credited also the use of machinery and the fact that less time was spent shifting from task to task.)

What we are discussing here involves a division of the resource called labour into different kinds of labour. The different kinds of labour are organized in such a way as to increase the amount of output possible from the fixed resources available. We can, therefore, talk about an organized division of labour within a firm leading to increased output.

CONCEPTS IN BRIEF

Learning Objective 2.4: Distinguish between absolute advantage and comparative advantage and use these concepts to explain how specialization and trade can increase production and consumption.

- Absolute advantage refers to the ability to produce one unit of a product at a lower labour cost than another producer. Comparative advantage refers to the ability to produce a unit of a product at a lower opportunity cost than another producer.
- With a given set of resources, specialization results in a higher output and, therefore, greater material well-being.

- Individuals must specialize in their areas of comparative advantage in order to reap the gains from specialization and trade.
- When individuals specialize in a subset of tasks related to a specific product, according to their comparative advantage, production is further enhanced. Such specialization is called division of labour.

2.5 Economic Systems

In the remainder of this chapter, we will study some of the established social arrangements that different nations use in choosing their production possibilities that, realistically, can include millions of goods and services being produced to satisfy the wants of millions of consumers.

Economic system The social arrangements or institutional means through which resources are used to satisfy human wants.

At any point in time, every nation has its own **economic system**, which can be defined as the social arrangements or institutional means through which resources are used to satisfy human wants. No matter what institutional means—marketplace or government—a nation chooses to use, the following three basic economic questions must always be answered because of the economic problem of scarcity.

1. *What and how much will be produced?* Literally billions of different things could be produced with society's scarce resources but not all at the same time. Some mechanism must exist that causes some things to be produced and others to remain as either inventors' pipe dreams or individuals' unfulfilled desires.
2. *How will it be produced?* There are many ways to produce a desired item. It is possible to use more labour and less capital or *vice versa*. It is possible to use more unskilled labour and fewer units of skilled labour. Somehow, in some way, a decision must be made as to the particular mix of inputs, the way they should be organized, and how they are brought together at a particular place.
3. *For whom will it be produced?* Once a commodity is produced, who should get it? In a modern economy, individuals and businesses purchase commodities with money income. The question then is what mechanism is there to distribute income, which then determines how commodities are distributed throughout the economy.

Not long ago, in response to the problem of scarcity, textbooks presented two extreme economic systems as possible polar alternatives for the industrialized nations to consider—the *pure command economy* versus the *pure capitalist economy*— in order to answer the three basic economic questions. Despite the fact that many countries have recently moved away from a command economy, it is appropriate to review both types of economic systems. This is because many informed citizens within Canada and other capitalist economies feel that elements of the command economy should prevail in the provision of important services, such as health care, education, and national security.

Pure Command Economy

Pure command economy An economic system characterized by public ownership of all property resources.

Public (government) ownership of all property resources characterizes a pure command economy. A **pure command economy** is an economic system characterized by public ownership of all property resources. The three basic economic questions—What, How, For Whom—are answered in a very centralized manner by government or the "state." Detailed five-year plans are formulated by the central authorities in order to respond to the three basic economic questions.

Until recently, such nations as Russia and China used the pure command economy to make their resource-allocation decisions. In the past, this type of system has typically been associated with nations practising communism or socialism.

Pure Capitalist Economy

Pure capitalist economy An economic system characterized by private ownership of all property resources.

In contrast to the pure command economy, a **pure capitalist economy** is an economic system characterized by private ownership of all property resources. Households and firms interacting through a system of markets answer the three basic economic questions—What, How, For Whom—in a decentralized manner. The pure capitalist economy goes by other names, such as *capitalism, market economy*, or *price system.*

Mixed Economic Systems

Mixed economy An economic system in which decisions about how resources are used are made partly by the private sector and partly by the public sector.

The pure command and the pure capitalist systems are extreme economic systems. Real world economies, which typically fall somewhere between these two extreme systems, are called mixed economies. In **mixed economies**, decisions about how resources are used are made partly by the private sector and partly by the public sector. As an example, Canada is referred to as a mixed capitalist system. This is because, while the majority of products are produced in the private sector, there are other goods and services provided by the government.

2.6 Capitalism in More Depth

Since there has been a global trend away from pure command economies toward capitalist economies, we will describe pure capitalism in more depth below.

Features of Capitalism

In elaborating on the pure capitalist economy, we will periodically refer to the Circular Flow Model presented in Figure 2–6.

Key features of pure capitalism include:

1. *Private ownership of resources:* Individual households and individual firms own the productive resources in pure capitalism. As described in Figure 2–6, households have two essential roles in capitalism—they supply resources to firms, and they demand goods and services with the income received from supplying resources. Firms, in turn, demand or hire resources in order to supply goods and services to households.
2. *Self-interest:* The primary motive underlying decisions made by households and firms in pure capitalism is the pursuit of self-interest. More specifically, firms attempt to maximize their own profit, when deciding what resources to demand or hire and what products to supply. Similarly, households are assumed to attempt to maximize individual wealth and other personal goals when deciding on where to

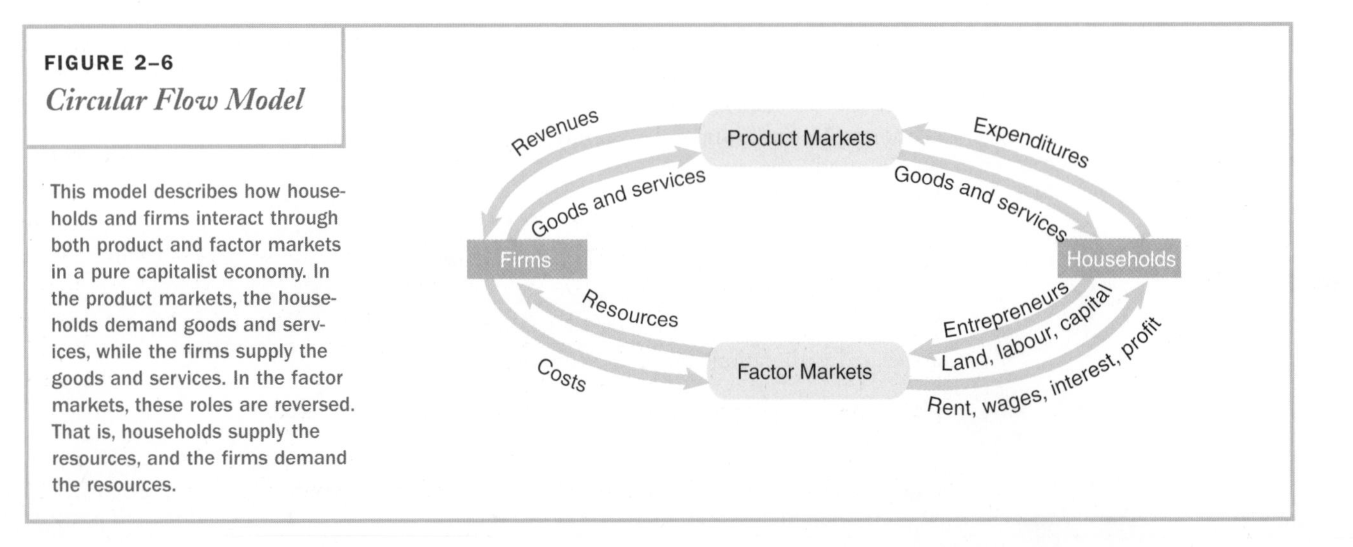

FIGURE 2–6
Circular Flow Model

This model describes how households and firms interact through both product and factor markets in a pure capitalist economy. In the product markets, the households demand goods and services, while the firms supply the goods and services. In the factor markets, these roles are reversed. That is, households supply the resources, and the firms demand the resources.

supply their resources. When demanding goods and services, households attempt to maximize self-satisfaction or utility.

3. *Consumer sovereignty:* The pure capitalist system is to serve the household in its consumer role. Operationally, this means that capitalism is to produce the mix of goods and services that consumers desire, at the lowest possible prices.
4. *Markets and prices:* The Circular Flow Diagram in Figure 2–6 indicates the two broad types of markets that exist in pure capitalism—product markets and factor (resource) markets. When consumer demand changes or resource availability changes, this sets off changes in relative prices in affected product and factor markets. These price changes ultimately reallocate resources in line with the change in consumer demand or resource availability. While we will examine how prices are determined in individual markets in the chapters that follow, we will provide a simple example below.

   Suppose that consumer demand for red wine increases and consumer demand for cigarettes decreases. Referring to the product markets in Figure 2–6, the price of red wine will increase, while the price of cigarettes will decrease. The higher price for red wine serves as a signal to firms that red wine is now relatively more profitable to produce than cigarettes.

   Driven by the profit motive, the red wine firms will increase their demand to hire resources, while the cigarette firms will decrease their demand for resources, to reduce their losses. Prices will now change in the factor markets in Figure 2–6. Prices (i.e., wages) of resources (i.e., employees) that engage in the production of red wine will increase relative to the prices offered to resources in the cigarette industry. Resources, guided by self-interest, will move out of cigarette production and into the production of red wine. Eventually, red wine production will increase. Note how this system of markets and prices operates to reallocate resources in line with changes in consumer demand, thus promoting consumer sovereignty.
5. *Competition:* In order to ensure that the self-interests of firms and resources work to the best interests of consumers, it is necessary that many independent sellers and buyers compete in each market. This will be more fully explained in the subsequent chapters of this text.
6. *Limited government:* To the extent that competition exists in each market, the "invisible hand" of self-interest will serve to promote consumer sovereignty. Hence, allocating resources to meet changes in consumer demand does not require the "heavy hand" of government. The French have termed this feature of capitalism **"laissez-faire,"** which means that the government should leave it (the economy) alone or "let it be."

Laissez-faire French term for "leave it alone"; the government should leave it (the economy) alone or "let it be."

One way to remember some of the important attributes of the market economy is by thinking of capitalism's **Three *P*s**: Private property, Profits, and Prices.

Three *Ps* Private property, Profits, and Prices inherent in capitalism.

Capitalism and the Three Economic Questions

Now that we have reviewed the essential features of pure capitalism, we can proceed to examine how this economic system operates to answer the three basic economic questions—What, How, For Whom.

WHAT AND HOW MUCH WILL BE PRODUCED? Since firms can enhance profits by producing what consumers are willing to buy, we can see that consumer demand plays an important role in deciding what goods and services are produced. In more formal terms, the profit motive and competition lead firms to promote allocative efficiency—that is, firms will produce the mix of goods and services most wanted by society. However, we must keep in mind that if the highest price that consumers are willing to pay for a good is less than the lowest resource cost at which the good can be produced, no profit will result, and none of this good will be produced. In other words, resource availability also plays a role in determining what goods and services are produced.

HOW WILL IT BE PRODUCED? The question of how output will be produced in a pure capitalist system relates to the efficient use of scarce inputs. Consider the possibility of using only two types of resources, capital and labour. A firm may have the options given in Table 2–2. It can use various combinations of labour and capital to produce the same amount of output.

TABLE 2–2

Production Costs for 100 Units of Product X

Technique A or B can be used to produce the same output. Obviously, B will be used because its total cost is less than A's. Using production technique B will generate a $2 savings for every 100 units produced.

		A		B	
Inputs	**Input Unit Price**	**Production Technique A (input units)**	**Cost**	**Production Technique B (input units)**	**Cost**
Labour	$10	5	$50	4	$40
Capital	8	4	32	5	40
Total cost of 100 units			82		80

Two hypothetical combinations are given in Table 2–2. How then is it decided which combination will be used? Under pure capitalism, the least cost combination (technique B, in our example) will be chosen by firms because it will maximize profits. In other words, in pure capitalism, competition and the profit motive encourage firms to achieve productive efficiency.

FOR WHOM WILL IT BE PRODUCED? This last question involves how households share in the consumption of the goods and services produced. This, in turn, is based on the distribution of money incomes and wealth among households. Households with higher levels of income and wealth will get to purchase and consume a greater portion of the goods produced in the economy.

What determines the distribution of wealth and money income among different households? This distribution is based on the quantities, qualities, and types of the various human and nonhuman resources that different households own and supply to the marketplace. Households that own large quantities of resources that are highly in demand in the marketplace will earn high levels of income.

It should be noted that many current debates regarding economic systems apply to individual industries within a national economy. The central question posed in this chapter's Issues and Applications is: "What economic system should be used to best provide auto insurance in Canada?" As this Issues and Applications section points out, different economic systems are currently being used to provide auto insurance in Canada, depending on the province one resides in.

As Policy Example 2–2 illustrates, Canadian school boards must choose from among different economic systems when providing education to our children.

POLICY EXAMPLE 2–2 **The Edmonton Revolution in Public Education**

The current Edmonton public school system has become a model for allocating limited educational resources in many public school districts in the United States. William Ouchi, the influential management studies professor at the University of California at Los Angeles (UCLA), in his 2003 book *Making Schools Work*, credits Edmonton as being the pioneer in delivering effective public education in North America.

The Edmonton revolution, as many are calling it, started a couple of decades ago, when, like other current school systems, all key decisions governing the use of resources in education were made by the central office of the school district. School boundaries were set by the central office, and parents had no choice but to have their children attend their neighbourhood school. The type of education offered in each school was fairly uniform throughout the district. If a teacher or school principal wanted something done, he or she had to win approval from a number of different departments at the central office. For instance, a school would go to the library specialist at the central office for books but had to go to the finance department to pay for them, and to the maintenance department for

continued

shelving. Anywhere along the way, someone could kill a request. Worst of all was the endless waiting for decisions. No wonder the parents and teachers started to turn toward private schools.

After the revolution, an open-boundary, school-based budgeting model emerged in the Edmonton Public School District. In the current Edmonton model, resource-use decisions have been decentralized so that principals and teachers at the school level control 92 percent of the district budget. School boundaries are now open so that parents can choose to send their children to schools anywhere in the district, room permitting.

A certain amount of budget dollars is now allocated to each student. If a school is successful in attracting additional students, it receives these additional budget dollars. As a result, different schools have focused on offering different alternative programs that meet the needs and wishes of children and parents. The 81 000-student Edmonton Public School District now has 29 alternative programs located at 80 of the board's 200 plus schools, with programs for ballet, hockey, soccer, Mandarin, Arabic, Spanish, performing arts, International Baccalaureate, Aboriginal culture, girls only, and numerous types of religious education. Since introducing this new model, Edmonton Public School District has gained students, while private school enrollment has shrunk.

For critical analysis:

1. What economic system, studied in this chapter, best relates to the way in which educational resources were allocated in Edmonton Public before the revolution?
2. What features of capitalism do you see in the current Edmonton Public School District model?

SOURCE: DAVID STAPLES, "THE ABCs OF A SCHOOL REVOLUTION.". *THE EDMONTON JOURNAL*, OCTOBER 19, 2003. P. D6.

CONCEPTS IN BRIEF

Learning Objective 2.5: Explain the differences between the pure capitalist, pure command, and mixed economic systems.

- In a pure command system, the government owns the resources, and the three basic questions—What, How, For Whom—are answered in a centralized manner by government. In pure capitalism, resources are privately owned, and the basic questions are answered in a decentralized manner by individual firms and households interacting in markets.
- In a mixed economic system, there is some private as well as some public ownership of resources. In some sectors of the economy, the government answers the three basic questions, while in other sectors, individual households and firms answer these questions.

Learning Objective 2.6: Describe the features of pure capitalism and explain how capitalism answers the three basic economic questions.

- The key features of pure capitalism include private ownership of resources, self-interest motives, consumer sovereignty, markets and prices, competition and limited government. In short, think of the three *P*s—Private property, Profits, and Prices.
- In capitalism, consumer demand and resource availability determine what goods and services will be produced. Due to the profit motive, the least cost method of production will be chosen when deciding how the goods will be produced. Who gets what is based on each consumer's level of wealth and income. This, in turn, depends on the degree to which individual households own marketable resources, and the price of these resources.

ISSUES AND APPLICATIONS

Private or Public Auto Insurance: What Is Best for Canada?

Concepts Applied: Capitalist, Command, and Mixed Systems; Productive Efficiency; Allocative Efficiency; and Equity

Ontario NDP Leader Howard Hampton points to a map of Canada to show that the gap between Ontario drivers and drivers in public auto insurance provinces is growing wider during a campaign stop in Peterborough, Ontario in September 2003.

In response to public outrage over skyrocketing car insurance premiums, the Consumers' Association of Canada completed a comprehensive report on auto insurance rates in Canada in September 2003. In presenting the report, the association noted that government-owned or public auto insurance systems offer the lowest premiums for Canadian drivers.

Provincial Automobile Insurance Rates

Figure 2–7, taken from the report, compares the average annual auto insurance premiums among provinces, assuming the same insurance coverage, vehicle, driving record, and claims history. The average premiums are based on over 7000 rate quotes across Canada. All quotes assume an insurance coverage of $2 million liability, $500 collision deductible, and $300 comprehensive deductible. As you can see from this figure, the annual car insurance premiums are significantly lower in the provinces of British Columbia, Saskatchewan, Manitoba, and Quebec, where the mandatory insurance is provided by a government monopoly.

The Consumers' Association of Canada's report also noted the differences in the annual rate of increase in premiums between the private and public insurance systems in 2003. While premiums were escalating by up to 70 percent per year in the six provinces where privately owned insurance companies operate, Manitoba's publicly run auto insurance system was increasing annual premiums by only 7.2 percent.

SOURCE: REVIEW OF AUTOMOBILE INSURANCE RATES. CONSUMERS' ASSOCIATION OF CANADA. SEPTEMBER 2003, P. 5. ACCESSED NOVEMBER 11, 2003. http://www.cacbc.com/reports/CAC%20National%20Auto%20Rates%20Study%202003%20.pdf

To add fuel to the fire, in provinces offering private insurance, individuals can pay significantly higher premiums based on such criteria as age, gender, and marital status, regardless of the driving record or type of vehicle being insured. In New Brunswick, in 2003, older drivers who drove newer, much more expensive cars, and who had driving convictions, pay up

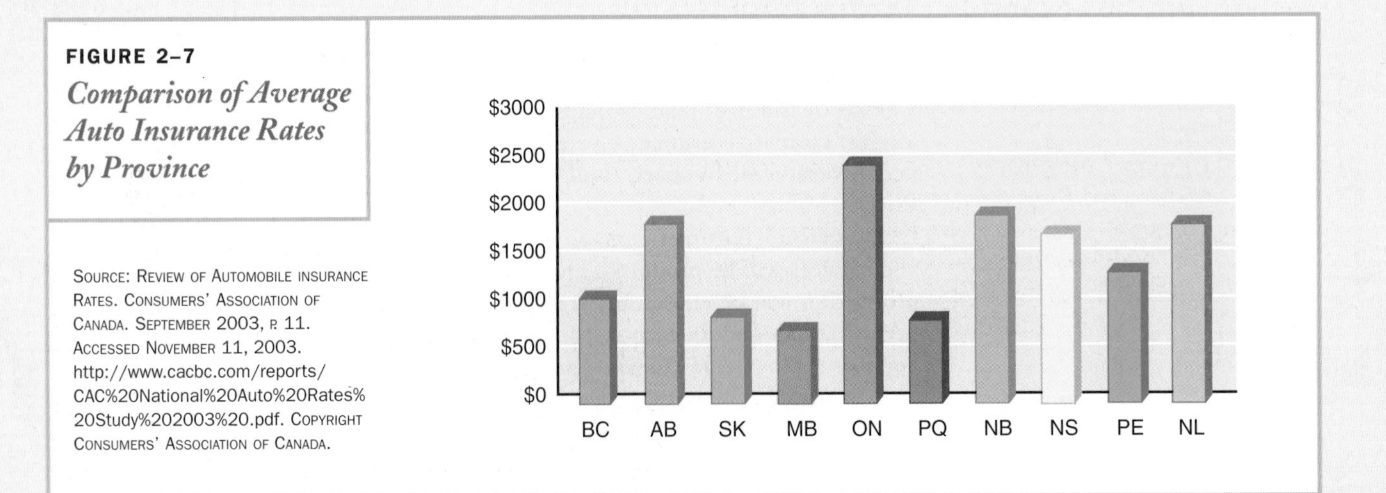

FIGURE 2–7
Comparison of Average Auto Insurance Rates by Province

SOURCE: REVIEW OF AUTOMOBILE INSURANCE RATES. CONSUMERS' ASSOCIATION OF CANADA. SEPTEMBER 2003, P. 11. ACCESSED NOVEMBER 11, 2003. http://www.cacbc.com/reports/CAC%20National%20Auto%20Rates%20Study%202003%20.pdf. COPYRIGHT CONSUMERS' ASSOCIATION OF CANADA.

to $2000 less for auto insurance, compared with young drivers with clean driving records. A 2002 Ford Taurus SE is more than $7000 cheaper for an 18-year-old male with a clean driving record to insure in Saskatoon's public insurance system than in Toronto or St John's, where private insurance companies operate. In provinces with public auto insurance, where rates are not based on age or gender, a young driver with a clean record pays a lower premium than an older driver with driving convictions.

SOURCE: AUTO INSURANCE RATE COMPARISON STUDY–JULY 28, 2003. CONSUMERS' ASSOCIATION OF CANADA. JULY 2003, P. 3. ACCESSED NOVEMBER 11, 2003. http://www.cacbc.com/reports/July%2028,2003%20Report%20Auto%20NB.pdf; SGI 2003 RATE COMPARISON PROFILES. ACCESSED NOVEMBER 11, 2003. http://www.sgi.sk.ca/sgi_internet/rates/2003_rate_profiles.html#.

Providing Auto Insurance: Two Extreme Models

To better understand the significant differences in automobile premiums being charged across provinces and across customers within the same province, we will first contrast the two extreme economic systems that are possible in the provision of car insurance.

Under the pure capitalist or pure market model, privately owned, for-profit insurance companies sell the mandatory auto insurance policies, and the claims are paid out according to a decentralized tort-based or fault-based system.

In a fault-based system, the injured party must first prove that the other party is at fault, and then the injured party can bring legal action for recovery of damages against the person who caused the accident. The claim for recovery of damages will typically include monies to replace lost wages, out of pocket expenses, medical expenses, damages to the vehicle, and an amount to compensate for the pain and suffering related to injuries sustained as a result of the accident. If the injured party and the party at fault cannot agree on the amount of the total claim, the matter will eventually go to court. The fault-based system awards damages in a very decentralized manner, as the amount of each accident claim is assessed on the merits of each individual situation.

At the other extreme, auto insurance can be delivered in a manner resembling a pure command economic system. In this model, the one government-owned Crown Corporation (public monopoly) provides all mandatory auto insurance for the entire province, and the claims are paid out on a pure no-fault basis.

In a pure no-fault system, one's own insurance company (or the government monopoly) pays for the damages that one incurs, regardless of fault. A comprehensive predetermined compensation schedule would dictate the maximum payment for specific types of losses, expenses, and injuries. In a pure no-fault system, one's individual right to sue for damages is eliminated.

The Advantages of Using the Command Model

It is interesting to note that Manitoba, the province that charges the lowest average annual auto insurance premiums, according to the Consumers' Association of Canada's study, operates an insurance system that most closely resembles the pure command model. That is, Manitoba Public Insurance (MPI), a government-owned monopoly, provides the mandatory car insurance, and the claims are paid out on a no-fault basis.

So, how can a pure command system result in lower auto insurance premiums when compared with the pure capitalist model? First, there are factors inherent in the public system that make it more productively efficient. Due to its no-fault feature, the system does not have to employ the expensive legal and court-related resources to establish fault and to establish the extent of the legal damages experienced by each injured party in each accident. As well, the amount of benefits paid out per claim to compensate an injured party for pain and suffering is significantly lower in the public system.

Since the government is the sole organization providing mandatory car insurance in the province, it does not have to employ resources to market its services to the customer. Moreover, as the sole provider, the public insurance organization is able to avoid the duplication in administrative resources that typically occurs when numerous private car insurance companies compete with each other in the same province. Because the public system can offer the same insurance coverage with minimal use of resources, it is able to keep its costs down and, in turn, charge low premiums.

A public insurance organization, such as Manitoba Public, does not have to raise premiums to a point where profits have to be earned on its operations, as is the case with privately run companies. Unlike the provincially owned public insurance providers, multinational private insurance corporations face the added pressure of raising premiums in order to recoup losses incurred in past global disasters, such as the September 11 terrorist attacks in the United States.

The Advantages of Using the Capitalist Model

In a series of recent studies, the Fraser Institute, a Canadian organization that promotes market-based policies, defends the use of the capitalist model in providing mandatory auto insurance. The Institute argues that a public auto insurance system results in more accidents and imposes greater burdens on the health-care system when compared with private insurance. After examining two private insurance provinces and three public insurance provinces, they note that the number of collisions and the number of collision related deaths, injuries, and hospital admissions is significantly higher, per 100 000 population or per vehicle kilometres travelled, in those provinces with public insurance. This difference is most pronounced for males between the ages of 16 and 25 years. The Institute suggests that since the public insurance system fails to charge higher premiums for certain high-risk classes, such as the younger male class, it encourages too many risky drivers to take to the road, and it shifts collision costs to other drivers—primarily female, safer, and older drivers. As well, the expensive lawsuits that accompany the fault system can provide incentives for safer driving.

SOURCE: MULLINS, MARK. " PUBLIC AUTO INSURANCE: A MORTALITY WARNING FOR MOTORISTS." FRASER INSTITUTE SEPT. 2003, PP. 1–4. ACCESSED NOVEMBER14, 2003. http://www.fraserinstitute.ca/admin/books/files/auto-insur.pdf.

Another benefit of the pure capitalist approach to auto insurance relates to the goal of allocative efficiency. A fault-based insurance system provides the opportunity for each injured individual to take the necessary legal action to ensure that the dollar value of the compensation resulting from an accident claim (marginal benefit) is sufficient to cover the full marginal cost related to the individual's injuries and losses sustained from the accident.

As an example, two individuals may suffer the same physical injury in an accident, but the pain and suffering experienced by one of the individuals would be significantly greater if that individual can no longer engage in his or her favourite hobby—playing the piano. The fault-based insurance system could enable the piano lover to receive a higher level of compensation based on the higher level of pain and suffering (i.e., the higher level of marginal cost). In contrast, the pure command model's no-fault system would likely pay out the same level of benefits to both injured individuals.

Using a Mixed System

Despite the potential benefits of using a pure capitalist approach in the provision of auto insurance, Canadians residing in the private insurance jurisdictions are putting political pressure on their provincial governments to play an active role in the auto insurance industry. Many of the private insurance provinces are moving toward a mixed economic system of providing auto insurance. While privately owned corporations continue to provide the car insurance in these provinces, the provincial governments are proposing to fix the premium rates and set maximum dollar limits for the payout of certain types of claims, such as pain and suffering. These governments have a difficult task ahead of them as they attempt to strike an acceptable balance between affordable premiums, public safety, equity, and their own political party's commitment to promote a capitalist provincial economy.

For critical analysis:

1. Explain how the pure command model of providing auto insurance can promote productive efficiency.
2. Explain how the pure capitalist model of providing auto insurance can promote the goals of public safety and allocative efficiency.
3. Explain what equity (fairness) trade-offs are involved when choosing the pure command model of providing auto insurance.
4. A provincial government freezes the premiums charged by private insurance companies but lets the fault system determine the payment of claims. What problems will likely occur with this mixed system policy?

SUMMARY DISCUSSION OF LEARNING OBJECTIVES

2.1 **The Production Possibilities Curve.** The production possibilities curve describes all possible combinations of two goods that can be produced assuming full and efficient employment of resources, a fixed time period, fixed quantity and quality of resources, and fixed technology.

2.2 **Applications of the Production Possibilities Curve.** The production possibilities curve illustrates the scarcity problem by acting as a production boundary in the face of unlimited wants. Its downward slope implies a trade-off—more of one good means less of another. An increasing opportunity cost situation is shown by a "bowed-out" production possibilities curve. Unemployment is reflected by a point inside the curve, signifying lost production. Any production combination on the curve is productively efficient and the one combination that society values the most is allocatively efficient. Economic growth shifts the production possibilities curve outward over time.

2.3 **Consumption Goods versus Capital Goods.** A production possibilities curve that involves capital goods and consumption goods illustrates that when we use more of our resources to produce capital goods that enhance future consumption, we must forgo present consumption goods.

2.4 **Specialization and Greater Productivity.** Absolute advantage refers to the ability to produce one unit of a product at a lower labour cost than another producer. Comparative advantage refers to the ability to produce a unit of a product at a lower opportunity cost than another producer. When individuals specialize in their areas of comparative advantage, this will enhance output and material well-being. Division of labour occurs when individuals specialize in a subset of tasks related to a specific product area.

2.5 **Economic Systems.** In a pure command system, the government owns the resources, and the three basic questions—What, How, For Whom—are answered in a centralized manner by government. In pure capitalism, resources are privately owned, and the basic questions are answered in a decentralized manner by individual firms and households interacting in markets. In a mixed economic system, where there is both private and public ownership of resources, the basic questions are partly answered by government and partly by individual firms and households in markets.

2.6 Capitalism in More Depth. The key features of pure capitalism include private ownership of resources, self-interest motives, consumer sovereignty, markets and prices, competition, and limited government. Consumer demand and resource availability determine *what* goods and services will be produced; the least costly method will be chosen in deciding *how* the goods will be produced; the degree to which households own marketable resources will determine *for whom* the goods are produced.

PROBLEMS

(Answers to the odd-numbered problems appear at the back of the book.)

LO 2.1, LO 2.2 Define the production possibilities curve and identify its assumptions; use the production possibilities curve to illustrate the concepts of scarcity, trade-offs, unemployment, productive efficiency, allocative efficiency, increasing opportunity cost, and economic growth.

1. The production possibilities curve for the nation of Epica for the two goods, factories and yachts, for 2006 is described in the accompanying graph.

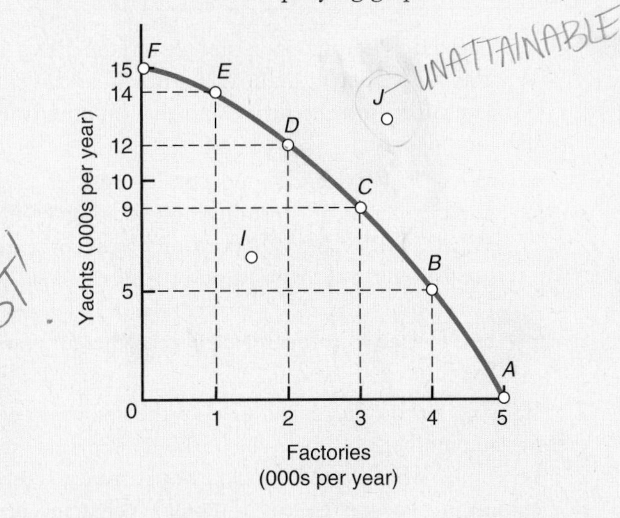

a. If Epica produces 12 000 yachts in 2006, what is the maximum amount of factories that can be produced in 2006?
b. If Epica devotes all its resources to the production of factories, what is the maximum amount of factories that can be produced in 2006?
c. What factors prevent Epica from producing the combination at point *J* in 2006?
d. If Epica is at point *I* in 2006, this situation could conflict with what two socioeconomic goals?
e. What is the opportunity cost of producing an additional factory when moving: (i) from point *E* to *D*? (ii) from point *C* to *B*?
f. What is the opportunity cost of producing an additional yacht when moving: (i) from point *A* to *B*? (ii) from point *E* to *F*?
g. What economic law is illustrated by your answers to parts (e) and (f) above?
h. If society values production combination *D* the most, but Epica is producing combination *C*, this situation conflicts with what socioeconomic goal?
i. How will economic growth affect Epica's production possibilities curve over time?

2. The production possibilities curve for the nation of Fantasia for the two goods, TVs and business machines, for 2005 is described in the accompanying graph.

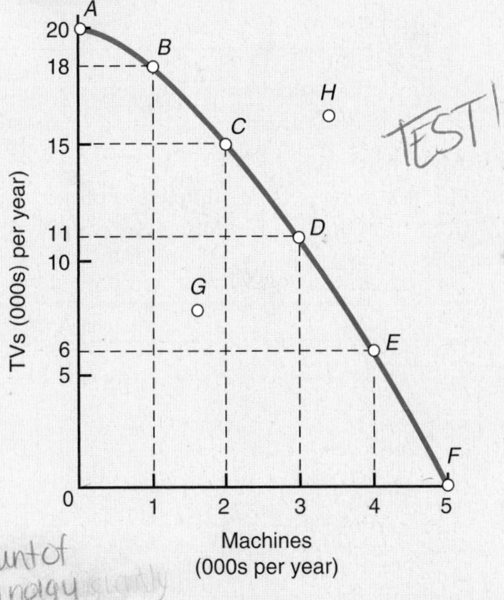

a. If Fantasia produces 2000 machines in 2005, what is the maximum number of TVs that can be produced in 2005?

b. What factors prevent Fantasia from producing the combination at point *H* in 2005?
c. If Fantasia completely specializes in the production of TVs in 2005, what maximum number of TVs could it produce per year?
d. If Fantasia is at point *G* in 2005, this situation could conflict with what two socioeconomic goals?
e. What is the opportunity cost of producing an additional machine when moving from: (i) point *A* to point *B*? (ii) point *D* to point *E*?
f. What economic law is illustrated by your answers to part (e) above?
g. Which of the points *A, B, C, D, E, F, G,* and *H* are productively efficient?
h. If society values the production combination at point *D* the most, but Fantasia is currently producing at point *C*, this situation conflicts with what socioeconomic goal?
i. Which one of the two points—*B* or *E*—would lead to a greater rate of economic growth? Why? What important trade-off is illustrated here?
j. How will economic growth affect Fantasia's production possibilities curve over time?

3. The following table illustrates the marks a student can earn on examinations in economics and biology if the student uses all available hours for study.

Economics	Biology
100	40
90	50
80	60
70	70
60	80
50	90
40	100

Plot this student's production possibilities curve. Does this PPC illustrate increasing or constant opportunity costs?

4. The following sets of numbers represent hypothetical production possibilities for a country in 2005. Plot these points on graph paper.

Cheese	Apples
4	0
3	1.6
2	2.4
1	2.8
0	3.0

Does the law of increasing relative cost seem to hold? Why? On the same graph, plot and draw the production possibilities curve that will represent 10 percent economic growth.

5. Construct a production possibilities curve for a country facing increasing opportunity costs for producing food and video games. Show how the PPC changes given the following events:
   a. A new and better fertilizer is developed.
   b. There is a surge in labour that can be employed in both the agriculture sector and the video game sector.
   c. A new programming language is invented that is less costly to code and is more memory-efficient, enabling the use of smaller games cartridges.
   d. A heat wave and drought result in a decrease of 10 percent in usable farmland.

LO 2.3 Use the production possibilities curve to explain the trade-off between consumption goods and capital goods.

6. Two countries, Workland and Playland, have similar populations and identical production possibilities curves but different preferences. The production possibilities combinations are as follows:

Point	Capital Goods	Consumption Goods
A	0	20
B	1	19
C	2	17
D	3	14
E	4	10
F	5	5

Playland is located at point *B* on the PPC, and Workland is located at point *E*. Assume that this situation continues into the future and that all other things remain the same.
   a. What is Workland's opportunity cost of capital goods in terms of consumption goods?
   b. What is Playland's opportunity cost of capital goods in terms of consumption goods?
   c. How would the PPCs of Workland and Playland be expected to compare with each other 50 years in the future?

7. If, by going to college, you give up the chance to work in your mother's business for 35 hours per week at $7 per hour, what would be your opportunity cost of earning a two-year college diploma? What incentives exist to make you incur that opportunity cost? What are you giving up today in order to have more in the future? Assume that you will need to spend 60 weeks in college to earn a diploma.

LO 2.4 Distinguish between absolute advantage and comparative advantage and use these concepts to explain how specialization and trade can increase production and consumption.

8. What two economic concepts presented in this chapter help explain the marriage premium described in Example 2–4, "Why Men Marry: Is It for Love or the Marriage Premium?"?

9. You can wash, fold, and iron a basket of laundry in two hours and prepare a meal in one hour. Your roommate can wash, fold, and iron a basket of laundry in three hours and prepare a meal in one hour. Should you and your roommate specialize in particular tasks? Why? And if so, who should specialize in which task? Calculate how much labour time you save if you choose to "trade" an appropriate task with your roommate, as opposed to doing it yourself.

LO 2.5, 2.6 Explain the differences between the pure capitalist, pure command, and mixed economic systems; describe the features of pure capitalism and explain how capitalism answers the three basic economic questions.

10. What type of economic system is the Edmonton Public School District currently using to allocate educational resources according to Policy Example 2–2, "The Edmonton Revolution in Public Education"? Explain your answer.
11. What features of capitalism help explain how consumer sovereignty can be achieved with limited government involvement?
12. Briefly explain how capitalism answers the three basic economic questions.
13. The table gives the production techniques and input prices for 100 units of product X.

		Production Technique		
Input	Input Unit Price	A (units)	B (units)	C (units)
Labour	$10	6	5	4
Capital	8	5	6	7

a. In a market system, which techniques will be used to produce 100 units of product X?
b. If the market price of a unit of X is $1, which technique will lead to the greatest profit?
c. The output of X is still 100 units, but the price of labour and capital changes so that labour is $8 and capital is $10. Which production technique will be used?
d. Using the information in part (c), what is the potential profit of producing 100 units of X?

APPENDIX B

THE PRODUCTION POSSIBILITIES CURVE AND COMPARATIVE ADVANTAGE

The gains from specialization and trade can be effectively illustrated by the production possibilities curve model. Let us assume that two Canadian family farms, the Pulets and the Dowbys, can produce chicken and perogies on each of their farm operations. The Pulets can produce one kilogram of chicken per hour or one kilogram of perogies per hour. The Dowbys can produce two kilograms of chicken per hour or eight kilograms of perogies per hour. Armed with this productivity information, we can proceed to construct production possibilities for each family farm.

Before Specialization and Trade

We will construct a daily production possibilities curve for the two products, chicken and perogies, for each family farm, by assuming that each family works an eight-hour day.

The Pulets' production possibilities curve in Figure B–1 part (a) shows that in a typical day, if they devote all eight hours to producing perogies, they can produce eight kilograms of perogies per day, which is at point *A* in Figure B–1 part (a). Alternatively, if the Pulets devote all of the eight hours to producing chicken, they can produce eight kilograms of chicken per day, which is at point *B* in Figure B–1 part (a). Currently, the Pulets are not specializing and trading, and so they are producing and consuming six kilograms of perogies and two kilograms of chicken on a daily basis, which is at point *C* in Figure B–1 part (a).

The Dowbys' production possibilities curve in Figure B–1 part (b) shows that in a typical day, if they devote all eight hours to producing perogies, they can produce 64 kilograms of perogies per day, which is at point *A* in Figure B–1 part (b). Alternatively, if the Dowbys devote all of the eight hours to producing chicken, they can produce 16 kilograms of chicken per day, which is at point *B* in Figure B–1 part (b). Currently, the Dowbys are not specializing and trading, and so they are producing and consuming 48 kilograms of perogies and four kilograms of chicken on a daily basis, which is at point *C* in Figure B–1 part (b).

You will notice that both production possibilities curves are assumed to be straight lines. This implies that the opportunity cost of production will stay constant as each farm specializes in the production of one of its products. This assumption will simplify our production possibilities illustration of the gains from trade and specialization.

Figure B–1 illustrates that the Dowbys can produce more of both products, when compared with the Pulets, despite the fact that both family farms are employing the same level of total labour input on a daily basis. This implies that the Dowbys can produce a kilogram of each product at a lower labour cost than the Pulets. In other words, the Dowbys have the absolute advantage in the production of chicken and in the production of perogies.

Since the Dowbys have the absolute advantage in the production of each product, it may appear that there would be no incentive for the Dowbys to specialize and trade with the Pulets. However, as we will explain below, the Pulets do have the comparative advantage in the production of chicken, and therefore, the Dowbys can increase their consumption possibilities by specializing and trading with the Pulets.

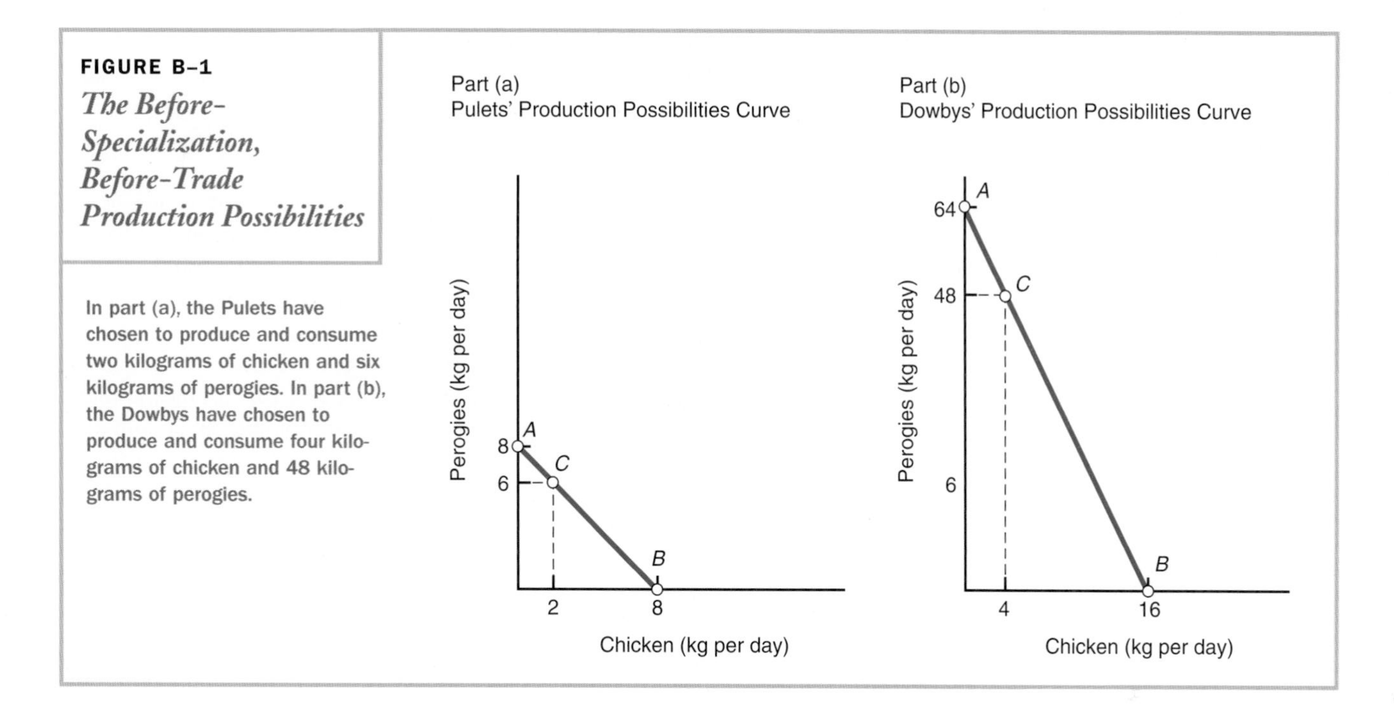

FIGURE B–1

The Before-Specialization, Before-Trade Production Possibilities

In part (a), the Pulets have chosen to produce and consume two kilograms of chicken and six kilograms of perogies. In part (b), the Dowbys have chosen to produce and consume four kilograms of chicken and 48 kilograms of perogies.

After Specialization and Before Trade

As noted in Chapter 2, we can identify the family farm that has the comparative advantage in each product by computing opportunity costs.

Opportunity Costs Incurred by the Pulets

According to Figure B–1 part (a), if the Pulets switch production possibilities from point *A* to point *B*, eight additional kilograms of chicken can be produced by giving up eight kilograms of perogies. Therefore, one additional kilogram of chicken has an opportunity cost or sacrifice of one kilogram of perogies on the Pulets' farm. If the Pulets switch production possibilities from point *B* to point *A* in Figure B–1 part (a), you can see that one additional kilogram of perogies has an opportunity cost of one kilogram of chicken. These opportunity costs are summarized in Table B–1.

Opportunity Costs Incurred by the Dowbys

According to Figure B–1 part (b), if the Dowbys switched production possibilities from point *A* to point *B*, 16 additional kilograms of chicken can be produced by giving up 64 kilograms of perogies. Therefore, one additional kilogram of chicken has an opportunity cost of four kilograms of perogies. If the Dowbys were to switch production possibilities from point *B* to point *A* in Figure B–1 part (b), you can see that one additional kilogram of perogies has an opportunity cost of one-quarter of a kilogram of chicken. These opportunity costs are summarized in Table B–1.

TABLE B–1

Opportunity Costs for Each Farm for Each Product

The Pulets can produce a kilogram of chicken at a lower opportunity cost than the Dowbys. The Dowbys can produce a kilogram of perogies at a lower opportunity cost than the Pulets.

	Opportunity cost of 1 kg of chicken:	**Opportunity cost of 1 kg of perogies:**
Pulets	1 kg of perogies	1 kg of chicken
Dowbys	4 kg of perogies	1/4 = 0.25 kg of chicken

Comparative Advantage Principle

Table B–1 indicates that the Pulets can produce an additional kilogram of chicken at a lower opportunity cost, one kilogram of perogies, than the Dowbys' opportunity cost of four kilograms of perogies. This implies that the Dowbys can produce an additional kilogram of the other product, perogies, at a lower opportunity cost than the Pulets (0.25 kilograms versus one kilogram of chicken). In other words, the Pulets have the comparative advantage in the production of chickens, and the Dowbys have the comparative advantage in the production of perogies.

Comparative Advantage Principle states that the combined production of two producers can be enhanced if each producer specializes in the product in which it has the comparative advantage.

The **Comparative Advantage Principle** states that the combined production of two producers can be enhanced if each producer specializes in the product in which it has the comparative advantage. According to this principle, the combined daily production of both family farms can be increased by having the Pulets specialize in the production of chicken and the Dowbys specialize in the production of perogies.

Figure B–1 part (a) reminds us that before specialization, the Pulets were producing two kilograms of chicken and six kilograms of perogies. Figure B–1 part (b) indicates that before specialization, the Dowbys were producing four kilograms of chicken and 48 kilograms of perogies. Therefore, the combined family farm production before specialization was 2 + 4 = 6 kilograms of chicken and was 6 + 48 = 54 kilograms of perogies.

According to Figure B–1 part (a), if the Pulets specialized in the production of chicken, they would switch production possibilities to point *B* and produce eight kilograms of chicken and zero kilograms of perogies per day. Figure B–1 part (b) indicates that if the Dowbys specialized in perogies, they would switch production possibilities to point *A* and produce 64 kilograms of perogies and zero kilograms of chicken per day. Note that by specializing according to comparative advantage, the combined family farm production of chicken has increased from six kilograms to eight kilograms per day. Similarly, the combined family farm production of perogies has increased from 54 kilograms to 64 kilograms per day.

After Specialization and After Trade

With each family farm specializing according to comparative advantage, the need will arise to trade the surplus production between family farms. Under specialization, the only way the Pulets can obtain perogies is by trading off some chicken. Similarly, the Dowbys will have to trade some of their perogies in order to consume some chicken. In trading with each other, the question now becomes, how much of one product should each farm trade away in order to get an additional kilogram of the other product?

The Terms of Trade Principle

Terms of trade The amount of one product that must be traded in order to obtain an additional unit of another product.

Terms of Trade Principle Each producer will gain from specialization and trade if the terms of trade is between the producers' opportunity costs of production.

The **terms of trade** for chicken is the amount of the other product, perogies, that must be traded in order to obtain one additional kilogram of chicken. The **Terms of Trade Principle** states that each producer will gain from specialization and trade if the terms of trade is between the producers' opportunity costs of production.

As an example, a mutually beneficial terms of trade for one kilogram of chicken would be anywhere between one kilogram of perogies (opportunity cost at the Pulets farm) and four kilograms of perogies (opportunity cost at the Dowbys farm). Thus, one acceptable terms of trade for one kilogram of chicken would be two kilograms of perogies. Assuming this terms of trade and assuming that the Pulets end up trading five kilograms of their chicken in exchange for 10 kilograms of perogies with the Dowbys, Table B–2 illustrates how both family farms can increase their consumption possibilities.

THE PULETS' GAIN FROM TRADE. According to Table B–2, if the Pulets specialize and produce eight kilograms of chicken and then trade away five kilograms of chicken for 10 kilograms of perogies, they end up consuming 8 − 5 = 3 kilograms of chicken and 0 + 10 = 10 kilograms of perogies, after specialization and after trade. On the basis of point *C* of Figure B–1, the Pulets produced and consumed only two kilograms of chicken and six kilograms of perogies, before specialization and trade. In other words, specialization and trade increased the Pulets' consumption of chicken and perogies by one kilogram and four kilograms per day, respectively.

Figure B–2 part (a) describes the Pulets' gain as a rightward shift from point *C* on the Pulets' production possibilities curve to point *C1* on the Pulets' new consumption possibilities curve. Note that the slope of the Pulets' new consumption possibilities curve is 2, which is based on the terms of trade for one kilogram of chicken.

THE DOWBYS' GAIN FROM TRADE. Table B–2 also describes how the Dowbys can enhance their consumption possibilities with the terms of trade of two kilograms of perogies for one kilogram of chicken. Before trade and specialization, the Dowbys produced and consumed four kilograms of chicken and 48 kilograms of perogies (point *C* in Figure B–1 part (b)). After trade and specialization, the Dowbys can consume five kilograms of chicken and 54 kilograms of perogies. Specialization and trade increased the Dowbys' consumption of chicken and perogies by one kilogram and six kilograms per day, respectively.

Figure B–2 part (b) describes the Dowbys' gain as a rightward shift from point *C* on the Dowbys' production possibilities curve to point *C1* on the Dowbys' new consumption possibilities curve. Again, note that the slope of the Dowbys' new consumption possibilities curve is 2, which is based on the terms of trade for one kilogram of chicken.

In summary, we have just shown how the Dowbys can benefit by specializing and trading with the Pulets, despite the fact that the Dowbys have the absolute advantage in both products. This is because the opportunity costs of production differ between both family farms. In other words, *the gains from specialization and trade are based on comparative advantage and not absolute advantage.*

TABLE B–2

Gains from Specialization and Trade

After specialization and trade, the Pulets gain one kilogram of chicken and four kilograms of perogies. The Dowbys gain one kilogram of chicken and six kilograms of perogies.

Farm	(1) Production Before Specialization	(2) Production After Specialization	(3) Trade: Sells (–) Buys (+)	(4) = (2) +(3) Consumption After Specialization and Trade	(5) = (4) –(1) Gains from Specialization and Trade
Pulets					
Chicken	2 kg	8 kg	-5 kg	8 - 5 = 3 kg	3 - 2 = +1 kg
Perogies	6 kg	0 kg	+10 kg	0 + 10 = 10 kg	10 - 6 = +4 kg
Dowbys					
Chicken	4 kg	0 kg	+5 kg	0 + 5 = 5 kg	5 - 4 = +1 kg
Perogies	48 kg	64 kg	-10 kg	64 - 10 = 54 kg	54 - 48 = +6 kg

FIGURE B–2

After-Specialization, After-Trade Consumption Possibilities

In part (a) and part (b), specialization and trade allow both the Pulets and the Dowbys to increase their consumption possibilities beyond their production possibilities.

Part (a)
Pulets' After-Specialization After-Trade, Consumption Possibilities Curve

Consumption Possibilities Curve After Trade and Specialization
Perogies (kg per day)
16
10
8
6
C1
C
B
2 3
8
Chicken (kg per day)

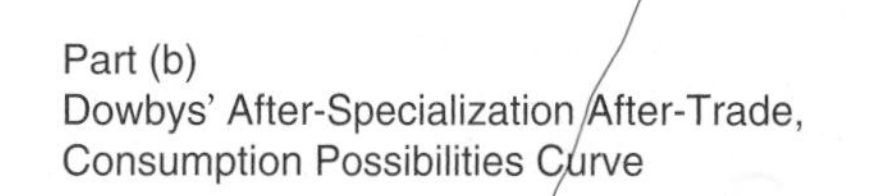

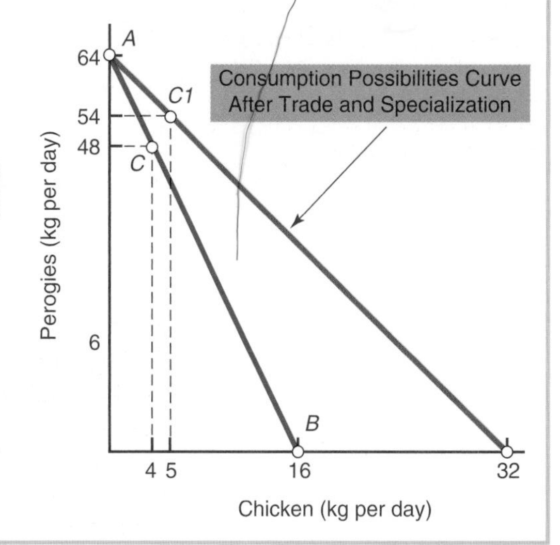

APPENDIX SUMMARY

1. Absolute advantage refers to the ability to produce one unit of a product at a lower labour cost than another producer. Comparative advantage refers to the ability to produce a unit of a product at a lower opportunity cost than another producer.
2. According to the Comparative Advantage Principle, the combined production of two producers can be increased if each producer specializes according to comparative advantage. This principle applies even in those cases where one producer has the absolute advantage in both product areas.
3. The terms of trade for one product, *A*, is the amount of the other product, *B*, that must be traded in order to obtain one additional unit of *A*.
4. The Terms of Trade Principle states that each producer will gain from specialization and trade if the terms of trade is between the producers' opportunity costs of production. In this case, consumption possibilities can exceed production possibilities.

APPENDIX PROBLEMS

(Answers to the odd-numbered problems appear at the back of the book.)

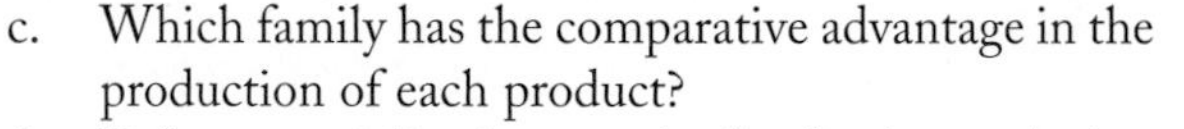

B–1. Answer each of the following on the basis of the before-specialization and trade production possibilities for the Martin and the Richard families described in the accompanying two graphs. Before specialization and trade, each family is producing and consuming production combination *C*.

a. Which family has the absolute advantage in the production of each product?

b. Compute the opportunity cost of producing one litre of beer for each family.

c. Which family has the comparative advantage in the production of each product?

d. Before specialization, each family is producing combination *C* on its respective production possibilities curve. Assuming that each family decides to specialize in its area of comparative advantage, compute the gains in total combined production for each product.

e. In order for both families to share the gains from specialization, the terms of trade for one litre of beer should be somewhere between ___ and ___ litres of wine.

Martins' Production Possibilities

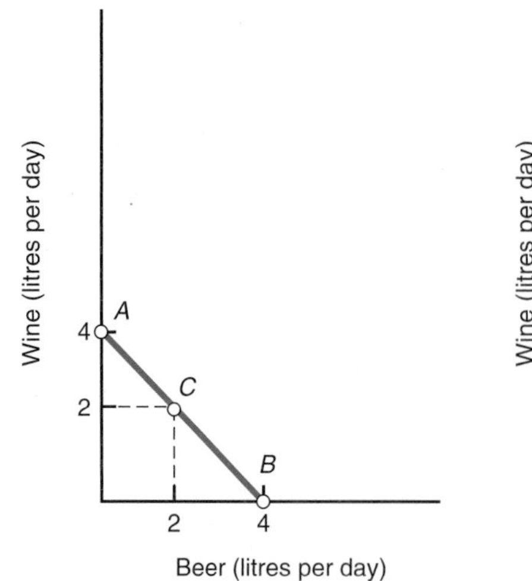

Richards' Production Possibilities

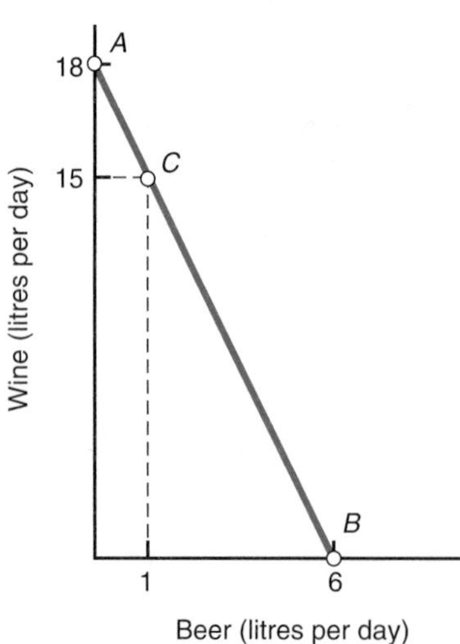

B-2. Answer each of the following on the basis of the before-specialization and trade production possibilities for the nations of Mazland and Attica for the two products, cell phones and digital cameras, as shown in the accompanying graphs. Before specialization and trade, each nation is producing and consuming production combination *C*.

a. Which nation has the absolute advantage in the production of each product?

b. Compute the opportunity cost of producing one camera for each nation.

c. Which nation has the comparative advantage in the production of each product?

d. Before specialization, both nations are producing combination *C* on their respective production possibilities curve. Assuming that each nation decides to specialize in its area of comparative advantage, compute the gains in total combined production for each product.

e. In order for both nations to share the gains from specialization, the terms of trade for one camera should be somewhere between ___ and ___ phones.

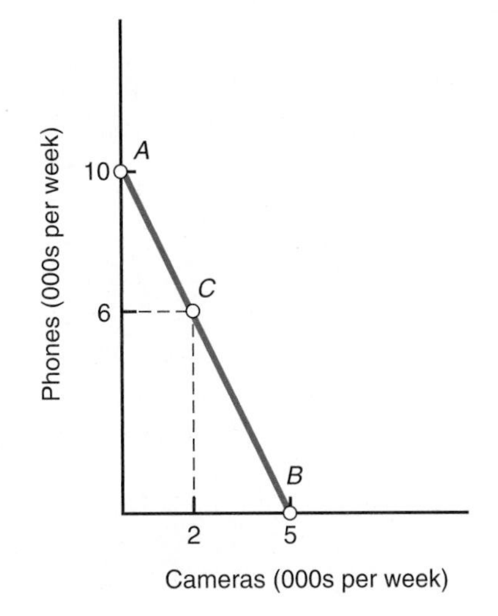

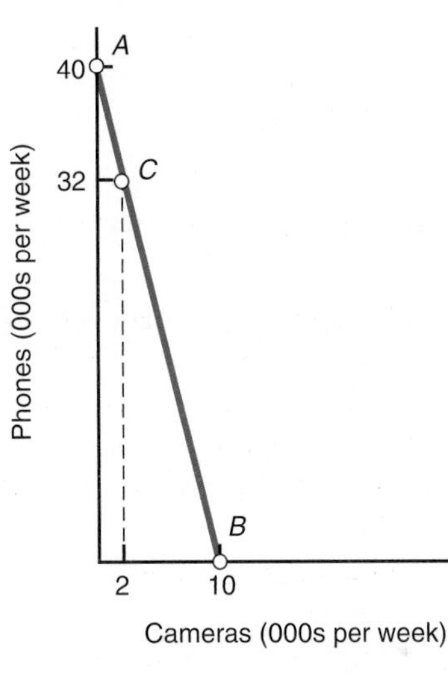

CHAPTER 3

Demand and Supply

It started, in 1999, with busloads of American seniors travelling to Canada to purchase low-priced prescription drugs. In 2003, it was estimated that 10 million American consumers would spend $1 billion on pharmaceuticals sold by Canadian Internet drugstores. For this Canadian export industry to flourish, Canadian health professionals had to cosign prescriptions for American patients they had not seen. While the United States congress pushed to expand this drug trade with Canada, multinational drug manufacturers were threatening to cut off the drug supply to Canadian Internet pharmacies.

The theory presented in this chapter will help you understand why selling drugs online is such a contentious issue in both Canada and the United States.

LEARNING OBJECTIVES

After reading this chapter, you should be able to:

3.1 Explain the law of demand.

3.2 Distinguish between a change in quantity demanded and a change in demand.

3.3 Explain the law of supply.

3.4 Distinguish between a change in quantity supplied and a change in supply.

3.5 Explain how the forces of demand and supply interact to determine equilibrium price and quantity.

3.6 Describe how changes in demand and supply can change equilibrium price and quantity.

? DID YOU KNOW THAT...

More than 140 million North American residences owned portable cellular phones in 2003. This is a huge jump from the mere 200 000 in 1985. Since 1992, two out of every three new telephone numbers in North America have been assigned to cellular phones. The 20-year wireless cell phone business has been growing so fast that it is predicted to overtake the regular wired phone business in North America by 2005.

There are several reasons for the spectacular growth in cellular phone use, not the least being the dramatic reduction in both price and size due to improved and cheaper computer chips that go into making them. There is something else at work, though. It has to do with crime. In a recent survey, 46 percent of new cellular phone users said that personal safety was the main reason they bought a portable phone. The tools of demand and supply, presented in this chapter, will help you better understand how prices can be declining in an industry that is experiencing explosive growth.

SOURCE: STEVE ROSENBUSH, ROGER CROCKETT, CHRISTOPHER PALMERI, AND PETER BURROWS. "A WIRELESS WORLD: IN A FEW YEARS MOBILE PHONES WILL DOMINATE U.S. COMMUNICATIONS." *BUSINESS WEEK*, ISSUE 3855, OCTOBER 27, 2003.; P. 110.

3.1 The Law of Demand

Demand Refers to the quantities of a specific good or service that individuals are willing to purchase at various possible prices, other things being constant.

Law of demand The observation that there is an inverse relationship between the price of any good and its quantity demanded, holding other factors equal.

Demand has a special meaning in economics. It refers to the quantities of specific goods or services that individuals, either singly or as a group, will purchase at various possible prices, other things being constant. We can, therefore, talk about the demand for microprocessor chips, French fries, compact disc players, and health care.

Associated with the concept of demand is the **law of demand**, which can be stated as follows:

When the price of a good goes up, people buy less of it, other things being equal. When the price of a good goes down, people buy more of it, other things being equal.

The law of demand tells us that the quantity demanded of any commodity is inversely related to its price, other things being equal. In an inverse relationship, one variable moves up in value when the other moves down. The law of demand states that a change in price causes the quantity demanded to change in the *opposite* direction.

Note that we tacked onto the end of the law of demand the statement "other things being equal." We referred to this in Chapter 1 as the *ceteris paribus* assumption. It means, for example, that when we predict that people will buy fewer CD players if their price goes up, we are holding constant the price of all other goods in the economy as well as people's incomes. Implicitly, therefore, if we are assuming that no other prices change when we examine the price behaviour of CD players, we are looking at the *relative* price of CD players.

The law of demand is supported by millions of observations of how people behave in the marketplace. Theoretically, it can be derived from an economic model based on rational behaviour, as was discussed in Chapter 1. Basically, if nothing else changes and the price of a good falls, the lower price induces us to buy more over a certain period of time. This is because we can enjoy additional net gains that were unavailable at the higher price. For the most part, if you examine your own purchasing behaviour, you will see that it generally follows the law of demand.

Relative Prices versus Money Prices

Relative price Any commodity's price in terms of another commodity.

Money price The actual price that you pay in dollars and cents for any good or service at any point in time.

The **relative price** of any commodity is its price in terms of another commodity. The actual price that you pay in dollars and cents for any good or service at any point in time is called its **money price**. Consider an example that you might hear quite often around older friends or relatives. "When I bought my first new car, it cost only $1500." The implication, of course, is that the price of cars today is outrageously high because the average new car might cost $20 000. But that is not an accurate comparison. What was the price of the average house during that same year? Perhaps it was only $12 000. By comparison, then, given that houses today average about $200 000, the current price of a new car does not sound so far out of line, does it?

The point is that comparing money prices during different time periods do not tell you much. You have to find out relative prices. Consider a simplified example of the price comparison of prerecorded DVDs versus prerecorded videocassettes between last year and this year. In Table 3–1, we show the money prices of DVDs and videocassettes for two years during which time both have gone up. That means that we have to pay out more for DVDs and more for videocassettes in today's dollars. If we look, though, at the relative prices of DVDs and videocassettes, we find that last year, DVDs were twice as expensive as videocassettes, whereas this year they are only 1.5 times as expensive. Conversely, if we compare videocassettes to DVDs, last year they cost only half as much as DVDs, but today they cost about 67 percent as much. In the one-year period, though both prices have gone up in money terms, the relative price of DVDs has fallen (and equivalently, the relative price of videocassettes has risen).

TABLE 3–1

Money Price versus Relative Price

The money prices of both DVDs and videocassettes have risen. But the relative price of DVDs has fallen (or conversely, the relative price of video cassettes has risen).

	Money Price		Relative Price	
	Last Year	**This Year**	**Last Year**	**This Year**
DVDs	$20	$24	$20 / $10 = 2.0	$24 / $16 = 1.5
Videocassettes	$10	$16	$10 / $20 = 0.5	$16 / $24 = 0.67

When evaluating the effects of price changes, we must always compare prices per *constant-quality unit.* Sometimes, relative price changes occur because the quality of a product improves, thereby bringing about a decrease in the item's effective price per constant-quality unit, as Policy Example 3–1 illustrates.

POLICY EXAMPLE 3–1

Price per Constant-Quality Unit and Teen Marijuana Use

Between 1981 and 1992, studies of teen marijuana use indicated that the percentage of high-school seniors who had purchased marijuana had declined from 46 percent to less than 22 percent. Private groups and government agencies that seek to educate teens about the ill-effects of drug use hailed this decline as evidence that those groups were succeeding in their efforts.

Today, however, more than 40 percent of high-school seniors are reporting marijuana purchases. Yet, teens also continue to indicate that they understand the potential harms of marijuana use. What happened? One part of the answer is that the market price of an ounce of marijuana has declined by nearly 20 percent since 1992. Another important factor, however, is that the potency of a typical ounce of marijuana sold on the street has increased by more than 50 percent. The combination of these two factors has translated into a decline in the price per constant-quality unit of more than 45 percent.

For critical analysis: Why has the relative price of marijuana fallen by more than 20 percent since 1992? How might the government apply the law of demand to create policies that reduce marijuana use in Canada?

SOURCE: ADAPTATION OF THE EXAMPLE FROM ROGER LEROY MILLER, *ECONOMICS TODAY: THE MICRO VIEW,* 12TH US ED., P. 52.

The Demand Schedule

Let us take a hypothetical demand situation to see how the inverse relationship between the price and the quantity demanded looks (holding other things equal). We will consider the quantity of rewriteable DVDs demanded *per year* by one person. Without stating the *time dimension*, we could not make sense out of this demand relationship because the numbers would be different if we were talking about the quantity demanded per month or the quantity demanded per decade.

In addition to implicitly or explicitly stating a time dimension for a demand relationship, we are also implicitly referring to constant-quality units of the good or service in question. Prices are always expressed in constant-quality units in order to avoid the problem of comparing commodities that are, in fact, not truly comparable.

In part (a) of Figure 3–1, we see that if the price were $1 per DVD, 50 of them would be bought each year by our representative individual, but if the price were $5 per DVD, only 10 would be bought each year. This reflects the law of demand. Part (a) is also simply called *demand*, or a *demand schedule*, because it gives a schedule of alternative quantities demanded per year at different possible prices.

The Demand Curve

Tables expressing relationships between two variables can be represented in graphical terms. To do this, we need only construct a graph that has the price per constant-quality DVD on the vertical axis, and the quantity measured in constant-quality DVDs per year on the horizontal axis. All we have to do is take combinations *A* through *E* from part (a) of Figure 3–1 and plot those points in part (b). Now we connect the points with a smooth line, and *voilà*, we have a *demand curve*.[1] It is downward-sloping (from left to right) to indicate the inverse relationship between the price of DVDs and the quantity demanded per year. Our presentation of demand schedules and curves applies equally well to all commodities, including toothpicks, hamburgers, textbooks, credit, and labour services. Remember, the **demand curve** is simply a graphical representation of the law of demand.

Demand curve A graphical representation of the law of demand.

Individual versus Market Demand Curves

The demand schedule shown in part (a) of Figure 3–1 and the resulting demand curve shown in part (b) are both given for one individual. As we shall see, determining price in the **market** (all of the arrangements that individuals have for exchanging with one another) depends on, among other things, the *market demand* for a particular commodity. The way in which we measure a **market demand** schedule and derive a market demand

Market All of the arrangements that individuals have for exchanging with one another.

Market demand Determined by adding the individual demand at each price for all the consumers in the market.

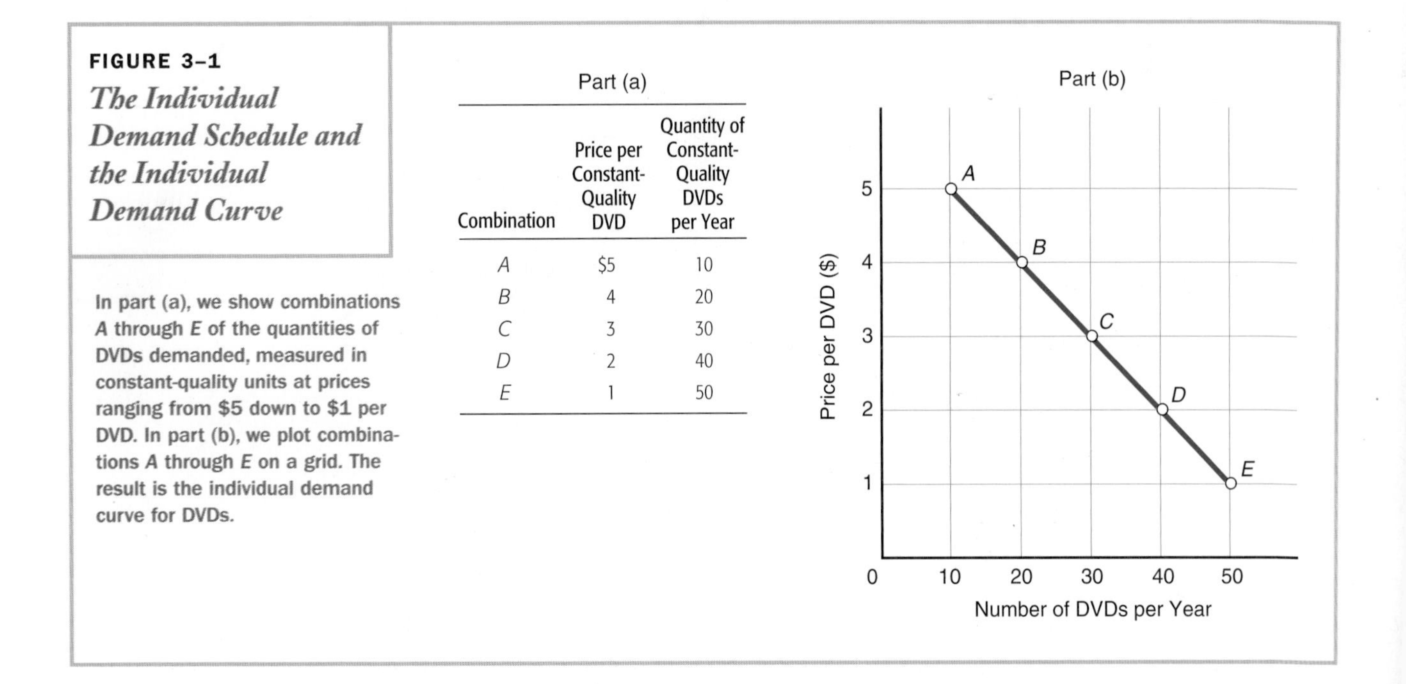

Part (a)

Combination	Price per Constant-Quality DVD	Quantity of Constant-Quality DVDs per Year
A	$5	10
B	4	20
C	3	30
D	2	40
E	1	50

FIGURE 3–1
The Individual Demand Schedule and the Individual Demand Curve

In part (a), we show combinations *A* through *E* of the quantities of DVDs demanded, measured in constant-quality units at prices ranging from $5 down to $1 per DVD. In part (b), we plot combinations *A* through *E* on a grid. The result is the individual demand curve for DVDs.

[1]Even though we call them "curves," for the purposes of exposition, we often draw straight lines. In many real-world situations, demand and supply curves will, in fact, be lines that do curve. To connect the points in part (b) with a line, we assume that for all prices in between the ones shown, the quantities demanded will be found along that line.

curve for DVDs or any other commodity is by adding the individual demand at each price for all those in the market. Suppose that the market for DVDs consists of only two buyers: buyer 1, for whom we have already shown the demand schedule in Figure 3–1, and buyer 2, whose demand schedule is displayed in Figure 3–2, part (a), column 3. Column 1 of Figure 3–2, part (a) shows the price, and column 2 gives the quantity demanded by buyer 1 (data taken directly from Figure 3–1). Column 4 states the total quantity demanded at each price, obtained by adding columns 2 and 3. Graphically, in part (d) of Figure 3–2, we add the demand curves of buyer 1 [part (b)] and buyer 2 [part (c)] to derive the market demand curve.

There are, of course, literally millions of potential consumers for DVDs. We will assume that the summation of all of the consumers in the market results in a demand schedule, given in part (a) of Figure 3–3, and a demand curve, given in part (b). The quantity demanded is now measured in millions of units per year. Remember, part (b) in Figure 3–3 shows the market demand curve for the millions of users of DVDs. The "market" demand curve that we derived in Figure 3–2 assumed that there were only two buyers in the entire market. This is why that demand curve is not a smooth line—whereas the true market demand curve in part (b) of Figure 3–3 is—and has no kinks.

FIGURE 3–2

The Horizontal Summation of Two Demand Schedules

Part (a) shows how to sum the demand schedule for one buyer with that of another buyer. Column 2 shows the quantity demanded by buyer 1, taken from part (a) of Figure 3–1. Column 4 is the sum of columns 2 and 3. We plot the demand curve for buyer 1 in part (b) and the demand curve for buyer 2 in part (c). When we add those two demand curves horizontally, we get the market demand curve for two buyers, shown in part (d).

Part (a)

(1) Price per DVD	(2) Buyer 1 Quantity Demanded	(3) Buyer 2 Quantity Demanded	(4) = (2) + (3) Combined Quantity Demanded per Year
$5	10	10	20
4	20	20	40
3	30	40	70
2	40	50	90
1	50	60	110

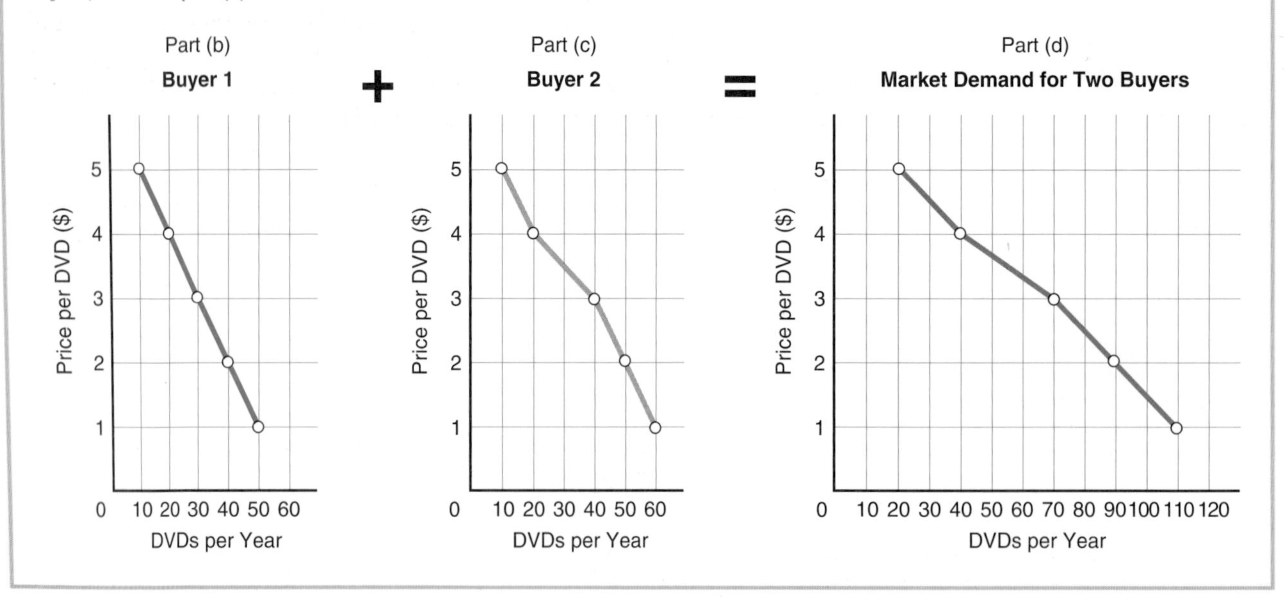

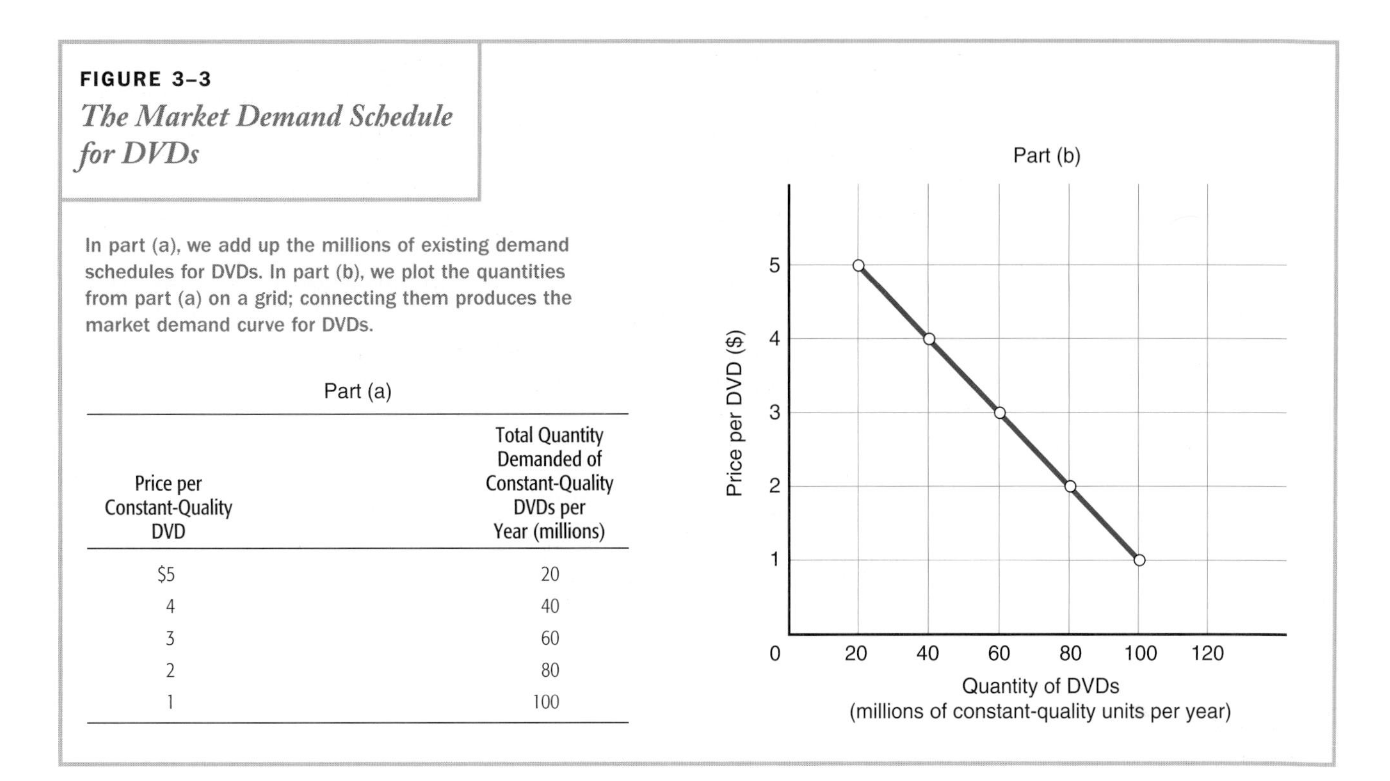

FIGURE 3–3

The Market Demand Schedule for DVDs

In part (a), we add up the millions of existing demand schedules for DVDs. In part (b), we plot the quantities from part (a) on a grid; connecting them produces the market demand curve for DVDs.

Part (a)

Price per Constant-Quality DVD	Total Quantity Demanded of Constant-Quality DVDs per Year (millions)
$5	20
4	40
3	60
2	80
1	100

3.2 *Shifts in Demand*

Assume that the federal government gives every student registered in a Canadian college, university, or technical school a personal computer that uses DVDs. The demand curve shown in part (b) of Figure 3–3 is no longer an accurate representation of the total market demand for DVDs. There will now be an increase in the number of DVDs demanded *at each and every possible price*. What we have to do is shift the curve outward, or to the right, to represent the rise in demand. The demand curve in Figure 3–4 will shift from D_1 to D_2. Take any price, say, $3 per DVD. Originally, before the federal government giveaway of personal computers, the amount demanded at $3 was 60 million DVDs per year. After the government giveaway, however, the quantity demanded at $3 is 100 million DVDs per year. What we have seen is a shift in the demand for DVDs.

FIGURE 3–4

A Shift in the Demand Curve

If some factor other than price changes, the only way we can show its effect is by moving the entire demand curve, say, from D_1 to D_2. We have assumed in our example that the move was precipitated by the government's giving a free personal computer to every registered college student in Canada. That meant that at all prices, a larger number of DVDs would be demanded than before. Curve D_3 represents reduced demand compared to curve D_1, caused by a law prohibiting computers on campus.

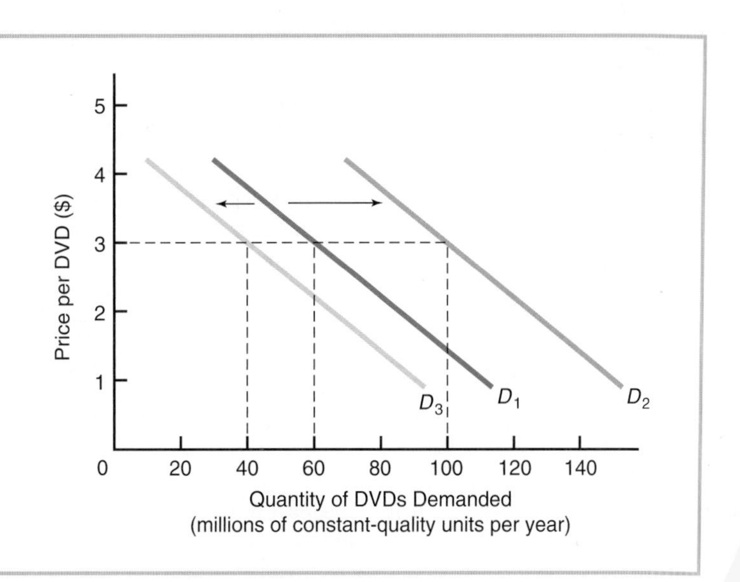

The shift can also go in the opposite direction. What if colleges uniformly outlawed the use of personal computers by students? Such a regulation would cause a shift inward—to the left—of the demand curve for DVDs. In Figure 3–4, the demand curve would shift to D_3; the amount demanded would now be less at each and every possible price.

If some factor other than price changes, the only way we can show its effect is by moving the entire demand curve, say, from D_1 to D_2. We have assumed in our example that the move was precipitated by the government's giving a free personal computer to every registered college student in Canada. That meant that at all prices, a larger number of DVDs would be demanded than before. Curve D_3 represents reduced demand compared to curve D_1, caused by a law prohibiting computers on campus.

The Other Determinants of Demand

The demand curve in part (b) of Figure 3–3 is drawn with other things held constant, specifically all of the other factors that determine how much will be bought. There are many such determinants. The major ones are income; tastes and preferences; the prices of related goods; expectations regarding future prices, future incomes, and future product availability; and population (market size). Let us examine each determinant more closely.

Normal goods Goods for which demand rises as income rises.

Inferior goods Goods for which demand falls as income rises.

INCOME. For most goods, an increase in income will lead to an increase in demand. The phrase *increase in demand* always refers to a comparison between two different demand curves. Thus, for most goods, an increase in income will lead to a rightward shift in the position of the demand curve from, say, D_1 to D_2 in Figure 3–4. You can avoid confusion about shifts in curves by always relating a rise in demand to a rightward shift in the demand curve and a fall in demand to a leftward shift in the demand curve. Goods for which the demand rises when income rises are called **normal goods**. Most goods, such as shoes, computers, and CDs, are "normal goods." For some goods, however, demand *falls* as income rises. These are called **inferior goods**. Beans might be an example. As households get richer, they tend to spend less and less on beans and more and more on meat. (The terms *normal* and *inferior* are merely part of the economist's terminology; no value judgments are implied by or associated with them.)

Remember, a shift to the left in the demand curve represents a fall in demand, and a shift to the right represents a rise, or increase, in demand. The changing demand for dental services is illustrated in Example 3–1.

EXAMPLE 3–1 Is Dental Care Becoming an Inferior Good?

A British health minister once claimed that the demand for health care is infinite because in the end everyone is in a losing battle against death. This is not so for Canadian dentistry, however. As aggregate Canadian income levels have risen during the past 25 years, overall spending on dental-care services has declined.

It is not that fewer Canadians are seeing dentists each year. They just do not require as many fillings or extractions. As incomes rose across the country, people purchased more expensive and effective toothpaste. More municipalities began to fluoridate their water as the relative price of the anticavity agent declined; thus, changing relative prices has also played a role. And higher incomes of their residents have permitted more municipalities to purchase fluoridation systems.

At every age, the average Canadian now has about two more teeth than 25 years ago. Unfortunately for dentists who specialize in treating decaying and diseased teeth, Canadians' teeth are healthier than ever before.

For critical analysis: Many new dentists have been specializing in "cosmetic dentistry" desired by patients with healthy but less than perfect teeth. Compared with traditional dental care services, is cosmetic dentistry more or less likely to be a normal good?

TASTES AND PREFERENCES. A change in consumer tastes in favour of a good can shift its demand curve outward to the right. When Frisbees® became the rage, the demand curve for them shifted outward to the right; when the rage died out, the demand curve shifted inward to the left. Fashions depend to a large extent on people's tastes and preferences. Economists have little to say about the determination of tastes; they have no "good" theories of taste determination or why people buy one brand of a product rather than others. Advertisers, however, do have various theories that they use in trying to make consumers prefer their products to those of competitors.

PRICES OF RELATED GOODS: SUBSTITUTES AND COMPLEMENTS. Demand schedules are always drawn with the prices of all other commodities held constant. In other words, when deriving a given demand curve, we assume that only the price of the good under study changes. For example, when we draw the demand curve for butter, we assume that the price of margarine is held constant. When we draw the demand curve for stereo speakers, we assume that the price of stereo amplifiers is held constant. When we refer to *related goods*, we are talking about goods for which demand is interdependent. If a change in the price of one good shifts the demand for another good, those two goods are related. There are two types of related goods: *substitutes* and *complements*. We can define and distinguish between substitutes and complements in terms of how the change in price of one commodity affects the demand for its related commodity.

Substitutes Two goods are substitutes when either one can be used to satisfy a similar want.

Two goods are **substitutes** when either one can be used to satisfy a similar want. Butter and margarine are substitutes. Let us assume that each originally cost $4 per kilogram. If the price of butter remains the same and the price of margarine falls from $4 to $2 per kilogram, people will buy more margarine and less butter. The demand curve for butter will shift inward to the left. If, conversely, the price of margarine rises from $4 to $6 per kilogram, people will buy more butter and less margarine. The demand curve for butter will shift outward to the right. An increase in the price of margarine will lead to an increase in the demand for butter, and an increase in the price of butter will lead to an increase in the demand for margarine. For substitutes, a price change in the substitute will cause a change in demand *in the same direction*.

Complements Two goods are complements if both are used together for consumption or enjoyment.

Two goods are **complements** if both are used together for consumption or enjoyment. For complements, the situation is reversed. Consider stereo speakers and stereo amplifiers. We draw the demand curve for speakers with the price of amplifiers held constant. If the price per constant-quality unit of stereo amplifiers decreases from, say, $500 to $200, that will encourage more people to purchase component stereo systems. They will now buy more speakers than before at any given price. The demand curve for speakers will shift outward to the right. If, by contrast, the price of amplifiers increases from $200 to $500, fewer people will purchase component stereo systems. The demand curve for speakers will shift inward to the left. To summarize, a decrease in the price of amplifiers leads to an increase in the demand for speakers. An increase in the price of amplifiers leads to a decrease in the demand for speakers. Thus, for complements, a price change in a product will cause a change in demand *in the opposite direction*.

Are new learning technologies complements or substitutes for university and college professors? Read Example 3–2 for further discussion.

EXAMPLE 3–2 Getting Your Degree via the Internet

In this class and others, you have probably been exposed to instructional technologies, such as videos, interactive computer software, CD-ROM learning systems, and websites that accompany your texts. Your professors have used these as complements to their teaching, but in the future, those technologies may, in fact, become a substitute for what your professors do in the classroom.

continued

Videotaped lectures, videoconferencing, Web-based course technology, high-speed Internet, and e-mail mean that more and more Canadian institutions can offer distance education courses, without having to hire additional instructors and professors.

Canadian Virtual University, a partnership of eleven Canadian universities, offers 250 degree, certificate, and diploma programs through the Internet or by distance education. When you enroll in one of these programs, you can select courses offered by any of the participating universities. This means 2000 courses to choose from, and the list is growing. Students can graduate from these programs without ever attending a class.

For critical analysis: What effect do online courses and distance education have on the demand curve for university and college professors?

EXPECTATIONS. Consumers' expectations regarding future prices, future incomes, and future availability may prompt them to buy more or less of a particular good without a change in its current money price. For example, consumers getting wind of a scheduled 100 percent price increase in DVDs next month may buy more of them today at today's prices. Today's demand curve for DVDs will shift from D_1 to D_2 in Figure 3–4 on page 65. The opposite would occur if a decrease in the price of DVDs were scheduled for next month.

Expectations of a rise in income may cause consumers to want to purchase more of everything today at today's prices. Again, such a change in expectations of higher future income will cause a shift in the demand curve from D_1 to D_2 in Figure 3–4. Finally, expectations that goods will not be available at any price will induce consumers to stock up now, increasing current demand.

POPULATION. An increase in the population in an economy (holding per-capita income constant) often shifts the market demand outward for most products. This is because an increase in population means an increase in the number of buyers in the market. Conversely, a reduction in the population will shift most market demand curves inward because of the reduction in the number of buyers in the market.

The rapid growth of Canadian Internet pharmacies selling prescription drugs to American consumers is highlighted in this chapter's Issues and Applications. Much of this growth can be explained in terms of some of the nonprice determinants mentioned above. That is, the higher prices of substitute products, such as prescription drugs sold by American pharmacies, have resulted in a significant increase in American consumer demand for the cheaper Canadian prescription drugs. As well, Internet and fax technology has made it very easy to promote and sell Canadian prescription drugs to virtually any location in the United States. This, in turn, has increased the population or number of American buyers wishing to purchase prescription drugs from Canadian online pharmacies. As a result of these changes in nonprice determinants, the market demand curve for prescription drugs sold by Canadian Internet pharmacies has been shifting to the right.

Changes in Demand versus Changes in Quantity Demanded

We have made repeated references to demand and to quantity demanded. It is important to realize that there is a difference between a *change in demand* and a *change in quantity demanded.*

Demand refers to a schedule of planned rates of purchase and depends on a great many nonprice determinants. Whenever there is a change in a nonprice determinant, there will be a change in demand—a shift in the entire demand curve to the right or to the left.

Quantity demanded is a specific quantity at a specific price, represented by a single point on a demand curve. When price changes, quantity demanded changes according to the law of demand, and there will be a movement from one point to another along the same demand curve. Look at Figure 3–5. At a price of $3 per DVD, 60 million DVDs per

FIGURE 3–5

Movement along a Given Demand Curve

A change in price changes the quantity of a good demanded. This can be represented as movement along a given demand schedule. If, in our example, the price of DVDs falls from $3 to $1 apiece, the quantity demanded will increase from 60 million to 100 million units per year.

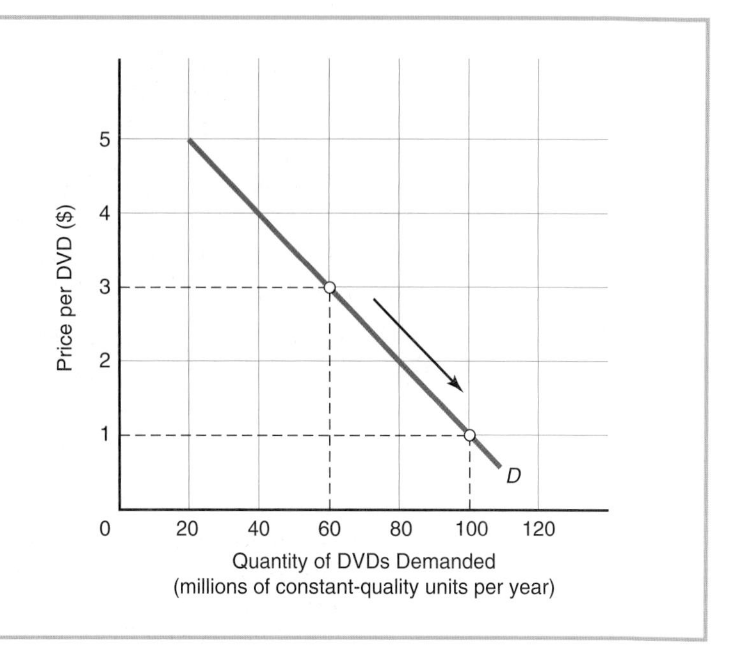

year are demanded. If the price falls to $1, quantity demanded increases to 100 million per year. This movement occurs because the current market price for the product changes. In Figure 3–5, you can see the arrow pointing down the given demand curve *D*.

When you think of demand, think of the entire curve. Quantity demanded, in contrast, is represented by a single point on the demand curve.

> **A change or shift in demand causes the *entire* curve to move. The *only* thing that can cause the entire curve to move is a change in a determinant *other than its own price*.**

In economic analysis, we cannot emphasize too much the following distinction that must constantly be made:

> **A change in a good's own price leads to a change in quantity demanded, for any given demand curve, other things held constant. This is a movement *along* the curve.**

A change in any other determinant of demand leads to a change in demand. This causes a shift *of* the curve.

As Example 3–3 explains, knowing the difference between a change in quantity demanded and a change in demand will help you understand the effects that a used or secondary market has on the market for a new good.

EXAMPLE 3–3 **Garth Brooks, Used CDs, and the Law of Demand**

A few years ago, country singer Garth Brooks tried to prevent his latest album from being sold to any retail chain or store that also sold used CDs. His argument was that the used-CD market deprived labels and artists of earnings. His announcement came after a giant American retailer started selling used CDs side by side with new releases, at half the price. Brooks, along with the distribution arms of Sony, Warner Music, Capitol-EMI, and MCA were trying to quash the used-CD market. This shows that none of these parties understood the law of demand.

continued

Let us say the price of a new CD is $15. The existence of a secondary used-CD market means that to people who choose to resell their CDs for $5, the net cost of a new CD is, in fact, only $10. Because we know that quantity demanded is inversely related to price, more copies of a new CD will be sold at a price of $10 than of the same CD at a price of $15. Taking only this force into account, eliminating the used-CD market will reduce the sale of new CDs.

But there is another force at work here, too. Used CDs are substitutes for new CDs. If used CDs are not available, some people who would have purchased them will instead purchase new CDs. If this second effect outweighs the incentive to buy less because of the higher effective price, then Brooks' attempt to suppress the used-CD market is correct.

For critical analysis: Sketch a demand curve for the product "new music CDs." On this same graph, describe the various effects that the used-CD market has on the "quantity demanded" and the "demand" for "new music CDs."

CONCEPTS IN BRIEF

Learning Objective 3.1: Explain the law of demand.

- The law of demand states that there is an inverse relationship between the quantity demanded of a good and its price.
- The law of demand applies when other nonprice determinants, such as income and the prices of all other goods, are held constant.
- Graphically, the law of demand is illustrated by a downward-sloping demand curve.
- The market demand curve is derived by summing the quantity demanded by all individuals in the market at each price.

Learning Objective 3.2: Distinguish between a change in quantity demanded and a change in demand.

- A change in quantity demanded occurs when there is a change in the good's own price. A change in quantity demanded is described as a movement along the good's demand curve.
- A change in demand occurs when there is a change in a determinant other than the good's own price. A change in demand is described as a shift in the entire demand curve. An increase in demand is shown as a rightward shift and a decrease in demand is shown as a leftward shift.
- Nonprice determinants that shift the demand curve for a good include (1) income, (2) tastes and preferences, (3) prices of related goods, (4) expectations about future prices or future incomes, and (5) population or number of buyers in the market.

3.3 The Law of Supply

The other side of the market for a product involves the quantities of goods and services that *firms* are prepared to *supply* to the market. The **supply** of any good or service is the amount that firms are willing to sell at various possible prices, other things being constant. The relationship between price and quantity supplied, called the **law of supply**, can be summarized as follows:

Supply Refers to the quantities of a specific good or service that firms are willing to sell at various possible prices, other things being constant.

Law of supply The observation that there is a direct relationship between the price of any good and its quantity supplied, holding other factors constant.

> **At higher prices, a larger quantity will generally be supplied than at lower prices, all other things held constant. At lower prices, a smaller quantity will generally be supplied than at higher prices, all other things held constant.**

There is generally a direct relationship between quantity supplied and price. Producers are normally willing to produce and sell more of their product at a higher price than at a lower price, other things being constant. At $5 per DVD, 3M, Sony, Maxell,

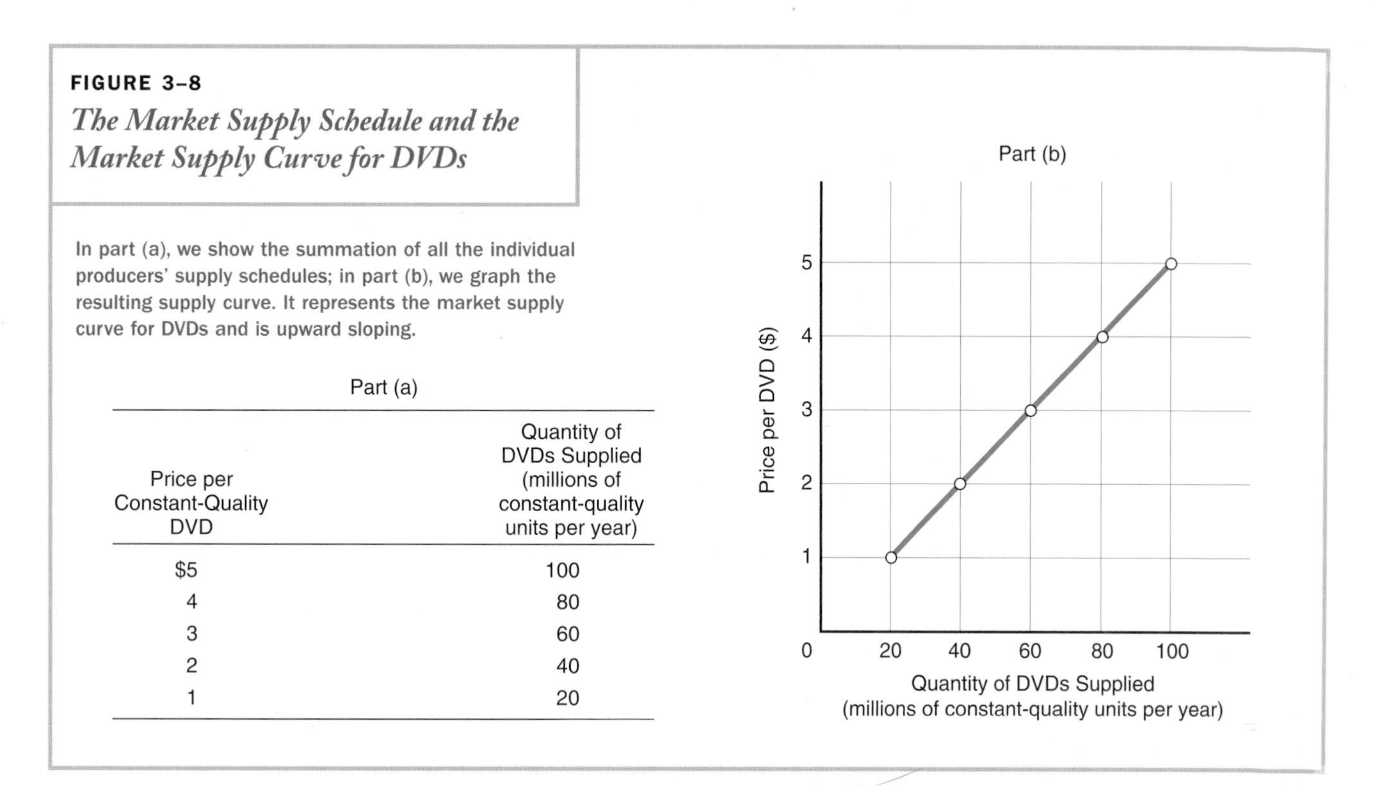

FIGURE 3-8

The Market Supply Schedule and the Market Supply Curve for DVDs

In part (a), we show the summation of all the individual producers' supply schedules; in part (b), we graph the resulting supply curve. It represents the market supply curve for DVDs and is upward sloping.

Part (a)

Price per Constant-Quality DVD	Quantity of DVDs Supplied (millions of constant-quality units per year)
$5	100
4	80
3	60
2	40
1	20

3.4 *Shifts in Supply*

When we looked at demand, we found out that any change in anything relevant other than the price of the good or service caused the demand curve to shift inward or outward. The same is true for the supply curve. If something relevant changes apart from the price of the product or service being supplied, we will see the entire supply curve shift.

Consider an example. A new method of putting magnetic material on DVDs has been invented. It reduces the cost of producing a DVD by 50 percent. In this situation, DVD producers will supply more of their product at all prices because their cost of so doing has fallen dramatically. Competition among DVD manufacturers to produce more at every price will shift the supply schedule of DVDs outward to the right from S_1 to S_2 in Figure 3–9. At a price of $3, the quantity supplied was originally 60 million DVDs per

FIGURE 3-9

A Shift in the Supply Curve

If the cost of producing DVDs were to fall dramatically, the supply curve would shift rightward from S_1 to S_2 such that at all prices, a larger quantity would be forthcoming from suppliers. Conversely, if the cost of production rose, the supply curve would shift leftward to S_3.

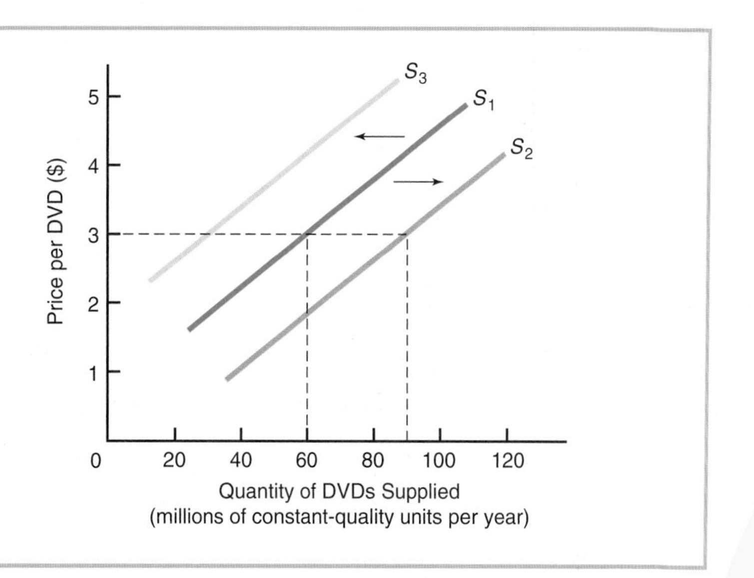

year, but now the quantity supplied (after the reduction in the costs of production) at $3 a DVD will be 90 million DVDs a year. (This is similar to what has happened to the supply curve of personal computers and fax machines in recent years as the price of the computer memory chip has fallen.)

Now, consider the opposite case. If the cost of the magnetic material needed for making DVDs doubles, the supply curve in Figure 3–9 will shift from S_1 to S_3. At each price, the number of DVDs supplied will fall due to the increase in the price of raw materials.

The Other Determinants of Supply

When supply curves are drawn, only the price of the good in question changes, and it is assumed that other things remain constant. The other things assumed constant are the costs of resources (inputs) used to produce the product, technology and productivity, taxes and subsidies, producers' price expectations, and the number of firms in the industry. These are the major nonprice determinants of supply. If any of them changes, there will be a shift in the supply curve.

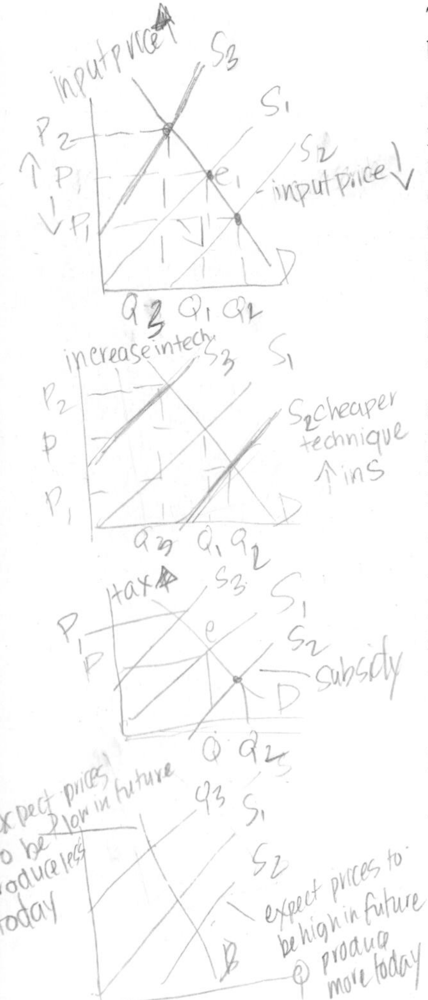

COST OF INPUTS USED TO PRODUCE THE PRODUCT. If one or more input prices fall, the supply curve will shift outward to the right; that is, more will be supplied at each price. The opposite will be true if one or more inputs become more expensive. For example, when we draw the supply curve of new cars, we are holding the cost of steel (and other inputs) constant. If the price of steel decreases, the supply curve for new cars will shift *outward to the right.* When we draw the supply curve of blue jeans, we are holding the cost of cotton fixed. The supply curve for blue jeans will shift inward to the left if the price of cotton *increases.*

TECHNOLOGY AND PRODUCTIVITY. Supply curves are drawn by assuming a given technology, or "state of the art." When the available production techniques change, the supply curve will shift. For example, when a better, cheaper, production technique for DVDs becomes available, the supply curve will shift to the right. A larger quantity will be forthcoming at every price because the cost of production is lower.

TAXES AND SUBSIDIES. Certain taxes, such as a per-unit tax, are effectively an addition to production costs and therefore reduce the supply. If the supply curve were S_1 in Figure 3–9, a per-unit tax increase would shift it to S_3. A subsidy would do the opposite; it would shift the curve to S_2. Every producer would get from the government a "gift" of a few cents for each unit produced.

PRICE EXPECTATIONS. A change in the expectation of a future relative price of a product can affect a producer's current willingness to supply, just as price expectations affect a consumer's current willingness to purchase. For example, DVD suppliers may withhold part of their current supply from the market if they anticipate higher prices in the future. The current amount supplied at all prices will decrease.

NUMBER OF FIRMS IN THE INDUSTRY. In the short run, when firms can only change the number of employees they use, we hold the number of firms in the industry constant. In the long run, the number of firms (or the size of some existing firms) may change. If the number of firms increases, the supply curve will shift outward to the right. If the number of firms decreases, it will shift inward to the left.

Example 3–4 describes how various nonprice determinants of supply have responded quickly in the global war against terrorism.

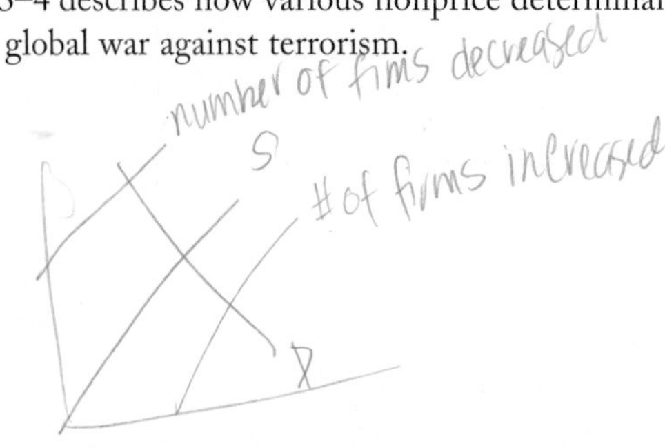

EXAMPLE 3–4 **Falling Costs of Fighting the War on Terror**

The world was taken by surprise when packages containing anthrax-laden powder began appearing in the mail in such locales as Washington, D.C.; New York City; and Karachi, Pakistan. Hardly anyone was prepared to detect whether individuals in affected workplaces had been exposed to the deadly toxin.

Until then, most people had been unwilling to pay the relatively high price of available systems for detecting anthrax and other deadly environmental pathogens. In 2001, firms that manufactured portable diagnostic systems permitting the testing of up to several dozen people offered the packages for sale at a price of nearly $200 000. Chemical equipment that the military could pack into a Humvee for transportation to sites where air quality was suspect was available at prices starting at about $250 000 per vehicle.

Following the terrorist attacks of September 11, 2001, companies accelerated their development of innovative new ways to monitor the air, water, and foods for pathogenic agents and of new lower-cost techniques for speedily diagnosing human exposure to such agents. In addition, biochemical companies that had not previously been involved in this business entered the market.

Improved technologies and the entry of new firms have steadily increased the supply of both monitoring devices and diagnostic equipment. As a result, government agencies, military organizations, and companies around the world are now much better prepared to battle bioterrorism than they were in 2001. They are also paying lower prices for the monitoring and diagnostic tools they wish to have on hand as they wage their war against terrorism.

For critical analysis: What has happened to the supply curve for the tools used to monitor and diagnose bioterror toxins? According to this example, what nonprice determinants of supply have been responsible for this change in supply?

SOURCE: ADAPTATION OF THE EXAMPLE FROM ROGER LEROY MILLER, *ECONOMICS TODAY: THE MICRO VIEW,* 12TH US ED., P. 65.

Changes in Supply versus Changes in Quantity Supplied

We cannot overstress the importance of distinguishing between a movement along the supply curve—which occurs only when the product's price changes—and a shift in the supply curve—which occurs only with changes in other nonprice factors. A change in price always brings about a change in quantity supplied along a given supply curve. We move from one point to another along the same supply curve. This is specifically called a *change in quantity supplied.*

When you think of *supply*, think of the entire curve. Quantity supplied is represented by a single point on the curve.

> A change in supply causes the entire curve to shift. The *only* thing that can cause the entire curve to shift is a change in a determinant *other than price*.

> Consequently,

> A change in the price leads to a change in the quantity supplied, other things being constant. This is a *movement along* the curve.

> A change in any other determinant of supply leads to a change in supply. This causes a *shift of* the curve.

CONCEPTS IN BRIEF

Learning Objective 3.3: Explain the law of supply.

- The law of supply states that there is a direct relationship between the quantity supplied of a good and its price.
- The law of supply applies when other things—such as technology and productivity, cost of inputs, government taxes and subsidies, expectations about future prices, and number of firms—are held constant.
- Graphically, the law of supply is illustrated by an upward-sloping supply curve.
- The market supply curve is derived by summing the quantity supplied by all firms in the market at each price.

Learning Objective 3.4: Distinguish between a change in quantity supplied and a change in supply.

- A change in quantity supplied occurs when there is a change in the good's own price. A change in quantity supplied is described as a movement along the good's supply curve.
- A change in supply occurs when there is a change in a determinant other than the good's own price. A change in supply is described as a shift in the entire supply curve. An increase in supply is shown as a rightward shift, and a decrease in supply is shown as a leftward shift.
- Nonprice determinants that shift the supply curve for a good include (1) cost of inputs, (2) technology and productivity, (3) taxes and subsidies, (4) expectations about future prices, and (5) number of firms in the market.

3.5 Putting Demand and Supply Together

In the sections on supply and demand, we tried to confine each discussion to supply or demand only. But you have probably already realized that we cannot view the world just from the supply side or just from the demand side. There is an interaction between the two. In this section, we will discuss how they interact and how that interaction determines the prices that prevail in our economy. Understanding how demand and supply interact is essential to understanding how prices are determined in our economy and other economies in which the forces of supply and demand are allowed to work.

Let us first combine the demand and supply schedules and then combine the curves.

Demand and Supply Schedules Combined

Let us place part (a) from Figure 3–3 (the market demand schedule) and part (a) from Figure 3–8 (the market supply schedule) together in part (a) of Figure 3–10. Column 1 shows the price; column 2, the quantity supplied per year at any given price; and column 3, the quantity demanded. Column 4 is merely the difference between columns 2 and 3, or the difference between the quantity supplied and the quantity demanded. In column 5, we label those differences as either excess quantity supplied (a surplus), or excess quantity demanded (a shortage). For example, at a price of $2, only 40 million DVDs would be supplied, but the quantity demanded would be 80 million. The difference is 40 million, which we label as excess quantity demanded (a shortage). At the other end of the scale, a price of $5 per DVD would elicit 100 million in quantity supplied, but quantity demanded would drop to 20 million. This leaves a difference of 80 million units, which we call excess quantity supplied (a surplus).

What do you notice about the price of $3? At that price, the quantity supplied and the quantity demanded per year are both 60 million. The difference, then, is zero. There is neither excess quantity demanded (shortage) nor excess quantity supplied (surplus). Hence the price of $3 is very special. It is called the **market clearing price**—it clears the market of all excess supply or excess demand. There are no willing consumers who want to pay $3 per DVD but are turned away by sellers, and there are no willing suppliers who want to sell DVDs at $3 who cannot sell all they want at that price. Another term for the market clearing price is the **equilibrium price**, the price at which there is no tendency for change. At that price, consumers are able to buy all they want and suppliers are able to sell the quantity that they desire.

Market clearing, or equilibrium, price The price at which quantity demanded equals quantity supplied.

FIGURE 3–10

Putting Demand and Supply Together

In part (a), we see that at the price of $3, the quantity supplied and the quantity demanded are equal, resulting in neither an excess in the quantity demanded nor an excess in the quantity supplied. We call this price the equilibrium, or market clearing, price. In part (b), the intersection of the supply and demand curves is at *E*, at a price of $3 per constant-quality DVD and a quantity of 60 million per year. At point *E*, there is neither an excess in the quantity demanded nor an excess in the quantity supplied. At a price of $1, the quantity supplied will be only 20 million DVDs per year, but the quantity demanded will be 100 million. The difference is excess quantity demanded at a price of $1. The price will rise, and so we will move from point *A* up the supply curve and point *B* up the demand curve to point *E*. At the other extreme, $5 elicits a quantity supplied of 100 million but a quantity demanded of only 20 million. The difference is excess quantity supplied at a price of $5. The price will fall, and so we will move down the demand curve and the supply curve to the equilibrium price, $3 per DVD.

Part (a)

(1) Price per Constant-Quality DVD	(2) Quantity Supplied (DVDs per year)	(3) Quantity Demanded (DVDs per year)	(4) Difference (2) — (3) (DVDs per year)	(5) Condition
$5	100 million	20 million	80 million	Excess quantity supplied (surplus)
4	80 million	40 million	40 million	Excess quantity supplied (surplus)
3	60 million	60 million	0	Market clearing price equilibrium (no surplus, no shortage)
2	40 million	80 million	−40 million	Excess quantity demanded (shortage)
1	20 million	100 million	−80 million	Excess quantity demanded (shortage)

Part (b)

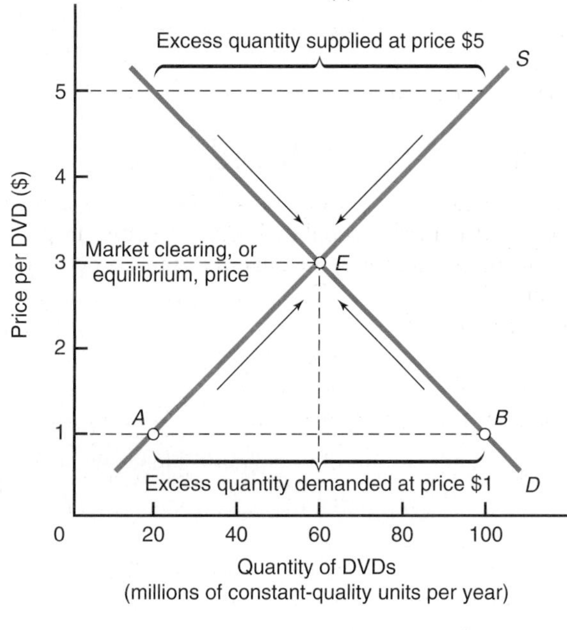

Equilibrium A point from which there tends to be no movement unless demand or supply changes.

We can define **equilibrium** in general as a point from which there tends to be no movement unless demand or supply changes. Any movement away from this point will set in motion certain forces that will cause movement back to it. Therefore, equilibrium is a stable point. Any point that is not at equilibrium is unstable and cannot be maintained.

The equilibrium point occurs where the supply and demand curves intersect. The equilibrium price is given on the vertical axis directly to the left of where the supply and demand curves cross. The equilibrium quantity demanded and supplied is given on the horizontal axis directly underneath the intersection of the demand and supply curves. Equilibrium can change whenever there is a *shock*.

A shock to the supply-and-demand system can be represented by a shift in the supply curve, a shift in the demand curve, or a shift in both. Any shock to the system will result in a new set of supply-and-demand relationships and a new equilibrium; forces will come into play to move the system from the old price–quantity equilibrium (now a disequilibrium situation) to the new equilibrium, where the new demand and supply curves intersect.

Part (b) from Figure 3–3 and part (b) from Figure 3–8 are combined as part (b) in Figure 3–10 on page 77. The only difference now is that the horizontal axis measures both the quantity supplied and the quantity demanded per year. Everything else is the same. The demand curve is labelled *D*, the supply curve *S*. We have labelled the intersection of the two curves as point *E*, for equilibrium. That corresponds to a market clearing price of \$3, at which both the quantity supplied and the quantity demanded are 60 million units per year. There is neither a surplus nor a shortage. Point *E*, the equilibrium point, always occurs at the intersection of the supply and demand curves. This is the price toward which the market price will automatically tend to gravitate.

Shortages

The demand and supply curves in Figure 3–10 represent a situation of equilibrium. But a non–market-clearing, or disequilibrium, price will bring into play forces that cause the price to change and move toward the market clearing price. Then, equilibrium is again sustained. Look once more at part (b) in Figure 3–10 on page 77. Suppose that instead of being at the market clearing price of \$3 per DVD, for some reason, the market price is \$1 per DVD. At this price, the quantity demanded (100 million), exceeds the quantity supplied (20 million). We have a situation of excess quantity demanded at the price of \$1. This is usually called a *shortage*. Consumers of DVDs would find that they could not buy all that they wished at \$1 apiece. But forces will cause the price to rise: Competing consumers will bid up the price, and suppliers will raise the price and increase output, whether explicitly or implicitly. (Remember, some buyers would pay \$5 or more, rather than do without DVDs. They do not want to be left out.) We would move from points *A* and *B* toward point *E*. The process would stop when the price again reached \$3 per DVD.

Shortage A situation in which the quantity demanded exceeds the quantity supplied at a price below the market clearing price.

At this point it is important to note that shortages and scarcity are not the same thing. A **shortage** is a situation in which the quantity demanded exceeds the quantity supplied at a price *below* the market clearing price. Our definition of scarcity in Chapter 1 was much more general and all-encompassing: a situation in which the resources available for producing output are insufficient to satisfy all wants. Any choice necessarily costs an opportunity, and the opportunity is lost. Hence we will always live in a world of scarcity because we must constantly make choices, but we do not necessarily have to live in a world of shortages.

Surpluses

Now, let us repeat the experiment with the market price at \$5 per DVD, rather than at the market clearing price of \$3. Clearly, the quantity supplied will exceed the quantity demanded at that price. The result will be an excess quantity supplied at \$5 per unit. This is often called a **surplus**, a situation in which quantity supplied is greater than quantity demanded at a price above the market clearing price. Given the curves in part (b) in Figure 3–10, however, there will be forces pushing the price back down toward \$3 per DVD: Competing suppliers will attempt to reduce their inventories by cutting prices and

Surplus A situation in which quantity supplied is greater than quantity demanded at a price above the ·rket clearing price.

reducing output, and consumers will offer to purchase more at lower prices. Suppliers will want to reduce inventories, which will be above their optimal level; that is, there will be an excess over what each seller believes to be the most profitable stock of DVDs. After all, inventories are costly to hold. But consumers may find out about such excess inventories and see the possibility of obtaining increased quantities of DVDs at a decreased price. It benefits consumers to attempt to obtain a good at a lower price, and they will therefore try to do so. If the two forces of supply and demand are unrestricted, they will bring the price back to $3 per DVD.

Shortages and surpluses are resolved in unfettered markets—markets in which price changes are free to occur. The forces that resolve them are those of competition: In the case of shortages, consumers competing for a limited quantity supplied drive up the price; in the case of surpluses, sellers compete for the limited quantity demanded, thus driving prices down to equilibrium. The equilibrium price is the only stable price, and all (unrestricted) market prices tend to gravitate toward it.

3.6 *Changes in Equilibrium*

Shifts in Demand or Supply

When a nonprice determinant of demand or supply changes, this will result in a shift in the demand or the supply curve for the product under study. In turn, this will cause the product's equilibrium price and equilibrium quantity to change. In certain situations, it is possible to predict in which direction the equilibrium price and equilibrium quantity will change. Specifically, whenever one curve is stable while the other curve shifts, we can tell what will happen to price and quantity. Consider the four possibilities in Figure 3–11. Each possibility starts with the equilibrium price of DVDs equal to $3.00 ($P_1$) and the equilibrium quantity equal to 60 million DVDs (Q_1).

INCREASE IN DEMAND. In Figure 3–11 part (a), the supply curve remains stable but *demand increases* from D_1 to D_2. Note that the result is both *an increase in the equilibrium price* of DVDs from P_1 to P_2 and an *increase in equilibrium quantity* from Q_1 to Q_2 ($P_e\uparrow Q_e\uparrow$).

Nonprice determinants that can cause an increase in demand include an increase in income with DVDs being a normal good; an increase in the price of a substitute good for DVDs; a decrease in the price of a complement good for DVDs; an increase in population or number of buyers, a change in tastes that favours DVDs; and expectations that DVD prices will increase in the future.

DECREASE IN DEMAND. In Figure 3–11 part (b), the supply curve remains stable but *demand decreases* from D_1 to D_3. Note that the result is both a *decrease in the equilibrium price* of DVDs from P_1 to P_3 and a *decrease in equilibrium quantity* from Q_1 to Q_3 ($P_e\downarrow Q_e\downarrow$).

INCREASE IN SUPPLY. In Figure 3–11 part (c), the demand curve remains stable but *supply increases* from S_1 to S_2. Note that the result is a *decrease in the equilibrium price* of DVDs from P_1 to P_2 and *an increase in equilibrium quantity* from Q_1 to Q_2 ($P_e\downarrow Q_e\uparrow$).

Nonprice determinants that can cause an increase in supply include a decline in the costs of inputs used to manufacture DVDs; a technological change increasing the productivity of manufacturing DVDs; a reduction in taxes imposed on DVD manufacturers; an increase in the subsidies enjoyed by DVD manufacturers; and an increase in the number of firms manufacturing DVDs.

DECREASE IN SUPPLY. In Figure 3–11 part (d), the demand curve remains stable but *supply decreases* from S_1 to S_3. Note that the result is both an *increase in the equilibrium price* of DVDs from P_1 to P_3 and *a decrease in equilibrium quantity* from Q_1 to Q_3 ($P_e\uparrow Q_e\downarrow$).

According to this chapter's Issues and Applications, Canadian Internet pharmacies have been making a lot of money buying prescription drugs from American drug manufacturers and then reselling these same drugs to American consumers at relatively low retail prices. As this practice grows, it threatens to reduce overall drug prices in the United

FIGURE 3–11

Shifts in Demand or Supply

In part (a), the supply curve is stable at S. The demand curve shifts outward, or increases, from D_1 to D_2. The equilibrium price increases from P_1 to P_2 and the equilibrium quantity increases from Q_1 to Q_2. In part (b), with the supply curve stable, the demand curve shifts to the left or decreases. In this case, the equilibrium price decreases from P_1 to P_3, while the equilibrium quantity decreases from Q_1 to Q_3. In part (c), the demand curve is stable at D. Now the supply curve shifts to the right or increases. This results in a decrease in the equilibrium price from P_1 to P_2 but an increase in equilibrium quantity from Q_1 to Q_2. In part (d), with the demand curve stable at D, there is a leftward shift, or a decrease in the supply. While this causes the equilibrium price to increase from P_1 to P_3, the equilibrium quantity decreases from Q_1 to Q_3.

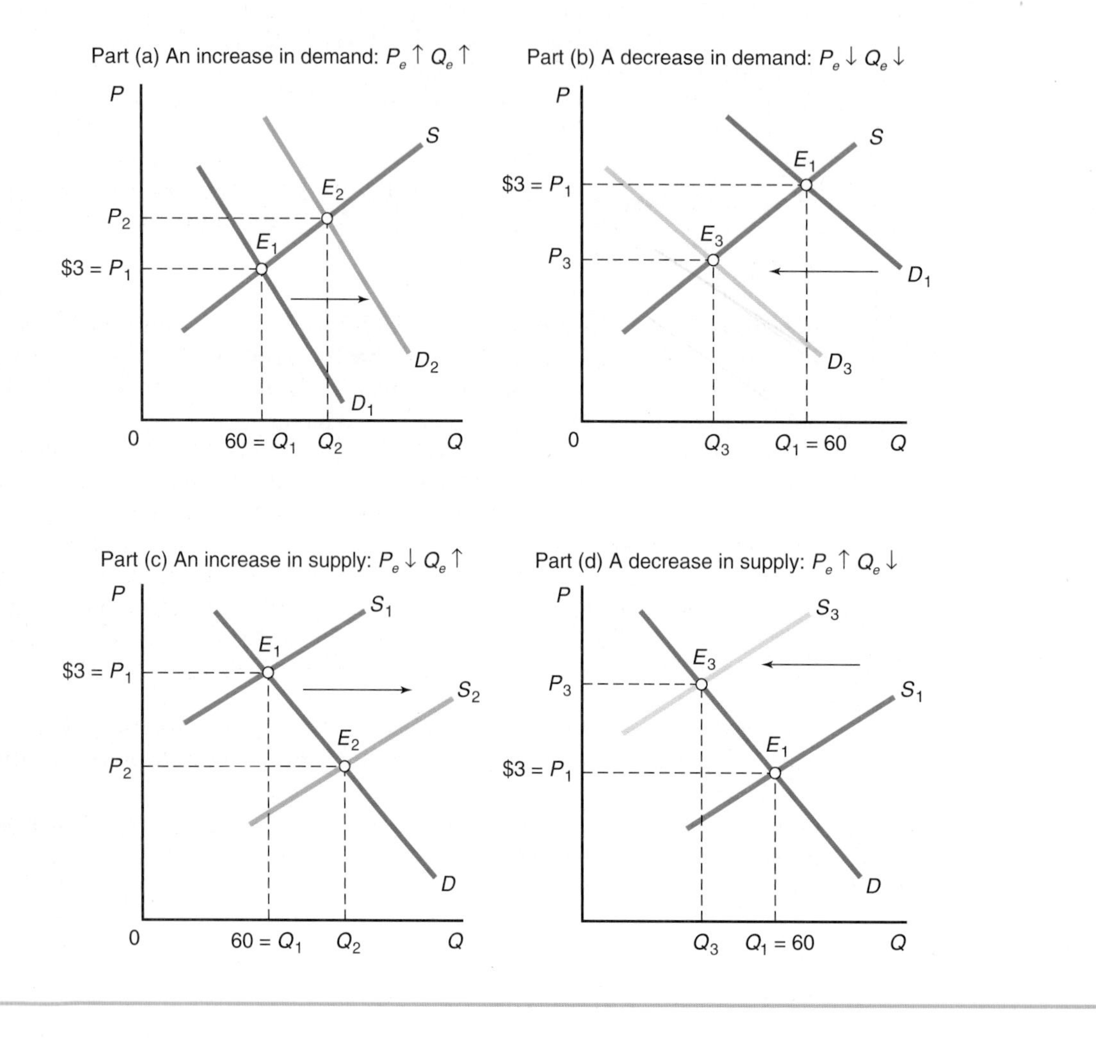

States, which, in turn, can reduce the profits earned by the American drug manufacturers. As a result, the American drug manufacturers are beginning to cut back the quantity of prescription drugs distributed to Canadian Internet pharmacies. To the extent that these cutbacks significantly reduce the supply of drugs available to Canadian pharmacies, this can result in higher equilibrium drug prices paid by Canadian consumers, as explained in Figure 3–11 part (d).

The principles of supply and demand presented above are powerful tools that will allow you to predict the future effects that current events will have on markets that affect you. Presumably, you will be able to react to these predictions in a manner that promotes your self-interest. As Policy Example 3–2 illustrates, supply and demand can also prove useful when evaluating government policies that interfere with market outcomes.

POLICY EXAMPLE 3–2 **Assisted Human Reproduction Not for Sale in Canada?**

On October 28, 2003, the Canadian House of Commons passed the third reading of Bill C-13, *The Assisted Human Reproduction Act*. Before this bill becomes law, it must be approved by the Canadian Senate. Among other things, this bill proposes to ban human cloning and will prohibit Canadian infertility clinics from offering monetary payments to sperm and egg donors. Only voluntary donations of sperm and ova will be permitted, if this bill is passed into law.

Critics of Bill C-13 have warned that it will significantly reduce hope for numerous infertile couples residing in Canada, especially those who fall in the lower-income brackets. Currently, before the passage of Bill C-13, many American companies are involved in the matching of American women willing to donate their eggs (for money) with Canadian couples planning to undergo in-vitro fertilization at a cost of up to U.S. $6000. These American companies arrange for the donor to travel to a Canadian clinic where her eggs are retrieved in a surgical procedure performed by a Canadian doctor. Under Bill C-13, this process will become illegal because the donor is paid.

If Bill C-13 is passed into law, many Canadian couples will find it much more expensive to undergo in-vitro fertilization, as they will be forced to travel to the United States to have the procedure completed. The Colorado Center for Reproductive Medicine, for example, has a clinic for international patients that charges a rate of U.S. $20 000 for the procedure, involving a weeklong stay.

Even without the passage of Bill C-13, Canada imports about one-third of the sperm used in reproductive technologies from the United States because running a sperm clinic is too expensive for nonprofit Canadian hospitals. Since the American sperm donors are financially compensated, this supply will be off-limits to Canadian clinics under Bill C-13.

While Bill C-13 is meant to promote the health and welfare of Canadians by prohibiting assisted reproduction for commercial ends, some medical practitioners are concerned that this legislation will do just the opposite. It will force Canadian couples to find their own doctors, clinics, and donors in an unregulated American market.

For critical analysis: Explain how the passage of Bill C-13 will affect the market for assisted human reproduction in Canada. What equity conflicts are likely to result from this type of legislation?

SOURCE: HEATHER SOKOLOFF. "FERTILITY TOURISTS EXPECTED TO FLOCK TO U.S CLINICS," *NATIONAL POST*, OCTOBER 31, 2000, P. A.5.

When Both Demand and Supply Shift

Each example given in Figure 3–11 shows a predictable outcome for equilibrium price and quantity based on a shift in either the demand curve holding the supply curve constant or the supply curve holding the demand curve constant. Often, we want to predict the changes in equilibrium price and quantity in market situations where *multiple nonprice determinants* are changing at the same time, resulting in shifts in *both* demand and supply. As you will see below, unless you know the full extent of each individual shift in demand and supply, the overall outcome will be *indeterminate* for *either* equilibrium price *or* equilibrium quantity.

INCREASE IN DEMAND AND INCREASE IN SUPPLY. Suppose the price of CDs, a substitute for DVDs, significantly increases, causing an *increase in demand* for DVDs. At the same time, new technology reduces the cost of manufacturing DVDs, resulting in an *increase in supply* of DVDs. To predict the overall effect on the equilibrium price and quantity of DVDs, we suggest that you begin by analyzing the effect of *each individual shift* on equilibrium price and quantity using the appropriate part in Figure 3–11.

According to part (a) in Figure 3–11, an *increase in demand* for DVDs will cause the *equilibrium price to increase* and the *equilibrium quantity to increase* ($P_e\uparrow Q_e\uparrow$). Similarly, part (c) in Figure 3.11 suggests that *an increase in supply* will cause *the equilibrium price to decrease* and the *equilibrium quantity to increase* ($P_e\downarrow Q_e\uparrow$).

If you now combine the effects of both shifts, you can conclude that the *equilibrium quantity will certainly increase*, but the overall effect on equilibrium price is *indeterminate*, meaning that it could go up or down or stay the same, depending on the extent of the shift in both curves. Figure 3–12 describes a situation where the supply shifts by a larger amount than the demand shifts, resulting in an overall decrease in the equilibrium price of DVDs.

At the start of this chapter, in the Did You Know That section, it was noted that cellular phone prices have been declining despite the fact that the demand for cellular phones has been significantly increasing worldwide. Now that you have been exposed to the tools of demand and supply, you are in a better position to understand the current trends in the cellular phone industry.

The smaller computer chips that have been invented have reduced the size and increased the portability of cellular phones, resulting in an increase in demand for cellular phones. As well, the concern for personal safety has increased the demand for cellular phones. At the same time, new technology has significantly reduced the cost of the computer chips used in the manufacture of cellular phones, and this has increased the supply of cellular phones. Since you know that the price of cellular phones has been declining, you can conclude that the increase in supply has exceeded the increase in demand in the cellular phone industry. As Figure 3–12 illustrates, this situation leads to a decline in equilibrium price and a substantial increase in equilibrium quantity, explaining what has often been called the " cellular phone explosion."

DECREASE IN DEMAND AND DECREASE IN SUPPLY. Suppose the average household income declines, causing a *decrease in demand* for DVDs. At the same time, the number of firms manufacturing DVDs declines, resulting in *a decrease in supply* of DVDs. On the basis of parts (b) and (d) of Figure 3–11, you can conclude that the *equilibrium quantity will certainly decrease*, but the overall *effect on equilibrium price is indeterminate*. If after further investigation, you determine that the decrease in demand (pulling the price down) far exceeds the decrease in supply (pushing the price up), you can predict that the equilibrium price will decline, as illustrated in Figure 3–13.

FIGURE 3–12

An Increase in Demand and Supply

The original equilibrium price is $3 per DVD, and the original equilibrium quantity is 60 million DVDs, which is determined by the intersection of D_1 and S_1. With an increase in demand and supply, the new demand curve is D_2, and the new supply curve is S_2. The new equilibrium price and quantity, located at the intersection of D_2 and S_2 is $2.50 and 120 million DVDs, respectively. The overall result is that the equilibrium price decreases and the equilibrium quantity increases significantly.

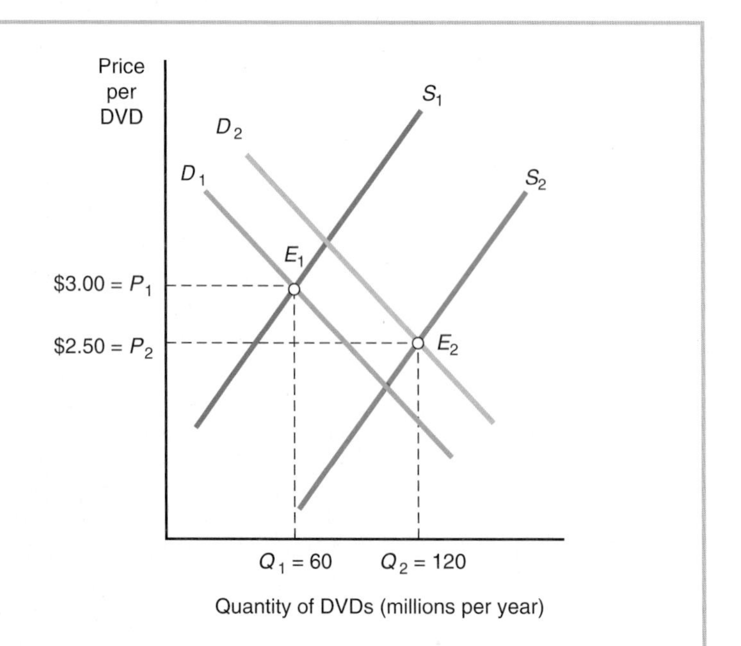

FIGURE 3–13

A Decrease in Demand and Supply

The original equilibrium price is $3 per DVD, and the original equilibrium quantity is 60 million DVDs, which is determined by the intersection of D_1 and S_1. With a decrease in demand and supply, the new demand curve is D_3 and the new supply curve is S_3. The new equilibrium price and quantity, located at the intersection of D_3 and S_3 is $2.75 and 20 million DVDs, respectively. The overall result is that the equilibrium price decreases and the equilibrium quantity decreases significantly.

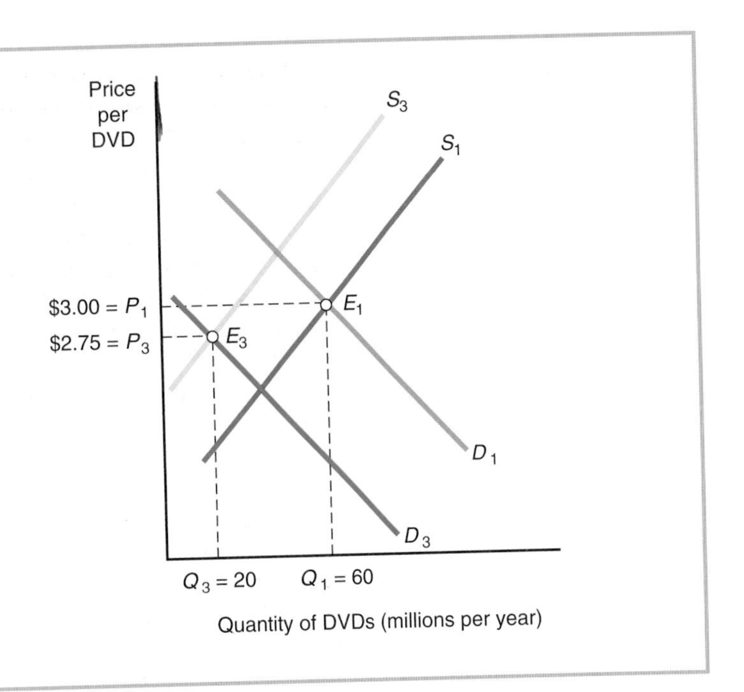

INCREASE IN DEMAND AND DECREASE IN SUPPLY. Suppose consumers, expecting the prices of DVDs to skyrocket in the future, increase their demand for DVDs in the current period. At the same time, the government imposes a new tax on DVD manufacturers, causing a *decrease in supply* of DVDs. On the basis of parts (a) and (d) of Figure 3–11, you can conclude that the *equilibrium price will certainly increase*, but the overall *effect on equilibrium quantity is indeterminate.*

DECREASE IN DEMAND AND INCREASE IN SUPPLY. Suppose the price of DVD players, a complement of DVDs, significantly increases, causing a decrease in demand for DVDs. At the same time, the government provides subsidies to Canadian DVD manufacturers, resulting in an increase in supply of DVDs. On the basis of parts (b) and (c) of Figure 3–11, you can conclude that the *equilibrium price will certainly decrease*, but the overall *effect on equilibrium quantity is indeterminate.*

As Example 3–5 explains, industry supply and demand trends can have a significant impact on the fortunes or misfortunes of major Canadian corporations.

EXAMPLE 3–5 **Air Canada Losses Are Flying High**

In the 12 months ending September 30, 2003, Air Canada mounted an annual loss exceeding $1 billion. Between July 2000 and December 2003, Air Canada's stock price nose-dived from $20 per share to $0.94 per share. Air Canada has been operating under bankruptcy-court protection from creditors since April 1, 2003. A review of the demand and supply trends affecting international air carriers helps explain, at least in part, the company's dismal financial situation.

The terrorist attacks of September 11, 2001, have significantly reduced air travel, globally. Due to these attacks, air carriers are now faced with increased security costs. Rising fuel and labour costs have also cut into airline profits. Many businesses are relying increasingly on video- and teleconferencing technologies in order to communicate across distances.

continued

Even as international airlines stake out their positions in the global market, they are not immune to competition in their own backyards. Regional airlines have gained new ground in regional routes, with the development of newer, smaller, more cost-efficient jets.

For critical analysis: According to this example, what is happening to the market demand and market supply for the air travel services provided by international air carriers? Explain. What is the predicted effect on the equilibrium quantity of air passengers and equilibrium airfares related to the international air carriers?

SOURCES: "AIR CANADA." GLOBEINVESTOR.COM. ACCESSED DECEMBER 13, 2003. http://investdb.theglobeandmail.com/invest/investSQL/gx.company_prof?company_id=168356; "AIRLINES INDUSTRY PROFILE. INDUSTRY CENTER." YAHOO!FINANCE. ACCESSED DECEMBER 13, 2003. http://biz.yahoo.com/ic/prof/4.html.

CONCEPTS IN BRIEF

Learning Objective 3.5: Explain how the forces of demand and supply interact to determine equilibrium price and quantity.

- Equilibrium price and quantity occur where market demand equals market supply. Graphically, equilibrium occurs where the market demand curve intersects the market supply curve.
- The forces of surpluses and shortages ensure that the market will stabilize at equilibrium. Whenever the price is greater than the equilibrium price, there is an excess quantity supplied (surplus). This surplus puts downward pressure on price. Whenever the price is below the equilibrium price, there is an excess quantity demanded (shortage). This shortage puts upward pressure on price.

Learning Objective 3.6: Describe how changes in demand and supply can change equilibrium price and quantity.

- An increase in demand will cause the equilibrium price and quantity to increase. A decrease in demand will cause the equilibrium price and quantity to decrease.
- An increase in supply will cause the equilibrium price to decrease and the equilibrium quantity to increase. A decrease in supply will cause the equilibrium price to increase and the equilibrium quantity to decrease.
- When both demand and supply change in the same direction, the equilibrium quantity will also change in the same direction, but the equilibrium price might increase, decrease, or remain the same.
- When both demand and supply change in opposite directions, the equilibrium price will change in the same direction as demand, but the equilibrium quantity might increase, decrease, or remain the same.

ISSUES AND APPLICATIONS

Is Canada the Prescription for Lower Drug Prices in the United States?

Concepts Applied: Changes in Demand and Supply, Changes in Equilibrium Price and Quantity

Americans show their demands while joining the RX Express, a group travelling by train from Miami to Toronto to buy medicine at prices 30 to 60 percent cheaper than in the United States.

The Dramatic Growth in the Canadian Internet Drug Export Industry

The Canadian prescription export industry started to attract international attention when busloads of American seniors travelled to drugstores, located just north of the American border, to purchase drugs in 1999. It was estimated that 10 million American consumers would spend $1 billion on prescription drugs sold through Canadian Internet pharmacies in 2003.

This rapidly growing Canadian export industry is based on the fact that many popular brand name prescription drugs sell for significantly lower prices in Canada than in the United States. Table 3–2 compares average Canadian and American list prices (in American dollars) taken from a sample of American and Canadian online pharmacies between October 1 and October 7, 2003, for a select number of brand name prescription drugs. As you can see, the average Canadian price for the eight selected drugs is $56.75, which is less than half (47%) the average American price ($121.97).

Why are brand name prescription drugs so much cheaper in Canada than in the United States? A number of factors help explain this difference.

In Canada, brand name prescription drugs are regulated by the Patent Medicine Prices Review Board to prevent excessive price gouging of the Canadian consumer. A new drug brought into the Canadian market, while protected by a 20-year patent, cannot cost more than the most expensive existing drug in its therapeutic class. If no similar drugs are sold in Canada, the board will ensure that the new drug's price will not exceed the average price charged in other countries where the drug is currently sold. In Canada, throughout the patent period, a drug's price cannot increase faster than the Canadian Consumer Price Index. Since there is no such form of government price control in the United States, prescription drug companies can charge higher prices to American consumers.

TABLE 3–2

Online Prices of Prescription Drugs in Canada and the United States

Prescription	Drug Description	American Online Price	Canadian Online Price
Clarinex 5 mg, 30 pills	Oral Antihistamine	$ 68.99	$ 24.99
Coumadin 5 mg, 100 pills	Blood Thinner	$ 69.99	$ 28.68
Lipitor 20 mg, 90 pills	Cholesterol Reducer	$275.97	$178.89
Mobic 15 mg, 30 pills	Anti-osteoarthritis	$ 87.89	$ 35.92
Prevacid 15 mg, 30 pills	Anti-acid	$120.99	$ 64.72
Risperdal 25 mg, 60 pills	Anti-psychotic	$167.99	$ 46.30
Synthroid 15 mg, 100 pills	Thyroid Treatment	$ 61.99	$ 17.73
Average Price		$121.97	$ 56.75

SOURCE: "DRUG PRICE COMPARISON." THE FIGHT FOR AFFORDABLE PRESCRIPTION DRUGS—STATE OF ILLINOIS. OCTOBER 2003. ACCESSED DECEMBER 20, 2003. http://www.affordabledrugs.il.gov/price.cfm.

In Canada, provincial governments pay for about 45 percent of outpatient drugs, about double what the American governments pay. This gives the provinces significant "buying power" over the drug companies selling the drugs. If the drug companies want to have their drugs covered by a provincial government drug insurance plan, they need to charge prices that are competitive with similar drugs insured by the plan.

Finally, Canadian income has increased at a lower rate than U.S. income over the past decade and this has caused a decrease in demand for prescription drugs in Canada, when compared to the U.S. As a result, prescription drug prices are lower in Canada.

SOURCE: JOHN GRAHAM. "PRESCRIPTION DRUG PRICES IN CANADA AND THE US—PART 4, CANADIAN PRESCRIPTIONS FOR AMERICAN PATIENTS ARE NOT THE SOLUTION." SEPTEMBER 2003. FRASER INSTITUTE. ACCESSED DECEMBER 20, 2003. http://www.fraserinstitute.ca/shared/readmore.asp?sNav=pb&id=580.

The Online Purchase Process: An Illegal Form of Reimportation

So, how do American consumers go about purchasing prescription drugs from Canadian Internet pharmacies? Canadian Internet pharmacies advertise the cheaper Canadian drug prices on the Web. After surfing the Web, American consumers choose the specific Canadian Internet pharmacies to import their drugs from. They then fax their American doctors' drug prescriptions to these Canadian pharmacies. Upon paying Canadian doctors a fee to cosign the American drug prescriptions, the Canadian Internet pharmacies mail out the drug orders directly to the homes of the American consumers.

Throughout the United States, American entrepreneurs recognized that there were many millions of people who did not have Internet access, and so they began opening up "storefront" operations in the United States that performed the Internet purchases and faxes on behalf of the American consumers. These storefront operations significantly expanded the imports of prescription drugs from Canada.

The online purchase process, described above, has frequently been referred to as drug reimportation. Many of the drugs sold by the Canadian Internet pharmacies are actually developed, patented, and manufactured in the United States by large multinational drug companies. The multinational companies distribute these drugs to large wholesalers, who, in turn, sell them to Canadian Internet pharmacies. When American consumers end up buying the drugs from Canadian Internet pharmacies, these goods are in essence reimported back into the United States.

American Opposition to Large-Scale Drug Reimportation

Strictly speaking, the reimportation of pharmaceuticals into the United States is illegal. The U.S. Food and Drug Administration (FDA) is responsible for enforcing this law. While the FDA continues to allow individual American consumers to import 90-day supplies of Canadian pharmaceuticals, it has recently been successful in getting the American courts to shut down many of the American storefront operations that were facilitating large-scale purchases from Canadian Internet suppliers. The FDA has justified these shutdowns by mounting publicity campaigns suggesting that Internet pharmacies can lead to the sale of counterfeit prescription drugs that threaten the safety of American consumers.

If drug reimportation is allowed to take place on a large-scale basis, this would serve to lower the price that the multinational drug companies get from selling their brand name prescription drugs on their home turf—in the United States. Hence, these multinational companies have supported the recent moves to shut down storefront operations facilitating reimportation. Moreover, six large American multinational drug companies have begun to restrict the sale of brand name drugs to Canadian Internet pharmacies.

American Support for Large-Scale Drug Reimportation

A number of American politicians have been promoting large-scale drug reimportation. Such a move would help ensure that necessary prescription drugs remain affordable for low-income American families. As well, drug reimportation would significantly improve the efficiency of numerous municipal and state insurance plans by lowering drug costs. The mayor of Springfield, Massachusetts, recently made the decision to purchase all the prescription drugs for his city's health insurance plan from Canadian Internet pharmacies. The states of Iowa, Illinois, Michigan, and Minnesota are all considering similar measures. The U.S. House of Representatives has passed a bill supporting large-scale drug reimportation. However, this bill is likely to be opposed by the American senate, which would prevent it from being passed into law.

Canadian Concerns with Large-Scale Drug Importation

Even in Canada, there have been recent moves to reduce the practice of drug reimportation. Provincial medical associations have been reprimanding some of the Canadian doctors who have facilitated reimportation by cosigning the American prescriptions faxed to Canadian Internet pharmacies. The actions of these doctors have been viewed as unethical in that they are authorizing prescriptions for American patients who have not been examined by them.

If drug reimportation is allowed to expand on a large-scale basis, this could have detrimental effects for Canadian drug consumers. The large American multinational drug companies will reduce their shipments of popular prescription drugs to the Canadian market, or they will pressure the Canadian government to relax the drug price controls, in exchange for resuming shipments of key drugs. Either way, Canada loses. Canadians could be deprived of much-needed medicines or wind up paying much higher prices for drugs.

SOURCE: BARRIE MCKENNA. "CANADIAN DRUGS NOT PRESCRIPTION FOR U.S. HEALTH ILLS." *THE GLOBE AND MAIL*. NOVEMBER 7, 2003.

For critical analysis:

1. According to the information provided in this Issues and Applications, are prescription drugs considered to be normal or inferior goods in Canada? Explain.
2. Identify the various nonprice determinants that result in an increase in demand for the prescription drugs sold by Canadian Internet pharmacies.
3. Identify the various nonprice determinants that result in a decrease in supply of the prescription drugs sold by Canadian Internet pharmacies.
4. Suppose the American government legalizes the reimportation of prescription drugs from Canadian Internet pharmacies. At the same time, suppose the multinational drug manufacturers significantly cut back the quantity of prescription drugs distributed to Canadian Internet pharmacies. Predict the effect that these two events will have on the equilibrium price and quantity of prescription drugs sold to Canadian consumers.

SUMMARY DISCUSSION OF LEARNING OBJECTIVES

3.1 **The Law of Demand.** According to the law of demand, other things being equal, households will purchase fewer units of a good at a higher price and more units of a good at a lower price. This law is described by a downward-sloping demand curve.

3.2 **Shifts in Demand.** A change in the good's own price causes a change in quantity demanded, which is a movement along the same demand curve. A change in demand is described as a shift in the entire demand curve caused by a change in a nonprice determinant, such as income, tastes, prices of related goods, expectations, and number of buyers. An increase in demand means that the demand curve shifts rightward, while a decrease in demand implies a leftward shift.

3.3 **The Law of Supply.** According to the law of supply, firms will produce and offer for sale more units of a good at a higher price and fewer units of a good at a lower price. This law is described by an upward-sloping supply curve.

3.4 **Shifts in Supply.** A change in the good's own price causes a change in quantity supplied, which is a movement along the same supply curve. A change in supply is described as a shift in the entire supply curve caused by a change in a nonprice determinant, such as input prices, technology and productivity, taxes and subsidies, price expectations, and number of sellers. An increase in supply means that the supply curve shifts rightward, while a decrease in supply implies a leftward shift.

3.5 **Putting Demand and Supply Together.** The equilibrium price and equilibrium quantity occur where market demand equals market supply. Graphically, equilibrium occurs where the market demand curve intersects the market supply curve. At this point, the plans of sellers and buyers match, meaning that shortages and surpluses are eliminated.

3.6 **Changes in Equilibrium.** An increase in demand will cause equilibrium price and quantity to increase, whereas a decrease in demand will cause equilibrium price and quantity to decrease. An increase in supply will cause equilibrium price to decrease and equilibrium quantity to increase, whereas a decrease in supply will cause equilibrium price to increase and equilibrium quantity to decrease. When both demand and supply change in the same direction, the equilibrium quantity will also change in the same direction, but the equilibrium price might increase, decrease, or remain the same. When both demand and supply change in opposite directions, the equilibrium price will change in the same direction as demand, but the equilibrium quantity might increase, decrease, or remain the same.

PROBLEMS

(Answers to the odd-numbered problems appear at the back of the book.)

LO 3.1, 3.2 Explain the law of demand; distinguish between a change in quantity demanded and a change in demand.

1. Examine the following table, and then answer the questions.

	Price per Unit Last Year	Price per Unit Today
Heating oil	$1.00	$2.00
Natural gas	$0.80	$3.20

What has happened to the absolute price of heating oil? Of natural gas? What has happened to the price of heating oil relative to the price of natural gas? What has happened to the relative price of natural gas? Will consumers, through time, change their relative purchases? If so, how?

2. Give an example of a complement and a substitute in consumption for each of the following items:
   a. Bacon
   b. Coffee
   c. Automobiles

3. Consider the market for Canadian beef. Explain whether each of the following events would cause an increase in demand, a decrease in demand, an increase in quantity demanded, or a decrease in quantity demanded. Also describe how each event will affect the demand curve for Canadian beef.
   a. The price of chicken decreases.
   b. Household income increases, and beef is a normal good.
   c. The price of Canadian beef decreases.
   d. A Canadian cow is found to have mad cow disease.
   e. The Canadian government raises the price of Canadian beef.

LO 3.3, 3.4 Explain the law of supply; distinguish between a change in quantity supplied and a change in supply.

4. Consider the market for newly constructed bungalow homes in Canada. Explain whether each of the following events would cause an increase in supply, a decrease in supply, an increase in quantity supplied, or a decrease in quantity supplied. Also describe how each event will affect the supply curve for new Canadian bungalow homes.
   a. The price of lumber skyrockets in Canada.
   b. The Canadian government lowers the price of new bungalow homes in Canada.
   c. New technology is developed that significantly reduces the cost of building new bungalows.
   d. The Canadian government provides subsidies to builders of new Canadian bungalows.
   e. The price of Canadian bungalows increases.

LO 3.5, 3.6 Explain how the forces of demand and supply interact to determine equilibrium price and quantity; describe how changes in demand and supply can change equilibrium price and quantity.

5. Suppose that, in a recent market period, an industry-wide survey determined the following relationship between the price of rock music CDs and the quantity supplied and demanded.

Price	Quantity Demanded	Quantity Supplied
$ 9	100 million	40 million
$10	90 million	60 million
$11	80 million	80 million
$12	70 million	100 million
$13	60 million	120 million

   a. What is the equilibrium price and equilibrium quantity?
   b. If the industry price is $13, is there a shortage or a surplus of CDs? How much is the shortage or surplus? Will the price stay at $13? Explain.
   c. If the industry price is $10, is there a shortage or a surplus of CDs? How much is the shortage or surplus? Will the price stay at $10? Explain.

6. With the aid of a supply-and-demand diagram, explain how the policy of banning the sale of sperm and ova will affect the market for assisted human reproduction in Canada, as described in Policy Example 3–2, "Assisted Human Reproduction Not for Sale in Canada?".

7. Suppose that a survey for a later market period indicates that the quantities supplied in the table in Problem 5 are unchanged. The quantity demanded, however, has increased by 30 million at each price. Construct the resulting demand curve in the illustration you made for Problem 5. Is this an increase or a decrease in demand? What is the new equilibrium quantity and the new market price? Give two examples that might cause such a change.

8. Suppose in Example 3–5, "Air Canada's Losses Are Flying High," the decrease in demand exceeds the decrease in supply for the airline services provided by international airlines, such as Air Canada. What will these market trends do to the fares that Air Canada charges its customers? In turn, what will this do to the magnitude of Air Canada's losses?

9. In the market for rock music CDs, explain whether the following events would cause an increase or decrease in

demand or an increase or decrease in the quantity demanded. Also explain what happens to the equilibrium quantity and the equilibrium price.

a. The price of CD packaging material declines.
b. The price of CD players declines.
c. The price of cassette tapes increases dramatically.
d. A booming economy increases the income of the typical CD buyer.
e. Many rock fans suddenly develop a fondness for country music.

10. Consider the market for laptop computers. Explain whether the following events would cause an increase or decrease in supply or an increase or decrease in the quantity supplied. Illustrate each, and show what would happen to the equilibrium market price, given a typical downward-sloping demand curve.

a. The price of memory chips used in laptop computers declines.
b. The price of memory chips used in desktop personal computers declines.
c. The number of manufacturers of laptop computers increases.
d. The prices of computer peripherals, printers, fax–modems, and scanners decrease.

11. The following diagram describes the hypothetical monthly demand and supply conditions for eggs in a small provincial market.

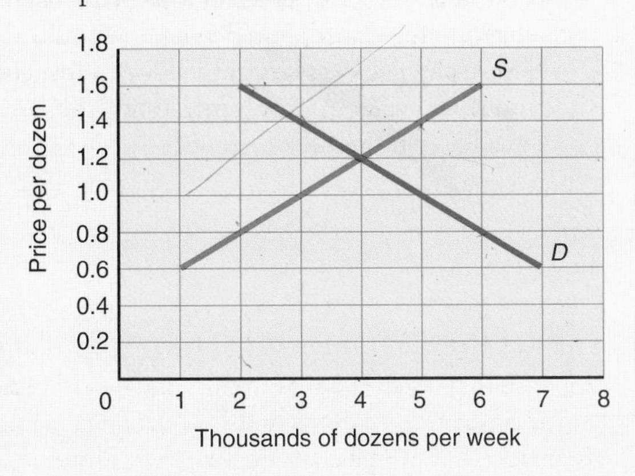

a. If the price in the egg market above was initially at $1.40 per dozen, there would be a (surplus or shortage) equal to ___ thousands of dozens of eggs per week. Will the price stay at $1.40?
b. If the price in the egg market above was initially at $0.80 per dozen, there would be a (surplus or shortage) equal to ___ thousands of dozens of eggs per week. Will the price stay at $0.80?
c. Determine the equilibrium price and equilibrium quantity in the egg market described above.
d. In the egg market described above, explain whether each of the following events would cause an increase or decrease in demand or supply. Also explain what happens to the equilibrium price and quantity.

i. Studies show that daily use of eggs reduces the risk of getting serious diseases.
ii. The cost of feeding chickens significantly increases.
iii. Average consumer income increases, and eggs are an inferior good.
iv. The government provides a subsidy to egg producers. A subsidy is a situation where the government pays the egg producers a set amount per dozen produced.

12. Airline routes are typically controlled by imposing a quota on the number of airline companies that may use the route and the number of flights on the route. Consequently, the government restricts the number of round-trip seats available on these flight routes. Suppose that the following table describes the daily demand and supply schedules for seats on round-trip flights between Toronto and Vancouver.

Price per seat ($)	Quantity Demanded (no. of seats)	Quantity Supplied (no. of seats)
200	2000	1200
300	1800	1400
400	1600	1600
500	1400	1800
600	1200	2000

a. What is the equilibrium price and quantity for the Toronto-to-Vancouver airline seats? How much, in total dollars, do passengers spend on this route each day?
b. Suppose the government limits the daily number of round-trip seats to ensure that only 1200 seats can be made available on the Toronto-to-Vancouver route. What will be the new price per round-trip seat on this route? With the quota policy, do passengers end up spending more or less each day on this same route in total dollars? Can you think of how this quota policy might actually benefit the passengers (consumers) in the longer run?

13. The following diagram describes the hypothetical monthly demand and supply for one-bedroom apartments in a small college town.

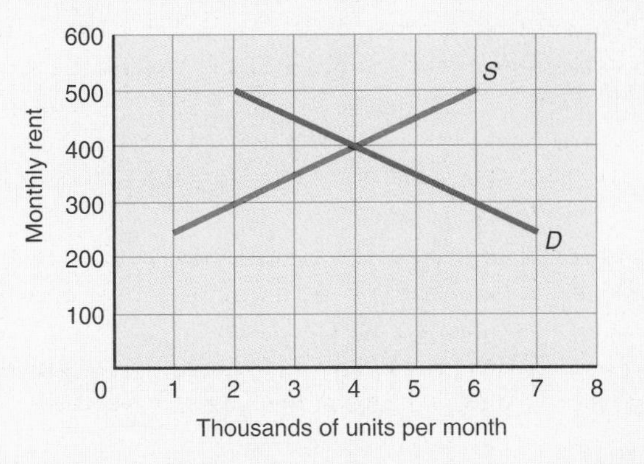

a. What is the equilibrium monthly rent (price) and equilibrium monthly quantity?

b. Suppose that the mayor of this town decides to make housing more affordable for the local college students by imposing a rent control that holds the price of a one-bedroom apartment to $300 per month.

This rent control policy will result in a (shortage or surplus) of ____ units per month.

c. What will this rent control policy do to the market for two-bedroom apartments that are not regulated by the government? What will happen to the equilibrium price and quantity for the unregulated two-bedroom apartments?

14. In May 2000, the Canadian government imposed a tax on bicycles imported from Taiwan and China. Show how this tax affects the market for Taiwanese and Chinese bicycles, shifting the appropriate curve and indicating a new market equilibrium quantity and price. In a separate graph, show the effect of the tax on Canadian-made bicycles, shifting the appropriate curve and indicating the new market equilibrium and price.

15. The following diagram describes the market for Canadian red wine. Explain how each of the following sets of events will affect the equilibrium price and equilibrium quantity of Canadian red wine. Note that in some cases, your answer will be "indeterminate," meaning that with the given information, you cannot predict the direction of change.

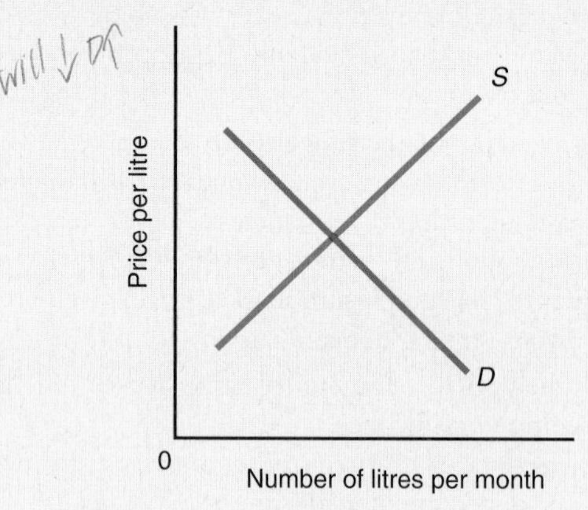

a. Studies indicate that Canadian red wine reduces the risk of heart disease. At the same time, the cost of the grapes used to produce red wine decreases.

b. Frost destroys a significant amount of the red grapes used to produce Canadian red wine. At the same time, the price of California red wine, a key substitute for Canadian red wine, increases.

c. New technology significantly lowers the cost of producing wine. At the same time, the price of Canadian white wine decreases.

PART 2
DIMENSIONS OF MICROECONOMICS

CHAPTER

Elasticity

Cigarette smoking is unhealthy, which is one reason that governments tax cigarettes. Cigarette consumption is relatively insensitive to price changes, however, and so higher cigarette taxes only moderately reduce cigarette purchases. Beer consumption tends to be more responsive to price changes. Thus, if beer drinking and cigarette smoking are complementary activities, boosting taxes on beer might do more to reduce cigarette consumption. How can we measure the responsiveness of consumption to a change in price? How can we determine whether cigarettes and beer are complements? In this chapter, you will learn the answers to these questions.

LEARNING OBJECTIVES

After reading this chapter, you should be able to:

4.1 Define price elasticity of demand and calculate it using two different methods.

4.2 Define the three price elasticity ranges and explain their effects on total revenues.

4.3 Discuss the three factors that determine the price elasticity of demand.

4.4 Describe the effects of substitutes, complements, and income on elasticity of demand.

4.5 Define price elasticity of supply and describe the difference between the long-run and short-run supply schedules.

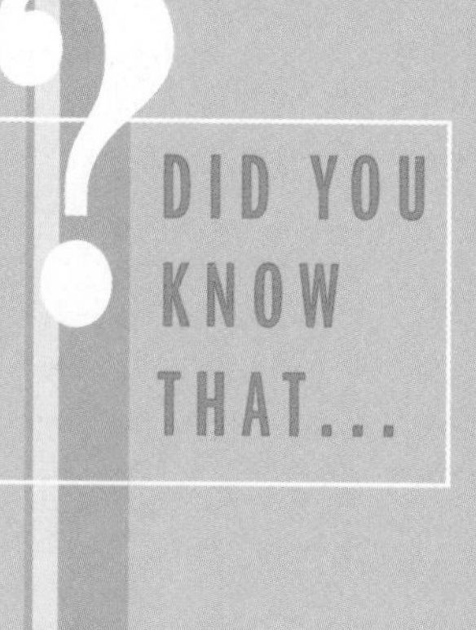

A fall in the price of beer might lead to an increase in campus violence. The law of demand indicates that a decline in the price of beer increases consumption. Economists have found that a 10 percent reduction in the price of beer is associated with an increase in the incidence of campus violence of just over 3.5 percent.

College officials are not alone in having to worry about how individuals respond to lower prices. Businesses must constantly take into account consumer response to changing prices. If McDonald's lowers its prices by 10 percent, will fast-food consumers respond by buying so many more Big Macs that the company's revenues will rise? At the other end of the spectrum, can Rolls Royce dealers "get away with" a 2 percent increase in prices? In other words, will Rolls Royce purchasers respond so little to the relatively small increase in price that the total revenues received for Rolls Royce sales will not fall and may actually rise? The only way to answer these questions is to know how responsive people in the real world will be to changes in prices. Economists have a special name for price responsiveness—*elasticity,* which is the subject of this chapter.

4.1 Price Elasticity

To begin to understand what elasticity is all about, just keep in mind that it means "responsiveness" or "sensitivity." Here, we are concerned with the price elasticity of demand and the price elasticity of supply. We wish to know the extent to which a change in the price of, say, petroleum products will cause the quantity demanded and the quantity supplied to change, other things held constant. Let us restrict our discussion at first to the demand side.

Price Elasticity of Demand

We will formally define price elasticity of demand, which we will label E_p, as follows:

$$E_p = \frac{\text{Percentage change in quantity demanded}}{\text{Percentage change in price}}$$

Price elasticity of demand (E_p) The relative amount by which the quantity demanded will change in response to a change in the price of a particular good.

Price elasticity of demand (E_p) is the relative amount by which the quantity demanded will change in response to a change in the price of a particular good.

What will price elasticity of demand tell us? It will tell us the relative amount by which the quantity demanded will change in response to a change in the price of a particular good.

Consider an example in which a 10 percent rise in the price of oil leads to a reduction in quantity demanded of only 1 percent. Putting these numbers into the formula, we find that the price elasticity of demand for oil, in this case, equals the percentage change in quantity demanded divided by the percentage change in price, or

$$E_p = \frac{-1\%}{+10\%} = -0.1$$

An elasticity of −0.1 means that a 1 percent *increase* in the price would lead to a mere 0.1 percent *decrease* in the quantity demanded. If you were now told, in contrast, that the price elasticity of demand for oil was −2, you would know that a 1 percent increase in the price of oil would lead to a 2 percent decrease in the quantity demanded.

RELATIVE QUANTITIES ONLY. Note that in our elasticity formula, we talk about *percentage* changes in quantity demanded divided by *percentage* changes in price. We are, therefore, not interested in the absolute changes, only in relative amounts. This means that it does not matter if we measure price changes in terms of cents, dollars, or hundreds of dollars. It also does not matter whether we measure quantity changes in bushels, grams, or litres. The percentage change will be independent of the units chosen. So, a $1 increase in a cup of coffee has more of an impact than a $1 increase in the price of a car.

ALWAYS NEGATIVE. The law of demand states that quantity demanded is *inversely* related to the relative price. An increase in the price of a good leads to a decrease in the quantity demanded. If a decrease in the relative price of a good should occur, the quantity demanded would increase by a certain percentage. The point is that price elasticity of demand will always be negative. By convention, *we will ignore the minus sign in our discussion from this point on.*

Basically, the greater the *absolute* price elasticity of demand (disregarding sign), the greater is the demand responsiveness to relative price changes—a small change in price has a great impact on quantity demanded. The smaller the absolute price elasticity of demand, the smaller is the demand responsiveness to relative price changes—a large change in price has little effect on quantity demanded. See Example 4–1 for further insight.

EXAMPLE 4–1 **"If They Doubled the Price, We'd Still Drink Coffee"**

Every time there is frost in Brazil, the price of coffee beans rises, and everyone fears a big rise in the prices of coffee. Members of the media interview coffee drinkers and ask how they will respond to the higher prices. Not surprisingly, even when coffee prices soared 150 percent a few years ago, some interviewees said they had to have their cup of coffee, no matter what. But if that were true for all coffee drinkers, why don't coffee prices rise as much as bean prices? If what coffee drinkers tell us were really true, their price elasticity of demand would be zero, and the retail price of coffee could skyrocket. But it never does. The truth is, interviewing coffee drinkers (or other consumers) about intentions tells us little. We need to examine the change in total market quantity demanded after an increase in price. The data make it clear: At least some people drink less coffee when the relative price goes up.

For critical analysis: Would the same be true for gas prices?

Calculating Elasticity

To calculate the price elasticity of demand, we have to compute percentage changes in quantity demanded and in price. To obtain the percentage change in quantity demanded, we divide the change in the quantity demanded by the original quantity demanded:

$$\frac{\text{Change in quantity demanded}}{\text{Original quantity demanded}}$$

To find the percentage change in price, we divide the change in price by the original price:

$$\frac{\text{Change in price}}{\text{Original price}}$$

There is an arithmetic problem, though, when we calculate percentage changes in this manner. The percentage change, say, from 2 to 3—50 percent—is not the same as the percentage change from 3 to 2—33⅓ percent. In other words, you would obtain a different value for the elasticity, depending on whether you looked at the change in demand when the price increased or when the price decreased.

To compute the average price elasticity of demand, we need to deal with the average change in quantity demanded caused by the average change in price. That means that we take the average of the two prices and the two quantities over the range we are considering and compare the change with these averages. For relatively small changes in price, the formula for computing the price elasticity of demand then becomes

$$E_p = \frac{\text{Change in quantity}}{\text{Sum of quantities / 2}} \div \frac{\text{Change in price}}{\text{Sum of prices / 2}}$$

We can rewrite this more simply if we do two things: (1) We can let Q_1 and Q_2 equal the two different quantities demanded before and after the price change and let P_1 and P_2 equal the two different prices. (2) Because we will be dividing a percentage by a percentage, we simply use the ratio, or the decimal form, of the percentages. Therefore,

$$E_p = \frac{\Delta Q}{(Q_1 + Q_2)/2} \div \frac{\Delta P}{(P_1 + P_2)/2}$$

where the Greek letter Δ stands for "change in." Example 4–2, below, provides a real-life example.

EXAMPLE 4–2 The Price Elasticity of Demand for World's Fair Tickets

Expo 2000, the world's fair for that year, was held in Hanover, Germany. Tickets to Expo 2000 were initially priced at $12 apiece, which generated sales of 60 000 tickets per day, well below the organizers' anticipations. During the second week of the fair, the organizers responded by setting a special $5 price for Wednesday tickets. Attendance on that day jumped to 100 000.

We can estimate the approximate price elasticity of demand for tickets to Expo 2000 by using the formula presented earlier (under the assumption, of course, that all other things, such as weather, were constant):

$$E_p = \frac{\Delta Q}{(Q_1 + Q_2)/2} \div \frac{\Delta P}{(P_1 + P_2)/2}$$

$$= \frac{100\,000 - 60\,000}{(100\,000 + 60\,000)/2} \div \frac{12 - 5}{(12 + 5)/2}$$

$$= \frac{40\,000}{80\,000} \div \frac{\$7.0}{\$8.5} = 0.61$$

The price elasticity of demand of 0.61 means that a 1 percent decrease in price would generate a 0.61 percent increase in the quantity of Expo 2000 tickets demanded.

For critical analysis: Would the estimated price elasticity of demand for Expo 2000 tickets have been different if we had *not* used the average-values formula? How?

CONCEPTS IN BRIEF

Learning Objective 4.1: Define price elasticity of demand and calculate it using two different methods.

- Elasticity is a measure of the price responsiveness of the quantity demanded and quantity supplied.
- The price elasticity of demand is equal to the percentage change in quantity demanded divided by the percentage change in price.
- Price elasticity of demand is calculated in terms of percentage changes in quantity demanded and in price. Thus, it is expressed as a unitless, dimensionless number.
- The law of demand states that quantity demanded and price are inversely related. Therefore, the price elasticity of demand is always negative because an increase in price will lead to a decrease in quantity demanded and a decrease in price will lead to an increase in quantity demanded. By convention, we ignore the negative sign in discussions of the price elasticity of demand.

4.2 Price Elasticity Ranges

We have names for the varying ranges of price elasticities, depending on whether a 1 percent change in price elicits more or less than a 1 percent change in the quantity demanded.

Elastic demand A demand relationship in which a given percentage change in price will result in a larger percentage change in quantity demanded.

Unit elasticity of demand A demand relationship in which the quantity demanded changes exactly in proportion to the changes in price.

Inelastic demand A demand relationship in which a given percentage change in price will result in a less than proportionate percentage change in the quantity demanded.

1. **Elastic demand** is a demand relationship in which a given percentage change in price will result in a larger percentage change in quantity demanded. We say that a good has an elastic demand whenever the price elasticity of demand is greater than 1. A 1 percent change in price causes a change of more than 1 percent in the quantity demanded.
2. **Unit elasticity of demand** is a demand relationship in which the quantity demanded changes exactly in proportion to the changes in price. In a situation of unit elasticity of demand, a 1 percent change in price causes a response of exactly a 1 percent change in the quantity demanded.
3. **Inelastic demand** is a demand relationship in which a given percentage change in price will result in a less than proportionate percentage change in the quantity demanded. In a situation of inelastic demand, a 1 percent change in price causes a response of less than a 1 percent change in the quantity demanded.

When we say a commodity's demand is elastic, we are indicating that consumers are relatively responsive to changes in price. When we say that a commodity's demand is inelastic, we are indicating that its consumers are relatively unresponsive to price changes. When economists say that demand is inelastic, it does not mean that quantity demanded is totally unresponsive to price changes. Remember, the law of demand suggests that there will be some responsiveness in quantity demanded to a price change. The question is how much. That is what elasticity attempts to determine. See Policy Example 4–1, below.

POLICY EXAMPLE 4–1 **To Cut Drug Abuse, Make the Price of a "High" Higher**

Recently, John Tauras of the University of Illinois at Chicago and Michael Grossman of the City University of New York conducted a study of teen use of cocaine. They found that, compared with adults, youthful drug abusers are three times more sensitive to price changes.

Whereas adult cocaine demand is inelastic, teen cocaine demand is nearly unit elastic over the range of market prices tabulated by the U.S. Drug Enforcement Administration. In other words, a 33 percent increase in the market price of cocaine likely would reduce the teen purchases and consumption of cocaine by a third. Undoubtedly, some teens would substitute other drugs. Nonetheless, cocaine and a derivative drug, crack cocaine, are considered addictive substances. Inducing teens to reduce cocaine use might, therefore, take a significant bite out of the nation's longer-term problems with drug abuse.

A policy implication of this study is that legal crackdowns on cocaine dealers that restrict the supply of the drug and push up its price might be an appropriate strategy in the war against drugs.

For critical analysis: According to the elasticity of demand results cited in this example, will a legal crackdown policy on cocaine dealers be more effective in reducing adult or teen abuse of cocaine? Explain. (Hint: You may wish to draw two separate demand and supply diagrams to think about this.)

Extreme Elasticities

Perfectly inelastic demand
A demand that exhibits zero responsiveness to price changes.

Perfectly elastic demand
A demand that has the characteristic that even the slightest increase in price will lead to zero quantity demanded.

There are two extremes in price elasticities of demand. One extreme represents total unresponsiveness of quantity demanded to price changes, which is referred to as **perfectly inelastic demand,** or zero elasticity—a demand that exhibits zero responsiveness to price changes. The other represents total responsiveness, which is referred to as infinitely elastic demand, or **perfectly elastic demand**—a demand that has the characteristic that even the slightest increase in price will lead to zero quantity demanded.

We show perfect inelasticity in part (a) of Figure 4–1. Note that the quantity demanded per year is 8 million units, no matter what the price. Hence, for any percentage price change, the quantity demanded will remain the same, and thus, the change in the quantity demanded will be zero. Look back at our formula for computing elasticity. If the change in the quantity demanded is zero, the numerator is also zero, and a nonzero number divided into zero results in an answer of zero, too. Hence, there is perfect inelasticity. At the opposite extreme is the situation depicted in part (b) of Figure 4–1. Here, we show that at a price of 30 cents, an unlimited quantity will be demanded. At a price that is only slightly above 30 cents, no quantity will be demanded. There is complete, or infinite, responsiveness here, and hence, we call the demand schedule in part (b) infinitely elastic or perfectly elastic.

Elasticity and Total Revenues

Suppose that you are in charge of the pricing decision for a cellular telephone service company. How would you know when it is best to raise or not to raise prices? The answer depends, in part, on the effect of your pricing decision on total revenues, or the total receipts of your company. (The rest of the equation is, of course, your cost structure, a subject we examine later.) It is commonly thought that the way to increase total receipts is to increase price per unit. But is this always the case? Is it possible that a rise in price per unit could lead to a decrease in total revenues? The answers to these questions depend on the price elasticity of demand.

Let us look at Figure 4–2. In part (a), column 1 shows the price of cellular telephone service in dollars per minute, and column 2 represents billions of minutes per year. In column 3, we multiply column 1 by column 2 to derive total revenue because total revenue is always equal to the number of units (quantity) sold times the price per unit, and in column 4, we calculate values of elasticity. Note what happens to total revenues throughout the schedule. They rise steadily as the price rises from 10 cents to 50 cents per minute; but when the price rises further to 60 cents per minute, total revenues remain

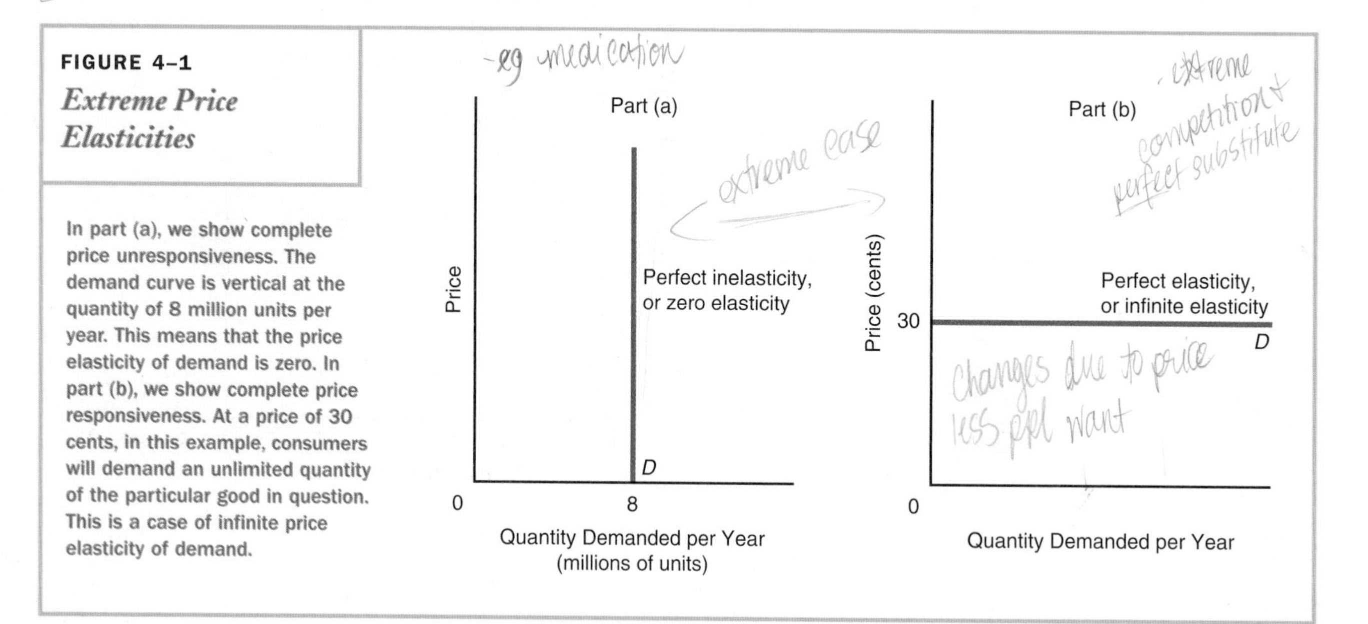

FIGURE 4–1
Extreme Price Elasticities

In part (a), we show complete price unresponsiveness. The demand curve is vertical at the quantity of 8 million units per year. This means that the price elasticity of demand is zero. In part (b), we show complete price responsiveness. At a price of 30 cents, in this example, consumers will demand an unlimited quantity of the particular good in question. This is a case of infinite price elasticity of demand.

FIGURE 4–2

The Relationship between Price Elasticity of Demand and Total Revenues for Cellular Phone Service

In part (a), we show the elastic, unit-elastic, and inelastic sections of the demand schedule according to whether a reduction in price increases total revenues, causes them to remain constant, or causes them to decrease, respectively. In part (b), we show these regions graphically on the demand curve. In part (c), we show them on the total revenue curve.

Part (a)

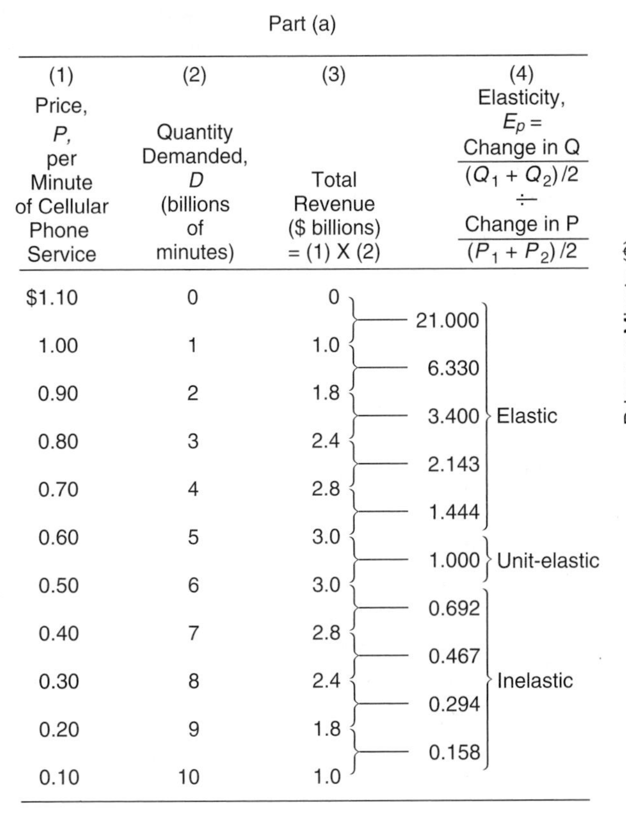

(1) Price, P, per Minute of Cellular Phone Service	(2) Quantity Demanded, D (billions of minutes)	(3) Total Revenue ($ billions) = (1) X (2)	(4) Elasticity, $E_p = \frac{\text{Change in Q}}{(Q_1 + Q_2)/2} \div \frac{\text{Change in P}}{(P_1 + P_2)/2}$	
$1.10	0	0		
			21.000	Elastic
1.00	1	1.0		
			6.330	Elastic
0.90	2	1.8		
			3.400	Elastic
0.80	3	2.4		
			2.143	Elastic
0.70	4	2.8		
			1.444	Elastic
0.60	5	3.0		
			1.000	Unit-elastic
0.50	6	3.0		
			0.692	Inelastic
0.40	7	2.8		
			0.467	Inelastic
0.30	8	2.4		
			0.294	Inelastic
0.20	9	1.8		
			0.158	Inelastic
0.10	10	1.0		

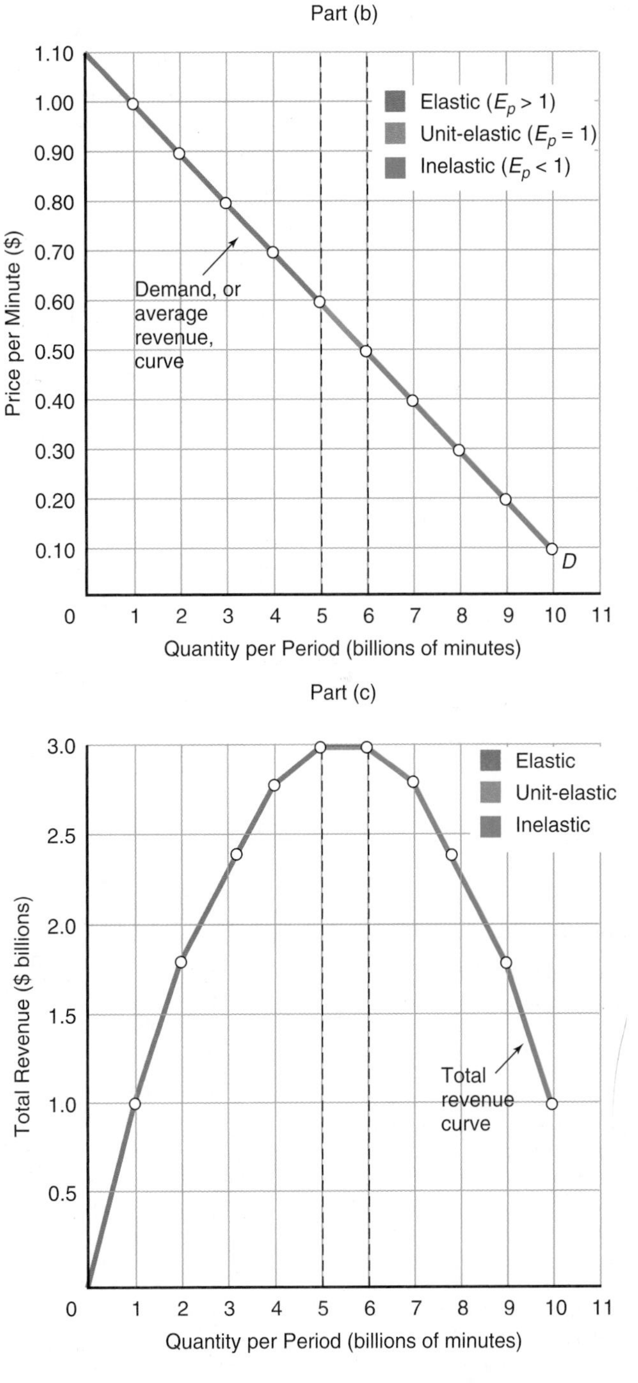

constant at $3 billion. At prices per minute higher than 60 cents, total revenues fall as price increases. Indeed, if prices are above 60 cents per minute, total revenues can be increased only by *cutting* prices, not by raising them.

Labelling Elasticity

The relationship between price and quantity on the demand schedule is given in columns 1 and 2 of part (a) in Figure 4–2. In part (b), the demand curve, *D*, representing that schedule is drawn. In part (c), the total revenue curve representing the data in column 3 is drawn. Note, first, the level of these curves at small quantities. The demand curve is at a maximum height, but total revenue is zero, which makes sense according to this demand schedule—at a price of $1.10 and above, no units will be purchased, and therefore, total revenue will be zero. As the price is lowered, we travel down the demand curve, and total revenues increase until the price is 60 cents per minute, remain constant from 60 cents to 50 cents per minute, and then fall at lower unit prices. Corresponding to those three sections, demand is elastic, unit-elastic, and inelastic. Hence, we have three relationships among the three types of price elasticity and total revenues.

1. *Elastic demand.* For some products, consumers are very price sensitive. If the price is lowered, total revenues will rise when the firm faces demand that is elastic, and if it raises the price, total revenues will fall. Consider another example. If the price of Diet Coke™ were raised by 25 percent and the price of all other soft drinks remained constant, the quantity demanded of Diet Coke™ would probably fall dramatically. The decrease in quantity demanded due to the increase in the price of Diet Coke™ would lead, in this example, to a reduction in the total revenues of the Coca-Cola Company. Therefore, if demand is elastic, price and total revenues will move in *opposite* directions.
2. *Unit-elastic demand.* Changes in price do not change total revenues. When the firm is facing demand that is unit-elastic, if it increases the price, total revenues will not change; if it decreases the price, total revenues will not change either.
3. *Inelastic demand.* For some products, consumers are not sensitive to price changes. When the firm is facing demand that is inelastic, if it raises the price, total revenues will go up; if it lowers the price, total revenues will fall. Consider another example. You have just invented a cure for the common cold, and the medication has been approved by Health Canada for sale to the public. You are not sure what price you should charge, and so you start out with a price of $1 per pill. You sell 20 million pills at that price over a year. The next year, you decide to raise the price by 25 percent, to $1.25. The number of pills you sell drops to 18 million per year. The price increase of 25 percent has led to a 10 percent decrease in quantity demanded. Your total revenues, however, will rise to $22.5 million because of the price increase. We therefore conclude that if demand is inelastic, price and total revenues move in the *same* direction.

The elastic, unit-elastic, and inelastic areas of the demand curve are shown in Figure 4–2. For prices from $1.10 per minute of cellular phone time to 60 cents per minute, as the price decreases, total revenues rise from zero to $3 billion. Demand is price-elastic. When the price changes from 60 cents to 50 cents, however, total revenues remain constant at $3 billion; demand is unit-elastic. Finally, when the price falls from 50 cents to 10 cents, total revenues decrease from $3 billion to $1 billion; demand is inelastic. In parts (b) and (c) of Figure 4–2, we have labelled the sections of the demand curve accordingly, and we have also shown how total revenues first rise, then remain constant, and finally fall.

The relationship between price elasticity of demand and total revenues brings together some important microeconomic concepts. Total revenues, as we have noted, are the product of price per unit times number of units sold. The law of demand states that along a given demand curve, price and quantity changes will move in opposite directions: One increases as the other decreases. Consequently, what happens to the product of price times quantity depends on which of the opposing changes exerts a greater force on total revenues. But this is just what price elasticity of demand is designed to measure—responsiveness of quantity demanded to a change in price. The relationship between price elasticity of demand and total revenues is summarized in Table 4–1 and illustrated in Example 4–3.

TABLE 4-1

Relationship between Price Elasticity of Demand and Total Revenues

Price Elasticity of Demand		Effect of Price Change on Total Revenues (TR)	
		Price Decrease	Price Increase
Inelastic	(E_p < 1)	TR ↓	TR ↑
Unit-elastic	(E_p = 1)	No change in TR	No change in TR
Elastic	(E_p > 1)	TR ↑	TR ↓

EXAMPLE 4-3 A Pricing Decision at Disneyland Paris

Several years after Disneyland Paris (formerly called EuroDisney) opened with great fanfare, the $4 billion American investment in it was in trouble. In an attempt to improve profits (actually, to decrease losses), Disney management decided to lower prices starting in the summer of 1995. Entrance fees during peak periods (April 1 to October 1) dropped from 250 francs (about $60) to 195 francs (about $48). Was this 22 percent reduction in ticket prices a good management strategy for Disney officials? That depends, in part, on what happened to total revenues. As it turned out, park attendance increased by 700 000 visitors. Thus, total revenues increased by more than 22 percent, indicating that the demand for Disneyland Paris is elastic in the price range between $48 to $60.

For critical analysis: What other factors may have affected attendance at Disneyland Paris?

CONCEPTS IN BRIEF

Learning Objective 4.2: Define the three price elasticity ranges and explain their effects on total revenues.

- Price elasticity of demand is related to total revenues (and total consumer expenditures).
- When demand is elastic, the change in price elicits a change in total revenues (and total consumer expenditures) in the direction opposite to that of the price change.
- When demand is unit-elastic, a change in price elicits no change in total revenues (or in total consumer expenditures).
- When demand is inelastic, a change in price elicits a change in total revenues (and in consumer expenditures) in the same direction as the price change.

4.3 Determinants of the Price Elasticity of Demand

We have learned how to calculate the price elasticity of demand. We know that, theoretically, it ranges numerically from zero (completely inelastic) to infinity (completely elastic). What we would like to do now is come up with a list of the determinants of the price elasticity of demand. The price elasticity of demand for a particular commodity at any price depends, at a minimum, on the following nonprice determinants:

1. The existence, number, and quality of substitutes
2. The percentage of a consumer's total budget devoted to purchases of that commodity
3. The length of time allowed for adjustment to changes in the price of the commodity

Existence of Substitutes

The closer the substitutes for a particular commodity and the more substitutes there are, the greater will be its price elasticity of demand. At the limit, if there is a perfect substitute, the elasticity of demand for the commodity will be infinite. Thus, even the slightest increase in the commodity's price will cause an enormous reduction in the quantity demanded: Quantity demanded will fall to zero. We are really talking about two goods that the consumer believes are exactly alike and equally desirable, like five-dollar bills whose only difference is serial numbers. When we talk about less extreme examples, we can only speak in terms of the number and the similarity of substitutes that are available. Thus, we will find that the more narrowly we define a good, the closer and greater will be the number of substitutes available. For example, the demand for Diet Coke™ may be highly elastic because consumers can switch to Diet Pepsi™. The demand for diet drinks in general, however, is relatively less elastic because there are fewer substitutes.

Share of Budget

We know that the greater the percentage of a total budget spent on the commodity, the greater is the person's price elasticity of demand for that commodity. The demand for pepper is thought to be very inelastic merely because individuals spend so little on it relative to their total budgets. In contrast, the demand for such things as transportation and housing is thought to be far more elastic because they occupy a large part of people's budgets—changes in their prices cannot be ignored so easily without sacrificing a lot of other alternative goods that could be purchased.

Consider a numerical example. A household earns $40 000 a year. It purchases $4 of pepper per year and $4000 of transportation services. Now, consider the spending power of this family when the price of pepper and the price of transportation both go up by 100 percent. If the household buys the same amount of pepper, it will now spend $8. It will, thus, have to reduce other expenditures by $4. This $4 represents only 0.01 percent of the entire household budget. By contrast, a doubling of transportation costs requires that the family spend $8000—$4000 more—on transportation, if it is to purchase the same quantity. That increased expenditure on transportation of $4000 represents 10 percent of total expenditures that must be switched from other purchases. We would, therefore, predict that the household will react differently to the doubling of prices for pepper than it will for transportation. It will buy almost the same amount of pepper but will spend significantly less on transportation.

Time for Adjustment

When the price of a commodity changes and that price change persists, more people will learn about it. Further, consumers will be better able to revise their consumption patterns the longer the time period they have to do so. And in fact, the longer the time they do take, the less costly it will be for them to engage in this revision of consumption patterns. Consider a price decrease. The longer the price decrease persists, the greater will be the number of new uses that consumers will discover for the particular commodity, and the greater will be the number of new users of that particular commodity.

It is possible to make a very strong statement about the relationship between the price elasticity of demand and the time allowed for adjustment:

> **The longer any price change persists, the greater is the elasticity of demand, other things held constant. Elasticity of demand is greater in the long run than in the short run.**

Let us take an example. Suppose that the price of electricity goes up by 50 percent. How do you adjust in the short run? You can turn the lights off more often, you can stop using the stereo as much as you do, and so on. Otherwise it is very difficult to cut back on your consumption of electricity. In the long run, though, you can devise methods to reduce your consumption. Instead of using electric heating, the next time you have a house built,

FIGURE 4–3

Short-Run and Long-Run Price Elasticity of Demand

Consider an equilibrium situation in which the market price is P_e and the quantity demanded is Q_e. Then, there is a price increase to P_1. In the short run, as evidenced by the demand curve D_1, we move from equilibrium quantity demanded, Q_e, to Q_1. After more time is allowed for adjustment, the demand curve rotates at original price P_e to D_2. Quantity demanded falls again, now to Q_2. After even more time is allowed for adjustment, the demand curve rotates at price P_e to D_3. At the higher price P_1, in the long run, the quantity demanded falls all the way to Q_3.

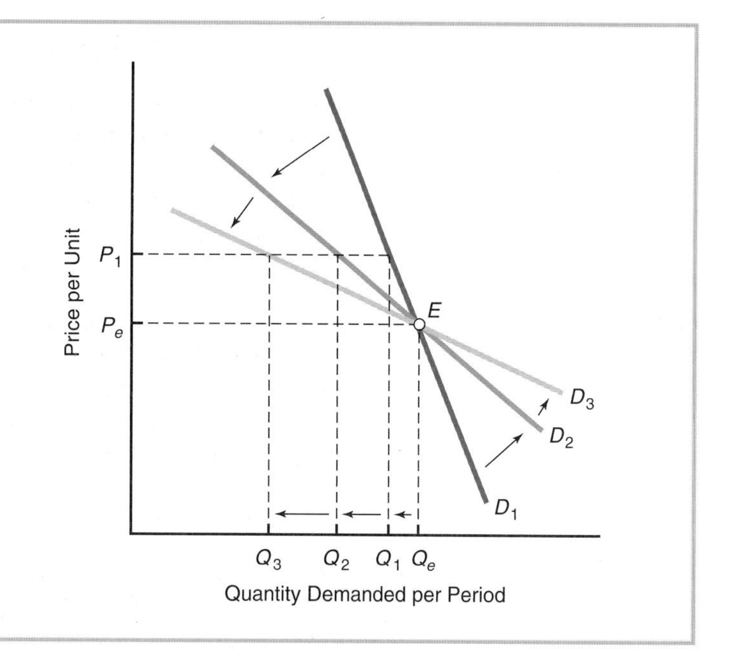

you might install solar heating. Instead of using an electric stove, the next time you move, you might have a gas stove installed. You might purchase fluorescent bulbs because they use less electricity. The more time you have to think about it, the more ways you will find to cut your electricity consumption. We would expect, therefore, that the short-run demand curve for electricity would be relatively inelastic (in the price range around P_e), as demonstrated by D_1 in Figure 4–3. However, the long-run demand curve may exhibit much more elasticity (in the neighbourhood of P_e), as demonstrated by D_3. Indeed, we can think of an entire family of demand curves, such as those depicted in that figure. The short-run demand curve is for the period when there is no time for adjustment. As more time is allowed, the demand curve goes first to D_2 and then all the way to D_3. Thus, in the neighbourhood of P_e, elasticity differs for each of these curves. It is greater for the less steep curves (but, slope alone does not measure elasticity for the entire curve).

HOW TO DEFINE THE SHORT RUN AND THE LONG RUN. We have mentioned the short run and the long run. Is the short run one week, two weeks, one month, or two months? Is the long run three years, four years, or five years? The answer is that there is no single answer. What we mean by the long run is the period of time necessary for consumers to make a full adjustment to a given price change, all other things held constant. In the case of the demand for electricity, the long run will be however long it takes consumers to switch over to cheaper sources of heating, to buy houses that are more energy-efficient, to purchase appliances that are more energy-efficient, and so on. The long-run elasticity of demand for electricity, therefore, relates to a period of at least several years. The short run—by default—is any period less than the long run.

EXAMPLE 4–4 **What Do Real-World Price Elasticities of Demand Look Like?**

In Table 4–2, we present price elasticity demand estimates for selected goods. Note that in all cases, we are leaving off the negative sign. Remember that these elasticities represent averages over given price ranges. Choosing different price ranges, over a different period, would likely result in different elasticity estimates.

continued

TABLE 4-2

Price Elasticity of Demand for Selected Goods

Good or Service	Elasticity	Good or Service	Elasticity
Metals	1.52	Chemicals	0.89
Electrical engineering products	1.39	Beverages (all types)	0.78
Mechanical engineering products	1.30	Clothing	0.64
Furniture	1.26	Tobacco	0.61
Motor vehicles	1.14	Banking and insurance services	0.56
Instrument engineering products	1.10	Housing services	0.55
Professional services	1.09	Agricultural and fish products	0.42
Transportation services	1.03	Books, magazines, and newspapers	0.34
Gas, electricity, and water	0.92	Food	0.12
Oil	0.91		

SOURCE: REPRINTED FROM HENRI THEIL, CHING-FAN CHUNG, AND JAMES L. SEALE JR., *ADVANCES IN ECONOMETRICS*, SUPPLEMENT I, 1989, INTERNATIONAL EVIDENCE ON CONSUMPTION PATTERNS (GREENWICH, CONN.: JAI PRESS, 1989), WITH PERMISSION FROM ELSEVIER SCIENCE.

For critical analysis: What determinants of price elasticity of demand explain the difference in the price elasticity estimates for food versus motor vehicles?

CONCEPTS IN BRIEF

Learning Objective 4.3: Discuss the three factors that determine the price elasticity of demand.

- Some determinants of price elasticity of demand are (1) the existence, number, and quality of substitutes, (2) the share of the total budget spent on the good in question, and (3) the length of time allowed for adjustment to a change in prices.

4.4 Cross-Elasticity of Demand

In an earlier chapter, we discussed the effect of a change in the price of one good on the demand for a related good. We defined substitutes and complements in terms of whether a reduction in the price of one caused a decrease or an increase, respectively, in the demand for the other. If the price of compact discs (CDs) is held constant, the amount of CDs demanded (at any price) will certainly be influenced by the price of a close substitute, such as MP3 players. If the price of stereo speakers is held constant, the amount of stereo speakers demanded (at any price) will certainly be affected by changes in the price of stereo amplifiers.

What we now need to do is come up with a numerical measure of the price responsiveness of demand to the prices of related goods. This is called the **cross-elasticity of demand (E_{xy})**, which is defined as the percentage change in the quantity demanded of one good (holding its price constant) divided by the percentage change in the price of the related good. In equation form, the cross-elasticity of demand for good X with respect to good Y is

Cross-elasticity of demand (E_{xy}) The percentage change in the quantity demanded of one good (holding its price constant) divided by the percentage change in the price of a related good.

$$E_{xy} = \frac{\text{Percentage change in quantity demanded of good X}}{\text{Percentage change in price of good Y}}$$

When two goods are substitutes, the cross-elasticity of demand will be positive. For example, when the price of margarine goes up, the demand for butter will rise, too, as consumers shift away from the now relatively more expensive margarine to butter. A producer of margarine could benefit from a numerical estimate of the cross-elasticity of demand between butter and margarine. For example, if the price of butter went up by 10 percent and the margarine producer knew that the cross-elasticity of demand was 1, the margarine producer could estimate that the demand for margarine would also go up by 10 percent at any given price. Plans for increasing margarine production could then be made.

When two related goods are complements, the cross-elasticity of demand will be negative (and we will not disregard the minus sign). For example, when the price of stereo amplifiers goes up, the demand for stereo speakers will fall. This is because as prices of amplifiers increase, the quantity of amplifiers demanded will naturally decrease. Because amplifiers and stereo speakers are often used together, the demand for speakers is likely to fall. Any manufacturer of stereo speakers must take this into account in making production plans. In this chapter's Issues and Applications, we look at whether increasing taxes on beer would lead to a decrease in cigarette consumption. If beer and cigarettes are complements, then the cross-elasticity of demand will be negative, and when the price of beer goes up the demand for cigarettes will fall.

If goods are completely unrelated, their cross-elasticity of demand will be zero. Read Policy Example 4–2 for further discussion on cross-elasticity.

POLICY EXAMPLE 4–2 **Should Public Libraries Be Shut Down?**

The public library has been an institution in Canada for years. Most public libraries are paid for out of property taxes. Some policy makers argue that there is no reason to subsidize public libraries anymore. Why? Because individuals are gradually shifting their demand from the use of *physical* public libraries to online information services, such as Netscape, and others available over the Internet. As the price of online information has fallen, the demand for traditional library services has dropped. Though no one has calculated the exact cross-elasticity of demand for traditional library services, the decrease in usage of such libraries shows that it is significant.

For critical analysis: Compare your costs of using a library with those for using online information services.

Income Elasticity of Demand

In Chapter 3, we discussed the determinants of demand. One of those determinants was income. Briefly, we can apply our understanding of elasticity to the relationship between changes in income and changes in demand. We measure the responsiveness of quantity demanded to income changes by the *income elasticity of demand* (E_i):

$$E_i = \frac{\text{Percentage change in quantity demanded}}{\text{Percentage change in income}}$$

holding relative price constant.

Income elasticity of demand refers to a *horizontal shift* in the demand curve in response to changes in income, whereas **price elasticity of demand** refers to a movement *along* the curve in response to price changes. Thus, income elasticity of demand is calculated at a given price, and price elasticity of demand is calculated at a given income.

Income elasticity of demand
A *horizontal shift* in the demand curve in response to changes in income.

Price elasticity of demand
A movement *along* the curve in response to price changes.

A simple example will demonstrate how income elasticity of demand can be computed. Table 4–3 gives the relevant data. The product in question is the compact disc (CD). We assume that the price of CDs remains constant relative to other prices. In period 1, six CDs per month are purchased. Income per month is \$400. In period 2, monthly income increases to \$600, and the quantity of CDs demanded per month increases to eight. Using the same mid-point formula that we used in computing the price elasticity of demand, we get:

$$E_i = \frac{(8-6)/7}{(600-400)/500} = \frac{2/7}{2/5} = \frac{5}{7} = 0.714$$

TABLE 4-3

How Income Affects Quantity of CDs Demanded

Period	Number of CDs Demanded per Month	Income per Month
1	6	$400
2	8	600

Note that the sign of the income elasticity of demand is positive. That is because as income rises, the quantity of CDs demanded also increases. In Chapter 3, we defined this kind of good as a "normal" good—one that we want more of as our income increases. An "inferior" good is one that we want less of as our income increases. The sign of the income elasticity of demand for an inferior good will therefore be negative, since quantity demanded will decrease as income increases. It is important to retain the negative sign on the income elasticity of demand for an inferior good, since the sign tells us whether the good is, in fact, normal or inferior.

You have just been introduced to three types of elasticities. Two of them—the price elasticity of demand (E_p), and income elasticity (E_i)—are the two most important factors in influencing the quantity demanded for most goods. Reasonably accurate estimates of these can go a long way toward making accurate forecasts of demand for goods or services. For an illustration of income elasticity, see Example 4–5, below.

EXAMPLE 4–5

Frequent Flyer Miles as Income

For the past 10 years, airlines have been discovering that consumers measure their incomes in more than one way. Most airlines now offer frequent flyer points for air travel, and many are affiliated with other carriers and businesses as well. For example, Air Canada gives frequent flyer points for travel on United Airlines and for renting cars from Budget Rent-a-Car. Travellers can also apply for a Visa card that gives them one frequent flyer mile for every dollar charged. The first of these programs began in 1981. Air Canada started its Aeroplan program in 1984 with 14 000 members; five months later, it had 62 000. Now there are over 2 million members. Worldwide, there are more than 42 million members of various plans, with over two trillion points outstanding.

At the same time, airlines have found the demand for their services increasing. Air Canada alone reported a 16 percent increase in passenger volumes between 1995 and 1996, with much of the increment attributed to "free flights" earned through frequent flyer programs. It appears that air travellers count their frequent flyer miles as part of their incomes, and thus, they demand more air travel as their incomes increase.

For critical analysis: The federal government has decided that the value of flights paid for with frequent flyer miles earned while travelling on business should be considered part of an individual's income—and thus be liable to income tax. What effect will this have on the income elasticity of demand for air travel?

CONCEPTS IN BRIEF

Learning Objective 4.4: Describe the effects of substitutes, complements, and income on elasticity of demand.

- Cross-elasticity of demand measures one good's demand responsiveness to another's price changes. For substitutes, it is positive; for complements, it is negative.
- Income elasticity of demand tells you by what percentage demand will change for a particular percentage change in income.

4.5 Elasticity of Supply

Price elasticity of supply (E_s) The responsiveness of the quantity supplied of a commodity to a change in its price.

The **price elasticity of supply (E_s)** is defined similarly to the price elasticity of demand—the responsiveness of the quantity supplied of a commodity to a change in its price. Supply elasticities are generally positive; this is because at higher prices, larger quantities will generally be forthcoming from suppliers. The definition of the price elasticity of supply is as follows:

$$E_s = \frac{\text{Percentage change in quantity supplied}}{\text{Percentage change in price}}$$

Classifying Supply Elasticities

Just as with demand, there are different types of supply elasticities. They are similar in definition to the types of demand elasticities.

Perfectly elastic supply When the slightest reduction in price will cause quantity supplied to fall to zero.

Perfectly inelastic supply When, no matter what the price, the quantity supplied remains the same.

If a 1 percent increase in price elicits a greater than 1 percent increase in the quantity supplied, we say that at the particular price in question on the supply schedule, *supply is elastic.* The most extreme elastic supply is called **perfectly elastic supply**—the slightest reduction in price will cause quantity supplied to fall to zero.

If, conversely, a 1 percent increase in price elicits a less than 1 percent increase in the quantity supplied, we refer to that as an *inelastic supply.* The most extreme inelastic supply is called **perfectly inelastic supply**—no matter what the price, the quantity supplied remains the same.

If the percentage change in the quantity supplied is just equal to the percentage change in the price, we call this *unit-elastic supply.*

We show in Figure 4–4 two supply schedules, S and S'. You can tell at a glance, without reading the labels, which one is infinitely elastic and which one is perfectly inelastic. As you might expect, most supply schedules exhibit elasticities that are somewhere between zero and infinity.

Price Elasticity of Supply and Length of Time for Adjustment

We pointed out earlier that the longer the time period allowed for adjustment, the greater the price elasticity of demand. It turns out that the same proposition applies to supply. The longer the time for adjustment, the more elastic is the supply curve. Consider why this is true:

> The longer the time allowed for adjustment, the more firms are able to figure out ways to increase (or decrease) production in an industry.

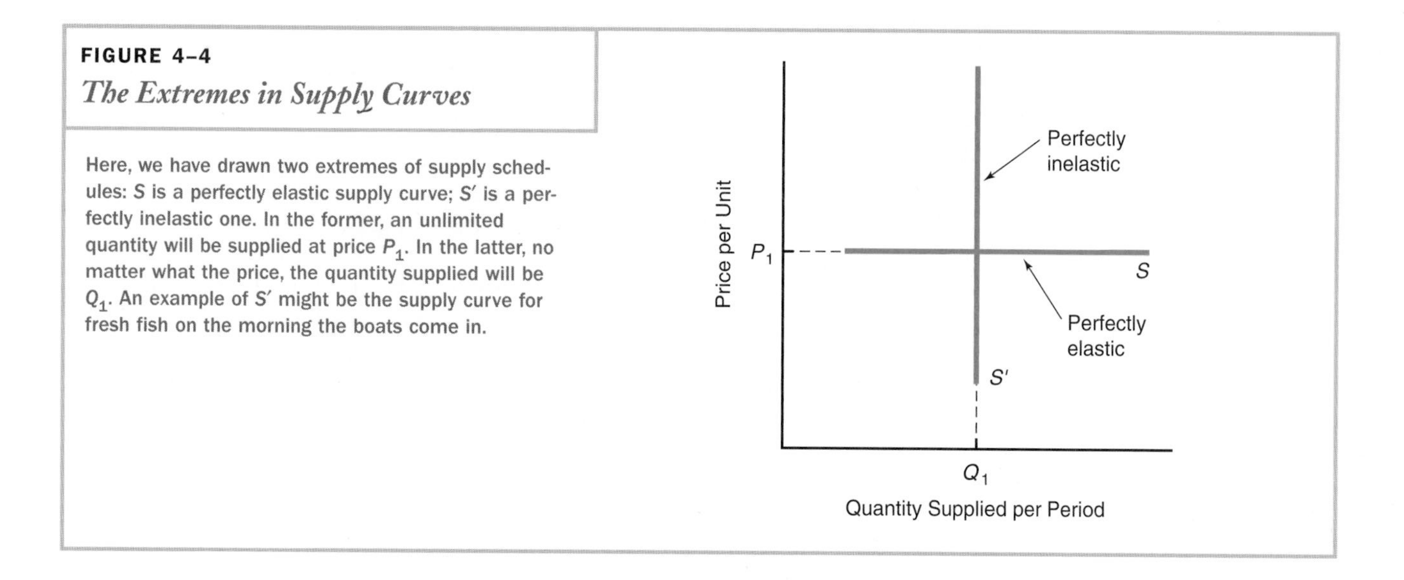

FIGURE 4–4

The Extremes in Supply Curves

Here, we have drawn two extremes of supply schedules: S is a perfectly elastic supply curve; S' is a perfectly inelastic one. In the former, an unlimited quantity will be supplied at price P_1. In the latter, no matter what the price, the quantity supplied will be Q_1. An example of S' might be the supply curve for fresh fish on the morning the boats come in.

The longer the time allowed for adjustment, the more resources can flow into (or out of) an industry through expansion (or contraction) of existing firms.

We therefore talk about short-run and long-run price elasticities of supply. The short run is defined as the time period during which full adjustment has not yet taken place. The long run is the time period during which firms have been able to adjust fully to the change in price.

Consider an increase in the price of housing. In the very short run, when there is no time allowed for adjustment, the amount of housing offered for rent or for sale is relatively inelastic. However, as more time is allowed for adjustment, current owners of the housing stock can find ways to increase the amount of housing they will offer for rent from given buildings. The owner of a large house can decide, for example, to have two children move into one room so that a "new" extra bedroom can be rented out. This can also be done by the owner of a large house who decides to move into an apartment and rent each floor of the house to a separate family. Thus, the quantity of housing supplied will increase. With more time, landlords will find it profitable to build new rental units.

We can show a whole set of supply curves similar to the ones we generated for demand. As Figure 4–5 shows, when nothing can be done in the short run, the supply curve is vertical, S_1. As more time is allowed for adjustment, the supply curve rotates to S_2 and then to S_3, becoming more elastic as it rotates.

CONCEPTS IN BRIEF

Learning Objective 4.5: Define price elasticity of supply and describe the difference between the long-run and short-run supply schedules.

- Price elasticity of supply is calculated by dividing the percentage change in quantity supplied by the percentage change in price.
- Usually, price elasticities of supply are positive—higher prices yield larger quantities supplied.
- Long-run supply curves are more elastic than short-run supply curves because the longer the time allowed, the more resources can flow into or out of an industry when price changes.

FIGURE 4–5

Short-Run and Long-Run Price Elasticity of Supply

Consider a situation in which the price is P_e and the quantity supplied is Q_e. In the short run, we hypothesize a vertical supply curve, S_1. With the price increase to P_1, therefore, there will be no change in the short run in quantity supplied; it will remain at Q_e. Given some time for adjustment, the supply curve will rotate to S_2. The new amount supplied will increase to Q_1. The long-run supply curve is shown by S_3. The amount supplied again increases to Q_2.

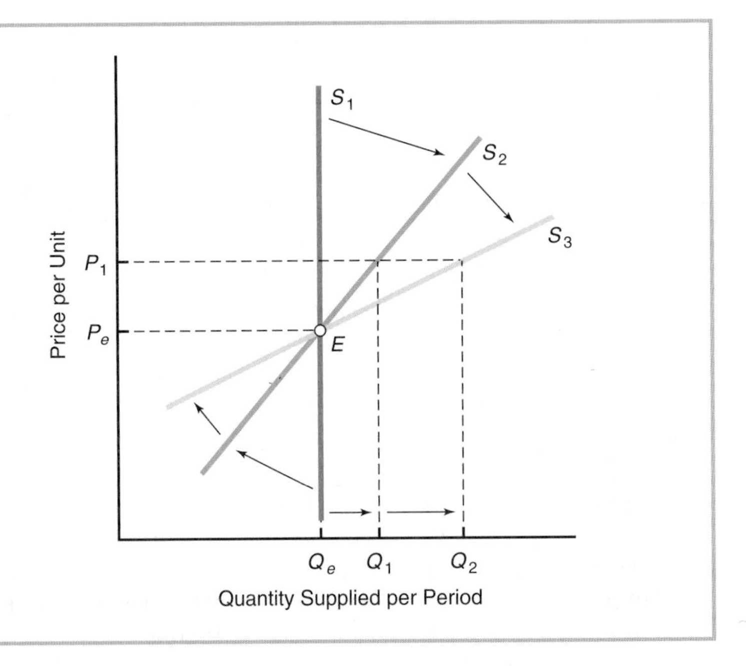

ISSUES AND APPLICATIONS

To Combat Cigarette Consumption, Should the Government Raise Taxes on Beer?

Concepts Applied: Price Elasticity of Demand; Cross-Elasticity of Demand

Smoking and drinking seem to go hand in hand.

According to the National Cancer Institute, cigarette smoking and other forms of tobacco use are directly responsible for at least one-third of all cancer deaths each year. Cigarette smoking contributes to the development of cancers of the lungs, head and neck, and throat. In addition, cigarette smoking contributes to cardiovascular disease and significantly raises the chance a heart attack. Smoking also poses problems for the fetus. Women who smoke during pregnancy are more likely to give birth to babies with below-average weights.

The Price Elasticity of Demand for Cigarettes

Why do so many people continue to smoke? One reason is that the average price of a cigarette sold in Canada is not much more than 40 cents. Among bad habits that people can pick up, smoking remains one of the least expensive.

In addition, cigarettes contain nicotine, which is a very addictive substance. This undoubtedly helps explain why the price elasticity of cigarette demand is approximately 0.3. Because the demand for cigarettes is relatively inelastic, relatively large price increases would be required to bring about a significant decline in cigarette consumption.

Taxation Policies to Combat Cigarette Consumption

Both the provincial and the federal governments levy taxes on cigarettes. Because the demand for cigarettes is inelastic, the market price of cigarettes reflects most of these taxes. Consequently, consumers pay the bulk of cigarette taxes, which account for about 77 percent of the average after-tax price of a pack of cigarettes.

Critics of the cigarette tax policy contend that in light of the relatively low price elasticity of demand for cigarettes, much higher taxes would be required to generate a significant drop in cigarette consumption. Canada raised taxes and found that teenage smoking fell from 42 percent to 16 percent, but smuggling of cigarettes increased.

Reducing Cigarette Consumption via Taxation of Alcohol?

Recently, some economists have proposed raising taxes on alcohol as another means of discouraging cigarette consumption. Their idea originates from the observation that bars are often smoke filled, which suggests that many people who drink regard alcoholic beverages, such as beer, as complements to cigarette smoking. Heavier taxes on alcohol would push up the price of alcoholic beverages, such as beer, thereby generating a reduction in cigarette consumption.

Estimates indicate that the cross elasticity of demand for cigarettes is approximately –0.2; each 10 percent increase in the price of beer thereby reduces cigarette demand by about 2 percent, and so cigarette smokers do, indeed, regard beer as a complement to cigarette consumption. Significant increases in taxes on beer could potentially supplement the use of cigarette taxes as a means of discouraging cigarette consumption.

Higher alcohol taxes would also help discourage the excessive use of alcohol, which imposes its own public health costs. The price elasticity of the demand for beer is only slightly less than 1, meaning that the demand for beer is nearly unit-elastic. This implies that a significant percentage increase in the price of beer due to higher taxes on beer would generate a nearly equal percentage reduction in beer consumption. In principle, therefore, higher taxes on beer and other alcoholic beverages could contribute to improved public health by reducing consumption of *both* cigarettes *and* alcohol.

For critical analysis:

1. On the basis of the information given here, would you expect that beer consumers pay a higher portion of the total tax on each unit of beer, compared with the fraction of the total tax that cigarette consumers pay on each pack of cigarettes? Why?
2. If both a beer producer and a cigarette producer raise their prices, which is more likely to experience an increase in total revenues? Explain.

SUMMARY DISCUSSION OF LEARNING OBJECTIVES

4.1 **Price Elasticity.** Price elasticity of demand is a measure of the percentage change in quantity demanded relative to the percentage change in price, given income, the prices of other goods, and time. Because of the law of demand, price elasticity of demand is always negative.

4.2 **Price Elasticity Ranges.** We classify demand as *elastic* if a 1 percent change in price leads to a more than 1 percent change in quantity demanded, *unit-elastic* if it leads to exactly a 1 percent change in quantity demanded, and *inelastic* if it leads to less than a 1 percent change in quantity demanded.

When facing a perfectly elastic demand, the slightest increase in price leads to zero quantity demanded; when facing a perfectly inelastic demand, no matter what the price, the quantity demanded remains unchanged. Perfect inelasticity means absolutely no price responsiveness.

Price elasticity of demand falls as we move down a straight-line demand curve. It goes from infinity to zero. Elasticity and slope are not equivalent; for example, the slope of a straight-line curve is always constant, whereas elasticity changes as we move along a linear curve. A vertical demand curve is perfectly inelastic; a horizontal demand curve is perfectly elastic.

4.3 **Determinants of the Price Elasticity of Demand.** Price elasticity of demand depends on (a) the existence, number, and quality of substitutes, (b) the share of total budget accounted for by the commodity, and (c) the length of time allowed for adjustment to changes in the price of the commodity.

4.4 **Cross-Elasticity of Demand.** Cross-elasticity of demand measures the responsiveness of the demand for one product, either a substitute or a complement, to changes in the price of another product. When the cross-elasticity of demand is negative, the two commodities under study are complements; when the cross-elasticity of demand is positive, they are substitutes.

Income elasticity of demand is given by the percentage change in quantity demanded divided by the percentage change in income, given the relative price. When the income elasticity of demand is positive, the good in question is a normal good; when the income elasticity of demand is negative, the good is an inferior good.

4.5 **Elasticity of Supply.** Price elasticity of supply is given by the percentage change in quantity supplied divided by the percentage change in price. The greater the time allowed for adjustment, the greater is the price elasticity of supply.

PROBLEMS

(Answers to the odd-numbered problems appear at the back of the book.)

LO 4.1 Define price elasticity of demand and calculate it using two different methods.

1. Use the following hypothetical demand schedule for tea to answer the questions.

Quantity Demanded per Week (kilograms)	Price per Kilogram	Elasticity
1000	$ 5	
800	10	
600	15	
400	20	
200	25	

a. Using the mid-point formula, determine the elasticity of demand for each price change. (Example:

When price changes from \$5 to \$10, quantity demanded changes from 1000 to 800 kilograms, so the elasticity of demand, using average values, is ⅓ or 0.33.)

b. Is the demand for this product income-elastic or income-inelastic?

c. Would you consider this commodity a luxury or a necessity?

2. Calculate the price elasticity of demand for the product in the table below using average values for the prices and quantities in your formula. Over the price range in question, is this demand schedule inelastic, unit-elastic, or elastic? Is total revenue greater at the lower price or the higher price?

Price per Unit	Quantity Demanded
\$4	22
6	18

3. A new mobile home park charges nothing whatsoever for water used by its inhabitants. Consumption is 100 000 litres per month. The decision is then made to charge according to how much each mobile home owner uses, at a rate of \$10 per 1000 litres. Consumption declines to 50 000 litres per month. What is the difficulty here in accurately estimating the price elasticity of the demand for water by these residents?

4. Suppose that the price of salt rises from 15 cents to 17 cents a kilogram. The quantity demanded decreases from 525 kilograms to 475 kilograms per month, and the quantity supplied increases from 525 kilograms to 600 kilograms per month. (Use averages in calculating elasticities.)

   a. Calculate the price elasticity of demand (E_p) for salt.

   b. Is the demand for salt price-elastic or price-inelastic?

5. Suppose that an automobile dealer cuts his car prices by 15 percent. He then finds that his car sales revenues have increased by 10 percent.

   a. What can you say about the price elasticity of demand for cars?

   b. What will happen to the dealer's total revenue?

LO 4.2 Define the three price elasticity ranges and explain their effects on total revenues.

6. Can any demand curve possibly be perfectly inelastic ($E_p = 0$) regardless of price? Explain. For Example 4–3, "A Pricing Decision at Disneyland Paris," if total revenues had dropped instead of increasing, what range would the price elasticity of demand be in?

LO 4.3 Discuss the three factors that determine the price elasticity of demand.

7. Given each example, determine whether price elasticity will tend to be elastic or inelastic.

   a. A 45-cent box of salt you buy once a year.

   b. A type of high-powered ski boat you can rent from any number of rental agencies.

   c. A 75-cent guitar pick for the lead guitarist of a major rock band.

   For Example 4–4, "What Do Real-World Price Elasticities of Demand Look Like?", food has a price elasticity of demand of around 0.12. Does the quality of substitutes affect this elasticity?

LO 4.4 Describe the effects of substitutes, complements, and income on elasticity of demand.

8. Calculate the income elasticity of demand for the product in the following table, using average values for incomes and quantities.

Quantity of VCRs per Year	Per Capita Annual Group Income
1000	\$15 000
2000	20 000

   a. Is the demand for this product income-elastic or income-inelastic?

   b. Would you consider this commodity a luxury or a necessity?

9. Which of the following cross-elasticities of demand would you expect to be positive and which to be negative?

   a. Tennis balls and tennis racquets

   b. Tennis balls and golf balls

   c. Dental services and toothpaste

   d. Dental services and candy

   e. Soft drinks and ice cubes

   f. Soft drinks and fruit juices

LO 4.5 Define price elasticity of supply and describe the difference between the long-run and short-run supply schedules.

10. Suppose that the price of salt rises from 15 cents to 17 cents a kilogram. The quantity demanded decreases from 525 kilograms to 475 kilograms per month, and the quantity supplied increases from 525 kilograms to 600 kilograms per month. (Use averages in calculating elasticities.)

    a. Calculate the elasticity of supply (E_s) for salt.

    b. Is the supply of salt price-elastic or price-inelastic?

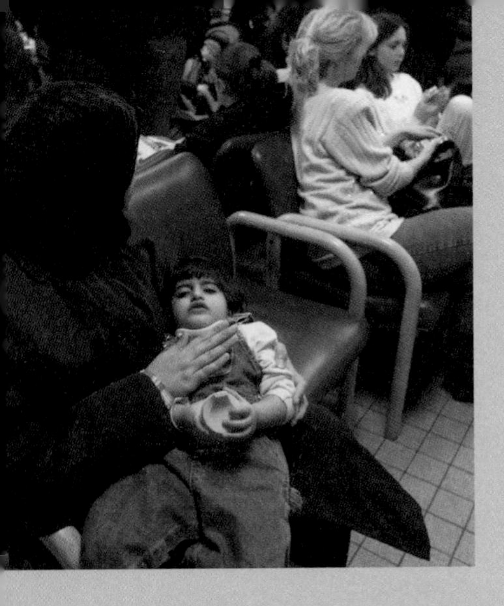

CHAPTER 5

Extensions of Demand, Supply, and Elasticity

Hospital and bed closures, crowded emergency rooms, health-care worker strikes, physician emigration to the United States, and growing waitlists for a variety of medical treatments have all become part of the daily news across Canada. Politicians, academics, and concerned citizens are debating the merits of using market incentives to address these reported problems.

The concepts presented in this chapter will enhance your ability to understand and evaluate the problems and proposed solutions relating to Canada's health-care system.

LEARNING OBJECTIVES

After reading this chapter, you will be able to:

5.1 Explain the role of markets, intermediaries, and prices in the price system.

5.2 Compare and contrast price ceiling and price floor policies.

5.3 Compare and contrast the offer-to-purchase and the marketing board price support policies.

5.4 Describe the various types of quantity restrictions that governments can impose on markets.

5.5 Explain how price elasticity governs the effects that a per-unit excise tax has on tax incidence, resource allocation, and government tax revenue collected.

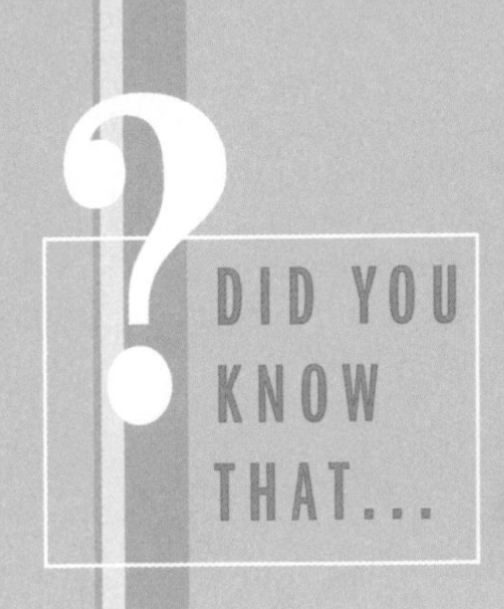

In 2002, an estimated 5.4 million Canadians, representing roughly 21 percent of the population aged 15 years and older, were current smokers, of which 18 percent reported smoking daily. Approximately 23 percent of men aged 15 years and older were current smokers, slightly higher than the 20 percent rate for women. The vast majority of Canadian smokers, 61 percent, reported consuming some type of "light" or "mild" cigarette, compared with 39 percent who smoke a "regular" type of cigarette. British Columbia reported the lowest prevalence of smoking, while Quebec reported the highest.

The rate of smoking has declined significantly since 1985 when 35 percent of the Canadian population aged 15 years and older were current smokers. Some of this decline in tobacco use can be attributed to policies that apply the principles of demand and supply, as this chapter illustrates.

5.1 The Price System

Price system An economic system in which relative prices are constantly changing to reflect changes in supply and demand for different commodities.

A **price system**, otherwise known as a *market system*, is one in which relative prices are constantly changing to reflect changes in supply and demand for different commodities. The prices of those commodities are the signals to everyone within the system as to what is relatively scarce and what is relatively abundant. Indeed, it is the *signalling* aspect of the price system that provides the information to buyers and sellers about what should be bought and what should be produced. In a price system, there is a clear-cut chain of events in which any changes in demand and supply cause changes in prices. Those price changes, in turn, affect the opportunities that businesses and individuals have for profit and personal gain. Such changes influence our use of resources.

Exchange and Markets

Voluntary exchange Acts of trading between individuals that make both parties to the trade subjectively better off.

Terms of exchange The prices we pay for the desired items.

The price system features **voluntary exchange**, acts of trading between individuals that make both parties to the trade subjectively better off. The **terms of exchange**—the prices we pay for the desired items—are determined by the interaction of the forces underlying supply and demand. In our economy, the majority of exchanges takes place voluntarily in markets. A market encompasses the exchange arrangements of both buyers and sellers that underlie the forces of supply and demand. Indeed, one definition of a market is a low-cost institution for facilitating exchange. A market in essence increases incomes by helping resources move to their highest-valued uses by means of prices. Prices are the providers of information.

Transaction Costs

Transaction costs The costs associated with finding out exactly what is being exchanged as well as the cost of enforcing contracts.

Individuals turn to markets because markets reduce the cost of exchanges. These costs are sometimes referred to as **transaction costs**, which are broadly defined as the costs associated with finding out exactly what is being exchanged as well as the cost of enforcing contracts. If you were Robinson Crusoe and lived alone on an island, you would never incur a transaction cost. For everyone else, transaction costs are just as real as the costs of production. High-speed large-scale computers have allowed us to reduce transaction costs by increasing our ability to process information and keep records.

Consider some simple examples of transaction costs. The supermarket reduces transaction costs relative to your having to go to numerous specialty stores to obtain the items you desire. Organized stock exchanges, such as the Toronto Stock Exchange, have reduced transaction costs of buying and selling shares and bonds. In general, the more organized the market, the lower are the transaction costs. One group of individuals who constantly attempt to lower transaction costs are intermediaries.

The Role of the Intermediary

As long as there are costs to bringing together buyers and sellers, there will be an incentive for intermediaries, often called middlemen, to lower those costs. This means that intermediaries specialize in lowering transaction costs. Whenever producers do not sell their products directly to the final consumer, there are, by definition, one or more intermediaries involved. Farmers typically sell their output to distributors, who are usually called wholesalers, who then sell those products to the retailers, or grocery stores.

Recently, technology has reduced the need, and hence the job prospects, for intermediaries, as seen in Example 5–1.

EXAMPLE 5–1 **Technology and the Death of Intermediaries**

For decades, most airline travellers bought their tickets from an independent travel agent, not from the airline itself. On August 27, 2001, Air Canada announced plans to slash the maximum commission it pays to travel agents by more than half, claiming that this was necessary to remain competitive with other North American airlines. The base commission will remain at 5 per cent but the maximum commission—the so called "cap"—will plunge from $60 for a round trip in Canada ($70 to the United States) to $28 for a round-trip ticket anywhere Air Canada flies in North America. This move comes after several American airlines also slashed maximum travel agent commissions from U.S.$50 to U.S.$20 for round-trip tickets south of the border. Two weeks prior to Air Canada's announcement, Air Canada had put on a seat sale that was restricted to people who booked their airline tickets online, bypassing travel agents entirely. Basically, the airlines have realized that there are high-tech alternatives to travel agents for the distribution of their tickets. The airlines' websites allow Web surfers to consult airline timetables and to reserve tickets from their home or office computers.

On May 13, 2002, the Canadian Standard Travel Agent Registry (CSTAR) filed a class action lawsuit, on behalf of Canada's 3700 travel agencies, against Air Canada and five American airlines. The CSTAR alleges that the major airlines in North America have jointly agreed to reduce and eliminate base commissions paid to Canadian travel agencies. According to the CSTAR, the ultimate motive for this joint agreement is to redirect the sale of airline tickets from travel agents to airline websites.

For critical analysis: Why might consumers prefer to book airline tickets through travel agents, rather than airline websites?

SOURCE: "TRAVEL AGENTS SUE OVER COMMISSION CUTS." CBC NEWS ONLINE STAFF. MARCH 5, 2003. http://cbc.ca/stories/2003/03/05/Consumers/travelagents_030305). (ACCESSED DEC. 31, 2003.)

The Rationing Function of Prices

A shortage creates a situation that forces price to rise toward a market clearing, or equilibrium, level. A surplus brings into play forces that cause the price of a product to fall toward its market clearing level. The synchronization of decisions by buyers and sellers that creates a situation of equilibrium is called the *rationing function of prices*. Prices are indicators of relative scarcity.

An equilibrium price clears the market. The plans of buyers and sellers, given the price, are not frustrated.[1] It is the free interaction of buyers and sellers that sets the price that eventually clears the market. Price, in effect, rations a commodity to demanders who are willing and able to pay the highest price. Whenever the rationing function of prices is frustrated by government-enforced price ceilings that set prices below the market clearing

[1]There is a difference between frustration and unhappiness. You may be unhappy because you cannot buy a Rolls Royce, but if you had sufficient income, you would not be frustrated in your attempt to purchase one at the current market price. By contrast, you would be frustrated if you went to your local supermarket and could get only two cans of your favourite soft drink when you had wanted to purchase a dozen and had the necessary income.

level, a prolonged shortage situation is not allowed to be corrected by the upward adjustment of the price.

You should note that if prices are not allowed to ration goods, services, or resources, other forms of rationing will have to be used. Admission to universities and colleges is often rationed not by tuition (a dollars and cents price) but by grade point average. The highest "bidders" for admission—those with the highest GPAs—are accepted.

There are other ways to ration goods. *First-come, first-served* is one method. *Political power* is another. *Physical force* is yet another. Cultural, religious, and physical differences have been and are used as rationing devices throughout the world.

Consider "first-come, first-served" as a rationing device. In countries that do not allow prices to reflect true relative scarcity, "first-come, first-served" has become a way of life. We call this *rationing by queues,* where *queue* means "line." Whoever is willing to wait in line the longest obtains meat that is being sold at less than the market clearing price. All who wait in line are paying a higher *total* price than the money price paid for the meat. Personal time has an opportunity cost. To calculate the total price of the meat, we must add up the money price plus the opportunity cost of the time spent waiting.

In this chapter's Issues and Applications, it is noted that Canada's current medicare system prohibits using prices to ration the services provided by doctors and hospitals. That is, patients are not allowed to pay a price or user fee to gain immediate access to the medical, diagnostic, or surgical services provided by specialist physicians. As a result, rationing by queues has become prevalent in the Canadian health-care system. Indeed, it is estimated that in 2003, Canadians waited an average of 17.8 weeks from the time they received a referral from their general practitioner to the time they received treatment from a medical specialist.

Lotteries are another way to ration goods. You may have been involved in a rationing-by-lottery scheme during your first year in college when you were assigned a parking pass for campus lots. Selling raffle tickets for popular college sweatshirts is also a method of rationing by lottery.

Rationing by *coupons* has also been used, particularly during wartime. In Canada, during World War II, families were allotted coupons that allowed them to purchase specified quantities of rationed goods, such as meat and gasoline. To purchase these goods, you had to pay a specified price *and* give up a coupon.

Rationing by *waiting* may occur in situations in which entrepreneurs are free to change prices to equate quantity demanded with quantity supplied but choose not to do so. This results in queues of potential buyers. The most obvious conclusion seems to be that the price in the market is being held below equilibrium by some noncompetitive force. That, however, is not true.

The reason is that queuing may also arise when the demand characteristics of a market are subject to large or unpredictable fluctuations, and the additional costs to firms (and ultimately to consumers) of constantly changing prices, or of holding sufficient inventories, or providing sufficient excess capacity to cover these peak demands are greater than the costs to consumers of waiting for the good. This is the usual case of waiting in line to purchase a fast-food lunch or to purchase a movie ticket a few minutes before the next show.

The Essential Role of Rationing

In a world of scarcity, there is, by definition, competition for what is scarce. After all, any resources that are not scarce can be had by everyone at a zero price in as large a quantity as everyone wants, such as air to burn in internal combustion engines. Once scarcity arises, there has to be some method to ration the available resources, goods, and services, as shown in Example 5–2. The price system is one form of rationing; the others that we mentioned are alternatives. Economists cannot say which system of rationing is the best. They can, however, say that rationing via the price system leads to the most efficient use of available resources. This means that generally in a price system, further trades could not occur without making somebody worse off. In other words, in a freely functioning price system, all of the gains from mutually beneficial trade will be exhausted.

EXAMPLE 5–2 Should Shortages in the Ticket Market Be Solved by Scalpers?

If you have ever tried to get tickets to a major league playoff game or a superstar's rock concert, you know about shortages. In many of these situations, ticket prices are initially set below the equilibrium price so that long line-ups develop at ticket counters. These queues serve to increase the media hype surrounding the event. As the day of the big event approaches, scalpers who paid the original price or "face value" for the tickets, end up selling these tickets at a much higher price, either online or just outside the coliseum gates.

For example, when tickets were first issued for the 2003 Heritage Classic, the NHL's first outdoor game and star-studded hall of famers'match, good seats were selling for $135 each. At this price, the event planners reported that they could have sold 700 000 seats, more than 10 times the capacity of Commonwealth Stadium, where the games were to be played. Just days before the big event, online scalpers were asking up to $2500 a ticket—almost 20 times the original price!

Figure 5–1 describes the market conditions for the Heritage Classic just days before game day. If there was no scalping of tickets, the price of each ticket would remain at the face value of $135, with a shortage of tickets equal to (Q_2 – Q_1). However, according to Figure 5–1, there are potential ticket buyers who are willing to pay up to $2500 per ticket to be part of a moment that may come only once in a lifetime. Ticket scalpers play the role of an intermediary that eliminates the shortage situation, by getting the Heritage Classic tickets into the hands of those consumers who tend to value the tickets the most (i.e., at a price of $2500).

In most Canadian provinces, scalping is illegal. In Ontario, convicted scalpers are fined around $500 for each infraction. For an economist, such legislation seems strange. The buying and selling of scalped tickets is purely voluntary. This implies that both the buyer and seller expect to gain from the exchange, or it would not occur. In other words, ticket scalping is simply the price system's way of efficiently rationing a scarce commodity.

SOURCE: BOB WEBER. "HOCKEY MAKES RETURN TO SIMPLER TIMES." *CANADIAN PRESS,* NOVEMBER 22, 2003. THE HALIFAX HERALD LIMITED. http://www.herald.ns.ca/stories/2003/11/22/f193.raw.html. (ACCESSED DECEMBER 31, 2003.)

For critical analysis: If on the day of the big event, there are lots of unsold seats for the Heritage Classic, what will happen to the value of the tickets still held by scalpers?

FIGURE 5–1

Shortage of Tickets for the 2003 Heritage Classic Hockey Event

No matter what the ticket price, the available total quantity of tickets is at Q_1, which is the stadium capacity. The Heritage Classic tickets were originally offered for sale at the "face value" of $135. Just days before the event, the quantity demanded at the ticket price of $135 is Q_2. Without ticket scalpers, there would be a shortage (Q_2 – Q_1). If ticket scalping occurs, the ticket price can increase to the equilibrium price of $2500.

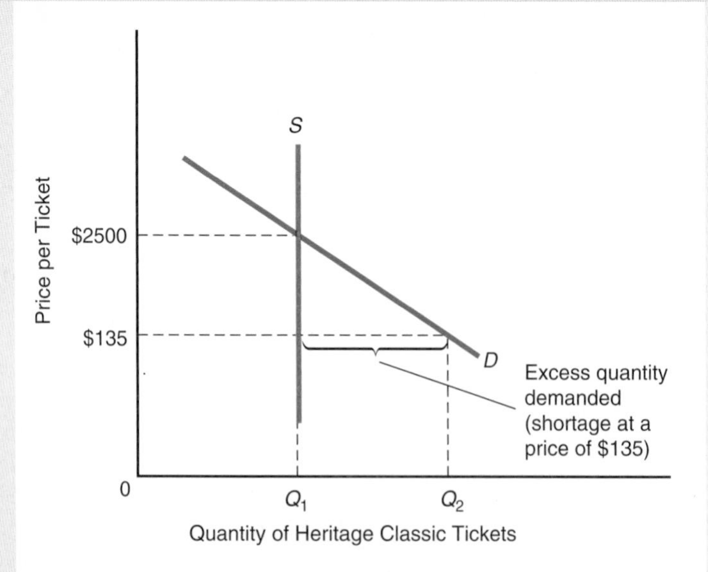

5.2 Price Ceilings and Price Floors

Price controls Government-mandated minimum or maximum prices that may be charged for goods and services.

Price ceiling The maximum price that may be allowed in an exchange.

Price floor A minimum price below which a good or service may not be sold.

The rationing function of prices is often not allowed to operate when governments impose price controls. **Price controls**—government-mandated minimum or maximum prices that may be charged for goods and services—typically involve setting a **price ceiling**—the maximum price that may be allowed in an exchange. The world has had a long history of price ceilings applied to some goods, wages, rents, and interest rates, among other things. Occasionally, a government will set a **price floor**—a minimum price below which a good or service may not be sold. These have most often been applied to wages and agricultural products. Let us consider price controls in terms of price ceilings.

Price Ceilings: Rent Controls

Rent control The placement of a price ceiling or maximum price on rents.

In order to understand and evaluate a price-ceiling situation, we will use the example of a rent control policy. **Rent control** refers to the placement of a price ceiling or maximum price on rents.

Figure 5–2 describes a hypothetical market situation relating to two-bedroom apartment units in a Canadian city. If there is no government intervention, the equilibrium monthly rental price of a two-bedroom unit is $800 per month. At this price, 60 000 quality two-bedroom units are being supplied and demanded for rental purposes each month.

In response to pressure due to public complaints that apartment rents are excessive, the provincial government decides to implement a price ceiling policy for two-bedroom apartment units. This rent control policy consists of legislating a maximum rental price of $650 per month. Any landlord who charges a monthly rent more than $650 for two-bedroom units would face large fines. The intent of the rent controls is to promote a more equitable distribution of income or simply "equity." That is, the government hopes to use the price ceiling policy as a means of ensuring that quality two-bedroom units remain affordable to lower-income families. By reducing the monthly rent charged, there will be a transfer of income from higher-income landlords to lower-income tenants (consumers).

What can we predict about the effects of the rent control policy, on the basis of the theory of supply and demand? In Figure 5–2, the price or rent of each two-bedroom unit is now set at $650 per month, which is below the equilibrium price. As is the case with any effective price ceiling policy, the maximum price will only replace the free market price if it is set below the equilibrium. As Figure 5–2 illustrates, at a monthly rent of $650 per month, 50 000 quality two-bedroom units will tend to be supplied per month (in the long

FIGURE 5–2

Price Ceiling Policy: Rent Controls on Two-Bedroom Apartments

If there is no government intervention in this apartment market, the equilibrium monthly rent will be $800 per month and the equilibrium quantity will be 60 000 units per month. Under rent controls, with a price ceiling of $650 per month, landlords will wish to supply only 50 000 quality two-bedroom rental units per month, while tenants will demand 70 000 units per month. A shortage of 20 000 units per month will eventually emerge. Moreover, once the quantity supplied is reduced to 50 000 units per month, according to the demand curve, there will be consumers who will pay a black market price up to $1000 per month.

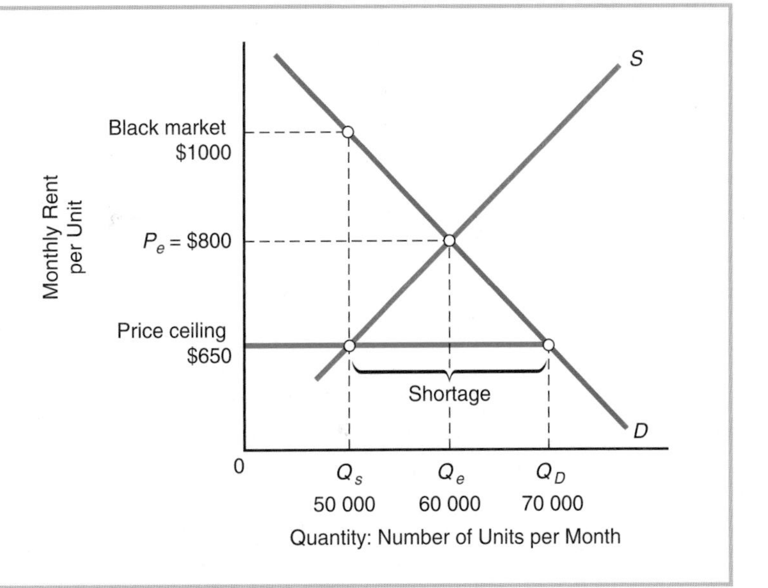

run), while 70 000 apartment units would be demanded per month. A shortage of 20 000 units per month will result, in the long run.

Nonprice-rationing devices Methods used to ration scarce goods that are price controlled.

The price ceiling policy leads to fewer exchanges and **nonprice-rationing devices**, which are methods used to ration scarce goods that are price controlled. With the rent controls imposed, the price system is no longer allowed to eliminate the shortage of apartment units. In other words, the available supply of apartment units is rationed according to nonprice criteria, such as "first-come, first-served," or "only rent to friends," or "rent to desirable-looking people," and so forth. Typically, queuing or long line-ups develop, which means that many of those potential tenants wishing to rent two-bedroom apartments may have a lengthy wait before a rental unit becomes vacant.

Black market A market in which the price-controlled good is sold at an illegally high price through various, under-the-table methods.

Typically, an effective price ceiling policy leads to a black market. A **black market** is a market in which the price-controlled good is sold at an illegally high price through various, under-the-table methods. In our rental apartment example, landlords may charge "key money," which can be a relatively large lump-sum illegal cash payment that must be made before a tenant is allowed to obtain the keys for the apartment. If the illegal key money is included in determining the actual monthly rent, we would call this monthly amount the black market price. As the demand curve in Figure 5–2 indicates, after the rent controls are imposed and a reduced supply of 50 000 units occurs, there will be tenants who will be willing to pay a black market price of up to $1000 per month. In other words, the actual monthly rent that is being charged (with the key money included) is more than the free market price of $800 per month!

It should be noted that black market behaviour is not limited to apartment units. In any market where price ceilings are imposed, there is the potential for black markets. If, due to an energy crisis, the price of gasoline is controlled, a hidden cash payment to the gas attendant may be required to gas up one's car. If beef shortages develop due to ceiling prices on beef, the butcher may give special service to a customer who offers the butcher free tickets for great seats at an upcoming rock concert. Indeed, the number of ways in which the true, implicit price of a price-controlled good or service can be increased is infinite, limited only by the imagination.

RENT CONTROLS AND EFFICIENCY. Let us return to the example of rent controls in order to describe how a price ceiling policy can result in an inefficient allocation of scarce resources. In housing markets, equilibrium rental prices can promote allocative efficiency by serving three functions: (1) to promote the construction of new housing in response to increased consumer demand, (2) to promote the efficient maintenance of the existing supply of housing, and (3) to ration the current supply of housing to the highest valued uses.

Rent controls have discouraged the construction of new rental units. Rents are the most important long-term determinant of profitability, and rent controls have artificially depressed them. Consider some examples. Halifax, with less than 15 percent of the population of Toronto, built proportionally more rental units than Toronto in 1995. This, in spite of a 7.2 percent vacancy rate in Halifax, compared with a 1.2 percent vacancy rate in Toronto. The major difference? There were no rent controls in Halifax, while rent increases were strictly controlled in Toronto. In the same year, Vancouver, with 70 percent of the population of Toronto, saw the construction of 11 000 rental units; only 4000 were built in Toronto. Again, the difference was that there were no rent controls in Vancouver.

When rental rates are held below equilibrium levels, property owners cannot use higher rents to recover the cost of maintenance, repairs, and capital improvements. Hence they curtail these activities. In the extreme situation, taxes, utilities, and the expenses of basic repairs exceed rental receipts. The result is abandoned and/or deteriorating buildings. It is estimated that over 15 percent of the rental units in Toronto will deteriorate so much by the early 2000s that many will be uninhabitable. In the 1970s, when Vancouver did have a system of rent controls, landlords, unable to increase rents, converted thousands of apartments into condominiums. The landlords then sold the condominiums and recouped their investment that way. This had the effect of severely reducing the supply of rental housing, thus making the housing shortage even worse.

Like any other price, rents serve the purpose of rationing output, in this case, the allocation of apartments among prospective tenants. When the rent is held at an arbitrarily low level, the number of prospective tenants increases, and excess demand develops. Students, for example, who might otherwise live with their families, decide they can afford to live on their own. In this situation, rationing of the available supply of rental housing is achieved through nonprice mechanisms, such as queuing or making "under-the-table" payments to landlords.

ATTEMPTS AT EVADING RENT CONTROLS. The distortions produced by rent controls lead to efforts by both landlords and tenants to evade the rules. This, in turn, leads to the growth of expensive government bureaucracies whose job it is to make sure that those rules are, indeed, followed. In 1995, the Ontario government spent about $1.8 million administering its *Residential Rent Regulation Act.*

In the 1980s, Ontario landlords had an incentive to speculate on the real estate market. They bought and sold apartment buildings, driving up prices and financing costs. Then, they applied for rent increases to cover the rising costs. Tenants, for their part, routinely tried to sublet all or part of their rent-controlled apartments at fees substantially above the rent they paid to the owner. They pocketed the difference, perhaps to help pay for a more expensive apartment.

RENT CONTROLS AND EQUITY. The big losers from rent controls are clearly landlords. But there is another group of losers—low-income individuals, especially single mothers, trying to find their first apartment. Some observers now believe that rent controls have worsened the problem of homeless people in such cities as Toronto.

Poor individuals cannot afford a hefty key money payment, nor can they assure the landlord that they will pay their rents on time or even regularly. Because controlled rents are usually below market clearing levels, there is little incentive for apartment owners to take any risk on low-income-earning individuals as tenants. As a result, economists question whether rent ceilings actually promote equity, especially in the long run.

Who benefits from rent control? Ample evidence indicates that upper-income professionals benefit the most. These are the people who can use their mastery of the bureaucracy and their large network of friends and connections to exploit the rent control system. These are also the people who can easily afford to pay key money or to pay an agency to locate an apartment for them.

Because the private sector was unwilling to finance construction of new rental units in an environment of rent controls, the Ontario government had to spend up to $3.5 billion per year subsidizing the building of nonprofit housing. Rents might have been controlled at lower-than-market levels, but renters and homeowners alike paid higher than necessary taxes to fund the government's subsidies.

Policy Example 5–1 explains how the Manitoba government designed its policy of rent controls so as to encourage the construction of new rental units.

POLICY EXAMPLE 5–1 **Rent Controls in Manitoba**

In 2004, the Manitoba NDP government was the only Canadian provincial government enforcing rent controls. The Manitoba rent control policy can be described as follows. Each year the Manitoba government sets a maximum allowable annual rent increase. In 2004, the maximum allowable increase was 1.5 percent over the previous year's monthly rental amount. As an example, if a landlord was charging $500 per month rent in 2003, the maximum this landlord can charge in 2004 would be $507.50 per month. Rents can only be increased once every 12 months. The rent controls apply to most rental units, including apartments, single rooms, houses, and duplexes.

continued

Critics of the Manitoba rent controls suggest that this policy has stifled new apartment construction and has led to the creation of a stock of run-down apartment buildings. Moreover, since rent controls reduce the profitability, supply, and market values of rental units, property taxes paid by landlords have decreased relative to the property taxes paid by homeowners. In other words, rent controls have increased the typical homeowner's property tax burden. In responding to these problems, the Manitoba government recently passed legislation that exempts newly constructed rental units from rent controls for a period of 15 years. Also exempt are rental units for which the monthly rent payable on December 31, 2002, was $970 or more.

For critical analysis: Using the appropriate economic concepts, explain the rationale for exempting newly constructed rental units and expensive rental units from rent control. What sources of the rental unit supply are largely ignored by the recently passed legislation?

SOURCES: "THE RESIDENTIAL RENT REGULATION." CONSUMER AND CORPORATE AFFAIRS. *MANITOBA FINANCE*, P. 4. http://web2.gov.mb.ca/laws/regs/pdf/r119-156.92.pdf. (ACCESSED JUNE 1, 2004); RICHARD MORANTZ. "LIFT RENT CONTROLS TO BENEFIT LOW INCOME RENTERS." DECEMBER 2002. FRONTIER CENTRE FOR PUBLIC POLICY. http://www.fcpp.org/publication_detail.php?PubID=463. (ACCESSED JANUARY 1, 2004.)

Price Floors: Minimum Wage

Minimum wage The lowest hourly wage rate that firms may legally pay their workers.

As we noted above, price controls can take the form of price floors, where a minimum price is fixed above the equilibrium price. An example of price floors currently in force in Canada are minimum wages set by provincial governments. The **minimum wage** is the lowest hourly wage rate that firms may legally pay their workers. Proponents want higher minimum wages to ensure low-income workers a "decent" standard of living. Opponents claim that higher minimum wages cause increased unemployment, particularly among unskilled teenagers.

Every province in Canada has a minimum wage. Figure 5–3 sets out the hourly minimum wage for each province. For many years, the federal government had a minimum wage of $4 per hour, which applied to federal workers. However, this legislated wage was

FIGURE 5–3

Provincial Minimum Wage Rates per Hour

Every province in Canada legislates a minimum wage rate per hour. At the beginning of 2004, the rate varied from a low of $5.90 in Alberta to a high of $8 in British Columbia. The average minimum wage was $6.82 per hour at the beginning of 2004.

SOURCE: "CURRENT MINIMUM WAGE LEVELS ACROSS CANADA." *SASKATCHEWAN LABOUR*. UPDATED MAY 1, 2004. http://www.labour.gov.sk.ca/minwage.htm). (ACCESSED JUNE 1, 2004.ACCESSED JUNE 1, 2004.)

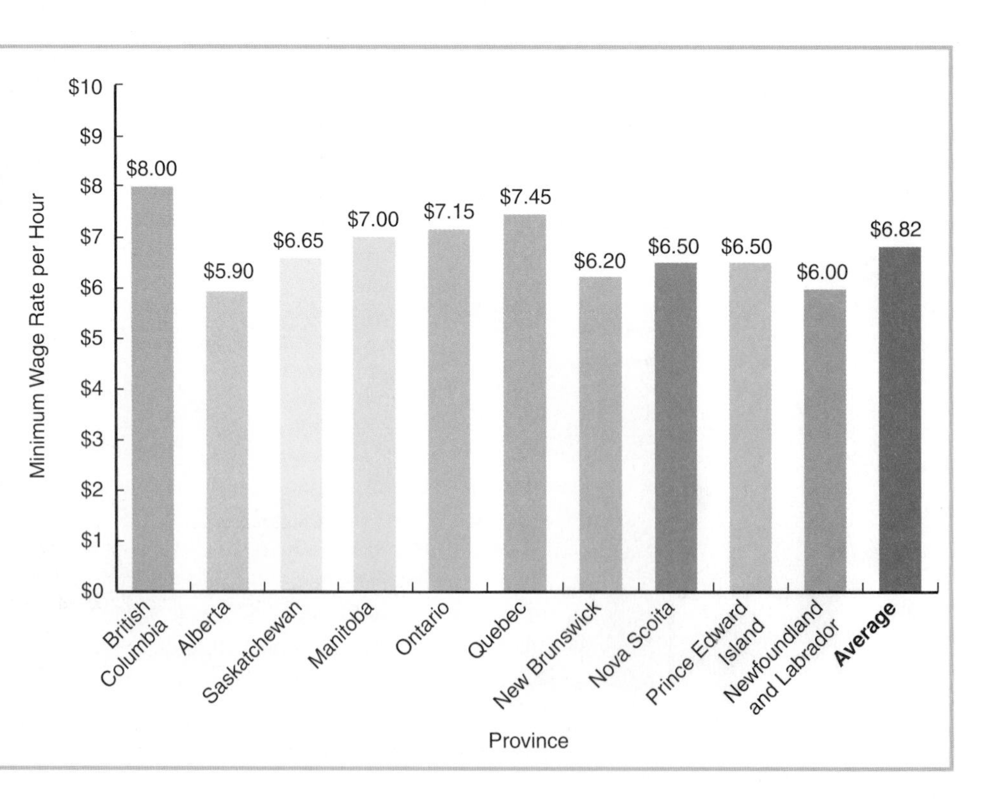

cancelled some time ago, since all workers were already earning more than the minimum anyway.

What happens when the government passes legislation setting a floor on wages? The effects can be seen in Figure 5–4. We start off in equilibrium with the equilibrium wage rate of W_e and the equilibrium quantity of labour demanded and supplied equal to Q_e. A minimum wage, W_m, higher than W_e, is imposed. At W_m, the quantity demanded for labour is reduced to Q_d, and some workers now become unemployed. Note that the reduction in employment from Q_e to Q_d, or the distance from *B* to *A*, is less than the excess quantity of labour supplied at wage rate W_m. This excess quantity supplied is the distance between *A* and *C*, or the distance between Q_d and Q_s. The reason the reduction in employment is smaller than the excess supply of labour at the minimum wage is that the latter also includes a second component, consisting of the additional workers who would like to work more hours at the new, higher minimum wage. Some workers may become unemployed as a result of the minimum wage, but others will move to sectors where minimum wage laws do not apply; wages will be pushed down in these uncovered sectors.

In the long run (a time period that is long enough to allow for adjustment by workers and firms), some of the reduction in labour demanded will result from a reduction in the number of firms, and some will result from changes in the number of workers employed by each firm. Economists estimate that a 10 percent increase in the real minimum wage decreases total employment of those affected by 1 to 2 percent.[2]

CONCEPTS IN BRIEF

Learning Objective 5.1: Explain the role of markets, intermediaries, and prices in the price system.

- Markets and intermediaries reduce the costs of obtaining mutually beneficial exchanges between buyers and sellers.
- Prices ration resources and goods in an efficient manner. When equilibrium prices are set, resources and goods are allocated to the highest valued uses, and all the gains from mutually beneficial trades are exhausted.

FIGURE 5–4

The Effect of Minimum Wages

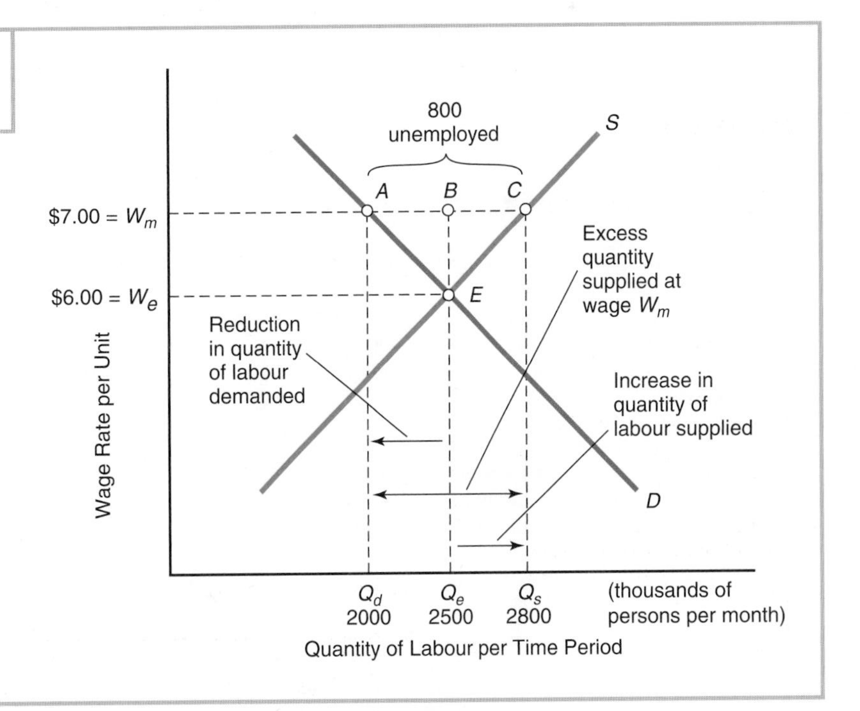

The market clearing wage rate is W_e = $6. The market clearing quantity of employment is Q_e = 2500, determined by the intersection of supply and demand at point *E*. A minimum wage equal to W_m = $7 is established. The quantity of labour demanded is reduced to Q_d = 2000; the reduction in employment from Q_e = 2000 to Q_d is equal to the distance between *B* and *A*. That distance is smaller than the excess quantity of labour supplied at wage rate W_m. The distance between *B* and *C* is the increase in the quantity of labour supplied that results from the higher minimum wage rate.

[2]Because we are referring to a long-run analysis here, the reduction in labour demanded would be demonstrated by an eventual shift inward to the left of the short-run demand curve, *D*, in Figure 5–4.

Learning Objective 5.2: Compare and contrast price ceiling and price floor policies.

- Effective price ceiling policies, such as rent controls, set a maximum legal price below the equilibrium price.
- Price ceilings lead to shortages, inefficient nonprice-rationing devices, and black markets.
- Effective price floor policies, such as minimum wages, set a minimum legal price above the equilibrium price that results in surpluses.

5.3 Price Supports: Offer to Purchase and Marketing Boards

Throughout the 20th century, governments around the world have implemented a variety of policies in support of farmers. Typically, the government initiatives have been in response to two well-publicized problems that plague the farm sector.

In the short run, on a year-to-year basis, a farmer's annual income can vary significantly due to uncontrollable supply factors, such as weather conditions and the uncoordinated production plans of the farmer's vast number of competitors. From a long-term viewpoint, due to high productivity and low income elasticity of demand, the increase in the supply of farm goods has significantly exceeded the increase in the demand for these same farm products, especially in the more developed nations. Therefore, the average annual income of farmers has lagged behind average incomes earned in nonfarm occupations. In response to the problems outlined above, governments have implemented policies in order to promote equity from the farmer's perspective.

In this section, we will apply the theory of demand, supply, and elasticity to understand and evaluate common types of farm **price support policies**, which aim to help the farmers by enhancing the prices they receive for the farm products they supply.

Price support policies Policies that aim to help the farmers by enhancing the prices they receive for the farm products they supply.

Offer to Purchase Policy

Offer-to-purchase policy A price floor policy reinforced by the purchase of surplus output by the government.

One type of price support policy used to enhance farm income is the **offer-to-purchase policy** that is a price floor policy reinforced by the purchase of surplus output by the government. Figure 5–5 describes a hypothetical market for apples in a Canadian province. Note that without government intervention, an equilibrium price of $500 per tonne and

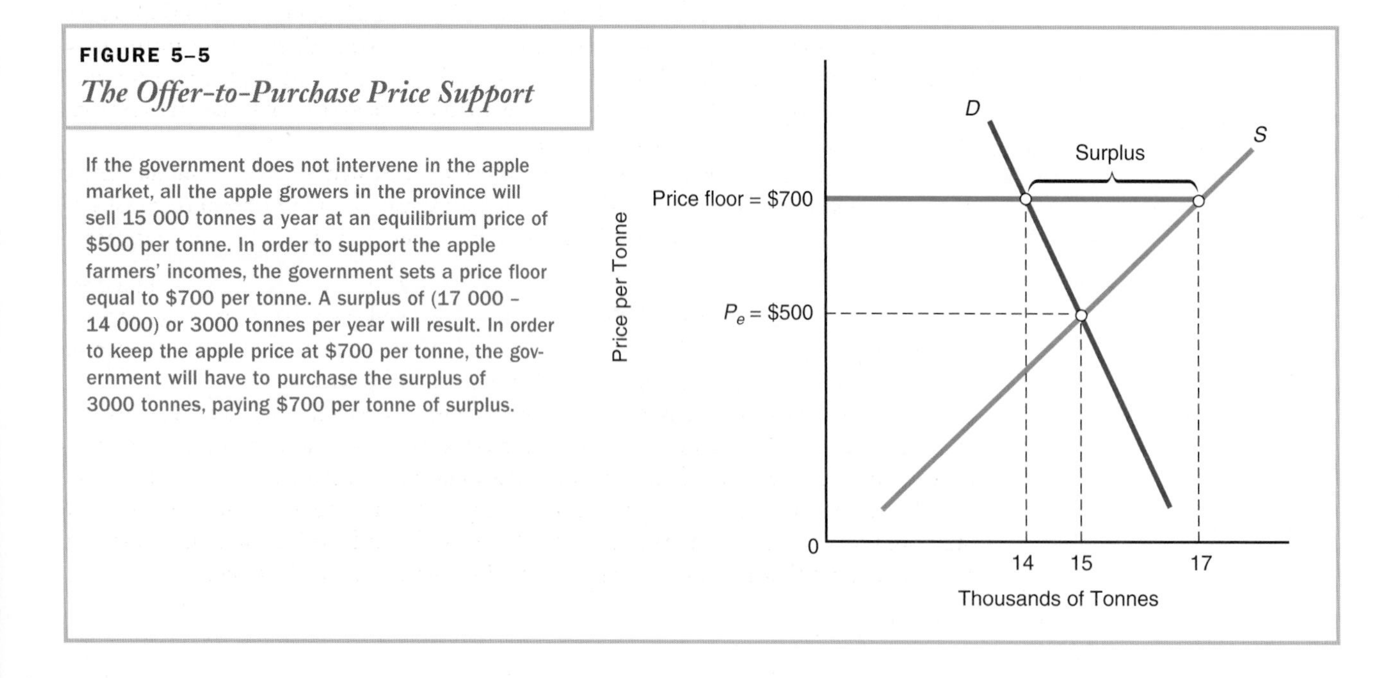

FIGURE 5–5
The Offer-to-Purchase Price Support

If the government does not intervene in the apple market, all the apple growers in the province will sell 15 000 tonnes a year at an equilibrium price of $500 per tonne. In order to support the apple farmers' incomes, the government sets a price floor equal to $700 per tonne. A surplus of (17 000 – 14 000) or 3000 tonnes per year will result. In order to keep the apple price at $700 per tonne, the government will have to purchase the surplus of 3000 tonnes, paying $700 per tonne of surplus.

an equilibrium of 15 000 tonnes (per year) would prevail. Annual total revenue for all the apple growers in the province would be ($500 × 15 000) = $7 500 000.

In order to promote the goal of a more equitable distribution of income for the apple farmers, the provincial government sets a minimum price floor of $700 per tonne. Since this price exceeds the equilibrium price, an annual surplus equal to (17 000 – 14 000) or 3000 tonnes results, as indicated in Figure 5–5. In order to maintain the price at $700 per tonne the government will also have to purchase this surplus at a total taxpayer cost of $700 × 3000 tonnes = $2 100 000. The apple growers' total revenue increases to $700 × 17 000 tonnes = $11 900 000. This means an increase in revenue of $11 900,000 – $7 500 000 = $4 400 000 for the apple growers!

While the offer-to-purchase policy, described above, does increase the total revenues of the apple growers, it accomplishes this at the expense of the consumer and the taxpayer. The consumer pays a higher price of $700 per tonne, compared with an equilibrium price of $500 per tonne. As well, taxpayers pay a total of $2 100 000 per year to purchase the surplus, which often rots in government storage bins. This policy results in allocative inefficiency due to the surplus output. Politically, the government becomes very unpopular if the voters find out that they are paying higher prices for apples that are rotting in storage. Finally, since the offer-to-purchase policy helps the farmers by securing a higher price per unit (per tonne), the largest, most affluent farms get the greatest benefit from the price supports.

Marketing Board Policy

Due to some of the problems related to the offer-to-purchase policy, provincial governments in Canada have preferred to aid the farmers by allowing them to form producer **marketing boards**—a policy that allows producers to band together to restrict total quantity supplied by using quotas. Returning to the apple growers example, if the majority of the apple growers agree to form a marketing board, the board will typically use quotas to restrict the quantity of apples sold to a level below the equilibrium quantity. This, in turn, will increase the price per tonne above the equilibrium price. If demand for apples is inelastic, the higher price will result in an increase in total revenue.

Marketing boards A policy that allows producers to band together to restrict total quantity supplied by using quotas.

Figure 5–6 describes how a marketing board can increase the apple growers' total revenue. We again note that without government intervention, the equilibrium price will be $500 per tonne and the equilibrium quantity will be 15 000 tonnes. Under a *laissez faire* policy, the apple growers' total revenue will be $500 × 15 000 tonnes = $7 500 000. The provincial government, not wanting to use taxpayer dollars to purchase surplus apples, decides to let the apple growers form a marketing board. The marketing board sets a quota on each of the apple growers, which results in a lower total quantity of 14 000 tonnes being sold to the consumer. Since the quantity sold is reduced, the price increases to $700 per tonne. With the marketing board, the total revenue for the apple growers is now $700 × 14 000 tonnes = $9 800 000. Despite a reduced quantity sold, the farmers' total revenue increases because demand is inelastic!

Over one-half of Canadian farmers' total sales are regulated by agricultural marketing boards. Chickens, turkeys, eggs, milk, butter, tobacco, grapes, and mushrooms are all sold through marketing boards that restrict the supply of these products to the marketplace.

WHO LOSES WHEN MARKETING BOARDS REGULATE SUPPLY? The consumer pays more for the regulated goods than necessary and is, therefore, the biggest loser. One estimate suggests that the average Canadian family pays $200 to $400 per year more than it would if all farm produce were sold at unregulated prices.

Prospective farmers lose, too. When quotas were first established, they were given to existing producers. New producers, however, have to purchase quotas from other farmers or from the appropriate marketing board. Some quotas have become prohibitively expensive. To buy a minimum-size quota for a chicken farm today would require $1 million; a minimum-size quota for a dairy farm in the Fraser Valley of British Columbia would take $3 million. And that is not counting the cost of the land and the livestock.

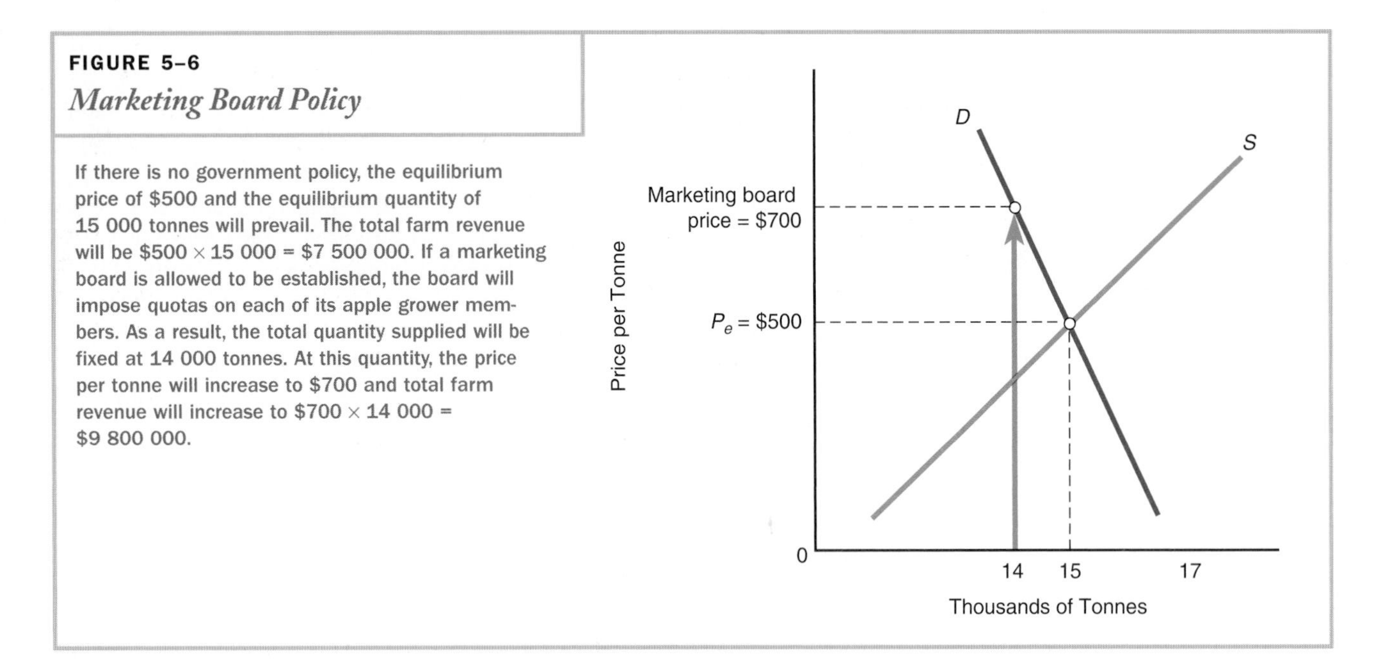

FIGURE 5–6
Marketing Board Policy

If there is no government policy, the equilibrium price of $500 and the equilibrium quantity of 15 000 tonnes will prevail. The total farm revenue will be $500 × 15 000 = $7 500 000. If a marketing board is allowed to be established, the board will impose quotas on each of its apple grower members. As a result, the total quantity supplied will be fixed at 14 000 tonnes. At this quantity, the price per tonne will increase to $700 and total farm revenue will increase to $700 × 14 000 = $9 800 000.

Another loser is the foreign farmer who would like to export farm products to Canada. The government restricts entry of foreign produce because the additional supply would reduce prices. Canada used to keep out foreign produce with import quotas, but the GATT (General Agreement on Tariffs and Trade) in its latest round of talks banned import quotas on agricultural goods. Thus, the federal government now uses import duties (i.e., taxes on imported produce) to restrict supply of foreign goods. The tariff on butter from the United States, for example, is 351 percent.

WHO WINS WHEN MARKETING BOARDS REGULATE SUPPLY? Existing farmers are clearly the major winners. The boards do stabilize their incomes, and so they can plan from one year to the next. To the extent that marketing boards restrict the supply of inelastic demand products, the total revenue of the existing farmers will increase. Supporters of marketing boards also point out that by guaranteeing a living for Canadian farmers, we are providing ourselves with a made-at-home food supply—something much more valuable than the costs associated with supply management. In addition, we are helping preserve a way of life that is disappearing elsewhere—the family farm.

Some farmers object to being regulated by marketing boards. They believe that they, as entrepreneurs, will be better salespeople for their products than a government bureaucracy. This is happening most clearly in the wheat industry, where a special form of marketing board exists. Policy Example 5–2 explains this policy.

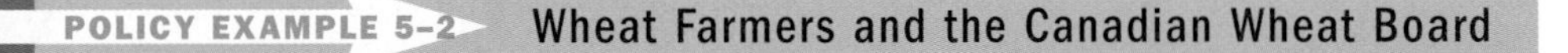

POLICY EXAMPLE 5–2 Wheat Farmers and the Canadian Wheat Board

The Canadian government has been involved in guaranteeing prices for wheat farmers since World War I. In 1917, to regulate the supply of wheat to troops in Europe and to Canadians at home, and to guarantee grain farmers a reasonable living, the government set up the Board of Grain Supervisors. After the war, the Board's name was changed to the Canadian Wheat Board. It still operates today.

The Canadian Wheat Board buys all the wheat a farmer produces and sells it on world markets. Farmers cannot sell their wheat independently. The Board advances 75 percent of the expected price to farmers in the spring, and then settles up with them after the wheat

continued

is sold in the fall. Farmers never receive less than the expected price, so if the world price is lower than predicted, the Wheat Board suffers a loss. But if the price is higher, farmers are paid more. This has the effect of reducing fluctuations in farm income by putting a floor under the price farmers receive.

Recently, some grain growers have been objecting to being forced to sell to the Wheat Board. They claim that by selling directly to the United States, they would earn \$2 to \$3 per bushel more, a significant price difference. But other farmers want the Wheat Board to remain. They fear that, as individual farmers, they would not have the leverage to stand up against major wheat buyers and demand a high price. In the end they fear their incomes would fall.

For critical analysis: What do you think would happen to the price of Canadian wheat if half the farmers sold independently, while half sold through the Canadian Wheat Board?

5.4 Quantity Restrictions

Governments can impose quantity restrictions on a market. The most obvious restriction is an outright ban on the ownership or trading of a good. It is presently illegal to buy and sell human organs. It is also currently illegal to buy and sell certain psychoactive drugs such as cocaine, heroin, and marijuana. It is illegal to open a new chartered bank without obtaining a government charter. This requirement effectively restricts the number of chartered banks in Canada. Policy Example 5–3 explains how an outright ban can create illegal markets that continue to supply the product—but at a much higher price.

POLICY EXAMPLE 5–3

Should the Legal Quantity of Cigarettes Supplied Be Set at Zero?

Nicotine has been used as a psychoactive drug by the Native Peoples of the Americas for approximately 8000 years. Five hundred years ago, Christopher Columbus introduced tobacco to the Europeans, who discovered that once they overcame the nausea and dizziness produced by chewing, snorting, or smoking the tobacco, they simply could not get along without it. Nicotine quickly joined alcohol and caffeine as one of the world's principal psychoactive drugs of choice.

In the century after Columbus returned from the Americas with tobacco, the use of and addiction to nicotine spread quickly around the world. There followed numerous efforts to quash what had become known as the "evil weed." In 1603, the Japanese prohibited the use of tobacco and repeatedly increased the penalties for violating the ban, which was not lifted until 1625. By the middle of the 17th century, similar bans on tobacco were in place in Bavaria, Saxony, Zurich, Turkey, and Russia, with punishments ranging from confiscation of property to the death penalty.

What if tobacco were ever completely prohibited today? Because tobacco is legal, the supply of illegal tobacco is zero. If the use of tobacco were restricted, the supply of illegal tobacco would not remain zero for long. Even if Canadian tobacco growers were forced out of business, the production of tobacco in other countries would increase to meet the demand. Consequently, the supply curve of illegal tobacco products would shift outward to the right as more foreign sources determined they wanted to enter the illegal Canadian tobacco market. The demand curve for illegal tobacco products would emerge almost immediately after the quantity restriction. The price people would pay to satisfy their nicotine addiction would go up.

For critical analysis: What other goods or services follow the same analysis as the one presented here?

Import quota A supply restriction that prohibits the importation of more than a specified quantity of a particular good in a one-year period.

Some of the most common quantity restrictions exist in the area of international trade. The Canadian government and many foreign governments impose import quotas on a variety of goods. An **import quota** is a supply restriction that prohibits the importation of more than a specified quantity of a particular good in a one-year period. Canada has had import quotas on cotton textiles, shoes, and immigrant labour. For many years, there were import quotas on dairy products coming into Canada from the United States. These import quotas were recently removed and replaced by tariffs, but the effect is still to limit the amount of dairy products that we import. There are also "voluntary" import quotas on certain goods. Japanese car makers, for example, have agreed since 1981 "voluntarily" to restrict the number of cars they send to Canada.

In many cases, import quotas are designed to increase the total amount spent by Canadians on domestically produced goods. However, if the Canadian demand for the foreign good being restricted is price inelastic, Canadian consumers may end up spending more dollars on the foreign product, resulting in a decrease in demand for the made-in-Canada good.

CONCEPTS IN BRIEF

Learning Objective 5.3: Compare and contrast the offer-to-purchase and the marketing board price support policies.

- High productivity, low income elasticity, and uncontrollable changes in supply have brought about low and unstable farm incomes. Offer-to-purchase and marketing board policies provide support to farm incomes by establishing farm product prices at levels that exceed equilibrium prices.
- The offer-to-purchase policy is a floor price policy in which the resulting surpluses are purchased by the government. The policy provides the greatest support to the largest farm operators at the expense of consumers and taxpayers.
- Marketing boards typically restrict the quantity supplied of farm products in order to support farm prices. When demand is inelastic, this strategy will increase total farm revenues. While this policy benefits the largest existing farmers the most, it is at the expense of consumers and prospective farmers.

Learning Objective 5.4: Describe the various types of quantity restrictions that governments can impose on markets.

- Quantity restrictions can take the form of outright government bans on the sale of certain goods, such as human organs or illicit drugs. They can also arise from licensing requirements or quotas, such as import quotas. Consumers may end up spending more dollars on the restricted goods if demand is price inelastic.

5.5 Elasticity and Excise Taxes

Excise tax A tax imposed on a particular commodity or service.

Canadian governments at both the federal and provincial levels can levy various taxes in order to affect market outcomes. One example is the **excise tax**, which is a tax imposed on a particular commodity or service, such as cigarettes, alcohol, gasoline, CDs, MP3 players, or hotel services. In the following section, we will apply the theory of demand, supply, and elasticity to predict the effects of a per-unit tax imposed on the firms manufacturing and supplying cigarettes in a Canadian province.

The Effects of a Per-Unit Tax on Market Supply

Suppose the federal government imposes an excise tax of $15 per carton of cigarettes on the firms manufacturing and supplying cigarettes in Ontario. To simplify the situation, we will assume that the manufacturers sell directly to cigarette consumers. In Figure 5–7, the pretax market supply and demand is S_1 and D_1.

Since the per-unit tax imposes an extra cost on the cigarette manufacturers at each price, this will cause a decrease in the supply of cigarettes.

FIGURE 5–7

The Effect of a Per-Unit Tax on Market Supply

The before-tax supply curve, S_1, shows the dollar amount per carton that cigarette manufacturers must receive, in their pockets, in order to be willing to supply each quantity. As an example, to be induced to supply 6 million cartons of cigarettes, the manufacturers must receive $55 per carton, in their pockets. After the tax, the supply curve shifts up vertically by the amount of the tax, or by $15 to S_2. After the tax, in order for the manufacturers to be willing to supply 6 million cartons of cigarettes, the price charged to the consumer must now be $70, based on S_2. At a $70 price, after paying the $15 tax to the government, the sellers will receive $55 per carton, which is the amount necessary to induce the 6 million carton supply.

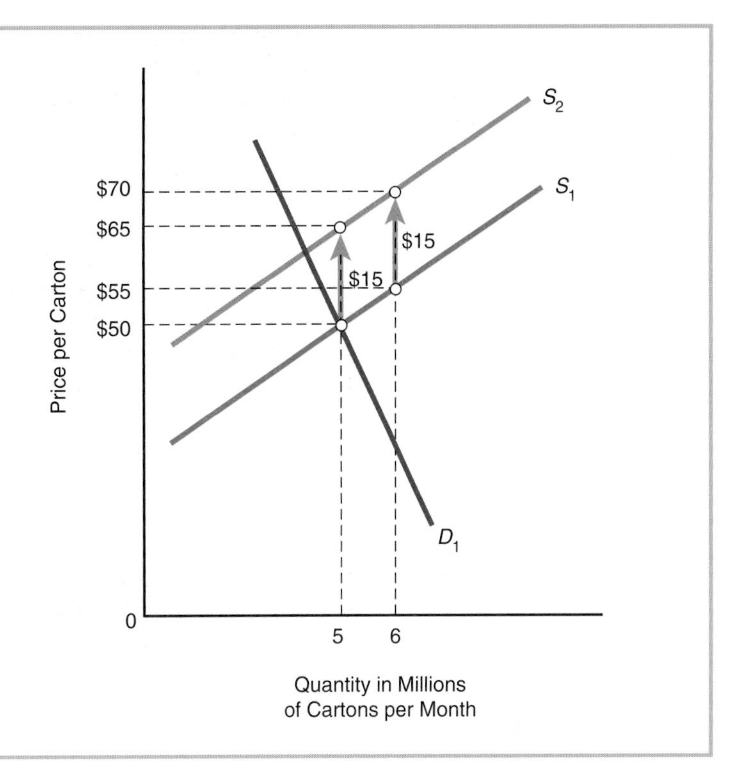

Graphically, the market supply curve will shift up vertically, at each quantity, by the amount of the per unit tax.

In Figure 5–7, this means that the supply curve will shift upward by a vertical amount of $15 (the per-unit tax) to form S_2, the new after-tax supply curve. This shift can be explained as follows.

According to S_1, the pretax supply curve, the manufacturers will be willing to supply 5 million cartons per month, if they receive $50 per carton, in their pockets. In order to coax the manufacturers to supply 6 million cartons of cigarettes per month, they will have to receive $55 per carton, in their pockets.

After a new tax of $15 per carton is imposed on the manufacturers, they will be willing to supply 5 million cartons per month, only if the price charged to the consumers is now $65 per carton, which is based on the new supply curve, S_2. If the manufacturers charge the consumers $65, they will receive, in their pockets, the $50 they require, after remitting to the government $15 for each carton sold.

Similarly, after the tax, the manufacturers will be willing to supply 6 million cartons per month, only if the price charged to the consumers is now $70 (on S_2). By charging $70 per carton, the manufacturers will be able to receive the necessary $55, in their pockets, after paying to the government a tax of $15 per carton. On the basis of this example, we can conclude that for each possible quantity, the after-tax supply curve will shift upward by $15, the amount of the per-unit tax.

Tax Incidence

Tax incidence The division of the burden of a tax between the buyer and the seller.

When the government imposes a per-unit excise tax, who bears the brunt of the tax—the buyer or the seller? This is a question relating to **tax incidence**, which is the division of the burden of a tax between the buyer and the seller. In our cigarette example above, the government imposes the tax on the manufacturers (sellers). However, the sellers can shift at least part of the tax to the buyers (consumers), to the extent that they can increase the equilibrium price charged for a carton of cigarettes.

In general, the buyer's portion of the tax burden equals the increase in equilibrium price that results from the tax. The seller's portion of the tax burden equals the per-unit tax minus the buyer's tax burden.

In Figure 5–8, the per-unit tax imposed on the cigarette manufacturers shifts the supply curve vertically upward by $15 (the tax per unit). This decrease in supply causes the equilibrium price to increase from $50 per carton to $62 per carton. The tax incidence can now be established as follows: The buyer's portion of the tax burden equals the increase in equilibrium price, which is $62 – $50 = $12 per carton. The seller's tax burden is the difference between the per-unit tax and the buyer's tax burden, which is $15 – $12 = $3 per carton.

The seller's tax burden of $3 per carton can be further explained by referring to Figure 5–8. Before the tax, the sellers received the equilibrium price of $50 in their pockets. After the tax, the sellers receive the new equilibrium price minus the per-unit tax that they have to remit to the government, which is $62 – $15 = $47. The sellers end up receiving $50 – $47 = $3 less, per carton, in their pockets, after the tax.

Elasticity and Tax Incidence

Elasticity of demand and supply affects the degree to which the burden of an excise tax is shared between the buyers and the sellers of the product being taxed. If demand is relatively elastic, buyers can easily escape the burden of a tax imposed on product A, by switching their consumption to close substitutes for product A. In this situation, sellers will be careful not to increase the equilibrium price too much for fear of scaring away the consumers of their product. Therefore, when demand is elastic, sellers will bear a greater portion of the tax burden.

On the other hand, if demand for product A is relatively inelastic, sellers can shift a larger portion of the tax burden to consumers by significantly increasing the price, as the consumers have few alternative goods to switch to. In Figure 5–8, the demand for cigarettes is relatively inelastic, which explains why the consumer's tax burden of $12 significantly exceeds the seller's tax burden of $3 per carton.

Elasticity of supply can also affect tax incidence. If supply is relatively elastic, sellers can easily escape the burden of a tax imposed on product A, by switching their production and supply to alternative products that are not taxed. As many sellers leave the market for product A, the price of A will increase significantly, shifting a large portion of the tax burden to consumers of product A. Therefore, when supply is elastic, buyers will bear a greater portion of the tax burden.

FIGURE 5–8

The Tax Incidence Related to a $15 Per-Carton Excise Tax

The before-tax equilibrium price equals $50 per carton, based on the intersection of D_1 and S_1. The $15 per-unit tax shifts the supply curve by $15 to S_2. The new after-tax equilibrium price is now $62 per carton, based on the intersection of D_1 and S_2. The buyer's portion of the tax burden equals the increase in equilibrium price, which is $62 - $50 = $12 per carton. The seller's portion of the tax burden is the per-unit tax minus the buyer's tax burden, which is $15 - $12 = $3 per carton. In other words, the seller receives $50 - $47 = $3 less for each carton sold, after the tax.

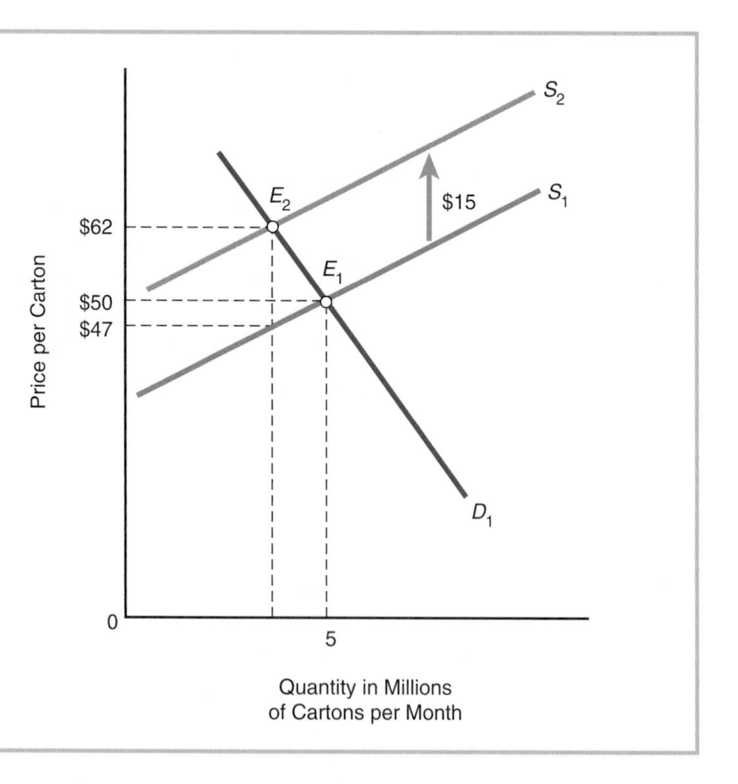

If the supply for product A is relatively inelastic, this means that the sellers cannot easily switch to producing and supplying other nontaxed products. In this situation, sellers will continue to supply a significant amount of product A, even if faced with a large tax burden. In Figure 5–9, the supply of cigarettes is relatively inelastic. Under these market conditions, the same $15 per-carton tax causes the equilibrium price to go up to $54 per carton. The buyer's tax burden equals the increase in equilibrium price, which is $54 – $50 = $4 per carton. The seller's burden is the per-unit tax minus the buyer's burden, which is $15 – $4 = $11 per carton. You can see that when supply is relatively inelastic, the seller bears the greater portion of the tax burden.

In general, the tax burden falls more heavily on the side of the market that is relatively more inelastic.

Elasticity and Resource Allocation

In many situations, an excise tax is imposed in order to discourage the production and consumption of a particular product that the government feels is detrimental to society. As an example, both the federal and provincial governments have imposed heavy excise taxes on cigarettes, which helps explain the significant decline in Canadian tobacco use noted in this chapter's Did You Know That. Under what elasticity conditions will the government be relatively successful in discouraging cigarette production and consumption?

When demand and/or supply is relatively elastic, a per-unit excise tax will significantly reduce the equilibrium quantity of cigarettes, thereby effectively reducing the amount of resources being used to produce this undesirable product.

Elasticity and Government Tax Revenue

Excise taxes provide tax revenues to both the federal and provincial governments in Canada. Elasticity affects the total amount of tax revenues that can be raised through these types of taxes.

FIGURE 5–9

The Tax Incidence When Supply is Inelastic

The before-tax equilibrium price equals $50 per carton, based on the intersection of D_1 and S_1. The $15 per-unit tax shifts the supply curve up by $15 to S_2. The new after-tax equilibrium price is now $54 per carton, based on the intersection of D_1 and S_2. The buyer's portion of the tax burden equals the increase in equilibrium price, which is $54 - $50 = $4 per carton. The seller's portion of the tax burden is the per-unit tax minus the buyer's tax burden, which is $15 - $4 = $11 per carton. In other words, the seller receives $50 - $39 = $11 less for each carton sold, after the tax.

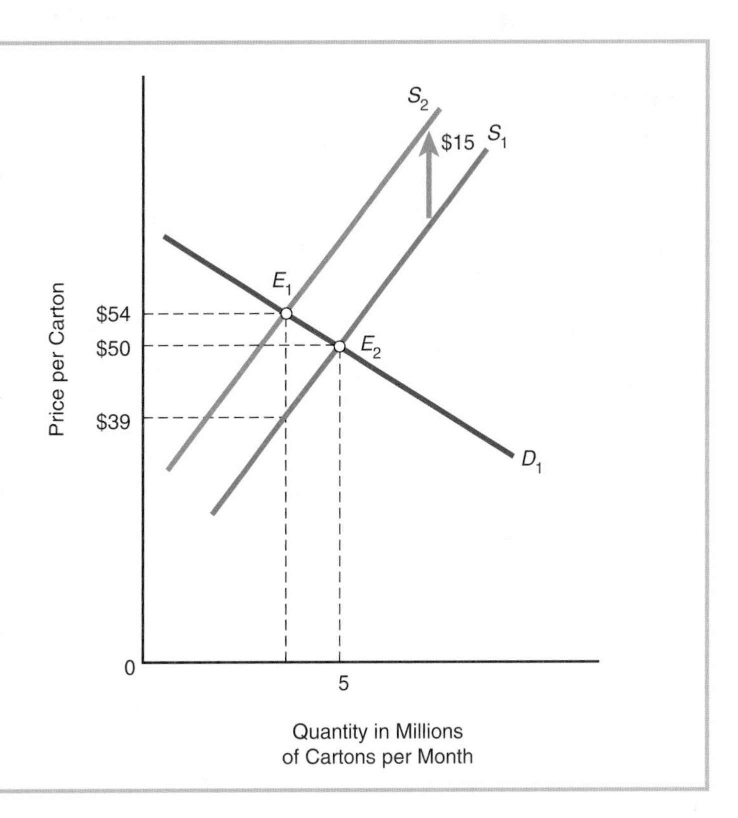

A per-unit excise tax will generate greater total tax revenues when the demand and/or supply of the taxed product is relatively inelastic.

In these situations, the equilibrium quantity of the taxed product will not significantly decrease, in response to a per-unit tax. If the after-tax equilibrium quantity remains relatively large, the total tax revenue generated will also be relatively large.

Policy Example 5–4 describes the private copying levies that the Canadian government uses to discourage the widespread downloading of music from the Internet and through the burning of CDs. The proceeds from these levies are used to compensate the Canadian music industry for the piracy of copyrighted music. By viewing each levy as a per-unit excise tax, you can use the theory of elasticity to evaluate this government policy.

POLICY EXAMPLE 5–4 An Excise Tax on Music Piracy?

On December 12, 2003, The Copyright Board of Canada introduced a new levy on nonremovable memory permanently embedded in digital audio recorders (such as MP3 players) at $2 for each recorder with a memory capacity of up to 1 Gigabyte (GB), $15 for each recorder with memory capacity of more than 1 GB and up to 10 GB, and $25 for each recorder with memory capacity of more than 10 Gbs. The Board also made the decision to maintain all existing private copying levies at their current levels. As a result, the current levies of 29¢ on audio cassette tapes of 40 minutes or longer, 21¢ on CD-Rs and CD-RWs, and 77¢ on CD-R Audio, CD-RW Audio, and MiniDiscs will remain in effect until the end of 2004. These levies represent the Canadian government's response to the flurry of free copying of copyrighted music through Internet downloads and CD burning.

Annual music sales from pre-recorded CDs in Canada have slipped by $450 million, or about 23 percent, since 1999. Music industry analysts attribute much of this decline to the widespread copying of music. The proceeds from the levies on private copying are to be distributed to music performers, songwriters, and music producers, as partial compensation for the loss of sales due to piracy.

For critical analysis: Explain how the price elasticity of demand and supply for blank media and for digital audio recorders will affect the total amount collected from the levies on private copying. How will elasticity affect the degree to which these levies discourage the copying of copyrighted music? Under what circumstances would consumers be unfairly "taxed" by these private-copying levies?

SOURCE: "TARIFF OF LEVIES TO BE COLLECTED BY CPCC IN 2003 AND 2004 ON THE SALE IN CANADA OF BLANK AUDIO RECORDING MEDIA." SUPPLEMENT TO THE *CANADA GAZETTE*, DECEMBER 13, 2003. COPYRIGHT BOARD OF CANADA, P. 5. http://www.cb-cda.gc.ca/tariffs/certified/c13122003-b.pdf.

CONCEPTS IN BRIEF

Learning Objective 5.5: Explain how price elasticity governs the effects that a per-unit excise tax has on tax incidence, resource allocation, and government tax revenue collected.

- A per-unit excise tax typically increases the equilibrium price and decreases the equilibrium quantity of the taxed good or service.
- The tax incidence resulting from a per-unit excise tax can be determined as follows: The buyer's portion of the tax burden equals the equilibrium price increase. The seller's portion of the tax burden equals the per-unit tax minus the buyer's portion of the tax burden.
- The excise tax burden falls more heavily on the side of the market that is relatively more inelastic.
- The resource allocation effects of an excise tax, in terms of a reduction in quantity produced, will be greatest when demand and/or supply is relatively price elastic.
- A per-unit excise tax will generate greater total tax revenues when the demand and/or supply of the taxed product is relatively price inelastic.

ISSUES AND APPLICATIONS

For-Profit Health Care in Canada?

Concepts Applied: Market versus Command Systems, Rationing Function of Prices, Price Ceilings, Allocative Efficiency, Productive Efficiency, and Equity

Is for-profit health care the way to reduce scenes like this?

In 2003, Canadians waited an average of 17.8 weeks from the time they received a referral from their general practitioner to the time they received treatment from a medical specialist. This represents an increase of over 90 percent when compared with 1993, when the typical waiting time was 9.3 weeks. In a recent study, 20 developed nations averaged 2.5 doctors per 1000 people. Canada ranked 17th out of these 20 countries, with 2.1 doctors per 1000 people. There continues to be an apparent shortage of medical services in Canada, even though the provincial governments have recently been spending an increasing portion of their budgets on health care.

These disturbing trends and statistics have renewed a debate over which type of system best suits the provision of health-care services—a market system or a command system. To appreciate the differing views we will begin by examining Canada's existing system of providing health-care services.

Canadian Medicare

Canada has a predominantly publicly financed, privately delivered health-care system that consists of 10 provincial (and three territorial) government health insurance plans. This mixed system of providing health-care services is frequently referred to as medicare.

The federal government's role in health care involves using financial incentives to ensure that each province provides equal access to universal, comprehensive coverage for medically necessary hospital, in-patient, and outpatient physician services.

Typically, each province makes each of its working residents pay into the medicare insurance fund, through compulsory taxation (or compulsory monthly premiums). When a Canadian consumer (patient) visits a physician (or hospital), monies from the medicare fund pay for the visit. This means that the patient does not incur any additional out-of-pocket expense each time he or she makes another visit to a physician or hospital.

In the Canadian medicare system, physicians typically operate their own private practices and are compensated from the medicare insurance fund on a fee-for-service basis. Since the majority of acute-care Canadian hospitals are operated by the public sector on a nonprofit basis, the only pressure to contain hospital costs is the annual hospital budget determined by government authorities.

A Market-Oriented Health-Care Model?

Those who support market solutions for our health-care system criticize Canadian medicare for its price ceiling policy for medical services. Under this policy, the federal government commands that a maximum price of zero be charged for both doctor and hospital visits. Figure 5–10 illustrates this view. There is no additional out-of-pocket charge each time a patient visits a doctor or a hospital. In other words, the Canadian government has imposed a maximum price ceiling of zero for doctor and hospital visits.

According to the market supporters, medicare's zero price ceiling policy has caused shortages, resulting in Canadian patients waiting long periods before receiving treatment or surgery. A zero price encourages many individuals to frequently visit doctors and hospitals, and take diagnostic tests for the most trivial reasons, resulting in an excess demand for medical services. As a result, patients experiencing really serious health problems are forced to wait a long time before receiving the badly needed treatment.

FIGURE 5–10
Zero Price Ceiling under Medicare

Since there is no additional charge per visit, there is a zero price ceiling policy under medicare. This results in a shortage, where the quantity of visits demanded exceeds the quantity of visits supplied. The shortage is reflected in significant waiting times before Canadian patients receive health-care services.

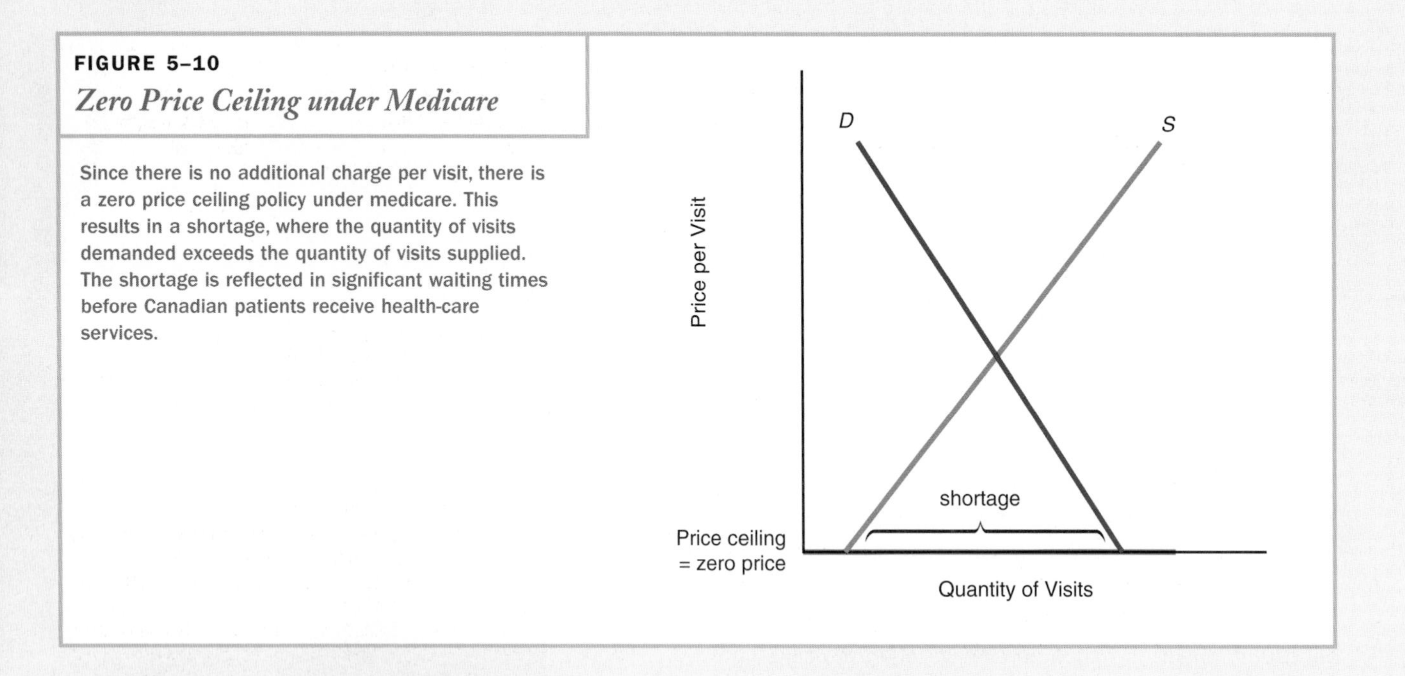

A second problem with Canadian medicare, according to market advocates, is that it essentially results in government-owned monopolies providing health insurance and hospital services in each province. The lack of competition and the absence of the profit incentive helps contribute to medical shortages, productive inefficiency, and escalating health-care costs.

The market system supporters propose that Canada adopt a number of market incentives currently present in the American health-care system. In the United States, health-care services are predominantly provided in the for-profit private sector. As Table 5–1 indicates, public expenditures constitute a much smaller portion of total health expenditures in the United States compared with Canada.

In order to finance their health-care costs, many American consumers voluntarily pay monthly premiums to private health insurance companies. In addition, consumers may have to pay a co-payment or user fee each time they visit a physician or hospital. Some private insurance plans may involve an experience rating, which is a situation where those who make more frequent visits to physicians may end up paying higher insurance premiums. According to market supporters, the user fees and experience ratings help eliminate waiting periods and ensure that those patients who value the medical services the most will be the ones visiting the health-care providers. The user fee will discourage frivolous use of scarce medical resources.

In the United States, large, private, for-profit health maintenance organizations (HMOs) operate hospitals, run diagnostic services, and hire physicians and nurses. In theory, one would expect to see a given quality of health care provided with minimal resource use in the United States, as it is in the interests of HMOs to contain the costs of providing health care, in order to enhance profits and stave off competition.

Evaluation of the Market-Based Solutions

Those who defend Canadian medicare argue that one cannot use the market model to analyze health care, which many consumers view as an extreme-necessity (highly inelastic) good. Consumers of health care (patients) lack the knowledge necessary to evaluate whether a contemplated visit to the doctor is trivial or not. Moreover, after the first visit to the general practitioner, it is typically the doctor who makes the decision, on behalf of the patient, to consume additional health-care resources. In this situation, it is meaningless to suggest that user fees paid by the patients will ensure a more efficient use of medical resources. Indeed, user fees and experience ratings will unfairly penalize the poor and the chronically ill.

TABLE 5–1
Annual National Health-Care Expenditures: Canada and the United States, 2001

Country	Total Health Expenditure as a Percent of GDP	Public Expenditures as a Percent of Total Health Expenditures
Canada	9.7%	70.8%
United States	13.9%	44.4%

SOURCES: "TABLE 10: TOTAL EXPENDITURE ON HEALTH, % GDP," "TABLE 11: PUBLIC EXPENDITURE ON HEALTH, % TOTAL EXPENDITURE ON HEALTH." OECD HEALTH DATA, 2003. OCTOBER 2003. http://www.oecd.org/document/16/0,2340,en_2825_495642_2085200_1_1_1_1,00.html). (ACCESSED DEC. 29, 2003.)

TABLE 5-2

Health Achievement Levels: Canada and the United States, 2002 and 2003

Country	Life Expectancy at Birth 2002 (Years)	Health Life Expectancy: Life Expectancy at Birth Adjusted for Time Spent in Poor Health 2002 (Years)	Infant Mortality Rate 2003
Canada	79.8	72	5.36 deaths per live 1000 births
United States	77.3	69.3	6.75 deaths per live 1000 births

SOURCES: "ANNEX TABLE 1: BASIC INDICATORS FOR ALL 191 MEMBER STATES IN 2002" AND "ANNEX TABLE 4: HEALTHY LIFE EXPECTANCY FOR ALL 191 MEMBERS STATES IN 2002." WORLD HEALTH REPORT 2003. WORLD HEALTH ORGANIZATION. http://www.who.int/whr/en/ (ACCESSED DEC. 28, 2003); "COUNTRY LISTING, THE WORLD FACTBOOK." 18 DECEMBER, 2003. CIA. http://www.odci.gov/cia/publications/factbook/geos/ca.html (ACCESSED 28 DEC. 2003.)

The view that private for-profit corporations will be more efficient than the government in providing health-care services can be challenged by comparing recent Canadian and American statistics. The data presented in Table 5–1 and Table 5–2 indicate that although Canada spends a smaller percentage of GDP (national income) on health care than the United States, Canada manages to achieve a higher level of health achievement in terms of life expectancy, life expectancy adjusted for time spent in poor health, and infant mortality rates. It seems that a much larger portion of every dollar spent on health care in the United States is spent on activities not directly related to patient health care, such as administration, marketing, and earning corporate profits.

In November 2002, the Romanow Report presented the findings and recommendations of the Commission on the Future of Health Care in Canada. The Commission rejected the notion of using additional market incentives to improve Canada's health-care system. The Commission attributes the recent shortcomings of various health-care services in Canada to a number of factors not related to medicare—a long-term decline in federal government cash transfers to the provinces for health-care spending; provincial budget cutbacks made during the early 1990s; the aging population; and the high income elasticity of demand for health care in Canada. The Commission recommended that Canada's health-care system be improved through an expanded public health sector financed by substantial increases in federal government cash transfers to the provinces.

SOURCES: NADEEM ESMAIL AND MICHAEL WALKER. "HOW GOOD IS CANADIAN HEALTH CARE?" AUGUST 2002. FRASER INSTITUTE. http://www.fraserinstitute.ca/shared/readmore.asp?sNav=pb&id=394 (ACCESSED DECEMBER 27, 2003.); NADEEM ESMAIL AND MICHAEL WALKER. "*WAITING YOUR TURN: HOSPITAL WAITING LISTS IN CANADA*." 13TH EDITION. OCTOBER 2003. FRASER INSTITUTE. http://www.fraserinstitute.ca/shared/readmore.asp?sNav=pb&id=587 (ACCESSED DECEMBER 27, 2003.); ROY ROMANOW, COMMISSIONER. "BUILDING ON VALUES: THE FUTURE OF HEALTH CARE IN CANADA." NOVEMBER 2002. PP. 100–106. http://www.hc-sc.gc.ca/english/pdf/care/romanow_e.pdf) (ACCESSED DECEMBER 28, 2003.)

For critical analysis:

1. According to those who promote market solutions in health care, what aspects of Canadian medicare encourage allocative inefficiency? Explain briefly.
2. According to those who promote market solutions in health care, what features of the American health-care system promote (a) allocative efficiency, and (b) productive efficiency?
3. According to the medicare supporters, why will user fees fail to promote allocative efficiency?
4. Explain how user fees for health-care services can conflict with equity.
5. Explain why it appears that the Canadian health-care system is more productively efficient than the American system.

SUMMARY DISCUSSION OF LEARNING OBJECTIVES

5.1 **The Price System.** In the price system, markets and intermediaries reduce the costs of obtaining mutually beneficial exchanges between buyers and sellers. Equilibrium prices ensure that resources and goods are allocated to the highest-valued uses and all the gains from mutually beneficial trades are exhausted.

5.2 **Price Ceilings and Price Floors.** Price ceilings, such as rent controls, set a maximum legal price below the equilibrium price. Ceilings lead to shortages, inefficient nonprice-rationing devices, and black markets. Price floors, such as minimum wages, set a minimum legal price above the equilibrium price that results in surpluses.

5.3 **Price Supports: Offer to Purchase and Marketing Boards.** Offer-to-purchase and marketing board policies provide support to low and unstable farm incomes by establishing farm product prices at levels that exceed equilibrium prices. The offer-to-purchase policy is a floor price policy in which the resulting surpluses are purchased by the government. The policy provides the greatest support to the largest farm operators at the expense of consumers and taxpayers. Marketing boards typically restrict the quantity supplied of farm products in order to support farm prices. When demand is inelastic, this strategy will increase total farm revenues at the expense of consumers and prospective farmers.

5.4 **Quantity Restrictions.** Examples of quantity restrictions include direct government bans, licensing restrictions, and quotas. Consumers may end up spending more dollars on the restricted goods if demand is price inelastic.

5.5 **Elasticity and Excise Taxes.** A per-unit excise tax typically increases the equilibrium price and decreases the equilibrium quantity of the taxed good or service. In terms of tax incidence, the buyer's portion of the tax burden equals the equilibrium price increase, while the seller's portion equals the per-unit tax minus the buyer's portion of the tax burden. The excise tax burden falls more heavily on the side of the market that is relatively more inelastic. The resource allocation effects of an excise tax, in terms of a reduction in quantity produced, will be greatest when demand and/or supply is relatively price elastic. The government will collect a larger amount of tax revenue when the demand and/or supply of the taxed product is relatively price inelastic.

PROBLEMS

(Answers to the odd-numbered problems appear at the back of the book.)

LO 5.1 Explain the role of markets, intermediaries, and prices in the price system.

1. Based on Example 5–2, "Should Shortages in the Ticket Market Be Solved by Scalpers?", explain the economic role that ticket scalpers play in the market for a sold-out event.
2. Under Canadian medicare, how are the diagnostic, medical, and surgical services of specialist physicians being rationed?

LO 5.2 Compare and contrast price ceiling and price floor policies.

3. Below is the market demand-and-supply schedule for lettuce in a Canadian city.

Price per crate	Quantity Demanded (crates per year)	Quantity Supplied (crates per year)
$1	10 million	0 million
2	9	1
3	8	4
4	7	7
5	6	8
6	4	9

a. Assuming no government intervention, what price and quantity would result in the lettuce market?

b. Suppose that the price of lettuce in part (a) was considered excessive. Consequently, the government legislates a maximum price of $3 per crate. At this maximum price, a (shortage or surplus) of __?__ million crates would develop. This policy is an example of a (price ceiling or price floor) policy.

c. Assuming the policy in part (b) above, what would be the maximum black market price?

d. Suppose that the price of lettuce in part (a) above was considered to be too low for lettuce farmers to make a decent living. Consequently, the government legislates a minimum price of $5 per crate. At this minimum price, a (shortage or surplus) of __?__ million crates would develop. This policy is an example of a (price ceiling or price floor) policy.

4. According to Policy Example 5–1, "Rent Controls in Manitoba," rent controls increase the taxes paid by homeowners. Explain.

5. This is a graph of the monthly demand for and supply of milk in a Canadian province.

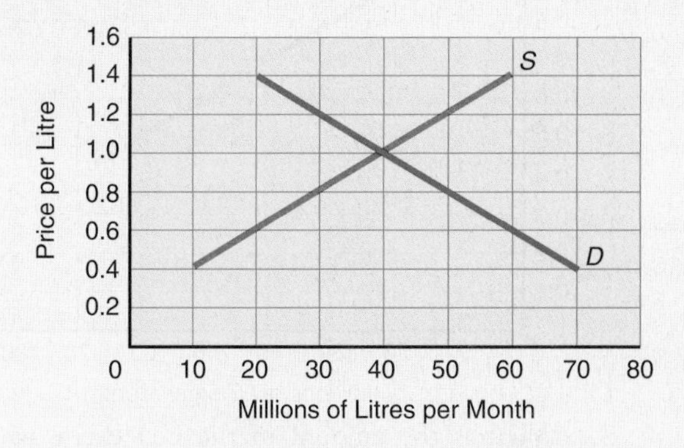

a. If the government does not intervene in the milk market, what price and quantity would result?
b. If the government imposes a maximum price policy of $0.80 per litre, this would result in a (shortage or surplus) of __?__ millions of litres of milk per month. This would be called a (price floor or price ceiling) policy.
c. For the policy described in part (b) above, what would be the black market price?
d. If the government imposes a minimum price policy of $1.40 per litre, this would result in a (shortage or surplus) of __?__ millions of litres of milk per month. This would be called a (price floor or price ceiling) policy.

6. "It is questionable whether a policy of rent controls promotes equity, despite leading to an inefficient allocation of resources." Fully explain the previous statement.

LO 5.3 Compare and contrast the offer-to-purchase and the marketing board price support policies.

7. For this problem, refer to the demand and supply schedules for lettuce provided in Problem 3 above.
a. Assuming that the market sets the price and quantity for lettuce, compute the total revenue received by the lettuce farmers.
b. If the government were to implement an offer-to-purchase policy to support the price of lettuce at $5 per crate, there would be a (shortage or surplus) equal to __?__ million crates per year. Compute the total revenue received by the lettuce farmers under this policy. What would be the total taxpayer cost associated with this policy?
c. Suppose that the government decided to support the price of lettuce by allowing a marketing board to develop and restrict the quantity of lettuce supplied to 6 million crates per year. What price per crate would develop? Compute the total revenue received by the lettuce farmers under this policy. Is the price elasticity of demand elastic or inelastic in the $4 to $5 price range? Explain.

8. Identify and explain both the short-run and long-run problems facing Canadian farmers.

9. For this problem, refer to the demand and supply curves for milk provided in Problem 5.
a. Assuming that the market sets the price and quantity for milk, compute the total revenue received by the milk farmers.
b. If the government were to implement an offer-to-purchase policy to support the price of milk at $1.20 per litre, there would be a (shortage or surplus) equal to __?__ million litres per month. Compute the total revenue received by the milk farmers under this policy. What would be the total taxpayer cost associated with this policy?
c. Suppose that the government decided to support the price of milk by allowing a marketing board to develop and restrict the quantity of milk supplied to 30 million litres per month. What price per litre would develop? What would be the total revenue received by the milk farmers under this marketing board policy? Is the price elasticity of demand elastic or inelastic in the $1 to $1.20 per litre price range? Explain.

LO 5.4 Describe the various types of quantity restrictions that governments can impose on markets.

10. Suppose the Canadian government imposes an import quota on Californian wines, in order to increase the demand for Canadian wines. Explain how the elasticity of demand for Californian wines will affect the outcome of the import quota policy.

LO 5.5 Explain how price elasticity governs the effects that a per-unit excise tax has on tax incidence, resource allocation, and government tax revenue collected.

11. The market demand and the before-tax market supply for gasoline sold in a Canadian province is described in the accompanying table. If the government imposes an excise tax of $0.20 per litre on the suppliers of gasoline in this market, answer the following:

Price (per litre)	Market Demand (millions of litres per day)	Before-Tax Market Supply (millions of litres per day)	After-Tax Market Supply (millions of litres per day)
$0.70	20	80	
$0.60	30	70	
$0.50	40	60	
$0.40	50	50	
$0.30	60	40	
$0.20	70	30	

a. In the accompanying table, fill in the after-tax market supply, at each price per litre.
b. Determine the after-tax equilibrium gas price and quantity.

c. Determine the tax incidence related to this $0.20 per litre excise tax.
d. Determine the total daily tax revenue that the government will receive from this gas excise tax.
e. Under what conditions will the tax revenue computed in part (d) increase—when the demand for gasoline becomes more elastic or less elastic? Explain.
f. Under what conditions will the excise tax more effectively reduce gas consumption—when the demand for gasoline becomes more elastic or less elastic?

12. Suppose the government imposes a per-litre excise tax on all the firms supplying vodka in Canada. For each of the following, pick the market conditions that would tend to increase the buyer's portion of the tax burden:
    a. Buyers have very few vodka substitutes available versus lots of good vodka substitutes available.
    b. Vodka makes up a large portion of each buyer's total monthly expenditures versus it makes up a very small portion of each buyer's total monthly expenditures.
    c. Buyers consider vodka to be a necessity item versus a luxury item.
    d. The firms supplying vodka can easily switch to supplying other products versus they cannot easily switch to supplying other products.

13. In order to raise funds for Canadian musicians, the Canadian government imposes a per-unit excise tax on all firms supplying blank recordable CDs in Canada. The accompanying graph describes the market demand, before-tax market supply, and after-tax market supply curves for the blank recordable CD market in Canada. Use the accompanying graph to answer each of the following:
    a. What is the before-tax equilibrium price and quantity?

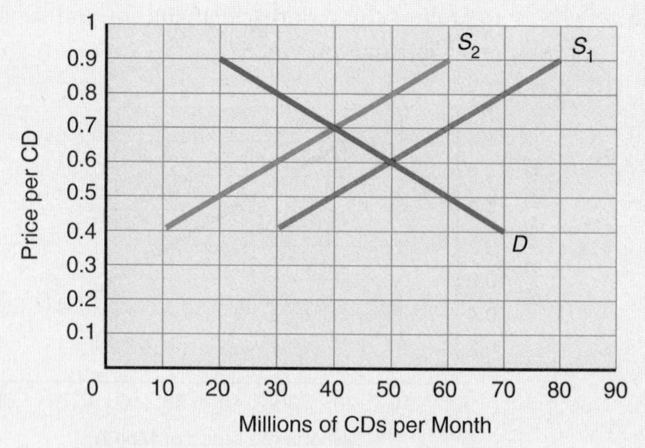

    b. What is the amount of the CD excise tax on a per-CD basis?
    c. What is the after-tax equilibrium price and quantity?
    d. Determine the tax incidence.
    e. Determine the total monthly tax revenue that the Canadian government will receive from this CD excise tax.
    f. Under what conditions will the tax revenue computed in part (e) increase—when the supply for CDs becomes more elastic or less elastic? Explain.
    g. Under what conditions will the CD excise tax more effectively discourage the use of CDs for illegal music downloads—when the supply for CDs becomes more elastic or less elastic?

14. Suppose a provincial government imposes an excise tax on all firms supplying beer in the province. Determine the tax incidence, under each of the following market conditions:
    a. The demand for beer is perfectly elastic.
    b. The demand for beer is perfectly inelastic.
    c. The supply of beer is perfectly elastic.
    d. The supply of beer is perfectly inelastic.

CHAPTER 6

Consumer Choice

In Canada, even if you live in the city, you can surely appreciate the existence of Banff National Park, the Rocky Mountains, and the great wilderness areas in the North and other parts of the country. And even if you have never seen a whale, you may receive some satisfaction from knowing that whales have not been made extinct. Therefore, you may feel a certain loss when an environmental disaster, such as a huge oil spill, occurs. Should your feelings of loss be taken into account when government officials attempt to determine the policy response to environmental damage? To answer this question, you need to know how consumers make choices and what values they place on those choices.

LEARNING OBJECTIVES

After reading this chapter, you should be able to:

6.1 Describe the utility theory and how it impacts the decisions of consumers.

6.2 Define the law of diminishing marginal utility and how it relates to consumer optimum.

DID YOU KNOW THAT...

In a typical year, a Canadian family spends about 15 percent of its income on food and about the same on housing. Within individual families, however, these relative percentages may be quite different. Some families devote a much higher percentage of their income to housing than do others. What determines how much each family spends on different items in its budget? One explanation is, simply, individual tastes—the values that family members place on different items on which they can spend their income. The saying "you can't argue with tastes" suggests that different individuals have different preferences on how to allocate their limited incomes. Although there is no real theory about what determines people's tastes, we can examine some of the behaviour that underlies how consumers react to changes in the prices of the goods and services that they purchase. Recall that people generally purchase less at higher prices than at lower prices. This is called the law of demand.

Because the law of demand is important, its derivation is useful as it allows us to arrange the relevant variables, such as price, income, and tastes, in a way that lets us understand the real world better and even perhaps generate predictions about it. One way of deriving the law of demand involves an analysis of the logic of consumer choice in a world of limited resources. In this chapter, therefore, we discuss what is called *utility analysis*.

6.1 Utility Theory

When you buy something, you do so because of the satisfaction you expect to receive from having and using that good. For everything that you like to have, the more you have of it, the higher the level of satisfaction you receive. Another term that can be used for satisfaction is **utility**, or want-satisfying power of a good or service. This property is common to all goods that are desired. The concept of utility is purely subjective, however. There is no way that we can measure the amount of utility that a consumer might be able to obtain from a particular good, for utility does not imply "useful" or "utilitarian" or "practical." For this reason, there can be no accurate scientific assessment of the utility that someone might receive by consuming a frozen dinner or a movie relative to the utility that another person might receive from that same good or service. Nevertheless, we can infer whether a person receives more utility from consuming one good versus another by that person's behaviour. For example, if an individual buys more coffee than tea (when both tea and coffee are priced equally), we are able to say that the individual receives more utility from consuming coffee than from consuming tea.

Utility The want-satisfying power of a good or service.

The utility that individuals receive from consuming a good depends on their tastes and preferences. These tastes and preferences are normally assumed to be given and stable for a particular individual. It is tastes that determine how much utility that individual derives from consuming a good, and this, in turn, determines how that individual allocates income. People spend a greater proportion of their incomes on goods they like. But we cannot explain why tastes are different among individuals. For example, we cannot explain why some people like yogurt but others do not.

We can analyze in terms of utility the way consumers decide what to buy, just as physicists have analyzed some of their questions about what they call "force." No physicist has ever seen a unit of force, and no economist has ever seen a unit of utility. In both cases, however, these concepts have proven useful for analysis.

Throughout this chapter, we will be discussing **utility analysis**, which is the analysis of consumer decision making based on utility maximization.

Utility analysis The analysis of consumer decision making based on utility maximization.

Utility and Utils

Economists once believed that utility could be measured. In fact, there is a school of thought based on utility theory called *utilitarianism*, developed by the English philosopher Jeremy Bentham (1748–1832). Bentham held that society should seek the greatest happiness for the greatest number. He sought to apply an arithmetic formula for measuring happiness. He and his followers developed the notion of measurable utility and invented the **util** to measure it. For the moment, we will also assume that we can measure

Util A representative unit by which utility is measured.

satisfaction using this representative unit. Our assumption will allow us to quantify the way we examine consumer behaviour.[1] Thus, the first chocolate bar that you eat might yield you four utils of satisfaction; the first peanut cluster, six utils; and so on. Today, no one really believes that we can actually measure utils, but the ideas forthcoming from such analysis will prove useful in our understanding of the way in which consumers choose among alternatives.

Total and Marginal Utility

Consider the satisfaction, or utility, that you receive each time that you rent and watch a video. To make the example straightforward, let us say that there are hundreds of videos to choose from each year and that each of them is of the same quality. Let us say that you normally rent one video per week. You could, of course, rent two, or three, or four per week. Presumably, each time you rent another video per week, you will get additional satisfaction, or utility. The question, though, that we must ask is, given that you are already renting one per week, will the next one rented that week give you the same amount of additional utility?

Marginal utility The change in total utility divided by the change in the number of units consumed.

That additional, or incremental, utility is called **marginal utility**, the change in total utility divided by the change in the number of units consumed, where *marginal,* as before, means "incremental" or "additional." (Marginal changes also refer to decreases, in which cases we talk about *decremental* changes.) The concept of marginality is important in economics because we make decisions at the margin. At any particular point, we compare additional (marginal) benefits with additional (marginal) costs.

Applying Marginal Analysis to Utility

The specific example presented in Figure 6–1 will clarify the distinction between total utility and marginal utility. The table in part (a) shows the total utility and the marginal utility of watching videos each week. Marginal utility is the difference between total utility derived from one level of consumption and total utility derived from another level of consumption. A simple formula for marginal utility is this:

$$\text{Marginal utility} = \frac{\text{Change in total utility}}{\text{Change in number of units consumed}}$$

In our example, when a person has already watched two videos in one week and then watches another, total utility increases from 16 utils to 19. Therefore, the marginal utility (of watching one more video after already having watched two in one week) is equal to three utils.

Graphic Analysis

We can transfer the information in part (a) of Figure 6–1 onto a graph, as we do in parts (b) and (c). Total utility, which is represented in column 2 of part (a), is transferred to part (b).

Total utility continues to rise until four videos are watched per week. This measure of utility remains at 20 utils through the fifth video, and at the sixth video per week it falls to 18 utils; we assume that at some quantity consumed per unit time period, boredom sets in. This is shown in part (b).

[1]What follows is typically called *cardinal utility analysis* by economists. It requires cardinal measurement. Numbers such as 1, 2, and 3 are cardinal numbers. We know that 2 is exactly twice as many as 1 and that 3 is exactly three times as many as 1. You will see in Appendix B at the end of this chapter a type of consumer behaviour analysis that requires only *ordinal* measurement of utility, meaning ranked or ordered. *First, second,* and *third* are ordinal numbers; nothing can be said about their exact size relationships. We can only talk about their importance relative to each other. Temperature, for example, is an ordinal ranking. One hundred degrees Celsius is not twice as warm as 50 degrees Celsius. All we can say is that 100 degrees Celsius is warmer than 50 degrees Celsius.

FIGURE 6-1

Total and Marginal Utility of Watching Videos

If we were able to assign specific values to the utility derived from watching videos each week, we could obtain a marginal utility schedule similar in pattern to the one shown in part (a). In column 1 is the number of videos watched per week; in column 2, the total utility derived from each quantity; and in column 3, the marginal utility derived from each additional quantity, which is defined as the change in total utility due to a change of one unit of watching videos per week. Total utility from part (a) is plotted in part (b). Marginal utility is plotted in part (c), where you see that it reaches zero where total utility hits its maximum at between four and five units.

Part (a)

(1) Number of Videos Watched per Week	(2) Total Utility (utils per week)	(3) Marginal Utility (utils per week)
0	0	
1	10	10 (10 – 0)
2	16	6 (16 – 10)
3	19	3 (19 – 16)
4	20	1 (20 – 19)
5	20	0 (20 – 20)
6	18	–2 (18 – 20)

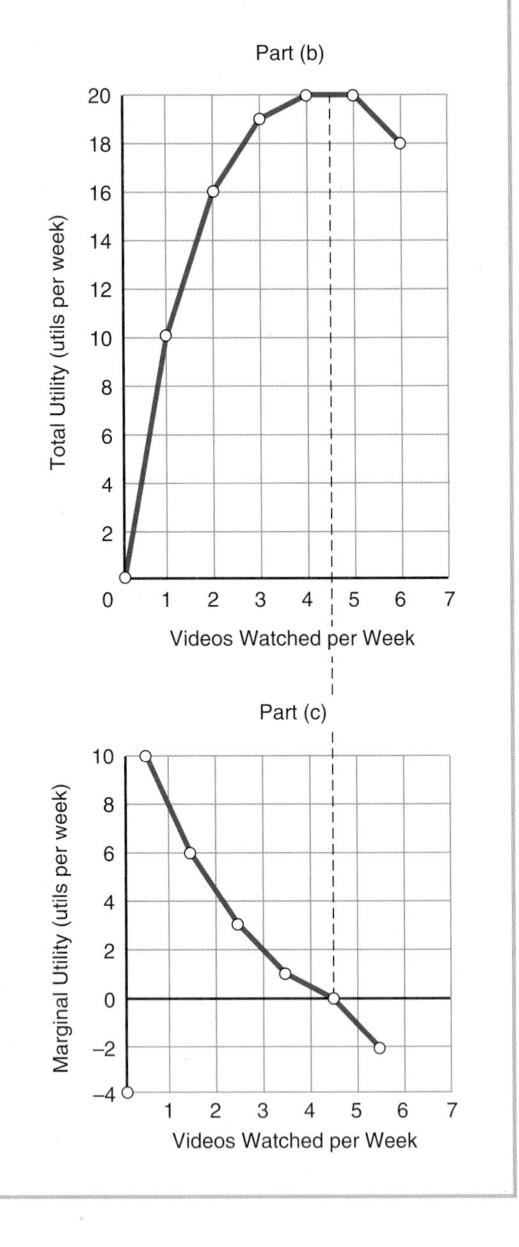

Marginal Utility

If you look carefully at parts (b) and (c) of Figure 6–1, the notion of marginal utility becomes very clear. In economics, the term *marginal* always refers to a change in the total. The marginal utility of watching three videos per week instead of two videos per week is the increment in total utility and is equal to three utils per week. All of the points in part (c) are taken from column 3 of the table in part (a). Note that marginal utility falls throughout the graph. A special point occurs after four videos are watched per week because the total utility curve in part (b) is unchanged after the consumption of the fourth video. That means that the consumer receives no additional (marginal) utility from watching the fifth video. This is shown in part (c) as *zero* marginal utility. After that point, marginal utility becomes negative.

In our example, when marginal utility becomes negative, it means that the consumer is fed up with watching videos and would require some form of compensation to watch any more. When marginal utility is negative, an additional unit consumed actually lowers total utility by becoming a nuisance. Rarely does a consumer face a situation of negative marginal utility. Whenever this point is reached, goods become in effect "bads." A rational consumer will stop consuming at the point at which marginal utility becomes negative, even if the good is free.

CONCEPTS IN BRIEF

Learning Objective 6.1: Describe the utility theory and how it impacts the decisions of consumers.

- Utility is defined as want-satisfying power; it is a power common to all desired goods and services.
- We arbitrarily measure utility in units called utils.
- It is important to distinguish between total utility and marginal utility. Total utility is the total satisfaction derived from the consumption of a given quantity of a good or service. Marginal utility is the change in total utility due to a one-unit change in the consumption of the good or service.

6.2 Diminishing Marginal Utility

Note that in part (c) of Figure 6–1, marginal utility is continuously declining. This property has been named *the principle of diminishing marginal utility*. It is not a concept that can be proven, but economists and others have believed in it for years and it has even been called a law. This supposed law concerns a psychological, or subjective, utility that you receive as you consume more and more of a particular good. Stated formally, the law of **diminishing marginal utility** is as follows:

Diminishing marginal utility
The principle that as an individual consumes more of a particular commodity, the total level of utility, or satisfaction, derived from that consumption usually increases. Eventually, however, the rate at which it increases diminishes as more is consumed.

> As an individual consumes more of a particular commodity, the total level of utility, or satisfaction, derived from that consumption usually increases. Eventually, however, the rate at which it increases diminishes as more is consumed.

Take a hungry individual at a dinner table. The first serving is greatly appreciated, and the individual derives a substantial amount of utility from it. The second serving does not have quite as much impact as the first one, and the third serving is likely to be even less satisfying. This individual experiences diminishing marginal utility of food and stops eating. This is true for most people. All-you-can-eat restaurants count on this fact; a second helping of ribs may provide some marginal utility, but the third helping would have only a little or even negative marginal utility. The fall in the marginal utility of other goods is even more dramatic. Try Example 6–1.

EXAMPLE 6–1 **Newspaper Vending Machines versus Candy Vending Machines**

Have you ever noticed that newspaper vending machines nearly everywhere in Canada allow you to put in the correct change—the cost of one newspaper—lift up the door, and take as many newspapers as you want? Contrast this type of vending machine with candy machines. They are completely locked at all times. You must designate the candy that you wish, normally by using some type of keypad. The candy then drops down to a place where you reach to retrieve it but from which you cannot grab any other candy. The difference between these two types of vending machines is explained by diminishing marginal utility. Newspaper companies dispense newspapers from coin-operated boxes that allow dishonest people to take more copies than they pay for. What would a dishonest person do with more than one copy of a newspaper, however? The marginal utility of a second newspaper is normally zero. The benefit of storing excessive newspapers is usually nil because yesterday's news has no value. But the same analysis does not hold for candy. The marginal utility of a second candy bar is certainly less than the first, but it is normally not zero. Moreover, one can store candy for relatively long periods of time at relatively low cost. Consequently, food vending machine companies have to worry about dishonest users of their machines and must make their machines much more theftproof than newspaper companies do.

For critical analysis: Can you think of a circumstance under which a substantial number of newspaper purchasers might be inclined to take more than one newspaper out of a vending machine?

Consider for a moment the opposite possibility—increasing marginal utility. Under such a situation, the marginal utility after consuming, say, one hamburger would increase. The second hamburger would be more valuable to you, and the third would be even more valuable yet. If increasing marginal utility existed, each of us would consume only one good or service! Rather than observing that "variety is the spice of life," we would see that monotony in consumption was preferred. We do not observe this, and therefore, we have great confidence in the concept of diminishing marginal utility.

Optimizing Consumption Choices

Every consumer has a limited income. Choices must be made. When a consumer has made all choices about what to buy and in what quantities, and when the total level of satisfaction, or utility, from that set of choices is as great as it can be, we say that the consumer has *optimized.* When the consumer has attained an optimum consumption set of goods and services, we say that individual has reached **consumer optimum.**[2]

Consumer optimum Reached when the consumer has attained an optimum consumption set of goods and services.

Consider a simple two-good example. The consumer has to choose between spending income on the rental of videos at $5 each and on purchasing deluxe hamburgers at $3 each. Let us say that the last dollar spent on hamburgers yields three utils of utility but the last dollar spent on video rentals yields 10 utils. Wouldn't this consumer increase total utility if some dollars were taken away from hamburger consumption and allocated to video rentals? The answer is yes. Given diminishing marginal utility, more dollars spent on video rentals will reduce marginal utility per last dollar spent, whereas fewer dollars spent on hamburger consumption will increase marginal utility per last dollar spent. The

[2]Optimization typically refers to individual decision-making processes. When we deal with many individuals interacting in the marketplace, we talk in terms of an equilibrium in the marketplace. Generally speaking, equilibrium is a property of markets rather than of individual decision making.

optimum—where total utility is maximized—might occur when the satisfaction per last dollar spent on both hamburgers and video rentals per week is equal for the two goods. Thus, the amount of goods consumed depends on the prices of the goods, the income of the consumers, and the marginal utility derived from each good.

Table 6–1 presents information on utility derived from consuming various quantities of videos and hamburgers. Columns 4 and 8 show the marginal utility per dollar spent on videos and hamburgers, respectively. If the prices of both goods are zero, individuals will consume each as long as their respective marginal utility is positive (at least five units of each and probably much more). It is also true that a consumer with infinite income will continue consuming goods until the marginal utility of each is equal to zero. When the price is zero or the consumer's income is infinite, there is no effective constraint on consumption.

Consumer optimum is attained when the marginal utility of the last dollar spent on each good is the same and income is completely exhausted. The individual's income is $26. From columns 4 and 8 of Table 6–1, maximum equal marginal utilities per dollar occur at the consumption level of four videos and two hamburgers (the marginal utility per dollar spent equals 7.3). Note that the marginal utility per dollar spent for both goods is also (approximately) equal at the consumption level of three videos and one hamburger, but here, total income is not completely exhausted. Likewise, the marginal utility per dollar spent is (approximately) equal at five videos and three hamburgers, but the expenditures necessary for that level of consumption exceed the individual's income.

Table 6–2 shows the steps taken to arrive at consumer optimum. The first video would yield a marginal utility per dollar of 10.0, while the first hamburger would yield a marginal utility of only 8.3 per dollar. Because it yields the higher marginal utility per dollar, the video is purchased. This leaves $21 of income. The second video yields a higher marginal utility per dollar (9.0, versus 8.3 for hamburgers), and so it is also purchased, leaving an unspent income of $16. At the third purchase, the first hamburger now yields a higher marginal utility per dollar than the next video (8.3 versus 8.0), and so the first hamburger is purchased. This leaves income of $13 to spend. The process continues until all income is exhausted and the marginal utility per dollar spent is equal for both goods.

To restate, consumer optimum requires the following:

> A consumer's money income should be allocated so that the last dollar spent on each good purchased yields the same amount of marginal utility (when all income is spent).

TABLE 6–1

Total and Marginal Utility from Consuming Videos and Hamburgers on an Income of $26

(1) Videos per Period	(2) Total Utility of Videos per Period (utils)	(3) Marginal Utility (utils) MU_v	(4) Marginal Utility per Dollar Spent (MU_v/P_v) (price = $5)	(5) Hamburgers per Period	(6) Total Utility of Hamburgers per Period (utils)	(7) Marginal Utility (utils) MU_h	(8) Marginal Utility per Dollar Spent (MU_h/P_h) (price = $3)
0	0.0	-	-	0	0	-	-
1	50.0	50.0	10.0	1	25	25	8.3
2	95.0	45.0	9.0	2	47	22	7.3
3	135.0	40.0	8.0	3	65	18	6.0
4	171.5	36.5	7.3	4	80	15	5.0
5	200.0	28.5	5.7	5	89	9	3.0

TABLE 6-2

Steps to Consumer Optimum

In each purchase situation described here, the consumer always purchases the good with the higher marginal utility per dollar spent (MU/P). For example, at the time of the third purchase, the marginal utility per last dollar spent on videos is 8.0, but it is 8.3 for hamburgers, and $16 of income remains, and so the next purchase will be a hamburger. Here, P_v = $5 and P_h = $3.

	Choices					
	Videos		Hamburgers			
Purchase	Unit	(MU_v/P_v)	Unit	(MU_h/P_h)	Buying Decision	Remaining Income
1	First	10.0	First	8.3	First video	$26 - $5 = $21
2	Second	9.0	First	8.3	Second video	$21 - $5 = $16
3	Third	8.0	First	8.3	First hamburger	$16 - $3 = $13
4	Third	8.0	Second	7.3	Third video	$13 - $5 = $ 8
5	Fourth	7.3	Second	7.3	Fourth video and second hamburger	$ 8 - $5 = $ 3 $ 3 - $3 = $ 0

A Little Math

We can state the rule of consumer optimum in algebraic terms by examining the ratio of marginal utilities and prices of individual products. This is sometimes called the *utility maximization rule.*

The rule simply states that a consumer maximizes personal satisfaction when allocating money income in such a way that the last dollars spent on good A, good B, good C, and so on, yield equal amounts of marginal utility. Marginal utility (*MU*) from good A is indicated by *MU* of good A. For good B, it is *MU* of good B.

Our algebraic formulation of this rule, therefore, becomes

$$\frac{MU \text{ of good A}}{\text{Price of good A}} = \frac{MU \text{ of good B}}{\text{Price of good B}} = \cdots = \frac{MU \text{ of good Z}}{\text{Price of good Z}}$$

The letters A, B,..., Z indicate the various goods and services that the consumer might purchase.

We know, then, that the marginal utility of good A divided by the price of good A must equal the marginal utility of any other good divided by its price in order for the consumer to maximize utility. Note, though, that the application of the utility maximization rule is not an explicit or conscious act on the part of consumers. Rather, this is a model of consumer optimum.

How a Price Change Affects Consumer Optimum

Consumption decisions are summarized in the law of demand, which states that the amount purchased is inversely related to price. We can now see why by using the law of diminishing marginal utility.

Purchase decisions are made such that the value of the marginal utility of the last unit purchased and consumed is just equal to the price that had to be paid. No consumer will, when optimizing, buy 10 units of a good per time period when the personal valuation placed on the tenth unit is less than the price of the tenth unit.

If we start out at consumer optimum and then observe a price decrease, we can predict that consumers will respond to the price decrease by consuming more. Now, with a lower price, it is possible to consume more than before and still not have the marginal utility be less than the price because the price has fallen. If the law of diminishing marginal utility holds, the purchase and consumption of additional units will cause marginal utility to fall. Eventually it will fall to the point at which it is equal to the price of the final good consumed. The limit to this increase in consumption is given by the law of diminishing marginal utility.

A hypothetical demand curve for video rentals per week for a typical consumer is presented in Figure 6–2. Because of the law of diminishing marginal utility—with the consumption of more videos, the marginal utility of the last unit of these additional videos is lower. What has happened is that at a lower price, the number of video rentals per week increased from two to three; marginal utility must have fallen. At a higher consumption rate, the marginal utility falls to meet the lower price for video rentals per week.

The Demand Curve Revisited

Linking the "law" of diminishing marginal utility and the utility maximization rule gives us a negative relationship between the quantity demanded of a good or service and its price. As the relative price of video rentals goes up, for example, the quantity demanded will fall; and as the relative price of video rentals goes down, the quantity demanded will rise. Figure 6–2 shows this demand curve for video rentals. As the price of video rentals falls, the consumer can maximize total utility only by renting more videos and vice versa. In other words, the relationship between price and quantity desired is simply a downward-sloping demand curve. Note, though, that this downward-sloping demand curve (the law of demand) is derived under the assumption of constant tastes and incomes. You must remember that we are keeping these important determining variables constant when we simply look at the relationship between price and quantity demanded.

Marginal Utility, Total Utility, and the Diamond–Water Paradox

Even though water is essential to life and diamonds are not, water is cheap and diamonds are dear. The economist Adam Smith in 1776 called this the "diamond–water paradox." The paradox is easily understood when we realize that the supply of water is abundant relative to demand and therefore carries a low price. Diamonds, however, are scarce relative to demand and therefore carry a high price. To better understand this, we must make the distinction between total utility and marginal utility. The total utility of water greatly exceeds the total utility derived from diamonds. What determines the price, though, is what happens on the margin. We have relatively few diamonds, and so the marginal utility of the last diamond consumed is high. The opposite is true for water. Total utility does not determine what people are willing to pay for a unit of a particular commodity; marginal utility does. Look at the situation presented graphically in Figure 6–3. We show the demand curve for diamonds, labelled $D_{diamonds}$. The demand curve for water is labelled D_{water}. We plot quantity in terms of kilograms per unit time period on the horizontal axis.

FIGURE 6–2

Video Rental Prices and Marginal Utility

A reduction in price from $5 to $4 per video rental causes consumers to increase consumption until marginal utility falls (because of the law of diminishing marginal utility).

Price per Unit ($)
5
4
0
1
2
3
D
Video Rentals per Week

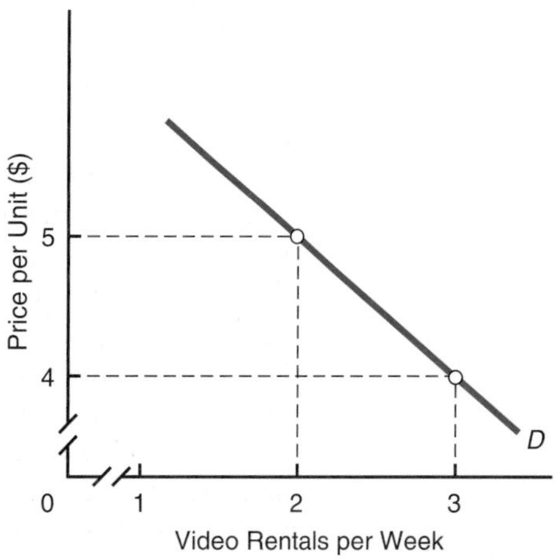

FIGURE 6–3

The Diamond–Water Paradox

We pick kilograms as a common unit of measurement for both water and diamonds. To demonstrate that the demand for and supply of water are immense, we have put a break in the horizontal quantity axis. Although the demand for water is much greater than the demand for diamonds, the marginal valuation of water is given by the marginal value placed on the last unit of water consumed. To find that, we must know the supply of water, which is given as S_1. At that supply, the price of water is P_{water}. But the supply for diamonds is given by S_2. At that supply, the price of diamonds is $P_{diamonds}$. The total valuation that consumers place on water is tremendous relative to the total valuation consumers place on diamonds. What is important for price determination, however, is the marginal valuation, or the marginal utility received.

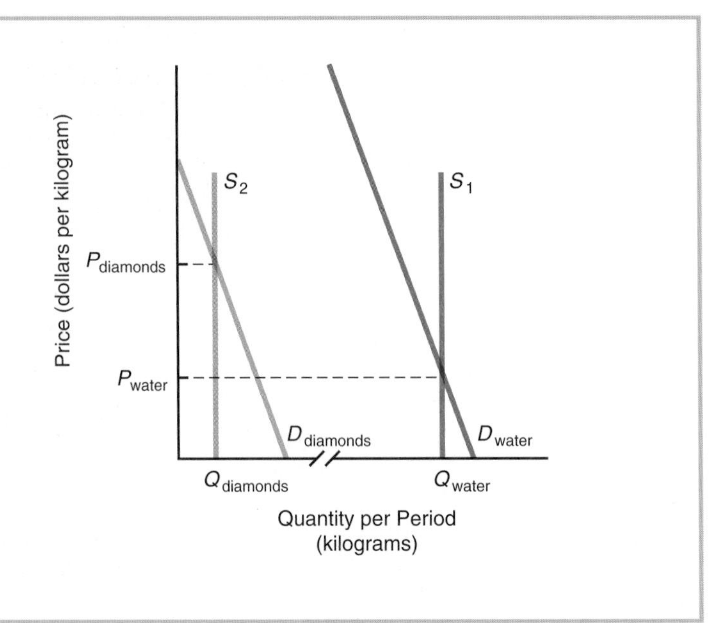

On the vertical axis, we plot price in dollars per kilogram. We use kilograms as our common unit of measurement for water and for diamonds. We could just as well have used gallons, acre-feet, or litres.

Note that the demand for water is many, many times the demand for diamonds. We draw the supply curve of water as S_1 at a quantity of Q_{water}. The supply curve for diamonds is given as S_2 at quantity $Q_{diamonds}$. At the intersection of the supply curve of water with the demand curve of water, the price per kilogram is P_{water}. The intersection of the supply curve of diamonds with the demand curve of diamonds is at $P_{diamonds}$. Note that $P_{diamonds}$ exceeds P_{water}. Diamonds sell at a higher price than water. See Example 6–2 for an illustration of the diamond–water paradox.

EXAMPLE 6–2 The World of Water in Saudi Arabia

The diamond–water paradox deals with the situation in which water, although necessary for life, may be much cheaper than some luxury item. In Saudi Arabia, as you might expect, the contrary can be true. A litre of water costs five times as much as a litre of gasoline, whereas a pair of custom-made British wool dress pants costs only $25. These relative prices are quite different from what we are used to seeing in Canada. Water costs next to nothing, a litre of gas costs about 95 cents, and custom-made wool pants costs at least $200. To understand what has happened in Saudi Arabia, simply substitute gasoline for water and water for diamonds in Figure 6–3.

For critical analysis: List some of the effects on human behaviour that such a high relative price of water would cause.

CONCEPTS IN BRIEF

Learning Objective 6.2: Define the law of diminishing marginal utility and how it relates to consumer optimum.

- The law of diminishing marginal utility tells us that each successive marginal unit of a good consumed adds less additional utility.
- Each consumer with a limited income must make a choice about the basket of commodities to purchase; economic theory assumes that the consumer chooses the basket of commodities that yields optimum consumption. The consumer maximizes total utility by equating the marginal utility of the last dollar spent on one good with the marginal utility per last dollar spent on all other goods. That is the state of consumer optimum.
- To remain in consumer optimum, a price decrease requires an increase in consumption; a price increase requires a decrease in consumption.

ISSUES AND APPLICATIONS

Contingent Valuation: Pricing the "Priceless"

Concepts Applied: Utility, Total Utility, Demand Curve

How much are we willing to pay to keep our national parks clean?

It is difficult to estimate the dollar amount an average citizen is willing to pay to keep Banff National Park's air clean. One way economists attempt to derive the demand for pristine wilderness is to use contingent valuation.

Obviously, not everything has a price. That is because not everything is bought and sold in the marketplace. Much of what occurs in the environment is outside the marketplace. A wilderness area so remote that hardly anyone visits it certainly has a value, but what is it? Just because only few people visit does not mean it has little worth. If the wilderness were privately owned and the owner received virtually no income from occasional visitors, that does not mean that it would have virtually no value.

When Disaster Occurs

When the wilderness area with few visitors is harmed by some disaster of human origin, such as an oil spill, what has been lost? If your house is burned down, you can get a pretty accurate idea of what the insurance company will give you by looking at the housing market for an alternative. Such is not the case with an oil-blighted wilderness area in the far reaches of the North.

Nonuse Satisfaction

Even people who never use the wilderness area may place a value on it. They may place a value on the opportunity to preserve the wilderness for their grandchildren and on the mere knowledge that such a pristine wilderness area exists. The question, then, is how do we get an accurate valuation of these nonuse values?

Contingent Valuation

Some economists believe that they can obtain an estimate of the demand curve for a wilderness area, for example, that includes nonuse values by conducting opinion polls. In this technique, called *contingent valuation*, people are asked what they are willing to pay for a particular benefit or what they would accept as compensation for its loss. This technique was used in developing multibillion-dollar damage claims against Exxon after its oil tanker, the *Exxon Valdez*, ran aground in Alaska in 1989. In essence, these contingent valuation surveys asked people *not* living in Alaska to place a value on the utility they lost by virtue of the fact that a part of Alaska's pristine beauty was harmed.

Criticisms of Opinion Data

Many economists are critical of opinion surveys conducted to estimate utility. They point out that such estimates of supposed willingness to pay are without strong meaning if individuals do not actually have to make the payments. One opinion survey estimated the average individual's willingness to pay to prevent the extinction of the whooping crane at $200 per year. That comes to almost $3 billion per year for all Canadian adults. Given that there are fewer than 170 whooping cranes in existence, this total represents about $23.6 million per bird *per year*. There are literally thousands of species that might be protected. Even if households' average willingness to pay is only $10 per year per endangered species, summing that amount over all environmental "goods" would exceed the average family's yearly income many times.

The way in which opinion survey questions are phrased also reveals their weaknesses. In one study, the people interviewed said they would be willing to pay $90 a year to preserve clean air in Banff National Park. In a follow-up survey, when they were asked about paying for competing claims of cleaner air in Toronto and in the eastern provinces as well, they were willing to spend only $16 a year to preserve clean air in Banff National Park.

Finally, when people are asked about their willingness to accept money in exchange for a harm to a resource, rather than their willingness to pay to prevent that very same harm, the dollar values they cite are substantially higher.

For critical analysis:

1. Why can't opinion polls be used effectively to estimate demand curves?
2. How do individuals normally express their perceived level of satisfaction for a good or a service in the marketplace?

SUMMARY DISCUSSION OF LEARNING OBJECTIVES

6.1 Utility Theory. As an individual consumes more of a particular commodity, the total level of utility, or satisfaction, derived from that consumption increases. However, the *rate* at which it increases diminishes as more is consumed. This is known as the law of diminishing marginal utility.

6.2 Diminishing Marginal Utility. An individual reaches consumer optimum when the marginal utility per last dollar spent on each commodity consumed is equal to the marginal utility per dollar spent on every other good.

When the price of a particular commodity goes up, to get back into an optimum position the consumer must reduce consumption of the now relatively more expensive commodity. As this consumer moves back up the marginal utility curve, marginal utility increases.

It is possible to derive a downward-sloping demand curve by using the principle of diminishing marginal utility.

PROBLEMS

(Answers to the odd-numbered problems appear at the back of the book.)

LO 6.1 Describe the utility theory and how it impacts the decisions of consumers.

1. Suppose that you are standing in the checkout line of a grocery store. You have five kilograms of oranges and three ears of corn. A kilogram of oranges costs 30 cents; so does an ear of corn. You have $2.40 to spend. You are satisfied that you have reached the highest level of satisfaction, or total utility. A friend comes along and tries to convince you that you have to put some of the corn back and replace it with oranges. From what you know about utility analysis, how would you explain this disagreement?
2. The campus pizzeria sells a single pizza for $12. If you order a second pizza, however, its price is only $5. Explain how this relates to marginal utility.
3. Assume that Alice Warfield's marginal utility is 100 utils for the last hamburger she consumed. If the price of hamburgers is $1 apiece, what is Warfield's marginal utility per dollar's worth of hamburger? What is her marginal utility per dollar's worth if the price is 50 cents per hamburger? If the price is $2? How do we calculate marginal utility per dollar's worth of specific commodities?

LO 6.2 Define the law of diminishing marginal utility and how it relates to consumer optimum.

4. A fall in the price of one good leads to more of that good being consumed, other things remaining constant. How might this increase in consumption be broken down?
5. Consider the table at the bottom of the page. Following the utility maximization rule, how much of each good will be consumed?
6. If total utility is increasing as more is consumed, what is happening to marginal utility?
7. Yesterday, you were consuming four eggs and two strips of bacon. Today, you are consuming three eggs and three strips of bacon. Your tastes did not change overnight. What might have caused this change? Are you better or worse off?
8. Complete the missing cells in the table below.

Number of Cheese-burgers	Total Utility of Cheese-burgers	Marginal Utility of Cheese-burgers	Bags of French Fries	Total Utility of French Fries	Marginal Utility of French Fries
0	0	–	0	0	–
1	20	–	1	–	8
2	36	–	2	–	6
3	–	12	3	–	4
4	–	8	4	20	–
5	–	4	5	20	–

9. If the price of a cheeseburger is $2 and the price of a bag of french fries is $1 and you have $6 to spend (and you spend all of it), what is the utility-maximizing combination of cheeseburgers and french fries?
10. In the Issues and Applications, "Contingent Valuation: Pricing the 'Priceless,'" some economists conduct opinion polls to place value on nonuse items such as national parks. What is this called?
11. In Example 6–1, "Newspaper Vending Machines versus Candy Vending Machines," newspaper vendors allow people to access more than one paper at a time. In Prince Edward Island, you will see potatoes left by the roadside for people to buy, on their honour. Farmers say they more than come out ahead at the end of the day. What does this say about the diminishing marginal utility of potatoes?

Quantity of Good A	Marginal Utility of Good A	Price of Good A	Quantity of Good B	Marginal Utility of Good B	Price of Good B
100	15	$4.51	9	7	$1.69
101	12	4.51	10	5	1.69
102	8	4.51	11	3	1.69
103	6	4.51	12	2	1.69

APPENDIX C

MORE ADVANCED CONSUMER CHOICE THEORY

It is possible to analyze consumer choice verbally, as we did for the most part in Chapter 6. The theory of diminishing marginal utility can be fairly well accepted on intuitive grounds and by introspection. If we want to be more formal and perhaps more elegant in our theorizing, however, we can translate our discussion into a graphic analysis with what we call indifference curves and the budget constraint. Here, we discuss these terms and their relationship and demonstrate consumer equilibrium in geometric form.

On Being Indifferent

What does it mean to be indifferent? It usually means that you do not care one way or the other about something—you are equally disposed to either of two alternatives. With this interpretation in mind, we will turn to two choices, video rentals and restaurant meals. In part (a) of Figure C–1, we show several combinations of video rentals and restaurant meals per week that a representative consumer considers equally satisfactory. That is to say, for each combination, *A, B, C,* and *D,* this consumer will have exactly the same level of total utility.

The simple numerical example that we have used happens to concern video rentals and restaurant meals per week. This example is used to illustrate general features of

FIGURE C–1

Combinations That Yield Equal Levels of Satisfaction

A, B, C, and *D* represent combinations of video rentals and restaurant meals per week that give an equal level of satisfaction to this consumer. In other words, the consumer is indifferent among these four combinations.

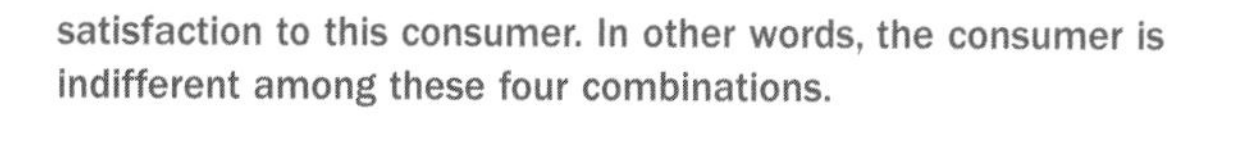

Part (a)

Combination	Video Rentals per Week	Restaurant Meals per Week
A	1	7
B	2	4
C	3	2
D	4	1

Part (b)

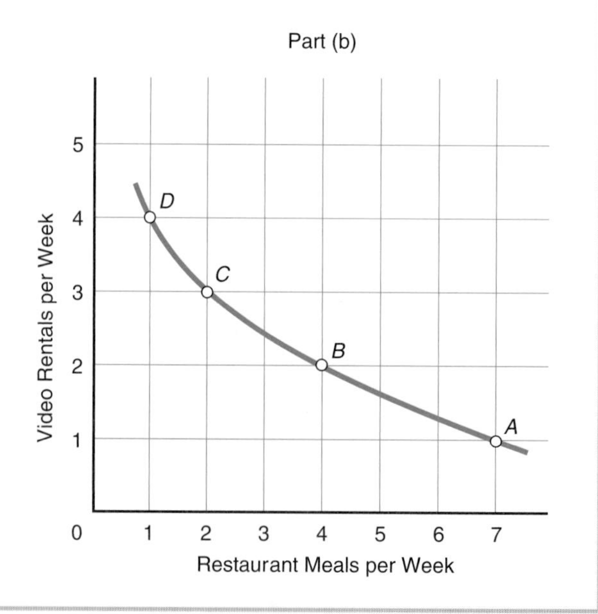

indifference curves and related analytical tools that are necessary for deriving the demand curve. Obviously, we could have used any two commodities. Just remember that we are using a *specific* example to illustrate a *general* analysis.

We can plot these combinations graphically in part (b) of Figure C–1, with restaurant meals per week on the horizontal axis and video rentals per week on the vertical axis. These are our consumer's indifference combinations—the consumer finds each combination as acceptable as the others. When we connect these combinations with a smooth curve, we obtain what is called the consumer's *indifference curve*. Along the **indifference curve**, every combination of the two goods in question yields the same level of satisfaction. Every point along the indifference curve is equally desirable to the consumer. For example, four video rentals per week and one restaurant meal per week will give our representative consumer exactly the same total satisfaction as two video rentals per week and four restaurant meals per week.

Indifference curve A curve where every combination of the two goods in question yields the same level of satisfaction.

Properties of Indifference Curves

Indifference curves have special properties relating to their slope and shape.

Downward Slope

The indifference curve shown in part (b) of Figure C–1 slopes downward; that is, it has a negative slope. Now, consider Figure C–2. Here, we show two points, *A* and *B*. Point *A* represents four video rentals per week and two restaurant meals per week. Point *B* represents five video rentals per week and six restaurant meals per week. Clearly, *B* is always preferred to *A* because *B* represents more of everything. If *B* is always preferred to *A*, it is impossible for points *A* and *B* to be on the same indifference curve because the definition of the indifference curve is a set of combinations of two goods that are equally preferred.

Curvature

The indifference curve that we have drawn in part (b) of Figure C–1 is special. Note that it is curved. Why didn't we just draw a straight line, as we have usually done for a demand curve? To find out why we do not posit straight-line indifference curves, consider the implications. We show such a straight-line indifference curve in Figure C–3. Start at point *A*. The consumer has no restaurant meals and five video rentals per week. Now the

FIGURE C–2
Indifference Curves: Impossibility of an Upward Slope

Point *B* represents a consumption of more video rentals per week and more restaurant meals per week than point *A*. *B* is always preferred to *A*. Therefore, *A* and *B* cannot be on the same indifference curve, which is positively sloped, because an indifference curve shows equally preferred combinations of the two goods.

FIGURE C–3

Implications of a Straight-Line Indifference Curve

If the indifference curve is a straight line, the consumer will be willing to give up the same number of video rentals (one for one in this simple example) to get one more restaurant meal per week, whether the consumer has no restaurant meals or a lot of restaurant meals per week. For example, the consumer at point *A* has five video rentals and no restaurant meals per week. He or she is willing to give up one video rental in order to get one restaurant meal per week. At point *C*, however, the consumer has only one video rental and four restaurant meals per week. Because of the straight-line indifference curve, this consumer is willing to give up the last video rental in order to get one more restaurant meal per week, even though he or she already has four.

consumer wishes to go to point *B*. He or she is willing to give up only one video rental in order to get one restaurant meal. Now, let us assume that the consumer is at point *C*, consuming one video rental and four restaurant meals per week. If the consumer wants to go to point *D*, he or she is again willing to give up one video rental in order to get one more restaurant meal per week.

In other words, no matter how many videos the consumer rents, he or she is willing to give up one video rental to get one restaurant meal per week—which does not seem plausible. Doesn't it make sense to hypothesize that the more videos the consumer rents per week, the less he or she will value an *additional* video rental? Presumably, when the consumer has five video rentals and no restaurant meals per week, he or she should be willing to give up more than one video rental in order to get one restaurant meal. Therefore, a straight-line indifference curve as shown in Figure C–3 no longer seems plausible.

In mathematical language, an indifference curve is convex with respect to the origin. Let us look at this in part (a) of Figure C–1. Starting with combination *A*, the consumer has one video rental but seven restaurant meals per week. To remain indifferent, the consumer would have to be willing to give up three restaurant meals to obtain one more video rental (as shown in combination *B*). However, to go from combination *C* to combination *D*, note that the consumer would have to be willing to give up only one restaurant meal for an additional video rental per week. The quantity of the substitute considered acceptable changes as the rate of consumption of the original item changes.

Consequently, the indifference curve in part (b) of Figure C–1 will be convex when viewed from the origin.

The Marginal Rate of Substitution

Instead of using marginal utility, we can talk in terms of the marginal rate of substitution between restaurant meals and video rentals per week. We can formally define the consumer's marginal rate of substitution as follows:

> **The marginal rate of substitution is equal to the change in the quantity of one good that just offsets a one-unit change in the consumption of another good, such that total satisfaction remains constant.**

We can see numerically what happens to the marginal rate of substitution in our example if we rearrange part (a) of Figure C–1 into Table C–1. Here, we show restaurant meals in the second column and video rentals in the third. Now we ask the question "What change in the consumption of video rentals per week will just compensate for a three-unit change in the consumption of restaurant meals per week and leave the consumer's total utility constant?" The movement from *A* to *B* increases video rental consumption by 1. Here, the marginal rate of substitution is 3:1—a three-unit decrease in restaurant meals requires an increase of one video rental to leave the consumer's total utility unaltered. Thus, the consumer values the three restaurant meals as the equivalent of one video rental. We do this for the rest of the table and find that as restaurant meals decrease further, the marginal rate of substitution goes from 3:1 to 1:1. The marginal rate of substitution of restaurant meals for video rentals per week falls as the consumer obtains more video rentals. That is, the consumer values successive units of video rentals less and less in terms of restaurant meals. The first video rental is valued at three restaurant meals; the last (fourth) video rental is valued at only one restaurant meal. The fact that the marginal rate of substitution falls is sometimes called the *law of substitution*.

TABLE C–1

Calculating the Marginal Rate of Substitution

As we move from combination *A* to combination *B*, we are still on the same indifference curve. To stay on that curve, the number of restaurant meals decreases by three and the number of video rentals increases by one. The marginal rate of substitution is 3:1. A three-unit decrease in restaurant meals requires an increase in one video rental to leave the consumer's total utility unaltered.

(1) Combination	(2) Restaurant Meals per Week	(3) Video Rentals per Week	(4) Marginal Rate of Substitution of Restaurant Meals for Video Rentals
A	7	1	
B	4	2	3:1
C	2	3	2:1
D	1	4	1:1

In geometric language, the slope of the consumer's indifference curve (actually, the negative of the slope) measures the consumer's marginal rate of substitution. Note that this marginal rate of substitution is purely subjective or psychological.

The Indifference Map

Let us now consider the possibility of having both more video rentals *and* more restaurant meals per week. When we do this, we can no longer stay on the same indifference curve that we drew in Figure C–1. That indifference curve was drawn for equally satisfying combinations of video rentals and restaurant meals per week. If the individual can now attain more of both, a new indifference curve will have to be drawn, above and to the right of the one shown in part (b) of Figure C–1. Alternatively, if the individual faces the possibility of having less of both video rentals and restaurant meals per week, an indifference curve will have to be drawn below and to the left of the one in part (b) of Figure C–1. We can map out a whole set of indifference curves corresponding to these possibilities.

Figure C–4 shows three possible indifference curves. Indifference curves that are higher than others necessarily imply that for every given quantity of one good, more of the other good can be obtained on a higher indifference curve. Looked at another way, if one goes from curve I_1 to I_2, it is possible to consume the same number of restaurant meals *and* be able to rent more videos per week. This is shown as a movement from point *A* to point *B* in Figure C–4. We could do it the other way. When we move from a lower to a higher indifference curve, it is possible to rent the same number of videos *and* to consume more restaurant meals per week. Thus, the higher a consumer is on the indifference map, the greater is that consumer's total level of satisfaction.

FIGURE C-4

A Set of Indifference Curves

An infinite number of indifference curves can be drawn. We show three possible ones. Realize that a higher indifference curve represents the possibility of higher rates of consumption of both goods. Hence, a higher indifference curve is preferred to a lower one because more is preferred to less. Look at points *A* and *B*. Point *B* represents more video rentals than point *A*; therefore, bundles on indifference curve I_2 have to be preferred over bundles on I_1 because the number of restaurant meals per week is the same at points *A* and *B*.

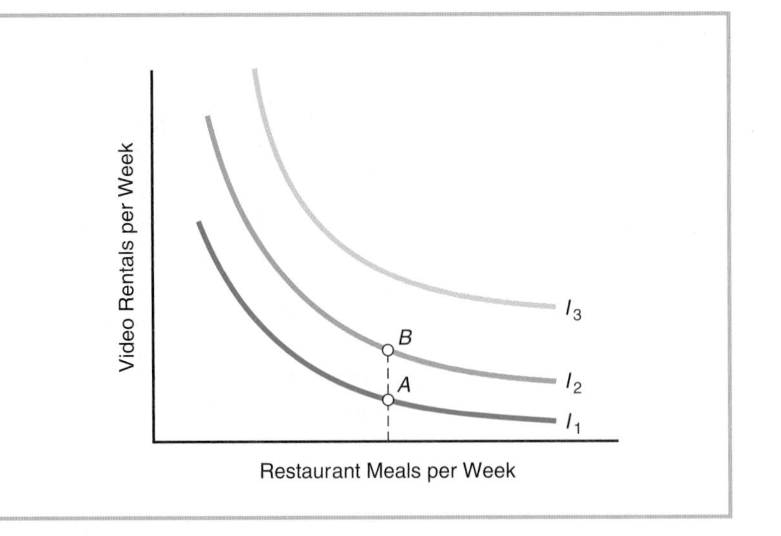

The Budget Constraint

Budget constraint All of the possible combinations of goods that can be purchased (at fixed prices) with a specific budget.

Our problem here is to find out how to maximize consumer satisfaction. To do so, we must consult not only our *preferences*—given by indifference curves—but also our *market opportunities*—given by our available income and prices, called our **budget constraint** (all of the possible combinations of goods that can be purchased [at fixed prices] with a specific budget). We might want more of everything, but for any given budget constraint, we have to make choices, or trade-offs, among possible goods. Everyone has a budget constraint; that is, everyone faces a limited consumption potential. How do we show this graphically? We must find the prices of the goods in question and determine the maximum consumption of each allowed by our budget. For example, let us assume that videos rent for $10 apiece and restaurant meals cost $20. Let us also assume that our representative consumer has a total budget of $60 per week. What is the maximum number of videos the consumer can rent? Six. And the maximum number of restaurant meals per week he or she can consume? Three. So, now, as shown in Figure C–5, we have two points on our budget line, which is sometimes called the *consumption possibilities curve.* These anchor points of the budget line are obtained by dividing money income by the price of each product. The first point is at *b* on the vertical axis; the second, at *b′* on the horizontal axis. The budget line is linear because prices are given.

Any combination along line *bb′* is possible; in fact, any combination in the coloured area is possible. We will assume, however, that the individual consumer completely uses up the available budget, and we will consider as possible only those points along *bb′*.

Slope of the Budget Constraint

The budget constraint is a line that slopes downward from left to right. The slope of that line has a special meaning. Look carefully at the budget line in Figure C–5. Remember in the discussion of graphs in Appendix A that we measure a negative slope by the ratio of the fall in *Y* over the run in *X*. In this case, *Y* is video rentals per week and *X* is restaurant meals per week. In Figure C–5, the fall in *Y* is −2 video rentals per week (a drop from 4 to 2) for a run in *X* of one restaurant meal per week (an increase from 1 to 2); therefore, the slope of the budget constraint is −2/1, or −2. This slope of the budget constraint represents the rate of exchange between video rentals and restaurant meals; it is the realistic rate of exchange, given their prices.

Now we are ready to determine how the consumer achieves the optimum consumption rate.

FIGURE C–5

The Budget Constraint

The line *bb′* represents this individual's budget constraint. Assuming that video rentals cost $10 each, restaurant meals cost $20 each, and the individual has a budget of $60 per week, a maximum of six video rentals or three restaurant meals can be bought each week. These two extreme points are connected to form the budget constraint. All combinations within the coloured area and on the budget constraint line are feasible.

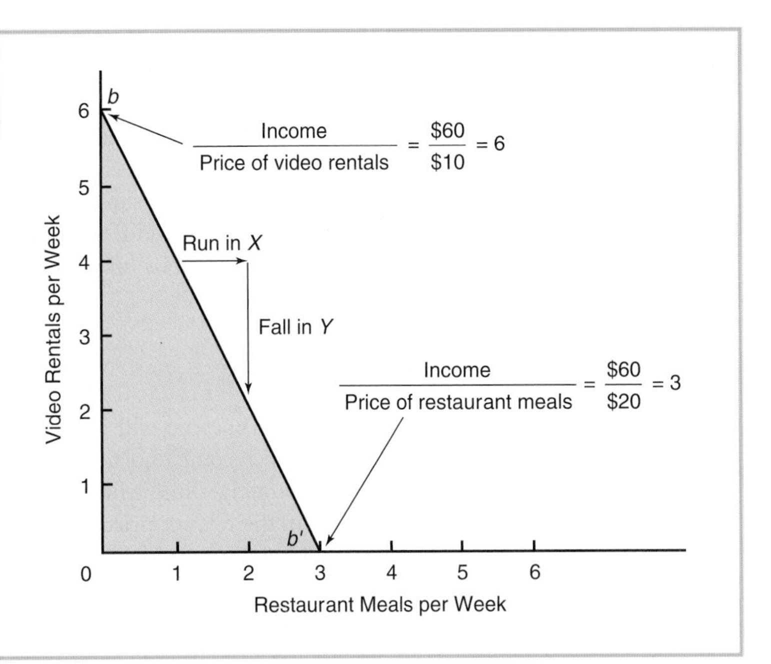

Consumer Optimum Revisited

Consumers will try to attain the highest level of total utility possible, given their budget constraints. How can this be shown graphically? We draw a set of indifference curves similar to those in Figure C–4, and we bring in reality—the budget constraint *bb′*. Both are drawn in Figure C–6. Because a higher level of total satisfaction is represented by a higher indifference curve, we know that the consumer will strive to be on the highest indifference curve possible. However, the consumer cannot get to indifference curve I_3 because the budget will be exhausted before any combination of video rentals and restaurant meals represented on indifference curve I_3 is attained. This consumer can maximize total utility, subject to the budget constraint, only by being at point E on indifference curve I_2 because here the consumer's income is just being exhausted. Mathematically, point E is called the tangency point of the curve I_2 to the straight line *bb′*.

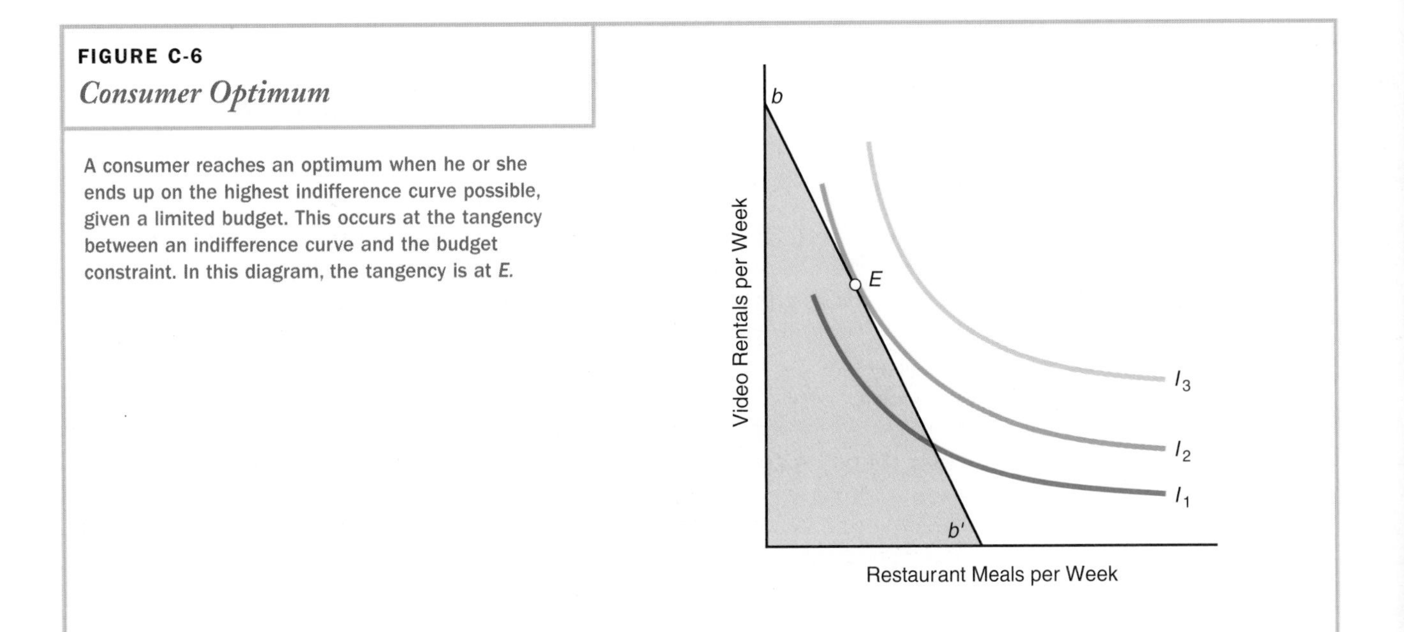

FIGURE C-6

Consumer Optimum

A consumer reaches an optimum when he or she ends up on the highest indifference curve possible, given a limited budget. This occurs at the tangency between an indifference curve and the budget constraint. In this diagram, the tangency is at *E*.

Consumer optimum is achieved when the marginal rate of substitution (which is subjective) is just equal to the feasible, or realistic, rate of exchange between video rentals and restaurant meals. This realistic rate is the ratio of the two prices of the goods involved. It is represented by the absolute value of the slope of the budget constraint. At point *E*, the point of tangency between indifference curve I_2 and budget constraint *bb′*, the rate at which the consumer wishes to substitute video rentals for restaurant meals (the numerical value of slope of the indifference curve) is just equal to the rate at which the consumer *can* substitute video rentals for restaurant meals (the slope of the budget line).

Effects of Changes in Income

A change in income will shift the budget constraint *bb′* in Figure C–6. Consider only increases in income and no changes in price. The budget constraint will shift outward. Each new budget line will be parallel to the original one because we are not allowing a change in the relative prices of video rentals and restaurant meals. We would now like to find out how an individual consumer responds to successive increases in income when relative prices remain constant. We do this in Figure C-7. We start out with an income that is represented by a budget line *bb′*. Consumer optimum is at point *E*, where the consumer attains the highest indifference curve I_1, given the budget constraint *bb′*. Now, we let income increase. This is shown by a shift outward in the budget line to *cc′*. The consumer attains a new optimum at point *E′*. That is where a higher indifference curve, I_2, is reached. Again, the consumer's income is increased so that the new budget line is *dd′*. The new optimum now moves to *E″*. This is where indifference curve I_3 is reached. If we connect the three consumer optimum points, *E*, *E′*, and *E″*, we have what is called an income-consumption curve. The **income–consumption curve** shows the set of optimum consumption points that would occur if income for that consumer were increased continuously, relative prices remaining constant. In our example, this means the prices of video rentals and restaurant meals remaining constant.

Income–consumption curve The set of optimum consumption points that would occur if income for a consumer were increased constantly, relative prices remaining constant.

The Price-Consumption Curve

In Figure C–8, we hold money income and the price of video rentals constant, while we lower the price of restaurant meals. As we keep lowering the price of restaurant meals, the

FIGURE C-7

Income–Consumption Curve

We start off with income sufficient to yield budget constraint *bb′*. The highest attainable indifference curve is I_1, which is just tangent to *bb′* at *E*. Next, we increase income. The budget line moves outward to *cc′*, which is parallel to *bb′*. The new highest indifference curve is I_2, which is just tangent to *cc′* at *E′*. We increase income again, which is represented by a shift in the budget line to *dd′*. The new tangency point of the highest indifference curve, I_3, with *dd′*, is at point *E″*. When we connect these three points, we obtain the income–consumption curve.

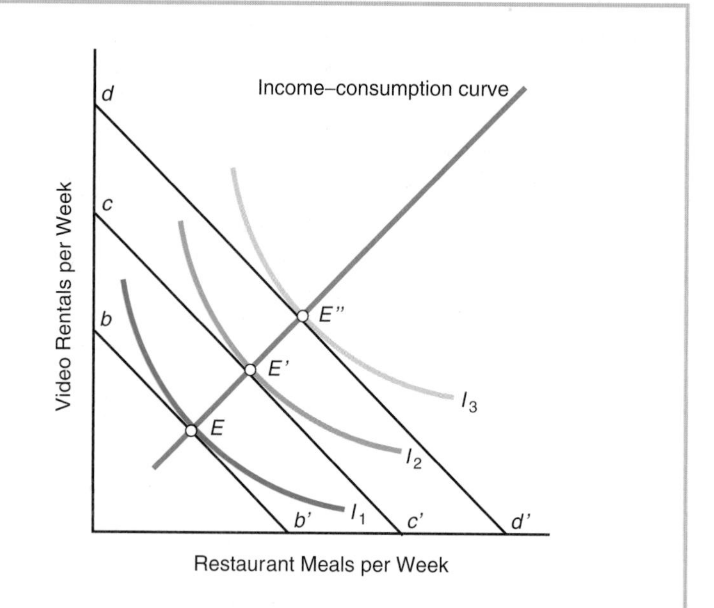

FIGURE C–8

Price–Consumption Curve

As we lower the price of restaurant meals, income measured in terms of restaurant meals per week increases. We show this by rotating the budget constraint from *bb′* to *bb″* and finally to *bb‴*. We then find the highest indifference curve that is attainable for each successive budget constraint. For budget constraint *bb′*, the highest indifference curve is I_1, which is tangent to *bb′* at point *E*. We do this for the next two budget constraints. When we connect the optimum points, *E*, *E′*, and *E″*, we derive the price–consumption curve, which shows the combinations of the two commodities that a consumer will purchase when money income and the price of one commodity remain constant while the other commodity's price changes.

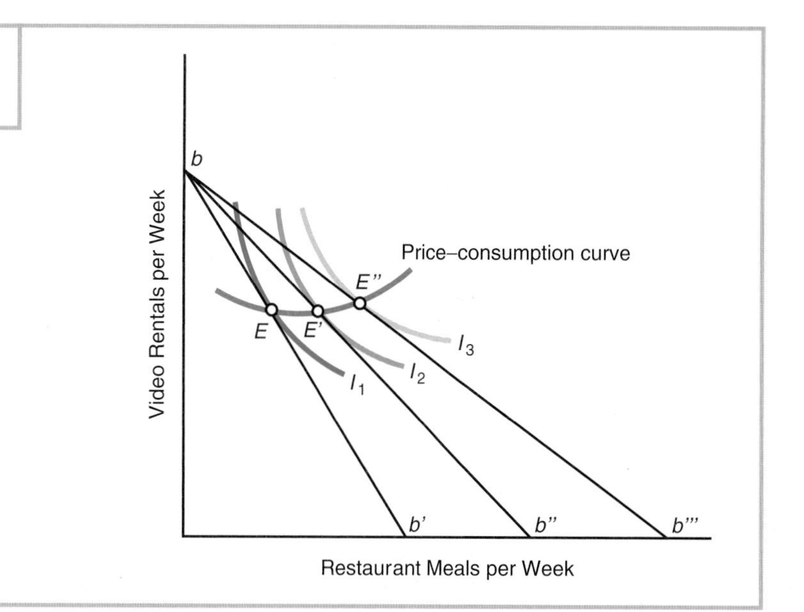

quantity of meals that could be purchased if all income were spent on restaurant meals increases; thus, the extreme points for the budget constraint keep moving outward to the right as the price of restaurant meals falls. In other words, the budget line rotates outward from *bb′* to *bb″* and *bb‴*. Each time the price of restaurant meals falls, a new budget line is formed. There has to be a new optimum point. We find it by locating on each new budget line the highest attainable indifference curve. This is shown at points *E*, *E′*, and *E″*. We see that as price decreases for restaurant meals, the consumer purchases more restaurant meals per week. We call the line connecting points *E*, *E′*, and *E″* the *price–consumption curve*. The **price–consumption curve** connects the tangency points of the budget constraints and indifference curves, thus showing the amounts of two goods that a consumer will buy when money income and the price of one commodity are held constant, while the price of the remaining good changes.

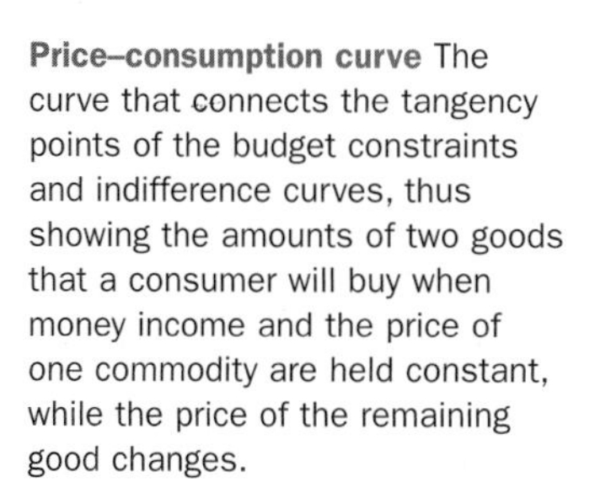

Price–consumption curve The curve that connects the tangency points of the budget constraints and indifference curves, thus showing the amounts of two goods that a consumer will buy when money income and the price of one commodity are held constant, while the price of the remaining good changes.

Deriving the Demand Curve

We are now in a position to derive the demand curve using indifference curve analysis. In part (a) of Figure C–9, we show what happens when the price of restaurant meals decreases, holding both the price of video rentals and income constant. If the price of restaurant meals decreases, the budget line rotates from *bb′* to *bb″*. The two optimum points are given by the tangency at the highest indifference curve that just touches those two budget lines. This is at *E* and *E′*. But those two points give us two price–quantity pairs. At point *E*, the price of restaurant meals is $20; the quantity demanded is 2. Thus, we have one point that we can transfer to part (b) of Figure C–9. At point *E′*, we have another price–quantity pair. The price has fallen to $10; the quantity demanded has increased to 5. We therefore transfer this other point to part (b). When we connect these two points (and all the others in between), we derive the demand curve for restaurant meals; it slopes downward.

FIGURE C-9
Deriving the Demand Curve

In part (a), we show the effects of a decrease in the price of restaurant meals from $20 to $10. At $20, the highest indifference curve touches the budget line *bb′* at point *E*. The quantity of restaurant meals consumed is 2. We transfer this combination—price, $20; quantity demanded, 2—down to part (b). Next, we decrease the price of restaurant meals to $10. This generates a new budget line, or constraint, which is *bb″*. Consumer optimum is now at *E′*. The optimum quantity of restaurant meals demanded at a price of $10 is five. We transfer this point—price, $10; quantity demanded, 5—down to part (b). When we connect these two points, we have a demand curve, *D*, for restaurant meals.

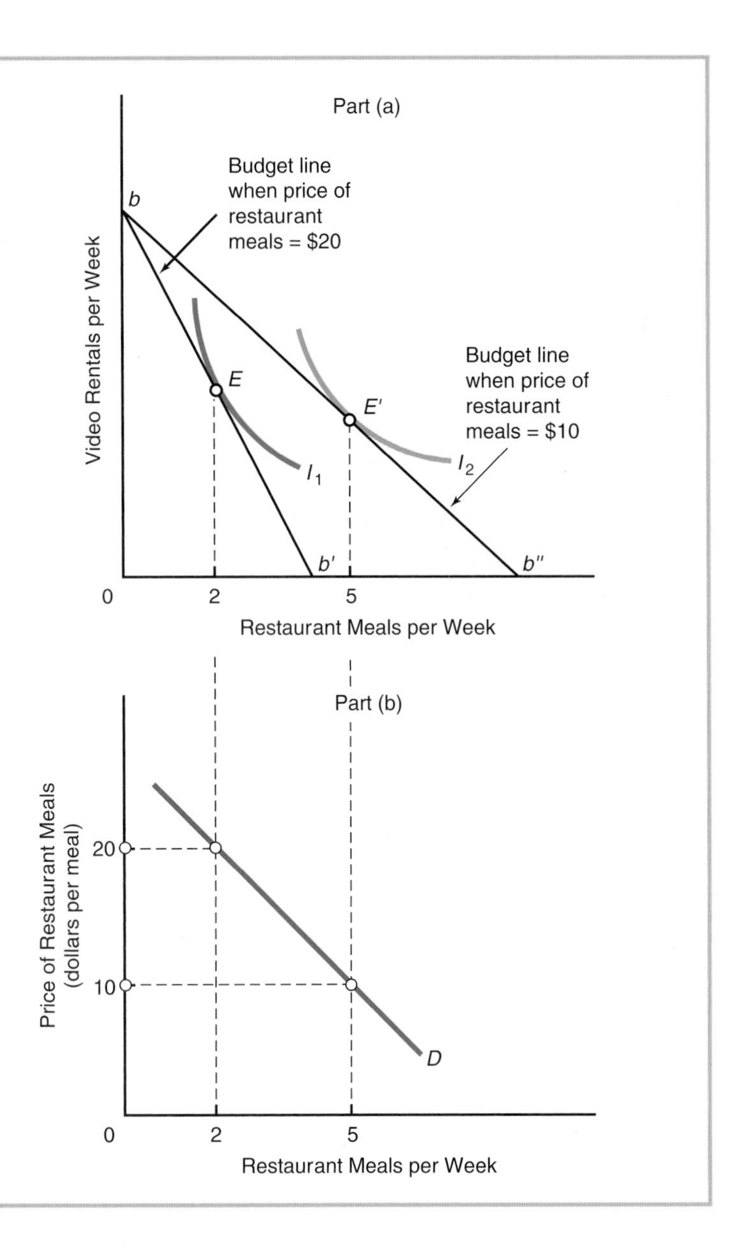

APPENDIX SUMMARY

1. Along an indifference curve, the consumer experiences equal levels of satisfaction. That is to say, along any indifference curve, every combination of the two goods in question yields exactly the same level of satisfaction.
2. Indifference curves usually slope downward and are usually convex to the origin.
3. To measure the marginal rate of substitution, we find out how much of one good has to be given up in order to allow the consumer to consume one more unit of the other good while still remaining on the same indifference curve. The marginal rate of substitution falls as one moves down an indifference curve.
4. Indifference curves represent preferences. A budget constraint represents opportunities—how much can be purchased with a given level of income. Consumer optimum is obtained when the highest indifference curve is just tangent to the budget constraint line; at that point, the consumer reaches the highest feasible indifference curve.
5. When income increases, the budget constraint shifts outward to the right, parallel to the previous budget constraint line.
6. As income increases, the consumer optimum moves up to higher and higher indifference curves. When we connect those points with a line, we derive the income–consumption curve.
7. As the price of one good decreases, the budget line rotates. When we connect the tangency points of the highest indifference curves to these new budget lines, we derive the price–consumption curve.

APPENDIX PROBLEMS

(Answers to the odd-numbered problems appear at the back of the book.)

C-1. Suppose that a consumer prefers A to B and B to C but insists that she also prefers C to A. Explain the logical problem here.

C-2. Suppose that you are indifferent among the following three combinations of food (f) and drink (d): $1f$ and $10d$, $2f$ and $7d$, $3f$ and $2d$. Calculate the marginal rate of substitution in consumption between the two goods. Does the substitution of the third f imply a greater sacrifice of d than the second did?

C-3. Construct a budget line from the following information: nominal income of \$100 per week; price of beef, P_b, \$2 per pound; price of shelter, P_s, \$20 per week; all income is spent on beef and shelter. Suppose that your money income remains constant, the price of beef doubles to \$4 per pound, and the price of shelter falls to \$10 per week. Draw the new budget line. Are you now better off or worse off? What do you need to know before deciding?

C-4. Given the following three combinations of goods, $A = 3x + 4y$, $B = 4x + 6y$, and $C = 5x + 4y$, answer the following questions:

a. Is any one bundle preferred to the other two?

b. Could a consumer possibly find B and C to be equally acceptable? How about A and C?

C-5. Calculate the marginal rate of substitution of burritos for yogurt for the following consumer's indifference schedule:

Servings of Yogurt per Week	Burritos per Week
10	1
6	2
3	3
1	4

C-6. Assume that you are consuming only yogurt (Y) and gymnasium exercise (G). Each serving of yogurt costs \$4, and each visit to the gym costs \$8. Given your food and exercise budget, you consume 15 servings of yogurt and five visits to the gym each week. One day, the price of yogurt falls to \$3 per serving and the price of gym visits increases to \$10. Now you buy 20 servings of yogurt and four gym visits per week.

a. Draw the old and new budget constraints, and show the two equilibrium bundles of yogurt servings and visits to the gym.

b. What is your weekly budget for food and exercise?

C-7. Explain why each of the following statements is or is not consistent with our assumptions about consumer preferences:

a. I cannot decide whether to go abroad this summer or to stay at home.

b. That is mine. You cannot have it. There is nothing you can do to make me change my mind.

c. I love hot pretzels with mustard at football games. If I had my way, I would never stop eating them.

CHAPTER 7

Rents, Profits, and the Financial Environment of Business

Brokerage firms conduct security analysis, which involves studying shares and bonds and forecasting the prospects for changes in their market prices. Clients who pay brokerage firms for this information believe they can gain from acting on it. In fact, it turns out that trading on the basis of *publicly available* investment suggestions of brokerage firms, including those that are available at no charge, could enable investors to earn higher *gross* returns on bonds and shares (but not higher *net* returns).

When brokerage firms develop their recommendations, the key factors they consider are market interest rates and the profitability of companies that issue shares and bonds. In this chapter, you will learn why information about these factors affects share and bond prices.

LEARNING OBJECTIVES

After reading this chapter, you will be able to:

7.1 Explain the concept of economic rent.

7.2 Explain the three forms of business an organization can choose.

7.3 Distinguish between accounting profits and economic profits.

7.4 Distinguish between real and nominal interest rates and calculate the present value of future sums.

7.5 Explain the three primary sources corporations use to finance their business.

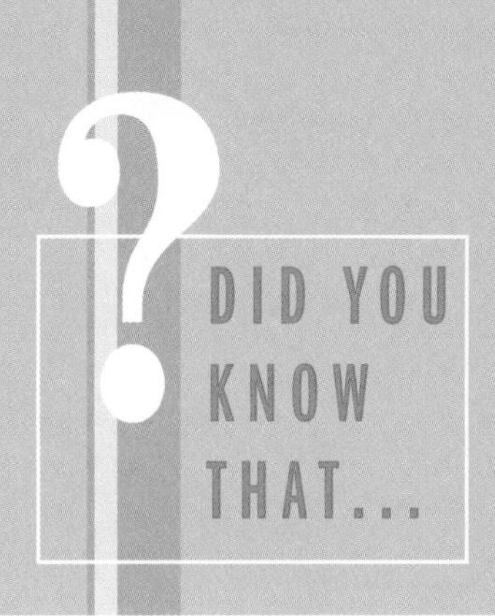

In Canada, one of the most industrialized countries in the world today, compensation for labour services makes up over 70 percent of national income every year. But what about the other 30 percent? It consists of compensation to the owners of the other factors of production. Somebody owns the real estate downtown for which the monthly commercial rents are higher for one square metre than you might pay to rent a whole apartment in the suburbs. Land, obviously, is a factor of production, and it has a market clearing price. Businesses also have to use capital. Compensation for that capital is interest, and it, too, has a market clearing level. Some of you may have entrepreneurial ability that you offer to the marketplace. Your compensation is called profit. In this chapter, you will learn about the sources and functions of profit. You will learn about different forms of business.

7.1 Economic Rent

Economic rent A payment to the owner of a resource in excess of its opportunity cost.

When you hear the term *rent,* you normally think it means the payment made to property owners for the use of land or apartments. But, the term *rent* has a different meaning in economics. **Economic rent** is payment to the owner of a resource in excess of its opportunity cost—the payment that would be necessary to call forth production of that amount of the resource. Economists originally used the term *rent* to designate payment for the use of land. What was thought to be important about land was that its supply is completely inelastic. Hence, the supply curve for land is a vertical line; no matter what the prevailing market price for land, the quantity supplied will remain the same.

Determining Land Rent

The concept of economic rent is associated with the British economist David Ricardo (1772–1823). He looked at two plots of land on which grain was growing, one of which happened to be more fertile than the other. The owners of these two plots sold the grain that came from their pieces of land, but the one who owned the more fertile land grew more grain and therefore made more profits. According to Ricardo, the owner of the fertile land was receiving economic rents that came about not because of the landowner's hard work or ingenuity but, rather, because of an accident of nature. Ricardo asked his readers to imagine another scenario, that of walking up a road that starts out flat with no rocks and then becomes steeper and rockier. The value of the land falls as one walks up the hill. If a different person owns the top of the hill, rather than the bottom, the highland owner will receive very little in payment from, say, a farmer who wants to cultivate land for wheat production.

Here is how Ricardo analyzed economic rent for land. He first simplified his model by assuming that all land is equally productive. Then, Ricardo assumed that the quantity of land in a country is *fixed.* Graphically, then, in terms of supply and demand, we draw the supply curve of land vertically (zero price elasticity). In Figure 7–1, the supply curve of land is represented by *S.* If the demand curve is D_1, it intersects the supply curve, *S,* at price P_1. The entire amount of revenues obtained, $P_1 \times Q_1$, is labelled "Economic rent." If the demand for land increased to D_2, the equilibrium price would rise to P_2. Additions to economic rent are labelled "More economic rent." Note that the quantity of land remains insensitive to the change in price. Another way of stating this is that the supply curve is perfectly inelastic.

Economic Rent to Labour

Land and natural resources are not the only factors of production to which the analysis of economic rent can be applied. In fact, the analysis is probably more often applicable to labour.

FIGURE 7–1

Economic Rent

If, indeed, the supply curve of land were completely price inelastic in the long run, it would be depicted by S. At the quantity in existence, Q_1, any and all revenues are economic rent. If demand is D_1, the price will be P_1; if demand is D_2, price will rise to P_2. Economic rent would be $P_1 \times Q_1$ and $P_2 \times Q_1$, respectively.

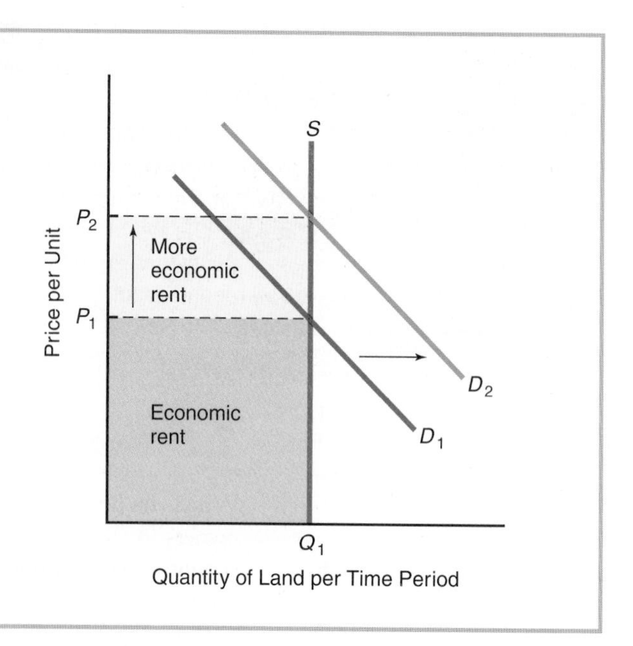

Here is a list of people who provide different labour services, some of whom probably receive large amounts of economic rent:

- Professional sports superstars
- Rock stars
- Movie stars
- World-class models
- Successful inventors and innovators
- World-famous opera stars

Just apply the definition of economic rent to the phenomenal earnings of these people. Undoubtedly, the amount of work they put in is not reflected in the money that they are paid. Therefore, much of their earnings constitutes economic rent (but not all, as we shall see). Economic rent occurs because specific resources cannot be replicated exactly. No one can duplicate today's most highly paid entertainment personalities, and therefore they receive economic rent.

Economic Rent and the Allocation of Resources

If an extremely highly paid movie star would make the same number of movies at half that individual's current annual earnings, does that mean that 50 percent of the star's income is unnecessary? To answer the question, consider first why the superstar gets such a high income. The answer can be found in Figure 7–1. Substitute *entertainment activities of the superstars* for the word *land.* The high "price" received by the superstar is due to the demand for that person's services. If Leonardo DiCaprio announces that he will work for a measly $1 million a movie and do two movies a year, how is he going to know which production company values his services the most highly? DiCaprio and other movie stars let the market decide where their resources should be used. In this sense, we can say the following:

Economic rent allocates resources to their highest-valued use.

In other words, economic rent directs resources to the people who can most efficiently use them.

A common counterexample involves rock stars who claim that their tickets are overpriced. Consequently, they agree to perform, say, five concerts with all tickets being sold at the same price, $15. Assume that a star performs these concerts in halls with 20 000 seats. A total of 100 000 individuals per year will be able to attend this particular performer's shows. This is represented by point *A* in Figure 7–2. By assumption, this performer is still receiving some economic rent because we are assuming that the supply curve of concerts is vertical at 100 000 seats per year. At a price per ticket of $15, however, the

FIGURE 7–2

The Allocative Function of Rent

If the performer agrees to give five concerts a year "at any price" and there are 20 000 seats in each concert hall, the supply curve of concerts, *S*, is vertical at 100 000 seats per year. The demand curve is given by *D*. The performer wants a price of only $15 to be charged. At that price, the quantity of seats demanded per year is 150 000. The excess quantity demanded is equal to the horizontal distance between points *A* and *B*, or 50 000 seats per year.

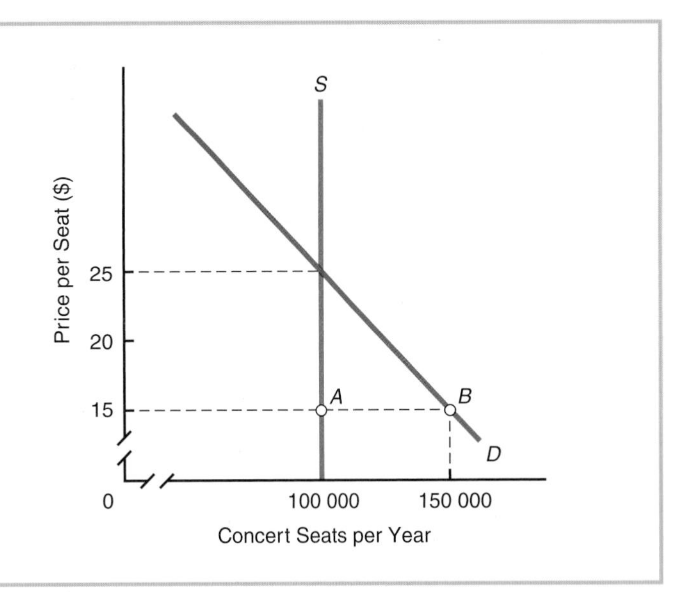

annual quantity of seats demanded will be 150 000, represented by point *B*. The difference between points *A* and *B* is the excess quantity of tickets demanded at the below-market-clearing price of $15 a seat. The *additional* economic rent that could be earned by this performer by charging the clearing price of $25 per seat in this graph would serve as the rationing device that would make the quantity demanded equal to the quantity supplied.

In such situations, which are fairly common, part of the economic rent that could have been earned is dissipated—it is captured, for example, by radio station owners in the form of promotional gains when they are allowed to give away a certain number of tickets on the air (even if they have to pay $15 per ticket) because the tickets are worth $25. Ticket holders who resell tickets at higher prices ("scalpers") also capture part of the rent. Conceivably, at 100 000 seats per year, this performer could charge the market clearing price of $25 per ticket and give away to charity the portion of the economic rent ($10 per ticket) that would be dissipated. Now, refer to Example 7–1.

EXAMPLE 7–1

Do Entertainment Superstars Make Super Economic Rents?

Superstars certainly do well financially. Table 7–1 shows the earnings of selected individuals in the entertainment industry as estimated by *Forbes* magazine. Earnings are totalled for a two-year period. How much of these earnings can be called economic rent? The question is not easy to answer because an entertainment newcomer would also almost certainly work for much less than he or she earns, thereby making high economic rents. The same cannot necessarily be said for entertainers who have been raking in millions for years. They probably have very large accumulated wealth and also a more jaded outlook about their work. It is, therefore, not clear how much they would work if they were not offered those huge sums of money.

continued

TABLE 7-1
Superstar Earnings

Name	Occupation	Annual Earnings
George Lucas	Director, producer, studio owner	$200 000 000
Oprah Winfrey	Talk show host	150 000 000
Steven Spielberg	Director, producer, studio owner	100 000 000
U2	Rock group	69 000 000
Mariah Carey	Pop singer	58 000 000
Dave Matthews Band	Rock band	50 000 000
Adam Sandler	Writer, producer	47 000 000
Bruce Willis	Actor	46 000 000
Tom Hanks	Actor	45 000 000
Madonna	Pop singer	43 000 000

SOURCE: *FORBES*, 2000.

For critical analysis: Even if some superstar entertainers would work for less, what forces cause them to make so much income anyway?

Taxing Away Economic Rent

Some people have argued in favour of imposing high taxes on economic rent. For example, drug companies that have developed *successful* patented drugs make large amounts of economic rent during the life of the patent. That is to say, the marginal cost of production is much less than the price charged. If the government taxed this economic rent completely, those successful drugs already on the market would, in fact, stay on the market. But there would be long-run consequences. Drug companies would invest fewer resources in discovering new successful drugs. So, economic rent is typically a *short-run* phenomenon. In the long run, it constitutes a source of reward for risk taking in society. This is true not only in the drug business but also in entertainment and professional sports.

CONCEPTS IN BRIEF

Learning Objective 7.1: Explain the concept of economic rent.

- Economic rent is defined as payment for a factor of production that is completely inelastic in supply. It is payment for a resource over and above what is necessary to keep that resource in existence at its current level in the long run.
- Economic rent serves an allocative function by guiding available supply to the most efficient use.

7.2 The Legal Organization of Firms

We all know that firms differ from one another. Some sell frozen yogurt, others make automobiles; some advertise, some do not; some have annual sales of a few thousand dollars, others have sales in the billions of dollars. The list of differences is probably endless. Yet for all this diversity, the basic organization of *all* firms can be thought of in terms of a few simple structures, the most important of which are the sole proprietorship, the partnership, and the corporation.

Sole proprietorship A business owned by a single individual who makes the business decisions, receives all the profits, and is legally responsible for all the debts of the firm.

Sole Proprietorships

The most common form of business organization is the *sole proprietorship*. A **sole proprietorship** is owned by a single individual who makes the business decisions, receives all the profits, and is legally responsible for all the debts of the firm. Although sole proprietorships are numerous, generally they are rather small businesses, with annual sales typically under $50 000. For this reason, even though there are more than a million sole proprietorships in Canada, they account for only a small percent of all business revenues.

ADVANTAGES OF SOLE PROPRIETORSHIPS. Sole proprietorships offer several advantages as a form of business organization. First, they are *easy to form and to dissolve.* In the simplest case, all one must do to start a business is to start working; to dissolve the firm, one simply stops working. Even a more complicated proposition, such as starting a restaurant or a small retail shop, involves only meeting broadly defined health and zoning rules and the payment of a modest business licence fee to the local government. To go out of business, one simply locks the front door. The second advantage of the sole proprietorship is that *all decision-making power resides with the sole proprietor.* The owner decides what and how much will be offered for sale, what the hours of operation will be, and who will perform what tasks. No partners, shareholders, or board of directors need be consulted. The third advantage is that its *profit is taxed only once.* All profit is treated by law as the net income of the sole proprietor and, as such, is subject only to personal income taxation.

Unlimited liability A legal concept whereby the personal assets of the owner of a firm can be seized to pay off the firm's debts.

DISADVANTAGES OF SOLE PROPRIETORSHIPS. The most important disadvantage of a sole proprietorship is that the sole proprietor faces **unlimited liability** *for the debts of the firm.* This means that the owner is personally responsible for all of the firm's debts. Thus, the owner's personal assets—home, car, savings account, coin collection—can be subject to seizure by the firm's creditors. The second disadvantage is that it has *limited ability to raise funds* to expand the business or even simply to help it survive bad times. Because the success of a sole proprietorship depends so heavily on the good judgment and hard work of but one person—the owner—many lenders are reluctant to lend large sums to a sole proprietorship. Thus, much of the financing of sole proprietorships often comes from the personal funds of the owner, which helps explain why sole proprietorships are usually small.

The third disadvantage of a sole proprietorship is that it normally *ends with the death of the sole proprietor.* This, of course, creates added uncertainty for prospective lenders or employees, for a freak accident or sudden illness can turn a prosperous firm into a bittersweet memory.

Partnerships

Partnership A business owned by two or more co-owners, or partners, who share the responsibilities of operating the firm and its profits, and they are *each* legally responsible for *all* of the debts incurred by the firm.

The second important form of business organization is the *partnership.* Partnerships are far less numerous than sole proprietorships but tend to be significantly larger, with average sales many times greater. A **partnership** differs from a sole proprietorship chiefly in that there are two or more co-owners, called partners, who share the responsibilities of operating the firm and its profits, and they are *each* legally responsible for *all* of the debts incurred by the firm. In this sense, a partnership may be viewed as a sole proprietorship with more than one owner. The partners may contribute equal or different amounts of financial capital to the firm, may have widely different operating responsibilities, and may share the profits in any way they see fit. Not surprisingly, partnerships share many of the advantages and disadvantages of sole proprietorships.

ADVANTAGES OF PARTNERSHIPS. The first advantage of a partnership is that it is *easy to form.* In fact, it is almost as easy as forming a sole proprietorship, except that it requires two or more participants. Second, partnerships, like sole proprietorships, often help *reduce the costs of monitoring job performance.* This is particularly true when interpersonal skills are important for successful performance and in lines of business where, even after the fact, it is difficult to measure performance objectively. Thus, lawyers and accountants often organize themselves as partnerships. In such professions as these, a spectacular success may consist of a greatly reduced jail term or a greatly reduced tax bill for a client. In such circumstances, partners have far more incentive to monitor their own work performance than they would as employees because the partners share in the profits of the firm. A third advantage of the partnership is that it *permits more effective specialization* in occupations where, for legal or other reasons, the multiple talents required for success are unlikely to be uniform across individuals. Finally, partnerships share with sole proprietorships the advantage that the income of the partnership is treated as personal income and, thus, is subject only to personal taxation.

DISADVANTAGES OF PARTNERSHIPS. Not surprisingly, partnerships also have their disadvantages. First, the *partners each have unlimited liability.* Thus, the personal assets of *each* partner are at risk due to debts incurred on behalf of the partnership by *any* of the partners. One partner's poor business judgment may impose substantial losses on all the other partners, a problem the sole proprietor need not worry about. Second, *decision making is generally more costly* in a partnership than in a sole proprietorship; there are more people involved in making decisions, and they may have differences of opinion that must be resolved before action is possible. Finally, *dissolution of the partnership is generally necessary* when a partner dies or voluntarily withdraws, or when one or more partners wish to remove someone from the partnership. As with sole proprietorships, this creates potential uncertainty for creditors and employees.

Corporations

Corporation A legal entity that may conduct business in its own name just as an individual does.

Limited liability A legal concept where if the corporation incurs debts that it cannot pay, creditors have no recourse to the shareholders' personal property.

A **corporation** is a legal entity that may conduct business in its own name just as an individual does. The owners of a corporation are called *shareholders* because they own shares of the profits earned by the firm. By law, shareholders enjoy **limited liability**, which means that if the corporation incurs debts that it cannot pay, creditors have no recourse to the shareholders' personal property. Corporations are far less numerous than sole proprietorships, but because of their large size, they are responsible for over 90 percent of all business revenues in Canada. Many, such as Seagram, Petro-Canada, McCain Foods Limited, and Canadian Tire, are so large that their annual sales are measured in billions of dollars and their names are household words.

ADVANTAGES OF CORPORATIONS. The fact that corporations conduct most of the nation's business suggests that the corporation offers significant advantages as a form of business organization. Perhaps the greatest of these is that the owners of a corporation (the shareholders) enjoy *limited liability.* The liability of shareholders is limited to the value of their shares. The second advantage arises because the law treats a corporation as a legal entity in and of itself; thus, the corporation *continues to exist* even if one or more owners cease to be owners. A third advantage of the corporation stems from the first two: Corporations are well positioned for *raising large sums of financial capital.* People are able to buy ownership shares or lend money to the corporation knowing that their liability is limited to the amount of money they invest and that the corporation's existence does not depend on the life of any one of the firm's owners.

Dividends Portion of a corporation's profits paid to its owners (shareholders).

DISADVANTAGES OF CORPORATIONS. The chief disadvantage of the corporation is the fact that corporate income is subject to *double taxation.* The profits of the corporation are subject first to corporate taxation. This is followed by **dividends**—a portion of a corporation's profits paid to its owners (shareholders). Such payments are treated as personal income to the shareholders and subject to personal taxation. The combined effect is that owners of corporations pay about twice as much in taxes on corporate income as they do on other forms of income.

A second disadvantage of the corporation is that corporations are potentially subject to problems associated with the *separation of ownership and control.* Specifically, it is common for the owners (shareholders) of corporations to have little, if anything, to do with the actual management of the firm. Instead, these tasks are handled by professional managers who may have little or no ownership interest in the firm. The objective of the shareholders is presumably to maximize the value of their holdings. Unless their sole compensation is in the form of shares in the corporation, however, the objective of the managers may differ from this. For example, managers may choose to have more luxurious offices than are needed for the efficient operation of the firm. If there are costs to the shareholders in preventing such behaviour, the result may be that the market value of the firm is not maximized.

In principle, such problems could arise with a partnership or a sole proprietorship if the owner or partners hired a manager to take care of day-to-day operations. Nevertheless, the separation of ownership and control is widely regarded as a more important problem for corporations; their attractiveness as a means of raising financial capital from many investors makes them subject to higher costs of agreement among owners with respect to penalties for managers who fail to maximize the value of the firm.

CONCEPTS IN BRIEF

Learning Objective 7.2: Explain the three forms of business an organization can choose.

- Sole proprietorships are the most common form of business organization. Each is owned by a single individual who makes all business decisions, receives all the profits, and has unlimited liability for the firm's debts.
- Partnerships are much like sole proprietorships, except that two or more individuals, or partners, share the decisions and the profits of the firm. In addition, each partner has unlimited liability for the debts of the firms.
- Corporations are responsible for the largest share of business revenues. The owners, called shareholders, share in the firm's profits but normally have little responsibility for the firm's day-to-day operations. They enjoy limited liability for the debts of the firm.

7.3 The Profits of a Firm

Most people think of a firm's profit as the difference between the amount of revenues the firm takes in and the amount it spends for wages, materials, and so on. In a bookkeeping sense, the following formula could be used:

$$\text{Accounting profit} = \text{Total revenue} - \text{Explicit costs}$$

Explicit costs Expenses that business managers must take account of because they must actually be paid out by the firm.

Accounting profit Total revenue minus total explicit costs.

Implicit costs Expenses that business managers do not have to pay out of pocket.

where **explicit costs** are expenses that business managers must take account of because they must actually be paid out by the firm. This definition of profit is known as **accounting profit**, total revenue minus total explicit costs. It is appropriate when used by accountants to determine a firm's taxable income. Economists are more interested in how firm managers react not just to changes in explicit costs but also to changes in **implicit costs**, defined as expenses that business managers do not have to pay out of pocket but are costs to the firm nonetheless because they represent an opportunity cost. They do not involve any direct cash outlay by the firm and must therefore be measured by the *alternative cost principle*. That is to say, they are measured by what the resources (land, capital) currently used in producing a particular good or service could earn in other uses. Economists use the full opportunity cost of all resources (including both explicit and implicit costs) as the figure to subtract from revenues to obtain a definition of profit. Another definition of implicit cost is therefore the opportunity cost of using factors that a producer does not buy or hire but already owns.

Opportunity Cost of Capital

Normal rate of return The amount that must be paid to an investor to induce investment in a business.

Firms enter or remain in an industry if they earn, at minimum, a **normal rate of return**—the amount that must be paid to an investor to induce investment in a business. People will not invest their wealth in a business unless they obtain a positive normal (competitive) rate of return—that is, unless their invested wealth pays off. Any business wishing to attract capital must expect to pay at least the same rate of return on that capital as all other businesses (of similar risk) are willing to pay. Put another way, when a firm requires the use of a resource in producing a particular product, it must bid against alternative users of that resource. Thus, the firm must offer a price that is at least as much as other potential users are offering to pay. For example, if individuals can invest their wealth in almost any publishing firm and get a rate of return of 10 percent per year, each firm in the publishing

Opportunity cost of capital The amount of income, or yield, that could have been earned by investing in the next-best alternative.

industry must *expect* to pay 10 percent as the normal rate of return to present and future investors. This 10 percent is a *cost to the firm*, the opportunity cost of capital. The **opportunity cost of capital** is the amount of income, or yield, that could have been earned by investing in the next-best alternative. Capital will not stay in firms or industries in which the expected rate of return falls below its opportunity cost, that is, what could be earned elsewhere. If a firm owns some capital equipment, it can either use it or lease it and earn a return. If the firm uses the equipment for production, part of the cost of using that equipment is the forgone revenue that the firm could have earned had it leased out that equipment.

Opportunity Cost of Owner-Provided Labour and Capital

Single-owner proprietorships often grossly exaggerate their profit rates because they understate the opportunity cost of the labour that the proprietor provides to the business. Here, we are referring to the opportunity cost of labour. Take, for example, people who run a small grocery store. These people will sit down at the end of the year and figure out what their "profits" are. They will add up all their sales and subtract what they had to pay to other workers, to their suppliers, in taxes, and so on. The end result they will call "profit." They normally will not, however, have figured into their costs the salary that they could have made if they had worked for somebody else in a similar type of job. By working for themselves, they become residual claimants—they receive what is left after all explicit costs have been accounted for. Part of the costs, however, should include the salary the owner-operator could have received working for someone else.

Consider a simple example of a skilled auto mechanic working 14 hours a day at his own service station, six days a week. Compare this situation with how much he could earn as a trucking company mechanic 84 hours a week. This self-employed auto mechanic might have an opportunity cost of about $20 an hour. For his 84-hour week in his own service station, he is forfeiting $1680. Unless his service station shows accounting profits of more than that per week, he is incurring losses in an economic sense.

Another way of looking at the opportunity cost of running a business is that opportunity cost consists of all explicit and implicit costs. Accountants only take account of explicit costs. Therefore, accounting profit ends up being the residual after only explicit costs are subtracted from total revenues.

This same analysis can apply to owner-provided capital, such as land or buildings. The fact that the owner owns the building or the land with which he or she operates a business does not mean that it is "free." Rather, use of the building and land still has an opportunity cost—the value of the next-best alternative use for those assets.

Some firms are nonprofit enterprises. Nevertheless, they face the same incentive to generate sufficient revenues or, in some cases, sufficient donations, to cover the opportunity cost of equipment and other capital resources.

POLICY EXAMPLE 7–1 **Nonprofit Firms Join in the Quest for Profits**

The American Medical Association and other leading medical societies are nonprofit organizations. This entitles them to special exemptions from taxes faced by for-profit companies.

The National Geographic Society now operates National Geographic Ventures, Inc., a for-profit firm that produces video documentaries, operates a mapping service, and manages retail outlets. The American Cancer Society earns millions of dollars each year in royalties from for-profit companies that it grants the right to use its name in for-profit marketing.

Profits earned by nonprofit organizations allow them to enlarge and facilitate their streams of cash inflows. This helps ensure that they cover the opportunity cost of capital. Nevertheless, profit-earning activities by nonprofit organizations are raising red flags. Are some of these organizations "nonprofit" only in name?

For critical analysis: Must nonprofit firms earn a normal rate of return?

Accounting Profits versus Economic Profits

The term profits in economics means the income that entrepreneurs earn, over and above all costs including their own opportunity cost of time, plus the opportunity cost of the capital they have invested in their business. Profits can be regarded as total revenues minus total costs—which is how accountants think of them—but we must now include *all* costs. Our definition of **economic profits** will be the following:

Economic profits Total revenues minus total opportunity costs of all inputs used, or total revenues minus the total of all implicit and explicit costs.

Economic profits = Total revenues − Total opportunity cost of all inputs used

or

Economic profits = Total revenues − (Explicit + Implicit costs)

Remember that implicit costs include a normal rate of return on invested capital. We show this relationship in Figure 7–3.

The Goal of the Firm: Profit Maximization

When we examined the theory of consumer demand, utility (or satisfaction) maximization by the individual provided the basis for the analysis. In the theory of the firm and production, *profit maximization* is the underlying hypothesis of our predictive theory. The goal of the firm is to maximize economic profits, and the firm is expected to try to make the positive difference between total revenues and total costs as large as it can.

Our justification for assuming profit maximization by firms is similar to our belief in utility maximization by individuals. To obtain labour, capital, and other resources required to produce commodities, firms must first obtain financing from investors. In general, investors are indifferent about the details of how a firm uses the funds they provide. They are most interested in the earnings on these funds and the risk of obtaining lower returns or losing the funds they have invested. Firms that can provide relatively higher risk-corrected returns will, therefore, have an advantage in obtaining the financing needed to continue or expand production. Over time, we would expect a policy of profit maximization to become the dominant mode of behaviour for firms that survive.

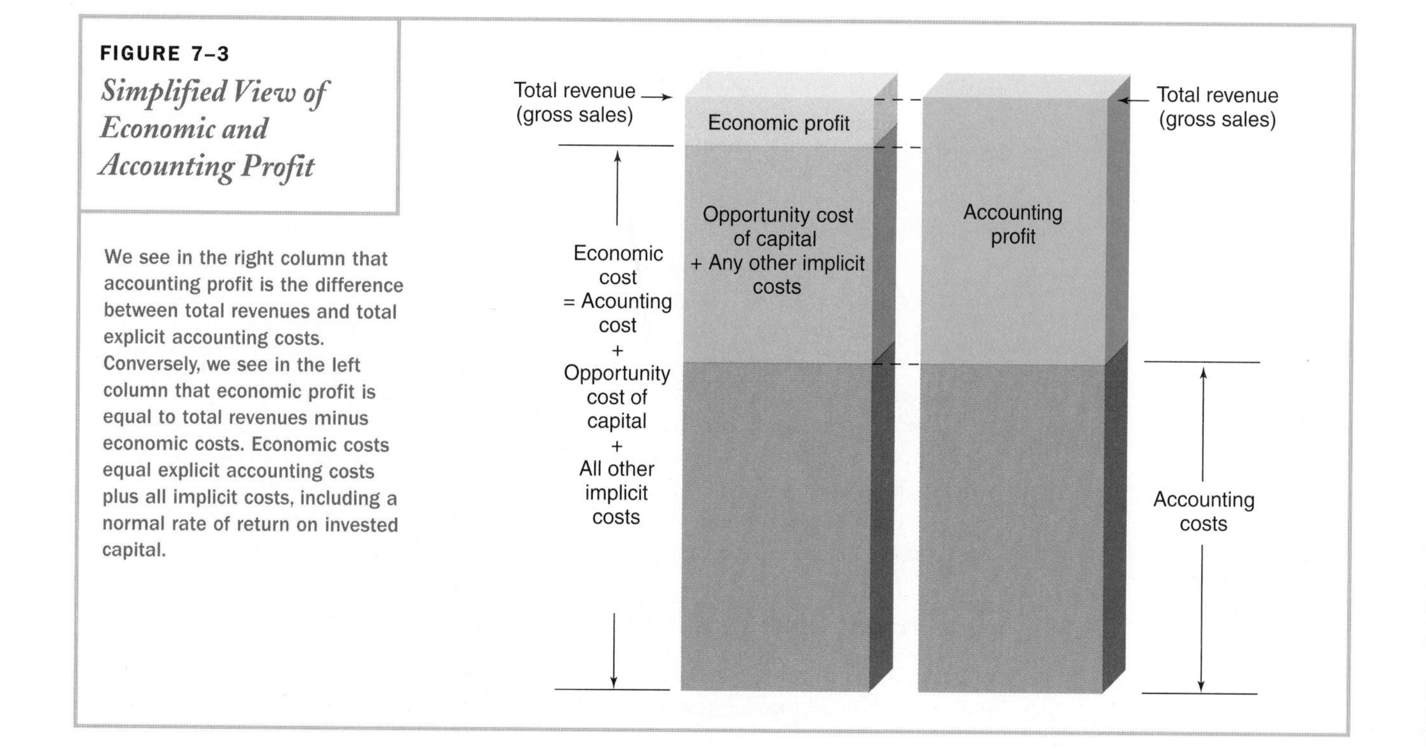

FIGURE 7–3
Simplified View of Economic and Accounting Profit

We see in the right column that accounting profit is the difference between total revenues and total explicit accounting costs. Conversely, we see in the left column that economic profit is equal to total revenues minus economic costs. Economic costs equal explicit accounting costs plus all implicit costs, including a normal rate of return on invested capital.

CONCEPTS IN BRIEF

Learning Objective 7.3: Distinguish between accounting profits and economic profits.

- Accounting profits differ from economic profits. Economic profits are defined as total revenues minus total costs, where costs include the full opportunity cost of all of the factors of production plus all other implicit costs.
- The full opportunity cost of capital invested in a business is generally not included as a cost when accounting profits are calculated. Thus, accounting profits often overstate economic profits. We assume throughout that the goal of the firm is to maximize economic profits.

7.4 Interest

Financial capital Funds used to purchase physical capital goods, such as buildings and equipment.

The term *interest* is used to mean two different things: (1) the price paid by debtors to creditors for the use of loanable funds and (2) the market return earned by (nonfinancial) capital as a factor of production. Owners of capital, whether directly or indirectly, obtain interest income. Often businesses go to credit markets to obtain so-called **financial capital**—funds used to purchase physical capital goods, such as buildings and equipment—from which they hope to make a satisfactory return. In other words, in our complicated society, the production of capital goods often occurs because of the existence of credit markets in which borrowing and lending take place. For the moment, we will look only at the credit market.

Interest and Credit

Interest The payment for current rather than future command over resources; the payment for obtaining credit. Also, the return paid to owners of capital.

When you obtain credit, you actually obtain funds to have command over resources today. We can say, then, that **interest** is the payment for current, rather than future, command over resources. Thus, interest is the payment for obtaining credit. If you borrow $100 from me, you have command over $100 worth of goods and services today. I no longer have that command. You promise to pay me back $100 plus interest at some future date. The interest that you pay is usually expressed as a percentage of the total loan, calculated on an annual basis. If you pay me back $105 at the end of one year, the annual interest is $5 ÷ 100, or 5 percent. When you go out into the marketplace to obtain credit, you will find that the interest rate charged differs greatly. A loan to buy a house (a mortgage) may cost you 6 to 9 percent in annual interest. An installment loan to buy an automobile may cost you 7 to 10 percent in annual interest. The federal government, when it wishes to obtain credit, may have to pay only 2 to 8 percent in annual interest. Variations in the rate of annual interest that must be paid for credit depend on the following factors.

1. *Length of loan.* In some (but not all) cases, the longer the loan will be outstanding, other things being equal, the greater will be the interest rate charged.
2. *Risk.* The greater the risk of nonrepayment of the loan, other things being equal, the greater is the interest rate charged. Risk is assessed on the basis of the creditworthiness of the borrower and whether the borrower provides collateral for the loan. Collateral consists of any asset that will automatically become the property of the lender should the borrower fail to comply with the loan agreement.
3. *Handling charges.* It takes resources to set up a loan. Papers have to be filled out and filed, credit references have to be checked, collateral has to be examined, and so on. The larger the amount of the loan, the smaller will be the handling (or administrative) charges as a percentage of the total loan. Therefore, we would predict that other things being equal, the larger the loan, the lower will be the interest rate.

Real versus Nominal Interest Rates

We have been assuming that there is no inflation. In a world of inflation—a persistent rise in an average of all prices—the *nominal rate of interest* will be higher than it would be in a

Nominal rate of interest The market rate of interest expressed in today's dollars.

world with no inflation. The **nominal rate of interest** is the market rate of interest expressed in today's dollars. Basically, nominal, or market, rates of interest rise to take account of the anticipated rate of inflation. If, for example, there is no inflation and no inflation is expected, the nominal rate of interest might be 5 percent for home mortgages. If the rate of inflation goes to 4 percent a year and stays there, everybody will anticipate that inflation rate. The nominal rate of interest will rise to about 9 percent to take account of the anticipated rate of inflation. If the interest rate did not rise to 9 percent, the principal plus interest earned at 5 percent would be worth less in the future because inflation would have eroded its purchasing power. We can, therefore, say that the nominal, or market, rate of interest is approximately equal to the real rate of interest plus the anticipated rate of inflation, or

$$i_n = i_r + \text{Anticipated rate of inflation}$$

where i_n equals the nominal rate of interest and i_r equals the real rate of interest. In short, you can expect to see high nominal rates of interest in periods of high inflation rates. The *real rate of interest* may not necessarily be high, though. The **real rate of interest** is the nominal rate of interest minus the anticipated rate of inflation. We must first correct the nominal rate of interest for the anticipated rate of inflation before determining whether the real interest rate is, in fact, higher than normal.

Real rate of interest The nominal rate of interest minus the anticipated rate of inflation.

The Allocative Role of Interest

We have talked about the price system and the role that prices play in the allocation of resources. Interest is a price that allocates loanable funds (credit) to consumers and to businesses. Within the business sector, interest allocates funds to different firms and therefore to different investment projects. Investment, or capital, projects with rates of return higher than the market rate of interest in the credit market will be undertaken, given an unrestricted market for loanable funds. For example, if the expected rate of return on the purchase of a new factory in some industry is 10 percent and funds can be acquired for 6 percent, the investment project may proceed. If, however, that same project had an expected rate of return of only 4 percent, it would not be undertaken. In sum, the interest rate allocates funds to industries whose investments yield the highest returns—where resources will be the most productive.

It is important to realize that the interest rate performs the function of allocating money capital and that this ultimately allocates real physical capital to various firms for investment projects.

Interest Rates and Present Value

Businesses make investments in which they often incur large costs today but do not make any profits until some time in the future. Somehow, they have to be able to compare their investment cost today with a stream of future profits. How can they relate present cost to future benefits?

Interest rates are used to link the present with the future. After all, if you have to pay $105 at the end of the year when you borrow $100, that 5 percent interest rate gives you a measure of the premium on the earlier availability of goods and services. If you want to have things today, you have to pay the 5 percent interest rate in order to have current purchasing power.

Present value The value of a future amount expressed in today's dollars.

The question could be put this way: What is the **present value** (the value of a future amount expressed in today's dollars) of $105 that you could receive one year from now? That depends on the market rate of interest, or the rate of interest that you could earn in some appropriate savings institution, such as in a savings account. To make the arithmetic simple, let us assume that the rate of interest is 5 percent. Now you can figure out the present value of $105 to be received one year from now. You figure it out by asking the question: "What sum must I put aside today at the market interest rate of 5 percent to receive $105 one year from now?"

Mathematically, we represent this equation as:

$$(1 + 0.05)PV_1 = \$105$$

where PV_1 is the sum that you must set aside now.

Let us solve this simple equation to obtain PV_1:

$$PV_1 = \frac{\$105}{1.05} = \$100$$

That is, \$100 will accumulate to \$105 at the end of one year with a market rate of interest of 5 percent. Thus, the present value of \$105 one year from now, using a rate of interest of 5 percent, is \$100. The formula for present value of any sums to be received one year from now thus becomes

$$PV_1 = \frac{FV_1}{1 + i}$$

where

PV_1 = Present value of a sum one year hence;

FV_1 = Future sum of money paid or received one year hence; and

i = Market rate of interest.

PRESENT VALUES FOR MORE DISTANT PERIODS. The present-value formula for figuring out today's worth of dollars to be received at a future date can now easily be seen. How much would have to be put in the same savings account today to have \$105 two years from now if the account pays a rate of 5 percent per year compounded annually?

The sum that would have to be set aside, PV_2, after one year would have grown to $PV_2 \times 1.05$. This amount during the second year would increase to $PV_2 \times 1.05 \times 1.05$, or $PV_2 \times (1.05)^2$. To find the PV_2 that would grow to \$105 over two years, let

$$PV_2 \times (1.05)^2 = \$105$$

and solve for PV_2:

$$PV_2 = \frac{\$105}{1.05^2} = \$95.24$$

Thus, the present value of \$105 to be paid or received two years hence, discounted at an interest rate of 5 percent per year compounded annually, is equal to \$95.24. In other words, \$95.24 put into a savings account yielding 5 percent per year compounded interest would accumulate to \$105 in two years.

THE GENERAL FORMULA FOR DISCOUNTING. The general formula for **discounting** becomes

Discounting The method by which the present value of a future sum or a future stream of sums is obtained.

$$PV_t = \frac{FV_t}{(1 + i)^t}$$

where t refers to the number of periods in the future the money is to be paid or received.

Table 7–2 gives the present value of \$1 to be received in future years at various interest rates. The interest rate used to derive the present value is called the **rate of discount**.

Rate of discount The interest rate used to derive the present value.

Each individual has his or her own *personal rate of discount*, which is the annual rate at which the individual discounts values to be received in future years. People with relatively low personal rates of discount are more willing to save funds today because they subjectively perceive a higher present value on future interest payments. Those with relatively high personal rates of discount are more likely to borrow because they perceive a lower present value on future interest payments. The market interest rate, therefore, lies between the upper and lower ranges of personal rates of discount.

TABLE 7-2

Present Value of a Future Dollar

This table shows how much a dollar received at the end of a certain number of years in the future is worth today. For example, at 5 percent a year, a dollar to be received 20 years in the future is worth 37.7 cents; if received in 50 years, it is not even worth a dime today. To find out how much $10 000 would be worth a certain number of years from now, just multiply the figures in the table by 10 000. For example, $10 000 received at the end of 10 years discounted at a 5 percent rate of interest would have a present value of $6140.

	Compounded Annual Interest Rate				
Year	3%	5%	8%	10%	20%
1	0.971	0.952	0.926	0.909	0.833
2	0.943	0.907	0.857	0.826	0.694
3	0.915	0.864	0.794	0.751	0.578
4	0.889	0.823	0.735	0.683	0.482
5	0.863	0.784	0.681	0.620	0.402
6	0.838	0.746	0.630	0.564	0.335
7	0.813	0.711	0.583	0.513	0.279
8	0.789	0.677	0.540	0.466	0.233
9	0.766	0.645	0.500	0.424	0.194
10	0.744	0.614	0.463	0.385	0.162
15	0.642	0.481	0.315	0.239	0.0649
20	0.554	0.377	0.215	0.148	0.0261
25	0.478	0.295	0.146	0.0923	0.0105
30	0.412	0.231	0.0994	0.0573	0.00421
40	0.307	0.142	0.0460	0.0221	0.000680
50	0.228	0.087	0.0213	0.00852	0.000109

CONCEPTS IN BRIEF

Learning Objective 7.4: Distinguish between real and nominal interest rates and calculate the present value of future sums.

- Interest is the price paid for the use of financial capital. It is also the cost of obtaining credit. In the credit market, the rate of interest paid depends on the length of the loan, the risk, and the handling charges, among other things.
- Nominal, or market, interest rates include a factor to take account of the anticipated rate of inflation. Therefore, during periods of high anticipated inflation, nominal interest rates will be relatively high.
- Payments received or costs incurred in the future are worth less than those received or incurred today. The present value of any future sum is lower the further it occurs in the future and the greater the discount rate used.

7.5 Corporate Financing Methods

When the Dutch East India Company was founded in 1602, it raised financial capital by selling shares of its expected future profits to investors. The investors thus became the owners of the company, and their ownership shares eventually became known as "shares of stock," or simply *stocks*. The company also issued notes of indebtedness, which involved borrowing funds in return for interest on the funds, plus eventual repayment of the principal amount borrowed. In modern parlance, these notes of indebtedness are called *bonds*. As the company prospered over time, some of its revenues were used to pay lenders the interest and principal owed them; of the profits that remained, some were paid to shareholders in the form of dividends, and some were retained by the company for reinvestment in further enterprises. The methods of financing used by the Dutch East India Company four centuries ago—shares, bonds, and reinvestment—remain the principal methods of financing for today's corporations.

Share A legal claim to a share of a corporation's future profits.

A **share** in a corporation is simply a legal claim to a share of the corporation's future profits. If there are 100 000 shares in a company and you own 1000 of them, you own the right to 1 percent of that company's future profits. If the shares you own are *common shares*, you also have the right to vote on major policy decisions affecting the company, such as the selection of the corporation's board of directors. Your 1000 shares would entitle you to cast 1 percent of the votes on such issues. If the shares you own are *preferred shares*, you own a share of the future profits of the corporation but do *not* have regular voting rights.

You do, however, get something in return for giving up your voting rights: preferential treatment in the payment of dividends. Specifically, the owners of preferred shares generally must receive at least a certain amount of dividends in each period before the owners of common shares can receive *any* dividends.

Bond A legal claim against a firm, entitling the owner of the bond to receive a fixed annual *coupon* payment, plus a lump-sum payment at the maturity date of the bond.

A **bond** is a legal claim against a firm, entitling the owner of the bond to receive a fixed annual *coupon* payment, plus a lump-sum payment at the maturity date of the bond.[1] Bonds are issued in return for funds lent to the firm; the coupon payments represent interest on the amount borrowed by the firm, and the lump-sum payment at maturity of the bond generally equals the amount originally borrowed by the firm. Bonds are *not* claims on the future profits of the firm; legally, bondholders must be paid whether the firm prospers or not. To help ensure this, bondholders generally receive their coupon payments each year, along with any principal that is due, before *any* shareholders can receive dividend payments.

Reinvestment When the firm uses some of its profits to purchase new capital equipment, rather than paying the profits out as dividends to shareholders.

Reinvestment takes place when the firm uses some of its profits to purchase new capital equipment, rather than paying the profits out as dividends to shareholders. Although sales of shares are an important source of financing for new firms, reinvestment and borrowing are the primary means of financing for existing firms. Indeed, reinvestment by established firms is such an important source of financing that it dominates the other two sources of corporate finance, amounting to roughly 75 percent of new financial capital for corporations in recent years. Also, small businesses, which are the source of much current growth, often cannot rely on the stock market to raise investment funds.

The Markets for Shares and Bonds

Securities Stocks and bonds.

Economists often refer to the "market for wheat" or the "market for labour," but these are concepts, rather than actual places. For **securities** (stocks and bonds), however, there really are markets—centralized, physical locations where exchange takes place. The largest stock exchange in Canada is the Toronto Stock Exchange (TSX), which accounts for over 80 percent of the value of shares traded on Canadian stock exchanges. Numerous other stock and bond markets, or exchanges, exist in various financial capitals of the world, such as London and Tokyo. Although the exact process by which exchanges are conducted in these markets varies slightly from one to another, the process used on the TSX is representative of the principles involved.[2]

More than 1700 companies' shares are traded on the TSX. Leading brokerage firms—about 100 of them—own seats on the TSX. These seats, which are actually rights to buy and sell shares on the floor of the TSX, are themselves regularly exchanged. In recent years, their value has fluctuated between $37 000 and $60 000 each. These prices reflect the fact that share trades on the TSX are ultimately handled by the firms owning these seats and the firms earn commissions on each trade.

As trading volume rises, as it did during the 1980s, the value of the seats rises. Read Example 7–2 for a better idea of how the market works.

---

[1]Coupon payments on bonds get their name from the fact that bonds once had coupons attached to them when they were issued. Each year, the owner would clip a coupon off the bond and send it to the issuing firm in return for that year's interest on the bond.

[2]A number of shares and bonds are traded in so-called over-the-counter (OTC) markets, which, although not physically centralized, otherwise operate in much the same way as the TSX and so are not treated separately in this text.

EXAMPLE 7-2 How to Read the Financial Press: Share Prices

Table 7–3, reproduced from *The Globe and Mail*, contains information about the shares of four companies. Across the top of the financial page are a series of column headings. Under the heading "Stock" we find the name of the company—in the first row, for example, is Molson Breweries, the beer maker. The two columns to the left of the company's name show the highest and lowest prices at which that company's shares traded during the past 52 weeks.

TABLE 7-3

Reading Share Quotes

52-week											
Hi	Lo	Stock	Sym	Div	Hi	Lo	Close	Chg	Vol (100s)	Yield	P/E Ratio
27.75	22.5	Molson	MOL.B	0.72	27.4	27.3	27.4	+0.15	40	2.6	62.3
11.75	9.75	Monrc Dv	MON	0.10	10.10	9.75	9.75	-0.25	655	1.0	16.8
0.65	0.115	Moneta Por j	ME	0.18	0.18		0.18		60		
32.00	23.10	Montrusco	MTA	0.84	29.50	29.00	29.00	-0.25	42	2.9	25.4

The summary of stock market information presented on the financial pages of many newspapers reveals the following:

52 weeks Hi/Lo: The highest and lowest prices, in dollars per share, of the shares during the previous 52 weeks

Stock: The name of the company (frequently abbreviated)

Sym: Highly abbreviated name of the company, as it appears on the stock exchange ticker tape

Div: Dividend paid, in dollars per share

Hi: Highest price at which the shares traded that day

Lo: Lowest price at which the shares traded that day

Close: Last price at which the shares traded that day

Chg: Net change in the share's price from the previous day's closing price

Vol (100s): Number of shares traded during the day, in hundreds of shares

Yield: Yield in percent per year; the dividend divided by the price of the share

P/E Ratio: Price–earnings ratio; the price of the shares divided by the earnings (profits) per share of the company

Immediately to the right of the company's name you will find the company's *symbol* on the TSX. This symbol (omitted by some newspapers) is simply the unique identifier used by the exchange when it reports information about the shares. For example, the designation MOL.B is used by the exchange as the unique identifier for the firm Molson Breweries.

The dividend column, headed "Div," shows the annual dividend (in dollars and cents) that the company has paid over the preceding year on each share. In Molson's case, this amounts to 72 cents per share.

The next four columns of information for each firm summarize the behaviour of the firm's share price on the latest trading day. On this particular day, the highest price at which Molson shares traded was $27.40, the lowest price was $27.30, and the last (or closing) price at which it traded was $27.40 per share. The *net change* in the price of Molson's shares was +$0.15, which means that it closed the day at a price of 15 cents per share higher than it *closed* the day before.

The "Yield" column is derived by dividing the dividend by the closing price of the shares. In Molson's case, the yield is 2.6 percent ($0.72 ÷ $27.40). In a sense, the company is paying interest on the shares at a rate of about 2.6 percent. The column heading "P/E" stands for *price–earnings ratio*. To obtain the entries for this column, the firm's total earnings (profits) for the year are divided by the number of the firm's shares in existence to give the earnings per share. When the price of the share is divided by the earnings per share, the result is the price–earnings ratio.

continued

The column to the left of the Yield column shows the total *volume* of the shares traded that day, measured in hundreds of shares.

For critical analysis: Is there necessarily any relationship between the net change in a share's price and how many shares have been sold on a particular day?

The Theory of Efficient Markets

At any point in time, there are tens of thousands, even millions, of persons looking for any bit of information that will enable them to forecast correctly the future prices of shares. Responding to any information that seems useful, these people try to buy low and sell high. The result is that all publicly available information that might be used to forecast share prices gets taken into account by those with access to the information and the knowledge and ability to learn from it, leaving no forecastable profit opportunities. And because so many people are involved in this process, it occurs quite swiftly. Indeed, there is some evidence that all information entering the market is fully incorporated into share prices within less than a minute of its arrival. One view is that any information about specific shares will prove to have little value by the time it reaches you.

Random walk theory The theory that the best forecast of tomorrow's price is today's price.

Consequently, share prices tend to follow a *random walk*, which is to say that the best forecast of tomorrow's price is today's price—called the **random walk theory**. Although large values of the random component of stock price changes are less likely than small values, nothing else about the magnitude or direction of a share price change can be predicted. Indeed, the random component of share prices exhibits behaviour much like what would occur if you rolled two dice and subtracted 7 from the resulting total. On average, the dice will show a total of 7, and so after you subtract 7, the average result will be zero. It is true that rolling a 12 or a 2 (resulting in a total of +5 or −5) is less likely than rolling an 8 or a 6 (yielding a total of +1 or −1). Nevertheless, positive and negative totals are equally likely, and the expected total is zero. See the Issues and Applications discussion on shares and bonds.

Inside Information

Inside information Information that is not available to the general public about what is happening in a corporation.

Isn't there any way to "beat the market"? The answer is yes—but normally only if you have **inside information**—information that is not available to the general public about what is happening in a corporation. Suppose that your best friend is in charge of new product development at the world's largest software firm, Microsoft Corporation. Your friend tells you that the company's smartest programmer has just come up with major new software that millions of computer users will want to buy. No one but your friend and the programmer—and now you—is aware of this. You could, indeed, make money using this information by purchasing shares of Microsoft and then selling them (at a higher price) as soon as the new product is publicly announced. There is one problem: stock trading based on inside information, such as this, is illegal, punishable by substantial fines and even imprisonment. So, unless you happen to have a stronger-than-average desire for a long vacation in a federal prison, you might be better off investing in Microsoft after the new program is publicly announced.

CONCEPTS IN BRIEF

Learning Objective 7.5: Explain the three primary sources corporations use to finance their business.

- The three primary sources of corporate funds are shares, bonds, and reinvestment of profits.
- A *share* is a share of ownership providing a legal claim to a corporation's future profits. A *bond* is a legal claim entitling the owner to a fixed annual coupon payment and to a lump-sum payment on the date the bond matures.

- Many economists believe that asset markets, especially the stock market, are efficient, meaning that one cannot make a higher-than-normal rate of return without having inside information (information that the general public does not possess). Share prices normally follow a random walk, meaning that you cannot predict changes in future share prices on the basis of information about share price behaviour in the past.

ISSUES AND APPLICATIONS

Can Investors Profit from Publicly Available Stock Tips?

Concepts Applied: Securities, Shares, Random Walk Theory

The trading floor can look inefficient at times.

When a stock market is efficient, all public information will be fully taken into account by stock traders. If traders act optimally with available information, therefore, share prices will fully reflect all information, and the best forecast of tomorrow's price of a share is the share's price today. The random walk theory will hold true.

Economists have found, however, that traders could earn higher gross returns—before subtracting transaction costs—if they were to buy and sell shares on the basis of publicly available recommendations of securities analysts. Does this mean that the stock market is not efficient?

Public Stock Recommendations and Unrealized Gains

Between the mid-1980s and late 1990s, more than 4000 securities market analysts associated with at least 250 brokerage firms issued public statements recommending shares to buy or sell. During this interval, an investor could have gained from following the suggestions of securities analysts at brokerage firms with the highest returns on trades the prior year. Suppose, for instance, that each year an investor had bought or sold shares recommended by the top fifth of brokerage firms with the best performances in the previous year. This individual would have earned an average annual gross rate of return at least 4 percentage points higher than if he or she had followed the suggestions of the lowest fifth of brokerage firms.

In addition, investors could have earned higher returns on their share holdings simply by following so-called consensus recommendations, the average publicly available suggestions of securities analysts at all brokerage firms. If any given investor had simply bought the shares with the most favourable consensus recommendations during these years, the average annual gross return would have been close to 19 percent. The average annual gross return that investors in the stock market actually earned, however, was about 14 percent.

On the face of it, investors apparently could have done better if they had traded on the basis of this freely available information. Evidently, there were available gains from using information that investors failed to realize.

Like Everything Else, Stock Trading Is Not Free

In an efficient stock market, people make the best possible use of information, and share prices reflect that fact. The failure of investors to buy or sell shares in response to consensus recommendations or on the basis of suggestions by the best-performing brokerage firms appears to contradict this condition.

There is a problem with this interpretation, however. Securities analysts issued more than 350 000 public recommendations between the mid-1980s and late 1990s. Earning the higher returns available from following public recommendations would have required investors to allocate more time to tracking recommendations and to conduct many more stock trades than they actually did. The brokerage fees investors would have incurred, it turns out, would have driven the *net* return from trying to follow analysts' recommendations down to or possibly even below the returns investors actually earned. Investors failed to follow all of the recommendations of securities analysts because doing so would not, in the end, have left them any better off. Share prices and returns, therefore, reflected all available information that investors could *profitably* use. This is fully consistent with the hypothesis that the stock market is efficient.

For critical analysis:

1. Why do you suppose that clients of brokerage firms are sometimes willing to pay for detailed recommendations about specific shares?
2. Why do you think that brokerage firms allow their securities analysts to make public statements about what shares to buy or sell? (Hint: Why might brokerage firms like for their analysts to be in the public spotlight?)

SUMMARY DISCUSSION OF LEARNING OBJECTIVES

7.1 **Economic Rent.** Resources that have a fixed supply are paid what is called economic rent. We therefore define economic rent as the payment over and above what is necessary to keep a resource of constant quality and quantity in supply at its current level.

Resource owners (including labour owners) of factors with inelastic supply earn economic rent because competition among potential users of those resources bids up the price offered.

7.2 **The Legal Organization of Firms.** Sole proprietorships are the most common form of business organization. Each is owned by a single individual who makes all business decisions, receives all the profits, and has unlimited liability for the firm's debts. Partnerships are much like sole proprietorships, except that two or more individuals, or partners, share the decisions and the profits of the firm; each partner has unlimited liability for the debts of the firm.

Corporations are responsible for the largest share of business revenues. The owners, called shareholders, share in the firm's profits but normally have little responsibility for the firm's day-to-day operations. Owners of corporations enjoy limited liability for the debts of the firm.

7.3 **The Profits of a Firm.** Accounting profits differ from economic profits. Economic profits are defined as total revenues minus total costs, where costs include the full opportunity cost of all factors of production plus all other implicit costs.

The full opportunity cost of capital invested in a business is generally not included as a cost. We assume throughout that the goal of the firm is to maximize profits.

7.4 **Interest.** Interest can be defined as the payment for command over resources today, rather than in the future. Interest is typically seen as the payment for credit, but it can also be considered the payment for the use of capital. Interest charged depends on length of loan, risk, and handling charges.

The nominal rate of interest includes a factor that takes account of the anticipated rate of inflation. In periods of high anticipated inflation, nominal interest rates will be high. Real interest rates may not actually be higher, however, because they are defined as the nominal rate of interest minus the anticipated rate of inflation.

The present value of any sum in the future is less than that same sum today. Present value decreases as the sum is paid or obtained further and further in the future and as the rate of discount increases.

7.5 **Corporate Financing Methods.** The three primary sources of corporate funds are shares, bonds, and reinvestment of profits.

A share is a share of ownership providing a legal claim to a corporation's future profits. A bond is a legal claim entitling the owner to a fixed annual coupon payment and to a lump-sum payment on the date the bond matures.

Share prices normally follow a random walk, meaning that you cannot predict changes in future share prices on the basis of information about share price behaviour in the past.

PROBLEMS

(Answers to the odd-numbered problems appear at the back of the book.)

LO 7.1 Explain the concept of economic rent.

1. Which of the following would you expect to have a high level of economic rent, and which would you expect to have a low level of economic rent? Explain why for each.
   a. Bob has a highly specialized medical skill that is in great demand.
   b. Sally has never attended school. She is 25 years old and is an internationally known supermodel.
   c. Tim is a high school teacher and sells insurance part-time.
2. Though he has retired from hockey, Wayne Gretzky still earns a sizable annual income from endorsements. Explain why, in economic terms, his level of economic rent is so high.
3. Michael Jordan once retired from basketball to play baseball. As a result, his annual dollar income dropped from the millions to the thousands. Eventually, Jordan quit baseball and returned to basketball. What can be said about the role of economic rents in his situation?
4. A British pharmaceutical company spent several years and considerable funds on the development of a treatment for HIV patients. Now, with the protection afforded by patent rights, the company has the potential to reap enormous gains. The government, in response, has threatened to tax away any economic rents the company may earn. Is this an advisable policy? Why, or why not?

LO 7.2 Explain the three forms of business an organization can choose.

5. Write a brief explanation of the difference between a sole proprietorship, a partnership, and a corporation. In addition, list one advantage and one disadvantage of a sole proprietorship, a partnership, and a corporation. Example 7–1, "Do Entertainment Superstars Make Super Economic Rents?", shows the salaries of various entertainers. Would these entertainers be better off setting themselves up as corporations? Why, or why not?

LO 7.3 Distinguish between accounting profits and economic profits.

6. After graduation, you face a choice. One option is to work for a multinational consulting firm and earn a starting salary (benefits included) of $40 000. The other option is to use $5000 in savings to start your own consulting firm. You could have earned an interest return of 5 percent on your savings. You choose to start your own consulting firm. At the end of the first year, you add up all of your expenses and revenues. Your total includes $12 000 in rent, $1000 in office supplies, $20 000 for office staff, and $4000 in telephone expenses. What are your total explicit costs and total implicit costs?
7. Suppose, as in Problem 6, that you choose to start your own consulting firm upon graduation. At the end of the first year, your total revenues are $77 250. On the basis of the information in Problem 6, what is the accounting profit, and what is your economic profit?
8. An individual leaves a college faculty, where she was earning $40 000 a year, to begin a new venture. She invests her savings of $10 000, which were earning 10 percent annually. She then spends $20 000 on office equipment, hires two students at $30 000 a year each, rents office space for $12 000, and has other variable expenses of $40 000. At the end of the year, her revenues are $200 000. What are her accounting profit and her economic profit for the year?

LO 7.4 Distinguish between real and nominal interest rates and calculate the present value of future sums.

9. Suppose that the interest rate in Japan is only 2 percent, while the comparable rate in Canada is 4 percent. Japan's rate of inflation is 0.5 percent, while the Canadian inflation rate is 3 percent. Which economy has the higher real interest rate?
10. You expect to receive a payment of $104 one year from now. Your discount rate is 4 percent. What is the present value of the payment to be received? Suppose that the discount rate is 5 percent. What is the present value of the payment to be received?

LO 7.5 Explain the three primary sources corporations use to finance their businesses.

11. Outline the differences between common shares and preferred shares.
12. Explain the basic differences between a share and a bond. Example 7-2, "How to Read the Financial Press: Share Prices," explains how to read share prices. If one of your friends informs you that he has developed a method of forecasting stock market returns based on past trends, should you invest with him?

CHAPTER 8

The Firm: Cost and Output Determination

Firms in any industry must always be aware of changing technologies. We have advanced from letters to e-mail, coal-burning furnaces to solar power, and gas-run automobiles to electric-powered, and still other advancements are just around the corner. What drives businesses to invest in new types of technology? What are the costs when technology fails, such as the blackout in the eastern seaboard of North America? To understand this issue, you must learn more about how businesses determine costs, profits, and output.

LEARNING OBJECTIVES

After reading this chapter, you should be able to:

8.1 Distinguish between the short run and the long run.

8.2 Calculate the various costs for the firm in the short run.

8.3 Explain why the long-run average cost curve is U-shaped.

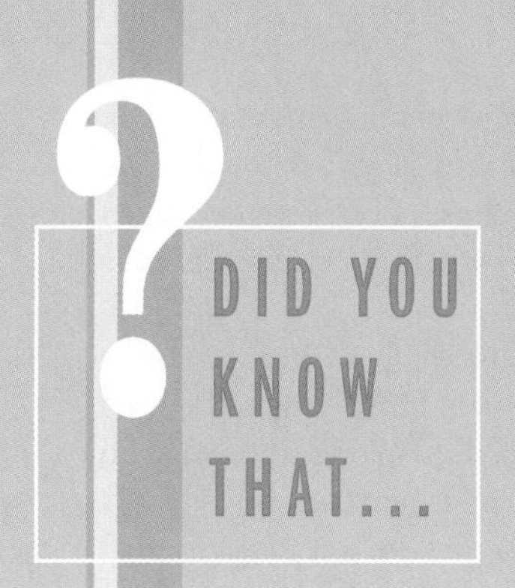

There are more than 25 steps in the process of manufacturing a simple lead pencil. In the production of an automobile, there are literally thousands. At each step, the manufacturer can have the job done by workers or machines or some combination of the two. The manufacturer must also figure out how much to produce each month. Should a new machine that can replace 10 workers be bought? Should more workers be hired, or should the existing workers be paid overtime? If the price of aluminum is rising, should the company try to make do with plastic? What you will learn about in this chapter is how producers can select the best combination of inputs for any given output that is desired.

Before we look at the firm's costs, we need to define a *firm*.

8.1 Short Run versus Long Run

The Firm

Firm An organization that brings together factors of production—labour, land, physical capital, human capital, and entrepreneurial skill—to produce a product or service that it hopes can be sold at a profit.

We define a business, or **firm**, as follows:

> A firm is an organization that brings together factors of production—labour, land, physical capital, human capital, and entrepreneurial skill—to produce a product or service that it hopes can be sold at a profit.

A typical firm will have an organizational structure consisting of an entrepreneur, managers, and workers. The entrepreneur is the person who takes the risks, mainly of losing personal wealth. In compensation, the entrepreneur will get any profits that are made. Entrepreneurs take the initiative in combining land, labour, and capital to produce a good or a service. Entrepreneurs are the ones who innovate in the form of new production and new products. The entrepreneur also decides whom to hire to manage the firm. Some economists maintain that the true quality of an entrepreneur becomes evident through the selection of managers. Managers, in turn, decide who should be hired or fired and how the business generally should be set up. The workers ultimately use the other inputs to produce the products or services that are being sold by the firm. Workers and managers are paid contractual wages. They receive a specified amount of income for a specified time period. Entrepreneurs are not paid contractual wages. They receive no reward specified in advance. The entrepreneurs make profits, if there are any, for profits accrue to those who are willing to take risks. Because the entrepreneur gets only what is left over after all expenses are paid, that individual is often referred to as a *residual claimant*. The entrepreneur lays claim to the residual—whatever is left. You might want to refer back to Section 7.3 in Chapter 7 for our discussion of explicit and implicit costs and the profits of a firm.

We have discussed short-run and long-run price elasticities of supply and demand. For consumers, the long run meant the time period during which all adjustments to a change in price could be made, and anything shorter than that was considered the short run. For suppliers, the long run was the time in which all adjustments could be made, and anything shorter than that was the short run.

Now that we are discussing firms only, we will maintain a similar distinction between the short and the long run, but we will be more specific. In the theory of the firm, the **short run** is defined as any time period that is so short that there is at least one input, such as current **plant size** (the physical size of the factories that a firm owns and operates to produce its output), that the firm cannot alter.[1] In other words, during the short run, a firm makes do with whatever big machines and factory size it already has, no matter how much more it wants to produce because of increased demand for its product. We consider the plant and heavy equipment, the size or amount of which cannot be varied in the short run, as fixed resources. In agriculture and in some other businesses, land may be a fixed resource.

Short run Any time period that is so short that there is at least one input that the firm cannot alter.

Plant size The physical size of the factories that a firm owns and operates to produce its output.

[1]There can be many short runs but only one long run. For ease of analysis, in this section we simplify the case to one short run and talk about short-run costs.

There are, of course, variable resources that the firm can alter when it wants to change its rate of production. These are called *variable inputs* or *variable factors of production.* Typically, the variable inputs of a firm are its labour and its purchases of raw materials. In the short run, in response to changes in demand, the firm can, by definition, vary only its variable inputs.

Long run The period of time in which *all* inputs can be varied.

The **long run** can now be considered the period of time in which *all* inputs can be varied. Specifically, in the long run, the firm can alter its plant size. How long is the long run? That depends on each individual industry. For Wendy's or McDonald's, the long run may be four or five months because that is the time it takes to add new franchises. For a steel company, the long run may be several years because that is how long it takes to plan and build a new plant. An electric utility might need over a decade to build a new dam, for example.

Short run and *long run* in our discussion are, in fact, management planning terms that apply to decisions made by managers. The firm can operate only in the short run in the sense that decisions must be made in the present. The same analysis applies to your own behaviour. You may have many long-run plans about graduate school, vacations, and the like, but you always operate in the short run—you make decisions every day about what you do every day.

The Relationship between Output and Inputs

A firm takes numerous inputs, combines them using a technological production process, and ends up with an output. There are, of course, a great many factors of production, or inputs. We classify production inputs in two broad categories (ignoring land)—labour and capital. The relationship between output and these two inputs is as follows:

Output per time period = Some function of capital and labour inputs

Mathematically, the production relationship can be written $Q = f(K, L)$, where Q = Output per time period, K = Capital, and L = Labour. What mix of capital and labour is used for production depends on many factors, as you can see from Example 8–1.

EXAMPLE 8–1 **Europeans Use More Capital**

Since 1970, the 15 nations of the European Union (EU) have increased their total annual output of goods and services about as much as that of Canada. But over this same time period, the EU has dramatically increased the amount of capital relative to the amount of labour it uses in its production processes. Business managers in the EU have substituted capital for labour much more than in Canada because the cost of labour (wages corrected for inflation) has increased by almost 60 percent in the EU but by only 25 percent in Canada.

For critical analysis: How does a firm decide when to buy more machines?

Production Any process by which resources are transformed into goods or services.

We have used the word *production* but have not defined it. **Production** is any process by which resources are transformed into goods or services. Production includes not only making things but also transporting them, retailing, repackaging them, and so on. Note that if we know that production occurs, we do not necessarily know the value of the output. The production relationship tells nothing about the worth or value of the inputs or the output.

The Production Function: A Numerical Example

Production function The relationship between the amount of physical output the firm can produce and the quantity of capital and labour used to produce it.

The relationship between the amount of physical output the firm can produce and the quantity of capital and labour used to produce it can be called a **production function**. The production function specifies the maximum possible output that can be produced with a given amount of inputs. It also specifies the minimum amount of inputs necessary to produce a given level of output. Firms that are inefficient or wasteful in their use of capital and labour will obtain less output than the production function in theory will show.

However, no firm can obtain more output than the production function shows. Since the production function is a technological relationship between inputs and output, it follows that an improvement in technology that allows the firm to produce more output with the same amount of inputs (or the same output with fewer inputs) results in a new production function.

Look at part (a) of Figure 8–1. It shows a production function relating the total output of pocket calculators in column 2 to the quantity of labour measured in workers in column 1. When there are zero workers, there is zero output. When there are five workers per hour of input (given the capital stock), there is a total output of 62 calculators per hour. (Ignore for the moment the rest of that part.) Part (b) of Figure 8–1 shows this particular production function graphically. Note again that it relates to the short run and that it is for an individual firm.

Part (b) shows a total physical product curve, or the maximum amount of physical output that is possible when we add successive equal-sized units of labour while holding all other inputs constant. The graph of the production function in part (b) is not a straight line. In fact, it peaks at seven workers per hour and then starts to go down. To understand why it starts to go down with an individual firm in the short run, we have to analyze in detail the **law of diminishing (marginal) returns**—the observation that after some point, successive equal-sized increases in a variable factor of production, such as labour, added to fixed factors of production, will result in smaller increases in output.

Law of diminishing (marginal) returns The observation that after some point, successive equal-sized increases in a variable factor of production, such as labour, added to fixed factors of production, will result in smaller increases in output.

But before that, let us examine the meaning of columns 3 and 4 of part (a) of Figure 8–1—that is, average and marginal physical product.

Average and Marginal Physical Product

Average physical product The total product divided by the number of workers expressed in output per hour.

The **average physical product** of labour is the total product divided by the number of workers expressed in output per hour. You can see in column 3 of part (a) of Figure 8–1 that the average physical product of labour first rises and then steadily falls after four workers are hired.

Remember that *marginal* means "additional." Hence the *marginal physical product* of labour (column 4 of part (a)) is the change in total product that occurs when a worker joins an existing production process. (The term *physical* here emphasizes the fact that we are measuring in terms of physical units of production, not in dollar terms.) It is also the *change* in total product that occurs when that worker quits or is laid off an existing production process. The **marginal physical product** of labour therefore refers to the *change in output caused by a one-unit change in the labour input*. (Marginal physical product is also referred to as *marginal productivity* and *marginal return*.)

Marginal physical product The change in output caused by a one-unit change in the labour input.

Diminishing Marginal Returns

The concept of diminishing marginal returns—also known as diminishing marginal product—applies to many situations. If you put a seat belt across your lap, a certain amount of safety is obtained. If you add another seat belt over your shoulder, some additional safety is obtained, but less than when the first belt was secured. When you add a third seat belt over the other shoulder, the amount of *additional* safety obtained is even smaller.

The same analysis holds for firms in their use of productive inputs. When the returns from hiring more workers are diminishing, it does not necessarily mean that more workers will not be hired. In fact, workers will be hired until the returns, in terms of the *value* of

FIGURE 8–1

Diminishing Returns, the Production Function, and Marginal Product: A Hypothetical Case of Pocket Calculator Production

Marginal product is the addition to the total product that results when one additional worker is hired. Thus, the marginal product of the fourth worker is 13 pocket calculators. With four workers, 52 calculators are produced, but with three workers, only 39 are produced; the difference is 13. In part (b), we plot the numbers from columns (1) and (2) of part (a). In part (c), we plot the numbers from columns (1) and (4) of part (a). When we go from zero workers to one, marginal product is eight. When we go from one worker to two, marginal product increases to 16. After two workers, marginal product declines, but it is still positive. Total product (output) reaches its peak at seven workers, so after seven workers marginal product becomes –5 calculators per hour.

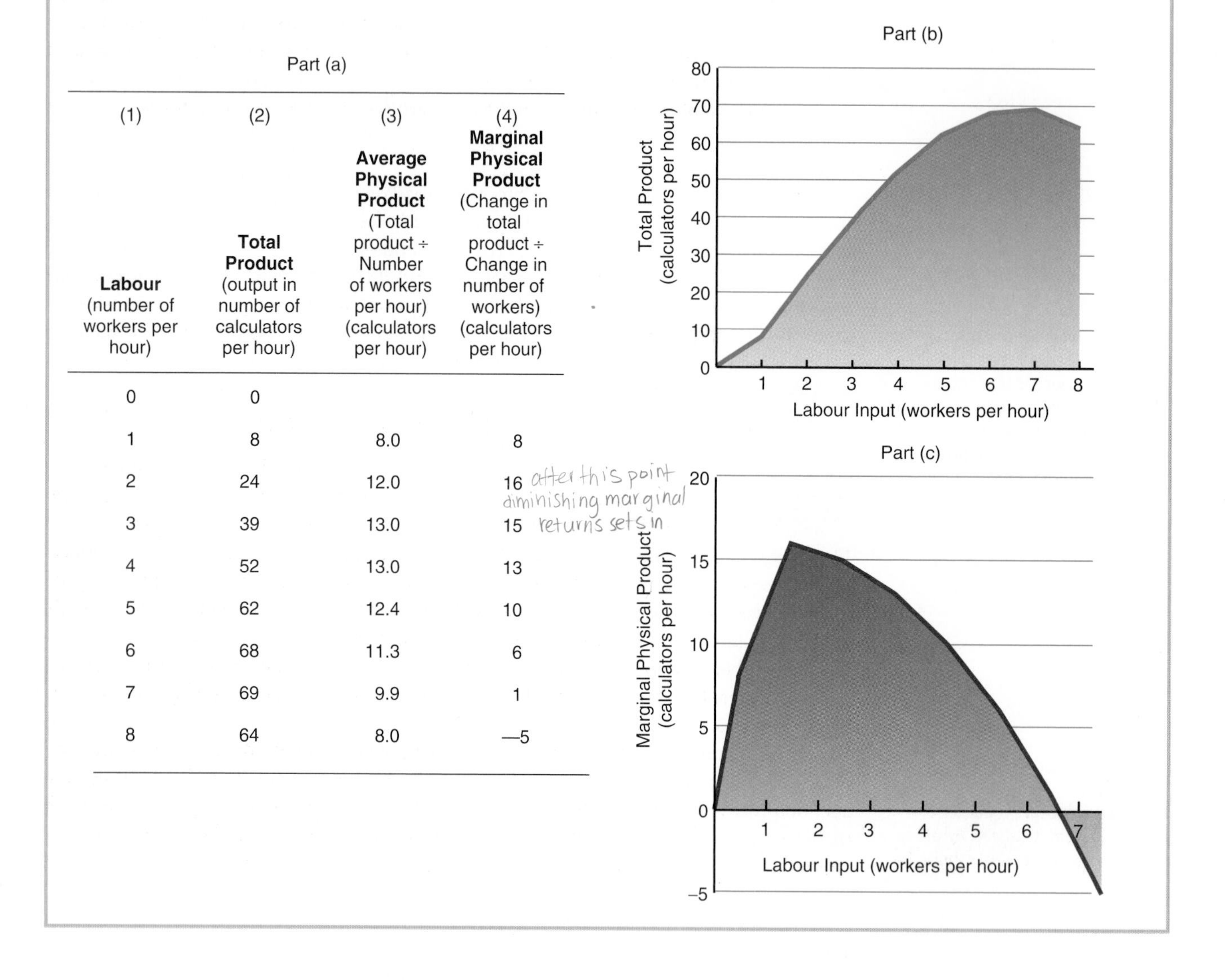

Part (a)

(1) Labour (number of workers per hour)	(2) Total Product (output in number of calculators per hour)	(3) Average Physical Product (Total product ÷ Number of workers per hour) (calculators per hour)	(4) Marginal Physical Product (Change in total product ÷ Change in number of workers) (calculators per hour)
0	0		
1	8	8.0	8
2	24	12.0	16
3	39	13.0	15
4	52	13.0	13
5	62	12.4	10
6	68	11.3	6
7	69	9.9	1
8	64	8.0	—5

the *extra* output produced, are equal to the additional wages that have to be paid for those workers to produce the extra output. Before we get into that decision-making process, let us demonstrate that diminishing returns can be represented graphically and can be used in our analysis of the firm.

Measuring Diminishing Returns

How do we measure diminishing returns? First, we limit the analysis to only one variable factor of production (or input)—let us say the factor is labour. Every other factor of production, such as machines, must be held constant. Only in this way can we calculate the marginal returns from using more workers and know when we reach the point of diminishing marginal returns.

The marginal productivity of labour may increase rapidly at the very beginning. A firm starts with no workers, only machines. The firm then hires one worker, who finds it difficult to get the work started. But when the firm hires more workers, each is able to specialize, and the marginal productivity of those additional workers may actually be greater than it was with the previous few workers. Beyond some point, however, diminishing returns must set in, not because new workers are less qualified but because each worker has (on average) fewer machines to work with (remember, all other inputs are fixed). In fact, eventually the firm will become so crowded that workers will start to get in each other's way. At that point, total production declines and marginal physical product becomes negative.

Using these ideas, we can define the law of diminishing returns as follows:

> **As successive equal increases in a variable factor of production are added to fixed factors of production, there will be a point beyond which the extra, or marginal, product that can be attributed to each additional unit of the variable factor of production will decline.**

Note that the law of diminishing returns is a statement about the *physical* relationships between inputs and outputs that we have observed in many firms. If the law of diminishing returns were not a fairly accurate statement about the world, what would stop firms from hiring additional workers forever?

An Example of the Law of Diminishing Returns

Look again at Figure 8–1. The numbers in part (a) illustrate the law of diminishing marginal returns and are presented graphically in part (c). Marginal productivity (returns from adding more workers) first increases, then decreases, and finally becomes negative.

When one worker is hired, total output goes from 0 to 8. Thus, marginal physical product is eight calculators per hour. When the second worker is hired, total product goes from 8 to 24 calculators per hour. Marginal physical product therefore increases to 16 calculators per hour. When a third worker is hired, total product again increases, from 24 to 39 calculators per hour. This represents a marginal physical product of only 15 calculators per hour. Therefore, the point of diminishing marginal returns occurs after two workers are hired.

Note that after seven workers per hour, marginal physical product becomes negative. That means that the hiring of an eighth worker would create a situation that reduces total product. Sometimes, this is called the *point of saturation*, indicating that given the amount of fixed inputs, there is no further positive use for more of the variable input. We have entered the region of negative marginal returns.

CONCEPTS IN BRIEF

Learning Objective 8.1: Distinguish between the short run and the long run.

- The short run is a time period when at least one input cannot be changed.
- In the long run, all factors of production can be varied by the firm.
- The technological relationship between output and input is called the production function. It relates output per time period to the several inputs, such as capital and labour.
- After some rate of output, the firm experiences diminishing marginal returns.
- The law of diminishing returns states that if all factors of production, except one, are held constant, equal increments in that one variable factor will eventually yield decreasing increments in output.

8.2 Short-Run Costs to the Firm

You will see that costs are the extension of the production ideas just presented. Let us consider the costs the firm faces in the short run. To keep our example simple, assume that there are only two factors of production—capital and labour. Our definition of the short run will be the time during which capital is fixed but labour is variable.

In the short run, a firm incurs certain types of costs. We label the sum of all costs incurred **total costs**. Then, we break total costs down into total fixed costs and total variable costs, which we will explain shortly. Therefore,

Total costs The sum of all costs incurred.

Total costs (TC) = Total fixed costs (TFC) + Total variable costs (TVC)

Remember that these total costs include both explicit and implicit costs, including the normal rate of return on investment.

After we have looked at the elements of total costs, we will find out how to compute average and marginal costs.

Total Fixed Costs

Let us look at an ongoing business, such as DaimlerChrysler Canada. The decision makers in that corporate giant can look around and see big machines, thousands of parts, huge buildings, and a multitude of other components of plant and equipment that have already been bought and are in place. DaimlerChrysler has to take into account the technological obsolescence of this equipment, no matter how many vehicles it produces. The payments on the loans taken out to buy the equipment will all be exactly the same. The opportunity costs of any land that DaimlerChrysler owns will all be exactly the same. These costs are more or less the same for the auto manufacturer, no matter how many automobiles it produces.

The opportunity cost (or normal rate of return) of capital must be included along with other costs. Remember that we are dealing in the short run, during which capital is fixed. If investors in DamlerChrysler Canada have already put $100 million into a new factory addition, the opportunity cost of that capital invested is now, in essence, a *fixed cost*. Why? Because in the short run, nothing can be done about that cost; the investment has already been made. This leads us to a very straightforward definition of fixed costs: All costs that do not vary—that is, all costs that do not depend on the rate of production—are called **fixed costs**.

Fixed costs All costs that do not vary—that is, all costs that do not depend on the rate of production.

Let us now take as an example the fixed costs incurred by our producer of pocket calculators. This firm's total fixed costs will equal the cost of the rent on its equipment and the insurance it has to pay. We see in part (a) of Figure 8–2 that total fixed costs per hour are $10.

In part (b), these total fixed costs are represented by the horizontal line at $10 per hour. They are invariant to changes in the output of calculators per hour—no matter how many are produced, fixed costs will remain at $10 per hour.

Total Variable Costs

Variable costs Costs whose magnitude varies with the rate of production.

Total **variable costs** are costs whose magnitude varies with the rate of production. One obvious variable cost is wages. The more the firm produces, the more labour it has to hire; therefore, the more wages it has to pay. Another variable cost is parts. In the assembly of calculators, for example, microchips must be bought. The more calculators that are made, the more chips must be bought. Part of the rate of depreciation (the rate of wear and tear) on machines that are used in the assembly process can also be considered a variable cost if depreciation depends partly on how long and how intensively the machines are used. Total variable costs are given in part (a) of Figure 8–2 in column 3. These costs are translated into the total variable cost curve in part (b). Note that the total variable cost curve lies below the total cost curve by the vertical distance of $10. This vertical distance represents, of course, total fixed costs.

FIGURE 8–2

Costs of Production: A Hypothetical Case of Pocket Calculator Production

In part (a), the deviation of columns (4) through (9) are given in parentheses in each column heading. For example, column 6, average variable costs, is derived by dividing column 3, total variable costs, by column 1, total output per hour. Note that marginal cost (MC) in part (c) intersects average variable costs (AVC) at the latter's minimum point. Also, MC intersects average total costs (ATC) at the latter's minimum point.

Part (a)

(1)	(2)	(3)	(4)	(5)	(6)	(7)	(8)	(9)
Total Output (Q/hour)	Total Fixed Costs (TFC)	Total Variable Costs (TVC)	Total Costs (TC) (4) = (2) + (3)	Average Fixed Costs (AFC) (5) = (2) (1)	Average Variable Costs (AVC) (6) = (3) : (1)	Average Total Costs (ATC) (7) = (4) (1)	Total Costs (TC) (4)	Marginal Costs (MC) (9) = Change in (8) / Change in (1)
0	$10	$ 0	$10				$10	
1	10	5	15	$10.00	$5.00	$15.00	15	$5
2	10	8	18	5.00	4.00	9.00	18	3
3	10	10	20	3.33	3.33	6.67	20	2
4	10	11	21	2.50	2.75	5.25	21	1
5	10	13	23	2.00	2.60	4.60	23	2
6	10	16	26	1.67	2.67	4.33	26	3
7	10	20	30	1.43	2.86	4.28	30	4
8	10	25	35	1.25	3.13	4.38	35	5
9	10	31	41	1.11	3.44	4.56	41	6
10	10	38	48	1.00	3.80	4.80	48	7
11	10	46	56	0.91	4.18	5.09	56	8

Part (b)

Total costs
Total variable costs
Total fixed costs
Total Costs (dollars per day)
Output (calculators per hour)

Part (c)

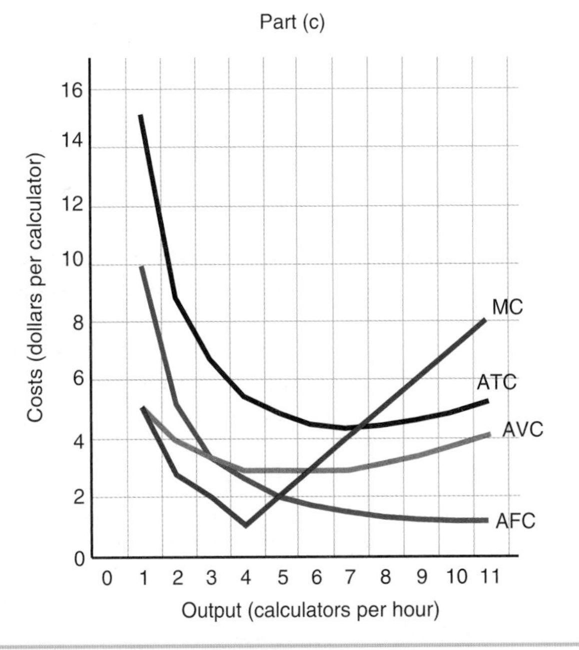

Short-Run Average Cost Curves

In part (b) of Figure 8–2, we see total costs, total variable costs, and total fixed costs. Now we want to look at average cost. The average cost concept is one in which we are measuring cost per unit of output. It is a matter of arithmetic to figure the averages of these three cost concepts. We can define them as follows:

$$\text{Average total costs (ATC)} = \frac{\text{Total costs (TC)}}{\text{Output } (Q)}$$

$$\text{Average variable costs (AVC)} = \frac{\text{Total variable costs (TVC)}}{\text{Output } (Q)}$$

$$\text{Average fixed costs (AFC)} = \frac{\text{Total fixed costs}}{\text{Output } (Q)}$$

The arithmetic is done in columns 5, 6, and 7 in part (a) of Figure 8–2. The numerical results are translated into a graphical format in part (c). Because total costs (TC) equal variable costs (TVC) plus fixed costs (TFC), the difference between average total costs (ATC) and average variable costs (AVC) will always be identical to average fixed costs (AFC). That means that average total costs and average variable costs move together as output expands.

Now let us see what we can observe about the three average cost curves in Figure 8–2.

Average fixed costs Total fixed costs divided by the number of units produced.

AVERAGE FIXED COSTS (AFC). **Average fixed costs**—total fixed costs divided by the number of units produced—continue to fall throughout the output range. In fact, if we were to continue the diagram farther to the right, we would find that average fixed costs would get closer and closer to the horizontal axis. That is because total fixed costs remain constant. As we divide this fixed number by a larger and larger number of units of output, the resulting AFC has to become smaller and smaller. In business, this is called "spreading the overhead."

Average variable costs Total variable costs divided by the number of units produced.

AVERAGE VARIABLE COSTS (AVC). The **average variable cost**—total variable costs divided by the number of units produced—curve takes a form that is U-shaped: First it falls; then it starts to rise. It is possible for the AVC curve to take other shapes in the long run.

Average total costs Total costs divided by the number of units produced; sometimes called per-unit total costs.

AVERAGE TOTAL COSTS (ATC). **Average total costs** are total costs divided by the number of units produced; sometimes called per-unit total costs. This curve has a shape similar to that of the AVC curve. However, it falls even more dramatically in the beginning and rises more slowly after it has reached a minimum point. It falls and then rises because average total costs are the summation of the AFC curve and the AVC curve. Thus, when AFC and AVC are both falling, ATC must fall, too. At some point, however, AVC starts to increase, while AFC continues to fall. Once the increase in the AVC curve outweighs the decrease in the AFC curve, the ATC curve will start to increase and will develop its familiar U-shape.

Marginal Cost

Marginal costs Costs that result from a one-unit change in the production rate.

We have stated repeatedly that the basis of decisions is always on the margin—decisions in economics are determined at the margin. This dictum also holds true within the firm. Firms, according to the analysis we use to predict their behaviour, are very interested in their *marginal costs*. Because the term *marginal* means "additional" or "incremental" (or "decremental," too) here, **marginal costs** refer to costs that result from a one-unit change in the production rate. For example, if the production of 10 calculators per hour costs a firm \$48, and the production of 11 calculators costs it \$56 per hour, the marginal cost of producing the eleventh calculator is \$8.

$$\text{Maginal cost} = \frac{\text{Change in total cost}}{\text{Change in output}}$$

We show the marginal costs of calculator production per hour in column 9 of part (a) in Figure 8–2, calculated according to the formula just given. A good example of the different costs is illustrated in Example 8–2.

This marginal cost schedule is shown graphically in part (c) of Figure 8–2. Just like average variable costs and average total costs, marginal costs first fall and then rise. The U-shape of the marginal cost curve is a result of increasing and then diminishing marginal returns. At lower levels of output, the marginal cost curve declines. The reasoning is that as marginal physical product increases with each addition of output, the marginal cost of this last unit of output must fall. Conversely, when diminishing marginal returns set in, marginal physical product decreases (and eventually becomes negative); it follows that the marginal cost of the last unit must rise. These relationships are clearly reflected in the geometry of parts (b) and (c) of Figure 8–2.

In summary:

As long as marginal physical product rises, marginal cost will fall, and when marginal physical product starts to fall (after reaching the point of diminishing marginal returns), marginal cost will begin to rise.

The Relationship between Average and Marginal Costs

Let us now look at the relationship between average costs and marginal costs. There is always a definite relationship between averages and marginals. Consider your grade point average. Say your GPA is currently a B. If you take an economics course and earn an A, what will happen to your GPA? It must increase. When your grade in a marginal course (the economics course) is higher than (above) your GPA, it pulls your average up. If you subsequently take an accounting course and earn a C, your GPA will fall.

There is a similar relationship between average variable costs and marginal costs. When marginal costs are less than average costs, the latter must fall. Conversely, when marginal costs are greater than average costs, the latter must rise. When you think about it, the relationship makes sense. The only way for average variable costs to fall is for the extra cost of the marginal unit produced to be less than the average variable cost of all the preceding units. For example, if the average variable cost for two calculators is $4, the only way the average variable cost of three calculators can be less than that of two is for the variable costs attributable to the last calculator—the marginal cost—to be less than the average of the previously produced calculators. In this particular case, if average variable cost falls to $3.33 per calculator, total variable cost for the three calculators would be three times $3.33, or almost exactly $10. Total variable costs for two calculators is two times $4, or $8. The marginal cost is therefore $10 minus $8, or $2, which is less than the average variable cost of $3.33.

A similar type of computation can be carried out for rising average variable costs. The only way for average variable costs to rise is for the cost of additional units to be more than that for units already produced. But the incremental cost is the marginal cost. In this particular case, the marginal costs have to be higher than the average variable costs.

There is also a relationship between marginal costs and average total costs. Remember that average total cost is equal to total cost divided by the number of units produced. Remember also that marginal cost does not include any fixed costs. Fixed costs are, by definition, fixed and cannot influence marginal costs. Our example can therefore be repeated substituting average total cost for average variable cost.

These rising and falling relationships can be seen in Figure 8–2, where MC intersects AVC and ATC at their respective minimum points.

Minimum Cost Points

At what rate of output of calculators per hour does our producer experience the minimum average total costs? Column 7 in part (a) of Figure 8–2 shows that the minimum average total cost is $4.28, which occurs at an output rate of seven calculators per hour. We can also find this minimum cost by finding the point in part (c) of Figure 8–2 at which the marginal cost curve intersects the average total cost curve. This should not be surprising. When marginal cost is below average total cost, average total cost falls. When marginal cost is above average total cost, average total cost rises. At the point where average total cost is neither falling nor rising, marginal cost must then be equal to average total cost. When we represent this graphically, the marginal cost curve will intersect the average total cost curve at the latter's minimum.

The same analysis applies to the intersection of the marginal cost curve and the average variable cost curve. When are average variable costs at a minimum? According to part (a) of Figure 8–2, average variable costs are at a minimum of $2.60 at an output rate of five calculators per hour. This is where the marginal cost curve intersects the average variable cost curve in part (c) of Figure 8–2. A good example of the relationship of costs is shown in Example 8–2.

EXAMPLE 8–2 The Cost of Driving a Car

Each year the Canadian Automobile Association publishes a study on the annual cost of owning and driving an automobile. The 2003 study found that driving a new 2003 Chevrolet Cavalier Z-24 four-door sedan (2.2 litre, four-cylinder) involved the following:

Costs per kilometre
Gasoline and oil: 8.99 cents
Maintenance: 2.90 cents
Tires: 1.86 cents

Annual costs
Insurance: $1962
Licence and registration: $130
Financing charges: $692
Depreciation: $4266

On the basis of an average annual driving distance of 18 000 kilometres, total costs amounted to $7050 per year, or $19.32 per day.

However, the average cost of driving a car varied depending on distance driven. At 18 000 kilometres per year, the cost was 52.9 cents per kilometre; at 24 000 kilometres per year, it was 46.5 cents; and at 32 000 kilometres per year, the cost was 41.6 cents per kilometre. (Depreciation was not factored into these numbers.)

For critical analysis: Which costs are total fixed costs, total variable costs, average total costs, and marginal costs?

The Relationship between Diminishing Marginal Returns and Cost Curves

There is a unique relationship between output and the shape of the various cost curves we have drawn. Let us consider specifically the relationship between marginal cost and the example of diminishing marginal physical returns in part (a) of Figure 8–3. It turns out that if wage rates are constant, the shape of the marginal cost curve in part (d) of Figure 8–3 is both a reflection of and a consequence of the law of diminishing returns. Let us assume that each unit of labour can be purchased at a constant price. Further assume that labour is the only variable input. We see that as more workers are hired, marginal physical product first rises and then falls after the point at which diminishing returns are encountered. Thus, the marginal cost of each extra unit of output will first fall as long as marginal physical product is rising, and then it will rise as long as marginal physical product is falling. Recall that marginal cost is defined as:

$$\text{MC} = \frac{\text{Change in total cost}}{\text{Change in output}}$$

Because the price of labour is assumed to be constant, the change in total cost is simply the constant price of labour, *W* (we are increasing labour by only one unit). The change in output is simply the marginal physical product (MPP) of the one-unit increase in labour. Therefore, we see that:

$$\text{Marginal cost} = \frac{W}{\text{MPP}}$$

This means that initially, when there are increasing returns, marginal cost falls (we are dividing *W* by increasingly larger numbers), and later, when diminishing returns set in and marginal physical product is falling, marginal cost must increase (we are dividing *W* by smaller numbers). As marginal physical product increases, marginal cost decreases, and as marginal physical product decreases, marginal cost must increase. Thus, when marginal physical product reaches its maximum, marginal cost necessarily reaches its minimum. To illustrate this, let us return to Figure 8–1. Assume that a worker at our pocket calculator factory is paid $5 per hour. When we go from zero labour input to one unit, output increases by eight calculators. Each of those eight calculators has a marginal cost of 63 cents. Now, the second unit of labour is hired, and it too costs $5 per hour. Output increases by 16. Thus, the marginal cost is $5 ÷ 16 = 31 cents. We continue the experiment. We see that the next unit of labour yields only 15 additional calculators, and so marginal cost starts to rise to 33 cents. The following unit of labour increases marginal physical product by only 13, so marginal cost becomes $5 ÷ 13 = 38 cents.

All of the foregoing can be restated in relatively straightforward terms:

> **Firms' short-run cost curves are a reflection of the law of diminishing marginal returns. Given any constant price of the variable input, marginal costs decline as long as the marginal product of the variable resource is rising. At the point at which diminishing marginal returns begin, marginal costs begin to rise as the marginal product of the variable input begins to decline.**

The result is a marginal cost curve that slopes down, hits a minimum, and then slopes up. The average total cost curve and average variable cost curve are of course affected. They will have their familiar U-shape in the short run. Again, to see this, recall that:

$$\text{AVC} = \frac{\text{Total variable costs}}{\text{Total output}}$$

As we move from zero labour input to one unit in part (a) of Figure 8–3, output increases from zero to eight calculators. The total variable costs are the price per worker, *W* ($5), times the number of workers (1). Because the average product of one worker

FIGURE 8–3

The Relationship between Physical Output and Costs

As the number of workers increases, the total number of calculators produced rises, as shown in parts (a) and (b). In part (c), marginal product (MP) first rises and then falls. Average product (AP) follows. The mirror image of part (c) is shown in part (d), in which MC and AVC first fall and then rise.

Part (a)

(1) Labour	(2) Total Product (number of calculators per hour)	(3) Average Physical Product (calculators per worker per hour) (3) = (2) ÷ (1)	(4) Marginal Physical Product (4) = Change in (2) ÷ Change in (1)	(5) Average Variable Cost (5) = (W = $5) ÷ (3)	(6) Marginal Cost (6) = (W = $5) ÷ (4)
0	0				
1	8	8	8	$0.63	$0.63
2	24	12	16	0.42	0.31
3	39	13	15	0.38	0.33
4	52	13	13	0.38	0.38
5	62	12.4	10	0.40	0.50
6	68	11.3	6	0.44	0.83
7	69	9.9	1	0.55	5.00

Part (b)

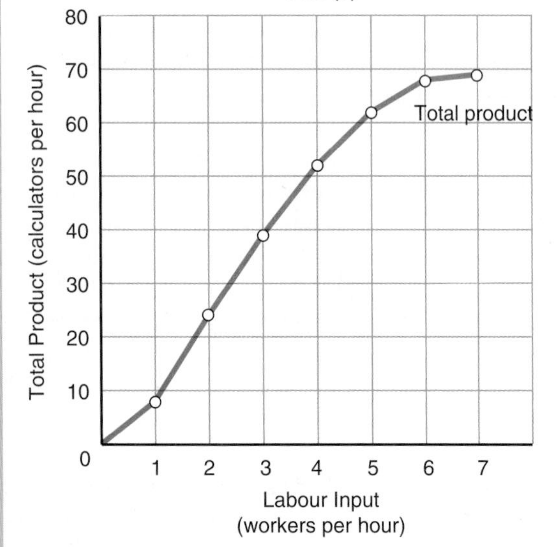

Part (c)

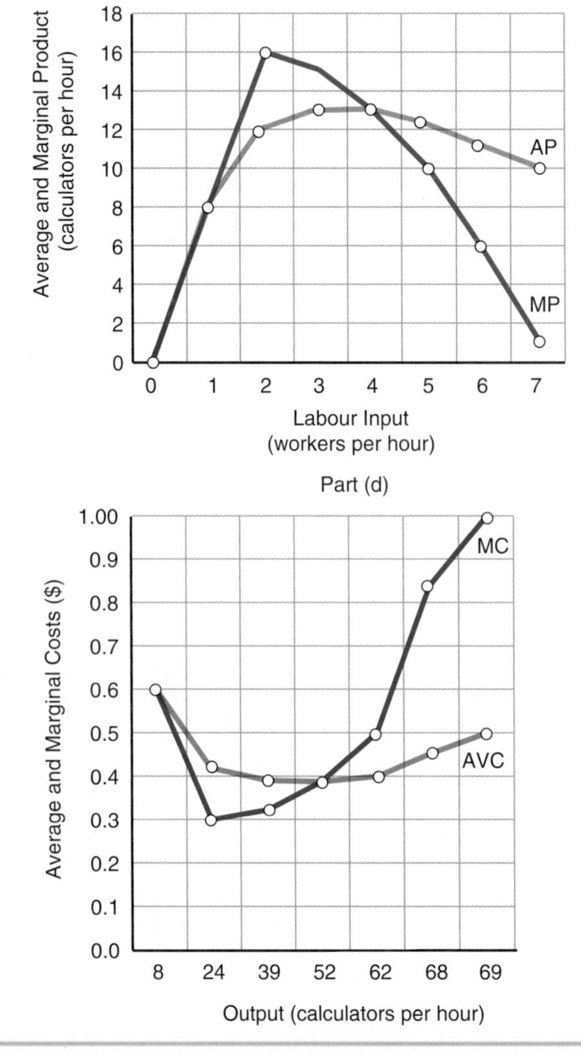

(column 3) is eight, we can write the total product, eight, as the average product, eight, times the number of workers, one. Thus we see that:

$$\text{AVC} = \frac{\$5 \times 1}{8 \times 1} = \frac{\$5}{8} = \frac{W}{\text{AP}}$$

From column 3 in part (a) of Figure 8–3, we see that the average product increases, reaches a maximum, and then declines. Because AVC = W / AP, average variable cost decreases as average product increases and increases as average product decreases. AVC reaches its minimum when average product reaches its maximum. Furthermore, because ATC = AVC + AFC, the average total cost curve inherits the relationship between the average variable cost and diminishing returns.

Breakeven Analysis

Breakeven The output that a firm must produce to reach the point where its profits are zero.

A very useful analysis that firms use is **breakeven**, the output that a firm must produce to reach the point where its profits are zero. The breakeven point will cover all fixed and variable costs. It helps managers make better decisions about what quantity has to be produced so that profits can be realized. Breakeven quantity (BQ) is the total fixed costs divided by the selling price minus the average variable costs.

$$\text{BQ} = \frac{\text{TFC}}{\text{Selling price} - \text{AVC}}$$

If a firm wants a specific profit, it can add the desired profit to the total fixed cost and then divide by the selling price minus the average variable costs.

CONCEPTS IN BRIEF

Learning Objective 8.2: Calculate the various costs for the firm in the short run.

- Total costs equal total fixed costs plus total variable costs.
- Fixed costs do not vary with the rate of production.
- Variable costs do vary with the rate of production.
- Average total cost equals total cost divided by quantity.
- Average variable cost equals total variable cost divided by quantity.
- Average fixed cost equals total fixed cost divided by quantity.
- Marginal cost equals the change in total cost divided by the change in quantity.
- Breakeven quantity equals the total fixed cost divided by selling price minus average variable cost.

Long-Run Cost Curves

Planning horizon The long run, during which all inputs are variable.

The long run is defined as a time period during which full adjustment can be made to any change in the economic environment. Long-run curves are sometimes called *planning curves,* and the long run, during which all inputs are variable, is sometimes called the **planning horizon**. We start out our analysis of long-run cost curves by considering a single firm contemplating the construction of a single plant. The firm has three alternative plant sizes from which to choose on the planning horizon. Each particular plant size generates its own short-run average total cost curve. Now that we are talking about the difference between long-run and short-run cost curves, we will label all short-run curves with an *S* and long-run curves with an *L;* short-run average (total) costs will be labelled SAC, and long-run average cost curves will be labelled LAC.

Part (a) of Figure 8–4 shows three short-run average cost curves for three successively larger plants. Which is the optimal size to build? That depends on the anticipated normal, sustained (permanent) rate of output per time period. Assume for a moment that the anticipated normal, sustained rate is Q_1. If a plant of size 1 is built, the average costs will be C_1. If a plant of size 2 is built, we see on SAC_2 that the average costs will be C_2, which

FIGURE 8–4

Preferable Plant Size and the Long-Run Average Cost Curve

If the anticipated permanent rate of output per unit time period is Q_1, the optimal plant to build would be the one corresponding to SAC_1 in part (a) because average costs are lower. However, if the permanent rate of output increases to Q_2, it will be more profitable to have a plant size corresponding to SAC_2. Unit costs fall to C_3.

If we draw all the possible short-run average cost curves that correspond to different plant sizes and then draw the envelope (a curve tangent to each member of a set of curves) to these various curves, SAC_1 to SAC_8, we obtain the long-run average cost curve, or the planning curve, as shown in part (b).

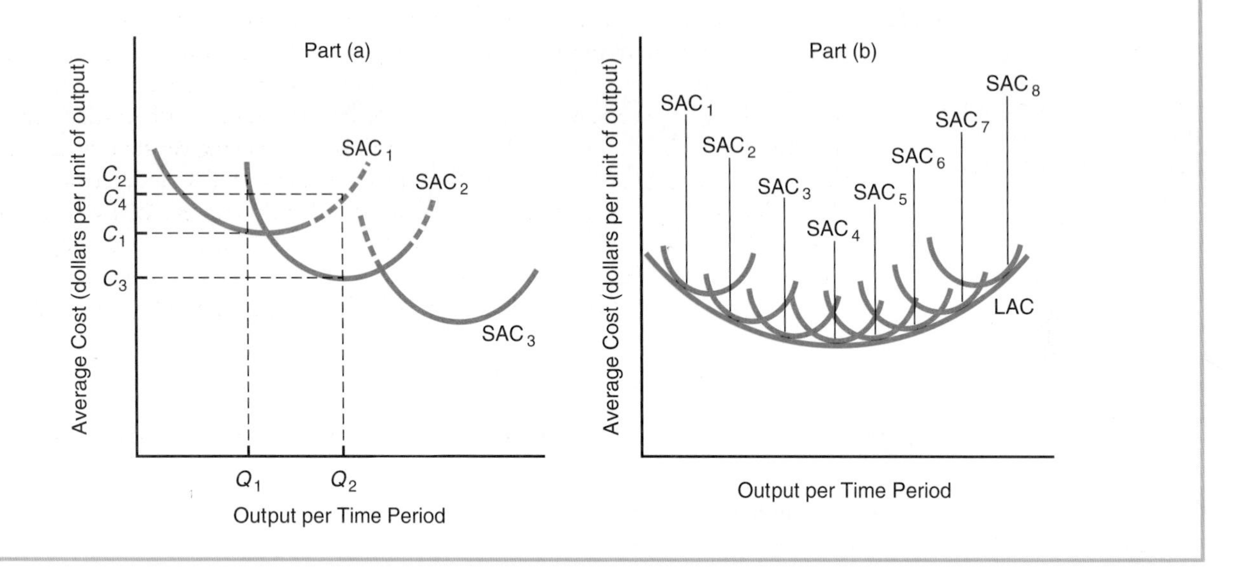

is greater than C_1. Thus, if the anticipated rate of output is Q_1, the appropriate plant size is the one from which SAC_1 was derived.

However, if the anticipated permanent rate of output per time period goes from Q_1 to Q_2 and a plant of size 1 had been decided on, average costs would be C_4. If a plant of size 2 had been decided on, average costs would be C_3, which is clearly less than C_4.

In choosing the appropriate plant size for a single-plant firm during the planning horizon, the firm will pick the size whose short-run average cost curve generates an average cost that is lowest for the expected rate of output.

Long-Run Average Cost Curve

Long-run average cost curve The locus of points representing the minimum unit cost of producing any given rate of output, given current technology and resource prices.

Planning curve The curve that represents the various average costs attainable at the planning stage of the firm's decision making.

If we now assume that the entrepreneur faces an infinite number of choices of plant sizes in the long run, we can conceive of an infinite number of SAC curves similar to the three in part (a) of Figure 8–4. We are not able, of course, to draw an infinite number; we have drawn quite a few, however, in part (b) of Figure 8–4. We then draw the "envelope" to all these various short-run average cost curves. The resulting envelope is the **long-run average cost curve**, which is the locus of points representing the minimum unit cost of producing any given rate of output, given current technology and resource prices. This long-run average cost curve is sometimes called the **planning curve**, for it represents the various average costs attainable at the planning stage of the firm's decision making. It represents the locus (path) of points giving the least unit cost of producing any given rate of output. Note that the LAC curve is *not* tangent to each individual SAC curve at the latter's minimum points. This is true only at the minimum point of the LAC curve. Then and only then are minimum long-run average costs equal to minimum short-run average costs.

Dec 11
7:30-9

8.3 *Why the Long-Run Average Cost Curve Is U-Shaped*

Note that the long-run average cost curve, LAC in part (b) of Figure 8–4, is U-shaped, similar to the U-shape of the short-run average cost curve developed earlier in this chapter. The reason behind the U-shape of the two curves is not the same, however. The short-run average cost curve is U-shaped because of the law of diminishing marginal returns. But the law cannot apply to the long run because in the long run, all factors of production are variable; there is no point of diminishing marginal returns because there is no fixed factor of production. Why, then, do we see the U-shape in the long-run average cost curve? The reason has to do with **economies of scale** (decreases in long-run average costs resulting from increases in output), **constant returns to scale** (no change in long-run average costs when output increases), and **diseconomies of scale** (increases in long-run average costs that occur as output increases). When the firm is experiencing economies of scale, the long-run average cost curve slopes downward—an increase in scale and production leads to a fall in unit costs. When the firm is experiencing constant returns to scale, the long-run average cost curve is at its minimum point such that an increase in scale and production does not change unit costs. When the firm is experiencing diseconomies of scale, the long-run average cost curve slopes upward—an increase in scale and production increases unit costs. These three sections of the long-run average cost curves are broken up into parts (a), (b), and (c) in Figure 8–5. Try doing Example 8–3 to check your understanding.

Economies of scale Decreases in long-run average costs resulting from increases in output.

Constant returns to scale No change in long-run average costs when output increases.

Diseconomies of scale Increases in long-run average costs that occur as output increases.

FIGURE 8–5

Economies of Scale, Constant Returns to Scale, and Diseconomies of Scale Shown with the Long-Run Average Cost Curve

Long-run average cost curves will fall when there are economies of scale, as shown in part (a). They will be constant (flat) when the firm is experiencing constant returns to scale, as shown in part (b). They will rise when the firm is experiencing diseconomies of scale, as shown in part (c).

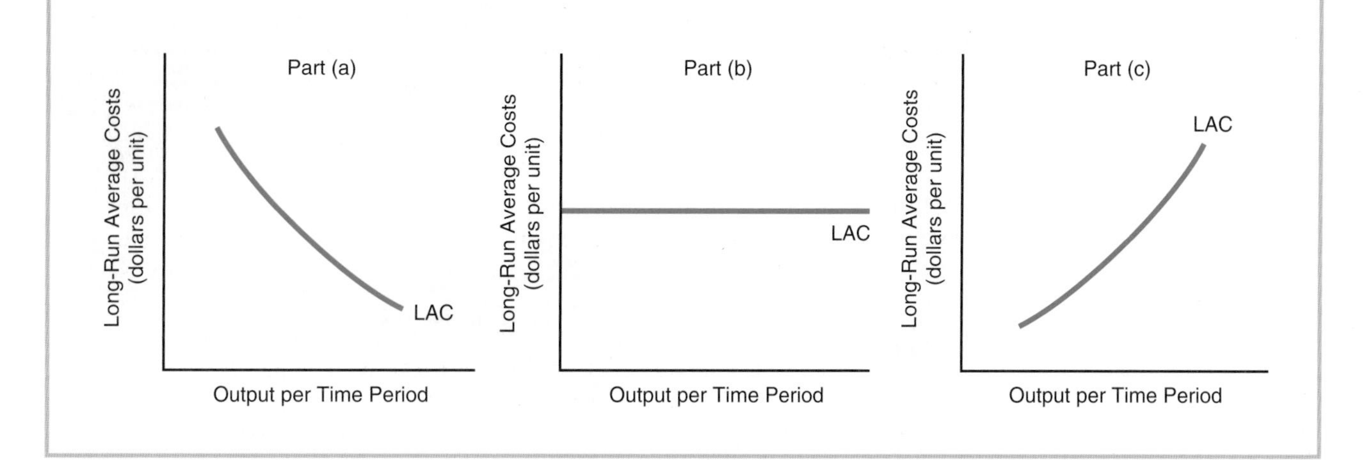

EXAMPLE 8–3 **Economies of Scale at Dell Computer Corporation**

In the mid-1990s, Dell Computer Corporation embarked on a plan to become the lowest-cost computer manufacturer in the world. Now, the company has factories that receive more than half of all customer orders via the Internet. These orders flow to a plant's so-called air-traffic control room, where procurement of parts, computer assembly, and shipping are managed.

At each point on the factory floor, which at some plants can be as large as 300 000 square feet, groups in charge of producing various computer components are linked via *intranets*, or internal computer networks. Each forklift truck contains a wireless computer that follows the paths of components to ensure that they reach the correct assembly points. Forklift trucks carrying completed computers are similarly equipped, to ensure that they reach the correct loading dock from among the dozens where trucks are waiting to be loaded.

In its newest and largest plants, Dell can produce more than 1000 computers per hour, which is almost twice as many as a typical plant could produce only half a dozen years ago. Even rival computer manufacturers agreed by the early 2000s that Dell had taken advantage of economies of scale to become the most cost-efficient manufacturer of personal computers.

For critical analysis: What has happened to Dell's short-run average cost curves as it has moved down along its long-run average cost curve?

Reasons for Economies of Scale

We shall examine three of the many reasons a firm might be expected to experience economies of scale: specialization, the dimensional factor, and improved productive equipment.

SPECIALIZATION. As a firm's scale of operation increases, the opportunities for specialization in the use of resource inputs also increase. This is sometimes called *increased division of tasks* or *operations*. Gains from such division of labour or increased specialization are well known. When we consider managerial staff, we also find that larger enterprises may be able to put together more highly specialized staff.

DIMENSIONAL FACTOR. Large-scale firms often require proportionately less input per unit of output simply because certain inputs do not have to be physically doubled in order to double the output. Consider the cost of storage of oil. The cost of storage is basically related to the cost of steel that goes into building the storage container; however, the amount of steel required goes up less than in proportion to the volume (storage capacity) of the container (because the volume of a container increases more than proportionately with its surface area).

IMPROVED PRODUCTIVE EQUIPMENT. The larger the scale of the enterprise, the more the firm is able to take advantage of larger-volume (output capacity) types of machinery. Small-scale operations may not be able profitably to use large-volume machines that can be more efficient per unit of output. Also, smaller firms often cannot use technologically more advanced machinery because they are unable to spread out the high cost of such sophisticated equipment over a large output.

For any of these reasons, the firm may experience economies of scale, which means that equal percentage increases in output result in a decrease in average cost. Thus, output can double, but total costs will less than double; hence average cost falls. Note that the factors listed for causing economies of scale are all *internal* to the firm; they do not depend on what other firms are doing or what is happening in the economy.

Why a Firm Might Experience Diseconomies of Scale

One of the basic reasons a firm can expect to run into diseconomies of scale is that there are limits to the efficient functioning of management. Moreover, as more workers are hired, a more than proportionate increase in managers and staff people may be needed, and this could cause increased costs per unit. This is so because larger levels of output imply successively larger *plant* size, which, in turn, implies successively larger *firm* size. Thus, as the level of output increases, more people must be hired, and the firm gets bigger. However, as this happens, the support, supervisory and administrative staff, and the general paperwork of the firm, increase. As the layers of supervision grow, the costs of information and communication grow more than proportionately; hence the average unit cost will start to increase.

Some observers of corporate giants claim that many of them are experiencing some diseconomies of scale today. Witness the problems that General Motors and IBM had in the early 1990s. Some analysts say that the financial problems that they have experienced are at least partly a function of their size relative to their smaller, more flexible competitors, who can make decisions faster and then take more rapid advantage of changing market conditions. This seems to be particularly true with IBM. It apparently adapted very slowly to the fact that the large mainframe computer business was declining as micro- and mini-computers became more and more powerful. Such companies as Dell Computers, Oracle, and eBay all enjoy economies of scale because of standardized products.

Minimum Efficient Scale

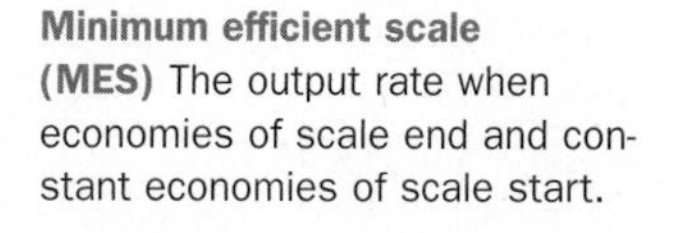
Minimum efficient scale (MES) The output rate when economies of scale end and constant economies of scale start.

Economists and statisticians have obtained actual data on the relationship between changes in all inputs and changes in average cost. It turns out that for many industries, the long-run average cost curve does not resemble that shown in part (b) of Figure 8–4. Rather, it more closely resembles Figure 8–6. What you observe there is a small portion of declining long-run average costs (economies of scale) and then a wide range of outputs over which the firm experiences relatively constant economies of scale. At the output rate when economies of scale end and constant economies of scale start, the **minimum efficient scale (MES)** for the firm is encountered. It occurs at point *A*. (The point is, of course, approximate. The more smoothly the curve declines into its flat portion, the more approximate will be our estimate of the MES.) The minimum efficient scale will always be the lowest rate of output at which long-run average costs are minimized. In any industry with a long-run average cost curve similar to the one in Figure 8–6, larger firms will have no cost-saving advantage over smaller firms as long as the smaller firms have at least obtained the minimum efficient scale at point *A*.

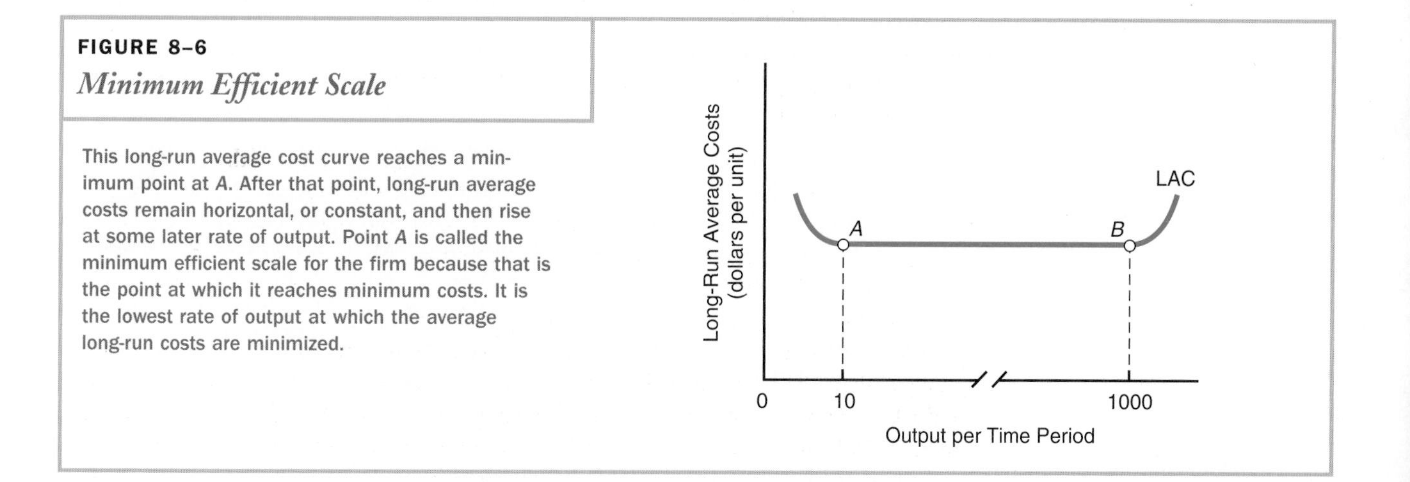

FIGURE 8–6
Minimum Efficient Scale

This long-run average cost curve reaches a minimum point at *A*. After that point, long-run average costs remain horizontal, or constant, and then rise at some later rate of output. Point *A* is called the minimum efficient scale for the firm because that is the point at which it reaches minimum costs. It is the lowest rate of output at which the average long-run costs are minimized.

Among its uses, the minimum efficient scale gives us a rough measure of the degree of competition in an industry. If the MES is small relative to industry demand, the degree of competition in that industry is likely to be high because there is room for many efficiently sized plants. Conversely, when the MES is large relative to industry demand, the degree of competition is likely to be small because there is room for a relatively small number of efficiently sized plants or firms. Looked at another way, if it takes a very large scale of plant to obtain minimum long-run average cost, the output of just a few of these very large firms can fully satisfy total market demand. This means that there is no room for a large number of smaller plants if maximum efficiency is to be obtained in the industry.

CONCEPTS IN BRIEF

Learning Objective 8.3: Explain why the long-run average cost curve is U-shaped.

- Economies of scale impact the shape of the long-run average cost curve. When a firm is experiencing economies of scale, the curve slopes downward. When constant returns to scale exist, the curve is at its minimum point. When diseconomies of scale exist, the curve slopes upward.

ISSUES AND APPLICATIONS

Technology and Costs

Concepts Applied: Short-Run Costs, Long-Run Costs, Minimum Efficient Scale of Production

When most of the eastern seaboard was plunged into darkness because of a power failure, it was obvious that technology is not without costs.

Some estimates of the cost of the blackout to Toronto alone are in the tens of millions. In the short run, many companies lost money when they were forced to close down. Perishables, such as meat, produce, and ice cream, had to be disposed of. Flights had to be cancelled, and transportation was brought to a standstill. There was an emotional cost that economists and accountants will find difficult to measure. The fear and stress that people endured must not be ignored. It will be a factor in how people react to proposed changes to the power system. Overall though, economists are saying that in the short run, the cost of the blackout is minimal.

Costs in the long run may be much greater, since Ontario's electrical grid and power system are in need of modernization. Before the blackout, many people were calling for a return to regulation of the industry. The blackout has forced even more people to be concerned about the state of the industry. People are looking at ways to save on electrical power.

One alternative that is being implemented at the Vancouver International Airport is a solar-powered hot water heating system. The system should save around $90 000 a year and will heat an average of 3000 litres of hot water a day. B.C. Hydro's Power Smart Program is partly funding the project. New initiatives are aimed at reducing power consumption with environmentally and socially acceptable technologies.

It is unlikely that solar power will totally replace electrical power in the near future. In the short run, solar power is still a more expensive alternative, but in the long run, as more investment capital becomes available and more companies become involved, economies of scale will occur.

For critical analysis:

1. Why would B.C. Hydro be interested in having companies use solar power?
2. Will the blackout change people's power usage?

SUMMARY DISCUSSION OF LEARNING OBJECTIVES

8.1 Short Run versus Long Run. The short run for the firm is defined as the period during which at least one input cannot be altered. The long run is the period during which all factors of production can be varied.

8.2 Short-Run Costs to the Firm. Fixed costs are costs that cannot be altered in the short run. Variable vosts are associated with input costs that vary as the rate of output varies.

- There are definitional relationships among average, total, and marginal costs.
- Total costs equal total fixed costs plus total variable costs.
- Fixed costs do not vary with the rate of production.
- Variable costs do vary with the rate of production.
- Average total cost equals total cost divided by quantity.
- Average variable cost equals total variable cost divided by quantity.
- Average fixed cost equals total fixed cost divided by quantity.
- Marginal cost equals the change in total cost divided by the change in quantity.
- Firms are also interested in how much they need to produce to reach breakeven.
- Breakeven quantity equals the total fixed cost divided by selling price minus average variable cost.

8.3 Why the Long-Run Average Cost Curve Is U-Shaped. Economies of scale impact the shape of the long-run average cost curve. When a firm is experiencing economies of scale, the curve slopes downward. When constant returns to scale exist, the curve is at its minimum point. When diseconomies of scale exist, the curve slopes upward.

PROBLEMS

(Answers to the odd-numbered problems appear at the back of the book.)

LO 8.1 Distinguish between the short run and the long run.

1. The short-run production function for a manufacturer of DVD drives is as follows:

Input of Labour (workers per week)	Total Output of DVD Drives
0	0
1	25
2	60
3	85
4	105
5	115
6	120

On the basis of this information, calculate the average physical product at each quantity of labour.

2. Using the information provided in Problem 1, calculate the marginal physical product labour at each quantity of labour.

3. Define long-run average total cost. In light of the fact that businesses are operated day to day in the short run, of what use is the concept of long-run average total cost to the entrepreneur?

LO 8.2 Calculate the various costs for the firm in the short run.

4. Your school's basketball team had a foul-shooting average of 0.800 (80 out of 100) before last night's game, during which they shot 5 for 10 at the foul line.
   a. What was their marginal performance last night?
   b. What happened to the team's foul-shooting average?
   c. Suppose that their foul shooting in the next game is 6 for 10. What is happening to their marginal performance? Now what is the team average foul-shooting percentage?

5. The cost structure of a manufacturer of cable modems is described in the following table:

Output (units)	Average Fixed Cost	Total Cost
0	–	$200
5	$40	300
10	20	380
20	10	420
40	5	520

   a. Find the average variable cost at each level of production.
   b. What is the marginal cost of increasing output from 10 to 20 units? From 20 to 40 units?
   c. Find the average total cost at each level of production.

6. You are given the following graph:

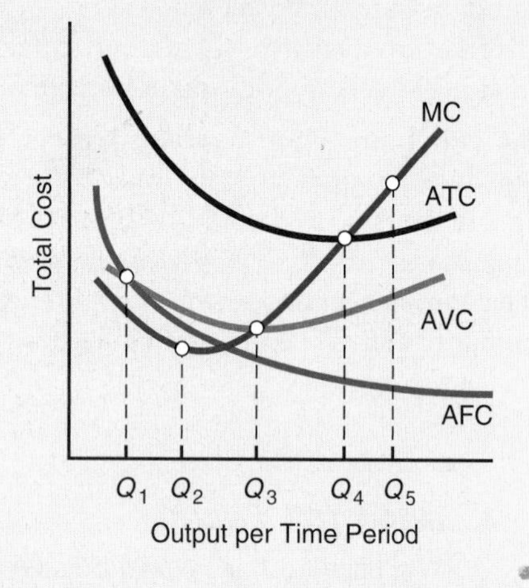

   a. At what output level is AVC at a minimum?
   b. At what output level is ATC at a minimum?
   c. At what output level is MC at a minimum?
   d. At what output level do the AVC and MC curves intersect?
   e. At what output level do the ATC and MC curves intersect?

LO 8.3 Explain why the long-run average cost curve is U-shaped.

7. A manufacturing firm with a single plant is contemplating changing its plant size. It must choose from among seven alternative plant sizes. In the table below, plant size A is the smallest it might build, and size G is the largest. Currently, the firm's plant size is B.

Plant Size	Average Total Cost ($)
A (smallest)	5000
B	4000
C	3500
D	3100
E	3000
F	3250
G (largest)	4100

   a. Is this firm currently experiencing economies of scale or diseconomies of scale?
   b. What is the firm's minimum efficient scale?

8. In Example 8–3, "Economies of Scale and Dell Computer Corporation," Dell was able to enter and compete in the computer market. Explain how this was possible given economies and diseconomies of scale.

9. In the Issues and Applications, "Technology and Costs," the cost of new technology was discussed. Why would people switch to solar power if it is initially expensive to make the change?

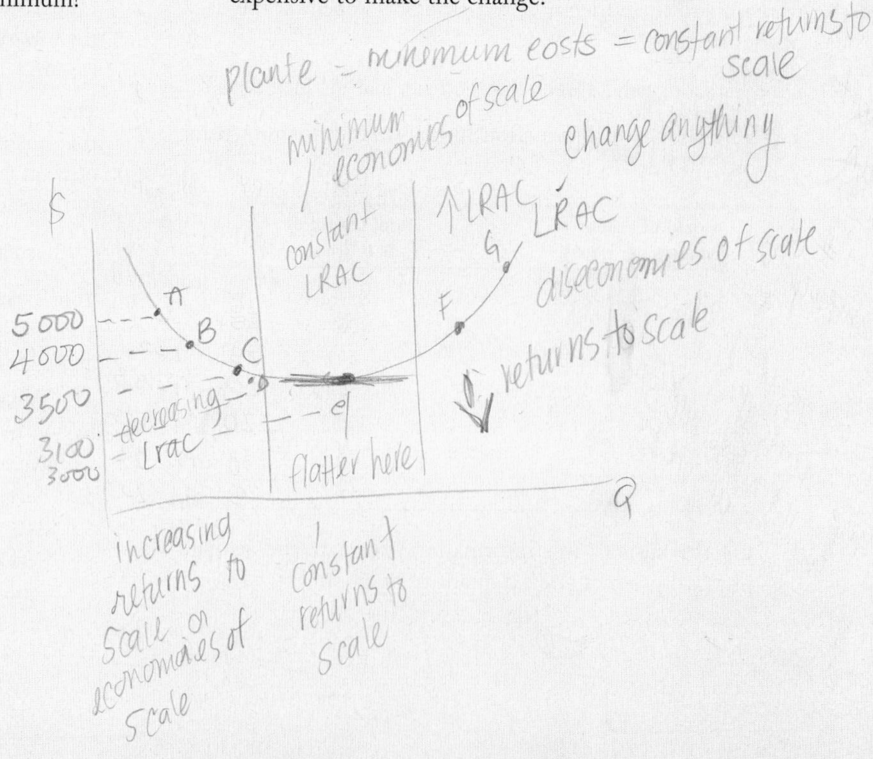

PART 3
MARKET STRUCTURE, RESOURCE ALLOCATION, AND REGULATION

CHAPTER 9

Perfect Competition

If you want to watch new-release or best-seller movies regularly in the comforts of your own home, you face just one problem: How should you pay for this? Should you remit extra monthly fees to your cable company to access video on demand? Should you buy DVD movies from a supermarket or big box retailer? Should you pay a fixed monthly subscription rate that will allow you to rent as many DVDs as you want over the Internet? Should you join an online video club by promising to buy so many DVDs per year? With all these options available, would you still consider visiting your local video store? An understanding of the model of perfect competition will help you appreciate the changing nature of the home video movie industry.

LEARNING OBJECTIVES

After reading this chapter, you should be able to:

- 9.1 Identify and explain the characteristics of a perfectly competitive market structure.
- 9.2 Using revenue and cost information, determine the firm's short-run profit-maximizing or loss-minimizing level of output and profit.
- 9.3 Derive the firm's short-run supply curve and explain how the short-run equilibrium price is determined in a perfectly competitive market.
- 9.4 Explain the features and long-run adjustments associated with long-run equilibrium in perfect competition.
- 9.5 Explain the three different long-run industry supply curve situations that are possible in perfect competition.
- 9.6 From a social viewpoint, evaluate the long-run behaviour in perfect competition.

DID YOU KNOW THAT...

Canada is the least costly place to locate a business, when one compares the set-up and operating costs of firms competing in 12 broad industrial sectors in 11 of the most industrialized nations in the world. In 2003, on average, Canadian businesses enjoyed a 9 percent cost advantage over similar firms situated in the United States. If one examines the costs of conducting business in cities with metropolitan populations in excess of 2 million people, Montreal stands out as the lowest-cost location, followed by Melbourne, Australia. Moncton, Halifax, and Edmonton are home to the least-cost businesses when comparing mid-sized cities in North America. The relatively low wages, salaries, benefits, utilities, land, construction, and office leasing expenses incurred by Canadian firms help explain Canada's global cost competitiveness.

As this chapter explains, for industries having what resembles perfect competition, low costs become a key factor contributing to business success, if not survival.

SOURCE: "THE CEO'S GUIDE TO INTERNATIONAL BUSINESS COSTS G7—2004 EDITION." KPMG. http://www.competitivealternatives.com/default.asp. (ACCESSED FEBRUARY 2004).

9.1 The Characteristics of Perfect Competition

The Field of Industrial Organization

Industrial organization The study of how the industry environment affects the behaviour and performance of the firm.

Market structure Characteristics of an industry—such as the number of sellers, the ease of entry of new firms, each firm's ability to set the price, and the degree to which each firm's product differs from its competitor's.

Our study of perfect competition introduces you to the field of economics called **industrial organization**—where we study how a firm's industry environment or **market structure** affects the firm's market behaviour and market performance.

In this text, we will study four distinct market structures—perfect competition, monopoly, monopolistic competition, and oligopoly. The vast majority of Canadian industries can be classified as being in one of these four types of market structures. As you will see, market structure affects a firm's market behaviour—price, profit, and nonprice competitive behaviour. In turn, for each of the four market structures studied, we will examine how the firm's market behaviour affects the public interest, which we call the firm's market performance.

Table 9–1 provides an overview of the four types of market structures we will study in the next three chapters.

The Perfectly Competitive Market Structure

Perfect competition A market structure in which each firm is such a small part of the industry that it cannot affect the price of the product in question.

Price taker A competitive firm that takes price as a given, something determined *outside* the individual firm.

In this chapter we are interested in studying how a firm acting within a perfectly competitive market structure makes decisions about how much to produce. In a situation of **perfect competition**, each firm is such a small part of the industry that it cannot affect the price of the product in question. That means that each perfectly competitive firm in the industry is a **price taker**—the firm takes price as a given, something determined *outside* the individual firm.

TABLE 9–1

Comparing Market Structures

Market Structure	Number of Sellers	Unrestricted Entry and Exit	Ability to Set Price	Long-Run Economic Profits Possible	Product Differentiation	Nonprice Competition	Examples
Perfect competition	Numerous	Yes	None	No	None	None	Agriculture, coal
Monopolistic competition	Many	Yes	Some	Not for most	Considerable	Yes	Restaurants, motels, retail trade
Oligopoly	Few	Partial	Some	Yes	Frequent	Yes	Cigarettes, steel, banks
Pure monopoly	One	No (for entry)	Considerable	Yes	None (product is unique)	Yes	Electric company, provincial telephone company, medicare

This definition of a competitive firm is obviously idealized, for in one sense, the individual firm *has* to set prices. How can we ever have a situation in which firms regard prices as set by forces outside their control? The answer is that even though every firm sets its own prices, a firm in a perfectly competitive situation will find that it will eventually have no customers at all if it sets its price above the competitive price. The best example is in agriculture. Although the individual farmer can set any price for a bushel of carrots, if that price does not coincide with the market price of a bushel of similar-quality carrots, no one will purchase the carrots at a higher price; nor would the farmer be inclined to reduce revenues by selling below the market price.

The following characteristics of perfect competition help us understand why a perfectly competitive firm is a price taker.

1. *Large numbers.* There must be a large number of buyers and sellers. When this is the case, no one buyer or one seller has any influence on price.
2. *Homogeneous product.* The product sold by each firm in the industry must be a perfect substitute for the product sold by another firm. Buyers must be able to choose from a large number of sellers of a product that the buyers believe to be the same.
3. *Easy entry and exit.* Firms in a competitive industry cannot be hampered in their ability to get resources or relocate resources. They move labour and capital in pursuit of profit-making opportunities to whatever business venture gives them their highest expected rate of return on their investment. New firms can easily enter the industry.
4. *Perfect market information.* Consumers are able to find out about lower prices charged by competing firms. Firms are able to find out about cost-saving innovations in order to lower production costs and prices, and they are able to learn about profitable opportunities in other industries.

In this chapter's Issues and Applications, it is noted that the Canadian home video movie industry that supplies new releases and best-seller movies closely resembles perfect competition. In a typical Canadian city, there are large numbers of video stores that rent an identical product—new releases and best-sellers. There are numerous close substitutes in the form of online movie rental firms, video on demand, and mass retailers who sell home-movie DVDs. It is relatively easy for a firm to enter or exit this industry.

Many Canadian mining industries possess the characteristics of perfect competition. As Example 9–1 illustrates, a Canadian coal producer must compete with numerous mines around the world. Since one mine in Canada makes up such a small portion of the global coal market, it can vary its mining production without affecting the world coal price.

EXAMPLE 9–1 The Global Coal Market

A good real-world example of perfect competition is the market for coal. Coal is a fossil fuel that started as luxurious vegetation growing in the swamps that covered much of the world about 300 million years ago. Today, coal is found in nearly every region of the world, although the most commercially important deposits are in Asia, Australia, Europe, and North America.

Throughout the world, coal is produced in thousands of different mines. The purchasers of coal, such as steel mills and electric utility generating companies, constantly keep track of the prices of coal output throughout the world. If the price of coal goes up, there are literally thousands of known untapped coal deposits that can be developed. If the price of coal drops, coal mines can be closed. So, the market for coal probably conforms as closely as possible to the assumptions underlining the model of perfect competition.

For critical analysis: There are actually several different grades of coal. Does this seriously violate the homogeneous product characteristic of a perfectly competitive industry?

The Demand Curve of the Perfect Competitor

When we discussed substitutes in Chapter 4, we pointed out that the more substitutes there were and the more similar they were to the commodity in question, the greater was the price elasticity of demand. Here, we assume for the perfectly competitive firm that it is producing a commodity that has perfect substitutes. That means that if the individual firm raises its price by one penny, it will lose all of its business. This, then, is how we characterize the demand schedule for a perfectly competitive firm: It is the going market price as determined by the forces of market supply and market demand—that is, where the market demand curve intersects the market supply curve. The single-firm demand curve in a perfectly competitive industry is perfectly elastic at the going market price. Remember that with a perfectly elastic demand curve, any increase in price leads to zero quantity demanded.

We show the market demand and supply curves in part (a) of Figure 9–1. Their intersection occurs at the price of $5. The commodity in question is recordable DVDs, and we assume for the purposes of this exposition that all DVDs are perfect substitutes for all others. At the going market price of $5 apiece, a hypothetical individual demand curve for a DVD producer who sells a very, very small part of total industry production is shown in part (b). At the market price, this firm can sell all the output it wants. At the market price of $5 each, which is where the demand curve for the individual producer lies, consumer demand for the DVDs of that one producer is perfectly elastic. This can be seen by noting that if the firm raises its price, consumers, who are assumed to know that this supplier is charging more than other producers, will buy elsewhere, and the producer in question will have no sales at all. Thus, the demand curve for that producer is perfectly elastic. We label the individual producer's demand curve *d,* whereas the *market* demand curve is always labelled *D.*

CONCEPTS IN BRIEF

Learning Objective 9.1: Identify and explain the characteristics of a perfectly competitive market structure.

- Four fundamental characteristics of perfect competition are (1) a large number of buyers and sellers, (2) a homogeneous product, (3) easy exit from and entry to the industry, and (4) perfect market information in the hands of both buyers and sellers.
- A perfectly competitive firm is a price taker. It has no control over price, and consequently it takes the price as given from the industry or market.

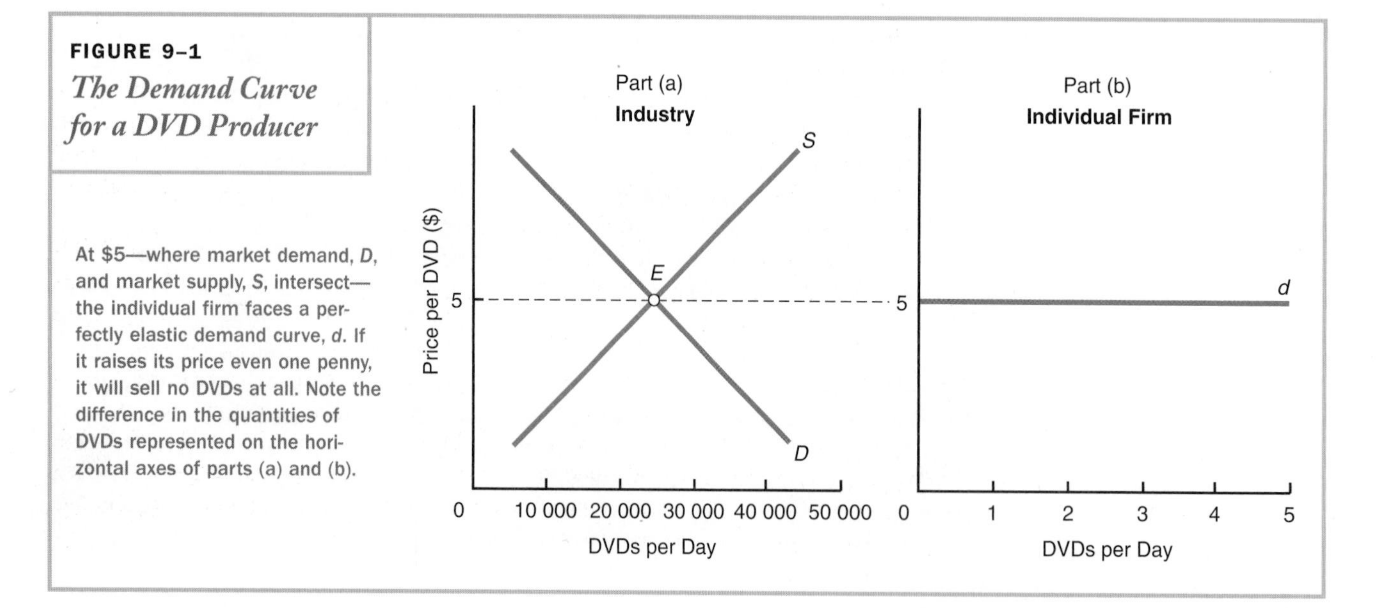

FIGURE 9–1

The Demand Curve for a DVD Producer

At $5—where market demand, *D*, and market supply, *S*, intersect—the individual firm faces a perfectly elastic demand curve, *d*. If it raises its price even one penny, it will sell no DVDs at all. Note the difference in the quantities of DVDs represented on the horizontal axes of parts (a) and (b).

- The individual firm's demand curve is horizontal or perfectly elastic. This implies that if any firm were to raise the price above the industry price, the firm would lose all of its sales. This also implies that the firm can sell all it wants at the given industry price.

9.2 Determining Output and Profit in the Short Run

As we have shown, a perfect competitor has to accept the price of the product as a "given." If the firm raises its price, it sells nothing; if it lowers its price, it makes less money per unit sold than it otherwise could. The firm has one decision left: How much should it produce? We will apply our model of the firm to this question to come up with an answer. We will use the *profit-maximization model,* which assumes that firms attempt to maximize their total profits—the positive difference between total revenues and total costs.

Total Revenues

Total revenues The quantity sold multiplied by the price.

Every firm has to consider its *total revenues,* or TR. **Total revenues** are defined as the quantity sold multiplied by the price. (They are the same as total receipts from the sale of output.) The perfect competitor must take the price as a given.

Look at Figure 9–2. Columns 1 and 2 show total output and sales per day and the total cost of producing that output. Column 3 is the market price, P, of $5 per DVD, which is also equal to average revenue (AR) because:

$$\text{AR} = \frac{\text{TR}}{Q} = \frac{PQ}{Q} = P$$

where Q stands for quantity. If we assume that all units sell for the same price, it becomes apparent that another name for the demand curve is the *average revenue curve* (this is true regardless of the type of market structure under consideration).

Column 4 shows the total revenues, or TR, as equal to the market price, P, times the total output in sales per day, or Q. Thus, TR = PQ. We are assuming that the market supply and demand schedules intersect at a price of $5 and that this price holds for all the firm's production. We are also assuming that because our DVD maker is a small part of the market, it can sell all that it produces at that price. Thus, part (b) of Figure 9–2 shows the total revenue curve as a straight line. For every unit of sales, total revenue is increased by $5.

Comparing Total Costs with Total Revenues

Total costs are also plotted in part (b). Remember, the firm's costs always include a normal rate of return on investment. So, whenever we refer to total costs, we are not talking about accounting costs but about economic costs. When the total cost curve is above the total revenue curve, the firm is experiencing economic losses. When it is below the total revenue curve, the firm is making economic profits.

Profit-maximizing rate of production The rate of production that maximizes total profits, or the difference between total revenues and total costs; also, the rate of production at which marginal revenue equals marginal cost.

By comparing total costs with total revenues, we can calculate the number of DVDs the individual competitive firm should produce per day. Our analysis rests on the assumption that the firm will attempt to maximize total profits. In part (a) of Figure 9–2, we see that total profits reach a maximum of $5.53 at a production rate of seven DVDs per day. We can see this graphically in part (b) of the figure. The firm will maximize profits where the total revenue curve exceeds the total cost curve by the greatest amount. That occurs at a rate of output and sales of seven DVDs per day; this rate is called the **profit-maximizing rate of production**—the rate of production that maximizes total profits, or the difference between total revenues and total costs; also, the rate of production at which marginal revenue equals marginal cost.

FIGURE 9–2

Profit Maximization

Given the firm's costs and the market price of $5, the daily quantity that results in the largest profit is seven DVDs per day. In the table in part (a), the profit-maximizing quantity occurs where (TR – TC) = $5.53, which is the maximum profit. Theoretically, this profit-maximizing quantity occurs where MR = MC. In part (b), we find the maximum profit at the quantity level, where the TR curve exceeds the TC curve by the largest vertical amount, at seven DVDs per day. In part (c), we find the maximum profit at the quantity level, where the MR curve intersects the MC curve, at seven DVDs per day.

Part (a)

(1) Total Output per Day (*Q*)	(2) Total Costs (TC)	(3) Market Price (*P*)	(4) Total Revenues (TR) = (3) × (1)	(5) Total Profit (TR – TC) = (4) – (2)	(6) Average Total Cost (ATC) = (2) ÷ (1)	(7) Average Variable Cost (AVC)	(8) Marginal Cost (MC) = Change (2) / Change (1)	(9) Marginal Revenue (MR) = Change (4) / Change (1)
0	$10.00	$5	$ 0	–$10.00				
1	14.00	5	5	–9.00	$14.00	$4.00	$ 4.00	$5.00
2	17.00	5	10	–7.00	8.50	3.50	3.00	5.00
3	19.00	5	15	–4.00	6.33	3.00	2.00	5.00
4	20.00	5	20	0.00	5.00	2.50	1.00	5.00
5	21.50	5	25	3.50	4.30	2.30	1.50	5.00
6	24.48	5	30	5.52	4.08	2.41	2.98	5.00
7	29.47	5	35	5.53	4.21	2.78	4.99	5.00
8	37.47	5	40	2.53	4.68	3.43	8.00	5.00
9	49.47	5	45	–4.47	5.50	4.39	12.00	5.00
10	66.47	5	50	–16.47	6.65	5.65	17.00	5.00

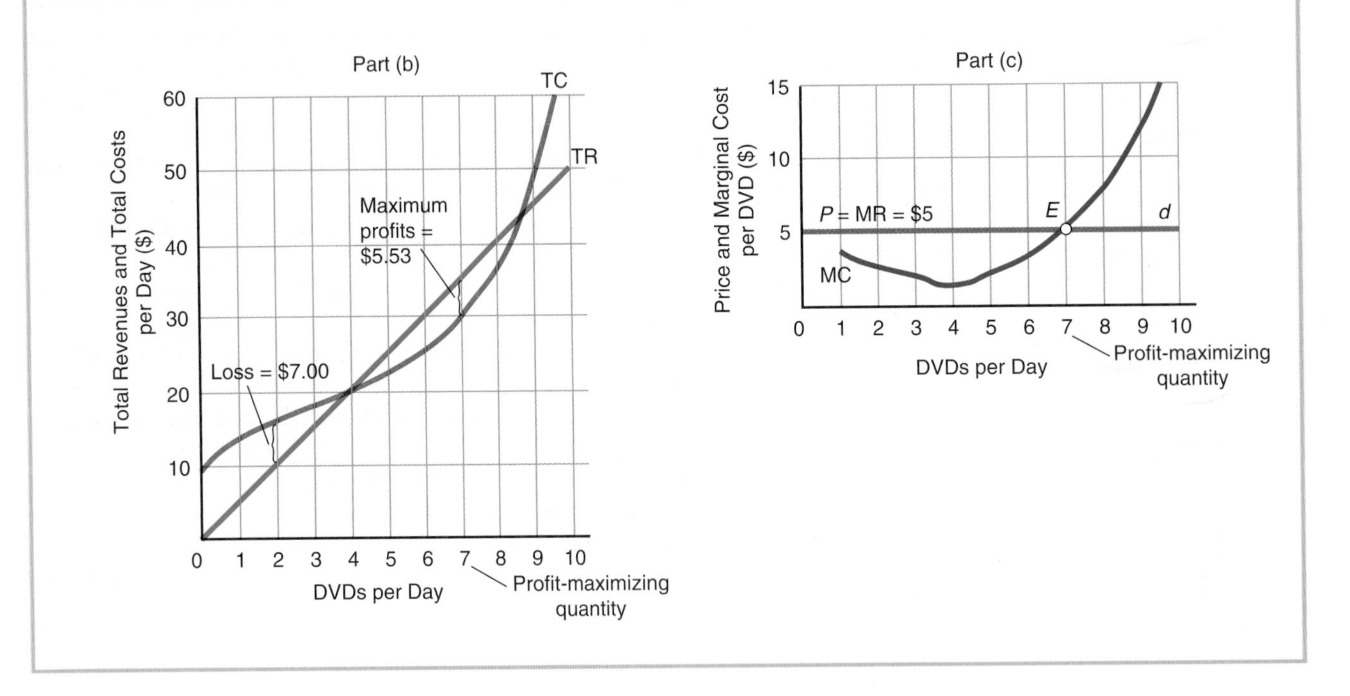

We can also find this profit-maximizing rate of production for the individual competitive firm by looking at marginal revenues and marginal costs.

Using Marginal Analysis to Determine the Profit-Maximizing Rate of Production

It is possible—indeed, preferable—to use marginal analysis to determine the profit-maximizing rate of production. We end up with the same results derived in a different manner, one that focuses more on where decisions are really made—on the margin. Managers examine changes in costs and relate them to changes in revenues. In fact, we almost always compare changes in cost with changes in benefits, where change is occurring at the margin, whether it be with respect to how much more or less to produce, how many more workers to hire or fire, or how much more to study or not study.

Marginal revenue The change in total revenues attributable to changing production by one unit of the product in question.

Marginal revenue represents the change in total revenues attributable to changing production by one unit of the product in question. Hence, a more formal definition of marginal revenue is:

$$\text{Marginal revenue} = \frac{\text{Change in total revenues}}{\text{Change in output}}$$

In a perfectly competitive market, the marginal revenue curve is exactly equivalent to the price line or the individual firm's demand curve, because the firm can sell all of its output (production) at the market price. Thus, in Figure 9–1, the demand curve, *d*, for the individual producer is at a price of $5—the price line is coincident with the demand curve. But so is the marginal revenue curve, for marginal revenue, in this case, also equals $5.

The marginal revenue curve for our competitive DVD producer is shown as a line at $5 in part (c) of Figure 9–2. Note, again, that the marginal revenue curve is equal to the price line, which is equal to the individual firm's demand, or average revenue, curve, *d*.

When Are Profits Maximized?

Now, we add the marginal cost curve, MC, taken from column 8 in part (a) of Figure 9–2. As shown in part (c) of that figure, the marginal cost curve first falls and then starts to rise because of the law of diminishing returns, eventually intersecting the marginal revenue curve and then rising above it. Note that column 8 in part (a) of Figure 9–2 indicates that the marginal cost of the first unit of output is $4; the second unit of output is $3; and so forth.

In part (c), the marginal cost curve intersects the marginal revenue curve at seven DVDs per day. The firm has an incentive to produce and sell until the amount of the additional revenue received from selling one more DVD just equals the additional costs incurred for producing and selling that DVD. This is how the firm maximizes profit. Whenever marginal cost is less than marginal revenue, the firm will always make more profit by increasing production.

Now, consider the possibility of producing at an output rate of eight DVDs per day. The marginal cost curve at that output rate is higher than the marginal revenue curve (or *d*). The firm would be spending more to produce that additional output than it would be receiving in revenues; it would be foolish to continue producing at this rate.

But how much should it produce? It should produce at point *E* in Figure 9–2 part (c), where the marginal cost curve intersects the marginal revenue curve from below.[1] The firm should continue production until the cost of increasing output by one more unit is just equal to the revenues obtainable from that extra unit. This is a fundamental rule in economics:

> **Profit maximization normally occurs at the rate of output at which marginal revenue equals marginal cost.**

For a perfectly competitive firm, this is at the intersection of the demand schedule, *d*, and the marginal cost curve, MC. When MR exceeds MC, each additional unit of output

[1]The marginal cost curve, MC, also cuts the marginal revenue curve, *d*, from above at an output rate of less than 1 in this example. This intersection should be ignored because it is irrelevant to the firm's decisions.

adds more to total revenues than to total costs, causing losses to decrease or profits to increase. When MC is greater than MR, each unit produced adds more to total cost than to total revenues, causing profits to decrease or losses to increase. Therefore, profit maximization occurs when MC equals MR. In our particular example, our profit-maximizing, perfectly competitive DVD producer will produce at a rate of seven DVDs a day.

In the first quarter of 2004, the Canadian government faced significant public pressure to implement policies that would restore international confidence in Canadian beef, due to the discovery of "mad cow disease" in Canada. Policy Example 9–1 encourages you to use marginal analysis to evaluate a policy proposal that would have every cow destined for Asia tested for "mad cow disease."

POLICY EXAMPLE 9–1 **Quelling Fears of "Mad Cow Disease" in Asia**

The Canada Beef Export Federation (CBEF) is an independent nonprofit organization committed to improving export results for the perfectly competitive Canadian cattle and beef industry. In the year ending 2002, according to the CBEF, the three key export markets for Canadian beef were the United States, Mexico, and East Asia—purchasing 72 percent, 15 percent, and 10 percent, respectively, of all Canadian beef exports.

On the basis of current market and profit trends, the Canada Beef Export Federation has established a marketing plan that would significantly increase Canadian beef exports to East Asia. According to this plan, by 2010, East Asia would purchase over 30 percent of Canadian beef exports, the United States 45 percent, with the remaining 25 percent going to Mexico and other nations. The Far East is an attractive market to target because its consumers eat nonprime beef cuts, such as tripe, that North Americans generally shun. That means that a carcass processed for Asia is worth up to $200 more than one killed for the North American market.

Since the discovery, in 2003, of two cases of bovine spongiform encephalopathy (BSE), or "mad cow disease," in cows raised in Canada, most nations around the world have closed their borders to Canadian beef and cattle. As of February 2004, the United States and Mexico were the only major export markets accepting beef from Canada.

Key East Asian markets, such as Japan, have demanded that Canada test for BSE all the cattle it slaughters, before they would consider buying Canadian beef. As of February 2004, Canada had resisted this demand, but some industry observers have suggested a policy of testing all animals destined for Asian consumption.

SOURCE: "CANADIAN BEEF AND VEAL PRODUCT EXPORTS." TRADE STATISTICS. CANADA BEEF EXPORT FEDERATION. http://www.cbef.com/PDF/Stats_1990-2010.pdf. (ACCESSED FEBRUARY 22, 2004).

For critical analysis: What maximum amount, per animal slaughtered, would Canadian beef producers be willing to pay, to ensure that all animals destined for the Asian markets are tested for BSE? Explain.

Short-Run Profits

To find what our competitive individual DVD producer is making in terms of profits in the short run, we have to add the average total cost curve to part (c) of Figure 9–2. That is, we take the information from column 6 in part (a) of Figure 9–2 and add it to part (c) of Figure 9–2 to get Figure 9–3.

In Figure 9–3, assuming a price of $5 per DVD, the profit-maximizing rate of output is seven DVDs per day, where marginal revenue equals marginal cost. At this output of seven DVDs, total revenue will equal price multiplied by quantity, which is $5 × 7 or $35 a day. Total cost, at an output level of seven DVDs, will be average total cost multiplied by the profit-maximizing rate of output, which is $4.21 × 7 = $29.47 a day. Total profit will then be total revenue minus total cost, or $35 − $29.47 = $5.53 a day.

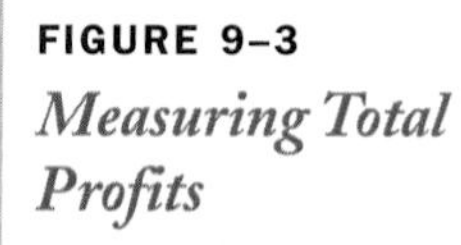

FIGURE 9–3
Measuring Total Profits

To determine the profits graphically, first find the profit-maximizing quantity = Q = 7 DVDs per day. This is where MR = MC. The maximum total profit = (P – ATC) × Q, where Q = 7 DVDs, P = given price = \$5 and ATC = \$4.21 at Q = 7 DVDs. Therefore, maximum total profit = (\$5 – \$4.21) × (7) = \$5.53 = shaded area of rectangle *abcd*.

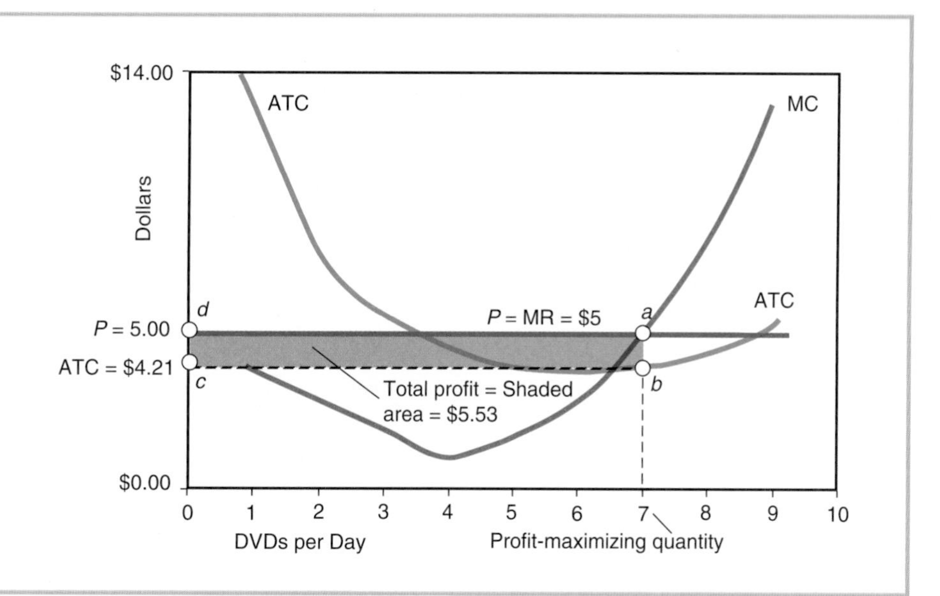

As Figure 9–3 illustrates, the maximum total profit of \$5.53 a day can be shown geometrically as the area of the shaded rectangle *abcd*. Recall that the area of a rectangle is the height multiplied by the length of the rectangle. The height of rectangle *abcd* equals the distance *dc*, which is the difference between the price (\$5) and the average total cost (\$4.21). That is, the height of the shaded rectangle *abcd* is \$5 – \$4.21 = \$0.79, which represents the *profit per unit* earned by the profit-maximizing firm. The length of rectangle *abcd* equals the profit-maximizing quantity of seven DVDs per day. Therefore, the area of the shaded rectangle, *abcd*, is the height multiplied by the length, or the profit per unit (\$0.79) multiplied by the number of units sold (7 DVDs), which equals the total profit of \$5.53 a day. Note that we are talking about an *economic profit* of \$5.53 per day because a normal rate of return on investment is included in the average total cost curve, ATC.

Minimizing Losses

It is certainly possible for the competitive firm to incur losses in the short run. We give an example in Figure 9–4, where the going market price has fallen from \$5 to \$3 per DVD because of changes in market demand or supply conditions (or both). The firm will always do the best it can by producing where marginal revenue equals marginal cost, assuming it continues to operate (a point explained below).

We see in part (b) of Figure 9–4 that the marginal revenue curve is intersected (from below) by the marginal cost curve at an output rate of six DVDs per day. The firm is no longer making an economic profit as its average total cost of \$4.08 per DVD exceeds the \$3 price it can charge. The firm's minimum loss is equal to the loss per unit of \$1.08 (\$4.08 – \$3) multiplied by the quantity of six DVDs, which equals a total loss of \$6.48 per day.

Should this firm go out of business when it faces a loss of \$6.48 per day? At this point, we should note that we are assuming a short-run situation, where the firm is stuck with meeting some of its fixed obligations, such as paying its monthly rent due to a lease agreement, or monthly interest on funds already borrowed from the bank. Also, in the short run, the firm is optimistic that the price will increase in the near future so that an economic profit can be earned during some of the days of the month. Therefore, we are assuming that the firm intends to stay in business in the short run.

Shutdown A short-run situation where the firm stays in business but temporarily produces at a zero quantity level.

Should this firm opt for a *shutdown*, with a loss of \$6.48 per day? By **shutdown** we mean that the firm stays in business but temporarily produces at a zero quantity level. If the firm were to shut down, it avoids incurring variable costs, but it would still have to pay for its total fixed costs. According to column 2 in part (a) of Figure 9–4, if the firm

FIGURE 9–4

Minimization of Short-Run Losses

To determine the losses graphically, first find the loss-minimizing quantity = Q = 6 DVDs per day. This is where MR = MC. The maximum total profit = (P – ATC) × Q, where Q = 6 DVDs, P = given price = \$3 and ATC = \$4.08 at Q = 6 DVDs. Therefore, total profit = (\$3 - \$4.08) × 6 = \$-6.48. This minimum total loss of \$6.48 equals the shaded area of rectangle abcd.

Part (a)

(1) Total Output per Day (*Q*)	(2) Total Costs (TC)	(3) Market Price (*P*)	(4) Total Revenues (TR) = (3) × (1)	(5) Total Profit (TR – TC) = (4) – (2)	(6) Average Total Cost (ATC) = (2) ÷ (1)	(7) Average Variable Cost (AVC)	(8) Marginal Cost (MC) = Change (2) / Change (1)	(9) Marginal Revenue (MR) = Change (4) / Change (1)
0	\$10.00	\$3	\$ 0	–\$10.00				
1	14.00	3	3	–11.00	\$14.00	\$4.00	\$4.00	\$3
2	17.00	3	6	–11.00	8.50	3.50	3.00	3
3	19.00	3	9	–10.00	6.33	3.00	2.00	3
4	20.00	3	12	–8.00	5.00	2.50	1.00	3
5	21.50	3	15	–6.50	4.30	2.30	1.50	3
6	24.48	3	18	–6.48	4.08	2.41	2.98	3
7	29.47	3	21	–8.47	4.21	2.78	4.99	3
8	37.47	3	24	–13.47	4.68	3.43	8.00	3
9	49.47	3	27	–22.47	5.50	4.39	12.00	3
10	66.47	3	30	–36.47	6.65	5.65	17.00	3

Part (b)

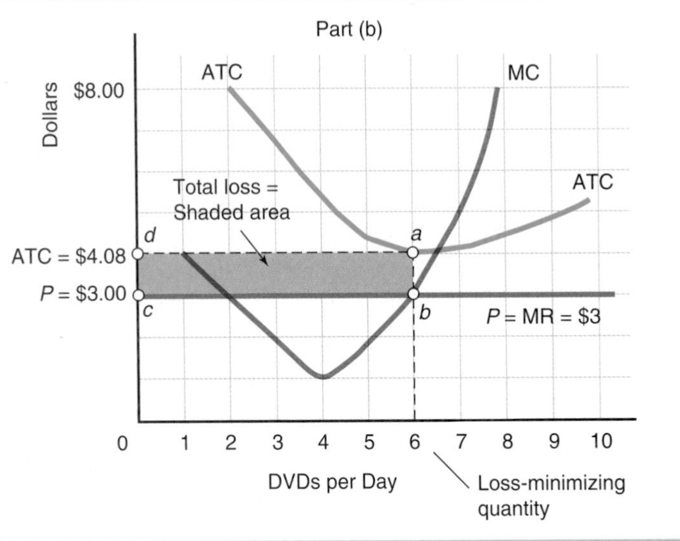

operates at a zero quantity level, it will still incur a total cost of \$10 per day. This means that its total fixed costs are \$10 per day. If the firm were to shut down in the short run, its total revenue would equal zero, its total costs would equal \$10, leaving a total loss of \$10 per day.

If, instead, the firm operates at an output rate of six DVDs per day, it minimizes its losses at \$6.48 per day, as described in Figure 9–4. As you can see, at a price of \$3 per DVD, this firm should not shut down.

In general, how do we know when it is best *not* to shut down in the face of economic losses? A firm should operate at a positive quantity level whenever the extra revenue it gets exceeds the extra costs incurred when operating at a positive quantity level, which are its *variable* costs. On a per-unit basis, as long as it is possible for the price of the product to exceed the firm's average variable cost, the firm should operate at a positive quantity level.

In the DVD example, at a quantity level of six DVDs per day, we can see that the price of \$3 per DVD exceeds the average variable cost of \$2.41 per DVD. By selling six DVDs per day, the firm gets a positive contribution toward recovering some of its fixed costs. Therefore, the firm should not shut down.

As long as the price per unit sold exceeds the average variable cost per unit produced, the firm will be recovering part of the opportunity cost of its investment in the business—that is, part of its fixed costs.

Once you appreciate the importance of having price exceed average variable cost in the short run, you can appreciate why big discounts are frequently offered in businesses that face a large amount of fixed costs, as Example 9–2 explains.

EXAMPLE 9–2

High Sunk Costs Can Mean Deep Discounts

Have you ever wondered why airline "standby" rates are so cheap? Or why you can pay half price to stay at a three-star hotel off-season? Or why restaurants frequently offer two-for-one entrees? Or why golf courses offer cheaper green fees during the quiet times of day or week? The answer to all of these questions is the same.

Whenever the production or sale of a product or service entails high sunk (fixed) costs and low variable costs, the marginal cost of supplying additional units of the service is very close to zero. This being the case, the firm can get some contribution toward its sunk costs by selling its service at deep discounts, as long as the discounted price more than covers the variable cost per unit. In this way, the firm can minimize its losses in the short run. Remember, if the firm shuts down in the short run, it is stuck with paying those large fixed monthly costs, which is why they are called sunk costs.

Consider the operation of a three-star hotel in a popular ski resort area during the off-season. Most of the costs incurred by the hotel's owners relate to the fixed monthly mortgage payment associated with the hotel's land, building, fixtures, and facilities. As well, the costs of furnishing each hotel room and bathroom are also fixed. The variable costs of renting out additional rooms would include such expenses as paying additional staff to clean the rooms and the extra laundry, which would result in a relatively low variable cost per room. In the off-season, when room vacancies become more common, the hotel owners can attract hotel guests by offering deep discounts, as long as the discounted daily room charge more than covers the relatively low variable cost per room.

For critical analysis: Suppose there is available seating on a popular jet flight between Vancouver and Toronto, moments before take-off. What is the marginal cost of allowing a passenger to fill one of these vacant seats? How large a discount can the airline give to this passenger? Explain.

Calculating the Short-Run Breakeven Price

Short-run breakeven price The price at which a firm's total revenues equal its total costs.

Look at demand curve d_1 in Figure 9–5. It just touches the minimum point of the average total cost curve, which is exactly where the marginal cost curve intersects the average total cost curve. At that price, which is about \$4, the firm will be making exactly zero short-run economic profits. That price, the **short-run breakeven price**, is the price at which a firm's total revenues equal its total costs. At the breakeven price, the firm is just making a normal rate of return on its capital investment. (It is covering its explicit and implicit costs.) Point E_1, therefore, occurs at the short-run breakeven price for a competitive firm. It is the point at which marginal revenue, marginal cost, and average total cost are all equal (that is, at which $P = \text{MC}$ and $P = \text{ATC}$). The breakeven price is the one that yields zero short-run economic profits or losses.

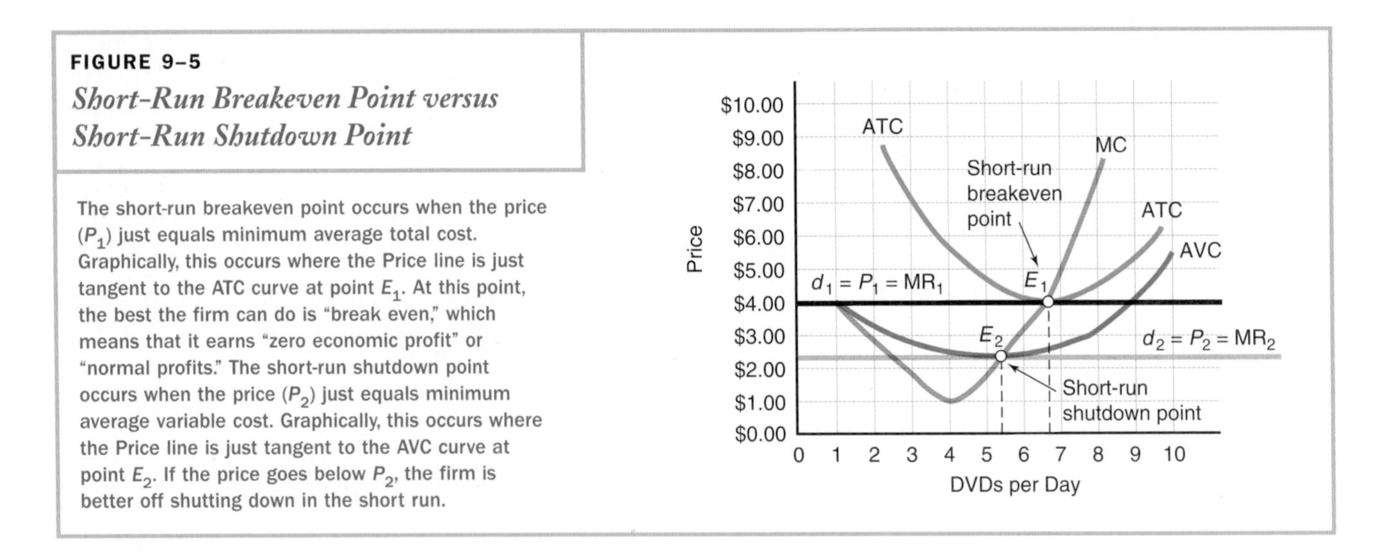

FIGURE 9–5

Short-Run Breakeven Point versus Short-Run Shutdown Point

The short-run breakeven point occurs when the price (P_1) just equals minimum average total cost. Graphically, this occurs where the Price line is just tangent to the ATC curve at point E_1. At this point, the best the firm can do is "break even," which means that it earns "zero economic profit" or "normal profits." The short-run shutdown point occurs when the price (P_2) just equals minimum average variable cost. Graphically, this occurs where the Price line is just tangent to the AVC curve at point E_2. If the price goes below P_2, the firm is better off shutting down in the short run.

Calculating the Short-Run Shutdown Price

To calculate the firm's shutdown price, we must introduce the average variable cost (AVC) to our graph. In Figure 9–5, we have plotted the AVC values from column 7 in part (a) of Figure 9–2. For the moment, consider two possible demand curves, d_1 and d_2, which are also the firm's respective marginal revenue curves. Therefore, if demand is d_1, the firm will produce at E_1, where that curve intersects the marginal cost curve. If demand falls to d_2, the firm will produce at E_2. The special feature of the hypothetical demand curve, d_2, is that it just touches the average variable cost curve at the latter's minimum point, which is also where the marginal cost curve intersects it. This price is the **short-run shutdown price**, which just equals minimum average variable cost. Why? Below this price, the firm would be paying out more in variable costs than it is receiving in revenues from the sale of its product. Each unit it sold would add to its losses. Clearly, the way to avoid incurring these additional losses, if price falls below the shutdown point, is, in fact, to shut down operations.

Short-run shutdown price The price that just equals minimum average variable cost.

As an example, suppose the price per DVD dropped to $2. As Table 9–2 indicates, the price is now below the average variable cost at every quantity. This indicates that the firm is better off shutting down in the short run. With this decision, the firm's total loss equals its total fixed costs of $10, which is the minimum loss displayed in Table 9–2. If, alternatively, the firm was to produce one DVD per day, the price of $2 would be $2 less than the average variable cost of $4 per DVD. In addition to the fixed costs of $10, the firm would lose an extra $2. Therefore, total losses would be $12 at an output of one DVD per day.

The Meaning of Zero Economic Profits

The fact that we labelled point E_1 in Figure 9–5 the breakeven point may have puzzled you. At point E_1, price is just equal to average total cost. If this is the case, why would a firm continue to produce if it were making no profits whatsoever? If we again make the distinction between accounting profits and economic profits, then at that price the firm has zero economic profits but positive accounting profits. Recall that accounting profits are total revenues minus total explicit costs. What is ignored in such accounting is the reward offered to investors—the opportunity cost of capital—plus all other implicit costs.

In economic analysis, the average total cost curve includes the full opportunity cost of capital. Indeed, the average total cost curve includes the opportunity cost of *all* factors of production used in the production process. At the short-run breakeven price, economic profits are, by definition, zero. Accounting profits at that price are not, however, equal to zero; they are positive. Consider an example. A clock manufacturer sells clocks at some

TABLE 9-2

Short-Run Shutdown Example: Price = $2.00 or Below Minimum Average Variable Cost

(1) Total Output per Day (*Q*)	(2) Total Costs (TC)	(3) Market Price (*P*)	(4) Total Revenues (TR) = (3) × (1)	(5) Total Profit (TR − TC) = (4) − (2)	(6) Average Total Cost (ATC) = (2) ÷ (1)	(7) Average Variable Cost (AVC)	(8) Marginal Cost (MC) = Change (2) / Change (1)	(9) Marginal Revenue (MR) = Change (4) / Change (1)
0	$10.00	$2	$ 0	−$10.00				
1	14.00	2	2	−12.00	$14.00	$4.00	$ 4.00	$2.00
2	17.00	2	4	−13.00	8.50	3.50	3.00	2.00
3	19.00	2	6	−13.00	6.33	3.00	2.00	2.00
4	20.00	2	8	−12.00	5.00	2.50	1.00	2.00
5	21.50	2	10	−11.50	4.30	2.30	1.50	2.00
6	24.48	2	12	−12.48	4.08	2.41	2.98	2.00
7	29.47	2	14	−15.47	4.21	2.78	4.99	2.00
8	37.47	2	16	−21.47	4.68	3.43	8.00	2.00
9	49.47	2	18	−31.47	5.50	4.39	12.00	2.00
10	66.47	2	20	−46.47	6.65	5.65	17.00	2.00

price. The owners of the firm have supplied all the funds in the business. They have borrowed no money from anyone else, and they explicitly pay the full opportunity cost to all factors of production, including any managerial labour that they themselves contribute to the business. Their salaries show up as a cost in the books and are equal to what they could have earned in the best alternative occupation. At the end of the year, the owners find that after they subtract all explicit costs from total revenues, they have earned $100 000. Let us say that their investment was $1 million. Thus, the rate of return on that investment is 10 percent per year. We will assume that this turns out to be equal to the rate of return that, on average, all other clock manufacturers make in the industry.

This $100 000, or 10 percent rate of return, is actually, then, a competitive, or normal, rate of return on invested capital in that industry or in other industries with similar risks. If the owners had made only $50 000, or 5 percent on their investment, they would have been able to make higher profits by leaving the industry. The 10 percent rate of return is the opportunity cost of capital. Accountants show it as a profit; economists call it a cost. We include that cost in the average total cost curve, similar to the one shown in Figure 9–5. At the short-run breakeven price, average total cost, including this opportunity cost of capital, will just equal that price. The firm will be making zero economic profits or a 10 percent *accounting* rate of return called "normal profits."

9.3 Short-Run Supply and Equilibrium

What does the supply curve for the individual firm in perfect competition look like? Actually, we have been looking at it all along. We know that when the price of DVDs is $5, the firm will supply seven of them per day. If the price falls to $3, the firm will supply six DVDs per day. And if the price falls to $2, the firm will shut down in the short run. Hence, in Figure 9–6, the firm's supply curve is the marginal cost curve above the short-run shutdown point. This is shown as the solid part of the marginal cost curve.

The definition, then, of the individual firm's supply curve in a competitive industry is its marginal cost curve equal to and above minimum average variable cost.

FIGURE 9–6

Individual Firm's Short-Run Supply Curve

In general, the firm's supply curve indicates what quantity the firm will supply at different prices. In this figure, we can see that at different possible prices, the firm will supply that quantity that maximizes profit or minimizes losses. That is, when the price is above minimum average variable cost, the firm will supply that quantity where P = MC or MR = MC. Therefore, the firm's supply curve is the portion of its marginal cost curve that is above minimum average variable cost.

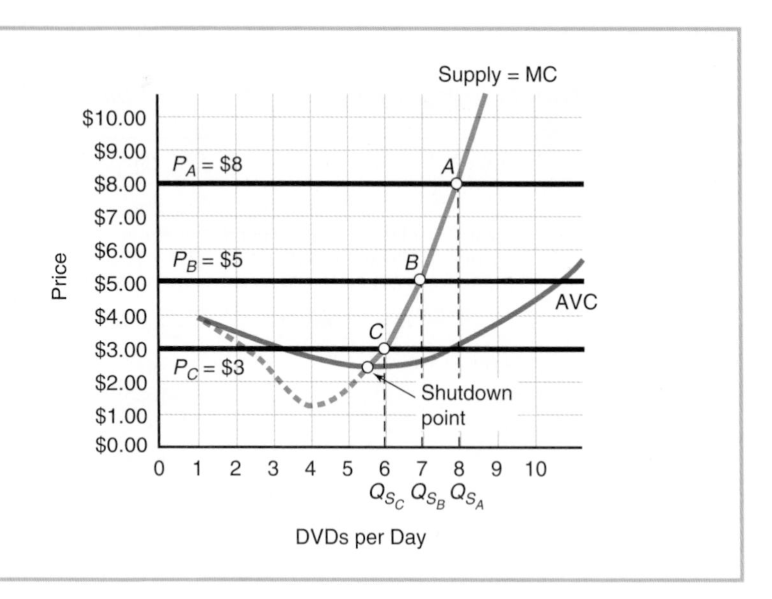

The Short-Run Industry Supply Curve

In Chapter 3, we indicated that the market supply curve was the summation of individual supply curves. At the beginning of this chapter, we drew a market supply curve in Figure 9–1. Now, we want to derive more precisely a market, or industry, supply curve to reflect individual producer behaviour in that industry. First, we must ask: "What is an industry?" It is merely a collection of firms producing a particular product. Therefore, we have a way to figure out the total supply curve of any industry: We add the quantities that each firm will supply at every possible price. In other words, we sum the individual supply curves of all the competitive firms *horizontally*. The individual supply curves, as we just saw, are simply the marginal cost curves of each firm.

Consider doing this for a hypothetical world in which there are only two DVD producers in the industry, firm A and firm B. These two firms' marginal cost curves are given in parts (a) and (b) of Figure 9–7. The marginal cost curves for the two separate firms are presented as MC_A in part (a) and MC_B in part (b). Those two marginal cost curves are drawn only for prices above the minimum average variable cost for each firm. Hence, we are not including any of the marginal cost curves below minimum average variable cost. In part (a), for firm A, at $5, the quantity supplied would be seven. At $10, the quantity supplied would be nine. In part (b), we see the two different quantities that would be supplied by firm B corresponding to those two prices. In part (c), for the $5 price, we add horizontally the quantities 7 and 10. This gives us one point, *F*, for our short-run **industry supply curve**, *S*—the locus of points showing the minimum prices at which given quantities will be forthcoming from the industry; also called the market supply curve. We obtain the other point, *G*, by doing the same horizontal adding of quantities at $10. When we connect points *F* and *G*, we obtain industry supply curve *S*, which is also marked ΣMC, indicating that it is the horizontal summation of the marginal cost curves (above the respective minimum average variable cost of each firm).[2]

Industry supply curve The locus of points showing the minimum prices at which given quantities will be forthcoming from the industry; also called the market supply curve.

Because the law of diminishing returns makes marginal cost curves rise, the short-run supply curve of a perfectly competitive industry must be upward sloping.

Factors That Influence the Industry Supply Curve

As you have just seen, the industry supply curve is the horizontal summation of all of the individual firms' marginal cost curves above their respective minimum average variable

[2]The capital Greek sigma, Σ, is the symbol for summation.

FIGURE 9–7

Deriving the Industry Supply Curve

Marginal cost curves above minimum average variable cost are presented in parts (a) and (b) for firms A and B. We horizontally sum the two quantities supplied, 7 and 10, at \$5. This gives us point *F* in part (c). We do the same thing for the quantities at \$10. This gives us point *G*. When we connect those points, we have the industry supply curve, *S*, which is the horizontal summation of the firms' marginal cost curves above their respective minimum average variable costs.

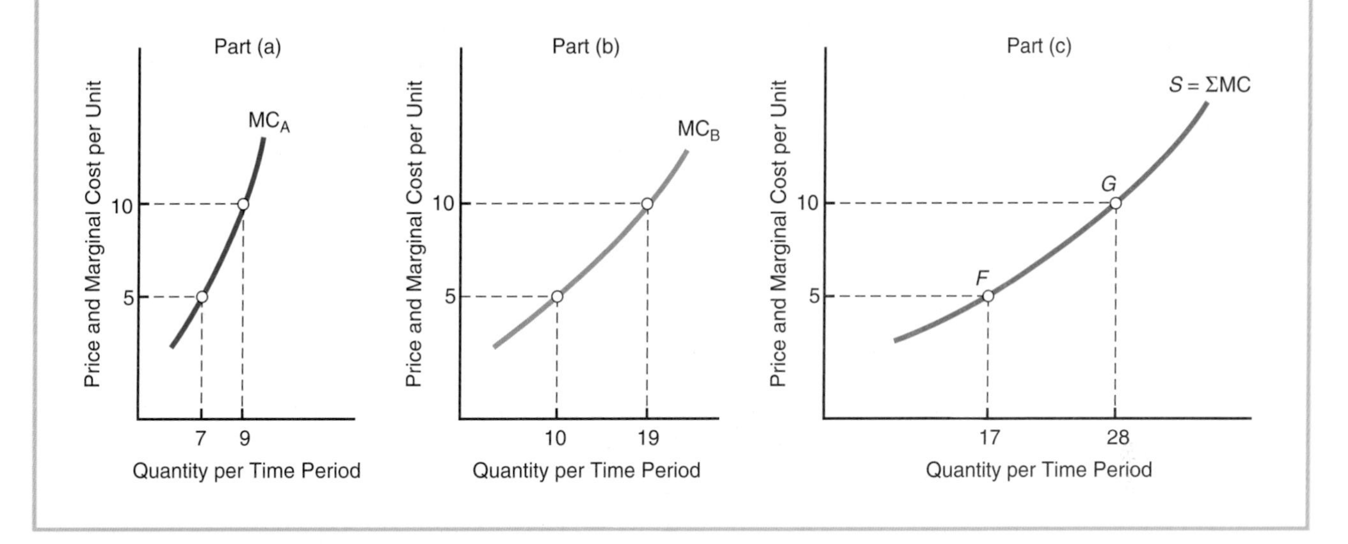

cost points. This means that anything that affects the marginal cost curves of the firm will influence the industry supply curve. Therefore, the individual factors that will influence the supply schedule in a competitive industry can be summarized as the factors that cause the *variable costs* of production to change. These are factors that affect the individual marginal cost curves, such as changes in the individual firm's productivity, in factor costs (wages paid to labour, prices of raw materials, and so on), in taxes, and in anything else that would influence the individual firm's marginal cost curve.

All of these are *ceteris paribus* conditions of supply. Because they affect the position of the marginal cost curve for the individual firm, they affect the position of the industry supply curve. A change in any of these will shift the market supply curve.

Short-Run Equilibrium

How is the market, or "going," price established in the short run in perfect competition? The short-run equilibrium price will occur where the short-run industry or market supply just equals the industry or market demand. We have just seen how the industry supply curve is the horizontal sum of the individual firms' marginal cost curves, assuming that firms maximize profits or minimize losses. This suggests that although no one single firm can affect the price, the supply plans of all the firms, combined, does play an important role in determining the industry price.

Short-Run Equilibrium for the Industry

Table 9–3 illustrates the process by which the competitive industry price is determined for the DVD market, on the basis of the following assumptions. The DVD industry comprises 100 identical perfectly competitive firms. Each firm has the total and per-units costs described in Figure 9–2. The industry or market demand schedule is given in column 4 in Table 9–3. While we will not attempt to derive the industry demand schedule, you may recall that it is the "horizontal sum" of all individual demand schedules for DVDs. Each individual demand schedule is based on the assumption that the consumer maximizes his or her utility, when responding to price.

TABLE 9-3

Short-Run Equilibrium in the DVD Industry

Price per DVD	Quantity Supplied Individual Firm	Quantity Supplied Industry (100 Firms)	Quantity Demanded Industry (all consumers)
$12	9	900	200
8	8	800	500
5	7	700	700
3	6	600	800

To determine the short-run industry equilibrium price in Table 9–3, we must first determine the individual firm's quantity supplied in column 2 of Table 9–3. To do this, we compare each price in column 1 of Table 9–3 with the marginal costs described in Figure 9–2. For example, at the price of $12 per DVD, the firm will maximize its profits if it supplies nine DVDs per day, where the marginal revenue of $12 just equals the marginal cost of $12. If the price falls to $8 per DVD, the firm will instead supply eight DVDs per day, where marginal revenue equals marginal cost.

After determining the individual firm's quantity supplied for all of the prices in Table 9–3, you are ready to derive the short-run industry supply schedule in column 3 of Table 9–3. At each price, the industry supply is simply 100 multiplied by the individual firm's quantity supplied at that same price. Once the industry supply schedule is determined for all prices in Table 9–3, you can see that the industry quantity supplied equals the industry quantity demanded at $5 per DVD. In other words, the short-run equilibrium industry price is $5 per DVD and the short-run equilibrium industry quantity is 700 DVDs per day.

Part (a) of Figure 9–8 provides a sketch of the graph of the short-run equilibrium in the DVD industry, on the basis of the industry demand in Table 9–3, and assuming that the industry comprises 100 identical firms. Each firm faces the total and per-unit costs described in Figure 9–2. Note that part (a) in Figure 9–8 shows how the short-run

FIGURE 9–8

Short-Run Equilibrium for the DVD Industry and Firm

In part (a) the horizontal sum of the 100 identical firm marginal cost curves determines the short-run industry supply curve. This short-run industry supply curve interacts with the industry demand curve, *D*, to establish an equilibrium industry price of $5 per DVD and an industry equilibrium quantity of 700 DVDs. In part (b), at the industry price of $5, each individual firm's equilibrium quantity will be seven DVDs per day with an economic profit of $5.53, which is equal to the shaded area.

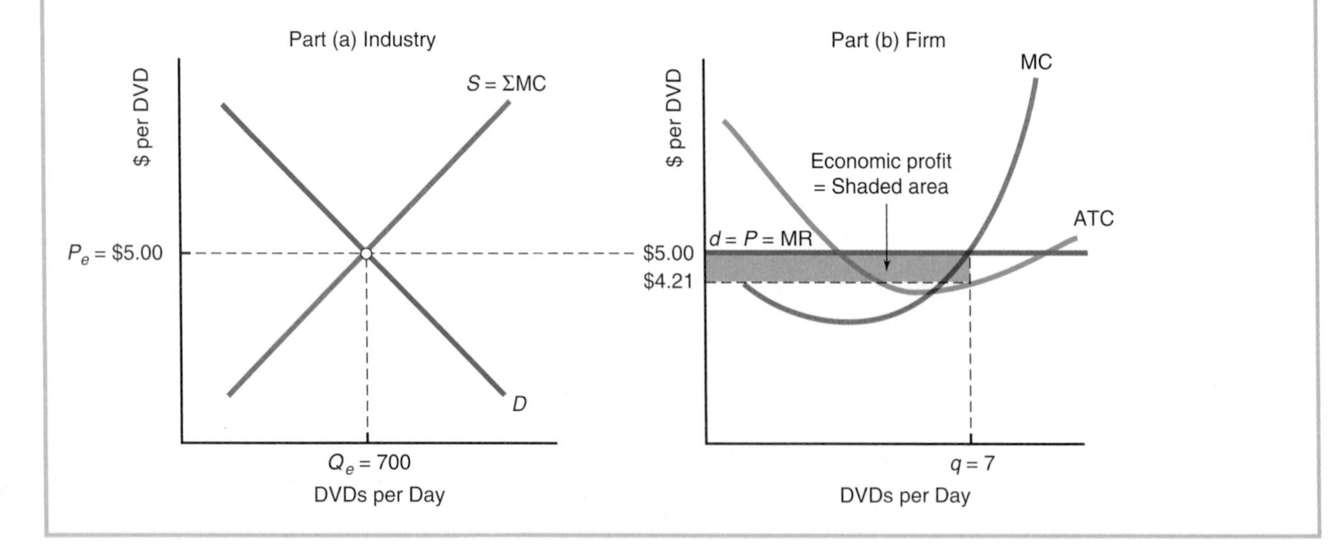

industry supply, made up of the horizontal sum of 100 identical marginal cost curves, interacts with the industry demand curve to establish an equilibrium price of $5 per DVD and an equilibrium industry quantity of 700 DVDs per day.

Short-Run Equilibrium for the Firm

Where will each individual DVD firm settle at in the short run? The individual firm's *equilibrium quantity* will be the quantity that maximizes profits or minimizes losses, given the industry equilibrium price. As part (b) of Figure 9–8 illustrates, the firm will maximize its profit at an output level of seven DVDs per day, where the industry equilibrium price of $5 per DVD is equal to the firm's marginal cost. Therefore, with an equilibrium industry price of $5 per DVD, the firm's equilibrium quantity is seven DVDs per day. As Figure 9–8 reveals, the firm's short-run total economic profit will be equal to its price minus average total cost multiplied by its equilibrium quantity, which equals ($5 – $4.21) × 7 = $5.53 per day.

In Figure 9–8, each firm earns a positive economic profit because at the firm's short-run equilibrium output level, price exceeds average total cost. If the industry demand for DVDs decreases so that the equilibrium price falls to a level equal to each firm's minimum average total cost, as described by point E_1 in Figure 9–5, then zero economic profits will prevail in short-run equilibrium. Further declines in industry demand will reduce the DVD price level below each firm's minimum average total cost. In these situations, each firm will operate at a loss or shut down with a loss, depending on whether price is above or below minimum average variable costs, as explained in Figures 9–4 and 9–5.

CONCEPTS IN BRIEF

Learning Objective 9.2: Using revenue and cost information, determine the firm's short-run profit-maximizing or loss-minimizing level of output and profit.

- Profit is maximized at the rate of output where the positive difference between total revenue and total cost is the greatest. Losses are minimized where the negative difference between total revenue and total cost is the smallest. We assume that each firm chooses the rate of output that maximizes profits or minimizes losses. This rate of output is called the firm's short-run equilibrium output level.
- If the industry price is below the firm's minimum average variable cost, the firm will minimize its losses by shutting down and will earn a negative economic profit (loss) equal to its total fixed costs.
- Graphically, the firm's shutdown point is where the price line is tangent to the minimum point on the average variable cost curve.
- When the industry price exceeds the firm's minimum average variable cost, the firm will maximize profits (minimize losses) by operating at the rate of output where marginal revenue or price equals marginal cost. The total amount of economic profit earned will depend on the following relation between price and average total cost at this rate of output: Total profit = (P – ATC) × Q. If price exceeds average total cost, the firm will earn a positive economic profit. If price is less than average total cost, the firm will earn a negative economic profit. If the price just equals average total cost, the firm will earn a zero economic profit (break even).
- Graphically, the firm's breakeven point is where the price line is tangent to the minimum point of the average total cost curve.

Learning Objective 9.3: Derive the firm's short-run supply curve and explain how the short-run equilibrium price is determined in a perfectly competitive market.

- The firm's short-run supply curve is the portion of its marginal cost curve at and above its minimum average variable cost.
- The industry's short-run supply curve is the horizontal sum of the individual firms' supply curves.
- In the short run, the equilibrium price occurs where short-run industry supply equals industry demand, in perfect competition.

9.4 Long-Run Equilibrium

We have just seen that a competitive firm can be in short-run equilibrium earning positive economic profits, or negative economic profits, or just breaking even, depending on the price. Only *one* situation, the breakeven, is possible in the long run, after sufficient time has passed to allow firms to change plant sizes and enter or exit the industry. This one situation is called *long-run equilibrium* and is explained below, using our DVD industry example.

Long-run equilibrium, as described in Figure 9–9, refers to the best situation that a competitive firm can look forward to in the long run. That is, in the long run, the industry supply, S_2, in conjunction with the industry demand, D, sets a price of P_2 = \$3 per DVD in part (a) of Figure 9–9. At this price, the firm's profit-maximizing quantity is q_2, where price equals marginal cost, in part (b) of Figure 9–9. At q_2, the typical firm is operating at minimum short-run and long-run average total cost, earning zero economic profits, as price equals average total cost.

Adjustments to Long-Run Equilibrium

Why does the typical firm in perfect competition end up in long-run equilibrium, as described in Figure 9–9? Suppose the initial industry supply is S_1 in part (a) of Figure 9–9, and the typical firm's plant size has a short-run average total cost equal to SAC_1 in part (b) of Figure 9–9. With the industry demand, D, the initial equilibrium price is \$5. At the price of \$5, the typical firm will be making positive economic profits, in short-run equilibrium (where the \$5 price will exceed SAC_1).

Due to the competitive characteristics of easy entry, large number of firms, and homogeneous product, the industry will not stay at the \$5 price in the long run. The positive economic profits earned by the typical competitive firm at the \$5 price will attract new firms to the DVD industry. As new firms enter, the short-run industry supply curve

FIGURE 9–9

Long-Run Equilibrium in Perfect Competition

In general, long-run equilibrium occurs when the industry equilibrium price just equals the typical firm's minimum long-run average total cost. This occurs when the industry supply curve is S_2 and the equilibrium price is \$3 per DVD in part (a). At the \$3 price, the typical firm in part (b) will maximize profit at q_2, where marginal revenue equals marginal cost. At q_2, the typical firm is operating at minimum short-run and long-run average total cost, earning zero economic profits, as price just equals average total cost.

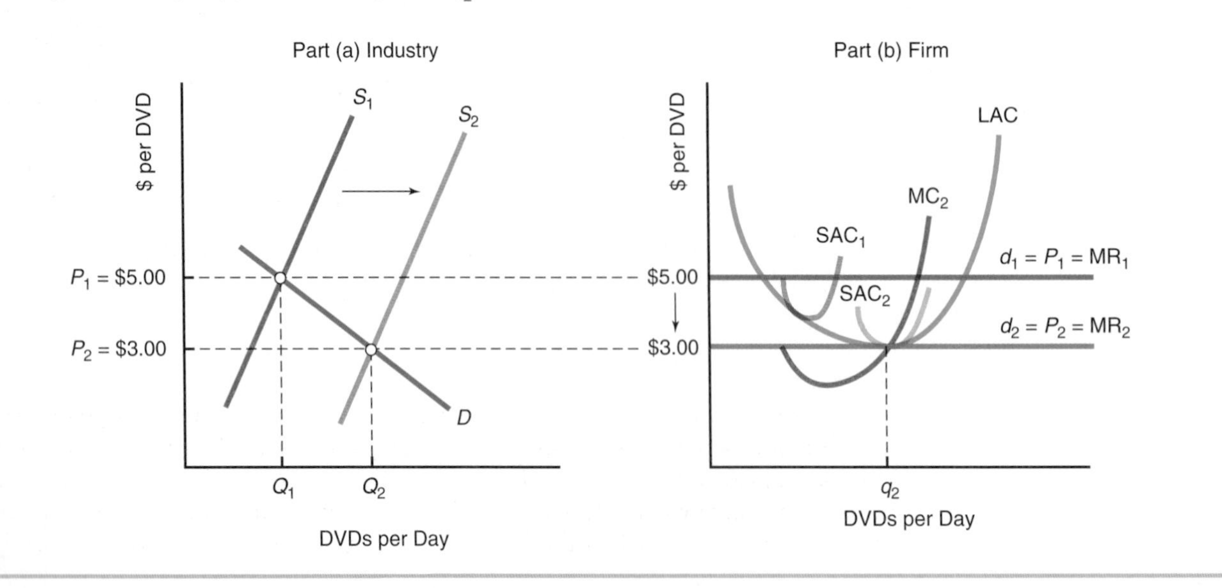

will increase or shift from S_1 toward S_2 in part (a) of Figure 9–9. As the industry supply increases, the industry price will decrease.

How do existing firms react to the increased competitive pressures stemming from the new entrants? Since their product is homogeneous, they cannot differentiate their product from their competitors'. Therefore, existing firms must attempt to lower costs per unit by adopting more efficient plant sizes. In part (b) of Figure 9–9, the existing firms are able to lower unit costs by changing the typical plant size from one with unit costs of SAC_1 to the larger plant size associated with SAC_2. As plant sizes expand, the short-run industry supply will continue to increase, leading to further declines in industry price. The price will continue to decrease until each firm earns zero economic profit (a normal profit) and each firm can no longer gain efficiencies by changing plant sizes. This occurs in long-run equilibrium, when the industry price falls to a level equal to the typical firm's minimum long-run average total cost, which is $3 in Figure 9–9.

Note that our explanation of long-run equilibrium began with the typical firm earning positive economic profit in the short run. What if, in the short run, the typical firm was facing economic losses? In this case, some firms will leave the industry in the long run, causing a decrease in short-run industry supply. As a result, the industry price will increase to a level where the price will just equal minimum long-run average total cost. That is, the same long-run equilibrium situation will result.

Example 9–3 explains how various e-commerce industries moved toward long-run equilibrium between late 1998 and early 2002.

EXAMPLE 9–3 **How the Dot-Com Boom Went Bust**

In 2000, if you wanted to shop for beauty supplies on the Internet, you could check out offerings at such sites as Beauty.com, BeautyJungle.com, Eve.com, Glass.com, or iBeauty.com. If you were looking for an engagement ring, you could compare the offerings at BlueNile.com, Diamond.com, Diamonds.com, and Modera.com, among others. If you desired assistance in planning a wedding, you could surf your way to websites that included Wedding.com, WeddingChannel.com, WeddingExpressions.com, and WeddingNetwork.com. If you or your spouse-to-be wished to buy supplies for your dog or cat on the Internet, you could visit pets.com, PETsMART.com, Petopia.com, PetStore.com, AllPets.com, Petco.com, PetWarehouse.com, or PetPlanet.com.

As the similarity of these website names implies, the basic business strategies of many Internet sellers could have been summed up in one exclamation: "Me, too!" Nearly all of these firms opened up websites after a number of early entrants proved that there was a potential to earn economic profits in the realm of electronic commerce. They were part of the dot-com boom that occurred between late 1998 and early 2000 as entrepreneurs rushed to the Internet in droves.

By the end of 2000, however, only one of three companies was earning positive accounting profits, and most of them were not covering the opportunity cost of capital. Adjustment toward a long-run competitive equilibrium, therefore, led numerous firms to exit electronic commerce, usually through bankruptcy. The result was a dot-com bust in 2001.

For critical analysis: Why might the owners of a new entrant to a market overestimate the economic profits they will earn?

It should be evident that perfectly competitive firms have no choice but to seek the most cost-efficient methods of operation in the long run. They do not have the luxury of controlling prices or differentiating their product. This implies that in the long run, competitive firms will seek to locate in geographical areas that minimize their production costs per unit. According to the Did You Know That section of this chapter, this may result in a more rapid rate of economic growth for Canada in the future. In 2003, Canada was found to be the least costly place to locate a business, when one compares the setup and operating costs of firms competing in 12 major industrial sectors in 11 of the most industrialized nations in the world. On average, Canadian businesses enjoyed a 9 percent cost advantage over similar firms situated in the United States.

9.5 Long-Run Industry Supply Curves

In part (a) of Figure 9–8, we drew the summation of all the portions of the individual firms' marginal cost curves, above each firm's respective minimum average variable costs, as the upward-sloping short-run supply curve for the competitive industry. We should be aware that a relatively steep upward-sloping supply curve might be appropriate only in the short run. In the long run, in perfect competition, further adjustments in quantity supplied will result, as firms adjust their plant size and enter or exit the industry.

Long-run industry supply curve A market supply curve showing the relationship between quantities supplied by the entire industry and prices, after sufficient time has passed to allow firms to change plant sizes and enter or exit the industry.

The **long-run industry supply curve** is a market supply curve showing the relationship between quantities supplied by the entire industry and prices, after sufficient time has passed to allow firms to change plant sizes and enter or exit the industry. In other words, the long-run supply curve describes the industry response to a change in prices, after long-run equilibrium has been re-established.

The long-run industry supply curve can take one of three shapes, depending on whether the input costs stay constant, increase, or decrease, as the size of the industry changes.

Constant-Cost Industries

Constant-cost industry An industry that can increase its output in the long run, without affecting input prices.

In principle, there are small enough industries that use such a small percentage of the total supply of inputs necessary for their production that the industry can expand without affecting input prices. In such a situation, we are dealing with a **constant-cost industry**. Since long-run per-unit costs stay constant, as the industry expands, the long-run industry supply curve is horizontal and is represented by S_L in part (a) of Figure 9–10.

FIGURE 9–10

Constant Cost, Increasing Cost, and Decreasing Cost Industries

In part (a), we show a situation in which the demand curve shifts from D_1 to D_2. Price increases from P_1 to P_2; however, in time, the short-run supply curve shifts outward because positive profits are being earned, and the equilibrium shifts from E_2 to E_3. The market clearing price is again P_1. If we connect such points as E_1 and E_3, we come up with the long-run supply curve S_L. This is a constant-cost industry. In part (b), unit costs are increasing for the industry, and therefore, the long-run supply curve slopes upward and long-run prices rise from P_1 to P_2. In part (c), unit costs are decreasing for the industry as it expands, and therefore, the long-run supply curve slopes downward such that long-run prices decline from P_1 to P_2.

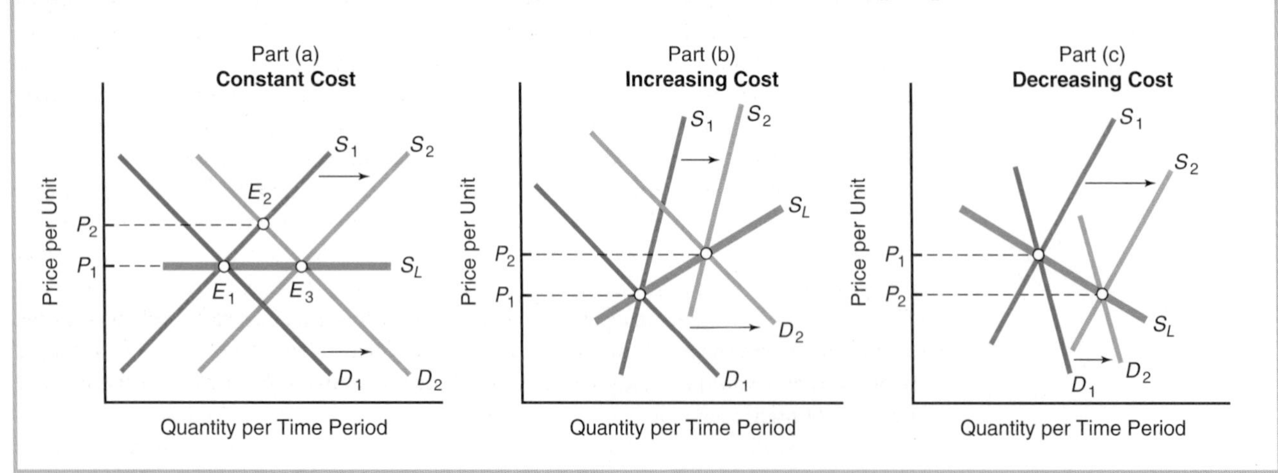

We can work through the case in which constant costs prevail. We start out in part (a) with demand curve D_1 and supply curve S_1. The equilibrium price is P_1. Market demand shifts rightward to D_2. In the short run, the equilibrium price rises to P_2. This generates positive economic profits for existing firms in the industry. Such economic profits induce resources to flow into the industry. The existing firms expand and/or new firms enter. The short-run supply curve shifts outward to S_2. The new intersection with the new demand curve is at E_3. The new equilibrium price is again P_1. The long-run supply curve is obtained by connecting the intersections of the corresponding pairs of demand and supply curves, E_1 and E_3. Labelled S_L, it is horizontal; its slope is zero. In a constant-cost industry, long-run supply is perfectly elastic. Any shift in demand is eventually met by an equal shift in supply so that the long-run price is constant at P_1.

Retail trade is often given as an example of such an industry because output can be expanded or contracted without affecting input prices.

Increasing-Cost Industries

Increasing-cost industry A situation where input prices increase as the industry expands in the long run.

In an **increasing-cost industry**, expansion by existing firms and the addition of new firms cause the price of inputs specialized within that industry to be bid up. As costs of production rise, the ATC curve and the firms' MC curve shift upward, causing short-run supply curves (each firm's marginal cost curve) to shift upward. The result is a long-run industry supply curve that slopes upward, as represented by S_L in part (b) of Figure 9–10. Examples are residential construction and coal mining—both use specialized inputs that cannot be obtained in ever-increasing quantities without causing their prices to rise.

Decreasing-Cost Industries

Decreasing-cost industry A situation where input prices decrease as the industry expands in the long run.

In a **decreasing-cost industry**, an expansion in the number of firms in an industry can lead to a reduction in input prices and a downward shift in the ATC and MC curves. When this occurs, the long-run industry supply curve will slope downward. This is described in part (c) of Figure 9–10. Examples are computers and long-distance phone service.

According to this chapter's Issues and Applications, the home-video movie industry is a good example of a decreasing-cost industry. As this industry has grown, the widespread use of DVDs has lowered the cost per unit of supplying these movies. Looking into the near future, the cost of supplying this product will continue to decrease, as the practice of downloading movies from the Internet becomes acceptable.

Long-Run Adjustments to Technological Change

In the previous section, we examined how perfect competition responds to changes in demand and prices in the long run. We now turn to examine the long-run adjustments that a competitive industry will incur, when faced with a cost-saving technological change.

Suppose new technology that lowers the per-unit cost of producing DVDs has just been discovered. In order to benefit from the new technology, new plants must be constructed, which implies a long-run response on the part of the DVD firms. As soon as some firms complete this new construction, their short-run and long-run average cost and marginal cost curves will shift downward and to the right. This implies that at the same DVD price, these firms can now supply a larger rate of output. Firms that adopt this new technology will make short-run positive economic profits, as average total cost slips below the industry price. These economic profits will induce new firms to enter the DVD industry.

As the new technology spreads throughout the DVD industry, the short-run market supply curve will increase, causing the industry price to decline. Eventually, the industry will reach a new long-run equilibrium, when the industry price falls to a level equal to the reduced minimum long-run average total cost curve. While the DVD firms will no longer enjoy positive economic profits, consumers will derive a long-term benefit in the form of lower DVD prices.

9.6 *Social Evaluation of Perfect Competition*

As we shall study in a subsequent chapter, the Canadian government has passed laws that encourage various industries to adopt a market structure and behaviour that more closely resemble perfect competition. This suggests that perfect competition must promote important socioeconomic goals. This is particularly the case when we focus on perfect competition in long-run equilibrium.

Perfect Competition and Productive Efficiency

Look again at Figure 9–9 part (b). In long-run equilibrium, the perfectly competitive firm finds itself producing at output rate q_2. At that rate of output, the price is just equal to the minimum long-run average cost as well as the minimum short-run average cost. In this sense, perfect competition results in the production of goods and services using the least costly combination of resources. This is called productive efficiency. This is an important attribute of a perfectly competitive long-run equilibrium, particularly when we wish to compare perfect competition with other market structures We will examine these other market structures in later chapters.

Perfect Competition and Allocative Efficiency

You may recall that allocative efficiency is concerned with producing the mix of goods and services that maximizes consumer satisfaction. Due to scarcity, it is crucial that economic resources are allocated to those uses that are most highly valued by consumers. In this section, we will explain how perfect competition promotes the goal of allocative efficiency.

We have seen that, in perfect competition, production takes place to the point where price just equals marginal cost. This is called **marginal cost pricing**, which is a system where the price charged to the consumer is equal to the opportunity cost to society of producing the last unit of the good in question. As we will explain below, marginal cost pricing promotes allocative efficiency.

Marginal cost pricing A system where the price charged to the consumer is equal to the opportunity cost to society of producing the last unit of the good in question.

ALLOCATIVE EFFICIENCY: A GRAPHIC ILLUSTRATION. In Figure 9–11, we illustrate how marginal cost pricing in the DVD industry promotes allocative efficiency. In this figure, we assume that the competitive industry is in long-run equilibrium with an equilibrium price of $3 per DVD and an equilibrium output of 800 DVDs per day.

At this point, it is appropriate to focus on the useful information that an industry demand curve provides us with. At any given quantity level, the height of the industry demand curve describes the maximum price that consumers are willing to pay for the last

FIGURE 9–11
Allocative Efficiency in the DVD Industry

In perfect competition, production takes place at the equilibrium level of 800 DVDs per day. At this equilibrium level, allocative efficiency is achieved, as the marginal benefit of the last DVD (800th DVD) produced, $3, just equals the marginal cost of the last DVD produced. If, instead, 700 DVDs were produced per day, resources would be underallocated to the DVD industry as the marginal benefit of the 700th DVD produced, $5, exceeds its marginal cost of $2.

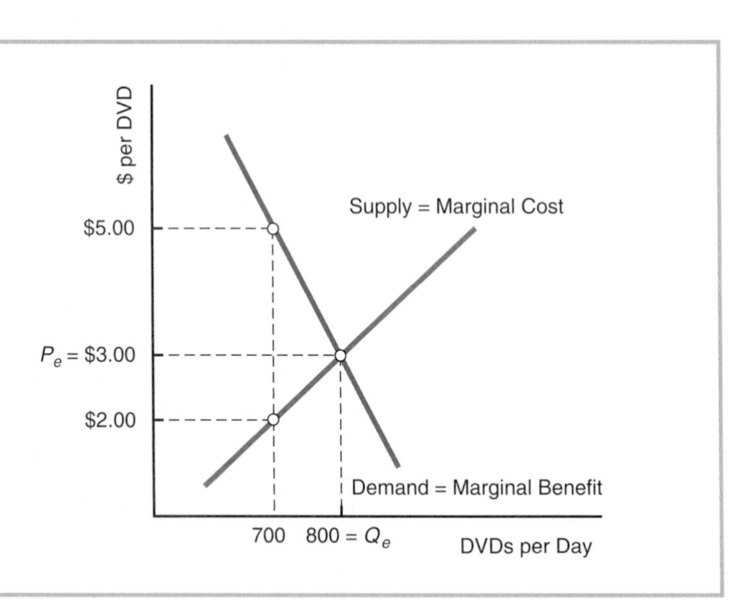

unit of output. As an example, in Figure 9–11, consumers are willing to pay a maximum price of $3 for the 800th DVD produced, as this is the height of the demand curve at the 800 DVD output level. This suggests that the marginal benefit or extra value that the household derives from consuming the 800th DVD is also $3. Once we appreciate that the demand curve provides us with price and marginal benefit information, we can proceed to examine how a perfectly competitive industry promotes allocative efficiency. As Figure 9–11 illustrates, the competitive DVD industry will end up at an equilibrium quantity of 800 DVDs per day. At this output, we have industry demand equal to industry supply. But industry demand reflects price and marginal benefit, and industry supply reflects marginal cost. Therefore, we can see that in a competitive industry, production takes place to the point where *price just equals marginal cost or, more significantly, marginal benefit just equals marginal cost.*

In our DVD example, this means that just the "right" quantity of DVDs is being produced, from society's viewpoint. The consumer value for the last DVD produced, $3, just equals the extra cost to society of producing this last DVD (800th DVD). This extra cost, or marginal cost, reflects the value of the output in other industries that is sacrificed (opportunity cost), when additional resources are used to produce the 800th DVD.

ALLOCATIVE INEFFICIENCY: A GRAPHIC ILLUSTRATION. To better understand how a competitive equilibrium situation promotes allocative efficiency, we will use Figure 9–11 to illustrate why an alternative situation results in allocative inefficiency.

Suppose the competitive industry produces 700 DVDs per day, which is not an equilibrium situation, according to Figure 9–11. At this quantity, the marginal benefit of the 700th DVD is $5 (height of the demand curve), while its marginal cost to society is $2 per DVD (height of the supply curve). This represents a situation where there is an underallocation of resources to the production of DVDs and an overallocation of resources to other industries, as far as society is concerned. If resources are taken away from producing goods in other industries and used to produce one additional DVD, the extra $5 value gained by the DVD consumer (marginal benefit) will exceed the $2 value of lost production in the other industries (marginal cost). From society's view, there will be a net gain in value of $3 by allocating more resources to the DVD industry. Clearly, allocative efficiency is not achieved when 700 DVDs are produced.

Perfect Competition and a Normal Profit

In long-run equilibrium, each firm operates at a quantity level where price equals average total cost. In other words, perfectly competitive firms earn zero economic or "normal" profits in the long run. This is due to the easy-entry feature of this market structure. One could look at this normal profit result as promoting an equitable distribution of income to the extent that corporate share ownership is concentrated in the hands of upper-income individuals. In other words, the shareholders are earning a rate of profit that is just necessary to maintain the current level of investment and output—no more and no less.

Possible Shortcomings of Perfect Competition

PERFECT COMPETITION AND MARKET FAILURE. Situations arise when competitive markets either overallocate or underallocate resources to a good or service. These situations are instances of **market failure**. One example is when the production of a product entails external costs.

Market failure A situation in which perfect competition either overallocates or underallocates resources to a good or service.

External costs Situations where the marginal social costs of producing a product exceed the marginal private costs of production.

External costs refer to situations where the marginal social costs of producing a product exceed the marginal private costs of production. In these cases, some of the costs resulting from the production of the product spill over to affect third parties. Third parties refer to individuals or organizations other than the buyer and seller of the product.

An example of an external cost situation would be when the production of DVDs results in air pollution that causes health problems for those individuals who are not directly involved as buyers or sellers of DVDs. The firms who manufacture the DVDs typically do not have to pay for these extra spillover costs. In this situation, the DVD firms' marginal cost curves do not include the extra spillover pollution costs borne by others. In fact, the true marginal social cost curves would be somewhat higher than the private marginal cost curves that govern the actual maximum profit production levels. Perfectly competitive firms would tend to overproduce DVDs relative to the socially desired production level.

External benefits A situation where the marginal social benefits from producing a product exceed the marginal private benefits.

Sometimes the production of a product results in **external benefits**, where the marginal social benefits from producing a product exceed the marginal private benefits. The production of the product results in spillover benefits to third parties. An example would be the discovery and production of a vaccine that prevents the spread of a contagious disease. The price that is charged to the consumers of this product does not reflect the extra spillover benefits. In this case, competitive marginal cost pricing will tend to underallocate resources to the product, from society's viewpoint.

Perfect Competition and Innovation

The rate of innovation and technological advance undertaken by perfectly competitive firms may prove to be socially sub-optimal. Activities related to such innovation as research and development are very expensive and entail significant risk. Since, in the long run, perfectly competitive firms can expect only normal profits, these firms may lack both the incentive and the level of funds necessary to engage in a socially desirable level of innovation.

CONCEPTS IN BRIEF

Learning Objective 9.4: Explain the features and long-run adjustments associated with long-run equilibrium in perfect competition.

- In long-run equilibrium, the industry supply adjusts to a level that sets an equilibrium price just equal to each firm's minimum long-run and short-run average total cost. Each firm produces an output level where the equilibrium price equals marginal cost and earns a zero economic profit.
- Long-run adjustments, such as changes in plant size and entry and exit of firms, bring about long-run equilibrium. If the typical firm is earning short-run economic profits, new firms will enter, driving the price down to equal minimum average total cost (normal profit). If the typical firm is earning short-run economic losses, existing firms will leave, driving the price up to equal minimum average total cost.

Learning Objective 9.5: Explain the three different long-run industry supply curve situations that are possible in perfect competition.

- The three different long-run supply situations are constant cost, increasing cost, and decreasing cost.
- In a constant-cost industry, the long-run supply curve is horizontal (perfectly elastic) because input prices do not change as the industry expands. In an increasing-cost industry, the long-run supply curve is upward-sloping because input prices increase as the industry expands. In a decreasing-cost industry, the long-run supply curve is downward sloping because input prices decrease as the industry expands.

Learning Objective 9.6: From a social viewpoint, evaluate the long-run behaviour in perfect competition.

- In long-run equilibrium, perfect competition promotes the socioeconomic goals of productive efficiency (minimum ATC), allocative efficiency (P = MC), and an equitable distribution of income (normal economic profit).
- Perfect competition will not lead to ideal results in situations of market failure or to the extent that it underallocates resources to research and innovation.

ISSUES AND APPLICATIONS

Does Your Local Video Store Have a Future?

Concepts Applied: Characteristics of Perfect Competition, Shutdown Price, Long-Run Equilibrium, Long-Run Supply Curve

Is the bricks-and-mortar video store here to stay?

The Bricks-and-Mortar Video Rental Stores

Fifteen years ago, the Canadian home-video movie rental industry was quite easy to describe. The movies rented for home viewing were typically in VHS tape format. While VHS tapes were rented primarily from numerous independent and chain video stores, the new releases and best-seller videos were also supplied by various small independent convenience outlets, gas stations, supermarkets, and department stores.

Today, the consumer wishing to watch movies at home faces many choices. Video rentals are still primarily supplied through many independent and chain bricks-and-mortar video stores. As an example, the Yellow Pages lists 140 video rental outlets operating in Toronto Central West, which is just one area within the city of Toronto. Most of the video stores rent movies in both VHS and DVD formats.

Since more than 60 percent of households in Canada and the United States own DVD players, movies rented in VHS format are quickly being replaced with DVD movie rentals. Reinforcing this trend is the fact that video stores actually make a greater amount of profit by renting DVD movies as opposed to VHS movies. DVDs now cost video rental stores about $25 to buy, compared with $100 or more for VHS titles.

Competition from Large Retail Chains Selling DVDs

Video movie rentals supplied by the bricks-and-mortar video stores now face competition stemming from a number of consumer alternatives. Attracted by a $3 billion Canadian home entertainment market—U.S.$20 billion for North America—big box retailers, department stores, supermarkets, and large music chains now provide Canadian consumers with the option to buy DVD movies. Wal-Mart, Best Buy, Costco, Future Shop, The Bay, Zellers, Real Canadian Superstore, HMV Canada, and A&B Sound are all examples of large retailers selling (not renting) movie DVDs. Typically, one has the option of buying DVD movies from these companies either in-store or online.

It is estimated that in North America, DVD movie sales, not including rentals, reached U.S.$12 billion in 2003, which was up 46 percent from 2002 sales. Retail prices for DVDs have been declining, prompting many consumers to buy movies at a rate that far outpaces that for videotapes during their peak. The average DVD buy rate in 2003 was 17 discs per machine, almost three times average VHS tape purchases in the mid-1990s.

There are a number of reasons why mass retailers can sell DVDs at relatively low prices. Since each of these large retailers purchases new-release and best-seller DVDs in large quantities, one would expect that they would be eligible to receive significant volume discounts from DVD suppliers.

The large retail chains, such as Wal-Mart, Best Buy, Costco, and Future Shop, carry many products other than DVDs. Because of their diversified inventories, they can afford to set low prices and earn low profit margins on such items as DVDs because of the profits earned on other items sold, such as computers, TVs, stereo systems, cameras, camcorders, phones, office products, and appliances. The low DVD prices can serve a promotional purpose for the large diversified retailer. It can be a way to increase in-store customer traffic on a regular basis. Consumers will set out to purchase small-ticket items such as DVDs on a more frequent basis than big-ticket items. Marketers call this type of pricing strategy "promotional pricing." If prices are set at a level below average total cost, the practice is called "loss leader" pricing.

Other Competitive Threats

The bricks-and-mortar video rental stores must now compete with cable and satellite TV companies that provide movie channels, pay-per-view TV movies, and video-on-demand to home subscribers. The video rental stores' ability to compete with the movie services of the cable and satellite TV companies depends, in part, on policies set by the movie studio executives in Hollywood. Currently, these studio executives have set the pecking order for new release movies in favour of the bricks-and-mortar video rental stores. That is, the video stores get new movie releases before the cable and satellite TV companies.

Such companies as Netflix Inc. (Netflix.com) in the United States and Movies For Me (moviesforme.com) in Canada use the Internet to rent DVD video movies to consumers. Netflix Inc. lists over 15 000 video titles on the Internet. After paying a monthly subscription fee of U.S.$19.95, American consumers can rent as many videos as they want—three movies allowed at any one time—and keep them for as long as they choose to without paying late fees. Each Netflix member picks his or her movies over the Internet and the DVD videos are delivered to his or her home within two days, via prepaid first-class mail service. In the last quarter of 2003, Netflix, which has 1.5 million subscribers, posted sales of U.S.$81.2 million. During 2003, its subscription membership grew by 74 percent.

Movies For Me, a Canadian company launched in 2002, provides an Internet video movie rental service similar to Netflix to Canadian consumers via Canada Post, for a monthly subscription fee of $24.95. Movies For Me was forecasting a 40 percent increase in subscribers during the first quarter of 2004.

The Changing Nature of Bricks-and-Mortar Video Rental Stores

How are the bricks-and-mortar video rental stores responding to all this competition? Many video rental outlets are now selling DVDs. Indeed, the rental stores have a lock on sales of previously viewed movies, which appeal to customers who appreciate the lower prices. So far, mass retailers have refrained from selling previously viewed movies.

In the United States, Blockbuster's DVD video sales grew to U.S.$331 million in the first nine months of 2003 compared with U.S.$220 million in the previous year. By contrast, video rentals were still significantly larger at U.S.$1.9 billion, up from U.S.$1.2 billion in 2002.

At Rogers Video, DVD sales account for about 10 percent of an average store's 6000 to 7000 titles. For 2004, Rogers predicts that video rentals will still contribute 76 percent of all of its stores' revenues.

Video stores are beginning to offer other products and services to their customers. In some of its video outlets, Rogers Video is selling its other products, such as mobile phones, mobile phone service, cable services, and Internet services. Many video stores rent video games for such game systems as Microsoft's Xbox and Sony's Playstation.

Some industry observers feel that video rental stores will survive despite the intense competition. No matter what the price, most consumers have a limit on the number of DVDs they wish to own. Currently, video on demand does not offer anywhere near the selection of titles found in a typical video store. As noted above, video stores are able to rent the new movie releases before they become available through video on demand.

Other analysts are not so optimistic about the bricks-and-mortar video stores. It is only a matter of time, they contend, before video movie suppliers begin to legally download their product over the Internet, in much the same manner as music is currently being distributed to households. Netflix Inc. has already indicated its interest in such a business proposition.

SOURCE: PETER BRIEGER. "VIDEO STORES: EVOLVE OR DIE." *FINANCIAL POST*, WEDNESDAY, JANUARY 28, 2004.

For critical analysis:

1. What characteristics of perfect competition relate to the industry that currently supplies new-release and best-seller home-video movies in a typical Canadian city?
2. In this Issue and Application, the practice of "loss leader" pricing was mentioned. Does it make economic sense to price a DVD movie at a level below average total cost?
3. If a firm specializes in renting new-release and best-seller movie videos, what amount of economic profit will it likely earn in the long run, and why?
4. What type of long-run supply curve best relates to the home-video movie industry?

SUMMARY DISCUSSION OF LEARNING OBJECTIVES

9.1 The Characteristics of Perfect Competition. The four fundamental characteristics of perfect competition are (1) a large number of buyers and sellers, (2) a homogeneous product, (3) easy exit from and entry to the industry, and (4) perfect market information in the hands of both buyers and sellers. A perfectly competitive firm is a price taker, meaning that the firm takes the price as given and outside of its control. The individual firm's demand curve is perfectly elastic (horizontal), which implies that the firm can sell all it wants at the given industry price, and so price equals marginal revenue.

9.2 Determining Output and Profit in the Short Run. Profit is maximized at the rate of output where the positive difference between total revenue and total cost is the greatest. Losses are minimized where the negative difference between total revenue and total cost is the smallest. We assume that each firm chooses the rate of output that maximizes profits or minimizes losses. This rate of output is called the firm's short-run equilibrium output level.

If the industry price is below the firm's minimum average variable cost, the firm will minimize its losses by shutting down and will earn a negative economic profit (loss) equal to its total fixed costs. Graphically, the firm's shutdown point is where the price line is tangent to the minimum point on the average variable cost curve.

When the industry price exceeds the firm's minimum average variable cost, the firm will maximize profits (minimize losses) by operating at the rate of output where marginal revenue or price equals marginal cost. The total amount of economic profit earned will depend on the following relation between price and average total cost at this rate of output: Total profit = $(P - \text{ATC}) \times Q$. If price exceeds average total cost, the firm will earn a positive economic profit. If price is less than average total cost, the firm will earn a negative economic profit. If the price just equals average total cost, the firm will earn a zero economic profit (break even). Graphically, the firm's breakeven point is where the price line is tangent to the minimum point of the average total cost curve.

9.3 Short-Run Supply and Equilibrium. The firm's short-run supply curve is the portion of its marginal cost curve at and above its minimum average variable cost. The industry short-run supply curve, which is the horizontal sum of the individual firms' supply curves, interacts with the industry demand curve to set the industry equilibrium price.

9.4 Long-Run Equilibrium. In long-run equilibrium, the industry supply adjusts to a level that sets an equilibrium price just equal to each firm's minimum long-run and short-run average total cost. Each firm produces an output level where the equilibrium price equals marginal cost and earns a zero economic profit.

Long-run adjustments, such as changes in plant size and entry and exit of firms, bring about long-run equilibrium. If the typical firm is earning short-run economic profits, new firms will enter, driving the price down to equal minimum average total cost (normal profit). If the typical firm is earning short-run economic losses, existing firms will leave, driving the price up to equal minimum average total cost.

9.5 Long-Run Industry Supply Curves. The three different long-run supply situations are constant-cost, increasing cost, and decreasing cost. In a constant-cost industry, the long-run supply curve is horizontal (perfectly elastic) because input prices do not change as the industry expands. In an increasing-cost industry, the long-run supply curve is upward sloping because input prices increase as the industry expands. In a decreasing-cost industry, the long-run supply curve is downward sloping because input prices decrease as the industry expands.

9.6 Social Evaluation of Perfect Competition. In long-run equilibrium, perfect competition promotes the socioeconomic goals of productive efficiency (minimum ATC), allocative efficiency (P = MC), and an equitable distribution of income (normal economic profit). Shortcomings will arise under perfect competition when there is a market failure or a sub-optimal rate of innovation.

PROBLEMS

(Answers to the odd-numbered problems appear at the back of the book.)

LO 9.1 Identify and explain the characteristics of a perfectly competitive market structure.

1. Explain why each of the following examples is not a perfectly competitive industry:
   a. The industry consists of one large firm and thousands of smaller firms, each selling an identical product. The large firm sets the price and the remaining firms take this price as a given. Firms can easily enter or exit the industry.
   b. There are many buyers and sellers in the industry. Consumers and firms have perfect information

about the prices of each competitor's product, which differ in quality from firm to firm.

c. There are many independently owned taxicabs that compete in a city. The city's government requires all taxicabs to provide identical service. All taxicabs operate the identical automobile model, with identical options. All drivers must wear a designated uniform. Through licensing, the government limits the number of taxicab companies that can operate within the city's boundaries.

2. Referring to Example 9–1, "The Global Coal Market," what characteristics of perfect competition apply to the coal industry?

3. Answer the following:
   a. Sketch a graph of both the industry and the firm to illustrate the following situations in the market for VHS video rentals, which is perfectly competitive. The industry supply and demand sets an equilibrium price of $4 per video rental per day. Illustrate the demand curve that a single independent video rental store faces, assuming the $4 price. Illustrate how a decrease in industry demand for VHS video rentals results in a new equilibrium price of $3 and a new demand curve for the firm.
   b. In general, explain the difference between the industry's demand curve and the firm's demand curve in perfect competition.

LO 9.2 Using revenue and cost information, determine the firm's short-run profit-maximizing or loss-minimizing level of output and profit.

4. Refer to the video rental example in Problem 3 above. Fill in the daily total, average, and marginal revenue table, below, assuming a price of $3 per video.

Daily Quantity (# videos)	1	2	3	4	5
Total revenue	—	—	—	—	—
Average revenue	—	—	—	—	—
Marginal revenue	—	—	—	—	—

5. The accompanying table represents the hourly output and cost structure for a local pizza outlet, which operates in perfect competition. Total fixed costs are $3 per hour.

Hourly Quantity (# pizzas)	0	1	2	3	4	5	6	7	8	9	10
Total Variable Costs per Hour ($)	0	6	8	9	11	15	21	29	40	54	71
Total Costs per Hour ($)	3	9	11	12	14	18	24	32	43	57	74

   a. If the price is $10 per pizza, compute the hourly total profit for each of the quantity levels in the accompanying table. What is the profit-maximizing (or loss-minimizing) quantity level? What is the maximum profit or minimum loss?
   b. Rework part (a) above, assuming that the price drops to $3 per pizza.
   c. Rework part (a) above assuming that the price drops to $2 per pizza.

6. Refer to Example 9–2, "High Sunk Costs Can Mean Deep Discounts." Suppose that you own a restaurant that currently offers meals in the evening. If you decide to open your restaurant during lunch hours, identify the relevant fixed and variable costs. If you offered two-for-one lunch coupons, you would have to ensure that the average price per meal exceeded what amount?

7. In the accompanying table, we list the per-unit costs for a perfectly competitive firm manufacturing and selling a standard-sized bookcase unit.

Output (units per hour)	Average Fixed Cost (AFC)	Average Variable Cost (AVC)	Average Total Cost (ATC)	Marginal Cost (MC)
1	$102.00	$40	$142	
2	51.00	$35	$ 86	30
3	34.00	$40	$ 74	50
4	25.50	$45	$ 70.50	60
5	20.40	$50	$ 70.40	70
6	17.00	$55	$ 72.00	80
7	14.57	$60	$ 74.57	90

   a. If the price per unit is $81, determine the profit-maximizing quantity level and the maximum profit.
   b. If the price per unit is $61, determine the profit-maximizing quantity level and the maximum profit. Should the firm shut down at this price, in the short run?
   c. If the price per unit is $31, determine the profit-maximizing quantity level and the maximum profit.
   d. The short-run breakeven point occurs at approximately what price?
   e. The short-run shutdown point occurs at approximately what price?

8. Consider the accompanying graph. Then answer the questions.

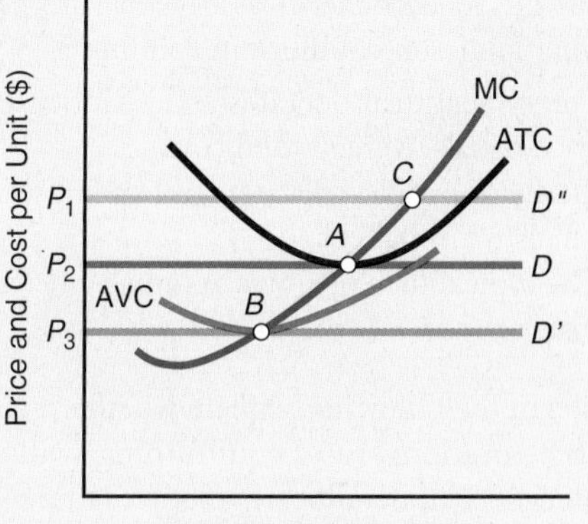

a. Which demand curve indicates that the firm is earning normal profits?
b. Which demand curve indicates that the firm is earning abnormal profits?
c. Which demand curve indicates that the firm is indifferent between shutting down and producing?
d. Which curve is the firm's supply curve?
e. Below which price will the firm shut down?

9. The accompanying graph is for firm J. Study it; then, answer the questions.

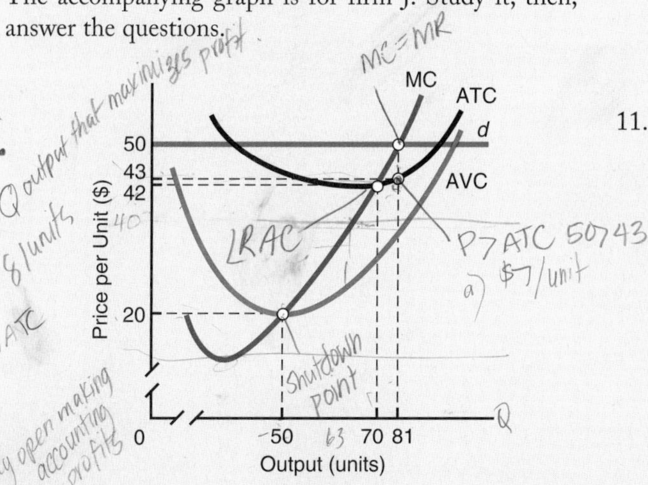

a. How many units will firm J sell in order to maximize profits?
b. What is firm J's total profit from selling the amount of output in part (a)?
c. At what price will firm J shut down in the short run?
d. If the cost curves shown represent production at the optimal long-run plant size, predict the long-run price.

LO 9.3 Derive the firm's short-run supply curve and explain how the short-run equilibrium price is determined in a perfectly competitive market.

10. The accompanying graph describes the marginal and average variable cost curves for a typical firm operating in a perfectly competitive industry. Assuming that the industry consists of 100 identical firms, use the graph information to fill in the accompanying short-run supply tables. What will be the short-run equilibrium price?

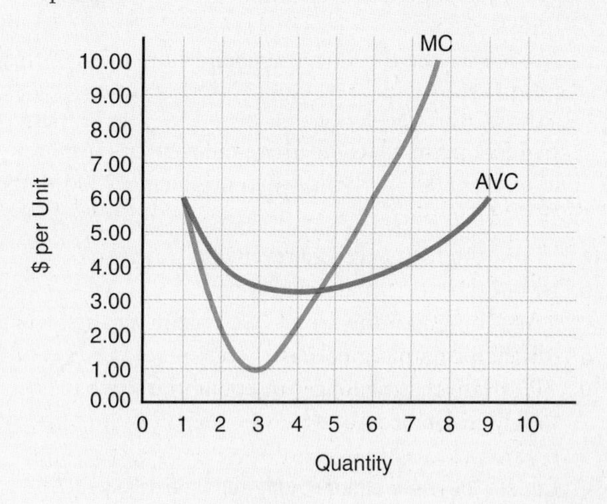

Price per Unit	Individual Quantity Supplied	Industry Supply	Industry Demand
$8	—	—	400
$6	—	—	600
$4	—	—	800
$2	—	—	1000

11. Use the perfectly competitive firm's per-unit cost data in Problem 7 above to fill in the accompanying short-run supply tables. Assume that the industry consists of 1000 firms identical to the firm in problem 7.

Price per Unit	Individual Quantity Supplied	Industry Supply	Industry Demand
$91	—	—	5000
$81	—	—	6000
$51	—	—	8000
$31	—	—	9000

a. On the basis of the information in the accompanying table, what will be the short-run equilibrium price?
b. At the short-run equilibrium price, what will be the typical firm's short-run equilibrium quantity? Determine the amount of total profit earned by the typical firm in equilibrium.

LO 9.4 Explain the features and long-run adjustments associated with long-run equilibrium in perfect competition.

12. Refer to the per-unit cost curves in Problem 9 above. Suppose that these costs relate to each firm's optimum long-run plant size. What will be the long-run equilibrium price in this industry?

13. Refer to the per-unit costs in Problem 7 above. Suppose that these costs relate to each firm's optimum long-run plant size.
    a. Suppose the current price is $81 per unit. Will this be the long-run equilibrium price? Why, or why not?
    b. What will be the long-run equilibrium price in this industry?

14. A firm in a perfectly competitive industry has total revenue of $200 000 per year, when producing 2000 units of output per year.
    a. Find the firm's average revenue or price.
    b. Find the firm's marginal revenue.
    c. Assuming that the firm is maximizing profits, what is the firm's marginal cost?
    d. If the firm is at long-run equilibrium, what is its average total cost?

LO 9.5 Explain the three different long-run industry supply curve situations that are possible in perfect competition.

15. What long-run supply situation best relates to each of the following? For each of the following situations, what will the long-run supply curve look like?
    a. As the number of active oil drilling rigs doubles, the extraction cost per barrel of oil increases.
    b. As the mobile phone industry explodes in size, the per-unit cost of manufacturing cellular phones decreases.

LO 9.6 From a social viewpoint, evaluate the long-run behaviour in perfect competition.

16. Explain the social benefits associated with each of the following long-run equilibrium conditions:
    a. The typical firm operates at a quantity level where price equals average total cost.
    b. Production takes place to the point where price equals marginal cost.
    c. The typical firm operates at minimum average total cost.

17. For each of the following, explain whether a competitive industry in long-run equilibrium will tend to overallocate or underallocate resources to the product it produces.
    a. Competitive research firms discover and supply a new drug that prevents the spread of a serious type of influenza.
    b. Competitive pulp producers pollute rivers and lakes, which increases the water treatment costs of nearby communities.

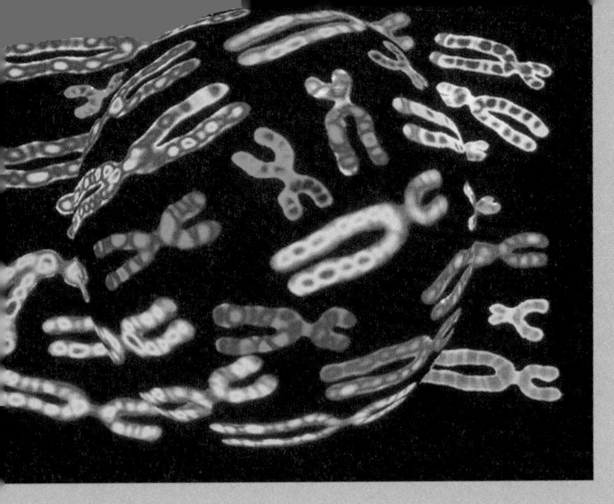

CHAPTER

Monopoly

10

Your genes make up your inherited physical characteristics. Genes are found in strands of genetic material called chromosomes. Each gene carries a "code" that is the chemical equation that translates hereditary information into proteins. Scientists are identifying new genes on a regular basis now. The discovery of new gene data has led, and will continue to lead, to the development of drugs necessary for the prevention, treatment, and cure of many life-threatening diseases. Much of the information relating to these new genetic data is owned by one drug company, GlaxoSmithKline. Does this company therefore have market power? To answer this question, you need to study the theory of monopoly.

LEARNING OBJECTIVES

After reading this chapter, you should be able to:

10.1 Identify and explain the characteristics of a monopoly market structure.

10.2 Using revenue and cost information, determine the monopolist's profit-maximizing or loss-minimizing level of output, price, and profit.

10.3 Explain why a monopoly firm engages in price discrimination.

10.4 Evaluate the long-run behaviour in monopoly, from a social viewpoint.

10.5 Compare and contrast the use of marginal cost pricing versus average cost pricing in the regulation of a natural monopoly.

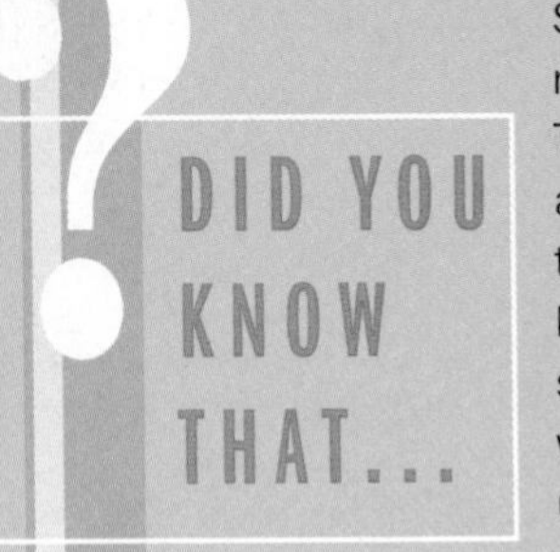

Single sellers of goods and services exist all around you. The company that equips your labs with new computers has probably been granted the exclusive right to do so by your college or university. The ski resort that offers you food at the top of the mountain does not allow anyone else to open a restaurant next to it. Just one drug manufacturer will typically supply the new prescription drug that you are eager to buy. If you book your wedding reception at a popular hotel ballroom, you will likely have to promise to use the hotel's expensive menu and wine list for this momentous occasion. No doubt, you will pay a high price if you want to enjoy your favourite beverage and snack while watching your home team play at the local coliseum. In this chapter, you will learn more about situations where competition is restricted to one supplier. We call such situations *monopoly*.

10.1 The Characteristics of Monopoly

The word *monopoly* probably brings to mind notions of large, corrupt business organizations that gouge the consumer. But if we are to succeed in analyzing and predicting the behaviour of a firm operating in a monopoly environment, we must be more objective in our description of this type of market structure. Whether applied to large or small businesses, monopoly situations typically have the following characteristics in common.

Monopolist A single supplier of a good or service for which there are no close substitutes.

Price searcher A firm that must determine the price–output combination that maximizes profit because it faces a downward-sloping demand curve.

1. *A monopoly firm is a single seller.* That is, we can define a **monopolist** as the single supplier of a good or service for which there are no close substitutes.
2. *A monopolist is a price searcher.* A **price searcher** is a firm that must determine the price–output combination that maximizes profit because it faces a downward-sloping demand curve. In a monopoly market structure, the firm and the industry are one and the same. Therefore, the firm's demand curve, d, is the same as the industry demand curve, D. Since the typical industry demand curve is downward sloping, the monopolist's demand curve is also downward sloping. When the monopoly firm increases its output sold per time period, this will decrease the price of the product. In contrast to perfect competition, where the price is given, in a monopoly the firm must "search" or determine the profit-maximizing price and output combination.
3. *Barriers to entry must exist in monopoly.* Since new businesses are started daily in Canada, there must be some reason why new firms are not successful in entering a monopoly industry. The types of barriers to entry may include: exclusive ownership of resources; problems in raising adequate capital; economies of scale; legal or government restrictions; and, possibly, predatory tactics of the monopolist.

What are some common examples of monopoly industries? In many large cities, there is often just one firm supplying all the natural gas, one utility firm selling electricity, and one firm providing local phone service. If one resides in a small city, one may regularly read the city's only daily newspaper; one may travel on the one available airline carrier to the nearest provincial capital; or one may stay at home and enjoy frequent visits to a local ski resort or a golf course owned by a monopolist.

Barriers to Entry

For any amount of monopoly power to continue to exist in the long run, the market must be closed to entry in some way. Either legal means or certain aspects of the industry's technical or cost structure may prevent entry. We will discuss several of the barriers to entry that have allowed firms to reap monopoly profits in the long run.

OWNERSHIP OF RESOURCES WITHOUT CLOSE SUBSTITUTES. Preventing a newcomer from entering an industry is often difficult. Indeed, some economists contend that no monopoly acting without government support has been able to prevent entry into the industry unless that monopoly has had the control of some essential natural resource. Consider the possibility of one firm's owning the entire supply of a raw material input that is essential to the production of a particular commodity. The exclusive ownership of such a vital resource serves as a barrier to entry until an alternative source of the raw material input is found or an alternative technology not requiring the raw material in question is developed. A good example of control over a vital input is the Aluminum Company of America, a firm that prior to World War II controlled the world's bauxite, which is the essential raw material in the production of aluminum. Such a situation is rare, though, and is usually temporary.

PROBLEMS IN RAISING ADEQUATE CAPITAL. Certain industries require a large initial capital investment. The firms already in the industry can, according to some economists, obtain monopoly profits in the long run because no competitors can raise the large amount of capital needed to enter the industry. This is called the "imperfect" capital market argument and is used to explain long-run, relatively high rates of return in certain industries. These industries are generally ones in which large fixed costs must be incurred merely to start production. Their fixed costs are generally for expensive machines necessary to the production process. Examples include industries that supply electricity, natural gas heating, cable TV, and local phone service using phone lines.

ECONOMIES OF SCALE. Sometimes it is not profitable for more than one firm to exist in an industry. This is so if, in order to realize lower unit costs, one firm would have to produce such a large quantity that there would be insufficient demand to warrant a second producer of the same product. Such a situation may arise because of a phenomenon we discussed in Chapter 8, economies of scale. When economies of scale exist, total costs increase less than proportionately to the increase in output. That is, proportional increases in output yield proportionately smaller increases in total costs, and per-unit costs drop. The advantage in economies of scale lies in the fact that larger firms (with larger output) have lower per-unit costs that enable them to charge lower prices, and that drives smaller firms out of business.

Natural monopoly The firm that first takes advantage of economies of scale in order to establish a monopoly position.

When long-run average costs decline as the scale of operation increases, a *natural monopoly* may develop. The **natural monopoly** is the firm that first takes advantage of economies of scale in order to establish a monopoly position. The natural monopolist is able to underprice its competitors and eventually force all of them out of the market.

In Figure 10–1, we have drawn a downward sloping long-run average cost curve (LAC). Recall that when average costs are falling, marginal costs are less than average costs. We can apply the same analysis in the long run. When the long-run average cost curve (LAC) is falling, the long-run marginal cost curve (LMC) will be below the LAC.

In our example, long-run average costs are falling over such a large range of production rates that we would expect only one firm to survive in such an industry. That firm would be the natural monopolist. It would be the first one to take advantage of the decreasing average costs; that is, it would construct the large-scale facilities first. As its average costs fell, it would lower prices and get an increasingly larger share of the market.

FIGURE 10–1

The Cost Curves That Might Lead to a Natural Monopoly: The Case of Electricity

Whenever long-run average costs are falling, so, too, will be long-run marginal costs. Also, long-run marginal costs (LMC) will always be below long-run average costs (LAC). A natural monopoly might arise in such a situation. The first firm to establish the low unit-cost capacity would be able to take advantage of the lower average total cost curve. This firm would drive out all rivals by charging a lower price than the others could sustain at their higher average costs.

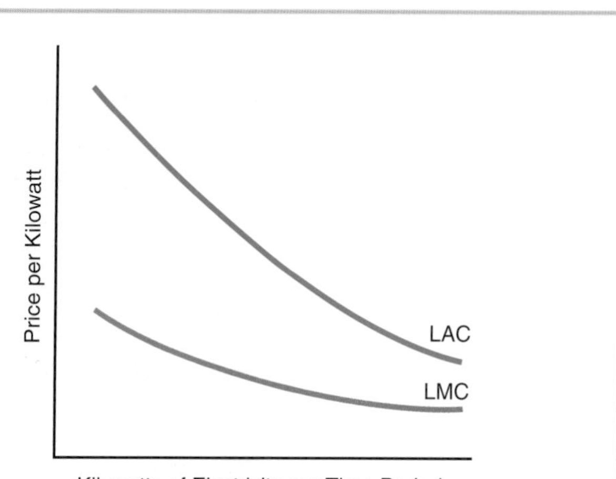

Once that firm had driven all other firms out of the industry, it would set its price to maximize profits.

PREDATORY BEHAVIOUR. It should be noted that a firm may establish a monopoly position in a market by engaging in behaviour that has already eliminated its competition and/or that has the effect of deterring new entrants to its industry. In some countries, such behaviour is considered to be illegal. For example, a criminal sanction against predatory pricing has been part of Canada's competition law for over 50 years.

The concept of predatory pricing is best illustrated by a dominant firm in a market setting its prices so low, over a long enough period of time, that it may drive one or more of its competitors from the market, deter other companies from entering the market, or both. Following the exit of competitors from the market, the predator is expected to raise prices significantly in an attempt to recover the profit lost during the period of predatory pricing. Example 10–1 provides examples of how Microsoft has gained near-monopoly positions in a number of different markets by engaging in predatory behaviour.

EXAMPLE 10–1 Microsoft's Abuse of Monopoly

On November 12, 2002, the U.S. Court of Appeals for the District of Columbia Circuit found Microsoft guilty of engaging in a series of exclusionary, anticompetitive, and predatory acts to maintain its monopoly power in the operating system software industry. At the time of the court decision, Microsoft's share of the worldwide market for Intel-compatible PC operating systems exceeded 90 percent.

On the basis of the dominance of its Windows operating system, Microsoft was in a position to unfairly dominate other industries, such as the Web browser market. In the early 1990s, Netscape Navigator controlled 70 percent of the Web browser market. Threatened by Netscape's dominance of the Internet, Microsoft created Internet Explorer and gave this new software away for free to Internet service providers and computer makers. Microsoft "packaged" Explorer as an integral part of Windows, which prevented computer manufacturers from modifying or deleting this browser software. Microsoft entered into agreements with computer manufacturers and Internet providers that restricted the distribution of competing software. Partly as a result of this predatory behaviour, the use of Internet Explorer has grown to the point of dominating the Web browser market worldwide.

Despite the fact that the Court of Appeals ruling in November 2002 prohibits Microsoft from engaging in predatory behaviour, it appears that it continues to employ similar tactics in other markets. On March 25, 2004, the European Union fined Microsoft U.S.$606 million for using its near monopoly in operating systems to dominate the markets for Internet media software, server software, and the software that will run next generation computing devices. As an example, the European Union's investigations support the view that Microsoft's Media Player has been bundled and sold with Microsoft Windows in a way that has unfairly restricted the growth of rival software, such as RealNetworks Inc.'s Real Player and Apple Computer's QuickTime player. In addition to the record fine assessed, the European Union has demanded that Microsoft create a new version of Windows that does not include its Media Player.

SOURCES: "UNITED STATES OF AMERICA, PLAINTIFF, V. MICROSOFT CORPORATION, DEFENDANT. UNITED STATES DISTRICT COURT FOR THE DISTRICT OF COLUMBIA. NOVEMBER 12, 2002. UNITED STATES DEPARTMENT OF JUSTICE. http://www.microsoft-antitrust.gov/pdf/Nov1202981232FinalJudgment.pdf; DAVID LAWSKY. "MICROSOFT ORDERED TO STRIP WINDOWS" *FINANCIAL POST*, THURSDAY MARCH 25, 2004, P. FP4.)

For critical analysis: Using this example, explain the various ways that Microsoft has engaged in predatory behaviour.

LEGAL OR GOVERNMENTAL RESTRICTIONS. The federal and provincial governments can also erect barriers to entry. These include public franchises, licences, patents, tariffs, and specific regulations that tend to limit entry.

In many industries, it is illegal to enter without a government *licence*. For example, you could not start a medical practice in Canada without first obtaining a licence from the Canadian College of Physicians and Surgeons. Standards are closely monitored by the government to protect the health and safety of consumers. By restricting entry to the profession and by agreeing to a common fee structure, doctors maintain a relatively high earnings level.

A *public franchise* is necessary to enter some markets, such as in the provision of cable television service. The Canadian Radio-television and Telecommunications Commission (CRTC) must approve all applications for entry and, in many cases, grants local, or geographical, monopolies to cable TV providers. Because these franchises are restricted, long-run monopoly profits might be earned by such firms as Rogers Cablesystems, which are already in the industry.

In some cases, government might license itself to be the sole provider of some product or service. In some Canadian provinces, liquor is sold only through government-owned retail outlets.

A *patent* is issued to an inventor to provide protection from having the invention copied or stolen for a period of 20 years. Suppose that engineers working for Northern Telecom discover a way to build fibre-optic cable that requires half the amount of inputs of regular cable, and transmits data twice as fast. If Nortel is successful in obtaining a patent on this discovery, it can (in principle) prevent others from copying it. The patent holder has a monopoly.

This chapter's Issues and Applications describes how privately owned profit-oriented pharmaceutical companies are able to obtain patents on genetic information that holds the key to discovering new treatments and drugs for numerous diseases. These patents serve as a barrier to entry in that they prevent other firms from developing competing drugs and treatments.

Tariffs Special taxes that are imposed on certain imported goods.

Tariffs are special taxes that are imposed on certain imported goods. They have the effect of making imports relatively more expensive than their domestic counterparts so that consumers switch to the relatively cheaper domestically made products. If the tariffs are high enough, imports become overpriced, and domestic producers gain monopoly advantage as the sole suppliers. Many countries have tried this protectionist strategy by using high tariffs to shut out foreign competitors.

Price and Revenue Behaviour under Monopoly

In this section, we will examine how price and revenue typically behave as a monopoly firm expands its production or quantity sold per time period. This will give you a better understanding of how the monopolist determines its profit-maximizing output level.

THE PERFECT COMPETITOR'S MARGINAL REVENUE: EQUAL TO PRICE. Let us first review the relation between demand, price, and revenue for a perfectly competitive firm. Recall that a perfectly competitive firm is a price taker. This means that the demand curve facing a perfectly competitive firm, *d*, is perfectly elastic. A perfectly competitive firm can increase its quantity sold without having to reduce the price per unit. In other words, the extra revenue received from selling one more unit is always the same as the price for the firm operating under perfect competition. No matter how many units the firm sells, the revenue per unit, or average revenue, will always equal the price that the perfectly competitive firm takes from the market. We can state all of this mathematically, as follows.

Under perfect competition:

Price set by the market = P = Average revenue = Marginal revenue, where

$$\text{Average revenue} = \frac{\text{Total revenue}}{\text{Total quantity sold}}$$

and

$$\text{Marginal revenue} = \frac{\text{Change in total revenue}}{\text{Change in quantity sold}}$$

Figure 10–2 part (a) graphs the behaviour of price, average, and marginal revenue for a small, perfectly competitive egg farmer at different daily quantities sold, assuming an industry set price of $2 per dozen. Note that in general, at each possible output level for this farmer, price equals marginal revenue equals $2 per dozen. If we now turn to a typical monopoly firm, we will see that price is not equal to marginal revenue!

THE MONOPOLIST'S MARGINAL REVENUE: LESS THAN PRICE. A monopolist is the sole supplier of one product, good, or service. This means that the monopoly firm faces the same demand curve as the overall industry demand curve. As the industry demand curve, *D*, is typically downward sloping, we can deduce that the monopoly firm's demand curve, *d*, is also downward sloping. In order for the monopoly firm to increase its quantity sold per time period, the firm will have to decrease the price of its product.

How is marginal revenue related to price under a monopoly situation? Consider an egg farmer who is the sole supplier of eggs to an entire city. If on Monday the monopoly farmer decides to hold back daily output sold to just seven dozen eggs, the farmer can command a high price of, say, $10 per dozen. Monday's total revenue will be $10 × 7 dozen eggs = $70. If the monopolist farmer wishes to increase the daily quantity sold on Tuesday to eight dozen eggs, the farmer will have to lower the price of each dozen sold on Tuesday to $9 per dozen. This means that Tuesday's total revenue is $9 × 8 = $72. What is the marginal revenue of the eighth or last dozen of eggs sold on Tuesday? We will compute this marginal revenue in two different ways.

First, the marginal revenue refers to the change in total revenue in selling one more unit. If we compare Monday's with Tuesday's total revenue, we can see that the eighth unit (dozen) sold changes total revenue from $70 to $72. The marginal revenue of the last or eighth dozen of eggs sold on Tuesday is $72 – $70 = $2. Note that while the price of the last or eighth unit (dozen) sold is $9, the marginal revenue of this last unit is only $2. Marginal revenue is less than the price for the eighth unit sold. In fact, if the same egg

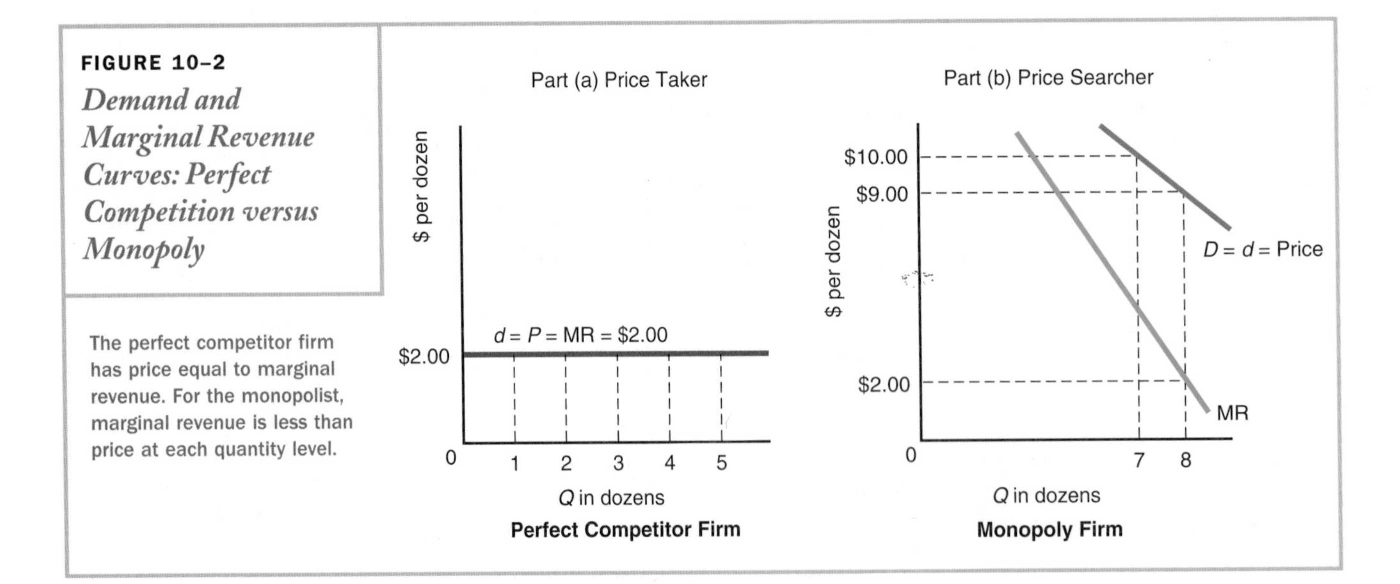

FIGURE 10–2
Demand and Marginal Revenue Curves: Perfect Competition versus Monopoly

The perfect competitor firm has price equal to marginal revenue. For the monopolist, marginal revenue is less than price at each quantity level.

farmer were to reduce the price of the eggs even further on Wednesday, we would again find that the marginal revenue of the last dozen sold on Wednesday would again be lower than Wednesday's price.

Figure 10–2 part (b) graphs the behaviour of price and marginal revenue for the monopoly egg farmer at different daily quantities sold. Note that in general, at each possible output level, marginal revenue is less than price.

Why is marginal revenue less than price in monopoly? Let us examine another way of computing the marginal revenue the monopoly farmer received from selling the last unit (eighth dozen eggs) on Tuesday. When the price per dozen was reduced from $10 on Monday to $9 on Tuesday, the farmer gained an extra $9 from selling one more dozen eggs (eighth dozen) when compared with Monday. However, in comparing both days, the farmer sold each of the first seven dozen eggs on Tuesday at $9 (compared to $10 on Monday). Therefore, on Tuesday, the farmer received $1 less for each of the first seven dozen eggs sold, or $7 less. If we combine the $9 gain from selling the eighth unit of eggs with the $7 loss incurred on the first seven dozen eggs sold, we also arrive at a marginal revenue of $9 − $7 = $2 for the eighth unit sold on Tuesday. Figure 10–3 uses a graph to illustrate this second way of determining the marginal revenue of the eighth unit of eggs sold.

Elasticity and Monopoly

The monopolist faces a downward-sloping demand curve (its average revenue curve). That means that it cannot charge just *any* price with no changes in quantity (a common misconception) because, depending on the price charged, a different quantity will be demanded.

Earlier we defined a monopolist as the single seller of a well-defined good or service with no *close* substitute. This does not mean, however, that the demand curve for a monopoly is vertical or exhibits zero price elasticity of demand. (Indeed, as we shall see, the profit-maximizing monopolist will never operate in a price range in which demand is inelastic.) After all, consumers have limited incomes and alternative wants. The downward slope of a monopolist's demand curve occurs because individuals compare the marginal satisfaction they will receive with the cost of the commodity to be purchased. Take the example of telephone service. Even if there were absolutely no substitute whatsoever for telephone service, the market demand curve would still slope downward. At lower prices, people will add more phones and separate lines for different family members.

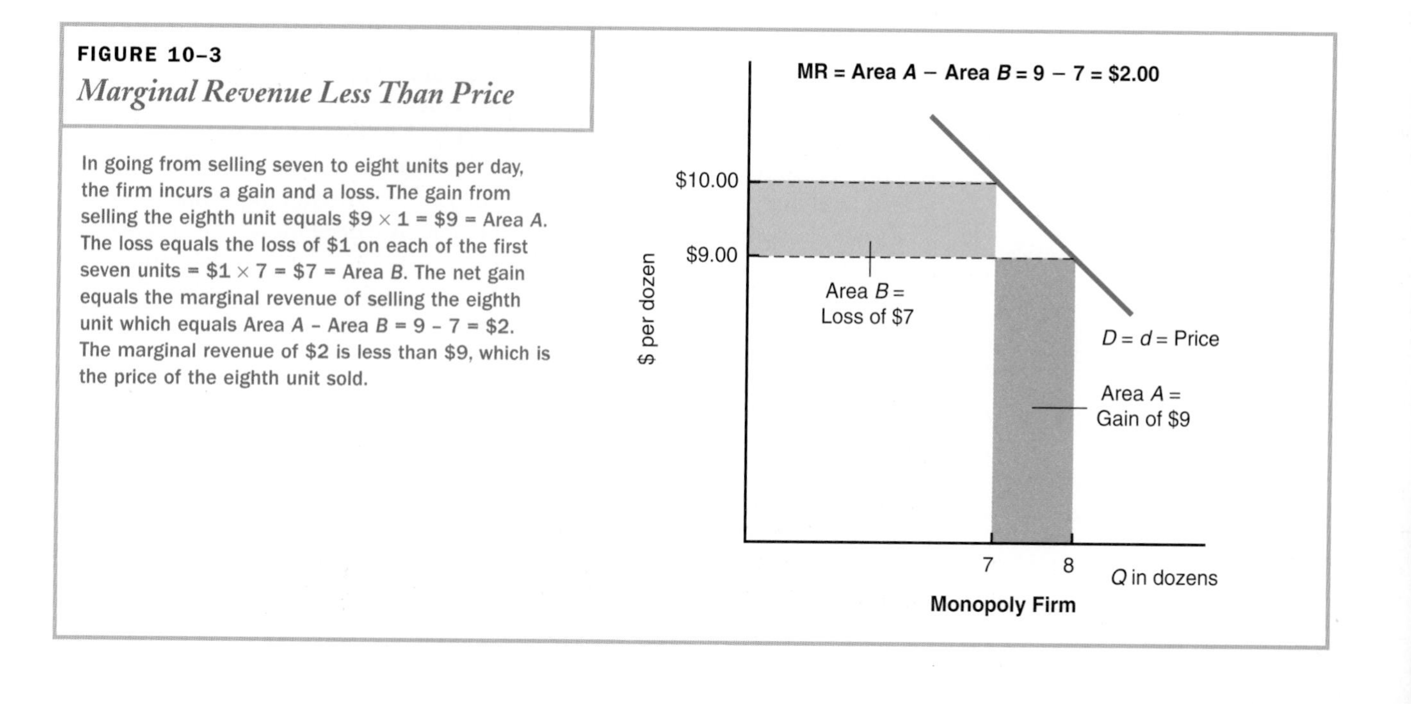

FIGURE 10–3
Marginal Revenue Less Than Price

In going from selling seven to eight units per day, the firm incurs a gain and a loss. The gain from selling the eighth unit equals $9 × 1 = $9 = Area *A*. The loss equals the loss of $1 on each of the first seven units = $1 × 7 = $7 = Area *B*. The net gain equals the marginal revenue of selling the eighth unit which equals Area *A* - Area *B* = 9 - 7 = $2. The marginal revenue of $2 is less than $9, which is the price of the eighth unit sold.

Furthermore, the demand curve for telephone service slopes downward because there are at least several *imperfect* substitutes, such as e-mail, letters, telegrams, in-person conversations, and CB and VHF-FM radios. Thus, even though we defined a monopolist as a single seller of a commodity with no *close* substitute, we can talk about the range of *imperfect* substitutes. The more such imperfect substitutes there are, the more elastic will be the monopolist's demand curve, all other things held constant.

Over time, the price elasticity of demand for the services provided by Canada Post, a legal monopoly, has changed, as explained by Policy Example 10–1.

POLICY EXAMPLE 10–1 **Should Canada Post Remain a Monopoly—Or Does it Matter?**

Canada Post has been granted a monopoly on basic letter mail by the government. Until fairly recently it had a de-facto monopoly on parcel delivery as well. Any monopoly power that Canada Post once had with respect to parcel delivery, however, has been whittled away by the growth of private couriers, such as United Parcel Service (UPS), Federal Express (FedEx), and Purolator. Over the last decade, technology has rendered the most fatal blow to Canada Post's position. Typically, a fax machine is faster than mailing a letter domestically or internationally. Now that fax modems are routinely installed or packaged with new personal computers, faxing is becoming ubiquitous. So, too, is the use of e-mail. With approximately 75 percent of all Canadians having access to the Internet, e-mail offers an almost free substitute for mailing a letter anywhere in the world.

For critical analysis: According to this example, what has happened to the price elasticity of demand for services provided by Canada Post, such as letter services and parcel deliveries? Explain. In what ways might Canada Post attempt to slow down the erosion of its monopoly position?

CONCEPTS IN BRIEF

Learning Objective 10.1: Identify and explain the characteristics of a monopoly market structure.

- A monopolist is defined as a single seller of a product or a good for which there is no close substitute.
- To maintain a monopoly, there must be barriers to entry. Barriers to entry include: ownership of resources without close substitutes; large capital requirements in order to enter the industry; economies of scale; legally required licences and public franchises; patents; tariffs; safety and quality regulations; and predatory behaviour.
- In a monopoly, the firm is a price searcher that must determine both the price and output level that maximizes profit, based on a downward-sloping demand curve.
- The price elasticity of demand for the monopoly firm depends on the number and similarity of substitutes. The more numerous and more similar the substitutes, the greater the price elasticity of demand of the monopolist's demand curve.
- Since the monopolist's demand curve is downward sloping, marginal revenue is less than price, for any given output level.

10.2 Determining Output, Price, and Profit in Monopoly

To find out the rate of output at which the perfect competitor would maximize profits, we had to add cost data. We will do the same thing now for the monopolist. We assume that profit maximization is the goal of the pure monopolist, just as for the perfect competitor. The perfect competitor, however, has only to decide on the profit-maximizing rate of output because price was given. The competitor is a price taker. For the pure monopolist, we must seek a profit-maximizing *price–output combination* because the monopolist is a price searcher. We can determine this profit-maximizing price–output combination with either of two equivalent approaches—by looking at total revenues and total costs or by looking at marginal revenues and marginal costs. We shall examine both approaches.

The Total Revenues–Total Costs Approach

We show hypothetical demand (rate of output and price per unit), revenues, costs, and other data in part (a) of Figure 10–4. In column 3, we see total revenues for our hypothetical monopolist, and in column 4, we see total costs. We can transfer these two columns to part (b). The difference between the total revenue and total cost diagram in part (b) and the one we showed for a perfect competitor in Chapter 9 is that the total revenue line is no longer straight. Rather, it curves. For any given demand curve, in order to sell more, the monopolist must lower the price. Thus, the basic difference between a monopolist and a perfect competitor has to do with the demand curve for the two types of firms. Monopoly market power is derived from facing a downward-sloping demand curve.

Profit maximization involves maximizing the positive difference between total revenues and total costs. This occurs at an output rate of nine units where the maximum profit equals $12.50.

The Marginal Revenue–Marginal Cost Approach

Profit maximization will also occur where marginal revenue equals marginal cost. This is as true for a monopolist as it is for a perfect competitor (but the monopolist will charge a higher price). When we transfer marginal cost and marginal revenue information from columns 6 and 7 in part (a) of Figure 10–4 to part (c), we see that marginal revenue approximately equals marginal cost at an output rate of nine units. Remember that a marginal cost of $3.70 refers to the extra cost of producing the ninth unit of output; a marginal revenue of $3.75 refers to the extra revenue earned by selling the ninth unit of output. Therefore, the monopolist will continue to add to profit by producing the ninth unit. Profit maximization occurs at nine units of output, which is the same output as in part (b).

WHY PRODUCE WHERE MARGINAL REVENUE EQUALS MARGINAL COST? If the monopolist goes past the point where marginal revenue equals marginal cost, marginal cost will exceed marginal revenue. That is, the incremental cost of producing any more units will exceed the incremental revenue. It just would not be worthwhile, as was true also in perfect competition. But if the monopolist produces less than that, it is also not making maximum profits. Look at an output rate of seven units in Figure 10–4. Here, the monopolist's marginal revenue is $4.75, but marginal cost is only $2.90. The monopolist would be foolish to stop at seven units of output because if output is expanded, marginal revenue will still exceed marginal cost, and therefore, total profits will rise. In fact, the profit-maximizing monopolist will continue to expand output and sales until marginal revenue approximately equals marginal cost, which is at nine units of output. The monopolist will not produce at an output rate of 10 because here, as we see, marginal cost is $4.20 and marginal revenue is $3.25. The difference of $0.95 represents the *reduction* in total profits from producing the tenth unit. Total profits will rise as the monopolist reduces its rate of output back toward nine units of output.

As Policy Example 10–2 describes, companies may employ marginal analysis when contemplating illegal actions.

FIGURE 10–4

Monopoly Costs, Revenues, and Profits

In part (a), we give hypothetical demand (rate of output and price per unit), revenues, and costs. As shown in part (b), the monopolist's maximum profit of $12.50 is where the positive difference between TR and TC is the greatest, at nine units. As part (c) indicates, this maximum profit occurs where MR = MC with a price of $5.75 per unit.

Part (a)

(1) Output (units)	(2) Price per Unit	(3) Total Revenues (TR) = (2) × (1)	(4) Total Costs (TC)	(5) Total Profit (TR – TC) = (3) – (4)	(6) Marginal Cost (MC)	(7) Marginal Revenue (MR) = Change in (3) / Change in (1)	(8) Average Total Cost (ATC) = (4) (1)
0	$8.00	$ 0.00	$10.00	–$10.00			
1	7.75	7.75	14.00	–6.25	$ 4.00	$7.75	$14.00
2	7.50	15.00	17.50	–2.50	3.50	7.25	8.75
3	7.25	21.75	20.75	1.00	3.25	6.75	6.92
4	7.00	28.00	23.80	4.20	3.05	6.25	5.95
5	6.75	33.75	26.70	7.05	2.90	5.75	5.34
6	6.50	39.00	29.50	9.50	2.80	5.25	4.92
7	6.25	43.75	32.40	11.35	2.90	4.75	4.63
8	6.00	48.00	35.55	12.45	3.15	4.25	4.44
9	5.75	51.75	39.25	12.50	3.70	3.75	4.36
10	5.50	55.00	43.45	11.55	4.20	3.25	4.35
11	5.25	57.75	48.55	9.20	5.10	2.75	4.41
12	5.00	60.00	54.85	5.15	6.30	2.25	4.57
13	4.75	61.75	62.65	–0.90	7.80	1.75	4.82
14	4.50	63.00	72.25	–9.25	9.60	1.25	5.16
15	4.25	63.75	83.95	–20.20	11.70	0.75	5.60

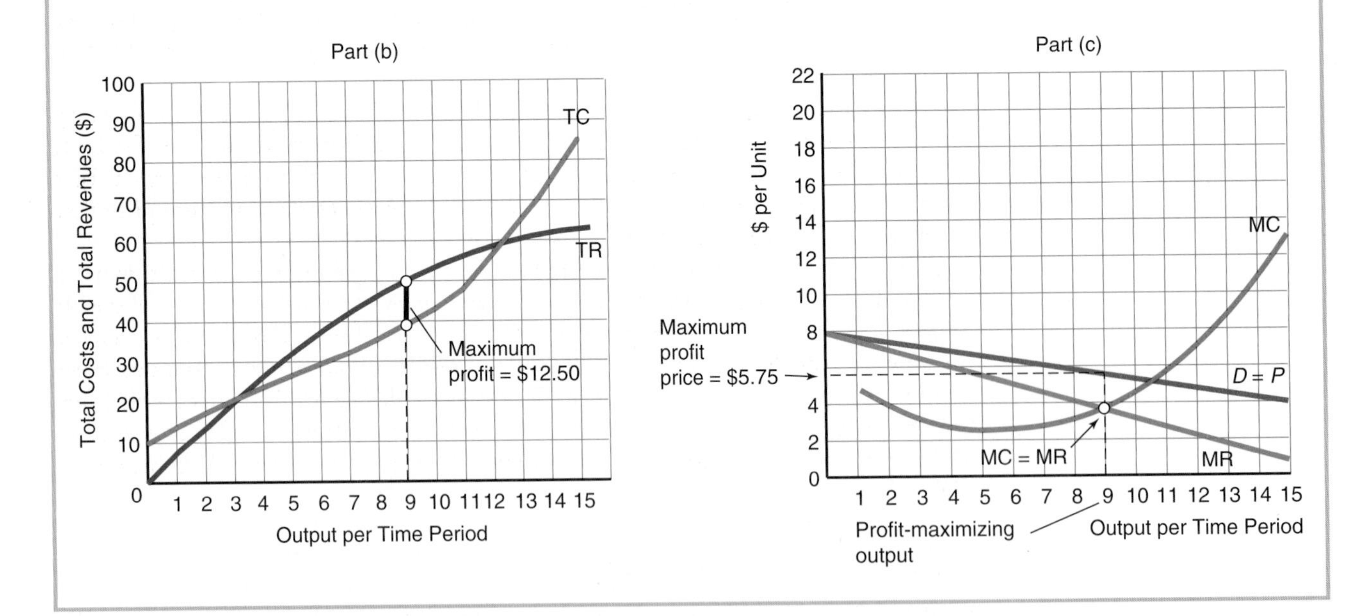

POLICY EXAMPLE 10–2 **In Germany, Watch Out– Your Price May Be Too Low**

In 2002, during the transition from Deutschmarks to euros as the official currency of Germany, C&A Mode KG, a clothing retailer known as C&A, had an idea for temporarily limiting the number of cash purchases. It held a special 20-percent-off sale that applied only to purchases using debit cards and credit cards. Immediately, retailer trade groups filed a lawsuit in a Düsseldorf court, claiming that C&A had violated a German law regulating when and under what conditions a business can hold a sale. Within days, the court threatened C&A with a 250 000-euro (nearly $250 000) fine if it continued the sale.

To the shock of other German retailers, C&A decided to pay the fine, extend its sale, and include purchases made with any form of payment. Nationwide media reports generated free publicity for the retailer, and consumers flocked to its 184 stores. Within days, retailer trade groups were lobbying the German government to enact even stiffer penalties for violating laws governing sales and thereby better "protect" consumers from "confusion" caused by sale prices.

For critical analysis: Why do you suppose that C&A was willing to tolerate higher operating costs by paying the fine for running an illegal sale?

What Price to Charge for Output?

How does the monopolist set prices? We know the quantity is set at the point at which marginal revenue equals marginal cost. The monopolist then finds out how much can be charged—how much the market will bear—for that particular quantity. We know that the demand curve is defined as showing the *maximum* price for which a given quantity can be sold. That means that our monopolist knows that to sell nine units, it can charge only $5.75 because that is the price at which that specific quantity is demanded according to Figure 10–4 part (c). This price is found by drawing a vertical line from the quantity to the market demand curve. Where that line hits the market demand curve, the price is determined. We find that price by drawing a horizontal line from the demand curve over to the price axis; that gives us the profit-maximizing price of $5.75, as described in Figure 10–4 part (c).

The basic procedure for finding the profit-maximizing short-run price–quantity combination for the monopolist is first to determine the profit-maximizing rate of output, by either the total revenue–total cost method or the marginal revenue–marginal cost method, and then to determine by use of the demand curve, D, the maximum price that can be charged to sell that output.

Do not get the impression that just because we are able to draw an exact demand curve in Figure 10–4, real-world monopolists have such perfect information. The process of price searching by a less than perfect competitor is just that—a process. A monopolist can only estimate the actual demand curve and therefore can only make an educated guess when it sets its profit-maximizing price. This is not a problem for the perfect competitor because price is given already by the intersection of market demand and market supply. The monopolist, in contrast, reaches the profit-maximizing output–price combination by trial and error.

Calculating Monopoly Profit

We have talked about the monopolist's profit, but we have yet to indicate how much profit the monopolist makes. We have actually shown total profits in column 5 of part (a) in Figure 10–4. We can also find total profits by adding an average total cost curve to part (c) of that figure. We do that in Figure 10–5. When we add the average total cost curve, we

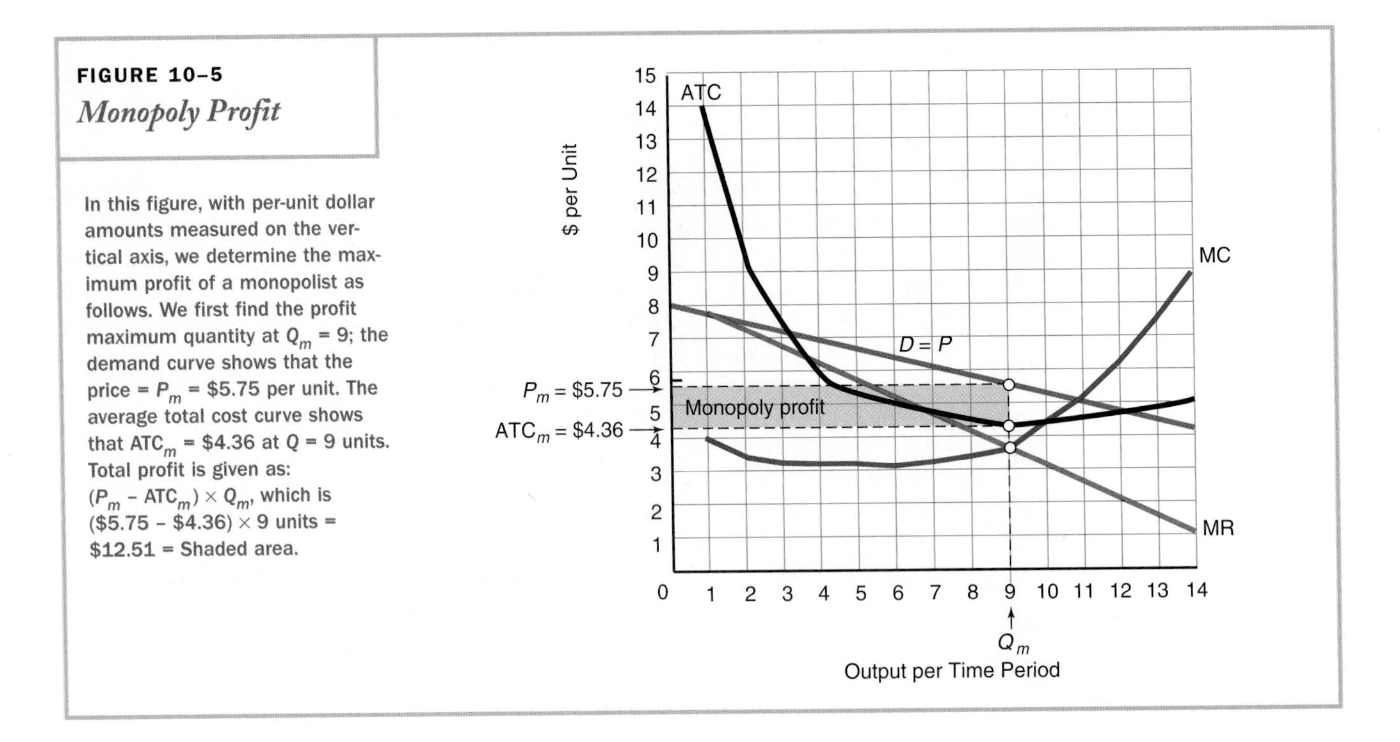

FIGURE 10–5
Monopoly Profit

In this figure, with per-unit dollar amounts measured on the vertical axis, we determine the maximum profit of a monopolist as follows. We first find the profit maximum quantity at $Q_m = 9$; the demand curve shows that the price = P_m = \$5.75 per unit. The average total cost curve shows that ATC_m = \$4.36 at $Q = 9$ units. Total profit is given as: $(P_m - ATC_m) \times Q_m$, which is (\$5.75 - \$4.36) × 9 units = \$12.51 = Shaded area.

find that the profit that a monopolist makes is equal to the shaded area which is $(P_m - ATC_m) \times Q_m$ or (\$5.75 – \$4.36) × 9 which equals \$12.51. Given the demand curve and a uniform pricing system (i.e., all units sold at the same price), there is no way for a monopolist to make greater profits than those shown by the shaded area.

The same is true of a perfect competitor. The competitor produces where marginal revenues equal marginal costs because it produces at the point where the marginal cost curve intersects the perfectly elastic firm demand curve. The perfectly elastic firm demand curve represents the marginal revenue curve for the pure competitor, for the same average revenues are obtained on all the units sold. Perfect competitors maximize profits at MR = MC, as do pure monopolists. But the perfect competitor makes no true economic profits in the long run; rather, all it makes is a normal, competitive rate of return.

It is possible for a monopoly firm to make positive economic profits in the long run. This is due to the existence of barriers to entry that prevents new firms from entering and eroding the monopolist's "excess" profit. The monopolist earns these positive economic profits by charging "excessive" prices—prices that exceed average total cost in the long run.

The Did You Know That section of this chapter provides examples of monopoly situations where one can expect to pay relatively high prices. Suppose a large computer manufacturer donates funds toward the construction of a new building on campus on the basis of an agreement that the university will purchase all of its computer equipment from this one manufacturer. In this situation, the university can expect to pay "top dollar" for all the computer equipment it purchases, as it faces a monopoly situation. Similarly, in order for you to book your wedding reception at your favourite hotel ballroom, you will likely have to promise to use the hotel's menu and wine list for this joyous event. Since you face a monopoly in terms of planning for the food and beverages for your wedding, you will pay high prices for these refreshments.

NO GUARANTEE OF PROFITS. The term *monopoly* conjures up the notion of a greedy firm ripping off the public and making exorbitant profits. However, the mere existence of a monopoly does not guarantee high profits. Numerous monopolies have gone bankrupt. Figure 10–6 shows the monopolist's demand curve as *D* and the resultant marginal revenue curve as MR. It does not matter at what rate of output this particular monopolist operates; total costs cannot be covered. Look at the position of the average total cost curve. It lies everywhere above *D* (the average revenue curve). Thus, there is no

FIGURE 10–6

Monopolies: Not Always Profitable

Some monopolists face the situation shown here. The average total cost curve, ATC, is everywhere above the average revenue, or demand, curve, *D*. In the short run, the monopolist will produce where MC = MR at point *E*. Output Q_m will be sold at price P_m, but cost per unit is C_1. Losses are the shaded rectangle. Eventually, the monopolist will go out of business.

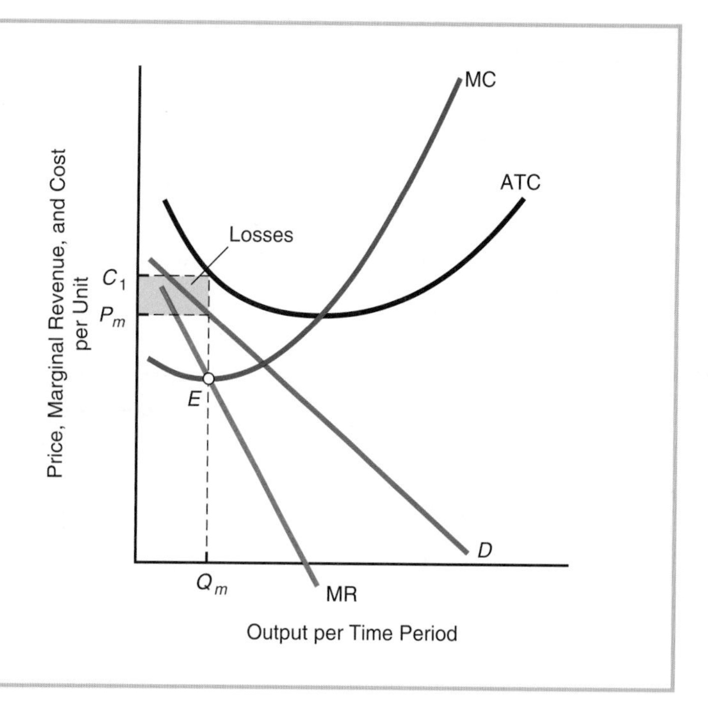

price–output combination that will allow the monopolist even to cover costs, much less earn profits. This monopolist will, in the short run, suffer economic losses as shown by the shaded area. The graph in Figure 10–6 depicts a situation for millions of typical monopolies that exist; they are called inventions. The owner of a patented invention or discovery has a pure legal monopoly, but the demand and cost curves may be such that production is not profitable. Every year at inventors' conventions, one can see many inventions that have never been put into production because they were deemed "uneconomic" by potential producers and users.

CONCEPTS IN BRIEF

Learning Objective 10.2: Using revenue and cost information, determine the monopolist's profit-maximizing or loss-minimizing level of output, price, and profit.

- The monopolist chooses the profit-maximizing price-output combination—the output at which marginal revenue equals marginal cost, and the highest price possible at this output level, as determined by the demand curve.
- The maximum amount of total profit equals the monopolist's maximum profit quantity level multiplied by the difference between the firm's price and its average total cost, at the maximum profit quantity level.
- It is possible for a monopoly firm to earn in excess of a normal profit in the long run due to barriers to entry.
- A monopolist does not necessarily earn a profit. If price is below average total cost at the quantity where marginal revenue equals marginal cost, the firm will incur an economic loss.

10.3 On Making Higher Profits: Price Discrimination

In a perfectly competitive market, each buyer is charged the same price for every unit of the particular commodity (corrected for differential transportation charges). Because the product is homogeneous and we also assume full knowledge on the part of the buyers, a difference in price cannot exist. Any seller of the product who tried to charge a price higher than the going market price would find that no one would purchase it from that seller.

In this chapter we have assumed until now that the monopolist charged all consumers the same price for all units. A monopolist, however, may be able to charge different people different prices or different prices for successive units sought by a given buyer. **Price discrimination** refers to the practice of charging different prices for units of the same product, not justified by cost differences. A firm will engage in price discrimination whenever feasible to increase profits.

Price discrimination The practice of charging different prices for units of the same product, not justified by cost differences.

Different Prices for Different Units of the Same Product

A negatively sloped demand curve suggests that consumers are willing to pay different amounts for different units of the same product. If a monopoly firm is able to charge the maximum amount that consumers are willing to pay for different units of the same product, the firm will enjoy a higher level of profit. Returning to Figure 10–4, you will recall that when our hypothetical monopolist charges a single price of $5.75 per unit, the firm earns an economic profit of $12.50. What amount of profit could be earned if this monopoly firm were to price discriminate?

A price-discriminating monopolist would, in the extreme, charge a different price for each unit of output according to the demand for its product. Thus, it would sell the first unit for $7.75, the second for $7.50, the third for $7.25 and so on, until the price it could charge for the next unit of output just equaled the marginal cost of producing it. In our example, therefore, the price discriminator would sell 11 units of output, with the 11th unit selling for $5.25, just equal to its marginal cost. How much extra profit would it make? Total revenue would be $71.50—the sum of all of the prices charged for the eleven units sold ($7.75 + $7.50 + $7.25 + $7 + $6.75 + $6.50 + $6.25 + $6 + $5.75 + $5.50 + $5.25). Total cost would be unchanged at $48.55, and the resulting profit would be $22.95. Figure 10–7 reproduces Figure 10–4 and highlights the extra revenues that accrue to the price-discriminating monopolist.

It is interesting to note that a monopolist that can price discriminate will usually produce a greater amount of output than a single-price monopoly. In fact, if the monopolist can perfectly price discriminate as in the above example, it will produce where price equals marginal cost—the perfectly competitive output.

Most monopolies, however, cannot charge a separate price for each unit of output. Instead, they sell blocks of output for different prices. For example, in some jurisdictions, electricity utility companies charge more for the first block of electricity consumed than for subsequent blocks used in the same month. For many years, when monopoly firms provided long-distance telephone service, consumers were charged a higher rate for the first minute of a long-distance telephone conversation compared with that for subsequent minutes. These practices reflect the fact that consumers typically place a higher marginal benefit on the first block of output than on subsequent blocks of output.

Different Prices for Different Groups of Buyers of the Same Product

Price discrimination is often found in situations where the consumers of a product (or service) can be separated into subgroups that exhibit different price elasticities of demand. In general, the monopoly firm can increase its profit by charging a higher price in the more inelastic market(s) and a lower price in the more elastic market(s).

For example, higher airfares are frequently charged to business travellers who, out of necessity, have to book a specific return flight. In contrast, leisure travellers, who do not have to travel on any specific flight, pay a lower airfare by agreeing to stay over a Saturday night before returning home. In this case, the business traveller constitutes an inelastic demand situation, while the leisure traveller is more price elastic.

People who go to see movie matinees are very price conscious (elastic demand) and therefore enjoy lower admission fees than those who go to the movies in the evenings.

FIGURE 10–7

Additional Profits from Perfect Price Discrimination: Part (a)

Under perfect price discrimination, the firm charges the maximum that consumers are willing to pay for each unit sold. This increases total revenue at each output level. Put differently, marginal revenue is now equal to price under discrimination.

The maximum profit quantity is now equal to 11 units, where price is just about equal to MC. The total maximum profit is now $22.95. This is higher than the total profit of $12.50 under the single-price monopoly.

(1) Output (units)	(2) Price per Unit (P)	(3) Total Revenue: Perfect Discrimination (TRd)	(4) Total Costs (TC)	(5) Total Profit: Perfect Discrimination	(6) Marginal Cost (MC)	(7) Marginal Revenue with Perfect Discrimination P = MR
0	$8.00	$ 0.00	$10.00	–$10.00		
1	7.75	7.75	14.00	–6.25	$ 4.00	$7.75
2	7.50	15.25	17.50	–2.25	3.50	7.50
3	7.25	22.50	20.75	1.75	3.25	7.25
4	7.00	29.50	23.80	5.70	3.05	7.00
5	6.75	36.25	26.70	9.55	2.90	6.75
6	6.50	42.75	29.50	13.25	2.80	6.50
7	6.25	49.00	32.40	16.60	2.90	6.25
8	6.00	55.00	35.55	19.45	3.15	6.00
9	5.75	60.75	39.25	21.50	3.70	5.75
10	5.50	66.25	43.45	22.80	4.20	5.50
11	5.25	71.50	48.55	22.95	5.10	5.25
12	5.00	76.50	54.85	21.65	6.30	5.00
13	4.75	81.25	62.65	18.60	7.80	4.75
14	4.50	85.75	72.25	13.50	9.60	4.50
15	4.25	90.00	83.95	6.05	11.70	4.25

FIGURE 10–7

Additional Profits from Perfect Price Discrimination: Part (b)

The single-price monopoly will sell Q_s = 9 units of output at a price of $5.75 per unit. The single-price monopoly has a total revenue of $5.75 × 9 = $51.75 = light shaded area. The price discriminating monopoly will sell Q_d = 11 units and will charge the maximum price for each of these units. Under price discrimination, the total revenue will be equal to the total revenue of the single-price monopolist (light shaded area) + dark shaded areas. Hence, for any cost structure, the price discriminator will earn a higher total revenue than the single-price monopoly.

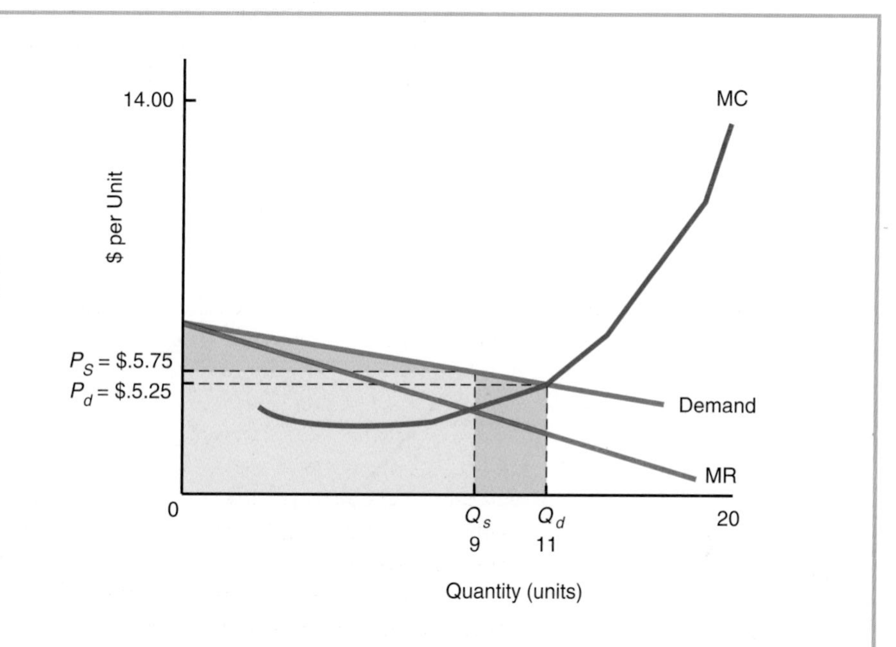

Similarly, people who carry around coupons will pay a lower rate per litre of gas compared with those consumers who never use coupons (inelastic users).

Example 10–2 illustrates how the Japanese film company, Fuji, practised price discrimination in order to maximize the profit it derived from selling to different groups of customers separated geographically. Again, differing price elasticities of demand served as the basis for the price discrimination.

EXAMPLE 10–2 Fuji Film Price Discrimination

For years, Kodak argued that the Japanese film company, Fuji, was "dumping" its film in North America. In effect, Kodak was arguing that Fuji was price discriminating. Because, according to Kodak, Fuji had effectively blocked Kodak from successfully competing in Japan, Fuji faced a less elastic demand for film in Japan than it did in North America, where Kodak dominated the market. Part (a) of Figure 10–8 shows the relatively inelastic demand curve, D_J, that Fuji faces domestically. In Canada and the United States, Fuji faces a relatively elastic demand curve, D_{NA}. For the sake of simplicity, marginal cost is assumed to be constant for Fuji. At profit maximization, marginal revenue must equal marginal cost. Here, we have a common marginal cost, MC. There are two sets of marginal revenue curves, however—MR_J and MR_{NA}. For profit maximization, $MR_J = MR_{NA} = MC$. (In essence, it is as if the Fuji film sold in Japan and in North America were two different goods having exactly the same marginal cost to produce.) The market for Fuji film in Japan is given in part (a) of Figure 10–8. MC = MR at Q_J, sold at price P_J. Buyers of Fuji film in Canada and the United States have a more elastic demand because of competition from Kodak. They ended up paying only P_{NA} for quantity Q_{NA}. P_{NA} is lower than P_J. (Since this analysis was completed, Kodak has been successful in having the courts force Fuji to raise its prices in North America.)

For critical analysis: Assuming that price discrimination was being undertaken by Fuji, who was benefiting?

FIGURE 10–8
Price Discrimination in Film by Fuji

The Japanese film industry is protected from foreign competition and therefore faces a relatively inelastic demand curve, D_J, in part (a). In North America, as shown in part (b), the industry faces competition such that its demand curve, D_{NA}, is more elastic. (For simplicity, the marginal cost curve is assumed to be horizontal.) Profit maximization occurs in each market where MC = MR. In Japan, that is at Q_J, at where the film can be sold at a price of P_J. In North America, profit maximization occurs at Q_{NA}, at which point film can be sold at a price of P_{NA}. Prices charged in Japan for the same film are higher than prices charged in North America.

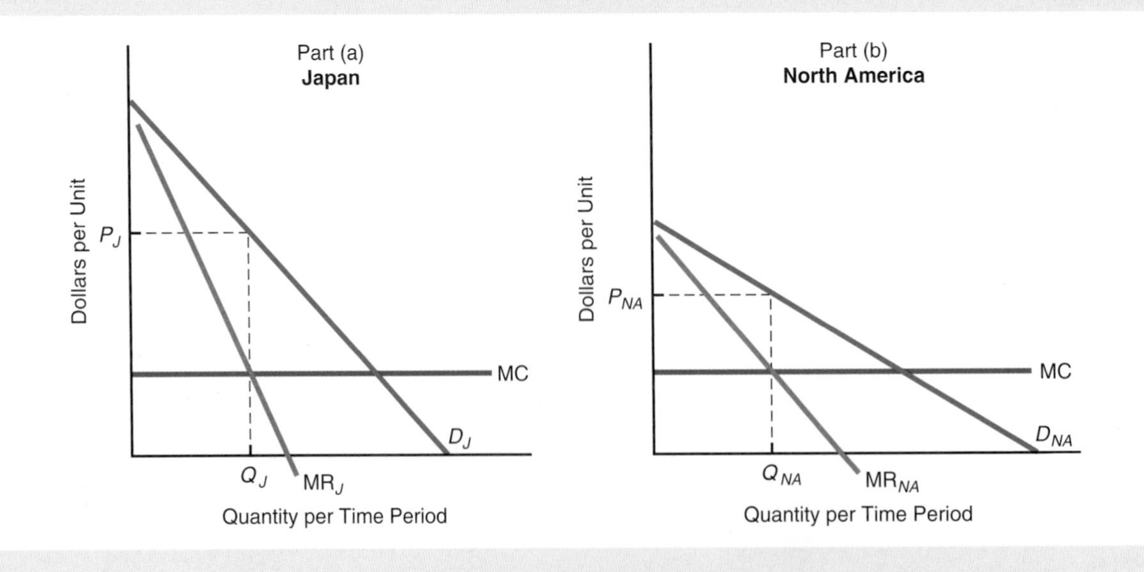

Necessary Conditions for Price Discrimination

Four conditions are necessary for price discrimination to exist:

1. *The firm must face a downward-sloping demand curve.* In order to charge different consumers different prices, the firm must have some control over price setting.
2. *The firm must be able to separate markets at a reasonable cost.* The monopoly must be able to determine in a relatively simple manner which consumers are willing to pay high prices and which are not. If the cost of segregating the market is high, it will offset the extra profit gained from price discrimination.
3. *The buyers in the various markets must have different price elasticities of demand.* Buyers who are willing to pay high prices typically have fewer substitutes to choose from; hence, their demand is relatively price inelastic. Consumers with more elastic demands usually are less willing to pay high prices for goods and services.
4. *The firm must be able to prevent resale of the product or service.* If the purchaser of the monopoly's product can resell it to a higher-price buyer, then the low-price purchaser, and not the firm, captures the profit that accrues from price discrimination.

For example, charging students a lower price for a movie can be done relatively easily. The cost of checking student IDs is apparently not significant. Also, it is fairly easy to make sure that students do not resell their tickets to nonstudents.

It must be made clear at the outset that charging different prices to different people or for different units that reflect differences in the cost of service to those particular people does not amount to price discrimination. If bus fares in the evening are higher than daytime fares because it is more costly to operate evening bus service, this is not price discrimination.

CONCEPTS IN BRIEF

Learning Objective 10.3: Explain why a monopoly firm engages in price discrimination.

- Price discrimination refers to the sale of the same product at different prices based on differences in consumers' willingness to pay. By price discriminating, the monopolist can increase its total profit by increasing total revenue.
- Under perfect price discrimination, the firm charges the maximum amount that consumers are willing to pay for each unit sold. In this case, the demand or price curve equals the marginal revenue curve.
- A monopoly firm may price discriminate when it sells to subgroups of customers with differing price elasticities of demand. The monopoly firm can increase its profit by charging a higher price in the more inelastic market(s) and a lower price in the more elastic market(s).
- Four conditions are necessary for price discrimination: (1) The firm must face a downward-sloping demand curve; (2) the firm must be able to separate different units sold or different customer groups at a reasonable cost; (3) different groups of customers exhibit differing price elasticities of demand; and (4) the resale of the product or service must be preventable.

10.4 Social Evaluation of Monopoly

In Canada, there are instances where monopoly situations are considered illegal. This, in itself, suggests that many monopoly firms may act against the public interest. To better understand the "evils" of monopoly, we should note that we are evaluating the long-run behaviour that may occur in a monopoly market structure.

Monopoly and Allocative Efficiency

Let us run a little experiment. We will start with a purely competitive industry that has numerous firms, each unable to affect the price of its product. The supply curve of the industry is equal to the horizontal sum of the marginal cost curves of the individual producers above their respective minimum average variable costs. In part (a) of Figure 10–9, we show the market demand curve and the market supply curve in a perfectly competitive situation. The competitive price in equilibrium is equal to P_e, and the equilibrium quantity at that price is equal to Q_e. Each individual competitor faces a demand curve (not shown) that is coincident with the price line P_e. No individual supplier faces the market demand curve, *D*.

Now, let us assume that a monopolist comes in and buys up every single competitor in the industry. In so doing, we will assume that the monopolist does not affect any of the marginal cost curves or demand. We can therefore redraw *D* and *S* in part (b) of Figure 10–9, exactly the same as in part (a).

How does this monopolist decide how much to charge and how much to produce? If the monopolist is maximizing profit, it is going to look at the marginal revenue curve and produce at the output where marginal revenue equals marginal cost. But what is the marginal cost curve in part (b) of Figure 10–9? It is merely *S* because we said that *S* was equal to the horizontal summation of the portions of the individual marginal cost curves above each firm's respective minimum average variable cost. The monopolist therefore produces quantity Q_m and sells it at price P_m. Note that Q_m is less than Q_e and that P_m is greater than P_e. A monopolist therefore produces a smaller quantity and sells it at a higher price. This is the reason usually given when economists criticize monopolists. Monopolists raise the price and restrict production compared with a competitive situation. For a

FIGURE 10–9

The Effects of Monopolizing an Industry

In part (a), we show a competitive situation in which equilibrium is established at the intersection of *D* and *S* at point *E*. The equilibrium price would be P_e, and the equilibrium quantity would be Q_e. Each individual competitive producer faces a demand curve that is a horizontal line at the market clearing price, P_e. What happens if the industry is suddenly monopolized? We assume that the costs stay the same; the only thing that changes is that the monopolist now faces the entire downward-sloping demand curve. In part (b), we draw the marginal revenue curve. Marginal cost is *S* because that is the horizontal summation of all the individual marginal cost curves. The monopolist therefore produces at Q_m and charges price P_m. P_m in part (b) is higher than P_e in part (a), and Q_m is less than Q_e. We see, then, that a monopolist charges a higher price and produces less than an industry in a competitive situation.

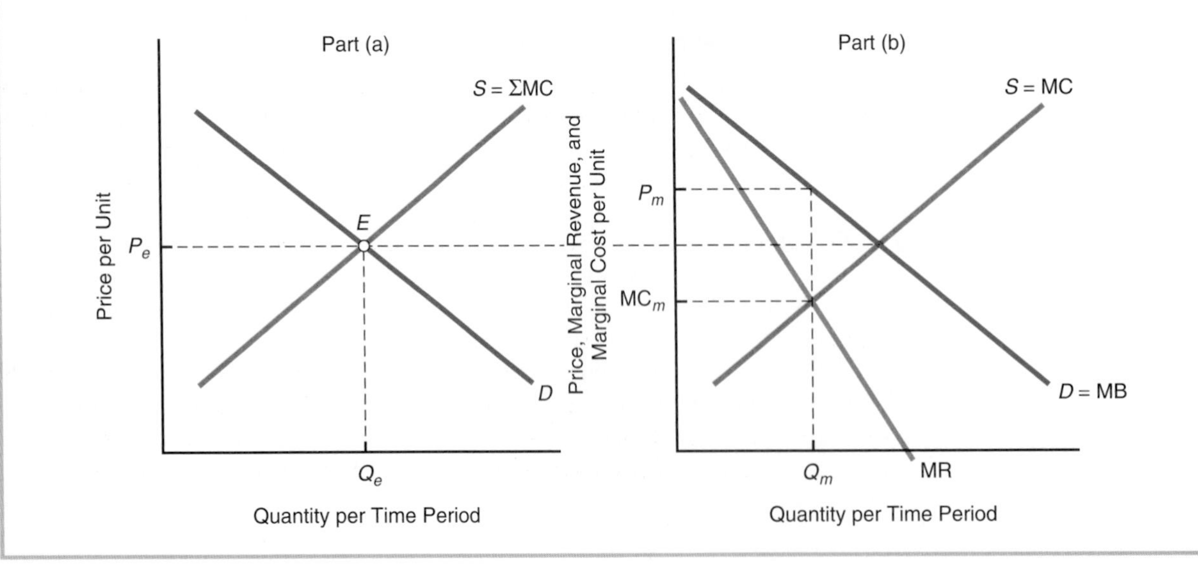

monopolist's product, consumers are forced to pay a price that exceeds the marginal cost of production. Resources are misallocated in such a situation—too few resources are being used in the monopolist's industry and too many are used elsewhere.

Note from Figure 10–9 that by setting MR = MC, the monopolist produces at a rate of output, Q_m, where the price exceeds marginal cost (compare P_m with MC_m). Suppose that $Q_m = 700$ units, $P_m = \$5$ per unit, and $MC_m = \$2$ per unit. The marginal cost of $2 per unit reflects the value of the output in other industries that is sacrificed (opportunity cost), when additional resources are used to produce the last unit or 700th unit in this monopoly industry. Price, by contrast, represents the marginal benefit that buyers derive from the last unit produced. Thus, society places a $5 value on the last unit (700th unit) produced in this monopoly industry.

The monopoly outcome of $P > MC$ means that the value to society of the last unit produced is greater than its additional cost; hence not enough of the good is produced. In our example, if one more unit of the monopoly good is produced, the extra $5 value gained in the monopoly industry will exceed the $2 value of lost production in other industries (marginal cost). From society's point of view, there will be a net gain in value of approximately $3 by allocating more resources to the monopoly industry. Clearly, monopoly conflicts with allocative efficiency, which is concerned with producing the mix of goods and services most valued by society.

Monopoly and Productive Efficiency

In theory, in long-run equilibrium, a perfectly competitive firm operates at minimum long-run average total cost. Being a price taker under intense competition, the perfectly competitive firm can survive only by being productively efficient.

Since a monopolist produces a product for which there is no close substitute, the firm can survive without having to operate at minimum average total cost. In cases where a monopolist is a very large corporation, the managers may pursue goals other than cost minimization. A manager may seek to enlarge the resources employed in his or her department as a way of obtaining a higher level of status and salary.

Monopoly and Long-Run Excess Profit

Due to barriers to entry, a monopoly firm can earn annual profits in excess of a normal profit. The excessive monopoly prices charged can be viewed as a "tax" on poorer consumers. To the extent that the shares of these monopoly firm(s) are concentrated in the hands of upper-income individuals, the proceeds of this "tax" are shared among affluent shareholders. In short, the existence of monopoly firms can result in a more inequitable distribution of income in our society.

Should All Monopolies Be Eliminated?

Before we leave the topic of the social cost of monopoly, we should recognize that some monopoly situations may benefit society as a whole. If large economies of scale exist in the monopoly industry, the monopolist can promote productive efficiency. If the government were to intervene to break up this one large efficient company into many smaller firms, average cost per unit may rise. Indeed, the consumers may end up paying more for the product under a more competitive structure! If the government were to try to eliminate a monopoly cable TV station in a small city by encouraging a second cable company to serve the city, think of the duplication of costs that could occur. As a start, two sets of cables would have to be laid throughout the city!

Monopolies created by patents may be socially desirable, to the extent that the promise of a monopoly encourages valuable inventions. Multinational drug companies have consistently argued that the lure of long-run "excess" profits, based on patent protection, serves as an excellent incentive to develop new and better prescription drugs.

Governments around the world bestow monopoly rights called *copyright* to those who originate, create, or produce various works, performances, and broadcasts. From an economics viewpoint, copyright means that authors, artists, and musicians have the right to collect royalties (monies) from any form of reproduction and sale of their works. Because a monopoly is granted to the originators, they are able to restrict the distribution of their works, in order to exact a higher price and maximize profits. In this way, copyright serves as an incentive to create high-quality literary, dramatic, artistic, and musical works that contribute to the enrichment and diversity of our culture, our freedom of expression, and our overall personal well being. In Canada, the monopoly right related to copyright is bestowed for a term of the life of the originator and 50 years following his or her death.

Under copyright law, it is illegal for any person to reproduce the works of others, without the consent of the owner of the copyright. This type of illegal behaviour constitutes an *infringement of copyright*. The widespread practice of freely downloading music through the Internet is a form of copyright infringement that threatens the livelihoods of many artists and companies that record and distribute music. However, as Policy Example 10–3 explains, this form of Internet piracy is difficult to curtail.

POLICY EXAMPLE 10–3

Swapping Songs on the Internet: Is It Really Free?

While the practice of music file sharing is escalating, music sales are on the decline. During one four-month period of 2002, the number of music files available on pirate sites nearly doubled from 500 million to 900 million, worldwide. At the same time global music sales in 2002 fell by 7 percent. As a result around 250 million fewer albums were sold in 2002 than in 2001.

The music industry, to date, has been unsuccessful in bringing legal charges against file-sharing software companies. On December 19, 2003, the Dutch Supreme Court ruled that the makers of Kazaa cannot be prosecuted for copyright infringement of music and movies downloaded using its software. In the United States, a federal judge had already dismissed charges made by the entertainment industry against two other file-sharing services-Grokster and StreamCast Networks (Morpheus). This decision is in the process of being appealed.

The file-sharing software makers have used two key arguments in their defence. The first is the Betamax doctrine, which states that products and services used for piracy are deemed legal if they are capable of substantial noninfringing uses. The Betamax doctrine is what Sony used, over two decades ago, to protect itself from charges that its videocassette recorders were infringing on the copyright of Hollywood actors and producers.

The second source of defence for the software makers is that file-sharing software, such as Kazaa, Grokster, and Morpheus (different from Napster), do not require a central company server. It is peer-to-peer software that allows users to search each other's hard drives for files they want. The files are downloaded right from each user's hard drive. This second line of defence has prompted the Recording Industry Association of America (RIAA) to launch lawsuits against individual users who are file-sharing a significant amount of copyrighted music over the Internet. Once the RIAA finds a user who is uploading copyrighted music files, it can obtain the identity of the user through the user's Internet provider, under American law.

Following the lead of the RIAA, the Canadian Recording Industry Association (CRIA) went to court to try to force Canadian Internet service providers to turn over the names of 29 large-volume file sharers. On March 31, 2004, a Canadian federal court denied the CRIA's request. The court ruled that placing files on a shared directory does not amount to active distribution of copyrighted music. In the decision, it was suggested that the actions

continued

of file sharers were no different from those of libraries that place photocopiers in a room full of copyrighted books. The court ruling is expected to be appealed.

SOURCES: THE CANADIAN RECORDING INDUSTRY ASSOCIATION. "THE FREE MUSIC MYTH." http://www.cria.ca/fmm.html. (ACCESSED MARCH 20, 2004).; CBC NEWS ONLINE. "CANADIAN RECORDING INDUSTRY TO IMITATE U.S. FILE-SHARING LAWSUITS.", DECEMBER.16, 2003. http://www.cbc.ca/arts/stories/CRIAtosue161203. (ACCESSED MARCH 20 2004).; ASSOCIATED PRESS WIRED NEWS. "DUTCH COURT THROWS OUT KAZAA CASE." DECEMBER 19, 2003. http://www.wired.com/news/digiwood/0,1412,61672,00.html. (ACCESSED MARCH 21, 2004).); JANET MCFARLAND. "RULING DEALS BLOW TO MUSIC INDUSTRY." *THE GLOBE AND MAIL*. APRIL 1, 2004, P. B3.

For critical analysis: Who really "pays" for the actions of those who freely upload music files over the Internet?

CONCEPTS IN BRIEF

Learning Objective 10.4: Evaluate the long-run behaviour in monopoly, from a social viewpoint.

- The social costs of monopoly include: (1) The firm is allocatively inefficient, to the extent that price exceeds marginal cost, for the last unit produced. (2) Due to the lack of competition the monopoly firm may be productively inefficient, to the extent that it does not produce at minimum long-run average total cost. (3) Due to barriers to entry, monopoly firms can charge excessive prices so as to enjoy positive economic profits in the long run. This can conflict with an equitable distribution of income to the extent that the excessive prices transfer real income from poorer consumers to already rich shareholders.
- The social benefits of monopoly may include: (1) In natural monopoly situations, a monopoly firm can be more productively efficient than a competitive firm. (2) The lure of long-run excess profits under monopoly may provide the incentive to invent or develop new products or services.

10.5 The Regulation of a Natural Monopoly

You will recall from our discussion of barriers to entry that whenever a single firm has the ability to produce all of the industry's output at a lower per-unit cost than other firms attempting to produce less than total industry output, a natural monopoly arises. Natural gas and electric utilities are examples. Long-run average costs for those firms typically fall as output increases. In a natural monopoly, economies of large-scale production dominate, leading to a single-firm industry.

The Pricing and Output Decision of the Natural Monopolist

We show data for a hypothetical natural monopoly in part (a) of Figure 10–10. Demand data is in columns 1 and 2, with marginal revenue in column 3. Total cost is in column 4. Notice that marginal cost in column 5 is constant over the range of demand provided. This might be typical of a hydroelectric utility—once the necessary dams are constructed, electricity can be produced at a relatively constant cost. Average total cost is in column 6.

Columns 1, 2, 3, 5, and 6 are graphed in part (b). The intersection of MR and MC is at $4. The monopolist will, therefore, produce 5000 units and charge a price of $8 per unit.

What do we know about a monopolist's solution to the price–quantity question? When compared with a competitive situation, we know that consumers end up paying more for the product, and consequently they purchase less of it than they would purchase under competition. The monopoly solution is economically inefficient from society's point of view; the price charged for the product is higher than the opportunity cost to society, and consequently there is a misallocation of resources. That is, the price does not equal

FIGURE 10–10

Profit Maximization and Regulation Through Marginal Cost Pricing

The profit-maximizing monopolist here would produce at the point in part (b) where marginal cost equals marginal revenue, which means production of 5000 units of output. The price charged would be $8. If a regulatory commission attempted to regulate natural monopolies so that price equalled long-run marginal cost, the commission would make the monopolist set production at the point where the marginal cost curve intersects the demand curve. This is shown in part (c). The quantity produced would be 9000 units, and the price would be $4. However, average costs at 9000 units are equal to $5.56. Losses would ensue, equal to the shaded area. It would be self-defeating for a regulatory commission to force a natural monopoly to produce at an output rate at which MC = P without subsidizing some of its costs because losses would eventually drive the natural monopolist out of business.

Part (a)

(1) Output (units)	(2) Price per Unit	(3) Marginal Revenue (MR)	(4) Long-Run Total Cost (TC)	(5) Long-Run Marginal Cost (MC)	(6) Long-Run Average Cost (ATC)
0	$13.00		$14 000		—
1 000	12.00	$12.00	18 000	$4.00	$18.00
2 000	11.00	10.00	22 000	4.00	11.00
3 000	10.00	8.00	26 000	4.00	8.67
4 000	9.00	6.00	30 000	4.00	7.50
5 000	8.00	4.00	34 000	4.00	6.80
6 000	7.00	2.00	38 000	4.00	6.33
7 000	6.00	0	42 000	4.00	6.00
8 000	5.00	–2.00	46 000	4.00	5.75
9 000	4.00	–4.00	50 000	4.00	5.56
10 000	3.00	–6.00	54 000	4.00	5.40
11 000	2.00	–8.00	58 000	4.00	5.27
12 000	1.00	–10.00	62 000	4.00	5.17

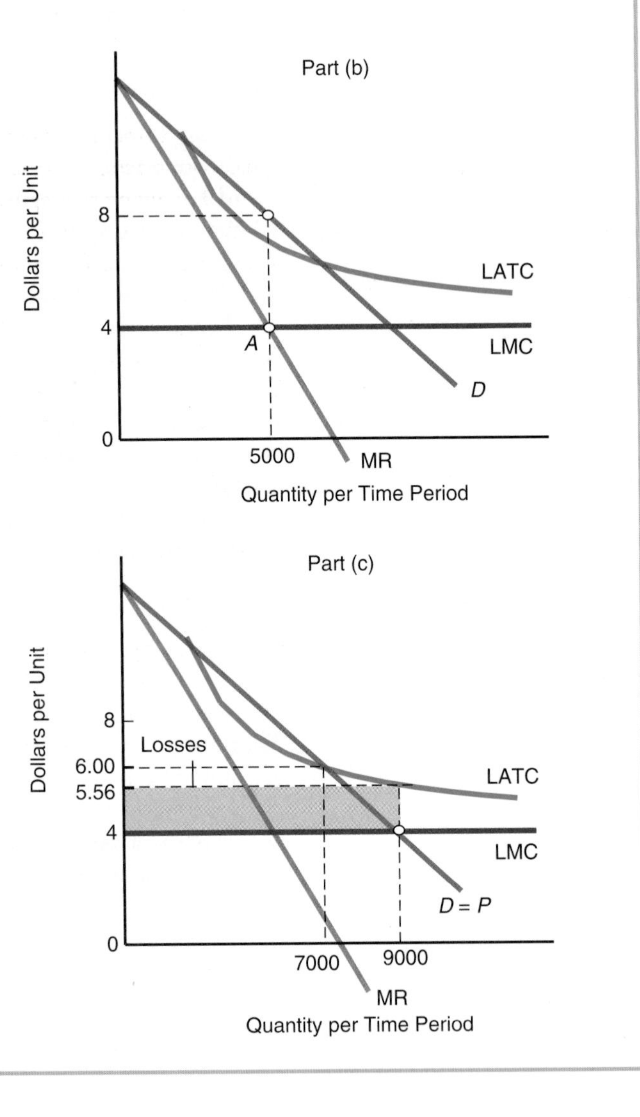

the true marginal cost of producing the good because the true marginal cost is at the intersection *A*, not at $8.

Regulation Using Marginal Cost Pricing

Assume that the government wants the natural monopolist to produce at an output at which price equals marginal cost, so that the value of the satisfaction that individuals receive from the marginal unit purchased is just equal to the marginal cost to society.

Marginal cost pricing Occurs when the monopoly firm is forced to set price equal to marginal cost.

Marginal cost pricing occurs when the monopoly firm is forced to set price equal to marginal cost. Where is that solution in part (c) of Figure 10–10? It is at the intersection of the marginal cost curve and the demand curve, where price equals $4. If a regulatory commission forces the natural monopolist to engage in *marginal cost pricing,* and hence to produce 9000 units to sell for $4 each, how large will the monopolist's profits be? Profits, of course, are the *positive* difference between total revenues and total costs. Total revenues equal price times output, and total costs equal average costs times output. At 9000 units, average cost is equal to $5.56, higher than the price that the regulatory commission forces our natural monopolist to charge. Profits turn out to be losses and are equal to the shaded area in part (c) of Figure 10–10. Thus, regulation that forces a natural monopolist to produce and price as if it were in a competitive situation would also force that monopolist into negative profits, or losses. Obviously, the monopolist would rather go out of business than be subject to such regulation.

Regulation Using Average Cost Pricing

Average cost pricing Occurs when the monopoly firm is forced to set price equal to average total cost.

As a practical matter, then, regulators cannot force a natural monopolist to engage in marginal cost pricing. Consequently, regulation of natural monopolies has often taken the form of allowing the regulated natural monopolist to set price where LAC intersects *D,* at 7000 units of output, in part (c) of Figure 10–10. This is called **average cost pricing**—when the monopoly firm is forced to set price equal to average total cost. Average cost includes what the regulators deem a "fair" rate of return on investment.

While average cost pricing is not socially optimal—at 7000 units of output, price is still $2 above marginal cost—it does result in more output being produced at a lower cost to consumers. Regulators must beware, however, of problems associated with average cost pricing. Unless there are safeguards in place to ensure that the monopoly is cost efficient, the firm has no incentive to keep average costs low. It is easier for the firm to condone inefficiencies in the form of very generous fringe benefits and large expense accounts for executives, all of which inflate average costs. In the extreme, the monopoly could allow its average costs, and hence its regulated price, to rise to the profit-maximizing level of $8.

CONCEPTS IN BRIEF

Learning Objective 10.5: Compare and contrast the use of marginal cost pricing versus average cost pricing in the regulation of a natural monopoly.

- Under marginal cost pricing the natural monopoly firm is forced to produce at the output level where price just equals marginal cost. While this promotes allocative efficiency, this will result in perpetual losses in a natural monopoly situation, as marginal cost is below average total cost.
- With average cost pricing the monopoly firm is forced to operate at a quantity level where price just equals average total cost. Compared with unregulated monopoly, average cost pricing will result in a lower price to consumers. As well, average cost pricing promotes an equitable distribution of income as the monopolist just earns a normal profit.

ISSUES AND APPLICATIONS

Should a Company Be Allowed to Monopolize Genetic Information?

Concepts Applied: Barriers to Entry, Allocative Efficiency, Economic Profit

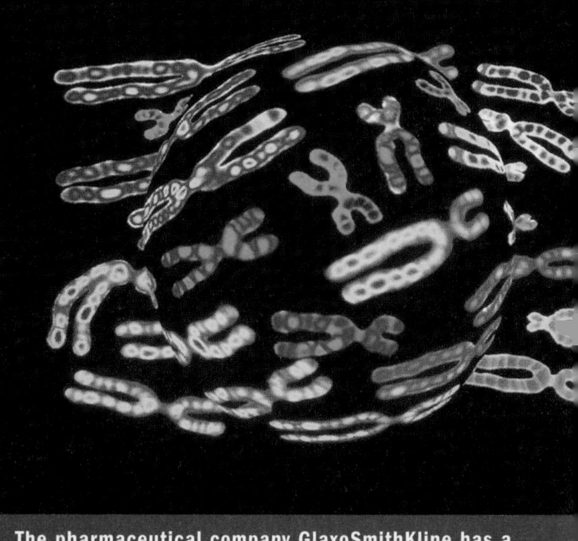

The pharmaceutical company GlaxoSmithKline has a monopoly over important information about the genes in human chromosomes.

The pharmaceutical company SmithKline Beecham, through a research pact with Human Genome Sciences, Inc., claimed to have isolated almost 50 000 human genes. Roche Holding of Switzerland and Glaxo Holdings of the United Kingdom have formed similar alliances, but none has been as successful as SmithKline. The question for each company is whether it should use its successful gene discoveries in developing its own drugs or sell or license the genetic sequences to other drug companies.

The Controversy

Because the area in question relates to health care, there is controversy. Doesn't SmithKline owe to humanity the valuable information it has? A few years ago, academic researchers called on SmithKline to make public its information on the molecular arrangement of a gene. The molecular sequence is the "biological blueprint" of a gene. Knowledge of it allows a company to make a drug that will enhance or block the gene's functioning in order to treat a disease. Researchers have already learned the molecular sequence for the gene that causes breast cancer, the gene that causes obesity, and the gene that causes type II (non–insulin-dependent) diabetes.

Monopoly Returns Needed

According to George Poste, SmithKline's research director, his company is not about to publish the initial information on the molecular arrangement of a gene. "The more people who get access to sequence data, the greater the number of competitors we have." After all, SmithKline paid U.S.$125 million for its association with Human Genome, Inc. SmithKline wants to make at least a normal rate of return on that investment.

The New Market in Genes

SmithKline decided to sell the rights to genetic information, rather than exploit the new information itself in the form of new drugs. The firm decided that even large pharmaceutical companies can handle only a small percentage of the genetic data that are available. SmithKline believes that it can earn higher profits by obtaining licensing royalties on the new drugs based on its genetic discoveries than by developing them itself. Presumably, it charges more than its marginal cost at all times. After all, it is in a classic monopoly position. It owns the rights to the genetic information. If it were to charge marginal cost, that would be effectively zero. That is the nature of many discoveries today. There are huge initial costs for the first unit but zero marginal costs for each additional unit. SmithKline could pass on genetic data over the Internet essentially free, if it chose to do so.

On December 27, 2000, SmithKline Beecham successfully merged with GlaxoWellcome to form the company currently named GlaxoSmithKline. This merger, while creating a world-leading research-based pharmaceutical company, strengthens one company's monopoly over valuable information concerning the genes in human chromosomes.

For critical analysis:

1. What type of barrier to entry is responsible for GlaxoSmithKline's monopoly relating to various genetic sequences?
2. Can we expect GlaxoSmithKline to distribute its rights to valuable genetic information in an allocatively efficient manner? Explain.
3. Will GlaxoSmithKline likely earn positive or normal economic profits when it distributes its rights to the genetic information? Explain.
4. On what grounds might one justify granting monopolies in cases where pharmaceutical companies discover new information or create new drugs? Explain.

SUMMARY DISCUSSION OF LEARNING OBJECTIVES

10.1 **The Characteristics of Monopoly.** A monopolist is a single seller of a product or a service for which there is no close substitute. To maintain a monopoly, there must be barriers to entry, which may include: (1) ownership of resources needed to enter the industry, (2) large capital outlays required for entry into the industry, (3) economies of scale, (4) legally required licences and public franchises, (5) patents, (6) tariffs, (7) safety and quality regulations, and (8) predatory behaviour. The monopoly firm is a price searcher, which means that it faces a downward-sloping demand curve, where marginal revenue is below the price at each quantity level.

10.2 **Determining Output, Price, and Profit in Monopoly.** The monopolist chooses the profit-maximizing price–output combination—the output at which marginal revenue equals marginal cost, and the highest price possible at this output level, as determined by the demand curve. Total maximum profit equals the monopolist's maximum profit quantity level multiplied by the difference between the firm's price and its average total cost. If, at the quantity where marginal revenue equals marginal cost, price is below average total cost, the firm will incur an economic loss.

10.3 **On Making Higher Profits: Price Discrimination.** Price discrimination refers to the sale of the same product at different prices based on differences in willingness to pay. By price discriminating, the monopolist can increase its revenue and profit. Under perfect price discrimination the firm charges the maximum amount that consumers are willing to pay for each unit sold. In this case, the demand or price curve equals the marginal revenue curve. The monopoly firm can increase its profit by charging a higher price in the market segment that is price inelastic, and a lower price in the market segment that is price elastic. Four conditions are necessary for price discrimination: (1) The firm faces a downward-sloping demand curve; (2) the firm must be able to separate different units sold or different customer groups at a reasonable cost; (3) different groups of customers exhibit differing price elasticities of demand; and (4) the resale of the product or service must be preventable.

10.4 **Social Evaluation of Monopoly.** The social costs of monopoly include the following: (1) The firm is allocatively inefficient, to the extent that price exceeds marginal cost; (2) due to the lack of competition the monopoly firm may be productively inefficient, to the extent that it does not produce at minimum long-run average total cost; and (3) due to barriers to entry, monopoly firms can charge excessive prices so as to enjoy positive economic profits in the long run. This can conflict with an equitable distribution of income to the extent that the excessive prices transfer real income from poorer consumers to already rich shareholders. The social benefits of monopoly may include these: (1) In natural monopoly situations, a monopoly firm can be more productively efficient than a competitive firm; and (2) the lure of long-run excess profits under monopoly may provide the incentive to invent or develop new products or services.

10.5 **The Regulation of a Natural Monopoly.** In order to encourage a natural monopolist to increase its output and lower its price, the government can impose regulation such as marginal cost pricing or average cost pricing. Under marginal cost pricing, the monopoly firm is forced to produce at the output level where price just equals marginal cost. While this promotes allocative efficiency, it will result in perpetual losses in a natural monopoly situation, as marginal cost is below average total cost. With average cost pricing, the monopoly firm is forced to operate at a quantity level where price just equals average total cost. Compared with unregulated monopoly, average cost pricing will result in a lower price to consumers. As well, average cost pricing promotes an equitable distribution of income as the monopolist just earns a normal profit.

PROBLEMS

(Answers to the odd-numbered problems appear at the back of the book.)

LO 10.1 Identify and explain the characteristics of a monopoly market structure.

1. For each of the following monopoly situations, state whether the barrier to entry is due to *economies of scale, predatory behaviour*, or *legal (government) restrictions.*
   a. A large supermarket maintains its monopoly position in a city subdivision by temporarily reducing prices every time a new competitor attempts to enter this market.
   b. A multinational drug company patents one of its new prescription drugs.
   c. The first company to bring cable television to a Canadian community eventually establishes itself as a natural monopoly in this market area.

2. Suppose that a monopolist faces the following demand schedule. Compute marginal revenue.

Price	Quantity Demanded	Marginal Revenue
$1000	1	$ ______
920	2	$ ______
840	3	$ ______
760	4	$ ______
680	5	$ ______
600	6	$ ______
520	7	$ ______
440	8	$ ______
350	9	$ ______
260	10	$ ______

In general, at each quantity level marginal revenue is ______ than price.

3. Explain the differences in the price elasticity of demand for an individual firm in a perfectly competitive industry as compared with a monopolist. Explain why the price elasticities differ.

4. A monopoly firm, being the sole supplier of its product, can charge any price it wants for the quantity level it decides to sell. Critically evaluate this statement.

LO 10.2 Using revenue and cost information, determine the monopolist's profit-maximizing or loss-minimizing level of output, price, and profit.

5. Use the graph to answer the questions.

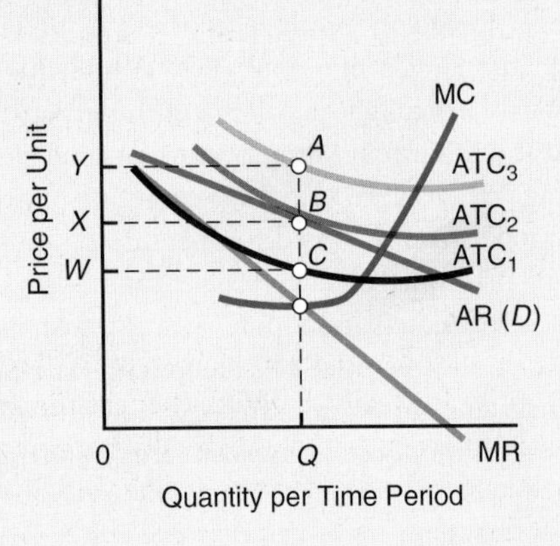

a. Suppose that a monopolist faces ATC_1. Define the rectangle that shows the monopolist's total costs at output rate Q. Also define the rectangle showing total revenue. Is the monopolist showing an economic loss, breakeven (normal profit), or an economic profit? What is the significance of the MC = MR output?

b. Suppose that the monopolist faces ATC_2. Define the rectangle that shows the monopolist's total costs at output rate Q. Also define the rectangle showing total revenue. Is the monopolist showing an economic loss, breakeven (normal profit), or an economic profit? What is the significance of the MC = MR output?

c. Suppose that the monopolist faces ATC_3. Define the rectangle that shows the monopolist's total costs at output rate Q. Also define the rectangle showing total revenue. Is the monopolist showing an economic loss, breakeven (normal profit), or an economic profit? What is the significance of the MC = MR output?

6. In the text, we indicated that a monopolist will produce at the rate of output at which MR = MC and will then charge the highest price consistent with that output level. What conditions would exist if the monopolist charged a lower price? A higher price?

7. Examine the revenue and cost figures for a monopoly firm in the table at the bottom of the page. For parts (a), (b), (c), and (d), assume a single-price monopoly.
   a. Fill in all the blank columns in the table below.
   b. At what rate of output would the firm maximize profits?
   c. What will be the profit-maximizing price?
   d. What would be the amount of the maximum profits?

Price	Quantity Demanded	Total Revenue	Marginal Revenue	Average Total Cost	Marginal Cost
$20	0	$______			
16	1	$______	$______	$ 8.00	$ 5.00
12	2	$______	$______	7.50	7.00
10	3	$______	$______	8.00	9.00
7	4	$______	$______	9.25	13.00
4	5	$______	$______	11.00	18.00
0	6	$______	$______	13.16	24.00

8. Explain why a monopolist will never set a price (and produce the corresponding output) at which the demand is price-inelastic.

9. Answer the questions based on the accompanying graph for a monopolist.

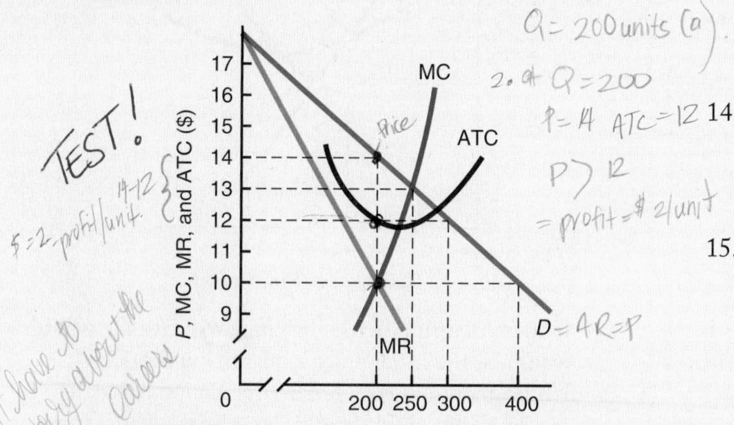

a. If this firm is a profit maximizer, how much output will it produce?

b. At what price will the firm sell its output?

c. How much profit or loss will this firm realize?

LO 10.3 Explain why a monopoly firm engages in price discrimination.

10. State the necessary conditions for price discrimination. Then, discuss how they might apply to the medical services of a doctor.

11. The accompanying table depicts the daily output, price, and costs of the only dry cleaner located near the campus of a small college town in a remote location. How much additional maximum profit can the monopoly dry cleaning firm earn by practising perfect price discrimination as opposed to charging a single price?

Output (suits cleaned)	Price per Suit ($)	Total Cost ($)	Marginal Cost ($)
0	8.00	3.00	
1	7.50	6.00	3.00
2	7.00	8.50	2.50
3	6.50	10.50	2.00
4	6.00	11.50	1.00
5	5.50	13.50	2.00
6	5.00	16.00	2.50
7	4.50	19.00	3.00
8	4.00	23.00	4.00

12. Referring to Example 10–2, "Fuji Film Price Discrimination," explain why Fuji can enhance total revenue, and therefore its profit, by charging a higher price in Japan than in North America.

13. Refer to Problem 7 above to answer the following:

a. If the monopoly firm practises perfect price discrimination, the new marginal revenue column would be the same as the ________ column.

b. Under perfect price discrimination, what rate of output would maximize profits?

c. What would be the amount of the maximum profit under perfect price discrimination?

14. Refer to Problem 9 above to answer the following. If the monopoly firm practises perfect price discrimination, what rate of output and what price would maximize profits?

15. For each of the following examples, explain how and why a monopoly would try to price discriminate:

a. A large hotel supplies the same hotel rooms for business purposes and leisure purposes.

b. A fast-food restaurant serves business people and retired people the same menu.

c. A theatre shows the same movie to large families with children and to individuals and couples who have no children.

LO 10.4 Evaluate the long-run behaviour in monopoly, from a social viewpoint.

16. Refer to Problem 9 above to answer the following. Assume that the monopoly firm does not price discriminate.

a. At the profit maximizing output level, is the firm being productively efficient? Explain.

b. At the profit maximizing output level, is the firm being allocatively efficient? Explain.

c. Explain how the profit behaviour of this monopoly firm can conflict with the goal of promoting a more equitable distribution of income.

17. What type of monopoly situation can

a. promote productive efficiency?

b. promote allocative efficiency?

18. Refer to Policy Example 10–3, "Swapping Songs on the Internet: Is It Really Free?" When is the practice of using the Internet to freely share files considered illegal? Who seems to be legally responsible for this practice? Explain how copyright can benefit society at large.

LO 10.5 Compare and contrast the use of marginal cost pricing versus average cost pricing in the regulation of a natural monopoly.

19. Unwired, Inc., has just obtained a patent on a satellite dish it invented that transmits TV programs and Internet services to homeowners. The table below describes the daily price and cost data for the satellite dishes it supplies, as a monopolist, to homeowners in the city of Digiton.

Quantity # dishes per day	Price per dish	Daily Total Revenue	Daily Marginal Revenue	Average Total Cost (per dish)	Marginal Cost (per dish)
1	$500		______	$500	______
2	450			350	$200
3	395			300	200
4	350			275	200
5	300			260	200
6	250			250	200
7	200			243	200

a. Assuming that Unwired, Inc., supplies the satellite dishes to Digiton residents without any government regulation, what would be Unwired's daily maximum profit quantity level? What would be Unwired's profit-maximizing price, assuming a single price monopoly? What would be the daily maximum profit?

b. If Unwired were forced by regulators to use marginal cost pricing, what daily quantity would Unwired supply to Digiton residents? What price would Unwired charge? What would be Unwired's daily profit (or loss) under marginal cost pricing?

c. If Unwired were forced by regulators to use average cost pricing, what daily quantity would Unwired supply to Digiton residents? What price would Unwired charge? What would be Unwired's daily profit (or loss) under average cost pricing?

d. From a social viewpoint, identify two reasons why average cost regulation would be preferred over unregulated monopoly.

20. The accompanying graph depicts a situation for a monopolist.

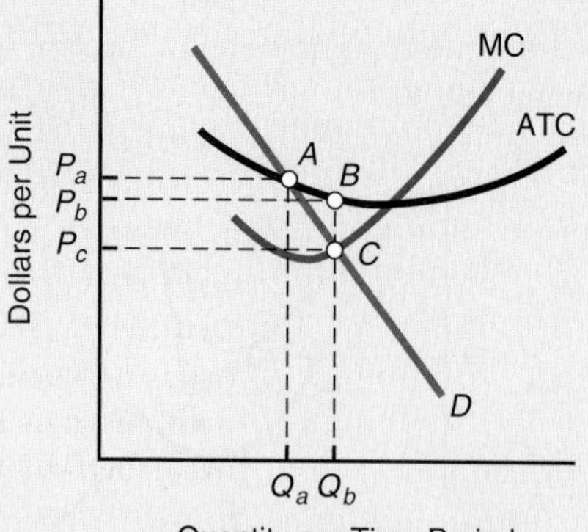

a. Under marginal cost pricing regulation, what would be the monopolist's quantity and price?

b. Under marginal cost pricing regulation, what rectangle in the graph would describe the firm's total losses?

c. Under average cost pricing regulation, what would be the monopolist's quantity and price?

d. What amount of profit (or loss) would the monopolist earn under average cost pricing?

e. In general, does average cost pricing encourage productive efficiency? Explain.

APPENDIX D

THE DEADWEIGHT LOSS DUE TO MONOPOLY

We have just studied how a monopoly situation can conflict with the goal of allocative efficiency. That is, when compared with perfect competition, monopoly misallocates society's resources by restricting output. In this appendix, we examine some concepts that will allow us to estimate the total loss in economic well-being resulting from the allocative inefficiency that occurs in a monopoly industry.

Consumer Surplus

Consumer surplus The difference between the maximum amount that consumers are willing to pay and the actual amount paid for all units of a product consumed.

If you think about what made you feel good about a recent purchase it is likely that you ended up paying less than the price at which you valued the product or service. When considering a specific market situation, **consumer surplus** refers to the difference between the maximum amount that consumers are willing to pay and the actual amount paid for all units of a product consumed.

For any given market situation, the consumer surplus can be determined once the market demand curve and the market price and quantity are known. For example, Figure D–1 describes the market for frying chickens in a Canadian province. If we assume that this a perfectly competitive market, the market price and quantity will be \$5 per kilogram and 3 million kilograms, respectively.

We can compute the consumer surplus in Figure D–1, as follows. The maximum that a consumer is willing to pay for the very first unit of chicken consumed is given by the height of the demand curve at a quantity of one kilogram, which is close to \$8 (note that since the scale is in millions, the very first kilogram is close to zero kilograms on the *x*-axis). Since the price actually paid for the first kilogram is \$5, the consumer derives a "surplus" of \$8 − \$5 = \$3. This \$3 "surplus" is described by the vertical distance between the demand curve and the \$5 price line at the quantity of one kilogram (the height of the line *AC* in Figure D–1). The consumer surplus for all 3 million kilograms of chicken consumed would be equal to the area of the triangle *ABC* in Figure D–1. Since the area of a

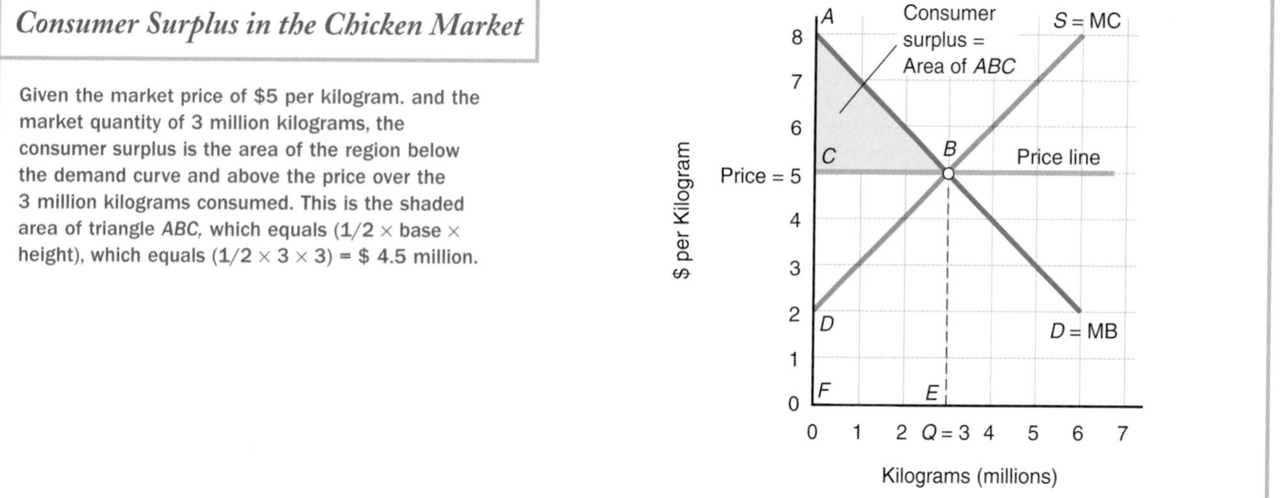

FIGURE D–1

Consumer Surplus in the Chicken Market

Given the market price of \$5 per kilogram. and the market quantity of 3 million kilograms, the consumer surplus is the area of the region below the demand curve and above the price over the 3 million kilograms consumed. This is the shaded area of triangle *ABC*, which equals (1/2 × base × height), which equals (1/2 × 3 × 3) = \$ 4.5 million.

triangle is (1/2 × base × height) the consumer surplus in this chicken market is (1/2 × 3 × \$3) = \$4.5 million. In general, the consumer surplus is the area of the region below the demand curve and above the price line. This surplus stems from a negatively sloped demand curve, which implies that there exists different willingness to pay for different units of the same product.

Another way of determining the consumer surplus from Figure D–1 is to subtract the total amount that consumers paid from the total consumer value derived from consuming the 3 million kilograms of chicken. The total consumer value equals the total area under the demand curve, over the 3 million kilogram quantity level, which equals the area of the region *ABEF.* The total amount paid by the consumers equals the area of region *BEFC.* The difference between the total consumer value (*ABEF*) and the total amount paid (*BEFC*) is the area of triangle ABC, which we now know is the consumer surplus.

Viewed in this way, we can see that the \$4.5 million consumer surplus represents the additional consumer value or net benefit derived from consuming chicken as opposed to alternative products. In this way, we can say that consumer surplus measures the net benefit (well-being) to buyers of participating in a specific market.

Producer Surplus

Producer surplus The difference between the actual amount that producers receive for a product and the lowest amount that they would be prepared to accept for it.

We now turn to examine the well-being of producers or suppliers in a specific market. **Producer surplus** refers to the difference between the actual amount that producers receive for a product and the lowest amount that they would be prepared to accept for it, which is equal to the marginal cost.

For any given market situation, the producer surplus can be determined once the market supply curve and the market price and quantity are known. In the chicken market, in Figure D–2, with the market price and quantity being \$5 per kilogram and 3 million kilograms, respectively, we can compute the producer surplus as follows.

In order to produce the first kilogram of chicken, a producer must receive a minimum amount equal to its marginal cost, which is \$2 (the height of the supply curve at a quantity of one kilogram). Since the price actually paid to a supplier for the first kilogram is \$5, the supplier derives a "surplus" of \$5 – \$2 = \$3. This \$3 "surplus" is described by the vertical distance between the supply curve and the \$5 price line at the quantity of one kilogram. The producer surplus related to all 3 million kilograms of chicken produced would be equal to the area of the triangle *BCD* in Figure D–2. Since the area of a triangle is (1/2 × base × height), the producer surplus in this chicken market is (1/2 × 3 × \$3) = \$4.5 million. In general, the producer surplus is the area of the region above the supply

FIGURE D–2

Producer Surplus in the Chicken Market

Given the market price of \$5 per kilogram. and the market quantity of 3 million kilograms, the producer surplus is the area of the region above the supply curve and below the price over the 3 million kilograms produced. This is the shaded area of triangle *BCD,* which equals (1/2 × base × height), which equals (1/2 × 3 × 3) = \$ 4.5 million.

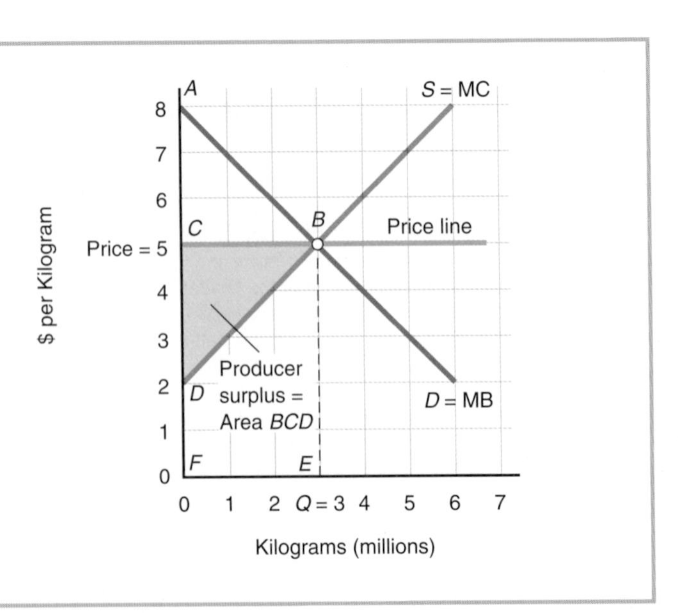

curve and below the price line. This surplus stems from a positively sloped supply curve, which implies that there exists a different marginal cost for different units of the same product. The producer surplus measures the benefit (well-being) to suppliers of participating in a specific market.

Allocative Efficiency and Perfect Competition

As was noted in Chapter 9, perfect competition establishes an equilibrium price and quantity where industry demand equals industry supply. This means that perfect competition promotes *allocative efficiency* as production takes place to the point where the marginal benefit of the last unit produced equals its marginal cost. At this allocatively efficient quantity, it can be shown that the sum of consumer and producer surpluses is maximized.

Allocative efficiency occurs when the sum of consumer and producer surpluses is maximized.

Figure D–3 describes a perfectly competitive chicken market, where the equilibrium price is \$5 (P_{pc}) and the equilibrium quantity is 3 million (Q_{pc}). At this equilibrium, the sum of consumer and producer surplus is maximized at (\$4.5 million + \$4.5 million) = \$9 million. Try as you might, you will not find a better quantity, in terms of maximizing consumer and producer surpluses. As you can see from Figure D–3, if the quantity is set at a level below 3 million kilograms, say, at 2 million kilograms, consumer surplus and producer surplus will be reduced by areas M and N, respectively. Similarly, if production is increased beyond 3 million kilograms, say, to 4 million, consumer and producer surpluses will be reduced by areas S and R, respectively.

Allocative Inefficiency and Monopoly

Suppose that all of the chicken producers in the province decide to form a marketing board that establishes a monopoly in terms of the sale of chicken. While marginal costs (the supply curve) stay the same, the monopoly's marginal revenue now lies below the demand curve, as shown in Figure D–4. In order to maximize profits, the chicken monopoly produces where marginal revenue equals marginal cost, which is at a quantity level of 2 million kilograms (Q_m) and at a price of \$6 per kilogram (P_m). Note that the monopoly quantity level is 1 million kilograms less than in perfect competition, and the monopoly price is \$1 higher than the competitive price.

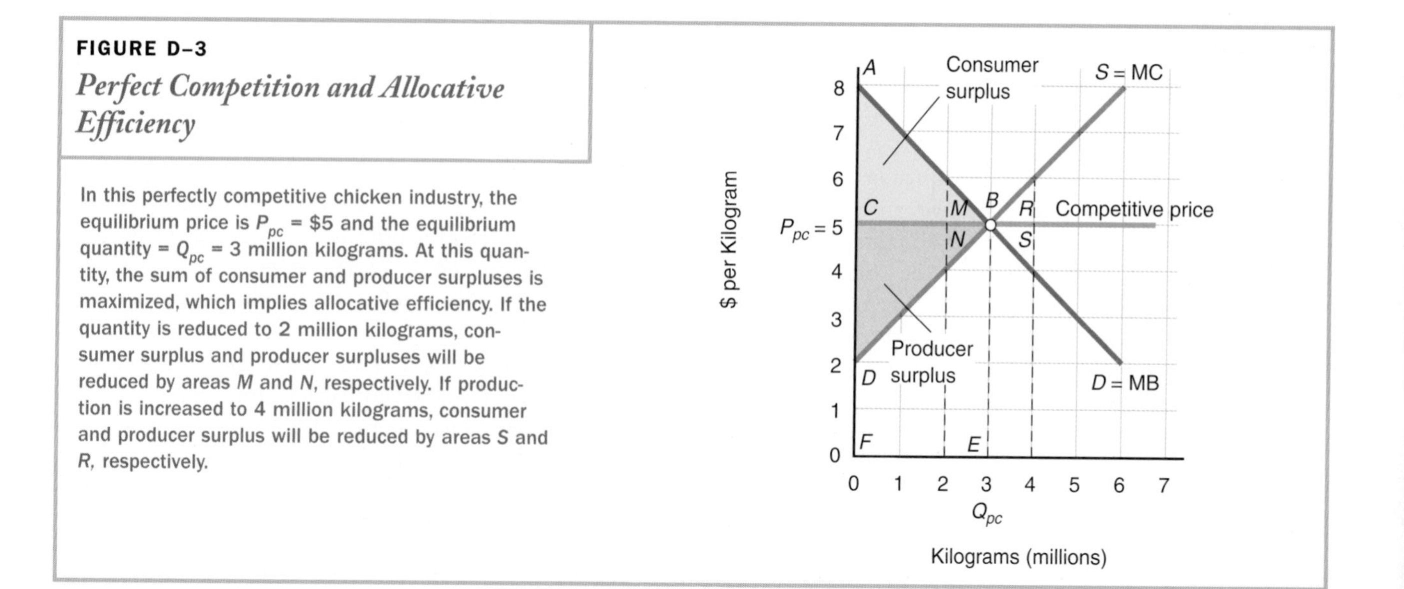

FIGURE D–3

Perfect Competition and Allocative Efficiency

In this perfectly competitive chicken industry, the equilibrium price is P_{pc} = \$5 and the equilibrium quantity = Q_{pc} = 3 million kilograms. At this quantity, the sum of consumer and producer surpluses is maximized, which implies allocative efficiency. If the quantity is reduced to 2 million kilograms, consumer surplus and producer surpluses will be reduced by areas M and N, respectively. If production is increased to 4 million kilograms, consumer and producer surplus will be reduced by areas S and R, respectively.

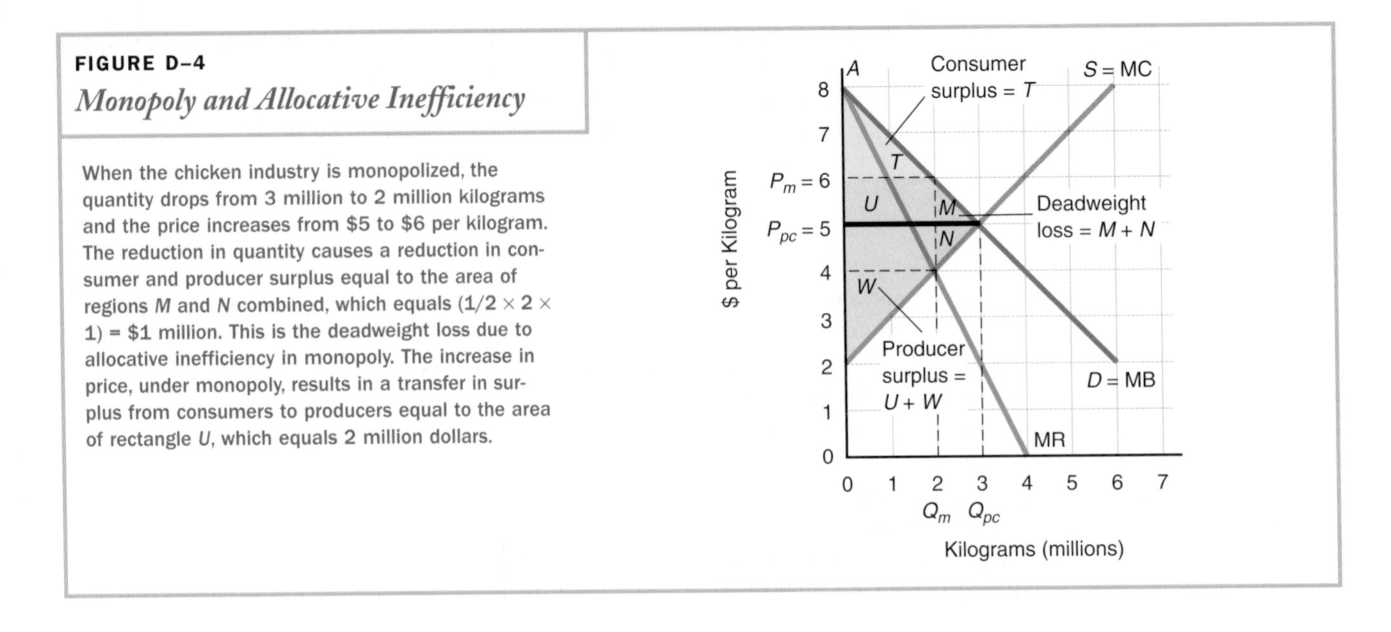

FIGURE D–4

Monopoly and Allocative Inefficiency

When the chicken industry is monopolized, the quantity drops from 3 million to 2 million kilograms and the price increases from $5 to $6 per kilogram. The reduction in quantity causes a reduction in consumer and producer surplus equal to the area of regions M and N combined, which equals $(1/2 \times 2 \times 1)$ = $1 million. This is the deadweight loss due to allocative inefficiency in monopoly. The increase in price, under monopoly, results in a transfer in surplus from consumers to producers equal to the area of rectangle U, which equals 2 million dollars.

The allocative efficiency loss due to monopoly is the loss in consumer and producer surpluses due to the reduction in quantity from 3 million to 2 million kilograms. The consumer surplus lost due to this reduction in quantity is the area of the triangle M, which equals $1/2 \times 1 \times 1$ = $0.5 million. Similarly, the loss in producer surplus due to the reduction in quantity is the area of the triangle N, which equals $1/2 \times 1 \times 1$ = $0.5 million. The allocative efficiency loss resulting from this monopoly equals the combined loss in consumer and producer surplus, which equals $0.5 + $0.5 = $1 million (area of regions M and N). We call this loss the **deadweight loss**—the combined loss in producer and consumer surplus resulting from the reduction in quantity under monopoly. The deadweight loss of $1 million is not recouped elsewhere in the economy, and so it is a loss to society as a whole.

Deadweight loss The combined loss in producer and consumer surplus resulting from the reduction in quantity under monopoly.

If you carefully examine Figure D–4, you will notice that under monopoly there is a loss in consumer surplus, in addition to the area of region M. The additional loss in consumer surplus is the area of rectangle U, which equals (height $\times$ length) = 1×2 = $2 million. This $2 million loss is due to the higher price charged, which translates to a $2 million gain for the monopolist in the form of additional producer surplus. Note that this $2 million loss in consumer surplus is not a deadweight loss, as it is recouped by another group in the economy—the chicken producers.

APPENDIX SUMMARY

1. Consumer surplus refers to the difference between the maximum amount that consumers are willing to pay and the actual amount paid for all units of a product consumed. It is described as the area under the demand curve and above the price line over the quantity of the product consumed. It exists due to a negatively sloped demand curve, which reflects the differences in willingness to pay for different units of the same product. Consumer surplus refers to the net benefit that consumers get in participating in a market—a benefit that they do not pay for.
2. Producer surplus refers to the difference between the actual amount that producers receive for a product and the lowest amount that they would be prepared to accept for it. It is described as the area over the supply curve and below the price line over the quantity of the product produced. It exists due to a positively sloped supply curve, which reflects the differences in marginal cost incurred when producing different units of the same product. Producer surplus refers to the net benefit that suppliers get in participating in a market—a benefit that they do not pay for.
3. A perfectly competitive industry is allocatively efficient as it sets a price and quantity that maximizes the sum of consumer and producer surplus.

4. A monopoly industry restricts quantity and charges a higher price, when compared with perfect competition. The deadweight loss refers to the loss in producer and consumer surplus resulting from the reduction in quantity supplied, under monopoly. This deadweight loss is used to measure the cost of allocative inefficiency in monopoly.
5. The higher price in monopoly causes a transfer in surplus from consumers to producers.

APPENDIX PROBLEMS

D-1. Refer to the data in Figure 10–4 in Chapter 10. Assume that the monopoly firm in Figure 10–4 operates at the profit-maximizing output level, and charges a single price for all units sold.

a. Compute the total consumer surplus.
b. Compute the total producer surplus.
c. Is this monopoly firm maximizing the sum of producer and consumer surpluses? Explain.

D-2. What happens to the consumer surplus in a market where a monopoly firm practises perfect price discrimination? Explain.

D-3. The following diagram describes the whole-wheat bagel market in a mid-size Canadian city.

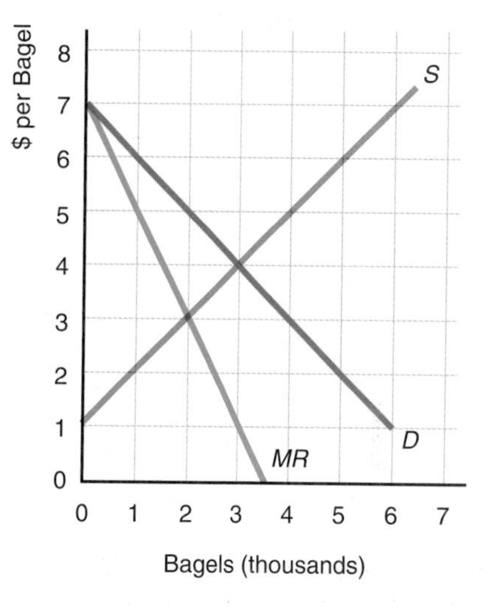

a. If the whole wheat bagels are supplied under perfect competition, compute the sum of the consumer and producer surpluses.
b. If the whole wheat bagels are supplied under monopoly, compute the total dollar loss due to allocative inefficiency.

Monopolistic Competition and Oligopoly

11

For most of this century, two firms have dominated the Canadian market for beer—John Labatt Ltd. and Molson Brewing Co. Ltd. Molson, Canada's largest brewer, accounted for 44 percent of all Canadian beer sales in 2003. Labatt Blue is the best-selling Canadian beer in the world. Over the past two decades, the big two breweries have increasingly been challenged by imported beers and by the entry of small microbreweries offering high quality "craft" beers. Labatt and Molson appear to have decided not to fight the entry of these competitors. To understand this strategic behaviour, you need to learn more about markets that are not perfectly competitive but, at the same time, are not pure monopolies.

LEARNING OBJECTIVES

After reading this chapter, you should be able to:

11.1 Identify and explain the characteristics of monopolistic competition.

11.2 Using revenue and cost information, determine the price, output, and profit for a firm in monopolistic competition in the short run.

11.3 Describe long-run equilibrium in monopolistic competition.

11.4 Identify and explain the characteristics of oligopoly.

11.5 Identify and explain the types of pricing behaviour that can occur in oligopoly.

11.6 Identify, explain, and evaluate the various nonprice forms of competition in oligopoly.

11.7 Evaluate the behaviour in oligopoly from a social viewpoint.

DID YOU KNOW THAT...

The so-called father of the modern department store, John Wanamaker, once said, "Half the money I spend on advertising is wasted. The trouble is, I don't know which half." Obviously, Canadian businesses do not know either, for they continue to advertise more each year. Total annual advertising expenditures in Canada amount to billions of dollars. The number of ads popping up on the Internet's World Wide Web shows that Canadian businesses will leave no stone unturned in their quest to let people know about their existence, what they have to sell, how they sell it, where it can be bought, and at what price.

Advertising did not show up in our analysis of perfect competition and monopoly. Nonetheless, it plays a large role in industries that lie somewhere between these two extreme types of market structures. A combination of consumers' preferences for variety and competition among producers has led to similar but differentiated products in the marketplace. This situation has been described as monopolistic competition, the subject of the first part of this chapter. In the second part of the chapter, we look at how firms in industries with a few major competitors make strategic decisions. Such decisions do not exist for pure monopolists, who do not have to worry about actual competitors. And clearly, perfect competitors cannot make any strategic decisions, for they must take the market price as given. We call firms that have the ability to make strategic decisions oligopolies, which we will define more formally later in this chapter.

11.1 The Characteristics of Monopolistic Competition

In the 1920s and 1930s, economists became increasingly aware that there were many industries for which both the perfectly competitive model and the pure monopoly model did not apply and did not seem to yield very accurate predictions. Theoretical and empirical research was instituted to develop some sort of middle ground. Two separately developed models of *monopolistic competition* resulted. American economist Edward Chamberlin published *The Theory of Monopolistic Competition* in 1933. The same year, Britain's Joan Robinson published *The Economics of Imperfect Competition*. In this chapter, we will outline the theory as presented by Chamberlin.

Monopolistic competition
A market structure in which there is a relatively large number of firms offering similar but differentiated products.

Chamberlin defined **monopolistic competition** as a market structure in which there is a relatively large number of firms offering similar but differentiated products. Monopolistic competition, therefore, has the following features:

1. Large numbers of sellers in a highly competitive market
2. Easy entry of new firms in the long run
3. Product differentiation

Even a cursory look at the Canadian economy leads to the conclusion that monopolistic competition is the dominant form of market structure in Canada. Indeed, that is true of all developed economies.

Number of Firms

In a perfectly competitive situation, there is an extremely large number of firms; in pure monopoly, there is only one. In monopolistic competition, there is a large number of firms, but not as many as in perfect competition. This fact has several important implications for a monopolistically competitive industry.

1. *Small share of market*. With so many firms, each firm has a relatively small share of the total market. Thus, it has only a very small amount of control over the market clearing price.
2. *Lack of collusion*. With so many firms, it is very difficult for all of them to get together to collude—to cooperate in setting a pure monopoly price (and output). Price fixing in a monopolistically competitive industry is virtually impossible. Also, barriers to entry are minor, and the flow of new firms into the industry makes collusive agreements less likely. The large number of firms makes the monitoring and detection of

cheating very costly and extremely difficult. This difficulty is compounded by differentiated products and high rates of innovation; collusive agreements are easier for a homogeneous product than for heterogeneous ones.

3. *Independence.* Because there are so many firms, each one acts independently of the others. No firm attempts to take into account the reaction of all of its rival firms—that would be impossible with so many rivals. Rivals' reactions to output and price changes are largely ignored.

Easy Entry

For any current monopolistic competitor, potential competitors are always lurking in the background. Substantial barriers to entry, such as economies of scale, patents, and large initial capital costs, do not exist in monopolistic competition.

Product Differentiation

Product differentiation The ways that the firm distinguishes its product, in a positive manner, from similar products or services offered by competitors.

Perhaps the most important feature of monopolistic competition is **product differentiation**, which refers to the ways that the firm distinguishes its product, in a positive manner, from similar products or services offered by competitors. The firm's product can be positively distinguished by consumers on the basis of its physical attributes; the bundle of services offered with the product; the product's superior location or accessibility; sales promotion and advertising; and by other qualities associated with the product, real or imagined.

Product differentiation means that the firm has some control over the price it charges. Unlike the perfectly competitive firm, the monopolistic competitive firm faces a downward-sloping demand curve, as shown in Figure 11–1. This means that the monopolistically competitive firm can increase the price of its product and still manage to attract loyal customers, due to product differentiation. For example, suppose that the typical daily rate charged to stay in a motel in a Canadian city is $75. One motel owner may decide to charge $100 per day. While this firm may end up renting fewer rooms per day than its competitors, some customers will still stay at this motel due to the motel's superior fitness facilities, convenient parking, and central location.

The elasticity of the monopolistically competitive firm's demand curve will depend on the degree to which the firm can positively differentiate its product in the eyes of the consumers in the industry. If the firm is very successful in establishing customer loyalty based on nonprice factors, then the firm's demand curve will be less elastic. Keep in mind, however, that the demand curve of the monopolistically competitive firm will still be relatively elastic compared with a monopoly situation, due to the presence of close substitutes.

A good example of a monopolistically competitive industry is the restaurant industry (excluding fast-food restaurants) in a Canadian city. Many small firms compete in the restaurant industry. Since the initial capital investment is not significant, it is relatively easy to enter this type of industry. Product differentiation in the restaurant industry can be established in a variety of ways. Any firm may choose to establish customer loyalty on the basis of the ethnic origin of the menu offerings, the superior service offered to patrons, the consistency of the quality of the meal established, the ease of parking at a convenient location, and the type of clientele attracted by the firm's advertising and brand image.

Monopolistically competitive industries are commonly found in the following sectors of the economy: retail apparel and gifts, personal services, entertainment and amusements, and hospitality. Example 11–1 describes a popular Canadian retail clothing firm operating under conditions of monopolistic competition.

FIGURE 11–1

Short-Run and Long-Run Equilibrium with Monopolistic Competition

In part (a), the typical monopolistic competitor is shown making economic profits. If that were the situation, there would be entry into the industry, forcing the demand curve for the individual firm to decrease and shift leftward. Eventually, firms would find themselves in the situation depicted in part (c), where zero economic profits are being made. In part (b), the typical firm is in a monopolistically competitive industry making economic losses. If that were the case, firms would leave the industry. Each remaining firm's demand curve would shift outward to the right. Eventually, the typical firm would find itself in the situation depicted in part (c).

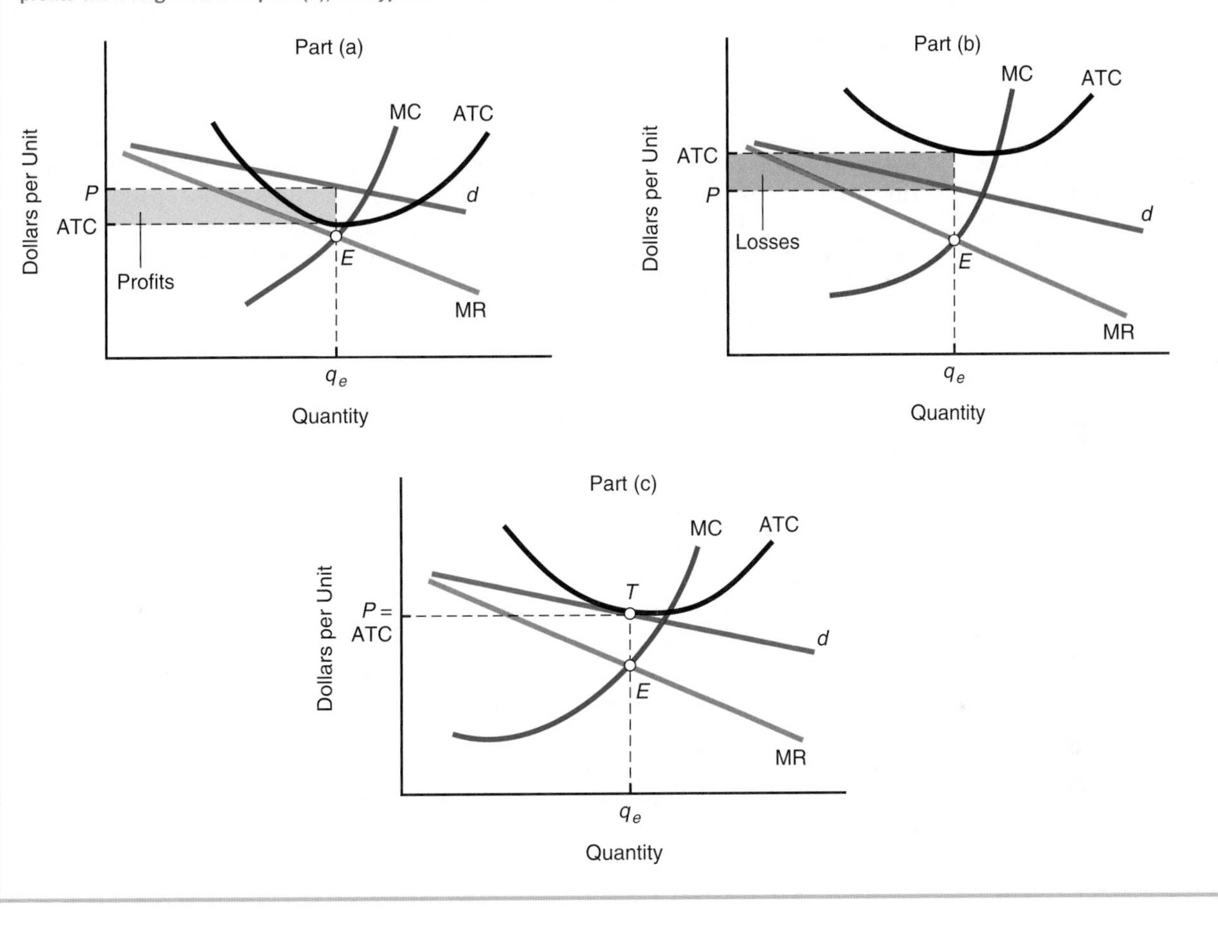

EXAMPLE 11–1 The Makeover of Bluenotes

After purchasing the Canadian jean chain Thriftys in 2000, American Eagle Outfitters proceeded to rename the stores Bluenotes, skewed its target to a younger clientele, changed to more fashionable product lines, and raised product prices by more than 15 percent. Unfortunately, sales at Bluenotes plunged by 25 percent in the fourth quarter, ended Feb. 2, 2003, compared with the year before. Industry observers say Bluenotes had been hurt by increased competition from specialty retailers getting into the jean category and by the arrival of Old Navy in Canada in 2001. As well, many contend, Bluenotes was made to appear too similar to its American Eagle parent.

continued

More recently, Bluenotes has been undergoing numerous changes aimed at improving sales performance. These changes are designed to make Bluenotes a really fun store for teens to hang out in. The company has signed on Canadian rock bands Lillix and Crowned King as pitch people to be featured in magazine ads. The rock bands will also participate in numerous in-store promotions and contests. Bluenotes will begin to sell compact discs and magazines (teen fashions, board sports, and music) to help connect to teens' interests.

Bluenotes will be putting more emphasis on denim clothing lines. Its prices will be lowered so that such items as jeans will sell for less than comparative items at The Gap or American Eagle. The firm will begin to feature new private labels, such as Sophia, National Velvet, Company Standard, and Monk Dot 5. Bluenotes will also be bringing in outside brands, such as Alphanumeric, 55 DSL, Blue Marlin, West Coast Choppers, and Dickies, in an effort to more closely link the firm to the "cool" world of extreme sports.

A new store design is being planned for many Bluenotes locations. The store of the future will have more window displays, more emphasis on the music sound system, and funkier dressing rooms.

For critical analysis: On the basis of this example, would the Canadian retail clothing industry be classified as perfect competition or monopolistic competition? Explain.

SOURCES: HOLLIE SHAW. "AMERICAN EAGLE INVESTORS WORRIED ABOUT CANADIAN CHAIN." *NATIONAL POST*, FEBRUARY 24, 2003. P. FP5; HOLLIE SHAW. "BLUENOTES SINGS NEW SONG: U.S. PARENT CUTS PRICES." *NATIONAL POST*, DON MILLS, ONT.: FEBRUARY 26, 2003. P. FP9.

CONCEPTS IN BRIEF

Learning Objective 11.1: Identify and explain the characteristics of monopolistic competition.

- Monopolistic competition is a market structure that lies between pure monopoly and perfect competition.
- A monopolistically competitive market structure has (1) a large number of sellers, (2) differentiated products, and (3) easy entry of firms in the long run.
- Because of the large number of firms, each has a small share of the market, making collusion difficult; the firms are independent.

11.2 Short-Run Price, Output, and Profit in Monopolistic Competition

Now that we are aware of the assumptions underlying the monopolistic competition model, we can analyze the price and output behaviour of each firm in a monopolistically competitive industry. We assume in the analysis that follows that the desired product type and quality have been chosen. We further assume that the budget and the type of promotional activity have already been chosen and do not change.

The Individual Firm's Demand and Cost Curves

Because the individual firm is not a perfect competitor, its demand curve slopes downward, as is shown in all three parts of Figure 11–1. Hence, it faces a marginal revenue curve that is also downward sloping and below the demand curve. To find the profit-maximizing rate of output and the profit-maximizing price, we go to the output where the marginal cost curve intersects the marginal revenue curve from below. That gives us the profit-maximizing output rate. Then, we draw a vertical line up to the demand curve. That gives us the price that can be charged to sell exactly that quantity produced. This is what we have done in Figure 11–1. In each part, a marginal cost curve intersects the marginal revenue curve at *E*. The profit-maximizing rate of output is q_e, and the profit-maximizing price is *P*.

Short-Run Equilibrium

In the short run, it is possible for a monopolistic competitor to make economic profits—profits over and above the normal rate of return or beyond what is necessary to keep that firm in that industry. We show such a situation in part (a) of Figure 11–1. The average total cost curve is drawn in below the demand curve, *d*, at the profit-maximizing rate of output, q_e. Economic profits are shown by the shaded rectangle in that part.

Losses in the short run are clearly also possible. They are presented in part (b) of Figure 11–1. Here, the average total cost curve lies everywhere above the individual firm's demand curve, *d*. The losses are marked as the shaded rectangle.

Just as with any market structure or any firm, in the short run, it is possible to observe either economic profits or economic losses. In either case, the price does not equal marginal cost but, rather, is above it. Therefore, there is some misallocation of resources, a topic that we will discuss later in this chapter.

11.3 Long-Run Equilibrium in Monopolistic Competition

What can we expect of the typical firm in monopolistic competition in the long run? Economic profits will be reduced to zero—either through the entry of new firms that see a chance to make a higher rate of return than elsewhere, or by changes in the product quality and advertising outlays of existing firms in the industry. (Profitable products will be imitated by other firms.) As for economic losses in the short run, they will disappear in the long run because the firms that suffer them will leave the industry. They will go into another business where the expected rate of return is at least normal. Parts (a) and (b) of Figure 11–1, therefore, represent only short-run situations for a monopolistically competitive firm. In the long run, the average total cost curve will just touch the individual firm's demand curve *d* at the particular price that is profit-maximizing for that particular firm. This is shown in part (c) of Figure 11–1. This situation is called long-run equilibrium in monopolistic competition.

A word of warning: This is an idealized, long-run equilibrium situation for each firm in the industry. It does not mean that even in the long run we will observe every single firm in a monopolistically competitive industry making exactly zero economic profits or just a normal rate of return. We live in a dynamic world. All we are saying is that if this model is correct, the rate of return will tend toward normal—economic profits will tend toward zero.

Comparing Monopolistic Competition with Perfect Competition

In the long run, there are similarities and differences between perfect competition and monopolistic competition.

LONG-RUN PROFITS? Due to easy entry, the typical firm operating in either perfect competition or monopolistic competition can expect to earn zero economic profit or just a normal profit. In Figure 11–2, we can see that at the profit-maximizing output level for both perfect competition and monopolistic competition, price equals average total cost. Some economists would view these normal profits as being consistent with the goal of an equitable distribution of income.

PRODUCTIVE EFFICIENCY? Figure 11–2 part (a) reminds us that, at the profit-maximizing level of output, q_1, the typical perfectly competitive firm operates at minimum

FIGURE 11–2

Comparison of the Perfect Competitor with the Monopolistic Competitor

In part (a), the perfectly competitive firm has zero economic profits in the long run. The price is set equal to marginal cost, and the price is P_1. The firm's demand curve is just tangent to the minimum point on its average total cost curve, which means that the firm is operating at an optimum rate of production. With the monopolistically competitive firm in part (b), there are also zero economic profits in the long run. The price is greater than marginal cost; the monopolistically competitive firm does not find itself at the minimum point on its average total cost curve. It is operating at a rate of output to the left of the minimum point on the ATC curve.

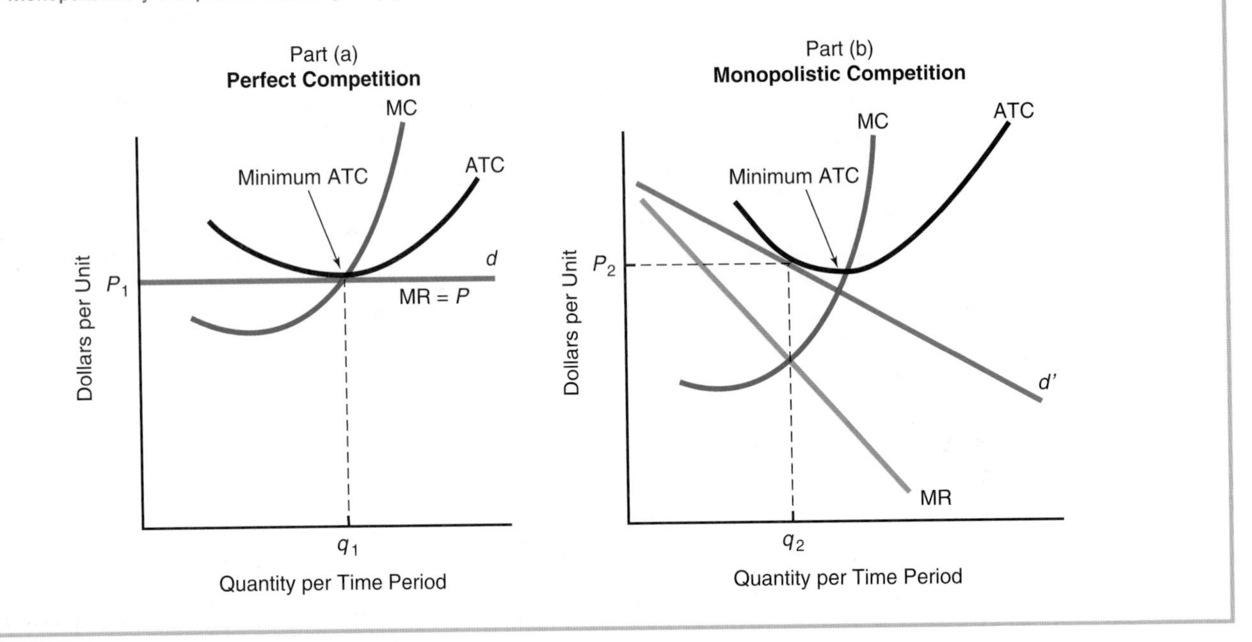

average total cost. That is, productive efficiency is being achieved in perfect competition, assuming the absence of economies of scale.

An examination of Figure 11–2 part (b) shows that at the profit-maximizing output level, q_2, the monopolistically competitive firm is operating at a quantity level that is less than the productively efficient level. Figure 11–2 part (b) should help you understand that because the demand curve is downward sloping in monopolistic competition, the long-run normal profit situation must occur to the left of the quantity where average total cost is at a minimum. This situation is one of **excess capacity**—a situation where the firm is operating at an output level below that required to achieve minimum average total cost. Such characteristics as easy entry and product differentiation result in a long-run situation where there are too many competitors, each saddled with excess capacity. As an example, the typical motel will have vacancy signs at frequent times of the year or the typical restaurant will have empty tables during many hours of each day. In other words, society's limited resources are being wasted!

Excess capacity A situation where the firm is operating at an output level below that required to achieve minimum average total cost.

CONSUMER CHOICE? Chamberlin contended that the higher average total cost typical in monopolistic competition, when compared with the perfectly competitive firm, represents what he called the cost of producing "differentness." Chamberlin argued that it is rational for consumers to be willing to pay more for a product in an industry that offers a variety of close, but not identical, substitutes. Put differently, a range of consumer choices adds value to consumers.

CONCEPTS IN BRIEF

Learning Objective 11.2: Using revenue and cost information, determine the price, output, and profit for a firm in monopolistic competition in the short run.

- Due to product differentiation, the demand curve for a firm in monopolistic competition is downward sloping, with marginal revenue below price.
- The firm in monopolistic competition chooses the profit-maximizing price–output combination—the output at which marginal revenue equals marginal cost, and the highest price possible at this output level, as determined by the demand curve.
- The maximum amount of total profit equals the firm's maximum profit quantity level multiplied by the difference between the firm's price and its average total cost. In the short run, the firm can be making a positive, negative, or zero economic profit.

Learning Objective 11.3: Describe long-run equilibrium in monopolistic competition.

- In long-run equilibrium the firm's downward-sloping demand curve is just tangent to its average total cost curve.
- Similar to perfect competition, in the long run, the monopolistically competitive firm will make zero economic profits—that is, it will make a normal rate of return.
- In the long run, the firm will operate at "excess capacity," which is at a quantity level that is less than the productively efficient, perfectly competitive quantity level.
- Chamberlin argued that the difference between the average cost of production for a monopolistically competitive firm and a perfectly competitive firm is the cost of "differentness."

11.4 The Characteristics of Oligopoly

There is another important market structure that we have yet to discuss. It involves a situation in which a few large firms dominate an entire industry. They are not competitive in the sense that we have used the term; they are not even monopolistically competitive. And because there are a few of them, a pure monopoly does not exist. We call such a situation an **oligopoly**, which consists of a small number of interdependent sellers. Each firm in the industry knows that other firms will react to its changes in prices, quantities, and qualities. An oligopoly market structure can exist for either a homogeneous or a differentiated product.

Oligopoly A market situation that consists of a small number of interdependent sellers.

Small Number of Firms

How many is "a small number of firms"? More than two but less than 100? The question is not easy to answer. Basically, though, oligopoly exists when a handful of firms dominate the industry enough to set prices. The top few firms in the industry account for an overwhelming percentage of total industry output.

Oligopolies usually involve three to five big companies dominating the industry. The Canadian banking industry is dominated by five large firms: the Royal Bank, the TD Canada Trust Bank, the Canadian Imperial Bank of Commerce, the Bank of Montreal, and the Bank of Nova Scotia. From World War II until the 1970s, the automobile industry was dominated by three large firms: General Motors, Chrysler, and Ford.

Interdependence

All markets and all firms are, in a sense, interdependent. When a few large firms dominate an industry they become strategically dependent on each others' actions. **Strategic dependence** is a situation in which one firm's actions with respect to price, quality, advertising, and related changes may be strategically countered by the reactions of

Strategic dependence A situation in which one firm's actions with respect to price, quality, advertising, and related changes may be strategically countered by the reactions of one or more other firms in the industry.

one or more other firms in the industry. Such dependence can exist only when there are a limited number of major firms in an industry. The firms must recognize that they are interdependent. Any action on the part of one firm with respect to output, price, quality, or product differentiation will cause a reaction on the part of other firms. A model of such mutual interdependence is difficult to build, but examples are not hard to find in the real world. Oligopolists in the supermarket industry, for example, are constantly reacting to each other.

Recall that in the model of perfect competition, each firm ignores the reactions of other firms because each is able to sell all that it wants at the going market price. At the other extreme, the pure monopolist does not have to worry about the reaction of current rivals because there are none. In an oligopolistic market structure, the managers of firms are like generals in a war: They must attempt to predict the reaction of rival firms. It is a strategic game.

Barriers to Entry

Why are some industries dominated by a few large firms? Since new businesses are formed on a daily basis, some type of barrier to entry must be preventing these new firms from entering oligopoly industries.

ECONOMIES OF SCALE. In some industries, economies of scale prevent the entry of new firms. Recall that, when economies of scale exist, the firm's long-run average total cost declines as the firm increases its size of operation. Consequently, larger firms have a cost advantage over smaller firms. Given a limited total market demand, this cost disadvantage may prevent smaller new firms from entering the industry. Due to the high fixed costs related to acquiring and maintaining airplanes, as well as expensive reservation systems, economies of scale have been a factor in explaining why we have oligopoly (and, in some cases, monopoly) situations in the provision of domestic flights to Canadian cities.

LEGAL BARRIERS. Legal barriers to entry such as patents and government regulation may explain why a few firms dominate a market. In Canada, many new prescription drugs are protected by patents. In these cases, the company owning the patent may permit other competitors to sell similar substitutes of the new drug in return for payment of royalties, resulting in an oligopoly situation. The Canadian Radio-television and Telecommunications Commission (CRTC) is the regulatory agency of the federal government, in charge of licensing certain industries, including television and radio broadcasting, cable distribution, and Direct-to-Home satellite systems. For many years, the commission's licensing practices have helped maintain oligopolies in such industries as cable TV distribution and national television network broadcasting.

MERGERS. Existing dominant firms situated in an industry may actively pursue practices that create and enhance an oligopoly market structure. One common way oligopolies develop is through mergers. A merger is the joining of two or more firms under single ownership or control. In situations where mergers result in a few large, dominant corporations operating in a market, other firms, faced with the prospect of raising large amounts of capital to compete successfully, are deterred from entering the industry.

There are three types of mergers: horizontal, vertical, and conglomerate. A **horizontal merger** involves the joining of firms that are producing or selling a similar product. If two daily newspapers in the same city merge, this is an example of a horizontal merger. A **vertical merger** is the joining of a firm with another to which it sells an output or from which it buys an input. When an oil refining company, such as Shell, purchases retail gas stations, this results in a vertical merger. A **conglomerate merger** is the joining of two firms from unrelated industries. If an automobile manufacturer purchases a chain of restaurants, this is an example of a conglomerate merger.

Horizontal merger The joining of firms that are producing or selling a similar product.

Vertical merger The joining of a firm with another to which it sells an output or from which it buys an input.

Conglomerate merger The joining of two firms from unrelated industries.

Primarily, we have been talking about oligopoly in theoretical terms. It is time to look at the actual picture of oligopolies in Canada.

Measuring Industry Concentration

Concentration ratio The percentage of total industry sales contributed by the four largest firms.

As we have stated, oligopoly is a situation where a few interdependent firms control a large part of the total output in an industry. In an attempt to identify the prevalence of oligopoly in Canadian industries, economists compute the **concentration ratio**—the percentage of total industry sales contributed by the four largest firms—for each industry.

Table 11–1 provides four-firm domestic concentration ratios for selected Canadian industries. In this table, you will notice that the concentration ratio for the beer industry is 90 percent. This means that the four largest Canadian breweries account for 90 percent of all annual Canadian beer sales. When an industry has a high concentration ratio, we refer to this industry as a highly concentrated industry.

TABLE 11–1

Four-Firm Domestic Concentration Ratios for Selected Canadian Industries

	Percentage of Value of Total Domestic Shipments Accounted for by the Top Four Firms
Tobacco products	99
Beer	90
Petroleum and coal products	75
Storage	72
Nonalcoholic beverages	69
Transportation equipment	68
Communications	65
Primary metals	63
Metal mining	59

SOURCE: ADAPTED FROM STATISTICS CANADA.

In general, for a given industry, the higher the level of concentration, the lower the level of industry competition. However, one must realize in computing concentration ratios that competing firms are identified assuming national market boundaries. In some cases, this may not accurately reflect the true state of competition in an industry. As an example, for a number of years the "Big Three" North American automakers—Ford, GM, and DaimlerChrysler—were the dominant firms actually manufacturing vehicles on Canadian soil. This situation would result in a relatively high domestic concentration ratio, suggesting a high level of concentration and a very low level of competition in the Canadian auto industry. However, to the extent that Canadian consumers were purchasing cars produced in other countries, then the industry definition used to compute the concentration ratio is inaccurate. In fact, if we expand the size of the industry to include foreign automakers, the level of concentration would be reduced.

What industries in Canada are oligopolistic in nature? If we recognize that some industries are local in nature while others can be defined at the national or international level, we can identify quite a few oligopoly industries. Some examples include motor vehicles, petroleum-refining products, tobacco products, beer products, soft drinks, pet foods, cereals, airline services, banking services, long-distance service, TV distribution services, credit card services, car rentals in airports, daily newspapers in a city, cement manufacturers in a city, and computer manufacturers.

CONCEPTS IN BRIEF

Learning Objective 11.4: Identify and explain the characteristics of oligopoly.

- An oligopoly is a market situation dominated by a few interdependent sellers.
- An oligopolistic market structure can exist for either a homogeneous or a differentiated product.
- Oligopolies develop in the long run due to some type of barrier to entry, such as economies of scale, legal restrictions, or merger behaviour.
- Oligopolistic industries exhibit high concentration ratios, which means that the top four firms account for a large percentage of industry sales.

11.5 Price Behaviour in Oligopoly

At this point, we should be able to show oligopoly price and output determination in the way we showed it for perfect competition, pure monopoly, and monopolistic competition, but we cannot. Whenever there are relatively few firms competing in an industry, each can and does react to the price, quantity, quality, and product innovations that the others undertake. The manner in which each firm reacts to its rival is called the oligopolist's **best response function**. Oligopolistic competitors are interdependent. Consequently, the decision makers in such firms must employ strategies. And we must be able to model their strategic behaviour if we wish to predict how prices and outputs are determined in oligopolistic market structures. In general, we can think of the reactions of other firms to one firm's actions as part of a game that is played by all firms in the industry. Not surprisingly, economists have developed *game theory* models to describe firms' rational interactions. **Game theory** is the analytical framework in which two or more individuals, companies, or nations compete for certain payoffs that depend on the strategy that the others employ.

Best response function The manner in which one oligopolist reacts to a change in price, output, or quality made by another competitor in the industry.

Game theory The analytical framework in which two or more individuals, companies, or nations compete for certain payoffs that depend on the strategy that the others employ.

Some Basic Notions about Game Theory

Games can be either cooperative or noncooperative. If firms get together to collude or fix prices, that is considered a **cooperative game**. Whenever it is too costly for firms to negotiate such collusive agreements and to enforce them, they are in a **noncooperative game** situation. Most strategic behaviour in the marketplace would be described as a noncooperative game.

Games can be classified by whether the payoffs are negative, zero, or positive. A **zero-sum game** is one in which one player's losses are offset by another player's gains; at any time, sum totals are zero. If two retailers have an absolutely fixed total number of customers, the customers that one retailer wins over are exactly equal to the customers that the other retailer loses. A **negative-sum game** is one in which players as a group lose at the end of the game (although one perhaps by more than the other, and it's possible for one or more players to win). A **positive-sum game** is one in which players as a group end up better off. Some economists describe all voluntary exchanges as positive-sum games. After an exchange, both the buyer and the seller are better off than they were prior to the exchange.

Cooperative game A game in which firms get together to collude or fix prices.

Noncooperative game A game in which it is too costly for firms to negotiate collusive agreements and to enforce them.

Zero-sum game A game in which one player's losses are offset by another player's gains; at any time, sum totals are zero.

Negative-sum game A game in which players as a group lose at the end of the game.

Positive-sum game A game in which players as a group end up better off.

Noncooperative Price Behaviour

Because oligopoly firms are mutually interdependent, each competitor (decision maker) has to devise a **strategy**, which is defined as a rule used to make a choice. The goal of the decision maker is, of course, to devise a strategy that is more successful than alternative strategies. Whenever a firm's decision makers can come up with certain strategies that are generally successful no matter what actions competitors take, these are called **dominant strategies**. The dominant strategy always yields the unique best action for the decision maker no matter what action the other "players" undertake. To better understand a noncooperative game and the notion of a dominant strategy, consider Example 11–2, "The Prisoners' Dilemma."

Strategy A rule used to make a choice.

Dominant strategies Whenever a firm's decision makers can come up with certain strategies that are generally successful no matter what actions competitors take.

EXAMPLE 11–2 The Prisoners' Dilemma

One real-world example of simple game theory involves what happens when two people, both involved in a bank robbery, are later caught. What should they do when questioned by police? The result has been called the prisoners' dilemma. The two suspects, Sam and Carol, are interrogated separately and confronted with alternative potential periods of imprisonment. The interrogator indirectly indicates to Sam and Carol the following:

continued

1. If both confess to the bank robbery, they will both go to jail for five years.
2. If neither confesses, they will each be given a sentence of two years on a lesser charge.
3. If one prisoner confesses, that prisoner goes free and the other one, who did not confess, will serve 10 years on bank robbery charges.

Payoff matrix A matrix of outcomes, or consequences, of the strategies available to the players in a game.

You can see the prisoners' alternatives in the **payoff matrix**—a matrix of outcomes, or consequences, of the strategies available to the players in a game—in Figure 11–3. The two options for each prisoner are "confess" and "don't confess." There are four possibilities:

1. Both confess.
2. Neither confesses.
3. Sam confesses, but Carol does not.
4. Carol confesses, but Sam does not.

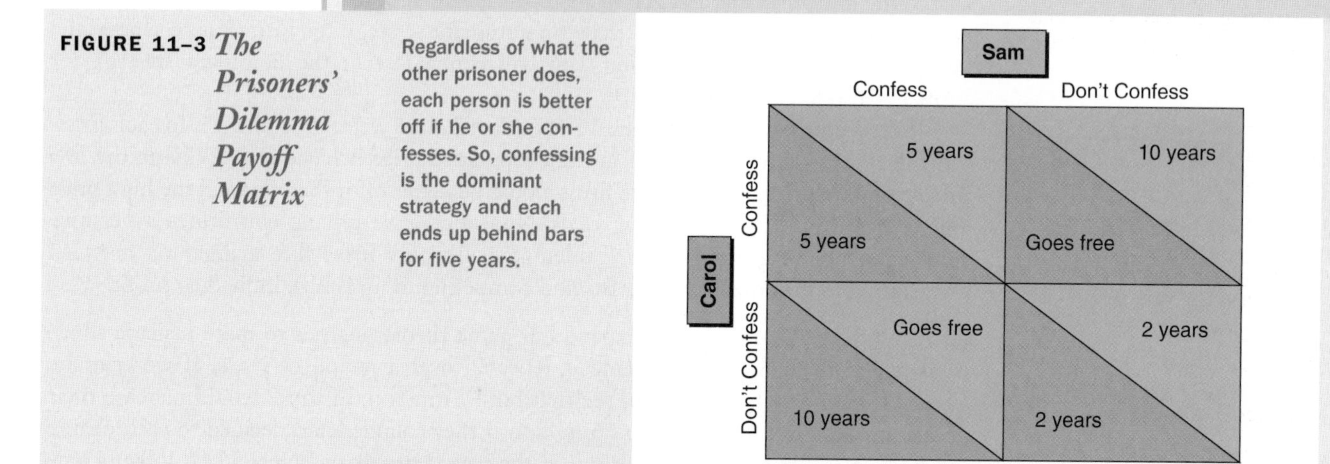

FIGURE 11–3 *The Prisoners' Dilemma Payoff Matrix*

Regardless of what the other prisoner does, each person is better off if he or she confesses. So, confessing is the dominant strategy and each ends up behind bars for five years.

In Figure 11–3, all of Sam's possible outcomes are shown on the upper half of each rectangle, and all of Carol's possible outcomes are shown on the lower half.

By looking at the payoff matrix, you can see that if Carol confesses, Sam's best strategy is to confess also—he will get only five years instead of 10. Conversely, if Sam confesses, Carol's best strategy is also to confess—she will get five years instead of 10. Now let us say that Sam is being interrogated and Carol does not confess. Sam's best strategy is still to confess because then he goes free instead of serving two years. Conversely, if Carol is being interrogated, her best strategy is still to confess even if Sam has not. She will go free instead of serving 2 years. To confess is a dominant strategy for Sam. To confess is also a dominant strategy for Carol. The situation is exactly symmetrical. So, this is the **prisoners' dilemma**—the strategic game in which two prisoners have a choice between confessing and not confessing to a crime; the game is used to understand why oligopoly firms may decide to engage in noncooperative pricing behaviour, even though it results in a negative-sum game. The prisoners know that both prisoners will be better off if neither confesses. Yet, it is in each individual prisoner's interest to confess, even though the collective outcome of each prisoner's pursuing his or her own interest is inferior for both.

Prisoners' dilemma The strategic game in which two prisoners have a choice between confessing and not confessing to a crime.

For critical analysis: Can you apply the prisoners' dilemma to the firms in a two-firm industry that agree to split the market by charging the same (high) price? (*Hint*: Think about the payoff to cheating on the market-splitting agreement.) Is there a dominant strategy?

Consider an oligopoly consisting of two firms with identical cost and demand curves. It can be shown that if each of these firms cooperates with the other to collectively produce the monopoly output and charges the *same* monopoly price, these two firms will maximize their joint profits. In Figure 11–4, this situation is displayed in the upper left hand portion of the payoff matrix, with both firms charging a *high* price resulting in each firm earning a profit of $6 million. The joint profit of $12 million is maximized with this cooperative pricing strategy.

The upper right (or lower left) portion of the payoff table shows that if one of the firms decides not to cooperate and, instead, lowers its price slightly below its competitor's, it is able to sell a larger quantity and earn a higher individual profit equal to $8 million. While this firm has increased its profit, the joint profit of the two firms will now been reduced to $10 million. The firm charging the higher monopoly price will clearly be the loser, selling a much lower quantity and earning a mere $2 million in profit. If both firms decide to lower their price, each of their profits will be $4 million, as shown on the lower right portion of the payoff table.

Given the payoff matrix in Figure 11–4, what would be the dominant strategy for Firm 2? If Firm 1 were to charge the high monopoly price, the best thing for Firm 2 to do is to charge the low price and earn a profit of $8 million. If, instead, Firm 1 were to charge the low price, the best action for Firm 2 is to also charge the low price and earn a profit of $4 million. You can see that the dominant strategy for Firm 2 is to charge the low price. Using similar reasoning, you will conclude that the dominant strategy for Firm 1 is also to charge a low price.

If the game described in Figure 11–4 is played once, we can see that it is in each firm's individual self-interest to engage in noncooperative price behaviour and charge the low price even though, collectively, the firms would be better off if they charged the high price and earned a profit of $6 million each. Noncooperative pricing constitutes a negative sum game. As with the prisoners' dilemma, oligopoly firms face a dilemma between cooperating to maximize joint profits and competing to maximize individual profit.

REPEATED GAMES. Let us expand our game theory analysis to more realistic situations where the same pricing game is repeated over a period of years. If we examine Figure 11–4 more closely, we can see that both Firm 1 and Firm 2 would increase their annual profits from $4 million to $6 million if they colluded and decided to each charge the high price—the upper left portion of the payoff matrix in Figure 11–4. When competing firms collude, this is classed as a form of cooperative pricing behaviour.

Let us assume that Firm 1 and Firm 2 decide to collude and keep prices high, repeatedly, over a period of years. Again, if we refer to Figure 11–4, we can see that there is a strong incentive for one of the two firms, say, Firm 1, to eventually "cheat" and lower the price, hoping that the other firm, Firm 2, continues to keep the price high. If this occurs the cheating firm will increase profit from $6 million to $8 million per year! This type of cheating is referred to as **opportunistic behaviour** as it focuses solely on short-run gains and ignores the benefits of cooperation in the long run.

Opportunistic behaviour Actions that focus solely on short-run gains and ignore the benefits of cooperation in the long run.

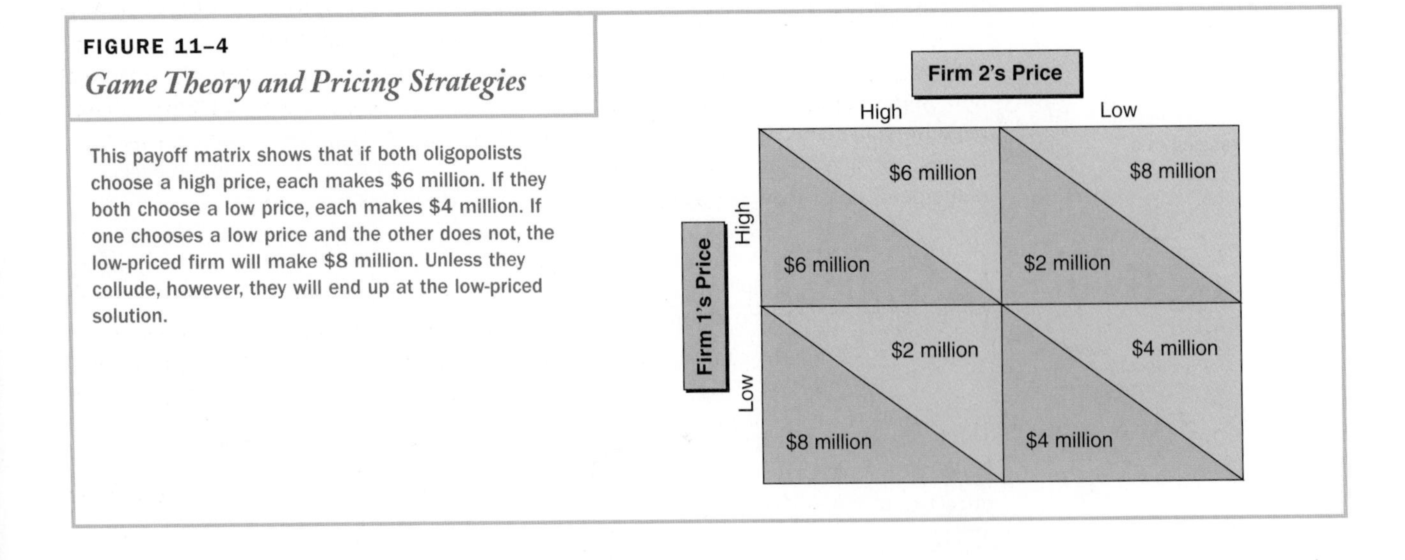

FIGURE 11–4
Game Theory and Pricing Strategies

This payoff matrix shows that if both oligopolists choose a high price, each makes $6 million. If they both choose a low price, each makes $4 million. If one chooses a low price and the other does not, the low-priced firm will make $8 million. Unless they collude, however, they will end up at the low-priced solution.

Tit-for-tat strategy A strategy in which a firm cheats in the current period if the rival firm cheated in the previous period but cooperates in the current period if the rival firm cooperated in the previous period.

As you might expect, if Firm 1 engages in opportunistic behaviour in one year, the competing firm, Firm 2, is likely to respond by punishing the cheater. One common oligopoly response to cheating is called the **tit-for-tat strategy**, in which a firm cheats in the current period if the rival firm cheated in the previous period but cooperates in the current period if the rival firm cooperated in the previous period. If both firms follow the tit-for-tat strategy, Firm 2 would respond to Firm 1's cheating by lowering the price in the next year, while Firm 1 goes back to raising the price. Figure 11–4 indicates that this would lower Firm 1's profits to $2 million, the worst possible result for Firm 1.Over the two-year period, Firm 1 achieves an average annual profit of (8 + 2) ÷ 2 = $5 million. This is lower than the annual $6 million profit resulting from the cooperative pricing situation.

Where does the tit-for-tat strategy lead in the long run? Suppose that both Firm 1 and Firm 2 pursue the tit-for-tat strategy, over a 10-year period. Assuming that the payoff matrix in Figure 11–4 applies to each of these 10 years, the average profit per year achieved by each firm will be $5 million (the simple average of the worst and best profits). Alternatively, if each firm had cooperated for each of the 10 years, the average yearly profit would be $6 million, a larger amount. In the long run, firms who experience the tit-for-tat strategy will likely see the benefits of pursuing some form of cooperative strategy. In other words, cooperative pricing is a positive-sum game.

Cooperative Price Behaviour

In the previous section, we noted that the largest industry payoffs accrue to oligopoly firms in cases where the competitors collude or pursue cooperative price behaviour. Cooperative price behaviour can take many forms. One example would be a formal price-fixing agreement among the oligopoly firms operating in the same industry.

PRICE FIXING. The most lucrative price-fixing situation would be where the oligopoly firms agree to raise the price of the product to the level where a monopolist would maximize profits. If all the firms agree to raise prices, the consumers have little choice but to buy the product at the higher price. From the oligopoly firms' viewpoint, this would be an example of a positive-sum game, where all the firms as a group end up achieving higher total profits. In Canada, formal agreements to fix prices are frequently deemed to be illegal, as the following Policy Example 11–1 illustrates.

POLICY EXAMPLE 11–1 Taxpayers Get Snowed in Quebec

On October 24, 2000, the Quebec Superior Court imposed a $1 million fine on five snow removal companies operating in the Greater Montreal area. These companies pleaded guilty to the charge of conspiring to share the market, fix prices, and unduly lessen competition in snow clearing, which is illegal under the *Canadian Competition Act*. The offence involved an agreement to share snow removal contracts awarded by the Ministère des Transports du Québec. While the total value of the contracts was about $4.6 million, it is estimated that the additional profit received by the five companies, due to the illegal behaviour, approximated $1 million. The price-fixing agreement encompassed major highways on the island of Montreal.

This is the second price-fixing agreement involving snow removal contracts awarded by the Ministère des Transports du Quebec. On January 15, 1999, the Competition Bureau, the Canadian government agency responsible for promoting competition in Canada, announced that eight snow removal companies had been fined close to $3 million following a conspiracy to fix prices in the Quebec City area. The offence involved an agreement to share the so-called "private" snow removal market, worth in excess of $16 million, which metropolitan Quebec City towns and municipalities north of the St. Lawrence River awarded to snow removal businesses.

continued

In both of the offences described above, the guilty firms agreed to take turns in submitting the winning bids on snow removal contracts awarded by the Ministère des Transports du Quebec. As a result of these conspiracies, the snow removal firms were able to significantly raise the prices that they charged for their services, when government contracts came up for renewal. Needless to say, Quebec taxpayers ended up paying the tab!

For critical analysis: If, in advance, the firms collude to decide which snow removal rival is to submit the winning bid for each contract tendered by the government, what type of market structure results? On the basis of the information provided in this example, is $1 million an appropriate fine for the price fixing agreement that covered the Greater Montreal area? Explain.

SOURCES: "$1 MILLION FINE IMPOSED IN MONTREAL AREA SNOW REMOVAL CONSPIRACY." NEWS RELEASES. COMPETITION BUREAU. OCTOBER 24, 2000. http://strategis.ic.gc.ca/epic/internet/incb-bc.nsf/en/ct02029e.html (ACCESSED APRIL 15, 2004).); "SNOW JOB ON ROADS." *THE GAZETTE MONTREAL QUE.* SEPTEMBER 1, 2000, P. B.2.

Cartel An association of suppliers in an industry that agree to set common prices and output quotas to prevent competition.

CARTEL. Perhaps the most comprehensive form of cooperative pricing occurs when the oligopoly firms in an industry join a cartel. A **cartel** is an association of suppliers in an industry that agree to set common prices and output quotas to prevent competition. The purpose of a cartel is to raise prices to monopoly levels in order to increase the total profits received by cartel members. Since cartels engage in a form of price fixing, they are generally illegal in Canada.

One of the most successful international cartels ever is the Organization of Petroleum Exporting Countries (OPEC), an association of the world's largest oil-producing countries. It is estimated that the eleven OPEC members, in total, possess about 78 percent of the world's total proven crude oil reserves. All of the members of OPEC meet regularly to establish daily production quotas. The long-term strategy of OPEC has been to restrict the daily production of oil in order to keep the price of oil significantly above competitive levels, as Example 11–3 describes.

EXAMPLE 11–3 OPEC Continues to Rule the World Oil Market

On April 1, 2004, the Organization of Petroleum Exporting Countries (OPEC) announced that its members will cooperatively reduce their combined daily crude oil production by a million barrels to 23.5 million barrels a day. In order to ensure this daily production target, each OPEC member (other than Iraq) has been allocated a daily production quota, as follows: Saudi Arabia 7 638 000 barrels, Iran 3 450 000, Venezuela 2 704 000, UAE 2 051 000, Nigeria 1 936 000, Kuwait 1 886 000, Libya 1 258 000, Indonesia 1 218 000, Algeria 750 000, and Qatar 609 000.

The OPEC production cut took place despite the fact that in the previous month crude oil prices reached a 13-year high of U.S.$38.18 per barrel, which is significantly above OPEC's stated target price of $22 to $28 a barrel.

What is driving this latest round of production cuts? Industry analysts contend that Saudi Arabia is enforcing the decrease in quotas in response to the falling American dollar, as oil is priced globally in American dollars. Will all OPEC nations abide by their decreased production quotas? Industry analysts are betting that they will, in light of the strategic behaviour followed by Saudi Arabia in the past. Repeatedly, Saudi Arabia has effectively said to other members of OPEC, "If you stick to your agreed-on production limits, so shall we; but if you expand production beyond those limits, so shall we."

continued

OPEC members have seen Saudi Arabia follow through on its threats of retaliation. In the 1980s when Iran and Iraq were selling in excess if their quotas, to finance their war, Saudi Arabia responded by significantly increasing its oil production. Oil prices collapsed. In just one year (1985 to 1986), crude oil prices plunged from U.S.$24.10 to U.S.$12.50 per barrel.

What are the consequences of this blatant display of market power by the world oil cartel? Subsequent to OPEC's announcement, the average price of a litre of gasoline hit an all-time high in North America. National airlines, faced with more costly fuel, are bracing themselves for yet another unprofitable year. Nations that are primarily oil consumers face renewed inflationary forces. Non-OPEC regions that are producers of oil receive unexpected rewards. In the spring of 2004, the Alberta government announced a $3.3 billion surplus, based on the increased taxes levied on the high-priced oil produced in that province. By the end of 2004, the Alberta government expects to be debt free.

For critical analysis: What game theory strategy is being employed by the OPEC cartel? Why is Saudi Arabia so effective in enforcing this strategy?

SOURCES: SCOT HAGGETT. "OPEC VOWS CUT IN OUTPUT: BUT PRICES HOLD DESPITE SUPPLY GLUT." *EDMONTON JOURNAL.* APRIL 1, 2004, P. G.1; OPEC. "OPEC QUOTA." APRIL 1, 2004. HTTP://WWW.OPEC.ORG. (ACCESSED APRIL 11, 2004).

Price leadership A practice in many oligopolistic industries in which the largest firm publishes its price list ahead of its competitors, who then match those announced prices. Also called *parallel pricing*.

PRICE LEADERSHIP. What if oligopolists do not actually collude to raise prices and share markets but do so implicitly? There are no formal cartel arrangements and no formal meetings. Nonetheless, there is tacit collusion. One example of this is the model of **price leadership**—a practice in many oligopolistic industries, in which the largest firm publishes its price list ahead of its competitors, which then match those announced prices.

In this model, the basic assumption is that the dominant firm, usually the biggest, sets the price and allows other firms to sell all they can at that price. The dominant firm then sells the rest. The dominant firm always makes the first move in a price leadership model. By definition, price leadership requires that one firm be the leader. Because of laws against collusion, firms in an industry cannot communicate this directly. That is why it is often natural for the largest firm to become the price leader. In the automobile industry, during the period of General Motors' dominance (until the 1980s), that company was traditionally the price leader. At various times in the breakfast-food industry, Kellogg was the price leader. In the banking industry, the Bank of Montreal has been the price leader in announcing changes in its prime rate, the interest rate charged on loans offered to the best credit risks. Typically, five or six hours after the Bank of Montreal would increase or decrease its prime rate, the other major banks would announce the same change in their prime rates.

Factors Conducive to Cooperative Price Behaviour

What factors are likely to prompt cooperative price behaviour, as opposed to noncooperative price behaviour, in oligopoly? Economic research does point to various industry characteristics as being important in determining whether cooperation or competition will ensue in an oligopoly situation.

There will be a greater tendency for cooperation the *smaller the number of firms* in the industry. In this situation, if one firm attempts to cheat, it can expect significant retaliation, as this cheating will have a very large negative effect on the remaining competitors. Moreover, it is easier to identify a cheater with just a few large firms in the industry.

Cooperative price behaviour is more likely to be sustained in a *growing industry* than in a shrinking market. When demand is increasing, firms can easily increase sales without resorting to noncooperative pricing practices that steal customers away from their rivals. Conversely, in recessions, price agreements frequently break down, as firms, facing declining sales, react in desperation by cutting prices.

The tendency toward joint pricing behaviour is greater for oligopoly firms supplying *identical* products as opposed to differentiated products. As an example, one would expect to see a greater degree of price cooperation in such industries as oil and steel refining where competitors' products are relatively homogeneous. In these cases, rival firms can quickly and easily punish a cheating firm through reciprocal price cuts.

Forms of cooperative pricing, such as price fixing and cartels, are more likely to occur in countries where *legal sanctions preventing this activity are largely absent*. It has already been noted that in such countries as Canada and the United States, many types of cooperative pricing strategies are deemed to be illegal and can result in significant fines being imposed.

Example 11–4 describes how DeBeers, the dominant supplier of the world's rough diamonds, has made recent moves away from price cooperation, partly due to industry trends and partly due to its desire to sell more finished diamond products in the United States.

EXAMPLE 11–4 **DeBeers Diamond Cartel: A Thing from the Past?**

"Diamonds are forever." For decades, the expression has applied not just to diamonds but also to South Africa's DeBeers diamond cartel. At the centre of the cartel's operations is DeBeers' marketing subsidiary, the Central Selling Organization (CSO). By restricting diamond sales each year, the CSO aimed to maximize profits earned by DeBeers and other members of a global cartel of diamond producers.

The CSO attempted to purchase most of the world's rough diamonds, even those that were not produced by the cartel firms. Using this strategy, the CSO controlled the diamond supply to the ultimate consumers. Each year, the CSO withheld from the marketplace stockpiles of $4 billion to $5 billion worth of uncut diamonds. Between 1986 and 1998, diamond prices increased by 50 percent!

Since 1998, things have not been going so smoothly for the cartel. Russia, Canada, and Australia have emerged as significant diamond producers, gradually loosening the DeBeers cartel's grip on global diamond supply and pricing. Better techniques for making artificial diamonds has also played a role in bringing new competition to the industry.

DeBeers has recently pledged to relinquish some of its practices intended to control the supply of rough diamonds. With diamond prices declining at the wholesale level, DeBeers is making efforts to establish premium brand name jewellery products at the retail level. On the basis of unresolved charges of price-fixing, DeBeers has been banned from competing in the lucrative American retail diamond jewellery industry. In 2004, the South African company was reportedly in secret negotiations to end its exile from the United States. There is speculation that DeBeers will agree to pay a significant fine in order to be able to sell its wares directly in the United States.

For critical analysis: What factors help explain why there may be a tendency away from cooperative pricing in the rough-diamond industry?

SOURCE: DAVID FINLAYSON. "RETURN OF DE BEERS MAY BOOST INDUSTRY: GUILTY PLEA TO PRICE FIXING WILL OPEN U.S. MARKET." *THE EDMONTON JOURNAL*. MARCH 3, 2004, P. G.3.

Deterring Entry into an Industry

Some economists believe that all decision making by existing firms in a stable industry involves some type of game playing. An important part of game playing does not have to do with how existing competitors might react to a decision by others. Rather, it has to do with how potential competitors might react. Strategic decision making requires that existing firms in an industry come up with strategies to deter entry into that industry. One important way is, of course, to get a municipal, provincial, or federal government to restrict entry. Another way is to adopt certain pricing and investment strategies that may deter entry.

Entry deterrence strategy A strategy to raise the cost of entry by a new firm.

INCREASING ENTRY COSTS. One **entry deterrence strategy** is to raise the cost of entry by a new firm. The threat of a price war is one technique. To sustain a long price war, existing firms might invest in excess capacity so that they can expand output if necessary. When existing firms invest in excess capacity, they are signalling potential competitors that they will engage in a price war.

Policy Example 11–2 explains how recent investigations conducted by the Competition Bureau, the federal government agency in charge of maintaining fair competition in Canada, support the view that Air Canada has engaged in entry deterrence strategies at the expense of smaller regional airlines.

POLICY EXAMPLE 11–2 Turbulence in the Canadian Airline Industry

For many years Canada was served by two national airlines—Air Canada and Canadian Airlines International. In January 2000, Air Canada purchased the financially plagued Canadian Airlines International, making Air Canada the dominant firm in the Canadian airline industry.

After the Air Canada–Canadian International merger, a number of regional airlines, such as WestJet and CanJet, have attempted to expand their services on a broader national scale. Both regional airlines have filed complaints with the Canadian government's Competition Bureau, claiming that Air Canada has been pursuing anti-competitive practices aimed at deterring entry into Eastern Canadian markets.

In March 2001, the Competition Bureau completed an investigation of Air Canada's response to the entry of WestJet Airlines and CanJet Airlines into seven Eastern Canadian routes—Halifax–Montreal, Halifax–Ottawa, Halifax–St. Johns, Toronto–Moncton, Toronto–Saint John, Toronto–Fredericton, and Toronto–Charlottetown. The Bureau concluded that in the seven eastern markets investigated, Air Canada was engaged in entry deterring predatory behaviour that included adding capacity and pricing below "avoidable cost." If these anti-competitive practices were to continue, this could cause WestJet and CanJet to abandon these routes, which would lead to higher airfares in the long run.

The Competition Bureau has asked the federal government's Competition Tribunal for a legal court order prohibiting Air Canada from engaging in various entry deterrence strategies. In July 2003, the Competition Tribunal filed a preliminary report that concluded that Air Canada did engage in predatory pricing behaviour in at least two of the seven routes investigated.

During the federal government investigations, CanJet was purchased by Canada 3000, a company that has subsequently gone out of business. WestJet, meanwhile, continues to bring forth new charges of predatory pricing behaviour by Air Canada. At one point, in 2003, Air Canada was offering one-way fares between Toronto and Ottawa for $12!

For critical analysis: Using this example, identify and explain two entry deterence strategies pursued by Air Canada.

SOURCES: COMPETITION BUREAU. "COMPETITION BUREAU SEEKS ORDER AGAINST ANTI-COMPETITIVE PRACTICES BY AIR CANADA." MARCH 5, 2001. HTTP://STRATEGIS.IC.GC.CA/EPIC/INTERNET/INCB-BC.NSF/EN/CT02136E.HTML; THE CANADIAN PRESS. "AIRLINE FLEW FOR LESS THAN COST, TRIBUNAL DECIDES." *DAILY NEWS*. HALIFAX, N.S., JULY 23, 2003, P. 23; NICOLAS VAN PRAET. "BEDDOE SAYS AIR CANADA PURSUING 'SCORCHED EARTH POLICY' PRICE WAR." *EDMONTON JOURNAL*. OCTOBER 21, 2003, P. F.3.

This chapter's Issues and Applications describes how game theory can be used in explaining entry deterring behaviour (or the lack of it) in Canada's oligopolic brewing industry. As the Issues and Applications explains, strategic behaviour on the part of the existing breweries can help explain the growth of the smaller microbreweries.

LIMIT-PRICING STRATEGIES. If existing firms make it clear to potential competitors that the existing firms will not change their market share after entry, this is a signal. It tells potential firms that the existing firm will simply lower its market price (moving down the firm demand curve) until it sells the same quantity as before the new entry came into the industry. The existing firms limit their price to be above competitive prices, but if there is a new entrant, the new limit price will be below the one at which the new firm can make a profit—this is called the **limit-pricing model.**

Limit-pricing model A model that hypothesizes that the existing firms will respond to new entrants by lowering the price below the one at which new firms can make a profit in order to maintain their market share.

RAISING CUSTOMERS' SWITCHING COSTS. If an existing firm can make it more costly for customers to switch from its product or service to a competitor's, the existing firm can deter entry. There are a host of ways in which existing firms can raise customers' switching costs. Makers of computer equipment have in the past produced operating systems and software that would not run on competitors' computers. Any customer wanting to change from one computer system to another faced a high switching cost. The Canadian banking industry provides a good illustration of high switching costs, as shown below in Example 11–5.

EXAMPLE 11–5 High Switching Costs in the Credit World

One way banks keep their customers is by raising the cost of switching to a different bank. The Royal Bank offers RBC Rewards to its Visa credit card holders. This incentive enables its Visa users to accumulate reward points on all credit card purchases. Once sufficient reward points have accumulated, the credit card user can redeem these points and obtain free travel services or free merchandise. A Royal Bank Visa holder who has accumulated a significant number of reward points will be reluctant to switch to another credit card, as this would entail a switching cost equal to the loss in reward points.

Similarly, the Canadian Imperial Bank of Commerce offers mortgages to its customers who accumulate Aeroplan Miles or Hbc Rewards Points for every dollar of mortgage interest paid. If a CIBC customer decides to renew a mortgage with CIBC, the customer receives a significant number of bonus Aeroplan Miles or bonus Hbc Rewards Points. Due to these incentives, a CIBC customer faces switching costs if he or she decides to renew a mortgage with another bank.

For critical analysis: Can you think of switching cost examples in other oligopolistic industries, besides banking?

Price Rigidity and the Kinked Demand Curve

Another noncooperative price model is the Kinked Demand Curve Theory. Let us hypothesize that the decision makers in an oligopolistic firm assume that rivals will react in the following way: They will match all price decreases (in order not to be undersold) but not price increases (because they want to capture more business). There is no collusion. The implications of this best-response function are rigid prices and a kinked demand curve.

NATURE OF THE KINKED DEMAND CURVE. In Figure 11–5, we draw a kinked demand curve, which assumes that oligopolists match price decreases but not price increases. We start off at a given price of P_0 and assume that the quantity demanded at the price for this individual oligopolist is q_0. The starting price of P_0 is usually the stable market price. If the oligopolist assumes that rivals will not react, it faces demand curve d_1d_1 with marginal revenue curve MR_1. Conversely, if it assumes that rivals will react, it faces demand curve d_2d_2 with marginal revenue curve MR_2. More than likely, the oligopoly firm will assume that if it lowers price, rivals will react by matching that reduction

FIGURE 11–5

The Kinked Demand Curve

If the oligopolist firm assumes that rivals will not match price changes, it faces demand curve d_1d_1 and marginal revenue curve MR_1. If it assumes that rivals will match price changes, it faces demand curve d_2d_2 and marginal revenue curve MR_2. If the oligopolist believes that rivals will not react to price increases but will react to price decreases, at prices above P_0 it faces demand curve d_1d_1 and at prices below P_0 it faces the other demand curve, d_2d_2. The overall demand curve will, therefore, have a kink, as is seen in part (b) at price P_0. The marginal revenue curve will have a vertical break, as shown by the dashed line in part (b).

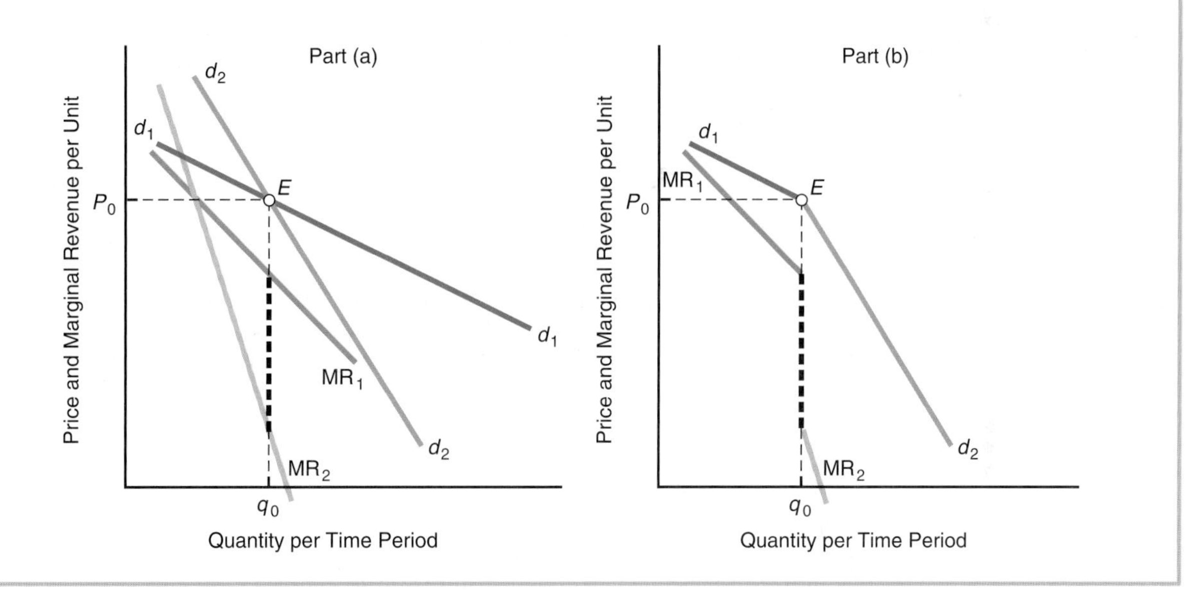

to avoid losing their respective shares of the market. The oligopolist that initially lowers its price will not greatly increase its quantity demanded. So, when it lowers its price, it believes that it will face demand curve d_2d_2. But if it increases price above P_0, rivals will probably not follow suit. Thus, a higher price than P_0 will cause quantity demanded to decrease rapidly. The demand schedule to the left of and above point E will be relatively elastic, as represented by d_1d_1. At prices above P_0, the relevant demand curve is d_1d_1, whereas below price P_0, the relevant demand curve will be d_2d_2. Consequently, at point E there will be a kink in the resulting demand curve. This is shown in part (b) of Figure 11–5, where the demand curve is labelled d_1d_2. The resulting marginal revenue curve is labelled MR_1MR_2. It has a discontinuous portion, or gap, represented by the boldfaced dashed vertical lines in both parts.

PRICE RIGIDITY. The kinked demand curve analysis may help explain why price changes might be infrequent in an oligopolistic industry without collusion. Each oligopolist can see only harm in a price change: If price is increased, the oligopolist will lose many of its customers to rivals who do not raise their prices. That is to say, the oligopolist moves up from point E along demand curve d_1 in part (b) of Figure 11–5. However, if an oligopolist lowers its price, given that rivals will lower their prices too, its sales will not increase very much. Moving down from point E in part (b) of Figure 11–5, we see that the demand curve is relatively inelastic. If the elasticity is less than 1, total revenues will fall, rather than rise, with the lowering of price. Given that the production of a larger output will increase total costs, the oligopolist's profits will fall. The lowering of price by the oligopolist might start a price war in which its rival firms will charge an even lower price.

The theoretical reason for price inflexibility under the kinked demand curve model has to do with the discontinuous portion of the marginal revenue curve shown in part (b)

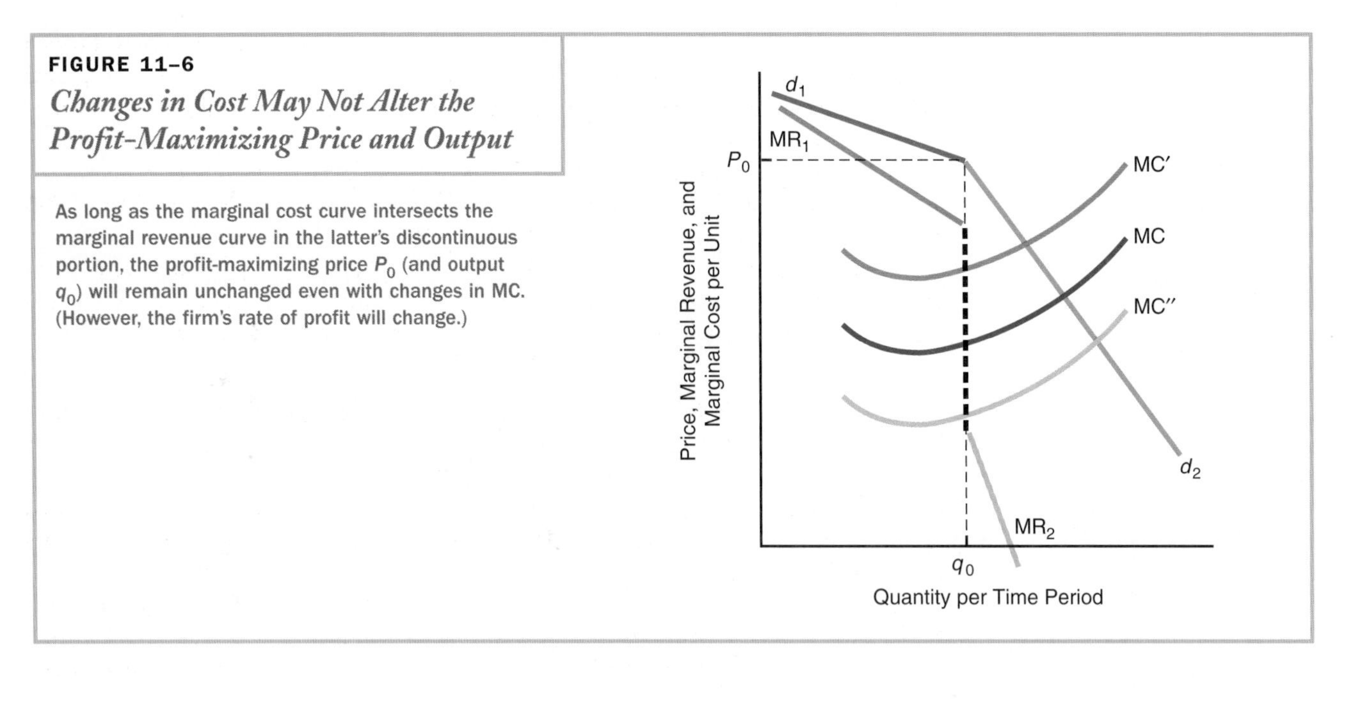

FIGURE 11–6

Changes in Cost May Not Alter the Profit-Maximizing Price and Output

As long as the marginal cost curve intersects the marginal revenue curve in the latter's discontinuous portion, the profit-maximizing price P_0 (and output q_0) will remain unchanged even with changes in MC. (However, the firm's rate of profit will change.)

of Figure 11–5, which we reproduce in Figure 11–6. Assume that marginal cost is represented by MC. The profit-maximizing rate of output is q_0, which can be sold at a price of P_0. Now, assume that the marginal cost curve rises to MC′. What will happen to the profit-maximizing rate of output? Nothing. Both quantity and price will remain the same for this oligopolist.

Remember that the profit-maximizing rate of output is where marginal revenue equals marginal cost. The shift in the marginal cost curve to MC′ does not change the profit-maximizing rate of output in Figure 11–6 because MC′ still cuts the marginal revenue curve in the latter's discontinuous portion. Thus, the equality between marginal revenue and marginal cost still holds at output rate q_0 even when the marginal cost curve shifts upward. What will happen when marginal costs fall to MC″? Nothing. This oligopolist will continue to produce at a rate of output q_0 and charge a price of P_0. Whenever the marginal cost curve cuts the discontinuous portion of the marginal revenue curve, fluctuations (within limits) in marginal cost will not affect output or price because the profit-maximizing condition MR = MC will hold. The result is that even when firms in such an oligopolistic industry as this experience increases or decreases in costs, their prices do not change as long as MC cuts MR in the discontinuous portion. Hence, prices are seen to be rigid in oligopolistic industries if oligopolists react the way we assume they do in this model.

Example 11–6 provides an example of pricing behaviour in the Canadian pet food industry, an oligopoly, that is consistent with the assumptions made in the Kinked Demand Curve model.

EXAMPLE 11–6 Do Pet Products Have Nine Lives?

A.J. Heinz's Pet Products Company knows all about the kinked demand curve. It makes 9-Lives cat food. To meet increased competition from Nestlé, Quaker, and Purina, Heinz dropped the wholesale price of a case of 9-Lives by 22 percent. Finally, Heinz had "had enough." It decided to buck the trend by raising the price of its 9-Lives to its original level. The result? A disaster, because none of Heinz's four major competitors increased its prices. Heinz's market share dropped from 23 percent to 15 percent.

For critical analysis: What does Heinz's experience with 9-Lives suggest about the price elasticity of demand for its product in the price ranges related to this example?

CRITICISMS OF THE KINKED DEMAND CURVE. One of the criticisms directed against the kinked demand curve is that we have no idea how the existing price, P_0, came to be. If every oligopolistic firm faced a kinked demand curve, it would not pay for it to change prices. The problem is that the kinked demand curve does not show us how demand and supply originally determine the going price of an oligopolist's product.

As far as the evidence goes, it is not encouraging. Oligopoly prices do not appear to be as rigid, particularly in the upward direction, as the kinked demand curve theory implies. During the 1970s and early 1980s, when prices in the economy were rising overall, oligopolistic producers increased their prices frequently. Evidence of price changes during the Great Depression showed that oligopolies changed prices much more frequently than monopolies.

PRICE WARS. Another potential criticism of the kinked demand curve prediction of rigid prices is the relatively frequent occurrence of a *price war* in oligopoly situations. A **price war** refers to a situation where competing firms respond to a rival's price cut with even larger price cuts. Many of us have witnessed price wars involving closely located supermarkets or gas price wars among gas retailers in a Canadian city. While most wars last for only a few days, some can drag into months and possibly even years.

Price war A situation where competing firms respond to a rival's price cut with even larger price cuts.

A price war can be caused by a variety of factors. It may be due to competing firms responding to opportunistic behaviour on the part of one rival attempting to steal market share. It may be part of an overall strategy to deter new firms from successfully entering the oligopoly industry.

CONCEPTS IN BRIEF

Learning Objective 11.5: Identify and explain the types of pricing behaviour that can occur in oligopoly.

- Since rival oligopolistic firms are very interdependent, each firm must engage in strategic behaviour, when determining its pricing strategy. One way to model this behaviour is to use game theory.
- The prisoners' dilemma game can be used to explain how an oligopolistic firm, acting in its own individual self-interest, might engage in *noncooperative pricing behaviour*, even though this can reduce the joint profits of all the firms in the industry.
- In repeated games, the tit-for-tat strategy can result in *cooperative pricing behaviour*.
- Cooperative pricing strategies can include overt collusion tactics, such as price fixing and cartels, or forms of tacit collusion, such as price leadership. To the extent that oligopolistic firms can cooperate and charge the monopoly price, joint profits will be maximized.
- There will be a greater tendency towards price cooperation (1) the smaller the number of rival firms, (2) in a growing industry situation, (3) the more identical the product supplied by all rivals, and (4) the lower the legal penalty attached to cooperative pricing behaviour.
- In some oligopoly situations the existing firms might engage in *price wars* or *limit pricing* in order to deter new firms from entering the industry.
- The *kinked demand curve theory* is a model that explains why, in some oligopoly situations, prices might remain rigid, even in the face of changing marginal costs.

11.6 Nonprice Forms of Competition in Oligopoly

Since price wars are costly and collusion can be illegal, many oligopoly firms have channelled their competitive energies into nonprice forms of competition. We will examine two forms of nonprice competition—product differentiation and innovation. Successful product differentiation and product improvements can often achieve more permanent gains in market share when compared with price-cutting opportunistic behaviour. These forms of nonprice competition cannot be duplicated as quickly and easily by rival firms as price reductions. Moreover, some forms of product differentiation and innovation can increase total industry sales and can be viewed by the firms as positive-sum games.

Product Differentiation

Recall that product differentiation refers to the distinguishing of products by physical attributes, bundling of services, location and accessibility, sales promotion and advertising, and other qualities, real or imagined.

To appreciate the degree of product differentiation that can exist in oligopoly, consider the motor vehicle manufacturing industry and the "big three"—GM, Ford, and DaimlerChrysler. For each type of motor vehicle product line, there are many differences in styling features, options offered, financing plans, sales promotion and advertising campaigns, warranties, sponsorship of entertainment and sporting events, and so on.

ADVERTISING. Perhaps the most socially contentious form of product differentiation is advertising. Those critical of the advertising activities undertaken by large oligopoly firms have frequently put forth the following arguments. While advertising adds to the cost of the product(s) to consumers, much of the advertising conveys little or no valuable information. Does a TV commercial featuring a new Jeep in the middle of the desert or on the top of a cliff really convey valuable consumer information?

When oligopoly firms engage in expensive advertising campaigns, this can serve as a barrier to entry to entrepreneurs considering the prospect of entering the industry. If a new firm were to consider entering the national beer industry in Canada, the extensive amount of advertising and sales promotion that would be required to keep up with Molson and Labatt may well be a discouraging factor.

To the extent that a firm's advertising efforts are successful in establishing substantial brand-name loyalty, the consumer faces disadvantages similar to monopolized markets. The price charged on the brand name product might significantly exceed marginal and average total cost, thus resulting in allocative inefficiency and excess profits.

Finally, some advertisements and sales promotions deliberately mislead consumers. One of the most common violations of the *Canadian Competition Act* relates to firms' misrepresenting the regular or ordinary price of a product or service in an advertised sale or in-store sales promotion. In recent years, national Canadian retailers have been fined hundreds of thousands of dollars for tagging merchandise with percentage discounts off a misleading regular price. In other words, the original price indicated on the tagged merchandise did not represent the regular price, since the sale item was never sold for this amount. In some cases, the articles of merchandise were already tagged "Special" before even entering the store.

What are the social benefits of advertising? To the extent that media advertisements contain objective information about product characteristics and prices, the consumer can make a rational purchase decision without having to spend several days visiting competing stores. One way new firms can make consumers aware of their new products is through advertising.

Individual companies can use advertising to engage in signalling behaviour that can benefit consumers. By establishing a strong brand name or trademark, a firm is sending a signal to consumers that it plans to stay in business for a long time. Moreover, the strong brand name is used to indicate that the firm undertakes to provide a consistently high level of product quality. This type of signalling behaviour is especially important to those consumers who prefer to buy products through the Internet.

Example 11–7 suggests that, in some cases, advertising can actually lower per-unit costs and thereby promote productive efficiency.

EXAMPLE 11-7 **Can Advertising Lead to Efficiency?**

Advertising budgets by major retailers may just seem like an added expense, not a step on the road to economic efficiency. According to research by economists Kyle Bagwell and Garey Ramey, just the opposite is true. When retailers advertise heavily, they increase the number of shoppers that come to their store. Such increased traffic allows retailers to offer a wider selection of goods, to invest in cost-reduction technology (such as computerized inventory and satellite communications), and to exploit manufacturers' quantity discounts. Such cost reductions can help explain the success of Wal-Mart, Zellers, Canadian Tire, and Home Depot. Consequently, Bagwell and Ramey conclude that advertising can help promote efficiency. Advertising signals to consumers where they can find big-company, low-priced, high-variety stores.

For critical analysis: Which is true: "We are bigger because we are better" or "We are better because we are bigger"?

Innovation

In the very long run, firms can benefit consumers by engaging in innovative activities that result in the development of more efficient methods of production or the creation of new and improved products. A number of theoretical arguments can be put forth to suggest that an oligopoly market structure can be conducive to technological innovation.

The large size of many oligopoly firms enables them to undertake expensive research and development activities. As well, due to barriers to entry and the lure of long-run excess profits, oligopoly firms have the incentive to innovate. Finally, interdependent oligopoly firms may prefer to channel their competitive energies in constructive product innovation as opposed to destructive price competition.

There is evidence to support the view that an oligopolistic industry, which consists of a few large firms competing with several highly innovative smaller firms, is conducive to the process of innovation. In many of these innovative industries, however, the scientific or technical nature of the industry may well be a more important factor than market structure in truly explaining the level of innovation taking place.[1] Thus, the fact that Nortel Networks Corporation is a leading Canadian innovator may be attributed more to the technological nature of its Internet and communications-related activities than its oligopolistic market environment.

11.7 Social Evaluation of Oligopoly

Since, in oligopoly, there are just a few major firms supplying a similar product, there is a danger that the lack of competitive pressure and the tendency toward nonprice competition can result in productive inefficiency. Moreover, due to barriers to entry, the existing oligopolistic firms can continue to enjoy excess profits in the long run. To the extent that an oligopolistic industry engages in cooperative behaviour and acts like a monopoly, the industry will tend to restrict output and drive up the price compared with a competitive industry.

Depending on the specific situation, an oligopolistic market structure may be socially preferred over a more competitive environment. If significant economies of scale exist and there are just a few large firms permitted to compete in the industry, the product can be produced at a lower cost per unit. As well, there is evidence to suggest that an oligopolistic market structure can be conducive to innovation. The challenge lies in

[1]Douglas F. Greer. *Industrial Organization and Public Policy,* 3d ed. (New York:Macmillan, 1992) pp. 680–87.

ensuring that the positive aspects of an oligopolistic market structure benefit the consumer and not just the large corporation.

CONCEPTS IN BRIEF

Learning Objective 11.6: Identify, explain, and evaluate the various nonprice forms of competition in oligopoly.

- Oligopolistic firms often engage in nonprice forms of competition including product differentiation and innovation. Types of product differentiation include differences in product features, consumer incentives, financing options, sales promotions, and advertising. These nonprice forms of competition can achieve more permanent gains in market share, when compared to price-cutting, opportunistic behaviour.
- Possible social disadvantages of advertising include: (1) it increases the cost of production without adding valuable consumer information, (2) acts as a barrier to entry, (3) results in greater monopoly power, and (4) can seriously mislead the consumer.
- Social benefits of advertising may include: (1) providing valuable technical and price information about a product, (2) serving as a valuable signalling device, and (3) promoting productive efficiency in cases where it increases the sales volume so that economies of scale can be achieved.

Learning Objective 11.7: Evaluate the behaviour in oligopoly from a social viewpoint.

- The social costs of oligopoly can include: productive inefficiency, allocative inefficiency, and excess profits.
- Oligopoly can benefit society if it results from economies of scale or if it contributes to innovation.

ISSUES AND APPLICATIONS

Game Theory: Opening Up the Brewing Industry

Concepts Applied: Game Theory, Strategic Behaviour, Entry Deterrence

Craft beers with exotic names like Warthog Cream Ale or Blanche de Chambly are slowly gaining a share of the beer market. The Labatt and Molson beer companies have found it too expensive to fight their entry.

In 2003, Canadians consumed about 6.25 billion bottles of beer. Together, Molson and Labatt produce the lion's share of this beer—about 87 percent of it. However, imports and small microbreweries have grown from virtually no sales in 1985 to capturing 13 percent of the Canadian beer market in 2003.

There are now 57 microbreweries in Canada producing craft beers with exotic names, such as Warthog Cream Ale, Moosehead Lager, Gastown Amber Ale, Blanche de Chambly, Classic Nut Brown Ale, and Alexander Keith's India Pale Ale.

Part of the reason for the success of microbreweries is that many of their brands are unpasteurized specialty beers brewed without preservatives. As Canadians have aged, they have begun to drink less and discriminate more, turning from the old standards—Labatt Blue and Molson Canadian—to the high-quality craft beers.

Industry analysts suggest that a 1 percent share of the beer market is worth about $16 million in profits. So, why have Molson and Labatt not fought the entry into the industry by the microbreweries and the import beers? We can use game theory to help us answer this question.

Constructing the Game

The two players in this game are: (1) Molson and Labatt, which currently dominate the market for beer; and (2) a representative microbrewery that wants to enter the market. Molson and Labatt can fight its entry or acquiesce. Fighting entry would cost each firm $1 million. The microbrewery's strategies are to enter the industry—which requires a $1 million fixed cost investment—or to stay out. If the firm successfully enters the market, it will capture a 1 percent market share worth $16 million. If it encounters a fight from the major breweries, however, it will lose the $1 million earmarked for setup costs.

The Payoffs

Figure 11–7 shows the payoff matrix for this game. If Molson and Labatt fight entry but are unsuccessful, they spend $2 million on the fight and lose $16 million in profits to the successful microbrewery, so they lose $18 million in total. If they fight and win, they spend $2 million fighting but retain the market share. If Molson and Labatt acquiesce, they lose a 1 percent market share to the microbrewery, for a payoff of negative $16 million. If they acquiesce and the microbrewery stays out, they spend nothing and lose nothing.

If the microbrewery chooses to enter the market and the major breweries fight, the firm spends $1 million on fighting off the two companies. If the microbrewery enters but Molson and Labatt acquiesce, the microbrewery earns a $16 million profit less the $1 million setup costs. If the microbrewery stays out, there are no profits and no costs involved.

The Solution

Molson and Labatt know that if the microbrewery wants to enter the market, fighting will cost them $18 million, while acquiescing will cost $16 million in lost profits. If the microbrewery decides to stay out of the market, then fighting will cost them $2 million, while acquiescing will cost nothing. In either case, the two breweries choose to acquiesce.

The microbrewery knows that if Labatt and Molson want to fight entry, it is better off staying out of the market and not losing its $1 million. If, however, Labatt and Molson want to acquiesce, the microbrewery is better off entering. Since Molson and Labatt's dominant strategy is to acquiesce, the microbrewery enters the market.

No Symmetrical Solution

This game is not symmetrical, since the microbrewery has no dominant strategy. If the major brewers decided to fight, the microbrewery would not enter the market. Nevertheless, Molson and Labatt choose not to fight, since fighting is an expensive undertaking. By behaving strategically, Molson and Labatt face increasing competition from small, high-quality brands.

For critical analysis:

1. Is this game a positive-sum, zero-sum, or negative-sum game? How do you know?
2. What strategies, besides fighting, could Labatt and Molson use to deter entry by the microbreweries?

FIGURE 11–7

Payoff Matrix

This payoff matrix shows that if the microbrewery enters the market, the best strategy for Molson and Labatt is to acquiesce. By acquiescing, the two dominant brewers lose $16 million, which is $2 million better than the $18 million loss that would occur if Molson and Labatt had fought the entry. If the microbrewery decides to stay out of the market, the best strategy of Molson and Labatt is also to acquiesce, as they would lose $0 compared to $2 million if they had fought the entry. Therefore the dominant strategy for Molson and Labatt is to acquiesce. Once Molson and Labatt decide to acquiesce, the best strategy for the microbrewery is to enter the market and earn $15 million in profit.

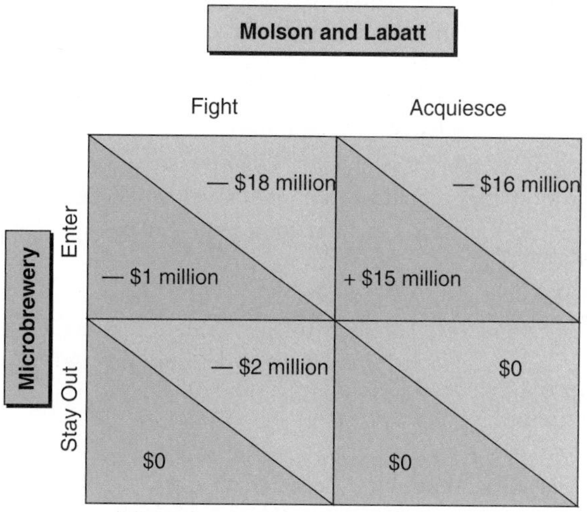

Microbrewery \ Molson and Labatt	Fight	Acquiesce
Enter	Molson and Labatt: — $18 million; Microbrewery: — $1 million	Molson and Labatt: — $16 million; Microbrewery: + $15 million
Stay Out	Molson and Labatt: — $2 million; Microbrewery: $0	Molson and Labatt: $0; Microbrewery: $0

SUMMARY DISCUSSION OF LEARNING OBJECTIVES

11.1 **The Characteristics of Monopolistic Competition.** Monopolistic competition, a market structure that lies between pure monopoly and perfect competition, has the following features: (1) a large number of sellers, (2) differentiated products, and (3) easy entry of firms in the long run. Each firm acts independently, as collusion is virtually impossible with a large number of competitors.

11.2 **Short-Run Price, Output, and Profit in Monopolistic Competition.** Due to product differentiation, the demand curve for a firm in monopolistic competition is downward sloping, with marginal revenue below price. The firm chooses the profit-maximizing price–output combination—the output at which marginal revenue equals marginal cost, and the highest price possible at this output level, as determined by the demand curve. Total maximum profit equals the firm's maximum profit quantity level multiplied by the difference between the firm's price and average total cost. In the short run, the firm can be making a positive, negative, or zero economic profit.

11.3 **Long-Run Equilibrium in Monopolistic Competition.** In the long run the typical firm will tend toward a situation where its downward-sloping demand curve is just tangent to its average total cost curve. Similar to perfect competition, a monopolistically competitive firm will make a normal profit in the long run. The monopolistically competitive firm will operate at "excess capacity," which is at a quantity level that is less than the productively efficient, perfectly competitive quantity level, in the long run. Chamberlin argued that the difference between the average cost of production for a monopolistically competitive firm and a perfectly competitive firm is the cost of "differentness."

11.4 **The Characteristics of Oligopoly.** An oligopoly is a market situation dominated by a few interdependent sellers. An oligopolistic market structure can exist for a homogeneous or a differentiated product. Oligopolies develop in the long run due to some type of barrier to entry, such as economies of scale, legal restrictions, or merger behaviour. Oligopolistic industries exhibit high concentration ratios, which means that the top four firms account for a large percentage of industry sales.

11.5 **Price Behaviour in Oligopoly.** Since rival oligopolistic firms are very interdependent, each firm must engage in strategic behaviour when determining its pricing strategy. One way to model this behaviour is to use game theory. The prisoners' dilemma game can be used to explain how an oligopolistic firm, acting in its own individual self-interest, might engage in *noncooperative pricing behaviour*, even though this can reduce the joint profits of all the firms in the industry. In repeated games, the tit-for-tat strategy can result in *cooperative pricing behaviour*. Cooperative pricing strategies can include overt collusion tactics, such as price fixing and cartels, or forms of tacit collusion, such as price leadership. To the extent that oligopolistic firms can cooperate and charge the monopoly price, joint profits will be maximized. There will be a greater tendency toward price cooperation (1) when the number of rival firms is small, (2) in a growing industry situation, (3) when the products supplied by all rivals are identical, and (4) when the legal penalty attached to cooperative pricing behaviour is lower. In some oligopoly situations, the existing firms might engage in *price wars* or *limit pricing* in order to deter new firms from entering the industry. The *kinked demand curve theory* is a model that explains why, in some oligopoly situations, prices might remain rigid, even in the face of changing marginal costs.

11.6 **Nonprice Forms of Competition in Oligopoly.** Oligopolistic firms often engage in nonprice forms of competition including product differentiation and innovation. Types of product differentiation include differences in product features, consumer incentives, financing options, sales promotions, and advertising. These nonprice forms of competition can achieve more permanent gains in market share, when compared with price-cutting, opportunistic behaviour. Possible social disadvantages of advertising include: (1) it increases the cost of production without adding valuable consumer information, (2) acts as a barrier to entry, (3) results in greater monopoly power, and (4) can seriously mislead the consumer. Social benefits of advertising may include: (1) it provides valuable technical and price information about a product, (2) serves as a valuable signalling device, and (3) promotes productive efficiency in cases where it increases the sales volume so that economies of scale can be achieved.

11.7 **Social Evaluation of Oligopoly.** The social cost of oligopoly can include productive inefficiency, allocative inefficiency, and excess profits. Oligopoly can benefit society if it results from economies of scale or if it contributes to innovation.

PROBLEMS

(Answers to the odd-numbered problems appear at the back of the book.)

LO 11.1 Identify and explain the characteristics of monopolistic competition.

1. Local night clubs in a large city typically operate under what type of market structure? Explain.
2. Compare and contrast the characteristics of monopolistic competition with perfect competition.
3. Explain why it is not rational for a perfectly competitive firm to incur significant advertising expenditures.
4. What aspects of a retail clothing business fit the description of a monopolistically competitive firm? Base your answer on Example 11–1, "The Makeover of Bluenotes," as well as your own experience.

LO 11.2 Using revenue and cost information, determine the price, output, and profit for a firm in monopolistic competition in the short run.

LO 11.3 Describe long-run equilibrium in monopolistic competition.

5. The table below describes the price, revenue, and cost information for a small motel firm that rents rooms on a daily basis under monopolistic competition. Note that the quantity level refers to the number of rooms rented per night. The price refers to the nightly rental rate charged per room. Recall that marginal revenue is the extra revenue per room received, or the change in total revenue divided by the change in quantity.
   a. Fill in the blanks in the table.
   b. How many rooms must be rented per night in order to maximize profits?
   c. What is the profit-maximizing price?
   d. What is the amount of the total maximum profit?
   e. Can this motel firm expect to earn these profits in the long run? Explain.
   f. Identify the different ways motels and hotels can differentiate their "product."
6. The graph below depicts long-run equilibrium for a monopolistic competitor.
   a. Which output rate represents equilibrium?
   b. Which price represents equilibrium?
   c. Which labelled point indicates that economic profits are zero?
   d. Which labelled point indicates minimum ATC?
   e. Is ATC at the equilibrium output rate above or at minimum ATC?
   f. Is the equilibrium price greater than, less than, or equal to the marginal cost of producing at the equilibrium output rate?
   g. At what quantity would a perfectly competitive firm operate in the long run? Explain. What would be the perfectly competitive firm's level of economic profit in the long run?

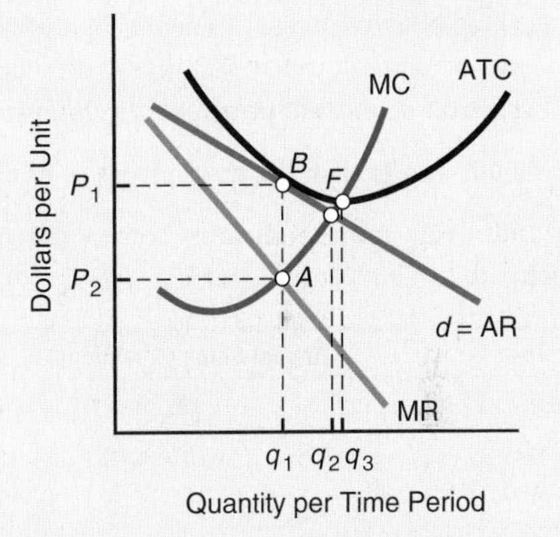

Quantity (# rooms)	Price (per room)	Total Revenue	Marginal Revenue	Marginal Cost	Average Total Cost
0	$95	$____			
4	90	$____	$____	$36	$86
8	85	$____	$____	34	60
12	80	$____	$____	33	51
16	75	$____	$____	34	46.75
20	70	$____	$____	36	44.60
24	65	$____	$____	39	43.67
28	60	$____	$____	43	43.57
32	55	$____	$____	48	44.13

7. The following table depicts the hourly quantity sold, prices, and costs for a popular used bookstore located close to a university campus. This store competes with numerous rival used bookstores but capitalizes on its location and the word-of-mouth reputation of the coffee it serves to its customers.

Quantity Sold (# Books)	Price ($)	Marginal Cost ($)	Average Total Cost ($)
0	6		
1	5.75	3.25	5.25
2	5.5	2.25	3.75
3	5.25	2.1	3.20
4	5	2.5	3.03
5	4.75	3.7	3.16
6	4.5	4.2	3.33
7	4	4.75	3.54

a. Why would this bookstore be classed as a firm in monopolistic competition?
b. In the short run, what would be the profit-maximizing hourly quantity, price, and total profit?
c. Suppose that after long-run equilibrium were achieved, the bookstore ended up selling two books per hour. What would be the long-run price and economic profit?
d. If this bookstore were operating in a perfectly competitive market, what would be the approximate price and economic profit, in the long run?

LO 11.4 Identify and explain the characteristics of oligopoly.

8. The following table indicates some information for industry A.

Firm	Annual Sales ($ millions)
1	200
2	150
3	100
4	75
5-30	300

a. What is the four-firm concentration ratio for this industry (with just 30 firms)?
b. Assume that industry A is the steel industry. What would happen to the concentration index if we redefined industry A as the cold rolled-steel industry? As the metals industry?

9. Classify each of the following as either a homogeneous product oligopoly or a differentiated product oligopoly.
a. Cement manufacturing
b. Auto manufacturing
c. Oil refining
d. Fast-food industry
e. Soft drink manufacturing

10. Which type of merger will have the effect of increasing an industry's concentration ratio—horizontal or vertical merger?

LO 11.5 Identify and explain the types of pricing behaviour that can occur in oligopoly.

11. Suppose there are only two equal-sized firms—Firm A and Firm B—competing in an oligopoly industry. Each firm can decide either to raise or to lower the price of the product. Each firm knows that the following outcomes will occur for each pricing decision, depending on how its rival reacts.
i. If both firms raise the price, each firm earns $5 million in annual profit.
ii. If both firms lower the price, each firm earns $3 million in annual profit.
iii. If one of the firms lowers the price while its rival raises the price, the firm with the low price will earn $7 million per year while the high-price firm will earn $1 million per year.

a. Construct a payoff matrix for these two oligopoly firms for all possible price decisions.
b. Assuming no collusion, what would be the dominant pricing strategy for each firm?
c. Suppose, in year 1, each firm decides to pursue cooperative pricing through collusion. What would be Firm A's annual profit?
d. Suppose, in year 2, Firm A decides to pursue opportunistic behaviour, while Firm B pursues a tit-for-tat strategy. What will be Firm A's profit in year 2?
e. If in year 3 both firms pursue a tit-for-tat strategy, what profit will Firm A earn in year 3?
f. In the long run, what would be the most profitable pricing strategy for each of these two firms?

12. Suppose two identical-sized oil refining firms, Apex and Petro, supply all the gasoline to a large city. If each firm agrees to limit its daily quantity to 20 000 litres a day, they will maximize their joint economic profits, with each firm earning $50 000 per day. If one of the firms increases its quantity to 40 000 litres, while the other firm supplies 20 000 litres, the economic profit earned by the firm with the larger quantity will increase to $75 000 per day, but the rival firm will be faced with an economic loss of $10 000 per day. If both companies increase their quantity so that each firm supplies 40 000 litres per day, zero economic profit will be earned by each competitor.
a. Construct a payoff matrix.
b. Assuming no collusion, in the short run, what would be the dominant quantity strategy for each firm?
c. If the tit-for-tat strategy is repeatedly used, in the long run, what quantity strategy would each firm employ?

13. Study the accompanying graph for a firm in an oligopolistic industry.

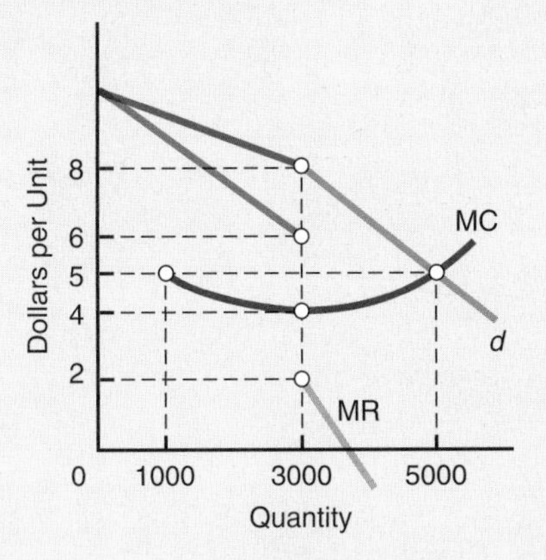

a. How much will this oligopolistic firm produce?
b. At what price will the firm sell this output?
c. How much can marginal cost vary without causing a change in price?

14. On the basis of the information provided in Example 11–3, "OPEC Continues to Rule the World Oil Market," explain why Saudi Arabia is the key oil supplier responsible for the cooperative pricing behaviour displayed in OPEC.

15. Explain whether each of the following will increase or decrease the tendency toward cooperative pricing in an oligopoly.
    a. The number of firms competing in the industry increases.
    b. All the firms produce an identical product.
    c. The industry sales are declining due to an economywide recession.

16. Referring to Example 11–4, "DeBeers Diamond Cartel: A Thing from the Past?", explain why diamonds are an attractive product to supply under a cartel arrangement.

LO 11.6 Identify, explain, and evaluate the various nonprice forms of competition in oligopoly.

17. When Coke increases its annual advertising expenses, it is likely that Pepsi will do the same. Can you explain how this apparent self-cancelling behaviour can actually result in a positive-sum game for Coke and Pepsi?

LO 11.7 Evaluate the behaviour in oligopoly from a social viewpoint.

18. According to Example 11–7, "Can Advertising Lead to Efficiency?", advertising can actually contribute to productive efficiency. Explain the argument used in this example.

CHAPTER 12

Regulation and Competition Policy

On November 3, 2000, The Competition Bureau announced that it would not challenge CanWest Global Corporation's $3.2 billion purchase of the majority of Conrad Black's Hollinger's Canadian media interests. As a result, CanWest became Canada's largest daily newspaper publisher. Not long after, the Canadian Radio-television and Telecommunications Commission (CRTC) approved of corporate acquisitions that entrenched Quebecor's dominant media position in Quebec and established Bell Canada Enterprises as the largest communications company in Canada. Is the concentration of ownership in Canadian media industries a social concern? To understand this issue, you need to know more about regulation and competition policy.

LEARNING OBJECTIVES

After reading this chapter, you should be able to:

12.1 Explain and evaluate the two broad types of government regulation of business.

12.2 Identify and contrast the various theories used to explain the behaviour of regulators.

12.3 Explain the short-run and long-run economic effects of deregulation.

12.4 Describe the various ways in which Canada's *Competition Act* benefits consumers.

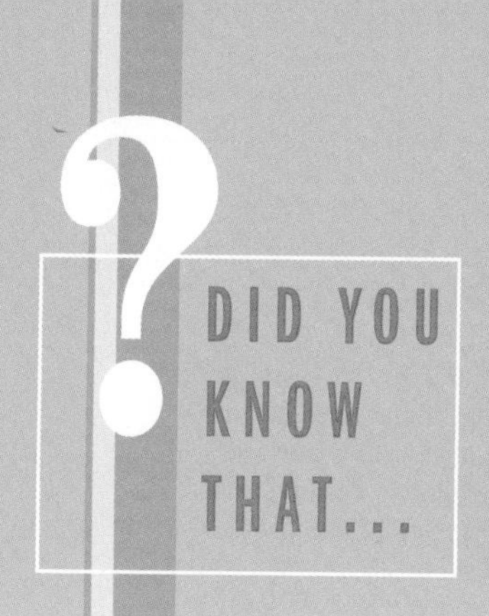

Each year thousands of pages of new or modified federal regulations are published. These regulations, found in the *Canada Gazette,* cover virtually every aspect of the way business can be conducted, products can be built, and services can be offered. In addition, every province and municipality publishes regulations relating to worker safety, restaurant cleanliness, and the number of lights needed in each room in a day-care centre. There is no question about it: Canadian business activities are highly regulated. Consequently, how regulators should act to promote the public's interest, and how they actually act are important topics for understanding today's economy.

Besides regulation, the Canadian government has an additional weapon it uses to encourage businesses to better serve consumers. It is called competition policy, and it is the subject of the latter part of this chapter.

12.1 Types of Government Regulation

The federal government began regulating economic and social activity early in Canadian history, but the amount of government regulation has significantly increased during the 20th century. There are two broad types of government regulation of Canadian business—economic regulation and social regulation.

Economic Regulation

Economic regulation Regulation that controls the prices that firms are allowed to change.

Economic regulation is intended to control the prices that regulated enterprises are allowed to charge. Various public utility commissions across the country regulate the rates (prices) of electricity and natural gas utilities and telephone operating companies. This is often referred to as *rate regulation.* The goal of rate regulation has, in principle, been to prevent monopoly firms from operating at inefficient levels of output and charging excessive prices.

Figure 12–1 describes a natural monopoly situation, where the long-run average total cost continues to decline over the relevant quantity levels of production. What type of price, quantity, and profit behaviour can we expect from the monopoly firm in Figure 12–1, if it is unregulated? As part (a) of Figure 12–1 describes, the unregulated monopolist will tend to restrict its supply to 5000 units of output and charge a relatively high price of $8 per unit, where marginal revenue equals marginal cost. At this output level, the monopoly firm earns an excess (economic) profit, as price exceeds average total cost. Since at 5000 units of output, the price, or marginal benefit, exceeds marginal cost, the monopolist is underallocating resources to the provision of this product or service. In other words, the monopolist is operating in an allocatively inefficient manner.

Would it be in the public's best interests to have government pursue a strategy of encouraging more firms to enter the industry described in Figure 12–1? Not necessarily, as in a natural monopoly situation the one existing firm can operate at a lower cost per unit than would be the case if a number of firms supplied this product or service. What, then, should government do?

One solution is to maintain the monopoly situation but have government regulate the rate (price) and quantity that the monopoly firm can establish. Ideally, in order to fully achieve allocative efficiency, government should encourage marginal cost pricing where the price is set at a level equal to the marginal cost of production. In Figure 12–1 part (b), this would imply setting the price and quantity at $4 per unit and 9000 units, respectively. However, at 9000 units of output, price is below average total cost so the firm would incur an economic loss. If the government were to enforce the $4 price over a long period of time, the firm would go out of business!

Cost-of-service regulation Regulation that allows the regulated companies to charge prices that reflect the actual average cost of providing the services, with a normal profit included in the assessment of these costs.

In order to maintain the viability of the natural monopolist, rate regulation policies have typically involved cost-of-service regulation and rate-of-return regulation. A regulatory commission using **cost-of-service regulation** allows the regulated companies to charge prices that reflect the actual average cost of providing the services, with a normal profit included in the assessment of these costs. In terms of Figure 12–1 part (b), cost-of-service regulation would result in the monopoly firm establishing a price and quantity

FIGURE 12–1

Profit Maximization and Regulation

The unregulated profit-maximizing monopolist will produce at the point in part (a) where marginal revenue equals marginal cost, which means production of 5000 units of output. The price charged would be $8 and the firm would be making excess or positive economic profit as price exceeds long-run average total cost (LATC). Referring to part (b), if the regulatory commission enforced marginal cost pricing, production would take place at the point where the demand curve just equals the marginal cost curve, which results in a price and quantity level of $4 and 9000 units, respectively. At the 9000 quantity level, the price of $4 is less than the long-run average total cost, and so the firm will incur an economic loss. If, instead, the regulatory commission pursued cost-of-service or rate-of-return regulation, the firm would set a price of $6 and a quantity level of 7000 units, where the demand curve just equals the long-run average total cost curve.

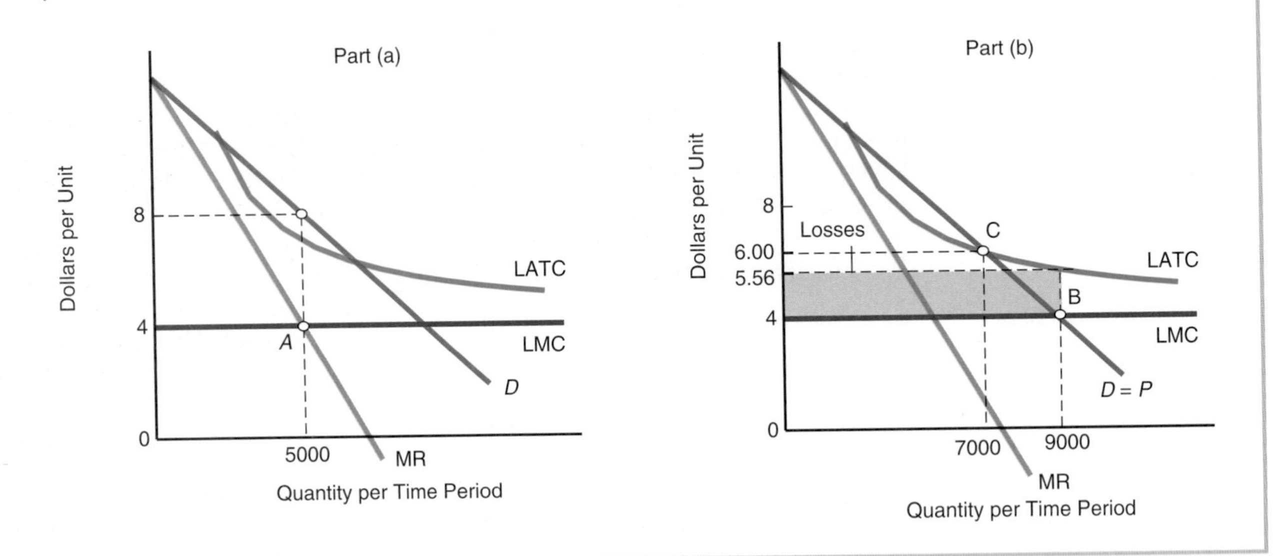

level of $6 per unit and 7000 units, respectively, where price just equals average total cost. Cost-of-service regulation is socially preferred over an unregulated monopoly situation in that the consumer enjoys a larger quantity at a lower price, and the monopolist just earns a normal profit.

From a practical point of view, cost-of-service regulation is difficult and expensive to administer. If you think of the large-scale operations related to electricity, natural gas, and phone companies, you can imagine that an army of government accountants would be required to constantly monitor the movement of thousands of service and cost items, in order to compute an accurate average cost of production for each service provided. To efficiently regulate these large monopolies, governments typically use the **rate-of-return regulation** method, which allows regulated companies to set prices that ensure a normal, or competitive, rate of return on the investment in the business. In terms of Figure 12–1 part (b) the rate-of-return method of regulation will, in theory, result in a price–quantity combination of $6.00 per unit and 7000 units, where price equals average total cost, similar to cost-of-service regulation.

Rate-of-return regulation
Regulation that allows regulated companies to set prices that ensure a normal, or competitive, rate of return on the investment in the business.

Critics of the rate-of-return method suggest that this form of regulation encourages regulated firms to "pad expenses" and therefore breeds inefficiency. For example, suppose that the regulator allows the monopoly firm to set its prices so that the firm achieves a 10 percent rate of return on its capital investment. Since the regulated company knows that it will be guaranteed a 10 percent rate of return, it can earn a larger dollar profit by overpurchasing capital equipment. What this suggests is that regulated firms have no incentive to keep costs at a minimum, under the rate-of-return method of regulation.

Another problem common to both cost-of-service and rate-of-return regulation concerns the quality of the service or product provided. Consider the many facets of telephone service: getting a dial tone, hearing other voices clearly, getting the operator to answer quickly, having out-of-order telephone lines repaired rapidly, putting through a long-distance call quickly and efficiently—the list goes on and on. But regulation of a telephone company usually deals with the prices charged for telephone service. Of course, regulators are concerned with the quality of service, but how could that be measured? Indeed, it cannot be measured very easily. Therefore, it is extremely difficult for any type of regulation to be successful in regulating the *price per constant-quality unit.* Certainly, it is possible to regulate the price per unit, but we do not really know that the quality remains unchanged when the price is not allowed to rise "enough." Thus, if regulation does not allow prices to rise, quality of service may be lowered, thereby raising the price per constant-quality unit.

Social Regulation

Social regulation Regulation that reflects concern for public welfare across all industries.

Social regulation reflects concern for public welfare across all industries. In other words, regulation is focused on the impact of production on the environment and society, the working conditions under which goods and services are produced, and sometimes the physical attributes of goods. The aim is a better quality of life for all through a less polluted environment, better working conditions, and safer and better products, and through the promotion of other valued social goals. For example, Health Canada attempts to protect consumers against impure and unsafe foods, drugs, cosmetics, and other potentially hazardous products; the Atomic Energy Control Board (AECB) controls the use and disposal of all radioactive materials to ensure the health, safety, and security of the public and the preservation of the environment; the Workers' Compensation Board attempts to protect workers against work-related injuries and illnesses; and the Canadian Human Rights Commission seeks to ensure fair access for all to jobs.

In this chapter's Issues and Applications, it is noted that the Canadian Radio-television and Telecommunications Commission (CRTC), Canada's broadcast regulator, has approved a number of company acquisitions that have significantly increased the concentration of economic power in Canada's media industries. As an example, in 2000, the CRTC allowed Bell Canada Enterprises (BCE) to buy the CTV network, a decision that created Canada's largest communications company. Similarly, in 2001, the CRTC let Quebecor purchase the TVA television network, making it a dominant firm in the Quebec television broadcasting market. This purchase was allowed, even though Quebecor already owned Videotron, Quebec's largest cable company, and Sun Media, the second-largest newspaper group in Canada. The CRTC approved these acquisitions on the condition that Bell and Quebecor undertake to create a significant amount of new Canadian television programming. These policy decisions are examples of social regulation where the policy goals include the encouragement of indigenous Canadian cultural activities and the promotion of jobs for Canadian artists, writers, and producers.

Table 12–1 lists some major federal regulatory agencies and their areas of concern. Although most people agree with the idea behind such social regulation, many disagree on whether we have too much regulation—whether it costs us more than the benefits we receive. Some contend that the costs that firms incur in abiding by regulations run into billions of dollars per year. The result is higher production costs, which are then passed on to consumers. Also, the resources invested in complying with regulatory measures could be invested in other uses. Furthermore, extensive regulation may have an anti-competitive effect because it may represent a relatively greater burden for smaller firms than for larger ones.

But the *potential* benefits of more social regulation are many. For example, the water we drink in some cities is known to be contaminated with cancer-causing chemicals; air pollution from emissions and toxic wastes from production processes cause many illnesses. Some contaminated areas have been cleaned up, but many other problem areas remain.

The benefits of social regulation may not be easy to measure and may accrue to society for a long time. Furthermore, it is difficult to put a dollar value on safer working conditions and a cleaner environment. In any case, the debate goes on. However, it should be pointed out that the controversy is generally not about whether we should have social

TABLE 12-1

Some Federal Regulatory Agencies

Agency	Jurisdiction	Date Formed	Major Regulatory Functions
Canadian Dairy Commission	Product Markets	1967	Sets support prices for milk used in making dairy products for the domestic market.
Canadian Radio-television and Telecommunications Commission	Product Markets	1976	Regulates broadcasting to balance interests of consumers, the creative community, and distribution industries.
Canada Industrial Relations Board	Labour Markets	1948	Enforces the *Canada Labour Code* where workers are direct employees of the federal government, or the employers fall within the authority of Parliament.
Bank of Canada	Financial Markets	1934	Regulates credit and currency and ensures the soundness of Canadian financial institutions.
Atomic Energy Control Board	Energy and Environment	1946	Enforces health, safety, security and environmental standards for the use of nuclear energy, and licenses users of radioactive material.
Canadian Food Inspection Agency	Health and Safety	1997	Sets and enforces standards for food quality and food delivery systems.
Transport Canada	Health and Safety	1936	Establishes and enforces regulations necessary for safety in civil aviation, marine transport, and rail transport.

regulation, but about when and how it is being done and whether we take *all* of the costs and benefits into account. For example, is regulation best carried out by federal, provincial, or local authorities? Is a specific regulation economically justified through a complete cost–benefit analysis?

Policy Example 12–1 points to yet another potential problem with social regulation. It may not be very effective in attaining its stated goals in situations where foreign firms operate in Canadian markets and provide services to Canadian consumers.

POLICY EXAMPLE 12–1 **Can the CRTC Effectively Regulate Cable TV?**

The Canadian Radio-television and Telecommunications Commission (CRTC) is a federal agency established to ensure that Canadian-made programs have a chance to be broadcast in Canada. The CRTC accomplishes this through its power to grant and renew broadcasting licences. The current standard is that Canadian broadcasters must include in their programming 60 percent Canadian content measured over a day, with at least 50 percent Canadian content in the evening hours. The CBC faces even greater content quotas.

Is the CRTC really ensuring that Canadians view Canadian-made programming? Not really. The spread of satellite dishes and pay-TV, for example, make American TV stations—such as WSBK in Boston, WGN in Chicago, and KTLA in Los Angeles—as accessible as Canadian stations. And the CRTC has no regulatory powers over those American broadcasters.

For critical analysis: Is there any way the CRTC could ensure that the American channels carried Canadian content?

Creative Response and Feedback Effects: Results of Regulation

Creative response A response that conforms to the letter of the law but undermines its spirit.

Regulated firms commonly try to avoid the effects of regulation whenever they can. In other words, the firms engage in **creative response**, which is a response that conforms to the letter of the law but undermines its spirit. Take federal laws requiring male–female pay equity: The wages of women must be on a par with those paid to men who are performing the same tasks. Employers that pay the same wages to both men and women are clearly not in violation of the law. However, wages are only one component of total employee compensation. Another component is fringe benefits, such as on-the-job training. Because on-the-job training is difficult to observe from outside the firm, employers could offer less on-the-job training to women and still not be in technical violation of pay-equity laws. This unobservable difference would mean that men were able to acquire skills that could raise their future income even though current wages among men and women were equal, in compliance with the law.

Individuals have a type of creative response that has been labelled a *feedback effect.* Regulation may alter individuals' behaviour after the regulation has been put into effect. If regulation requires fluoridated water, then parents know that their children's teeth have significant protection against tooth decay. Consequently, the feedback effect on parents' behaviour is that they may be less concerned about how many sweets their children eat. Example 12–1 shows that in the case of auto safety, the feedback effect may not always work to the consumer's advantage.

EXAMPLE 12–1 The Effectiveness of Auto Safety Regulation

A good example of the feedback effect has to do with automotive safety regulation. Since the 1960s, the federal government has required automobile manufacturers to make cars increasingly safer. Some of the earlier requirements involved nonprotruding door handles, collapsible steering columns, and shatterproof glass. More recent requirements involve daytime running lights, better seat belts, and airbags. The desired result was fewer injuries and deaths for drivers involved in accidents. According to economist Sam Peltzman, however, due to the feedback effect, drivers have gradually started driving more recklessly. Automobiles with more safety features have been involved in a disproportionate number of accidents.

For critical analysis: The feedback effect has also been called the law of unintended consequences. Why?

CONCEPTS IN BRIEF

Learning Objective 12.1: Explain and evaluate the two broad types of government regulation of business.

- The two broad types of regulation are economic and social regulation.
- In economic regulation, government controls the prices that regulated enterprises can charge. This prevents monopoly firms from restricting output and charging excessive prices. In natural monopoly situations, consumers can be better served by a regulated monopoly as opposed to an unregulated competitive situation, where per-units costs could be greater.
- Two common types of economic regulation are cost-of-service and rate-of-return regulation. Cost-of-service regulation can be expensive to administer in large-scale companies. Rate-of-return regulation can encourage regulated companies to overcapitalize and pad their costs. A problem common to both types of regulation is that it is very difficult to regulate the price per constant-quality unit.
- Social regulation seeks to promote public welfare across all industries. The aim of social regulation is a better quality of life through a less polluted environment, better working conditions, less discrimination, better-quality and safer products, and the promotion of valued social goals. A major concern with social regulation focuses on whether governments conduct appropriate cost–benefit analyses when creating their various regulations.
- Regulation can have undesirable consequences. Regulated firms may engage in creative responses and individuals may elicit a feedback effect due to regulation.

12.2 Explaining Regulators' Behaviour

Regulation has usually been defended by contending that government regulatory agencies are needed to correct market imperfections. We are dealing with a nonmarket situation because regulators are paid by the government and their decisions are not determined or constrained by the market. A number of theories have been put forward to describe the behaviour of regulators. These theories can help us understand how regulation has often harmed consumers through higher prices and less choice and benefited producers through higher profits and fewer competitive forces. Two of the best-known theories of regulatory behaviour are the *capture hypothesis* and the *share-the-gains, share-the-pains theory.*

The Capture Hypothesis

Capture hypothesis A theory of regulatory behaviour that predicts that the regulators will eventually be captured by the special interests of the industry being regulated.

It has been observed that with the passage of time, regulators often end up adopting the views of the regulated. According to the **capture hypothesis**[1]—a theory of regulatory behaviour that predicts that the regulators will eventually be captured by the special interests of the industry being regulated—no matter what the reason for a regulatory agency's having been set up, it will eventually be captured by the special interests of the industry that is being regulated. Consider the reasons.

Who knows best about the industry that is being regulated? The people already in the industry. Who, then, will be asked to regulate the industry? Again, people who have been in the industry. And people who used to be in the industry have allegiances and friendships with others in the industry.

Also consider that whenever regulatory hearings are held, the affected consumer groups will have much less information about the industry than the people already in the industry, the producers. Additionally, the cost to any one consumer to show up at a regulatory hearing to express concern about a change in the rate structure will certainly exceed any perceived benefit that consumer could obtain from going to the rate-making hearing.

Because they have little incentive to do so, consumers and taxpayers will not be well organized, nor will they be greatly concerned with regulatory actions. But the special interests of the industry are going to be well organized and well defined. Political entrepreneurs within the regulatory agency see little payoff in supporting the views of consumers and taxpayers anyway. After all, few consumers understand the benefits deriving from regulatory agency actions. Moreover, how much could a consumer directly benefit someone who works in an agency? Regulators have the most incentive to support the position of a well-organized special-interest group within the industry that is being regulated.

"Share the Gains, Share the Pains"

Share-the-gains, share-the-pains theory A theory of regulatory behaviour in which the regulators must take account of the demands of three groups: legislators, members of the regulated industry, and consumers of the regulated industry's products or services.

A somewhat different view of regulators' behaviour is given in the **share-the-gains, share-the-pains theory**[2], a theory of regulatory behaviour in which the regulators must take account of the demands of three groups: legislators, who established and who oversee the regulatory agency; members of the regulated industry; and consumers of the regulated industry's products or services. This theory looks at the specific aims of the regulators. It argues that a regulator simply wants to continue in the job.

Under the capture hypothesis, only the special interests of the industry being regulated had to be taken into account by the regulators. The share-the-gains, share-the-pains model contends that such a position is too risky because customers who are really hurt by improper regulation will complain to legislators, who might fire the regulators. Thus, each regulator has to attach some weight to these three separate groups. What happens if there is an abrupt increase in fuel costs for electrical utilities? The capture theory would predict that regulators would relatively quickly allow for a rate increase in order to maintain the

[1]See George Stigler. *The Citizen and the State: Essays on Regulation.* Chicago: University of Chicago Press, 1975.

[2]See Sam Peltzman. "Towards a More General Theory of Regulation." *Journal of Law and Economics,* 19 (1976), pp. 211–40.

profits of the industry. The share-the-gains, share-the-pains theory, however, would predict that there will be an adjustment in rates, but not as quickly or as completely as the capture theory would predict. The regulatory agency is not completely captured by the industry; it has to take account of legislators and consumers.

Deregulation

There is no truly accurate way to measure the costs of regulation. However, in recent years, that cost has been growing, and more and more complex regulations are passed into law. In 1994, for example, it took 1000 more pages to print the federal government's 818 new regulations than it did to print the 844 new regulations passed in 1974. But actual direct costs to taxpayers are only a small part of the overall cost of regulation. Pharmaceutical manufacturing safety standards raise the prices of drugs. Automobile safety standards raise the prices of cars. Environmental controls on manufacturing raise the prices of manufactured goods. All of these increased prices add to the cost of regulation. Studies suggest that the cost of administering federal regulations is about $50 billion per year. When you add the cost of enforcing regulations at the municipal and provincial levels, the total rises to $86 billion, or about 12 percent of each year's GDP!

Despite the fact that all levels of government devote a significant amount of our limited resources to the regulation of businesses, it is not clear as to what extent these government policies effectively achieve their stated goals. As we have just seen, rate-of-return regulation can encourage natural monopolies to be inefficient. Due to behaviour consistent with the capture hypothesis and creative response, the regulated firms may continue to operate to the detriment of public interest. Not surprisingly, the increasing cost of regulation on occasion has brought about cries for **deregulation**, the elimination of regulations on economic activity.

Deregulation The elimination of regulations on economic activity.

12.3 Short-Run versus Long-Run Effects of Deregulation

The short-run effects and the long-run effects of deregulation are quite different. In the short run, a regulated industry that becomes deregulated may experience numerous temporary adjustments. One is the inevitable shakeout of higher-cost producers with the accompanying removal of excess monopoly profits. Another is the sometimes dramatic displacement of workers who have laboured long and hard in the formerly regulated industry. The level of service for some consumers may fall; for example, after the deregulation of the Canadian National Railway (CNR), service to many small communities was eliminated, as the CNR off-loaded over 2000 kilometres of track. The power of unions in the formerly regulated industry may decrease. And bankruptcies may cause disruptions, particularly in the local economy where the headquarters of the formerly regulated firm are located.

Those who support deregulation, or at least less regulation, contend that there are long-run, permanent benefits. These include lower prices that are closer to marginal cost. Furthermore, lower monopoly profits are made in the deregulated industry. Such proponents argue that deregulation has positive *net* benefits.

Policy Example 12–2 describes how the Ontario government pursued a policy of electricity deregulation in order to bring about a more secure supply of power, lower electricity rates, and a reduced level of provincial government debt. Unfortunately, the short-run response to deregulation has caused the provincial government to pursue policies that work against the successful implementation of this type of deregulation in the long run.

POLICY EXAMPLE 12–2

Ontario's Feeble Attempt at Energy Deregulation

The *Energy Competition Act* was passed by the Ontario government in November 1998, beginning the process of deregulating Ontario's electricity industry. Under this Act, the former Ontario Hydro monopoly was replaced by two separate commercial operations—Ontario Power Generation (OPG) and Hydro One Inc. OPG was to focus on the generation of electricity in Ontario, while Hydro One was responsible for the transmission and distribution of electricity in the province. Deregulation was to apply to the firms generating the electricity, thanks to small-turbine technology and the power grid. The distribution and transmission of electricity in Ontario was to continue as a regulated monopoly situation.

Why energy deregulation in Ontario? Prior to deregulation, all of the province's electricity was generated by one large government-owned monopoly firm, Ontario Hydro. By the late 1990s, Ontario Hydro had accumulated a massive debt of approximately $38.1 billion, which was about a third of the total provincial government debt. Ontario Hydro's financial woes were largely due to major cost overruns in the construction of large-scale nuclear generation facilities, many of which are currently out of operation. Moreover, despite the growing Ontario Hydro debt, industry analysts were projecting serious power shortages for the province within the next 10 to 15 years.

With the advent of new technology conducive to small-scale electricity generation, it seemed appropriate for the Ontario government to slowly get out of the electricity generation business. Private competitors would ultimately take over the responsibility for producing electricity in the province. In the long run, deregulation would yield the benefits of a more secure energy supply, lower energy prices, and a reduced provincial debt.

The Ontario electricity deregulation policy was not actually implemented until May 1, 2002. When the market opened up to competition the average wholesale price was 3.01 cents per kilowatt-hour. By July 2002, the wholesale price had risen to 6.2 cents per kilowatt-hour. In September 2002, the price peaked at $1.03 per kilowatt-hour. In response to public outrage over escalating electricity bills, the Ontario government lowered and froze the retail price of electricity for low-volume consumers (residential users) at 4.3 cents per kilowatt-hour, the price that existed before deregulation. The freeze covered about half of all electricity consumed in the province. In March 2003, the provincial government extended the price freeze to consumers purchasing up to 250 000 kWh of electricity per year.

In order to quell mounting fears of future power shortages, the recently elected Ontario Liberal government has hinted that it might again have to consider investing additional public funds so as to ensure secure sources of power. For the sake of Ontario consumers and taxpayers, one can only hope that history does not repeat itself, especially when it comes to the province's electricity market.

For critical analysis: Can you explain how the actions of the Ontario government tended to work against the successful implementation of electricity deregulation in Ontario?

SOURCE: MICHAEL TREBILCOCK AND ROY HRAB. "WHAT WILL KEEP THE LIGHTS ON IN ONTARIO." C.D. HOWE INSTITUTE COMMENTARY. NO. 191 DECEMBER 2003. ISSN 0824-8001. PP. 1–6. http://www.cdhowe.org/pdf/commentary_191.pdf.

Deregulation and Contestable Markets

Theory of contestable markets A hypothesis that most of the outcomes predicted by the theory of perfect competition will occur in certain industries with relatively few firms, due to easy entry.

A major argument in favour of deregulation is that when government-imposed barriers to entry are removed, competition will cause firms to enter markets that previously had only a few firms with market power due to those entry barriers. Potential competitors will become actual competitors, and prices will fall toward a competitive level. Recently, this argument has been bolstered by a relatively new model of efficient firm behaviour that predicts competitive prices in spite of a lack of a large number of firms. This model is called the *theory of contestable markets*. Under the **theory of contestable markets**, most of the outcomes predicted by the theory of perfect competition will occur in certain industries with relatively few firms. Specifically, where the theory of contestable markets is applicable, the few firms may still produce the output at which price equals marginal cost in both the short run and the long run. These firms will receive zero economic profits in the long run.

UNCONSTRAINED AND RELATIVELY COSTLESS ENTRY AND EXIT. For a market to be perfectly contestable, firms must be able to enter and leave the industry easily. Freedom of entry and exit implies an absence of nonprice constraints and of serious fixed costs associated with a potential competitor's decision to enter a contestable market. Such an absence of important fixed costs results if the firm need buy no specific durable inputs in order to enter, if it uses up all such inputs it does purchase, or if all of its specific durable inputs are saleable upon exit without any losses beyond those normally incurred from depreciation. The important issue is whether potential entrants can easily get their investment out at any time in the future.

The mathematical model of perfect contestability is complex, but the underlying logic is straightforward. As long as conditions for free entry prevail, any excess profits or any inefficiencies on the part of incumbent firms will serve as an inducement for potential entrants. By entering, new firms can temporarily profit at no risk to themselves from the less-than-competitive situation in the industry. Once competitive conditions are again restored, these firms will leave the industry just as quickly.

BENEFITS OF CONTESTABLE MARKETS. Contestable markets have several desirable characteristics. One has to do with profits. Profits that exceed the opportunity cost of capital will not exist in the long run because of freedom of entry, just as in a perfectly competitive industry. The elimination of "excess" profits can occur even with only a couple of firms in an industry. The threat of entry will cause them to expand output to eliminate excess profit.

Also, firms that have cost curves that are higher than those of the most efficient firms will find that they cannot compete. These firms will be replaced by entrants whose cost curves are consistent with the most efficient technology. In other words, in contestable markets, there will be no cost inefficiencies in the long run.

Rethinking Regulation Using Cost–Benefit Analysis

Rather than considering deregulation as the only solution to "too much" regulation, some economists argue that regulation should simply be put to a cost–benefit test, as demonstrated in Example 12–2. Specifically, the cost of existing and proposed regulations should be compared with the benefits. Unless it can be demonstrated that regulations generate net positive benefits (benefits greater than costs), such regulations should not be in effect.

EXAMPLE 12–2 Cutting Through the "Red Tape"

Since 1975, governments at every level in Canada have collectively implemented approximately 100 000 regulations dealing with everything from land use and environmental protection to building codes and packaging. In many cases, provincial regulations overlap federal regulations, leaving businesses with mounds of "red tape" to cut through each year. Governments in Canada have recognized the need to simplify regulatory procedures, and many of them are working on it now.

The federal government has adopted a cost–benefit approach to reviews of current regulations. Every federal regulatory agency must use a software-based business impact test to measure the effect on the private sector of proposed changes to its regulations. This is

continued

no small task—the Treasury Board estimates that between 1993 and 1998, over 800 regulatory revisions took place.

The provinces, too, are looking to streamline their regulations. Alberta has introduced "sunset" schedules, which trigger reviews of the effectiveness of regulations every three years. Saskatchewan has committed to review all its regulations for necessity and efficiency, and to reduce overall regulation by 25 percent within the next 10 years. Other governments are developing cost-saving targets: New Brunswick reduced its regulatory costs by 25 percent in 1996 alone!

While these governments recognize the importance of regulating certain industries to provide safety and security for consumers, they are trying to do so without unduly penalizing the business community. In this way, they hope to achieve, as one Treasury Board booklet put it, "smarter" regulatory management.

For critical analysis: What costs are attached to reviewing and revising regulations?

CONCEPTS IN BRIEF

Learning Objective 12.2: Identify and contrast the various theories used to explain the behaviour of regulators.

- The capture hypothesis holds that regulatory agencies will eventually be captured by special interests of the industry. This is because consumers are a diffuse group who individually are not affected greatly by regulation, whereas industry groups are well focused and know that large amounts of potential profits are at stake and depend on the outcome of regulatory proceedings.
- In the share-the-gains, share-the-pains theory of regulation, regulators must take account of the interests of three groups: the industry, legislators, and consumers.

Learning Objective 12.3: Explain the short-run and long-run economic effects of deregulation.

- The short-run effects of deregulation often include bankruptcy and disrupted service. The long-run results in deregulated industries can include better service, more variety, and lower costs. One argument in favour of deregulation involves the theory of contestable markets—if entry and exit are relatively costless, the number of firms in an industry is irrelevant in terms of determining whether consumers pay competitive prices.

12.4 How Competition Policy Benefits the Consumer

It is the express aim of our government to foster efficiency and competition in the economy. To this end, numerous attempts have been made to legislate against business practices that seemingly destroy the competitive nature of the system. This is the general idea behind anticombines legislation: If the courts can prevent collusion among sellers of a product, monopoly prices will not result; there will be no restriction of output if the members of an industry are not allowed to join together in restraint of trade. Remember that the competitive solution to the price–quantity problem is one in which the price of the item produced is equal to its marginal social opportunity cost. Also, no *economic* profits are made in the long run.

The History of Anticombines Legislation

Anticombines legislation has a long history in Canada. *An Act for the Protection and Suppression of Combinations in Restraint of Trade* was passed by the federal government in

1889 and amended in 1892 to become Section 502 of the *Criminal Code*. This new law made it a criminal offence to act to unduly restrict competition in the marketplace. Over the next 100 years, the Act was amended many more times.

THE *ANTICOMBINES ACT* OF 1910. The *Anticombines Act* of 1910 expanded and clarified the powers bestowed under the 1889 Act. It set out procedures for initiating and investigating complaints of restrictive trade practice. On petition from any six persons, a judge could now order investigation of an alleged crime.

In 1915, the government established a board whose duties included regulating prices and preventing persons or firms from hoarding necessities in order to drive up price and increase profits. The courts, however, declared in 1922 that this board was unconstitutional under the terms of the *British North America Act*. Accordingly, in 1923, the government again amended the *Anticombines Act* to allow for a constitutional investigative body.

EVOLUTION OF ANTICOMBINES LAW. Over the first half of the 20th century, the interpretation of anticombines law evolved to apply to three main offences: price fixing that unduly restricted competition; mergers or monopolies acting contrary to the public interest; and unfair trade practices. Convictions under the anticombines legislation were difficult to obtain, however, because of the *Criminal Code* requirement of proof beyond a reasonable doubt. Thus, in 1960, government passed an amendment to the *Combines Investigation Act* making offences under the Act civil, rather than criminal, matters. By applying the less restrictive burden of proof required in civil cases, the Restrictive Trade Practices Commission won many more convictions of offending companies.

The federal government added to the scope and power of the *Combines Investigation Act* in 1976. The Act was extended to cover service industries that had hitherto been exempt, and sections were added dealing with misleading advertising. The Restrictive Trade Practices Commission was given power to protect consumers by keeping suppliers from refusing to supply without good reason and from restricting the way in which a good is sold.

THE *COMPETITION ACT* OF 1986. In June 1986, the government repealed the *Combines Investigation Act* and replaced it with the *Competition Act* and the *Competition Tribunal Act*. The purpose of this new legislation is to "maintain and encourage competition in Canada in order to promote the efficiency and adaptability of the Canadian economy." The Competition Bureau provides the administrative and enforcement support necessary to carry out the provisions of the Act. The Commissioner of Competition heads the Competition Bureau.

The new Act contains both criminal and noncriminal provisions. Criminal offences include conspiracy, bid rigging, discriminatory and predatory pricing, price maintenance, and deceptive marketing practices. Where the Commissioner believes a criminal offence has occurred, the matter is referred to the Attorney General for prosecution before criminal courts. The courts may impose fines, order imprisonment, issue prohibition orders and interim injunctions or any combination of these remedies.

Mergers, abuse of dominant position, exclusive dealing, and tied selling are practices that relate to the noncriminal provisions, which are called "reviewable matters." To address these matters, the Commissioner of Competition can apply to the Competition Tribunal for an interim order or final order to stop the undesirable activities. Under this new legislation, Canada's anticombines legislation now applies to all economic activities, except collective bargaining, amateur sports, securities underwriting, and government-regulated industries.

BILL C-20: AN ACT TO AMEND THE *COMPETITION ACT*. On March 11, 1999, the Canadian Parliament assented to Bill C-20, an act to amend the *Competition Act*. Under the new act, the Competition Bureau can apply for civil court orders to halt misleading advertising and deceptive marketing practices quickly, rather than seek conviction in the criminal courts (which can be a lengthy process). For effective enforcement, the new law provides such tools as judicially authorized interception (through wiretap without consent) of private communications to deal with deceptive telemarketing practices. As well, deceptive telemarketing now becomes a criminal offence.

Bill C-20 gives the courts more scope and flexibility in the use of prohibition orders issued against persons convicted or suspected of engaging in criminal misconduct, such as bid rigging, conspiracy to fix prices or share markets, and misleading advertising with intent. Provisions of the new bill will improve and speed up the merger review process. Finally, the amendments to the *Competition Act* protect the identity of persons who report criminal offences under the Act to the Competition Bureau.

BILL C-23: AN ACT TO AMEND THE *COMPETITION ACT* AND THE *COMPETITION TRIBUNAL ACT*. On June 4, 2002, the Canadian parliament passed Bill C-23: *An Act to Amend the Competition Act* and the *Competition Tribunal Act*. The amendments include new provisions that facilitate greater cooperation with foreign competition authorities, prohibit deceptive notices of winning prizes, streamline the Competition Tribunal processes, and broaden the scope of the Competition Tribunal.

In an increasingly global economy, it is very important that competition agencies around the globe have the means to share information to gather evidence. Cooperation agreements between Canadian and foreign competition agencies will have the effect of strengthening Canada's *Competition Act*.

The creation of a new offence prohibiting deceptive notices of a prize is aimed at eliminating scam artists who send notices through the mail and the Internet. These notices deceive people into believing that they have won a prize when, in fact, there is some cost attached.

The new provisions designed to streamline Competition Tribunal processes will enhance the tribunal's ability to expeditiously resolve disputes. The amendments will allow some disputes to be settled without the need for a full hearing. Cost awards will enable the Tribunal to penalize a party that brings forth proceedings in order to delay the resolution of a dispute.

Anti-Competitive Behaviour Prohibited by Competition Policy

Canada's current *Competition Act* prohibits a variety of business practices on the basis that they significantly reduce competition. *Some* of the business practices that are potentially illegal under Canada's *Competition Act* are abuse of dominant position; mergers detrimental to the public interest; anti-competitive conspiracies; price discrimination; resale price maintenance and refusal to supply; exclusive dealing and tied selling; and deceptive marketing practices. We will briefly explain each of these restrictive practices below.

ABUSE OF DOMINANT POSITION. Under the *Competition Act*, it is illegal for a dominant firm in an industry to pursue strategies that are aimed at reducing competition substantially in the market. These strategies might include selling a product or service at unreasonably low prices; using fighting brands introduced on a temporary basis in order to restrain or eliminate a competitor; squeezing, by a vertically integrated dominant supplier, of the margin available to an unintegrated customer who competes with the supplier; requiring a supplier to sell primarily to certain customers, or to refrain from selling to a competitor; and purchasing a supplier firm or customer firm in order to restrict competition in either the customer's market or the supplier's market.

In a previous chapter, we noted that in 2001, the Competition Bureau had asked the Competition Tribunal for an order prohibiting Air Canada from abusing its dominant position in the Canadian airlines market. It was the Bureau's view that Air Canada was charging unreasonably low prices—air fares below avoidable or variable costs—in an attempt to restrict competition from WestJet and CanJet on various routes in Eastern Canada. The Competition Tribunal is still investigating this situation.

MERGERS DETRIMENTAL TO THE PUBLIC INTEREST. Mergers that significantly reduce competition in a market may be illegal under the *Competition Act*. It should be noted, however, that the Competition Tribunal might allow a merger to take place even if it causes the industry's concentration ratio to substantially increase. That is, before prohibiting a proposed merger, the Tribunal would look at such factors as the extent to which foreign suppliers are likely to provide effective competition to the businesses of the parties to the merger; the extent to which good substitutes for products supplied by the parties to the merger are likely to be available; and the extent to which the merger results in significant gains in efficiency that will be passed on to consumers.

ANTI-COMPETITIVE CONSPIRACIES. Under the conspiracy provisions of the *Competition Act,* it is a crime for competitors to agree on the prices that they will charge their customers, where it unduly lessens competition or unreasonably raises prices. These provisions apply to formal cartel arrangements, price-fixing agreements, and the rigging of bids.

PRICE DISCRIMINATION. It is illegal for a firm to charge different prices to its different customers where the rationale is to substantially lessen competition or eliminate a competitor. For example, suppose a large computer manufacturer sells the same computer model to a number of different computer retail firms. The largest retailer, due to its sheer size and bargaining power, is able buy the computer model at a lower price than its competitors, and this lower price is not justified by cost saving due to the larger volume purchased. To the extent that this practice significantly reduces competition in the computer retail market, this would constitute price discrimination under the *Competition Act.*

RESALE PRICE MAINTENANCE AND REFUSAL TO SUPPLY. The *Competition Act* prohibits the manufacturer or supplier of a product from attempting to control the resale price of its product at the wholesale or retail level. For example, it is illegal for a jeans manufacturer to put pressure on a jeans retailer to resell its jeans at a set price. This set price hurts consumers, as it prevents the retailer from offering discounts to its customers. It is also an offence, under the *Competition Act,* for the jeans manufacturer to threaten to refuse to continue supplying its jeans to a retailer, should the retailer decide to discount these jeans at the retail level.

EXCLUSIVE DEALING AND TIED SELLING. Exclusive dealing refers to a situation where a firm supplies its product to a customer on condition that the customer not buy similar products from competitive suppliers. If a petroleum refining company agreed to sell its gas to a gas station only if the gas station promised not to buy gas from other refiners, this would be an example of exclusive dealing. This practice reduces competition as it prevents gas retailers from contacting competing refiners in order to secure a lower cost price. This exclusionary tactic can further restrict competition, to the extent that it prevents other retailers from securing an adequate supply of the product.

As Example 12–3 illustrates, exclusive dealing must substantially lessen competition in order to be considered illegal under Canada's *Competition Act.*

EXAMPLE 12–3 HMV Boycotts Rolling Stones Products

In October 2003, HMV Canada removed all Rolling Stones merchandise from its store shelves to protest an exclusive agreement that allowed only Best Buy stores to carry the Rolling Stones' Four Flicks DVD box set between October 2003 and March 2004. One month later, HMV filed a complaint with the Competition Bureau, arguing that the exclusive agreement between Best Buy and TGA Entertainment Ltd., the company responsible for the distribution of the Rolling Stones DVD, contravened Canada's *Competition Act*. HMV claimed that by preventing other retailers from reselling the Four Flicks DVD set, the exclusive agreement had the effect of reducing competition at the retail DVD level.

The Competition Bureau subsequently examined whether the exclusive agreement violated a number of provisions of the *Competition Act*, including exclusive dealing, refusal to supply, and abuse of dominance. After completing its investigation, the Bureau concluded that the agreement in question did not contravene the *Competition Act*, for reasons explained below.

continued

To be considered illegal, exclusive dealing must substantially lessen competition. In the Four Flicks DVD example, the exclusive agreement covered only one DVD set released by just a single artist over a very limited period of time. As a result, the Bureau concluded that the agreement between Best Buy and TGA did not significantly reduce competition in the DVD music retail industry.

The Competition Bureau also investigated whether the exclusionary agreement constituted an offence under the refusal to supply provision of the *Competition Act*. For this to be the case, the firm being refused the supply (HMV) would have to prove that it was substantially negatively affected or that it was precluded from carrying on business as a result of the exclusionary arrangement. Since the agreement covered just one DVD from a single artist, the Bureau concluded that the refusal to supply provision was not violated.

Finally, the Bureau examined whether the exclusionary agreement could be viewed as an abuse of dominance situation under the Act. Under this provision, it must be shown that a dominant supplier is engaging in practices that are substantially reducing competition at the distribution or retail industry level. Since there are a multitude of producers, distributors, and retailers of DVD music products, the Competition Bureau ruled that neither Best Buy nor TGA was in a position to control the markets in which it competes. Since neither party to the agreement was in a dominant position, the abuse of dominance provision was considered to be irrelevant to the exclusionary agreement.

In response to thousands of customer complaints, HMV lifted its ban on Rolling Stones products in March 2004. While it was unsuccessful in bringing legal action against Best Buy and TGA, HMV felt that it was successful in sending a message to those considering similar exclusionary agreements in the future.

For critical analysis: On the basis of the information provided in this example, when would an exclusive agreement made between a specific manufacturer and a specific retailer likely contravene the *Competition Act*?

SOURCES: BACKGROUNDERS. "EXAMINATION OF THE DISTRIBUTION AGREEMENT FOR THE ROLLING STONES FOUR FLICKS DVD SET." COMPETITION BUREAU. DECEMBER 18, 2003. http://competition.ic.gc.ca/epic/internet/incb-bc.nsf/en/ct02780e.html. (ACCESSED MAY 22, 2004); PETER BRIEGER. "HMV CANADA LIFTS ITS BAN ON ROLLING STONES PRODUCTS." *NATIONAL POST*. DON MILLS, ONTARIO, MARCH 4, 2004, P. FP.07.

Tied selling refers to the practice of supplying a product only if the purchaser agrees to buy other products from the same supplier. For example, if a petroleum refinery agreed to supply its gas to a gas station on the condition that the gas station bought all of its petroleum products from the same refiner, this would constitute tied selling.

DECEPTIVE MARKETING PRACTICES. We will describe only a few of the deceptive marketing practices considered illegal under the *Competition Act*. Perhaps the most common offence is for a supplier to misrepresent the original price of an article, when the article is sold at a discounted rate. If a shoe retailer offered a brand of shoes at a discounted price of $90 and advertised the offer as being "50% off," the implied regular price is $180. However, the "50% off" advertisement would be considered to be illegal if the shoe retailer never sold the shoes at the $180 price. As Example 12–4 illustrates, the merchandise that is being promoted in a discounted price advertisement must have sold, at one time, at the implied regular price in significant quantities over a reasonable period of time.

EXAMPLE 12–4 **Suzy Shier Pays $1 Million to Settle Misleading Advertising Dispute**

When is a bargain not a bargain? When it is always a bargain. Suzy Shier learned this lesson the hard way. On June 13, 2003, Suzy Shier reached a $1 million settlement with the Competition Bureau to resolve concerns over the company's discount pricing practices.

After completing an investigation, the Bureau charged that Suzy Shier placed discount price tags on garments that suggested misleading regular prices, as the advertised merchandise never sold at the implied regular prices in any significant quantity for any reasonable time period. According to the Bureau, Suzy Shier inflated the true regular prices of the garments, thereby overstating the savings realized by consumers who purchased the merchandise at the "discounted prices."

In addition to paying the $1 million, Suzy Shier filed a civil Consent Agreement that commits the company to ensure that all future price representations comply with the Ordinary Selling Price provisions of the *Competition Act*, over the next 10 years. In a public statement, La Senza Corporation suggested that it did not act contrary to the *Competition Act* but, nevertheless, agreed to the fine. Hours after the settlement was announced, La Senza sold the Suzy Shier chain to YM Inc., the Toronto company that owned Stitches.

For critical analysis: Visit the website that displays the Deceptive Marketing Practices section of Canada's *Competition Act*. After visiting this site, explain the Ordinary Price provisions, as they pertain to a supplier's own product. In your description, make sure that you explain the conditions under which a representation pertaining to a regular price is considered a reviewable offence.

SOURCES: COMPETITION BUREAU. "COMPETITION BUREAU INVESTIGATION LEADS TO A $1-MILLION SETTLEMENT WITH SUZY SHIER INC." NEWS RELEASES. JUNE 13, 2003. http://competition.ic.gc.ca/epic/internet/incb-bc.nsf/en/ct02578e.html. (ACCESSED MAY 22, 2004); SUSAN LAZARUK. "SUZY SHIER FINED $1-MILLION FOR MISLEADING SALES." *THE PROVINCE*. VANCOUVER, BC. JUNE 15, 2003, P. A19. (ACCESSED MAY 22, 2004).

Bait-and-switch selling, another deceptive marketing practice, is where a supplier advertises a product at a bargain price but does not supply the discounted product in reasonable quantities, having regard to the nature of the market. The intent of this deceptive practice is to lure customers to the store so that the supplier can promote its higher-priced products.

CONCEPTS IN BRIEF

Learning Objective 12.4: Describe the various ways in which Canada's *Competition Act* benefits consumers.

- The purpose of Canada's *Competition Act* is to maintain and encourage competition in Canadian industries. The increased competition serves Canadian consumers by promoting allocative and productive efficiency.
- Some of the anti-competitive business practices that are potentially illegal under Canada's *Competition Act* are abuse of dominant position; mergers detrimental to the public interest; anti-competitive conspiracies; price discrimination; resale price maintenance and refusal to supply; exclusive dealing and tied selling; and deceptive marketing practices.

ISSUES AND APPLICATIONS

Media Concentration in Canada: A Public Concern?

Concepts Applied: Regulation, Competition Policy, Media Concentration and the Public Interest

CanWest Global's newspaper, *The National Post*, competes with Canada's only other major national newspaper, *The Globe and Mail*, owned by BCE. CanWest and BCE have substantial media holdings in Canada. Does media concentration threaten editorial diversity?

In mid-1996, Conrad Black, publisher of almost 650 newspapers worldwide, approached the Bureau of Competition Policy for approval of his plan to acquire 50.7 percent of Southam Inc., publisher of 32 Canadian daily papers. After the Bureau gave its consent, Mr. Black and his company, Hollinger Inc., became the largest newspaper publisher in Canada. Subsequent to the acquisition, Hollinger Inc. owned 59 of the 105 daily newspapers in Canada in 1996, including all of the dailies in Saskatchewan, Prince Edward Island, and Newfoundland.

The Controversy

Hollinger's purchase of Southam brought forth howls of outrage from the Council of Canadians. The Council, a 60 000-member, nonprofit national lobby group, feared that freedom of the press and editorial diversity would be seriously threatened by this growing concentration of ownership. The Council filed an appeal of the Bureau's decision but had missed the deadline for submitting appeals. It then sued the federal government, arguing that the Canadian Constitution guarantees freedom of expression for newspaper readers and asking the federal government to step in to regulate the newspaper business. The federal court ruled that the lawsuit did not have grounds to proceed.

The Decision

The Bureau of Competition Policy defended its decision by declaring that Hollinger Inc. was not unduly restricting competition with its purchase of Southam Inc. The Bureau looked strictly at the competitive aspects of the newspaper business and particularly at the effect of the purchase on advertising space. Since the purchase of Southam Inc. meant only a change of ownership and not a change in the number of newspapers, the availability of advertising space was not affected. Thus, the Bureau approved the purchase. Later, the Bureau noted that its mandate did not include passing judgment on editorial diversity.

The Response

Mr. Black, for his part, brushed off his critics. Since, in addition to the print media, there are 60 or more television channels and hundreds of radio stations across Canada, he explained that he could not possibly control editorial diversity. Mr. Black then expressed an interest in going national. He purchased *The Financial Post* and incorporated it in his new national newspaper, *The National Post*, which debuted on October 27, 1998.

The Issue Revisited?

On November 3, 2000, The Competition Bureau announced that it would not challenge the $3.2 billion acquisition by CanWest Global Communications Corporation of the majority of Hollinger's Canadian media interests. As a result, on November 15, 2000, CanWest became the largest daily newspaper publisher in Canada and one of the country's leading international multimedia news, information, and entertainment providers. Immediately after its Hollinger purchase, CanWest owned 14 English-language metropolitan daily newspapers in Canada, as well as 120 daily and weekly newspapers and shoppers in smaller communities all across Canada. Newspapers operated by CanWest Global, just after the acquisition, include *The National Post*, *Montreal Gazette*, *Ottawa Citizen*, *Windsor Star*, *Regina Leader-Post*, *Saskatoon Star Pheonix*, *Calgary Herald*, *Edmonton Journal*, *Vancouver Sun*, *Vancouver Province*, and *Victoria Times-Colonist*.

In addition to its newspaper holdings, CanWest Global owns Canada's Global Television Network, which broadcasts over-the-air via 11 television stations, licensed in eight provinces, and reaches 94 percent of English-speaking Canada. CanWest also owns canada.com, which is one of Canada's largest Internet news sites.

In reviewing the CanWest acquisition, the Competition Bureau focused on the impact on advertisers. As a result of its review, the Bureau concluded that there is no evidence that newspapers, Internet, and television are competing directly for retail advertising normally found in newspapers. Therefore, it has concluded that there is no evidence that the transaction would likely lead to a substantial lessening of competition in such markets. It should be noted that the Bureau did not investigate the merger's possible effects in terms of reducing editorial diversity.

In December 2000, the Canadian Radio-television and Telecommunications Commission (CRTC), Canada's broadcast regulator, allowed Bell Canada Enterprises (BCE) to buy the CTV network, a decision that created Canada's largest communications company. The CTV purchase closely followed BCE's acquisition of *The Globe and Mail*. In securing the ownership of CTV, BCE promised the CRTC that it would pump over $200 million into Canadian broadcasting during the next seven years. The CRTC has stipulated that $140 million of these monies should go into drama and documentary production created by independent Canadian writers and producers.

On July 5, 2001, the CRTC approved Quebecor Inc.'s purchase of the TVA television network, the dominant firm in the Quebec television broadcasting market. Prior to the CRTC decision, Quebecor had already accumulated significant Canadian media assets including Videotron, the largest cable TV producer in Quebec, and Sun Media, the second-largest newspaper group in Canada, with eight metropolitan dailies, eight community dailies, and 175 local weeklies and specialty publications. As in the BCE decision, the CRTC has made the Quebecor acquisition conditional on commitments by TVA to create additional independent Canadian productions.

The concentration of all forms of Canadian media, including newspaper, radio, television and the Internet, in the hands of a few large corporations, such as CanWest Global, BCE, and Quebecor, has renewed concerns regarding the maintenance and encouragement of freedom of expression and editorial diversity in Canada. On June 16, 2002, Russell Mills, former publisher of the *Ottawa Citizen*, was fired by the newspaper's owner, CanWest Global Communications Ltd. Mills claimed that his dismissal was for, among other things, not asking the owners of CanWest Global for their approval of the publication of an editorial calling for the resignation of Prime Minister Jean Chrétien.

In preparation for the 2004 federal election, a top member of BCE's Bell Globemedia's editorial team took a leave of absence to help mastermind the Liberal party's multi-million dollar election advertising campaign. The campaign includes ads that depict the leader of the opposition party as one who lacks Canadian values. This particular leave of absence has brought forth the criticism that the BCE media giant is prone to side with the incumbent Liberal party throughout its media coverage of the 2004 federal election. As one can see, the issues relating to media concentration include the very preservation of values and behaviour consistent with a democratic society.

For critical analysis:

1. As this Issues and Applications explains, the CRTC has approved of significant Canadian media acquisitions involving CanWest, BCE, and Quebecor. Are these policy decisions examples of economic regulation or social regulation?
2. Explain how increased media concentration can operate against the interests of the Canadian public.

SOURCES: CRTC. "CRTC APPROVES QUEBECOR ACQUISITION OF TVA ON THE CONDITION IT SELL TQS, RENEWS TVA'S LICENCE FOR ANOTHER SEVEN YEARS." NEWS RELEASE. JULY 5, 2001. http://www.crtc.gc.ca/eng/NEWS/RELEASES/2001/R010705.htm. (ACCESSED MAY 29,2004); CRTC. "CRTC APPROVES ACQUISITION OF CTV BY BCE." NEWS RELEASE. DECEMBER 7, 2000. http://www.crtc.gc.ca/ENG/NEWS/RELEASES/2000/R001207.htm. (ACCESSED MAY 29, 2004); "FIRED PUBLISHER SETTLES WITH CANWEST GLOBAL." *EDMONTON JOURNAL*. EDMONTON, ALBERTA. DECEMBER 14, 2002. P. A8; GILLIAN COSGROVE. "BELL GLOBEMEDIA UNDER LIBERAL THUMB? ROBTV CHIEF TAKES LEAVE TO RUN LIBERAL AD CAMPAIGN." *NATIONAL POST*. DON MILLS, ONTARIO. MAY 14, 2004,. P. A.10; COMPETITION BUREAU."COMPETITION BUREAU AND CANWEST RESOLVE CONCERNS ABOUT ROBTV."NEWS RELEASES. NOVEMBER 3, 2000. MEDIA ROOM. http://competition.ic.gc.ca/epic/internet/incb-bc.nsf/en/ct02067e.html. (ACCESSED MAY 29, 2004).

SUMMARY DISCUSSION OF LEARNING OBJECTIVES

12.1 **Types of Government Regulation.** The two broad types of regulation are economic and social regulation. In economic regulation, the government controls the prices that regulated enterprises can charge. This prevents monopoly firms from restricting output and charging excessive prices. In natural monopoly situations, consumers can be better served by a regulated monopoly as opposed to an unregulated competitive situation, where per-unit costs could be greater. Two common types of economic regulation are cost-of-service and rate-of-return regulation. Cost-of-service regulation can be expensive to administer in large-scale companies. Rate-of-return regulation can encourage regulated companies to overcapitalize and pad their costs. A problem common to both types of regulation is that it is very difficult to regulate the price per constant quality unit. Social regulation seeks to promote public welfare across all industries. The aim of social regulation is a better quality of life through a less polluted environment, better working conditions, less discrimination, better quality and safer products, and the promotion of valued social goals. A major concern with social regulation focuses on whether governments conduct appropriate cost–benefit analyses, when creating their various regulations. Regulation can have undesirable consequences. Regulated firms may engage in creative responses and individuals may elicit a feedback effect due to regulation.

12.2 **Explaining Regulators' Behaviour.** The capture hypothesis holds that regulatory agencies will eventually be captured by special interests of the industry. This is because consumers are a diffuse group who individually are not affected greatly by regulation, whereas industry groups are well focused and know that large amounts of potential profits depend on the outcome of regulatory proceedings. In the share-the-gains, share-the-pains theory of regulation, regulators must take account of the interests of three groups: the industry, legislators, and consumers.

12.3 **Short-Run versus Long-Run Effects of Deregulation.** The short-run effects of deregulation often include bankruptcy and disrupted service. The long-run results in deregulated industries can include better service, more variety, and lower costs. One argument in favour of deregulation involves the theory of contestable markets—if entry and exit are relatively costless, the number of firms in an industry is irrelevant in terms of determining whether consumers pay competitive prices.

12.4 **How Competition Policy Benefits the Consumer.** The purpose of Canada's *Competition Act* is to maintain and encourage competition in Canadian industries. The increased competition serves Canadian consumers by promoting allocative and productive efficiency. Some of the anti-competitive business practices that are potentially illegal under Canada's *Competition Act* are abuse of dominant position; mergers detrimental to the public interest; anti-competitive conspiracies; price discrimination; resale price maintenance and refusal to supply; exclusive dealing and tied selling; and deceptive marketing practices.

PROBLEMS

(Answers to the odd-numbered problems appear at the back of the book.)

LO 12.1: Explain and evaluate the two broad types of government regulation of business.

1. Under what conditions would a regulated monopoly bring about lower costs and prices, when compared with the alternative of establishing a competitive industry?
2. Compare and contrast cost-of-service regulation and rate-of-return regulation.
3. The following table depicts the cost and demand structure a natural monopoly faces.

Quantity	Price	Long-Run Total Cost
0	100	0
1	95	92
2	90	177
3	85	255
4	80	331
5	75	406
6	70	480

a. If the government pursued economic regulation in the form of marginal cost pricing, what would be the price and quantity level? What problem would arise, if the government enforced this type of regulation in the long term? Explain.

b. If the government imposed rate-of-return regulation on this monopoly firm, what would be the price and quantity level? What would be the amount of economic profit?
c. Critics suggest that rate-of-return regulation can breed inefficiency. Explain their argument.

4. Contrast the major objectives of economic regulation and social regulation.

LO 12.2: Identify and contrast the various theories used to explain the behaviour of regulators.

5. In 2003, the American government banned the importation of Canadian beef products into the United States, on the basis of fears related to "mad cow disease." Assuming that the scientific evidence suggested that there was no significant health risk related to human consumption of Canadian beef, what theory of regulator behaviour best explains this situation?

LO 12.3: Explain the short-run and long-run economic effects of deregulation.

6. Referring to Policy Example 12–2, "Ontario's Feeble Attempt at Energy Deregulation," explain why the Ontario government was eager to deregulate its electricity generation industry. What economic reason explains why the government continued to operate the electricity distribution industry as a regulated monopoly?
7. Why is the right of free entry insufficient to prevent sustained economic profits in a deregulated natural monopoly situation?
8. "Philosophically, I am vehemently opposed to government interference in the marketplace. As the owner of a neighbourhood pub, however, I can tell you that deregulation will be bad for the citizenry. You would not want a neighbourhood pub on every corner, would you?" Why would you predict that a neighbourhood pub owner would defend regulation of the liquor industry in this way?

LO 12.4: Describe the various ways in which Canada's *Competition Act* benefits consumers.

9. What anti-competitive business practice, as defined under Canada's *Competition Act*, best relates to each of the following:
   a. A manufacturer will supply its popular leather jackets to a clothing retailer, only under the condition that the retailer sells the jackets at the manufacturer's suggested list price.
   b. In order to maintain its monopoly position in a large subdivision, a supermarket chain lowers the prices of its products below each item's average variable cost. These low prices deter the entry of rival supermarket stores.
   c. In order to be able to sell a manufacturer's line of computers, a computer retailer agrees to purchase all of its computer accessories from the same computer manufacturer.
   d. A large golf equipment retailer advertises a popular brand of clubs at 50 percent off, available only during its Canada Day sale. After the first 30 minutes of the sale, the retailer sold out all units of this brand of golf clubs.
   e. A leading soft drink manufacturer will allow large supermarkets to resell its cola products, only under the condition that the supermarkets refrain from selling the cola products produced by rival manufacturers.
10. Explain why Canada's *Competition Act* might approve of a merger that significantly increased an already high industry concentration ratio.
11. According to Example 12–3, "HMV Boycotts Rolling Stones Products," the Competition Bureau investigated whether the exclusive agreement between Best Buy and TGA Entertainment violated at least one of three provisions of the *Competition Act*. What three provisions were examined? Why did the Bureau rule that the exclusive agreement did not violate the *Competition Act*?

PART 4

PRODUCTIVE FACTORS, POVERTY, THE ENVIRONMENT, AND THE PUBLIC SECTOR

CHAPTER 13

Labour Demand and Supply

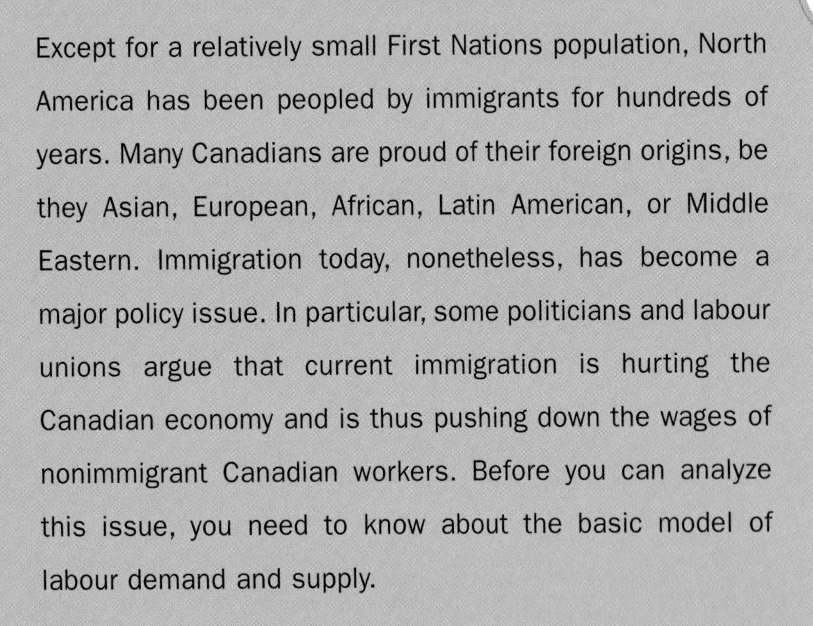

Except for a relatively small First Nations population, North America has been peopled by immigrants for hundreds of years. Many Canadians are proud of their foreign origins, be they Asian, European, African, Latin American, or Middle Eastern. Immigration today, nonetheless, has become a major policy issue. In particular, some politicians and labour unions argue that current immigration is hurting the Canadian economy and is thus pushing down the wages of nonimmigrant Canadian workers. Before you can analyze this issue, you need to know about the basic model of labour demand and supply.

LEARNING OBJECTIVES

After reading this chapter, you should be able to:

13.1 Explain the demand for labour using the marginal physical product, marginal revenue product, and price elasticity of demand concepts.

13.2 Analyze the impact on the labour market when shifts occur in the demand for and supply of labour.

13.3 Discuss how other factors of production affect the labour market.

DID YOU KNOW THAT...

Some CEOs are paid as much as $5 000 000 in salaries and benefits. In contrast, if you are a typical college or university student, the most you can hope to make during the first year after graduating is between $25 000 and $40 000. Besides the question of whether the CEO is worth it, to understand why firms pay different workers different wages requires an understanding of the demand for and supply of labour.

A firm's demand for inputs can be studied in much the same manner as we studied the demand for output in different market situations. Again, various market situations will be examined. Our analysis will always end with the same commonsense conclusion: A firm will hire employees up to the point beyond which it is not profitable to hire any more. It will hire employees to the point at which the marginal benefit of hiring a worker will just equal the marginal cost. Basically, in every profit-maximizing situation, it is most profitable to carry out an activity up to the point at which the marginal benefit equals the marginal cost. Remembering that guideline will help you in analyzing decision making at the firm level. We will start our analysis under the assumption that the market for input factors is perfectly competitive. We will further assume that the output market is perfectly competitive. This provides a benchmark against which to compare other situations in which labour markets or product markets are not perfectly competitive.

13.1 Demand for Labour

Competition in the Product Market

Let us take as our example a compact disc (CD) manufacturing firm that is in competition with many companies selling the same kind of product. Assume that the labourers hired by our CD maker do not need any special skills. This firm sells its product in a perfectly competitive market. A CD manufacturer also buys labour (its variable input) in a perfectly competitive market. A firm that hires labour under perfectly competitive conditions hires only a tiny proportion of all the workers who are potentially available. By "potentially available," we mean all the workers in a given geographical area who possess the skills demanded by our perfect competitor. In such a market, it is always possible for the individual firm to pick up extra workers without having to offer a higher wage. Thus, the supply of labour to the firm is perfectly elastic—that is, represented by a horizontal line at the going wage rate established by the forces of supply and demand in the entire labour market. The firm is a price taker in the labour market.

Marginal Physical Product

Look at part (a) of Figure 13–1. In column 1, we show the number of workers per week that the firm can hire. In column 2, we show total physical product (TPP) per week, the total *physical* production that different quantities of the labour input (in combination with a fixed amount of other inputs) will generate in a week's time. In column 3, we show the additional output gained when a CD maker adds workers to its existing manufacturing facility. This column, the **marginal physical product (MPP) of labour**, represents the change in output resulting from the addition of one more worker. If this firm adds a seventh worker, the MPP is 118. The law of diminishing marginal returns predicts that additional units of a variable factor will, after some point, cause the MPP to decline, other things being held constant.

Marginal physical product (MPP) of labour The change in output resulting from the addition of one more worker.

Why the Decline in MPP?

We are assuming all other nonlabour factors of production are held constant. So, if our CD maker wants to add one more worker to its production line, it has to crowd all the existing workers a little closer together because it does not increase its capital stock (the production equipment). Therefore, as we add more workers, each one has a smaller and smaller fraction of the available capital stock with which to work. If one worker uses one machine, adding another worker usually will not double the output because the machine

FIGURE 13–1

Marginal Revenue Product

In part (a), column 4 shows marginal revenue product (MRP), which is the amount of additional revenue the firm receives for the sale of additional output produced by one worker. Marginal revenue product is simply the amount of money the additional worker brings in—the combination of that worker's contribution to production and the revenue that production will bring to the firm. For this perfectly competitive firm, marginal revenue is equal to the price of the product, or $6 per unit. At a weekly wage of $498, the profit-maximizing employer will pay for only 12 workers because then the marginal revenue product is just equal to the wage rate or weekly salary.

In part (b), we find the number of workers the firm will want to hire by observing the wage rate that is established by the forces of supply and demand in the entire labour market. We show that this employer is hiring labour in a perfectly competitive labour market and therefore faces a perfectly elastic supply curve represented by *s* at $498 per week. As in all other situations, we basically have a supply and demand model; in this example, the demand curve is represented by MRP, and the supply curve is *s*. Equilibrium occurs at their intersection.

Part (a)

(1) Labour Input (workers per week)	(2) Total Physical Product (TPP) CDs per Week	(3) Marginal Physical Product (MPP) CDs per Week	(4) Marginal Revenue (MR = *P* = $6 net) x MPP = Marginal Revenue Product (MRP) ($ per additional worker)	(5) Wage Rate ($ per week) = Marginal Factor Cost (MFC) = Change in Total Costs / Change in Labour
6	882			
7	1000	118	708	498
8	1111	111	666	498
9	1215	104	624	498
10	1312	97	582	498
11	1402	90	540	498
12	1485	83	498	498
13	1561	76	456	498

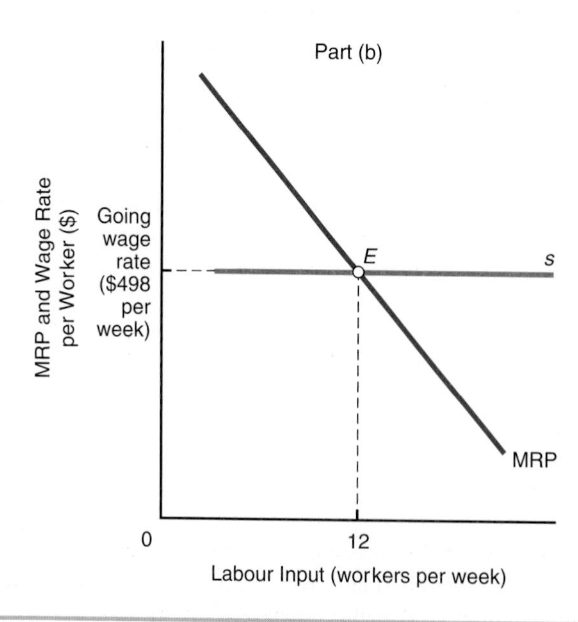

can run only so fast and for so many hours per day. In other words, MPP declines because of the law of diminishing marginal returns.

Marginal Revenue Product

Marginal revenue product (MRP) The marginal physical product (MPP) times marginal revenue.

We now need to translate into a dollar value the physical product that results from hiring an additional worker. This is done by multiplying the marginal physical product by the marginal revenue of the firm. Because our CD firm is selling its product in a perfectly competitive market, marginal revenue is equal to the price of the product. If the seventh worker's MPP is 118 and the marginal revenue is $6 per CD, the **marginal revenue product (MRP)**—the marginal physical product (MPP) times marginal revenue—is $708 (118 × $6). The MRP is shown in column 4 of part (a) of Figure 13–1. *The marginal revenue product represents the worker's contribution to the firm's total revenues.*

When a firm operates in a competitive product market, the marginal physical product times the product price is also sometimes referred to as the *value of marginal product (VMP).* Because price and marginal revenue are the same for a perfectly competitive firm, the VMP is also the MRP.

Marginal factor cost (MFC) The cost of using an additional unit of an input.

In column 5 of part (a) of Figure 13–1, we show the wage rate, or *marginal factor cost,* of each worker. The marginal cost of workers is the extra cost of using an additional unit of an input. We call that cost the **marginal factor cost (MFC)**—the cost of using an additional unit of an input. Otherwise stated,

$$\text{Marginal factor cost} = \frac{\text{Change in total cost}}{\text{Change in amount of resource used}}$$

Because each worker is paid the same competitively determined wage of $498 per week, the MFC is the same for all workers. And because the firm is buying labour in a perfectly competitive labour market, the wage rate of $498 per week really represents the firm's supply curve of labour. That curve is perfectly elastic because the firm can purchase all labour at the same wage rate, considering that it is a minuscule part of the entire labour-purchasing market. (Recall the definition of perfect competition.) We show this perfectly elastic supply curve as *s* in part (b) of Figure 13–1.

General Rule for Hiring

Virtually every optimizing rule in economics involves comparing marginal benefits with marginal cost. The general rule, therefore, for the hiring decision of a firm is this:

> The firm hires workers up to the point at which the additional cost associated with hiring the last worker is equal to the additional revenue generated by that worker.

In a perfectly competitive situation, this is the point at which the wage rate just equals the marginal revenue product. If the firm hired more workers, the additional wages would not be covered by additional increases in total revenue. If the firm hired fewer workers, it would be forfeiting the contributions that those workers could make to total profits.

Therefore, referring to columns 4 and 5 in part (a) of Figure 13–1, we see that this firm would certainly employ the seventh worker because the MRP is $708, while the MFC is only $498. The firm would continue to employ workers up to the point at which MFC = MRP because as workers are added, they contribute more to revenue than to cost.

The MRP Curve: Demand for Labour

We can also use part (b) of Figure 13–1 to find how many workers our firm should hire. First, we draw a straight line across from the going wage rate, which is determined by demand and supply in the labour market. The straight line is labelled *s* to indicate that it is the supply curve of labour for the *individual* firm purchasing labour in a perfectly competitive labour market. That firm can purchase all the labour it wants of equal quality at

\$498 per worker. This perfectly elastic supply curve, *s*, intersects the marginal revenue product curve at 12 workers per week. At the intersection, *E*, the wage rate is equal to the marginal revenue product. Equilibrium for the firm is obtained when the firm's demand curve for labour, which turns out to be its MRP curve, intersects the firm's supply curve for labour, shown as *s*. The firm in our example would not hire the 13th worker, who will add only \$456 to revenue but \$498 to cost. If the price of labour should fall to, say, \$456 per worker, it would become profitable for the firm to hire an additional worker; there is an increase in the quantity of labour demanded as the wage decreases.

Derived Demand

Derived demand Input factor demand derived from demand for the final product being produced.

We have identified an individual firm's demand for labour curve as its MRP curve. Under conditions of perfect competition in both product and labour markets, MRP is determined by multiplying MPP times the product's price. This suggests that the demand for labour is a **derived demand**. That is to say that our CD firm does not want to purchase the services of labour just for the services themselves. Factors of production are rented or purchased not because they give any intrinsic satisfaction to the firms' owners but because they can be used to manufacture output that is expected to be sold for profit.

We know that an increase in the market demand for a given product raises the product's price (all other things held constant), which, in turn, increases the marginal revenue product, or demand for the resource. Figure 13–2 illustrates the effective role played by changes in product demand in a perfectly competitive product market. The MRP curve shifts whenever there is a change in the price of the final product that the workers are making. If, for example, the market price of CDs goes down, the MRP curve will shift downward to the left from MRP_0 to MRP_1. We know that MRP = MPP × MR. If marginal revenue (here the output price) falls, so, too, does the demand for labour; at the same going wage rate, the firm will hire fewer workers. This is because at various levels of labour use, the marginal revenue product of labour falls so that at the initial equilibrium, the price of labour (here the MFC) becomes greater than MRP. Thus, the firm would reduce the number of workers hired. Conversely, if the marginal revenue (output price) rises, the demand for labour will also rise, and the firm will want to hire more workers at each and every possible wage rate.

We just pointed out that MRP = MPP × MR. Clearly, then, a change in marginal productivity, or in the marginal physical product of labour, will shift the MRP curve. If the marginal productivity of labour decreases, the MRP curve, or demand curve for labour

FIGURE 13–2

Demand for Labour, a Derived Demand

The demand for labour is derived from the demand for the final product being produced. Therefore, the marginal revenue product curve will shift whenever the price of the product changes. If we start with the marginal revenue product curve MRP at the going wage rate of \$498 per week, 12 workers will be hired. If the price of CDs goes down, the marginal product curve will shift to MRP_1, and the number of workers hired will fall to 10. If the price of CDs goes up, the marginal revenue product curve will shift to MRP_2, and the number of workers hired will increase to 15.

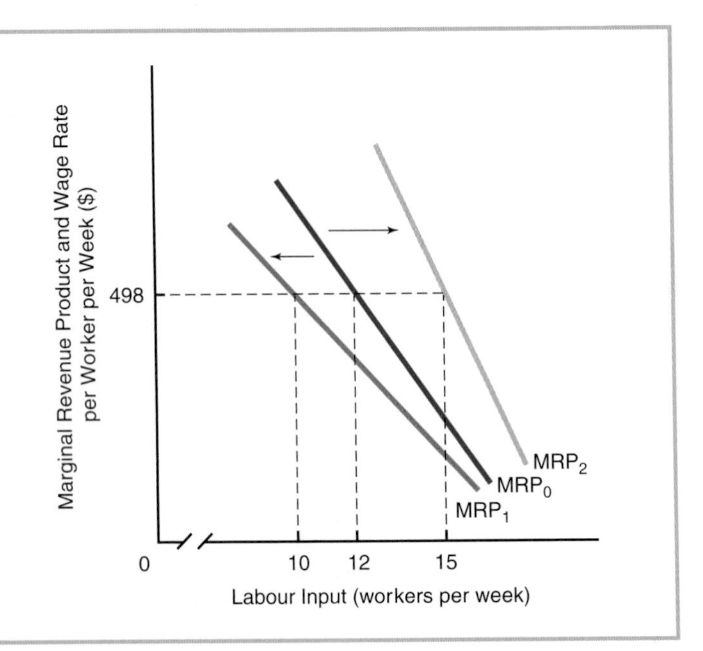

will shift inward to the left. Again, this is because at every quantity of labour used, the MRP will be lower. A lower quantity of labour will be demanded at every possible wage rate.

The Market Demand for Labour

The downward-sloping portion of each individual firm's marginal revenue product curve is also its demand curve for the one variable factor of production—in our example, labour. When we go to the entire market for a particular type of labour in a particular industry, we find that quantity of labour demanded will vary as the wage rate changes. Given that the market demand curve for labour is made up of the individual firms' demand curves for labour, we can safely assume that the market demand curve for labour will look like *D* in part (b) of Figure 13–3: It will slope downward. That market demand curve for labour in the CD industry shows the quantities of labour demanded by all of the firms in the industry at various wage rates.

It is important to note that the market demand curve for labour is not a simple horizontal summation of the labour demand curves of all individual firms. Remember that the demand for labour is a derived demand. Even if we hold labour productivity constant, the demand for labour still depends on both the wage rate and the price of the final output. Assume that we start at a wage rate of $20 per hour and employment level 10 in part (a) of Figure 13–3. If we sum all such employment levels—point *a* in part (a)—across firms, we get a market quantity demanded of 2000—point *A* in part (b)—at the wage rate of $20. A decrease in the wage rate to $10 per hour induces individual firms' employment levels to increase toward a quantity demanded of 22. As all firms simultaneously increase employment, however, there is a shift in the product supply curve such that output increases. Hence, the price of the product must fall. The fall in the output price, in turn, causes a downward shift of each firm's MRP curve (d_0) to MRP_1 (d_1) in part (a). Thus, each firm's employment of labour increases to 15, rather than to 22, at the wage rate of

FIGURE 13–3

Derivation of the Market Demand Curve for Labour

The market demand curve for labour is not simply the horizontal summation of all individual firms' demand curves for labour. If wage rates fall from $20 to $10, all firms will increase employment and therefore output, causing the price of the product to fall. This causes the marginal revenue product curve of each firm to shift inward, as from d_0 to d_1 in part (a). The resulting market demand curve, *D*, in part (b) is therefore less elastic than it would be if output price remained constant.

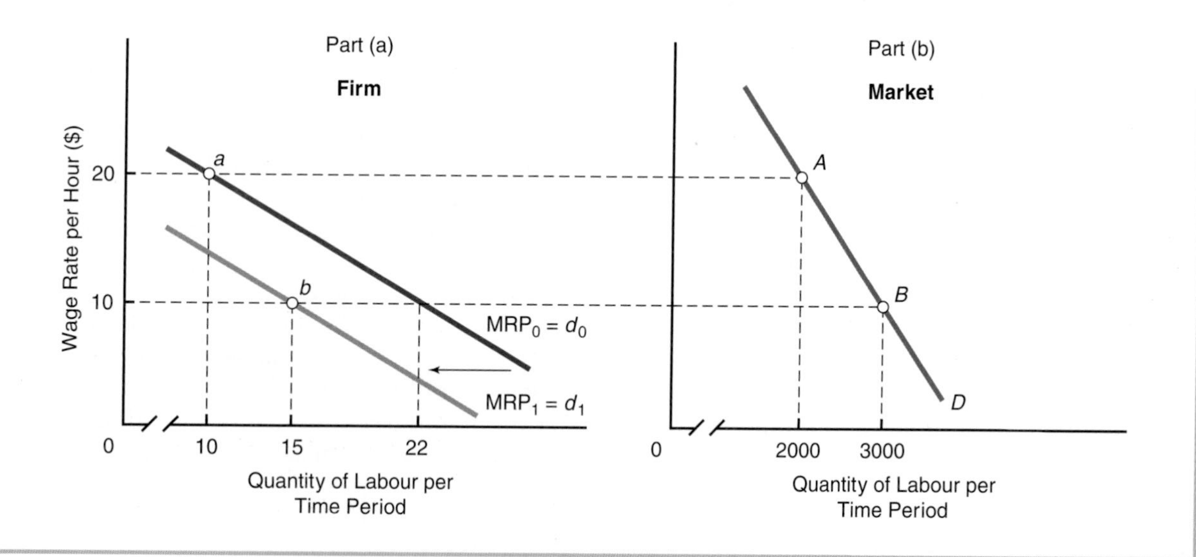

$10 per hour. A summation of all such employment levels gives us 3000—point *B*—in part (b).

Determinants of Demand Elasticity for Inputs

Just as we were able to discuss the price elasticity of demand for different commodities, we can discuss the price elasticity of demand for inputs. The price elasticity of demand for labour is defined in a manner similar to the price elasticity of demand for goods: the percentage change in quantity demanded divided by the percentage change in the price of labour. When the numerical value of this ratio is less than 1, it is inelastic; when it is 1, unit-elastic; and when it is greater than 1, elastic.

There are four principal determinants of the price elasticity of demand for an input. The price elasticity of demand for a variable input will be greater:

1. The greater the price elasticity of demand for the final product
2. The easier it is for a particular variable input to be substituted for by other inputs
3. The larger the proportion of total costs accounted for by a particular variable input
4. The longer the time period being considered

Consider some examples. An individual radish farmer faces an extremely elastic demand for radishes, given the existence of many competing radish growers. If the farmer's labourers tried to obtain a significant wage increase, the farmer would not be able to pass on the resultant higher costs to radish buyers. So, any wage increase to the individual radish farmer would lead to a large reduction in the quantity of labour demanded.

Clearly, the easier it is for a producer to switch to using another factor of production, the more responsive that producer will be to an increase in an input's price. If plastic and aluminum can easily be substituted in the production of, say, car bumpers, then a price rise in aluminum will cause car makers to greatly reduce their quantity of aluminum demanded.

When a particular input's costs account for a very large share of total costs, any increase in that input's price will affect total costs relatively more. If labour costs are 80 percent of total costs, a company will cut back on employment more aggressively than if labour costs were only 8 percent of total costs, for any given wage increase.

Finally, over longer periods, firms have more time to figure out ways to economize on the use of inputs whose prices have gone up. Furthermore, over time, technological change will allow for easier substitution in favour of relatively cheaper inputs and against inputs whose prices went up. At first, a pay raise obtained by a strong telephone company union may not result in many layoffs, but over time, the telephone company will use new technology to replace many of the now more expensive workers.

CONCEPTS IN BRIEF

Learning Objective 13.1: Explain the demand for labour using the marginal physical product, marginal revenue product, and price elasticity of demand concepts.

- The change in total output due to a one-unit change in one variable input, holding all other inputs constant, is called the marginal physical product (MPP). When we multiply marginal physical product times marginal revenue, we obtain the marginal revenue product (MRP).
- A firm will hire workers up to the point at which the additional cost of hiring one more worker is equal to the additional revenues generated. For the individual firm, therefore, its MRP of labour curve is also its demand for labour curve.
- The demand for labour is a derived demand, derived from the demand for final output. Therefore, if the price of final output changes, this will cause a shift in the MRP curve (which is also the firm's demand for labour curve).
- Input price elasticity of demand depends on final product elasticity, the ease of other input substitution, the relative importance of the input's cost in total costs, and the time allowed for adjustment.

13.2 *Shifts in the Demand for and Supply of Labour*

Wage Determination

Having developed the demand curve for labour (and all other variable inputs) in a particular industry, let us turn to the labour supply curve. By adding supply to the analysis, we can come up with the equilibrium wage rate that workers earn in an industry. We can think in terms of a supply curve for labour that slopes upward in a particular industry, as illustrated in part (b) of Figure 13–4. At higher wage rates, more workers will want to enter that particular industry. The individual firm, however, does not face the entire *market* supply curve. Rather, in a perfectly competitive case, the individual firm is such a small part of the market that it can hire all the workers that it wants at the going wage rate as illustrated in part (a) of Figure 13–4. We say, therefore, that the industry faces an upward-sloping supply curve but that the individual *firm* faces a perfectly elastic supply curve for labour.

The demand curve for labour in the CD industry is D in Figure 13–5, and the supply curve of labour is S. The equilibrium wage rate of $498 a week is established at the intersection of the two curves. The quantity of workers both supplied and demanded at that rate is Q_1. If for some reason the wage rate fell to $400 a week, in our hypothetical example, there would be an excess number of workers demanded at that wage rate. Conversely, if the wage rate rose to $600 a week, there would be an excess quantity of workers supplied at that wage rate.

We have just found the equilibrium wage rate for the entire CD industry. The individual firm must take that equilibrium wage rate as given in the competitive model used here because the individual firm is a very small part of the total demand for labour. Thus, each firm purchasing labour in a perfectly competitive market can purchase all of the input it wants at the going market price. See Policy Example 13–1 for more discussion on the minimum wage.

FIGURE 13–4
Supply of Labour

The individual firm faces a perfectly elastic supply curve for labour as illustrated in part (a). The industry faces an upward-sloping supply curve as illustrated in part (b).

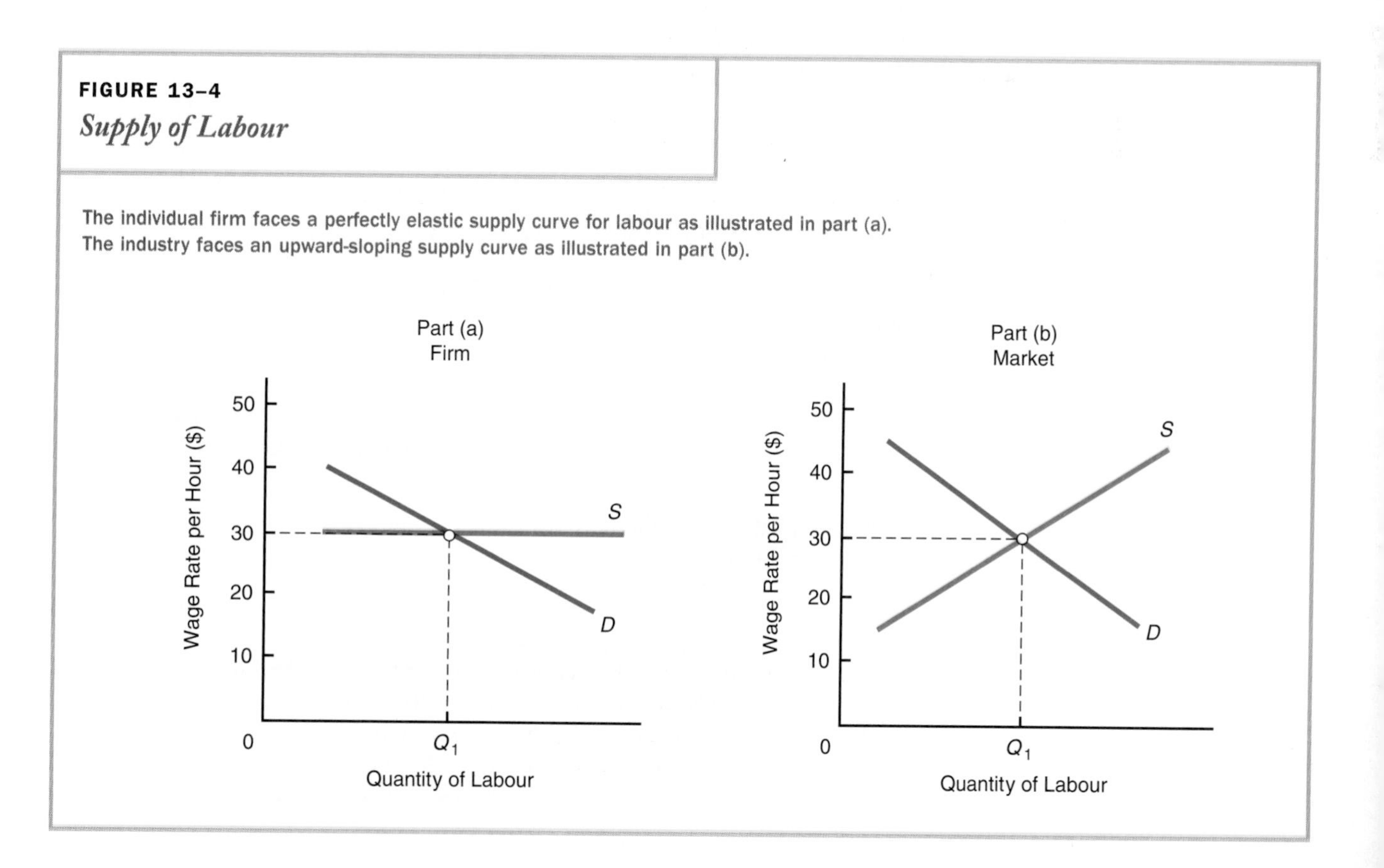

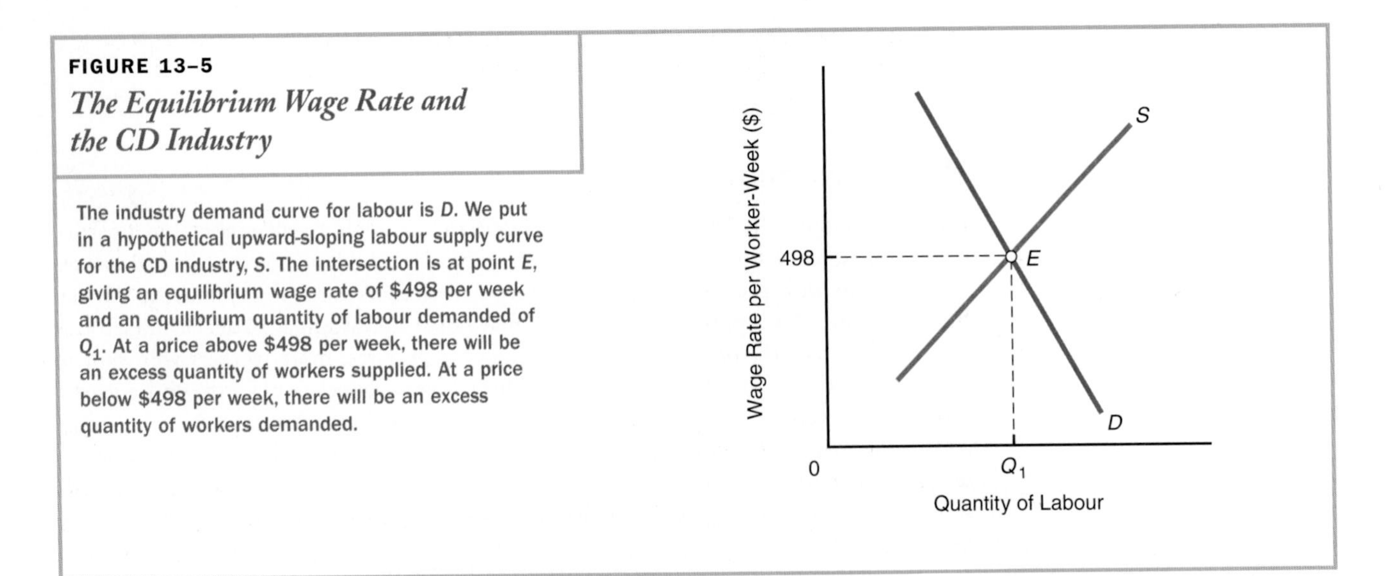

FIGURE 13–5
The Equilibrium Wage Rate and the CD Industry

The industry demand curve for labour is *D*. We put in a hypothetical upward-sloping labour supply curve for the CD industry, *S*. The intersection is at point *E*, giving an equilibrium wage rate of $498 per week and an equilibrium quantity of labour demanded of Q_1. At a price above $498 per week, there will be an excess quantity of workers supplied. At a price below $498 per week, there will be an excess quantity of workers demanded.

Shifts in the Market Demand for and Supply of Labour

Just as we discussed shifts in the supply curve and the demand curve for various products, we can discuss the effects of shifts in supply and demand in labour markets.

Reasons for Labour Demand Curve Shifts

Many factors can cause the demand curve for labour to shift. We have already discussed a number of them. Clearly, because the demand for labour or any other variable input is a derived demand, the labour demand curve will shift if there is a shift in the demand for the final product. There are two other important determinants of the position of the demand curve for labour: changes in labour's productivity and changes in the price of related factors of production (substitutes and complements).

CHANGES IN DEMAND FOR FINAL PRODUCT. The demand for labour or any other variable input is derived from the demand for the final product. The marginal revenue product is equal to marginal physical product times marginal revenue. Therefore, any change in the price of the final product will change MRP. This happened when we derived the market demand for labour. The general rule of thumb is as follows:

> **A change in the demand for the final product that labour (or any other variable input) is producing will shift the market demand curve for labour in the same direction.**

CHANGES IN LABOUR PRODUCTIVITY. The second part of the MRP equation is MPP, which relates to labour productivity. We can surmise, then, that, other things being equal,

> **A change in labour productivity will shift the market labour demand curve in the same direction.**

Labour productivity can increase because labour has more capital or land to work with, because of technological improvements, or because labour's quality has improved. Such considerations explain why the real standard of living of workers in Canada is higher than in most countries. Canadian workers generally work with a larger capital stock, have more natural resources, are in better physical condition, and are better trained than workers in many countries. Hence, the demand for labour in Canada is, other things held constant, greater. Conversely, labour is relatively scarcer in Canada than it is in many other countries. One result of relatively greater demand and relatively smaller supply is a relatively higher wage rate. See Example 13–1 for further discussion.

POLICY EXAMPLE 13–1

Should the Minimum Wage Be Raised to Help Young People?

The equilibrium wage rate model shown in Figure 13–5 does not apply when the government sets a minimum wage rate below which employers are not allowed to pay workers and workers are not allowed to offer their services. Recall that in general, a minimum wage (if set above equilibrium) creates an excess quantity of labour supplied (a surplus) at that legal minimum. Thus, young people probably would not be helped by an increase in minimum wages. Look at Figure 13–6. There, you see the unemployment rate for young people aged 15 to 24. As minimum wages across the country rose during the 1990s, so did the rate of unemployment for young people. It started falling again only around 1993. Why? In part because what is important is the real, inflation-corrected minimum wage rate. In real terms, the minimum wage fell until about 1989. Then, it rose until 1993 and started falling again, exactly coincident with the reduction in the unemployment rate for young people. So, to answer the policy question, raising the minimum wage probably would not help young people as a group, although it might help some young people who retain their jobs at the higher wage rate.

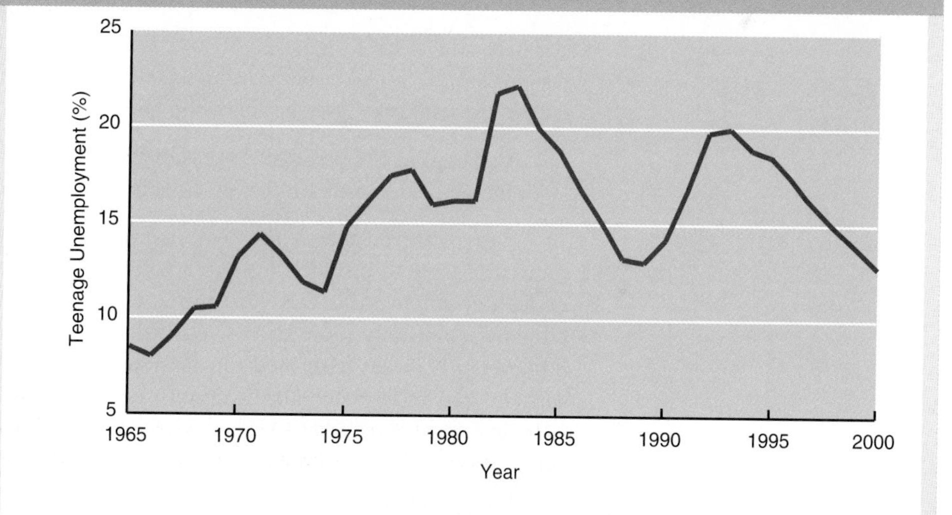

FIGURE 13–6

Teenage Unemployment and the Real Minimum Wage

Although the minimum wage has risen over the past 30 years, the real minimum wage has fallen since 1993, leading to a decrease in the rate of youth unemployment since then.

SOURCE: ADAPTED FROM THE STATISTICS CANADA WEBSITE, http://www.statcan.ca/english/freepub/82-221-XIE/00502/tabels/html/2242.htm.

For critical analysis: Why are young people most affected by changes in the minimum wage? (*Hint*: Which workers have the lowest MRP?)

EXAMPLE 13–1 **Does It Pay to Study?**

One way to increase labour productivity is to increase skill level. One way to do that, of course, is to go to college or university. Is there a big payoff? According to a recent study of identical twins carried out by economists Orley Ashenfelter and Alan Krueger, the answer is a resounding yes. They studied the earning patterns of more than 250 identical twins. In this manner, they were able to hold constant heredity, early home life, and so on. They focused on differences in the number of years of schooling. They discovered that each additional year of schooling increased wages almost 16 percent. Four years of postsecondary education yielded a 67 percent increase in monthly wages compared with none at all.

Some economists believe that a university degree is part of *labour market signalling*. Employers do not have much information about the future productivity of job applicants. Typically, the only way to find out is to observe someone working. Employers attempt to reduce the number of bad choices that they might make by using a job applicant's amount of higher education as a signal. According to the **labour market signalling** theory, even if higher education does not change productivity, it acts as an effective signal of greater individual abilities.

Labour market signalling The theory that even if higher education does not change productivity, it acts as an effective signal of greater individual abilities.

For critical analysis: Why does studying identical twins' earnings hold constant many of the factors that can determine differences in wages?

CHANGE IN THE PRICE OF RELATED FACTORS. Labour is not the only resource used. Some resources are substitutes and some are complements. If we hold output constant, we have the following general rule:

> A change in the price of a substitute input will cause the demand for labour to change in the same direction. This is typically called the *substitution effect*.

Note, however, that if the cost of production falls sufficiently, the firm will find it more profitable to produce and sell a larger output. If this so-called *output effect* is great enough, it will override the substitution effect just mentioned, and the firm will end up employing not only more of the relatively cheaper variable input but also more labour. This is exactly what happened for many years in the Canadian automobile industry. Car makers used more machinery (capital), but employment continued to increase in spite of rising wage rates. The reason: Markets were expanding and the marginal physical productivity of labour was rising faster than its wage rate.

With respect to complements, we are referring to inputs that must be used jointly. Assume now that capital and labour are complementary. In general, we predict the following:

> A change in the price of a complementary input will cause the demand for labour to change in the opposite direction.

If the cost of machines goes up but they must be used with labour, fewer machines will be purchased and therefore fewer workers will be used.

Determinants of the Supply of Labour

There are a number of reasons labour supply curves will shift in a particular industry. For example, if wage rates for factory workers in the CD industry remain constant while wages for factory workers in the computer industry go up dramatically, the supply curve of factory workers in the CD industry will shift inward to the left as these workers move to the computer industry.

Changes in working conditions in an industry can also affect its labour supply curve. If employers in the CD industry discover a new production technique that makes working conditions much more pleasant, the supply curve of labour to the CD industry will shift outward to the right.

Job flexibility also determines the position of the labour supply curve. For example, in an industry in which workers are allowed more flexibility, such as the ability to work at home via computer, the workers are likely to work more hours. That is to say, their supply curve will shift outward to the right. Some industries in which firms offer *job sharing*, particularly to people raising families, have found that the supply curve of labour has shifted outward to the right. See the Issues and Applications for this chapter to read about the impact of immigration.

CONCEPTS IN BRIEF

Learning Objective 13.2: Analyze the impact on the labour market when shifts occur in the demand for and supply of labour.

- The individual competitive firm faces a perfectly elastic supply curve—it can buy all the labour it wants at the going market wage rate. The industry supply curve of labour slopes upward.
- By plotting an industrywide supply curve for labour and an industrywide demand curve for labour on the same coordinate system, we obtain the equilibrium wage rate in this industry.
- The labour demand curve can shift because (1) the demand for the final product shifts, (2) labour productivity changes, or (3) the price of a related (substitute or complementary) factor of production changes.

13.3 The Impact of Other Factors of Production

Monopoly in the Product Market

So far, we have considered only a perfectly competitive situation, both in selling the final product and in buying factors of production. We will continue our assumption that the firm purchases its factors of production in a perfectly competitive factor market. Now, however, we will assume that the firm sells its product in an *imperfectly* competitive output market. In other words, we are considering the output market structures of monopoly, oligopoly, and monopolistic competition. In all such cases, the firm, be it a monopolist, an oligopolist, or a monopolistic competitor, faces a downward-sloping demand curve for its product. Throughout the rest of this chapter, we will simply refer to a monopoly output situation for ease of analysis. The analysis holds for all industry structures that are less than perfectly competitive. In any event, the fact that our firm now faces a downward-sloping demand curve for its product means that if it wants to sell more of its product (at a uniform price), it has to lower the price, *not just on the last unit, but on all preceding units.* The *marginal revenue* received from selling an additional unit is continuously falling (and is less than price) as the firm attempts to sell more and more. This is certainly different from our earlier discussions in this chapter in which the firm could sell all it wanted at a constant price. Why? Because the firm we discussed until now was a perfect competitor.

Constructing the Monopolist's Input Demand Curve

In reconstructing our demand schedule for an input, we must account for the facts that (1) the marginal *physical* product falls because of the law of diminishing returns as more workers are added, and (2) the price (and marginal revenue) received for the product sold also falls as more is produced and sold. That is, for the monopolist, we have to account for both the diminishing marginal physical product and the diminishing marginal revenue. Marginal revenue is always less than price for the monopolist. The marginal revenue curve is always below the downward-sloping demand curve.

Marginal revenue for the perfect competitor is equal to the price of the product because all units can be sold at the going market price. In our CD example, we assumed that the perfect competitor could sell all it wanted at $6 per compact disc. A one-unit change in sales always led to a $6 change in total revenues. Hence, marginal revenue was always equal to $6 for that perfect competitor.

The monopolist, however, cannot simply calculate marginal revenue by looking at the price of the product. To sell the additional output from an additional unit of input, the monopolist has to cut prices on all previous units of output. As output is increasing, then, marginal revenue is falling. The underlying concept is, of course, the same for both the perfect competitor and the monopolist. We are asking exactly the same question in both cases: When an additional worker is hired, what is the benefit? In either case, the benefit is obviously the change in total revenues due to the one-unit change in the variable input, labour. In our discussion of the perfect competitor, we were able simply to look at the marginal physical product and multiply it by the *constant* per-unit price of the product because the price of the product never changed (for the perfect competitor, $P = \text{MR}$).

A single monopolist ends up hiring fewer workers than all of the competitive firms added together. To see this, we must calculate the marginal revenue product for the monopolist. To make it simple, we will look at it as simply the change in total revenues due to a one-unit change in the labour input for a monopolist. This is what we do in part (a) of Figure 13–7, which shows the change in total revenues. Column 6, headed "Marginal Revenue Product," gives the monopolistic firm a quantitative notion of how profitable additional workers and additional production actually are. The marginal revenue product curve for this monopolist has been plotted in part (b) of the figure. To emphasize the steeper slope of the monopolist's MRP curve, MRP_m, the MRP curve for the perfect competitor in Figure 13–1, labelled MRP_c, has been plotted on the same graph.

Why does MRP_m represent the monopolist's input demand curve? As always, our profit-maximizing monopolist will continue to hire labour as long as additional profits result. Profits are made as long as the additional cost of more workers is outweighed by the additional revenues made from selling the output of those workers. When the wage rate equals these additional revenues, the monopolist stops hiring. That is, it stops hiring when the wage rate is equal to the marginal revenue product because additional workers would add more to cost than to revenue.

Why the Monopolist Hires Fewer Workers

Because we have used the same numbers as in Figure 13–1, we can see that the monopolist hires fewer worker-weeks than the perfect competitor. That is to say, if we could magically change the CD industry in our example from one in which there is perfect competition in the output market to one in which there is monopoly in the output market, the amount of employment would fall. Why? Because the monopolist must take account of the declining product price that must be charged in order to sell a larger number of CDs. Remember that every firm hires up to the point at which marginal benefit equals marginal cost. The marginal benefit to the monopolist of hiring an additional worker is not simply the additional output times the price of the product. Rather, the monopolist faces a reduction in the price charged on all units sold in order to be able to sell more. So, the monopolist ends up hiring fewer workers than all of the perfect competitors taken together, assuming that all other factors remain the same for the two hypothetical examples. But this should not come as a surprise. In considering product markets, by implication we saw that a monopolized CD industry would produce less output than a competitive one. Therefore, the monopolized CD industry would want fewer workers.

Other Factors of Production

The analysis in this chapter has been given in terms of the demand for the variable input labour. The same analysis holds for any other variable factor input. We could have talked about the demand for fertilizer or the demand for the services of tractors by a farmer instead of the demand for labour and reached the same conclusions. The entrepreneur will hire or buy any variable input up to the point at which its price equals the marginal revenue product.

FIGURE 13–7

A Monopolist's Marginal Revenue Product

The monopolist hires just enough workers to make marginal revenue product equal to the going wage rate. If the going wage rate is $498 per week, as shown by the labour supply curve, *s*, the monopolist would want to hire between 9 and 10 workers per week. That is the profit-maximizing amount of labour. The MRP curve for the perfect competitor from Figure 13–1 is also plotted (MRP_c). The monopolist's MRP curve will always be less elastic than it would be if marginal revenue were constant.

Part (a)

(1) Labour Input (workers per week)	(2) Total Physical Product (TPP) CDs per week	(3) Marginal Physical Product (MPP) CDs per week	(4) Price of Product (*P*)	(5) Total Revenue (TR) = (2) x (4)	(6) Marginal Revenue Product (MRP_m) $= \frac{\text{Change in (5)}}{\text{Change in (1)}}$
7	1000		$8.00	$ 8 000.00	
8	1111	111	7.80	8 665.80	$665.80
9	1215	104	7.60	9 234.00	568.20
10	1312	97	7.40	9 708.80	474.80
11	1402	90	7.20	10 094.40	385.60
12	1485	83	7.00	10 395.00	300.60
13	1561	76	6.80	10 614.80	219.80

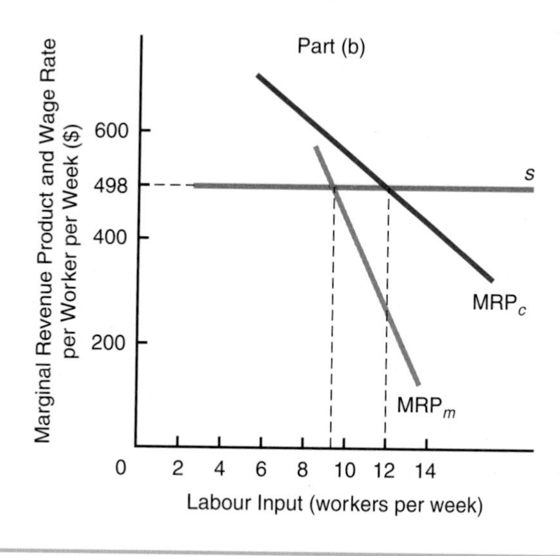

A further question remains: How much of each variable factor should the firm use when all the variable factors are combined to produce the product? We can answer this question by looking at either the profit-maximizing side of the question or the cost-minimizing side.[1]

[1]Many economic problems involving maximization of profit or other economic variables have duals, or precise restatements, in terms of *minimization*, rather than maximization. The problem "How do we maximize our output, given fixed resources?" for example, is the dual of the problem "How do we minimize our cost, given fixed output?" Noneconomists sometimes confuse their discussions of economic issues by mistakenly believing that a problem and its dual are two problems, rather than one. Asking, for example, "How can we maximize our profits while minimizing our costs?" makes about as much sense as asking, "How can we cross the street while getting to the other side?"

Profit Maximization Revisited

If a firm wants to maximize profits, how much of each factor should be hired (or bought)? As we just saw, the firm will never hire a factor of production unless the marginal benefit from hiring that factor is at least equal to the marginal cost. What is the marginal benefit? As we have pointed out, the marginal benefit is the change in total revenues due to a one-unit change in use of the variable input. What is the marginal cost? In the case of a firm buying in a competitive market, it is the price of the variable factor—the wage rate if we are referring to labour.

The profit-maximizing combination of resources for the firm will be where, in a perfectly competitive situation,

$$\text{MRP of labour} = \text{Price of labour (wage rate)}$$

$$\text{MRP of land} = \text{Price of land (rental rate per unit)}$$

$$\text{MRP of capital} = \text{Price of capital (cost per unit of service)}$$

Alternatively, we can express this profit-maximizing rule as:

$$\frac{\text{MRP of labour}}{\text{Price of labour}} = \frac{\text{MRP of land}}{\text{Price of land}} = \frac{\text{MRP of capital}}{\text{Price of capital}}$$

The marginal revenue product of each of a firm's resources must be exactly equal to its price. If the MRP of labour were $20 and its price were only $15, the firm would be underemploying labour.

Cost Minimization

From the cost minimization point of view, how can the firm minimize its total costs for a given output? Assume that you are an entrepreneur attempting to minimize costs. Consider a hypothetical situation in which if you spend $1 more on labour, you would get 20 more units of output, but if you spend $1 more on machines, you would get only 10 more units of output. What would you want to do in such a situation? Most likely you would wish to hire more workers or sell off some of your machines, for you are not getting as much output per last dollar spent on machines as you are per last dollar spent on labour. You would want to employ factors of production so that the marginal products per last dollar spent on each are equal. Thus, the least-cost, or cost minimization, rule will be as follows:

> **To minimize total costs for a particular rate of production, the firm will hire factors of production up to the point at which the marginal physical product per last dollar spent on each factor of production is equalized.**

That is,

$$\frac{\text{MRP of labour}}{\begin{array}{c}\text{Price of labour}\\\text{(wage rate)}\end{array}} = \frac{\text{MRP of land}}{\begin{array}{c}\text{Price of land}\\\text{(rental rate per unit)}\end{array}} = \frac{\text{MRP of capital}}{\begin{array}{c}\text{Price of capital}\\\text{(cost per unit of service)}\end{array}}$$

All we are saying here is that the profit-maximizing firm will always use *all* resources in such combinations that cost will be minimized for any given output rate. This is commonly called the *least-cost combination of resources.* There is an exact relationship between the profit-maximizing combination of resources and the least-cost combination of resources. In other words, either rule can be used to yield the same cost-minimizing rate of use of each variable resource.[2] See Example 13–2 for a real-life example of cost minimization.

[2]This can be proved as follows: Profit maximization requires that the price of every input must equal that input's marginal revenue product (the general case). Let i be the input. Then $P_i = \text{MRP}_i$. But MRP_i is equal to marginal revenue times marginal physical product of the input. Therefore, $P_i = \text{MR} \times \text{MPP}_i$. If we divide both sides by MPP_i, we get $P_i/\text{MPP}_i = \text{MR}$. If we take the reciprocal, we obtain $\text{MPP}_i/P_i = 1/\text{MR}$. That is another way of stating our cost minimization rule.

EXAMPLE 13–2 Cost Minimization and the Substitution of Software for Labour

The computer revolution, while it is increasing employment in one sector of the economy, may at the same time be decreasing the use of labour in other sectors. In particular, accounting software (capital) is replacing certified general accountants (labour) at an increasing rate. Accounting software has become more plentiful, less costly, easier to use, and more sophisticated in the past several years. Nonetheless, the number of CGAs has risen virtually every year since 1970. A prediction would be that the relative salaries of CGAs should therefore fall in the future (all other things held constant).

The same analysis holds for lawyers. Legal software has proliferated, grown more sophisticated, dropped in price, and become easier to use. Consequently, paralegals are now able to do many of the jobs that lawyers used to do. Not surprisingly, the paralegal profession is expanding rapidly, while the growth in the number of lawyers is starting to slow down.

For critical analysis: Can you apply the same analysis to doctors?

CONCEPTS IN BRIEF

Learning Objective 13.3: Discuss how other factors of production affect the labour market.

- When a firm sells its output in a monopoly market, marginal revenue is less than price.
- Just as the MRP is the perfectly competitive firm's input demand curve, the MRP is also the monopolist's demand curve.
- For a less than perfectly competitive firm, the profit-maximizing combination of factors will occur where each factor is used up to the point where its MRP is equal to its unit price.
- To minimize total costs for a given output, the profit-maximizing firm will hire each factor of production up to the point where the marginal physical product per last dollar spent on each factor is equal to the marginal physical product per last dollar spent on each of the other factors of production.

ISSUES AND APPLICATIONS

Are Immigrants Pushing Down Canadian Wages?

Concepts Applied: Demand for and Supply of Labour, Shifts in the Supply Curve of Labour, Real Wages, Productivity

New Canadians swear an oath of allegiance to the Queen at a citizenship ceremony in Toronto. Economists have found that the traditional view that immigrants push down real wages and take advantage of social programs is not borne out by the evidence.

Immigration has been on the upsurge since the 1930s, but the number of immigrants as a percentage of the population is still less than it was 80 years ago. Thus, any notion that immigration is posing an increased threat to Canadian culture certainly does not stand up to the facts.

A Worldwide Phenomenon

Immigration into Canada is just a small part of a worldwide phenomenon of human migration. Today, at least 100 million people live outside the country in which they were born. Most of this migration is not to the richer industrialized countries. Consequently, by 2000, fully 17 of the world's biggest cities will be in the developing world with Mexico City, Mexico (26 million), and São Paulo, Brazil (22 million), in first and second places. New York City will rank fifth.

Just because human migration occurs everywhere does not mean that it is "good" or "bad" for the Canadian economy.

Costs and Benefits of Immigration

One of the basic criticisms of immigrants is that they use the social welfare system more than in proportion to their numbers. This and other issues are currently being investigated by the four federally funded Centres for Excellence for the Study of Immigration and Integration.

Existing data show, however, that the percentage of immigrant households receiving social assistance is less than Canadian households, 12.5 percent compared with 13.8 percent. After all, immigrants usually arrive when they are young and healthy, as you can see in part (a) of Figure 13–8. Consequently, they generally need fewer welfare services than Canadian-born families. More importantly, because they are young, they do not require much medical care, nor do they receive Old Age Security payments, two significant government expenditures. Moreover, several studies have found that immigrant families contribute more to government coffers, by way of taxes, than they take out in social services.

Employment and Wages

Another major question with respect to immigration is whether immigrants will force down wages and create unemployment. According to numerous studies, there is virtually no statistically significant change in unemployment rates when immigration increases. But data on the level of education, as you can see in part (b) of Figure 13–8, shows a high level of education.

The data on wage rates are inconclusive. While immigrants definitely increase the supply curve of labour, they mainly affect specific parts of the labour market, and then for only a short time. On an empirical basis, given that Canada has been peopled by immigrants since the 17th century and that real wage rates have been rising more or less steadily, immigration cannot have reduced real wage rates. What has happened is that all labour has become increasingly productive in spite of large increases in the labour force due to both Canadian births and net immigration.

For critical analysis:

1. While immigrants increase the supply of labour, they also increase the demand for goods and services. What impact will this increase in demand for goods and services have on the *wage rate*?
2. Canada's population growth rate without immigration is approximately 1.2 children per couple. In the absence of immigration, what effect will this replacement rate have on the labour market and the quantity of output produced?

FIGURE 13–8

Immigrants in Canada

Most immigrants arriving in Canada are young and healthy as seen in part (a). They are also well educated, which means more tax dollars for the government as seen in part (b).

SOURCE: REPRODUCED WITH THE PERMISSION OF THE MINISTER OF PUBLIC WORKS AND GOVERNMENT SERVICES, 2004.

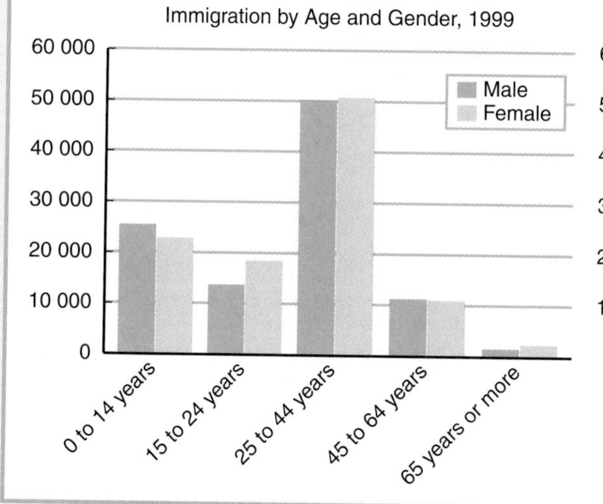

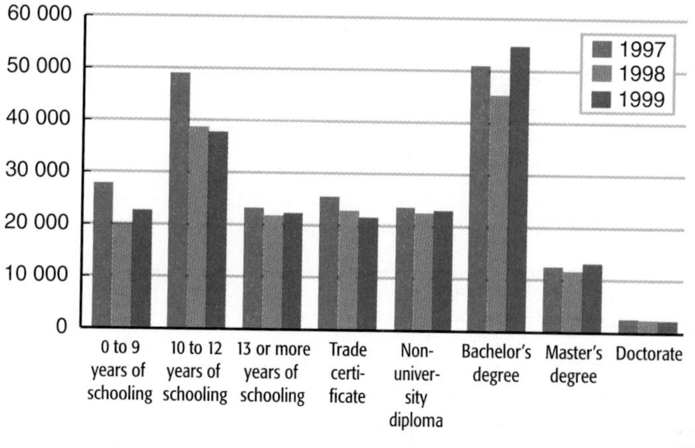

SUMMARY DISCUSSION OF LEARNING OBJECTIVES

13.1 **Demand for Labour.** In a competitive situation in which the firm is a very small part of the entire product and labour market, the firm will want to hire workers up to the point at which the marginal revenue product just equals the going wage rate.

The marginal revenue product curve for the individual competitive firm is the input demand curve. The competitive firm hires up to the point at which the wage rate equals the MRP.

The summation of all the MRP curves does not equal the market demand curve for labour. The market demand curve for labour is less elastic than the sum of the MRP curves because as more workers are hired, output is increased and the price of the product must fall, lowering the MRP.

The demand for labour is derived from the demand for the product produced.

The elasticity of demand for an input is a function of several determinants, including the elasticity of demand for the final product. Moreover, the price elasticity of demand for a variable input will usually be larger in the long run than it is in the short run because there is time for adjustment.

13.2 **Shifts in the Demand for and Supply of Labour.** The firm buying labour in a perfectly competitive labour market faces a perfectly elastic supply curve at the going wage rate because the firm can hire all it wants at that wage rate. The industry supply curve of labour slopes upward.

The demand curve for labour will shift if (a) the demand for the final product shifts, (b) labour productivity changes, or (c) the price of a substitute or a complementary factor of production changes.

13.3 **The Impact of Other Factors of Production.** The MRP curve is also the monopolist's input demand curve. Because marginal revenue is less than the price of the product for a monopolist, the monopolist's input demand curve is steeper.

A firm minimizes total costs by equating the ratio of marginal physical product of labour divided by the price of labour with the ratio of marginal physical product of machines to the price of capital with all other such ratios for all the different factors of production. This is the mirror of profit maximization.

PROBLEMS

(Answers to the odd-numbered problems appear at the back of the book.)

LO 13.1 Explain the demand for labour using the marginal physical product, marginal revenue product, and price elasticity of demand concepts.

1. Assume that the product in the table is sold by a perfectly competitive firm for $2 per unit.
   a. Use the information in the table to derive a demand schedule for labour.
   b. What is the most that this firm would be willing to pay each worker if five workers were hired?
   c. If the going salary for this quality of labour is $200 per week, how many workers will be hired?

Quantity of Labour	Total Physical Product per Week	MPP	MRP
1	250	______	______
2	450	______	______
3	600	______	______
4	700	______	______
5	750	______	______
6	750	______	______

2. The table presents some production function data for a firm in which the only variable input is capital; the labour input is fixed. First fill in the other columns. What quantity of capital will the firm use if the price of capital is $90 per machine-week? If the price of capital is $300 per machine-week, what quantity of capital will the firm use? Explain.

LO 13.2 Analyze the impact on the labour market when shifts occur in the demand for and supply of labour.

3. The accompanying graph indicates labour supply and demand in the construction industry.

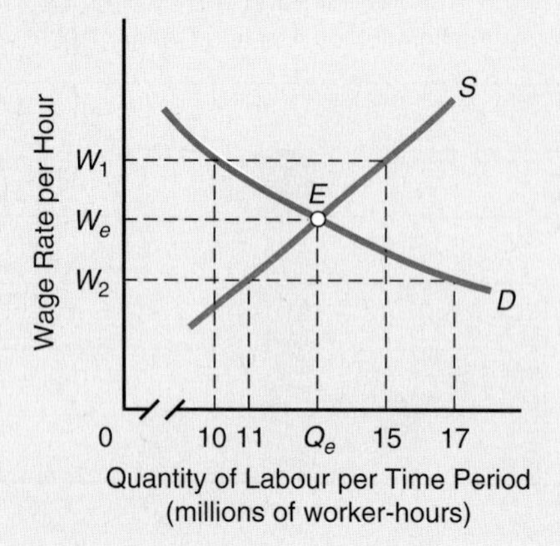

   a. When wage rates are W_1 per hour, how many worker-hours do workers intend to offer per unit?
   b. How much do businesses intend to buy at this wage rate?
   c. Which group can realize its intentions, and which cannot?
   d. What forces will be set in motion at wage rate W_1, given a free market for labour?

4. Using the graph in Problem 3, answer the following questions:
   a. At wage rate W_2, how many worker-hours do workers intend to offer?
   b. At W_2, how many worker-hours do businesses intend to purchase?
   c. Which group can realize its intentions, and which cannot?
   d. What forces will be set in motion at W_2 if a free market for labour exists in this industry?
   e. What will the equilibrium wage rate be?

Quantity of Capital (machine-weeks)	Total Physical Product per Week	Marginal Physical Product of Capital per Week	Marginal Revenue (product price) per Unit	Marginal Revenue Product per Week
0	0		$10	
1	25	______	10	$______
2	45	______	10	______
3	60	______	10	______
4	70	______	10	______
5	75	______	10	______

5. The price elasticity of demand for the final output product directly affects the elasticity of demand for the input factor. Why?

6. Suppose that you are seeking to maximize output for a given outlay. If the marginal physical product of input x is 10 and that of input y is 20, and the prices of the two inputs are $3 and $7, respectively, how should you alter your input mix in order to increase output and profit?

LO 13.3 Discuss how other factors of production affect the labour market.

7. Suppose that you are a monopolist and labour is the only variable input you employ. You are currently producing 150 units of output and selling them for $20 apiece. You are considering the possibility of hiring an additional full-time employee. You estimate that daily output would increase to 160 units if you hired this additional person and that you would be able to sell all of those units at a price of $19 each. What is the MRP of labour (per worker-day)? Assuming that you take the price of labour as a given, what is the maximum daily wage that would make it in your interest to hire this additional employee?

8. When there is only one variable input, how does a monopoly seller's demand for that input differ from that of a perfectly competitive seller?

9. According to Policy Example 13–1, "Should the Minimum Wage Be Raised to Help Young People?", it pays to study. Assume that you have graduated from university. You decide to look for a job, rather than go for further schooling. Indicate how the following criteria might affect the salary that you will receive and the type of job you may end up taking after you graduate.
   a. You want to stay near your family, and so you do not consider moving out of your immediate geographical area to find a job.
   b. You look only for jobs that allow you to apply the knowledge and skills you have learned in your major.
   c. You now live in the city but decide that you will only work in a rural area.

CHAPTER 14

Unions and Labour Market Monopoly Power

The average major-league baseball player today earns about $1.8 million a year. The average professional hockey player earns about $1.2 million a year. The average professional basketball player earns about $3 million a year. At the same time, professional sports team owners continue to buy and sell professional franchises for tens and hundreds of millions of dollars.

For many years, players' salaries grew relatively slowly. Only since 1989 have they increased significantly. To understand the market for professional sports league players, you have to acquire an understanding of various restrictions in the labour market.

LEARNING OBJECTIVES

After reading this chapter, you should be able to:

14.1 Explain the history of the labour movement in Canada.

14.2 Discuss the three main union goals and the five benefits of labour unions.

14.3 Determine the impact on pricing and employment under various market conditions.

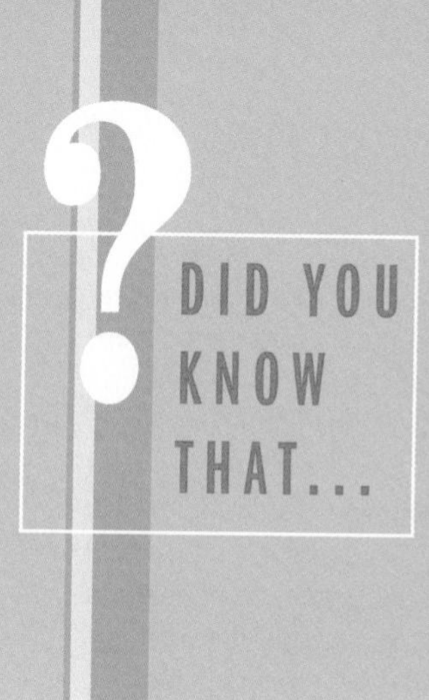

In 1976, more than 1.5 million Canadian workers were involved in strikes. In the past few years, however, fewer than 70 000 have participated. More than 12 times the number of workdays were lost to strikes in the 1950s than are lost today. The labour landscape has been changing in Canada. Some workers are able to earn more than they would in a competitive labour market because they have obtained a type of monopoly power. These are members of effective **labour unions**, worker organizations that seek to secure economic improvements for their members; they also seek to improve safety, health, and other benefits (such as job security) for their members.

In forming unions, a certain monopoly element enters into the supply of labour equation. That is because we can no longer talk about a perfectly competitive labour supply situation when active and effective unions bargain as a single entity with management. The entire supply of a particular group of workers is controlled by a single source. Later in the chapter, we will examine the opposite—a single employer who is the sole user of a particular group of workers.

Labour unions Worker organizations that seek to secure economic improvements for their members.

Craft unions Labour unions composed of workers who engaged in a particular trade or skill, such as shoemaking, printing, or baking.

Industrial unions Labour unions whose membership came from an entire industry, such as steel or automobile manufacturing.

Collective bargaining Bargaining between the management of a company, or a group of companies, and the management of a union, or a group of unions, for the purpose of setting a mutually agreeable contract on wages, fringe benefits, and working conditions for all employees in all the unions involved.

14.1 The Canadian Labour Movement

The Canadian labour movement started with local **craft unions**—labour unions composed of workers who engaged in a particular trade or skill, such as shoemaking, printing, and baking. Initially, workers struggled for the right to band together to bargain as a unit. Until 1872, that right did not exist.

Between 1875 and 1907, the American-based Knights of Labor, an organized group of both skilled and unskilled workers, demanded a nine-hour workday, equal pay for men and women, and the replacement of free enterprise with the socialist system. In 1883, the Trades and Labour Congress (TLC) formed as a meeting ground for craft unions and the Knights of Labor. Several years later, during the last decade of the 19th century, a rapid expansion of American branch plants took place in Canada. Paralleling this growth was international unionism; by 1911, there were 135 000 Canadian members of the American Federation of Labour (AFL).

During World War I, overall union membership grew rapidly but fell off amidst the prosperity of the 1920s. In response to declining membership, the All-Canadian Congress of Labour (ACCL) was formed to rival the TLC and divorce Canadian unionism from the United States. In contrast to the TLC, the ACCL was composed of **industrial unions**—labour unions whose membership came from an entire industry, such as steel or automobile manufacturing.

Then came the Great Depression. It was a time of both economic and labour turmoil. The American Congress of Industrial Organizations (CIO), a committee of the AFL, joined the TLC but was subsequently expelled from both the AFL and the TLC due to conflicting ideologies with respect to partnerships with business. The CIO then joined the ACCL, which dropped the "A" for "All" and became simply the Canadian Congress of Labour (CCL).

World War II was another time of significant union activity, and in 1944, the federal government enfranchised the public sector with the *Trade Union Act*. In 1946, a Supreme Court decision gave unions the legal right to organize, to engage in *collective bargaining*, and to strike. **Collective bargaining** is bargaining between the management of a company, or a group of companies, and the management of a union, or a group of unions, for the purpose of setting a mutually agreeable contract on wages, fringe benefits, and working conditions for all employees in all the unions involved. The "Rand formula" also guaranteed the solvency of unions by ensuring a union check-off—a law stipulating that employees in a union shop must pay dues whether or not they choose to join the union. Look at Example 14–1 for another way of collective bargaining.

EXAMPLE 14–1 Europe's Management-Labour Councils

Unionization rates are much higher in the European Union (EU) than in Canada, averaging 48 percent. Perhaps more importantly, most EU countries have institutionalized the concept of management–labour councils. In Germany, legislation dating back to the early 1950s created such councils, requiring that management and labour reach decisions jointly and unanimously. German management–labour councils use up a significant amount of management time. At H.C. Asmussen, a small German distilling company with 300 workers, there are five work councils, some of which meet weekly.

A directive from the EU has forced 1500 of the European Union's largest companies to set up Europe-wide worker–management consultative committees. In Canada, no such legislation exists, although there is a management desire to create more "quality circles" (to improve quality and to reduce costs) that involve workers and management. Many unions view these quality circles as a threat and are active in their opposition to them.

For critical analysis: Why do you think unions might be against quality circles involving management and workers?

In 1956, the TLC and the CCL merged to form the Canadian Labour Congress (CLC), which today has over 2 million members organized into almost 9000 locals across the country. Other labour congresses, such as the Canadian Federation of Labour (CFL), the Confederation of National Trade Unions (CNTU) in Quebec, and the AFL-CIO in Canada, boast a further 630 000 members. In 2003, total union membership in Canada consisted of 4 million workers.

The Current Status of Labour Unions

Union membership grew quite rapidly from the 1940s to the late 1950s. Since 1967, union membership has been fairly stable, and is currently hovering around 30 percent of the civilian labour force. If you remove labour unions in the public sector—federal, provincial, and municipal government workers—private-sector union membership in Canada is about 18 percent of the working-age population.

As you can see from Figure 14–1, unionization increased in 11 of the 16 major industry groups from 1999 to 2000. High union rates were found in employees aged 45 to 54, employees with university degrees, and workers in Newfoundland and Quebec. Low union rates were recorded by youths 15 to 24 years old, workers in Alberta, and agricultural workers.

CONCEPTS IN BRIEF

Learning Objective 14.1: Explain the history of the labour movement in Canada.

- The Trades and Labour Congress (TLC), composed primarily of craft unions, was formed in 1883. Membership increased until after World War I.
- The Canadian Congress of Labour (CCL), formerly the All-Canadian Congress of Labour, was formed in 1927 by industrial unions.
- In 1946, the Rand formula gave unions the right to strike, to bargain collectively, and to collect dues from both members and nonmembers.
- The TLC and the CCL merged in 1956 to form the Canadian Labour Congress (CLC).

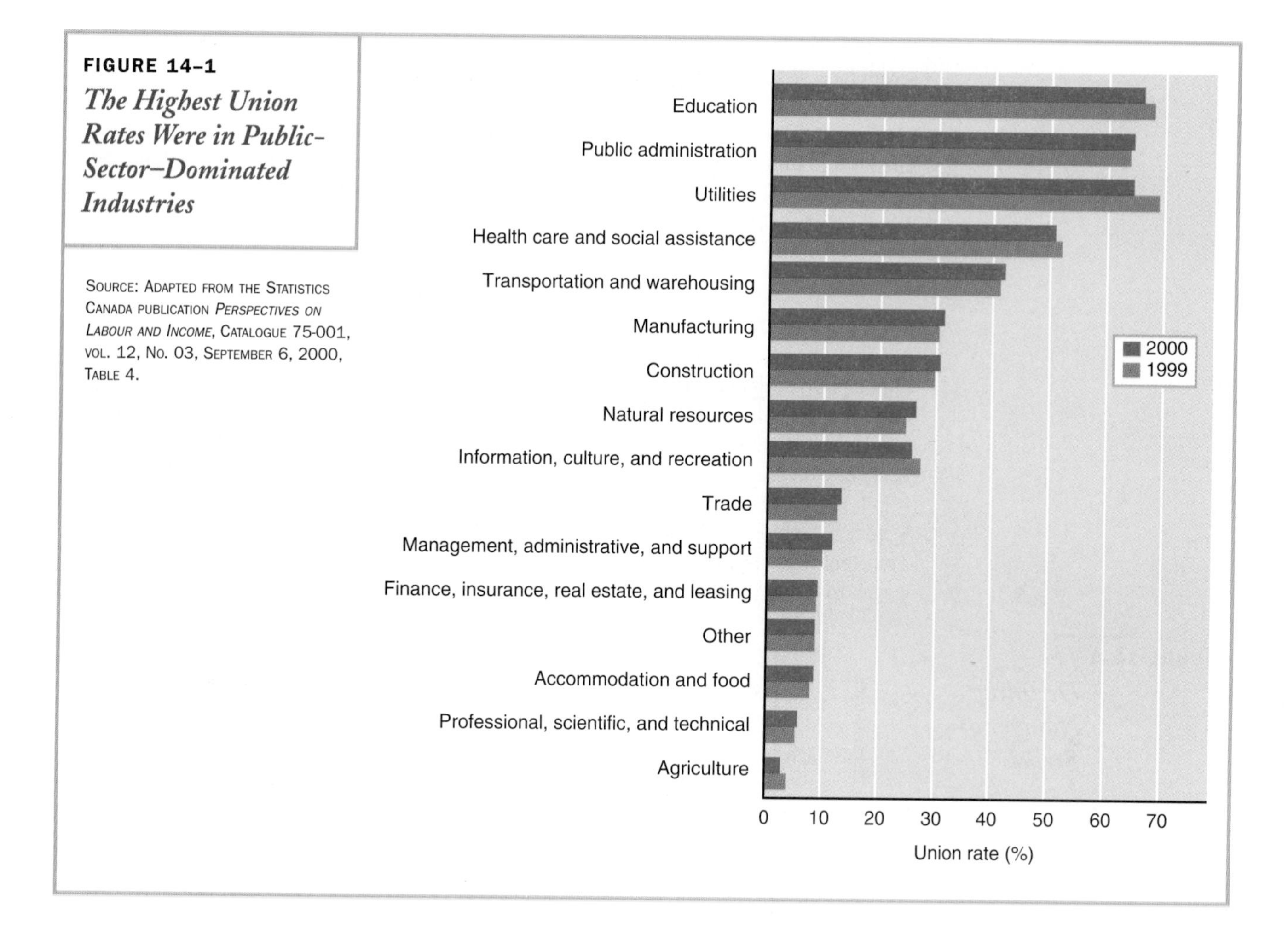

FIGURE 14–1

The Highest Union Rates Were in Public-Sector–Dominated Industries

SOURCE: ADAPTED FROM THE STATISTICS CANADA PUBLICATION *PERSPECTIVES ON LABOUR AND INCOME*, CATALOGUE 75-001, VOL. 12, NO. 03, SEPTEMBER 6, 2000, TABLE 4.

14.2 Union Goals and Labour Unions

Unions and Collective Bargaining Contracts

Unions can be regarded as setters of minimum wages. Through collective bargaining, unions establish minimum wages below which no workers can offer their services. Each year, collective bargaining contracts covering wages as well as working conditions and fringe benefits for about 2 million workers are negotiated. Union negotiators act as agents for all members of the bargaining unit. They bargain with management about the provisions of a labour contract. Once union representatives believe that they have an acceptable collective contract, they will submit it to a vote of the union members. If approved by the members, the contract sets wage rates, maximum workdays, working conditions, fringe benefits, and other matters, usually for the next two or three years. Typically, collective bargaining contracts between management and the union apply also to nonunion members who are employed by the firm or the industry.

Strike: The Ultimate Bargaining Tool

Whenever union–management negotiations break down, union negotiators may turn to their ultimate bargaining tool—the threat, or the reality, of a strike. The first recorded strike in Canadian history occurred in 1671 when shipyard workers in Quebec conducted a slowdown to secure better wages and working conditions. Strikes make headlines, but in only 4 percent of all labour–management disputes does a strike occur before the contract is signed. In the other 96 percent of cases, contracts are signed without much public fanfare.

The purpose of a strike is to impose costs on stubborn management to force its acceptance of the union's proposed contract terms. Strikes disrupt production and interfere with a company's or an industry's ability to sell goods and services. The strike works both ways, though. Workers draw no wages while on strike (they may be partly compensated out of union strike funds) and are not eligible to claim Employment Insurance benefits. Effects of this are illustrated in Example 14–2.

EXAMPLE 14–2 **Strike Activity in Canada**

Although unionization rates have been fairly stable in Canada, the number of strikes and lockouts has decreased. As you can see from Figure 14–2, the highest number of strikes took place in the early 1980s and peaked again in the mid-1980s. Strike activity has declined sharply since then.

Typically, in a strike situation, the workers will lose wages, while companies' costs will increase. A gain for one union is likely to cause losses for other unions. Some economists even feel that the best wage-setting arrangement might be the automatic adjustments of wages to firm profitability.

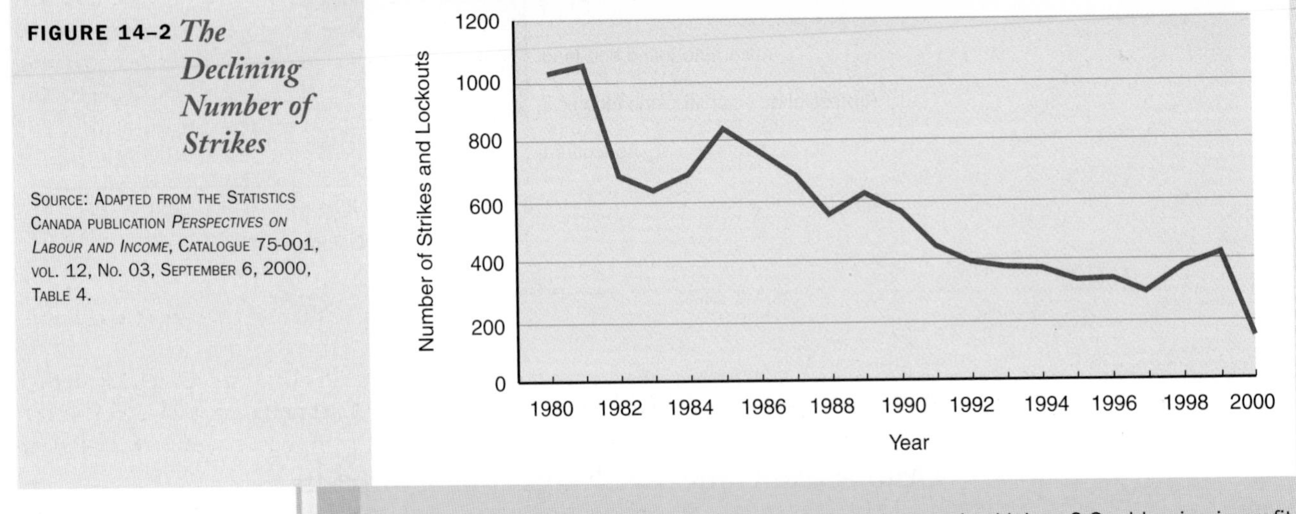

FIGURE 14–2 *The Declining Number of Strikes*

SOURCE: ADAPTED FROM THE STATISTICS CANADA PUBLICATION *PERSPECTIVES ON LABOUR AND INCOME*, CATALOGUE 75-001, VOL. 12, NO. 03, SEPTEMBER 6, 2000, TABLE 4.

For critical analysis: In what way might a strike help organized labour? Could a rise in profit-sharing have caused the declines in strikes that we see in Figure 14–2? How?

The impact of a strike is closely related to the ability of striking unions to prevent nonstriking (and perhaps nonunion) employees from continuing to work for the targeted company or industry. Therefore, steps are usually taken to prevent others from working for the employer. **Strikebreakers** (temporary or permanent workers hired by a company to replace union members who are on strike) can effectively destroy whatever bargaining power rests behind a strike. Numerous methods—including violence on the picket lines—have been used to deter strikebreakers.

Strikebreakers Temporary or permanent workers hired by a company to replace union members who are on strike.

Union Goals

We have already pointed out that one of the goals of unions is to set minimum wages. In many situations, any wage rate set higher than a competitive market clearing wage rate will reduce total employment in that market. This can be seen in Figure 14–3. We have a competitive market for labour. The market demand curve is *D*, and the market supply curve is *S*. The market clearing wage rate will be W_e; the equilibrium quantity of labour

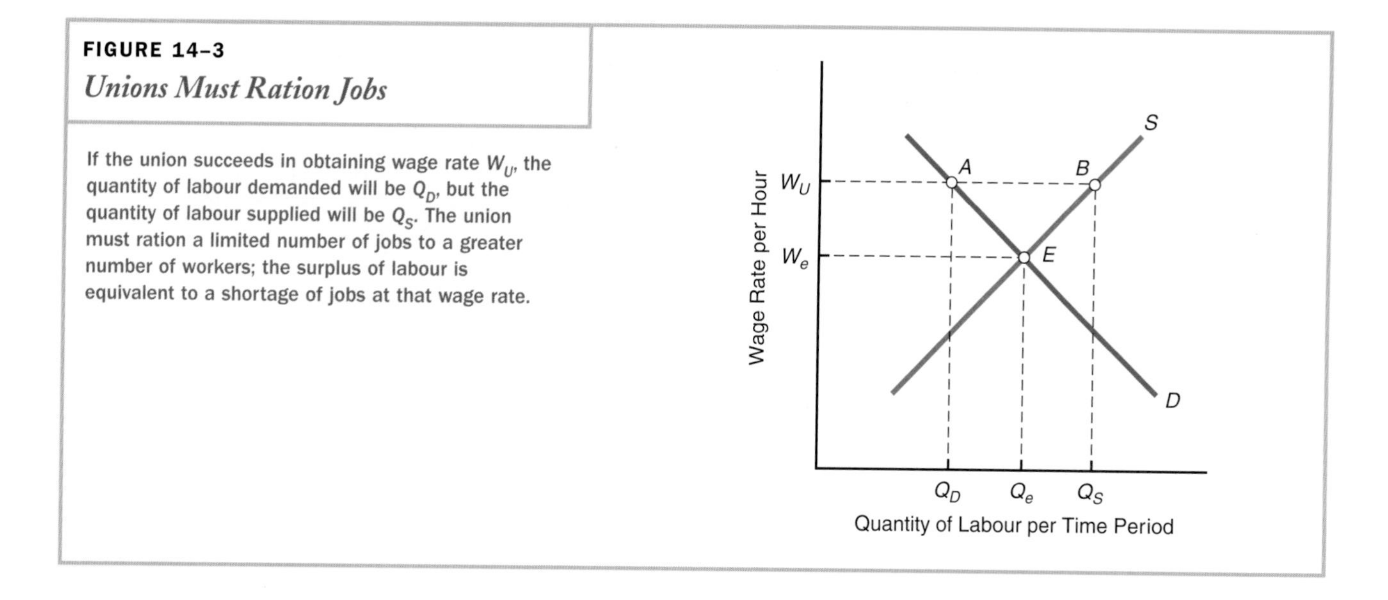

FIGURE 14–3

Unions Must Ration Jobs

If the union succeeds in obtaining wage rate W_U, the quantity of labour demanded will be Q_D, but the quantity of labour supplied will be Q_S. The union must ration a limited number of jobs to a greater number of workers; the surplus of labour is equivalent to a shortage of jobs at that wage rate.

will be Q_e. If the union establishes by collective bargaining a minimum wage rate that exceeds W_e, an excess quantity of labour will be supplied (assuming no change in the labour demand schedule). If the minimum wage established by union collective bargaining is W_U, the quantity supplied would be Q_S; the quantity demanded would be Q_D. The difference is the excess quantity supplied, or surplus. Hence, the following point becomes clear:

> **One of the major roles of a union that establishes a wage rate above the market clearing wage rate is to ration available jobs among the excess number of workers who wish to work in unionized industries.**

Note also that the surplus of labour is equivalent to a shortage of jobs at wage rates above equilibrium.

The union may use a system of seniority, a lengthening of the apprenticeship period to discourage potential members from joining, and other such rationing methods. This has the effect of shifting the supply of labour curve to the left in order to support the higher wage, W_U.

There is a trade-off here that any union's leadership must face: Higher wages inevitably mean a reduction in total employment, as more persons are seeking a smaller number of positions. (Moreover, at higher wages, more workers will seek to enter the industry, thereby adding to the surplus that occurs because of the union contract.) Facing higher wages, management may replace part of the workforce with machinery.

Union Strategies

If we view unions as monopoly sellers of a service, we can identify three different wage and employment strategies that they use: ensuring employment for all members of the union, maximizing aggregate income for all workers, and maximizing wage rates for some workers.

EMPLOYING ALL MEMBERS IN THE UNION. Assume that the union has Q_1 workers. If it faces a labour demand curve such as D in Figure 14–4, the only way it can "sell" all of those workers' services is to accept a wage rate of W_1. This is similar to any other demand curve. The demand curve tells the maximum price that can be charged to sell any particular quantity of a good or service. Here, the service happens to be labour.

MAXIMIZING MEMBER INCOME. If the union is interested in maximizing the gross income of its members, it will normally want a smaller membership than Q_1—namely, Q_2 workers, all employed and paid a wage rate of W_2. The aggregate income to all

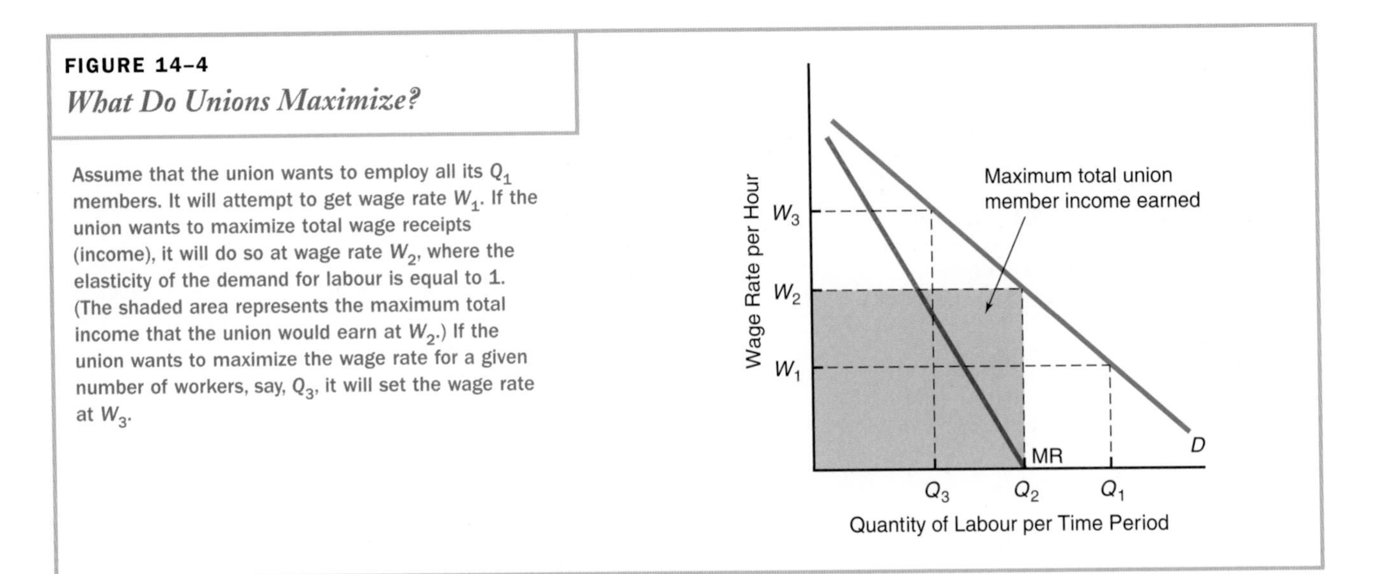

FIGURE 14–4
What Do Unions Maximize?

Assume that the union wants to employ all its Q_1 members. It will attempt to get wage rate W_1. If the union wants to maximize total wage receipts (income), it will do so at wage rate W_2, where the elasticity of the demand for labour is equal to 1. (The shaded area represents the maximum total income that the union would earn at W_2.) If the union wants to maximize the wage rate for a given number of workers, say, Q_3, it will set the wage rate at W_3.

members of the union is represented by the wages of only the ones who work. Total income earned by union members is maximized where the price elasticity of demand is numerically equal to 1. That occurs where marginal revenue equals zero. In Figure 14–4, marginal revenue equals zero at a quantity of labour Q_2. So, we know that if the union obtains a wage rate equal to W_2, and therefore Q_2 workers are demanded, the total income to the union membership will be maximized. In other words, $Q_2 \times W_2$ (the shaded area) will be greater than any other combination of wage rates and quantities of union workers demanded. It is, for example, greater than $Q_1 \times W_1$. Note that in this situation, if the union started out with Q_1 members, there would be $Q_1 - Q_2$ members out of *union* work at the wage rate W_2. (Those out of union work either remain unemployed or go to other industries, which has a depressing effect on wages in nonunion industries due to the increase in supply of nonunion workers there.)

MAXIMIZING WAGE RATES FOR CERTAIN WORKERS. Assume that the union wants to maximize the wage rates for some of its workers—perhaps those with the most seniority. If it wanted to keep a quantity of Q_3 workers employed, it would seek to obtain a wage rate of W_3. This would require deciding which workers should be unemployed and which should work, as well as for how long each week or each year they should be employed.

Limiting Entry over Time

One way to raise wage rates without specifically setting wages is for unions to limit the size of their membership to the extent of their employed workforce when the union was first organized. No workers are put out of work at the time the union is formed. Over time, as the demand for labour in the industry increases, there is no net increase in union membership, and so larger wage increases are obtained than would otherwise be the case. We see this in Figure 14–5. Union members freeze entry into their union, thereby obtaining a wage rate of $16 per hour instead of allowing a wage rate of $15 per hour with no restriction on labour supply.

Altering the Demand for Union Labour

Another way in which unions can increase wages is to shift the demand curve for labour outward to the right. This approach compares favourably with the supply restriction approach because it increases both wage rates and employment level. The demand for union labour can be increased by increasing worker productivity, increasing the demand for union-made goods, and decreasing the demand for nonunion-made goods.

FIGURE 14–5

Restricting Supply over Time

When the union was formed, it did not affect wage rates or employment, which remained at $14 and Q_1 (the equilibrium wage rate and quantity). However, as demand increased—that is, as the demand schedule shifted outward to D_2 from D_1—the union restricted membership to its original level of Q_1. The new supply curve is S_1S_2, which intersects D_2 at E_2, or at a wage rate of $16. Without the union, equilibrium would be at E_3 with a wage rate of $15 and employment of Q_2.

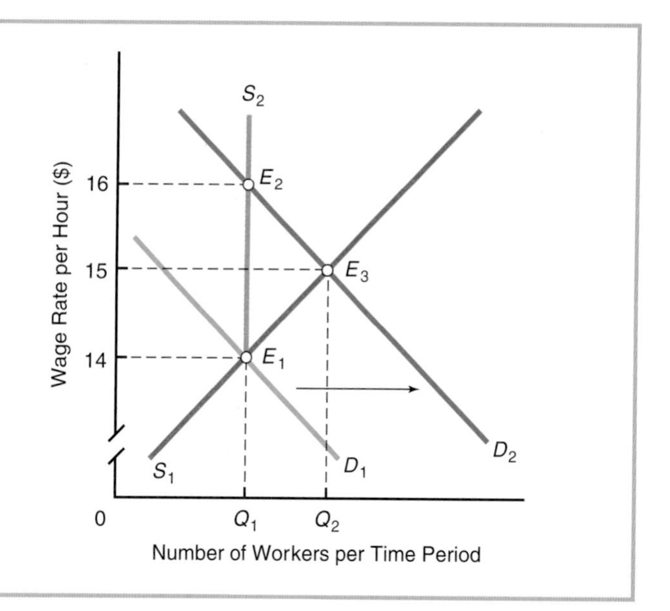

INCREASING WORKER PRODUCTIVITY. Supporters of unions have argued that unions provide a good system of industrial jurisprudence. The presence of unions may induce workers to feel that they are working in fair and just circumstances. If so, they work harder, increasing labour productivity. Productivity is also increased when unions resolve differences and reduce conflicts between workers and management, thereby providing a smoother administrative environment.

INCREASING DEMAND FOR UNION-MADE GOODS. Because the demand for labour is a derived demand, a rise in the demand for products produced by union labour will increase the demand for union labour itself. One way in which unions attempt to increase the demand for union labour–produced products is by advertising "Look for the union label."

DECREASING THE DEMAND FOR NONUNION-MADE GOODS. When the demand for goods that are competing with (or are substitutes for) union-made goods is reduced, consumers shift to union-made goods, increasing the demand. A good example is when various unions campaign against imports. The result is greater demand for goods "made in Canada," which, in turn, presumably increases the demand for Canadian union (and nonunion) labour.

Have Unions Raised Wages?

We have seen that unions are able to raise the wages of their members if they are successful at limiting the supply of labour in a particular industry. They are also able to raise wages above what wages would otherwise be to the extent that they can shift the demand for union labour outward to the right. This can be done using the methods we have just discussed, including collective bargaining agreements that require specified workers for any given job—for example, by requiring a pilot, a co-pilot, and an engineer in the cockpit of a jet airplane, even if an engineer is not really needed on short flights.

Economists have done extensive research to determine the actual increase in union wages relative to nonunion wages. They have found that in certain industries, such as construction, and in certain occupations, such as commercial airline pilot, the union wage differential can be 50 percent or more. That is to say, unions have been able in some industries and occupations to raise wage rates 50 percent or more above what they would be in the absence of unions.

In addition, the union wage differential appears to increase during recessions. This is because unions often, through collective bargaining, have longer-term contracts than nonunion workers so that they do not have to renegotiate wage rates, even when overall demand in the economy falls.

On average, unions appear to be able to raise the wage rates of their members relative to nonunion members by 10 to 20 percent. Note, though, that when unions increase wages beyond what productivity increases would permit, some union members will be laid off. A redistribution of income from low- to high-seniority union workers is not equivalent to higher wages for *all* union members.

Can Unions Increase Productivity?

Featherbedding Unions' tendency to bargain for excessive use of workers.

A traditional view of union behaviour is that unions decrease productivity by artificially shifting the demand curve for union labour outward through excessive staffing and make-work requirements. For example, some economists have traditionally felt that unions tend to bargain for excessive use of workers—referred to as **featherbedding**—as when requiring an engineer on all flights. Many painters' unions, for example, resisted the use of paint sprayers and required that their members use only brushes. They even specified the maximum width of the brush. Moreover, whenever a union strikes, productivity drops, and this reduction in productivity in one sector of the economy can spill over into other sectors.

This view of unions has recently been countered by one that unions can actually increase productivity. The new labour economists argue that unions act as a collective voice for their members. In the absence of a collective voice, any dissatisfied worker either simply remains at a job and works in a disgruntled manner or quits. But unions, as a collective voice, can listen to worker grievances on an individual basis and then apply pressure on the employer to change working conditions and other things. The individual worker does not run the risk of being singled out by the employer and harassed. Also, the individual worker does not have to spend time trying to convince the employer that some change in the working arrangement should be made. Given that unions provide this collective voice, worker turnover in unionized industries should be less, and this should contribute to productivity. Indeed, there is strong evidence that worker turnover is reduced when unions are present. Of course, this evidence may also be consistent with the fact that wage rates are so attractive to union members that they will not quit unless working conditions become truly intolerable.

The Benefits of Labour Unions

It should, by now, be clear that there are two opposing views about unions. One portrays them as monopolies whose main effect is to raise the wage rate of high-seniority members at the expense of low-seniority members. The other contends that they can increase labour productivity through a variety of means. Economists Richard B. Freeman and James L. Medoff argue that the truth lies somewhere in between. They came up with the following conclusions:

1. Unionism probably raises social efficiency, thereby contradicting the traditional monopoly interpretation of what unions do. Even though unionism reduces employment in the unionized sector, it does permit labour to develop and implement workplace practices that are more valuable to workers. In some settings, unionism is associated with increased productivity.
2. Unions appear to reduce wage inequality.
3. Unions seem to reduce profits.
4. Internally, unions provide a political voice for all workers, and unions have been effective in promoting general social legislation.
5. Unions tend to increase the stability of the workforce by providing such services as arbitration proceedings and grievance procedures.

Freeman and Medoff take a positive view of unionism. But critics of the two economists point out they may have overlooked the fact that many of the benefits that unions provide do not require that unions engage in restrictive labour practices, such as refusing to allow nonmembers to work in any particular company. Unions could still do positive things for workers without restricting the labour market.

CONCEPTS IN BRIEF

Learning Objective 14.2: Discuss the three main union goals and the five benefits of labour unions.

- When unions raise wage rates above market clearing prices, they face the problem of rationing a restricted number of jobs to a more-than-willing supply of workers.
- Unions may pursue any one of three goals: (1) to employ all members in the union, (2) to maximize total income of the union's workers, or (3) to maximize wages for certain, usually high-seniority, workers.
- Unions can increase the wage rate of members by engaging in practices that shift the union labour supply curve inward or shift the demand curve for union labour outward (or both).
- Some economists believe that unions can increase productivity by acting as a collective voice for their members, thereby freeing members from the task of convincing their employers that some change in working arrangements should be made. Unions may reduce employee turnover, thus improving productivity.

14.3 Pricing and Employment in Various Market Conditions

Monopsony: A Buyer's Monopoly

Let us assume that a firm is a perfect competitor in the product market. The firm cannot alter the price of the product it sells, and it faces a perfectly elastic demand curve for its product. We also assume that the firm is the only buyer of a particular input. Although this situation may not occur often, it is useful to consider. Let us think in terms of a factory town, like those dominated by textile mills or in the mining industry. One company not only hires the workers but also owns the businesses in the community, owns the apartments that workers live in, and hires the clerks, waiters, and all other personnel. This buyer of labour is called a **monopsonist**, the single buyer of a factor of production.

Monopsonist The single buyer of a factor of production.

What does an upward-sloping supply curve mean to a monopsonist in terms of the costs of hiring extra workers? It means that if the monopsonist wants to hire more workers, it has to offer higher wages. Our monopsonist firm cannot hire all the labour it wants at the going wage rate. If it wants to hire more workers, it has to raise wage rates, including the wage of all its current workers (assuming a nonwage-discriminating monopsonist). It therefore has to take account of these increased costs when deciding how many more workers to hire. See why cheating by colleges and universities would occur as a result of monopsony, as illustrated in Example 14–3.

EXAMPLE 14–3 Monopsony in College Sports

How many times have you read stories about American colleges and universities violating National Collegiate Athletic Association (NCAA) rules? If you keep up with the sports press, these stories about alleged violations occur every year. About 600 four-year colleges and universities in the United States belong to the NCAA, which controls more than 20 sports. In effect, the NCAA operates an intercollegiate cartel that is dominated by universities that

continued

operate big-time athletic programs. It operates as a cartel with monopsony (and monopoly) power in four ways:

1. It regulates the number of student athletes that universities can recruit.
2. It often fixes the prices that the university charges for tickets to important intercollegiate sporting events.
3. It sets the prices (wages) and the conditions under which the universities can recruit these student athletes.
4. It enforces its regulations and rules with sanctions and penalties.

The NCAA rules and regulations expressly prohibit bidding for college athletes in an overt manner. Rather, the NCAA requires that all athletes be paid the same for tuition, fees, room, board, and books. Moreover, the NCAA limits the number of athletic scholarships that can be given by a particular university. These rules are ostensibly to prevent the richest universities from "hiring" the best student athletes.

Not surprisingly, from the very beginning of the NCAA, individual universities and colleges have attempted to cheat on the rules in order to attract better athletes. The original agreement among the colleges was to pay no wages. Almost immediately after this agreement was put into effect, colleges switched to offering athletic scholarships, jobs, free room and board, travel expenses, and other enticements. It was not unusual for athletes to be paid $10 an hour to rake leaves when the going wage rate for such work was only $5 an hour. Finally, the NCAA had to agree to permit wages up to a certain amount per year.

If all American universities had to offer exactly the same money wages and fringe benefits, the academically less-distinguished colleges in urban areas (with a large potential number of ticket-buying fans) would have the most inducement to violate the NCAA agreements (to compensate for the lower market value of their degrees). They would figure out all sorts of techniques to get the best student athletes. Indeed, such schools have, in fact, cheated more than other universities and colleges, and their violations have been detected and punished with a relatively greater frequency than those of other colleges and universities.

For critical analysis: American college and university administrators argue that the NCAA rules are necessary to "keep business out of higher education." How can one argue that college athletics is related to academics?

Marginal Factor Cost

The monopsonist faces an upward-sloping supply curve of the input in question because as the only buyer, it faces the entire market supply curve. Each time the monopsonist buyer of labour, for example, wishes to hire more workers, it must raise wage rates. Thus, the marginal cost of another unit of labour is rising. In fact, the marginal cost of increasing its workforce will always be greater than the wage rate. This is because in the situation in which the monopsonist pays the same wage rate to everyone in order to obtain another unit of labour, the higher wage rate has to be offered not only to the last worker but also to all its other workers. We call the additional cost to the monopsonist of hiring one more worker the marginal factor cost (MFC).

The marginal factor cost for the last worker is therefore that individual's wages plus the increase in the wages of all other existing workers. As we pointed out, marginal factor cost is equal to the change in total variable cost due to a one-unit change in the one variable factor of production—in this case, labour. Marginal factor cost was simply the competitive wage rate because the employer could hire all workers at the same wage rate.

Derivation of a Marginal Factor Cost Curve

Part (a) of Figure 14–6 shows the quantity of labour purchased, the wage rate per hour, the total cost of the quantity of labour purchased per hour, and the marginal factor cost per hour for the additional labour bought.

FIGURE 14–6

Derivation of a Marginal Factor Cost Curve

The supply curve, S, in part (b) is taken from columns 1 and 2 of part (a). The marginal factor cost curve (MFC) is taken from columns 1 and 4. It is the increase in the total wage bill resulting from a one-unit increase in labour input.

Part (a)

(1) Quantity of Labour Supplied to Management	(2) Required Hourly Wage Rate	(3) Total Wage Bill (3) = (1) x (2)	(4) Marginal Factor Cost (MFC) = $\frac{\text{Change in (3)}}{\text{Change in (1)}}$
0			
1	$1.00	$ 1.00	$1.00
2	2.00	4.00	3.00
3	2.40	7.20	3.20
4	2.80	11.20	4.00
5	3.60	18.00	6.80
6	4.20	25.20	7.20

Part (b)

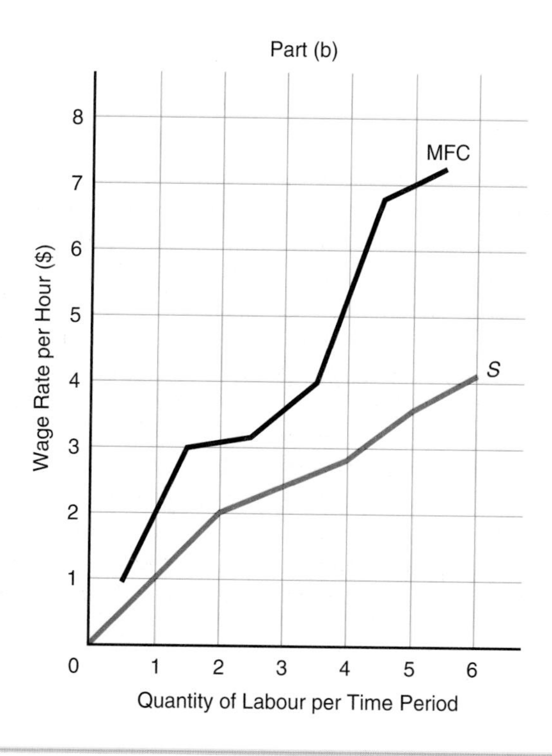

We translate the columns from part (a) to the graph in part (b) of the figure. We show the supply curve as S, which is taken from columns 1 and 2. (Note that this is the same as the *average* factor cost curve; hence you can view Figure 14–6 as showing the relationship between average factor cost and marginal factor cost.) The marginal factor cost curve (MFC) is taken from columns 1 and 4. The MFC curve must be above the supply curve whenever the supply curve is upward sloping. If the supply curve is upward sloping, the firm must pay a higher wage rate in order to attract a larger amount of labour. This higher wage rate must be paid to all workers; thus the increase in total costs due to an increase in the labour input will exceed the wage rate. Note that in a perfectly competitive input market, the supply curve is perfectly elastic and the marginal factor cost curve is identical to the supply curve.

Employment and Wages under Monopsony

To determine the number of workers that a monopsonist desires to hire, we compare the marginal benefit with the marginal cost of each hiring decision. The marginal cost is the marginal factor cost curve, and the marginal benefit is the marginal revenue product curve. In Figure 14–7 we assume competition in the output market and monopsony in the input market. A monopsonist finds its profit-maximizing quantity of labour demanded at E, where the marginal revenue product is just equal to the marginal factor cost.

How much is the firm going to pay these workers? In a nonmonopsonistic situation, it would face a given wage rate in the labour market, but because it is a monopsonist, it faces the entire supply curve, S.

A monopsonist faces an *upward-sloping* supply curve for labour. Firms do not usually face the market supply curve; most firms can hire all the workers they want at the going wage rate and thus usually face a perfectly elastic supply curve for each factor of production. The market supply curve, however, slopes upward.

The monopsonist therefore sets the wage rate so that it will get exactly the quantity, Q_m, supplied to it by its "captive" labour force. We find that wage rate is W_m. There is no reason to pay the workers any more than W_m because at that wage rate, the firm can get exactly the quantity it wants. The actual quantity used is established at the intersection of the marginal factor cost curve and the marginal revenue product curve for labour—that is, at the point at which the marginal revenue from expanding employment just equals the marginal cost of doing so.

FIGURE 14–7

Marginal Factor Cost Curve for a Monopsonist

The monopsonist firm looks at a marginal cost curve, MFC, that slopes upward and is above its labour supply curve, S. The marginal benefit of hiring additional workers is given by the firm's MRP curve. The intersection of MFC with MRP, at point E, determines the number of workers hired. The firm hires Q_m workers but has to pay them only W_m in order to attract them. Compare this with the competitive solution, in which the wage rate would have to be W_e and the quantity of labour would be Q_e.

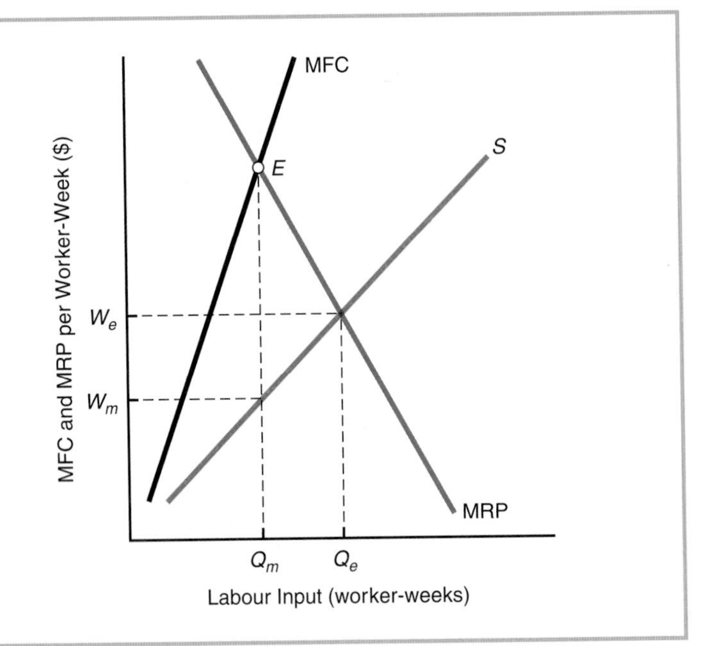

Monopsonistic exploitation Monopsonistic exploitation is the difference between marginal revenue product and the wage rate.

Bilateral monopoly A market structure in which a single buyer faces a single seller.

Note that the profit-maximizing wage rate paid to workers (W_m) is lower than the marginal revenue product. That is, workers are paid a wage that is less than their contribution to the monopsonist's revenues. This is sometimes referred to as **monopsonistic exploitation** of labour—the difference between marginal revenue product and the wage rate. The monopsonist is able to do this because each individual worker has little power in bargaining for a higher wage. The organization of workers into a union, though, creates a monopoly supplier of labour, which gives the union some power to bargain for higher wages.

What happens when a monopsonist meets a union? This is the situation called **bilateral monopoly**, defined as a market structure in which a single buyer faces a single seller. An example is a provincial Ministry of Education facing a single teachers' union in the labour market. Another example is a professional players' union facing an organized group of team owners. Such bilateral monopoly situations have, indeed, occurred in professional baseball and hockey. To analyze bilateral monopoly, we would have to look at the interaction of both sides, buyer and seller. The price outcome turns out to be indeterminate.

We have studied the pricing of labour in various situations, including perfect competition in both the output and input markets and monopoly in both the output and input markets. Figure 14–8 shows four possible situations graphically.

CONCEPTS IN BRIEF

Learning Objective 14.3: Determine the impact on pricing and employment under various market conditions.

- A monopsonist is a single buyer. The monopsonist faces an upward-sloping supply curve of labour.
- Because the monopsonist faces an upward-sloping supply curve of labour, the marginal factor cost of increasing the labour input by one unit is greater than the wage rate. Thus, the marginal factor cost curve always lies above the supply curve.
- A monopsonist will hire workers up to the point at which marginal factor cost equals marginal revenue product. Then the monopsonist will find what minimal wage is necessary to attract that number of workers. This is taken from the supply curve.

FIGURE 14–8

Summary of Pricing and Employment under Various Market Conditions

In part (a), the firm operates in perfect competition in both input and output markets. It purchases labour up to the point where the going rate W_e is equal to MRP_c. It hires quantity Q_e of labour. In part (b), the firm is a perfect competitor in the input market but has a monopoly in the output market. It purchases labour up to the point where W_e is equal to MRP_m. It hires a smaller quantity of labour, Q_m, than in part (a). In part (c), the firm is a monopsonist in the input market and a perfect competitor in the output market. It hires labour up to the point where MFC = MRP_c. It will hire quantity Q_1 and pay wage rate W_c. Part (d) shows bilateral monopoly. The wage outcome is indeterminate.

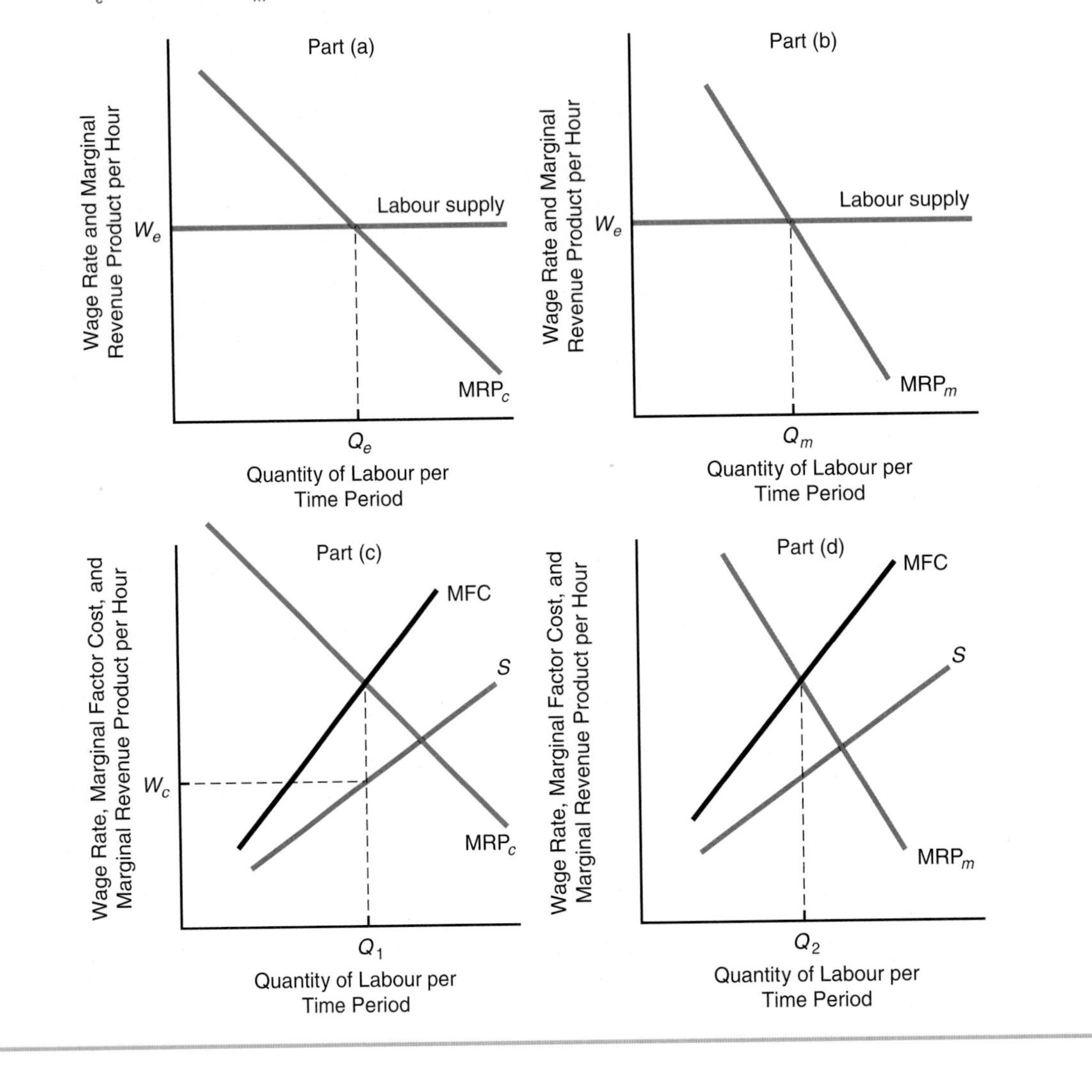

ISSUES AND APPLICATIONS

Pro Sports Means Big Bucks

Concepts Applied: Monopoly, Monopsony, Bilateral Monopoly, Collusion, Marginal Revenue Product, Marginal Factor Cost

Blue Jays' pitcher Roy Halliday has benefited from membership in the baseball players' union. High players' salaries and team profits are made possible, in part, by subsidies provided by taxpayers.

A year does not go by without a headline in the sports news that involves multimillion-dollar figures—either a new contract for a professional player that breaks all records or a team franchise that was just sold for $140 million. For many years, though, the big dollar figures were all on the side of the team owners; professional players faced classic monopsony power by the owners.

The Era of Monopsony Power

Through a variety of restrictions, professional team owners in baseball, basketball, and hockey acted in concert as single buyers of the labour services of players. The result was salaries below players' marginal revenue product. Economists Lawrence Kahn and Peter Sherer estimated that a popular NBA star, such as Wilt Chamberlain, could have earned about $3 million per year (in 1996 dollars) in the early 1970s had he been able to sell his services to the highest bidder. Instead, he was paid about $1.7 million (in 1996 dollars). A similar study done by Gerald Scully found that star hitters in baseball were paid almost $3 million per year less than their marginal revenue product in the late 1960s.

Look at Figure 14–9. In part (a), you see what happened to baseball players' income during a four-year period of strong collusion by baseball team owners. In part (b), you see what happened to profits during the same period.

The Era of Bilateral Monopoly

Through the formation of stronger and stronger players' unions, professional sports have become more of a bilateral monopoly situation. The wage rate is now higher than under pure monopsony, but it is theoretically indeterminate because it depends on the respective bargaining power of the two opposing sides. Strikes in professional baseball and hockey resulted when bargaining did not yield satisfactory results for both sides.

Taxpayers' Dollars, Too

One little-known fact concerning both high salaries for professional sports players and large profits for owners of professional teams is that both phenomena are, in part, the result of taxpayer subsidies. Taxpayers do not give money directly to baseball, hockey, and basketball players or to team owners. Rather, taxpayers give them money indirectly by subsidizing new stadiums and arenas. Just consider that in 1950, not a single stadium for baseball's National League was owned by the public; today, more than 80 percent of the league's stadiums are publicly owned. For the American League, the comparable numbers are 12 percent in 1950 and almost 90 percent today. For basketball, the number went from 46 to 76 percent and for hockey from 0 to 52 percent.

All in all, just since 1992, about $8.5 billion of Canadian and American taxpayers' money has been spent on professional sports stadiums and arenas.

For critical analysis:

1. Distinguish between a monopoly, a monopsony, and a bilateral monopoly.
2. What arguments are there to justify subsidizing professional sports?

FIGURE 14–9

The Effect of Monopsony Power on Baseball Players' Salaries and the Incomes of Team Owners

The salaries of professional baseball players remained almost flat from 1985 through 1988, the four years during which team owners successfully colluded, as shown in part (a). In part (b), you see that team owners experienced rising net incomes during that same period.

SOURCE: NATIONAL LEAGUE.

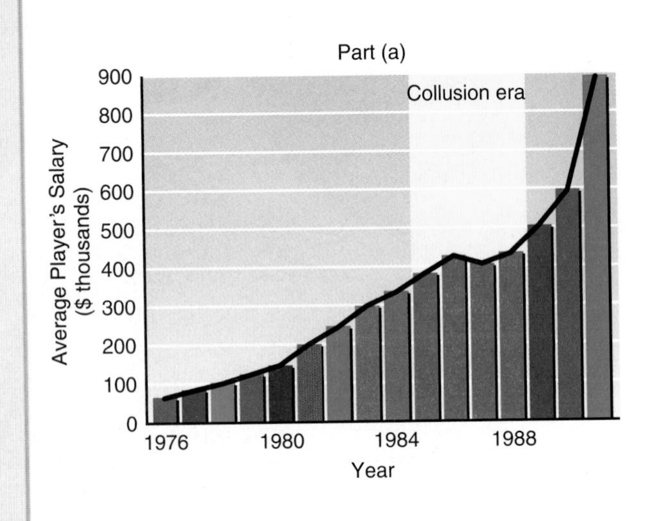

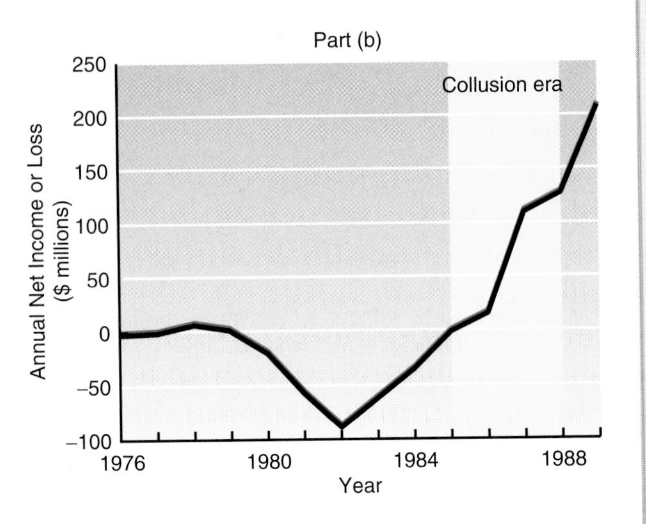

SUMMARY DISCUSSION OF LEARNING OBJECTIVES

14.1 **The Canadian Labour Movement.** The Canadian labour movement started with local craft unions but was very small until the 20th century. Important organizations in the history of labour in Canada are the Knights of Labor, the Trades and Labour Congress, the Canadian Congress of Labour and the Canadian Labour Congress.

In 1946, unions won the right to bargain collectively, to strike, and to collect dues from both members and nonmembers working in organized establishments. This right flowed from a Supreme Court decision referred to as the Rand formula.

14.2 **Union Goals and Labour Unions.** Unions raise union wage rates relative to nonunion wages. The union wage differential increases during recessions because of the longer-term nature of union collective bargaining contracts.

Because unions act as a collective voice for individual employees, they may increase productivity by reducing the time that employees spend trying to alter unproductive working arrangements. Unions may also increase productivity by reducing turnover.

14.3 **Pricing and Employment in Various Market Conditions.** Monopsony is a situation in which there is only one buyer of a particular input. The single buyer faces an upward-sloping supply curve and must therefore pay higher wage rates to attract additional workers. The single buyer faces a marginal factor cost curve that is upward-sloping and above the supply curve. The buyer hires workers up to the point at which the marginal revenue product equals the marginal factor cost. Then the labour buyer will find out how low a wage rate can be paid to get that many workers.

When a single buyer faces a single seller, a situation of bilateral monopsony exists.

PROBLEMS

(Answers to the odd-numbered problems appear at the back of the book.)

LO 14.1 Explain the history of the labour movement in Canada.

1. In Example 14–1, "Europe's Management–Labour Councils," in the European Union, management–labour councils exist. Would these work in Canada? Why, or why not?
2. Did unions protect workers during the Great Depression?

LO 14.2 Discuss the three main union goals and the five benefits of labour unions.

3. What are the three union goals?
4. What are the five benefits of labour unions?
5. Example 14–2, "Strike Activity in Canada," shows that the number of strikes has been decreasing in Canada. Explain why this might be happening.

LO 14.3 Determine the impact on pricing and employment under various market conditions.

6. The accompanying graph indicates a monopsonistic firm that is also a perfect competitor in the product market.

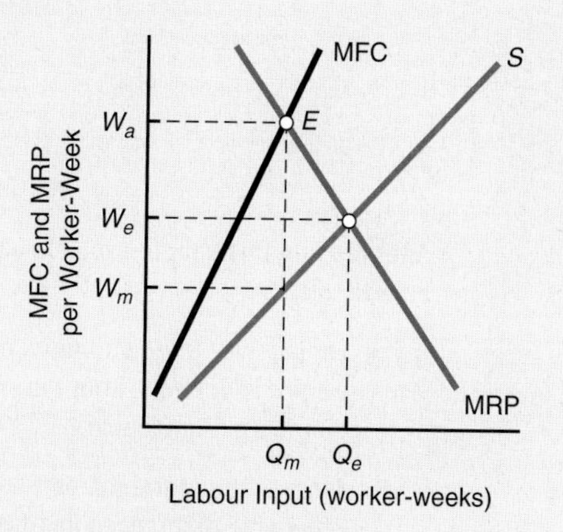

   a. What does MRP stand for?
   b. Which is the supply of labour curve?
   c. How many labourers will this firm voluntarily hire?
   d. Given the profit-maximizing employment rate, what is the lowest wage rate that this firm can offer to get this quantity of labour?

7. Imagine yourself managing a plant that is a monopsony buyer of its sole input and is also the monopoly seller of its output. You are currently employing 30 people, producing 20 units of output per day, and selling them for $100 apiece. Your current wage rate is $60 per day. You estimate that you would have to raise your wage scale for all workers to $61 per day in order to attract one more person to your firm. The 31 employees would be able to produce 21 units of output per day, which you would be able to sell at $99.50 apiece. Should you hire the thirty-first employee?
8. A firm finds that the price of its product changes with the rate of output. In addition, the wage it pays its workers varies with the amount of labour it employs. The price and wage structure that the firm faces is depicted in the following table:

Labour Supplied	Total Physical Product	Required Hourly Wage Rate ($)	Product Price ($)
10	100	5	3.11
11	109	6	3.00
12	116	7	2.95
13	121	8	2.92
14	124	9	2.90
15	125	10	2.89

This firm maximizes profits. How many units of labour will it hire? What wage will it pay?

CHAPTER 15

Income and Poverty

By some measures, Canada is one of the richest nations in the world, not only in terms of total annual national income but also in terms of average annual income per person. Despite such riches, almost 1.1 million Canadian children under the age of 18 live in poverty. Over 40 percent of people who use food banks are children. In fact, Canada ranks second among the industrialized countries, behind only the United States, for the highest rate of child poverty. Can something be done to eradicate child poverty? To answer this question, you need to know more about the distribution of income and the facts about poverty in this country.

LEARNING OBJECTIVES

After reading this chapter, you should be able to:

15.1 Explain why the distribution of wealth is different from the distribution of income.

15.2 Discuss the four main determinants of income differences and two ways that income should be distributed.

15.3 Define poverty and the four major federal income support programs.

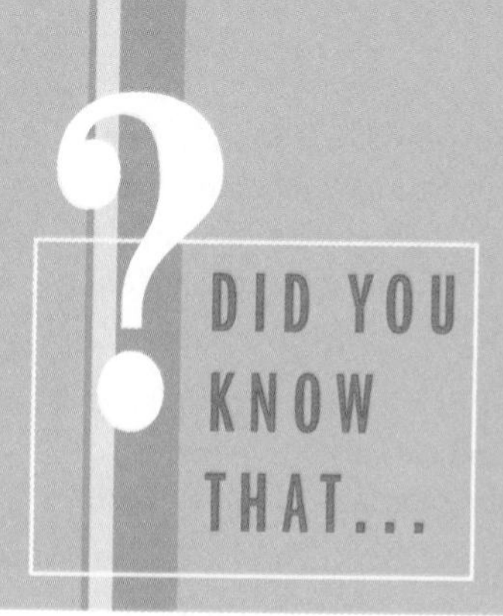

Over 300 000 Canadians earn more than $100 000 per year. That constitutes 1 percent of the Canadian population. When you go further up the income ladder, there are only about 2400 who earn more than $1 million per year, or about 0.008 percent. At the same time, over 5 million Canadians live in poverty. Why is the **distribution of income**, the way income is allocated among the population, the way it is? Economists have devised various theories to explain this distribution. We present some of these theories in this chapter. We also present some of the more obvious institutional reasons why income is not distributed equally in Canada.

Distribution of income The way income is allocated among the population.

15.1 The Distribution of Wealth and Income

Income

Income provides each of us with the means of consuming and saving. Income can be derived from a payment for labour services or a payment for ownership of one of the other factors of production besides labour—land, physical capital, human capital, and entrepreneurship. In addition, individuals obtain spendable income from gifts and government transfers. (Some individuals also obtain income by stealing, but we will not treat this matter here.) Right now, let us examine how money income is distributed across classes of income earners within Canada.

Measuring Income Distribution: The Lorenz Curve

Lorenz curve A geometric representation of the distribution of income.

The **Lorenz curve**, named after American-born statistician, Max Otto Lorenz, who proposed it in 1905, is a geometric representation of the distribution of income. The Lorenz curve shows what portion of total money income is accounted for by different proportions of the country's households. Look at Figure 15–1. On the horizontal axis, we measure the *cumulative* percentage of households, lowest-income households first. Starting at the left corner, there are zero households; at the right corner, we have 100 percent of households; and in the middle, we have 50 percent of households. The vertical axis represents the cumulative percentage of money income. The 45-degree line represents complete equality: 50 percent of the households obtain 50 percent of total income, 60 percent of the households obtain 60 percent of total income, and so on. Of course, in no real-world situation

FIGURE 15–1
The Lorenz Curve

The horizontal axis measures the cumulative percentage of households from 0 to 100 percent. The vertical axis measures the cumulative percentage of money income from 0 to 100 percent. A straight line at a 45-degree angle cuts the box in half and represents a line of complete income equality, along which 25 percent of the families get 25 percent of the money income, 50 percent get 50 percent, and so on. The Lorenz curve, showing actual money income distribution, is not a straight line but rather a curved line as shown. The difference between complete money income equality and the Lorenz curve is the inequality gap.

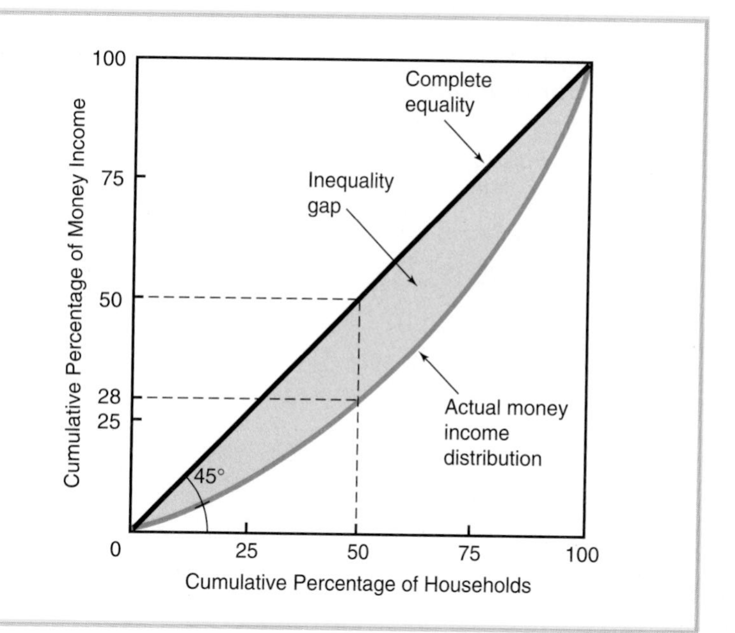

is there such complete equality of income; no actual Lorenz curve would be a straight line. Rather, it would be some curved line, like the one labelled "Actual money income distribution" in Figure 15–1. For example, the bottom 50 percent of households in Canada receive about 28 percent of total money income. In Figure 15–2, we show the actual money income distribution Lorenz curve for 1996.

CRITICISMS OF THE LORENZ CURVE. In recent years, economists have placed less and less emphasis on the shape of the Lorenz curve as an indication of the degree of income inequality in a country. There are five basic reasons the Lorenz curve has been criticized:

Income in kind Income received in the form of goods and services.

1. The Lorenz curve is typically presented in terms of the distribution of *money* income only. It does not include **income in kind**, income received in the form of goods and services, such as health care, public school education, and goods or services produced and consumed in the home or on the farm.
2. The Lorenz curve does not account for differences in the size of households or the number of wage earners they contain.
3. It does not account for age differences. Even if all families in Canada had exactly the same *lifetime* incomes, chances are that young families would have lower incomes, middle-aged families would have relatively high incomes, and retired families would have low incomes. Because the Lorenz curve is drawn at a moment in time, it could never tell us anything about the inequality of *lifetime* income.
4. The Lorenz curve ordinarily reflects money income *before* taxes.
5. It does not measure unreported income from the underground economy, a substantial source of income for some individuals.

Income Distribution in Canada

We could talk about the percentage of income earners within specific income classes—those earning between $20 001 and $30 000 per year, those earning between $30 001 and $40 000 per year, and so on. The problem with this type of analysis is that we live in a growing economy. Income, with some exceptions, is going up all the time. If we wish to make comparisons of the relative share of total income going to different income classes, we cannot look at specific amounts of money income. Instead, we talk about a distribution of income over five groups. Then, we can talk about how much the bottom fifth (or quintile) makes compared with the top fifth, and so on. In Table 15–1, we see the

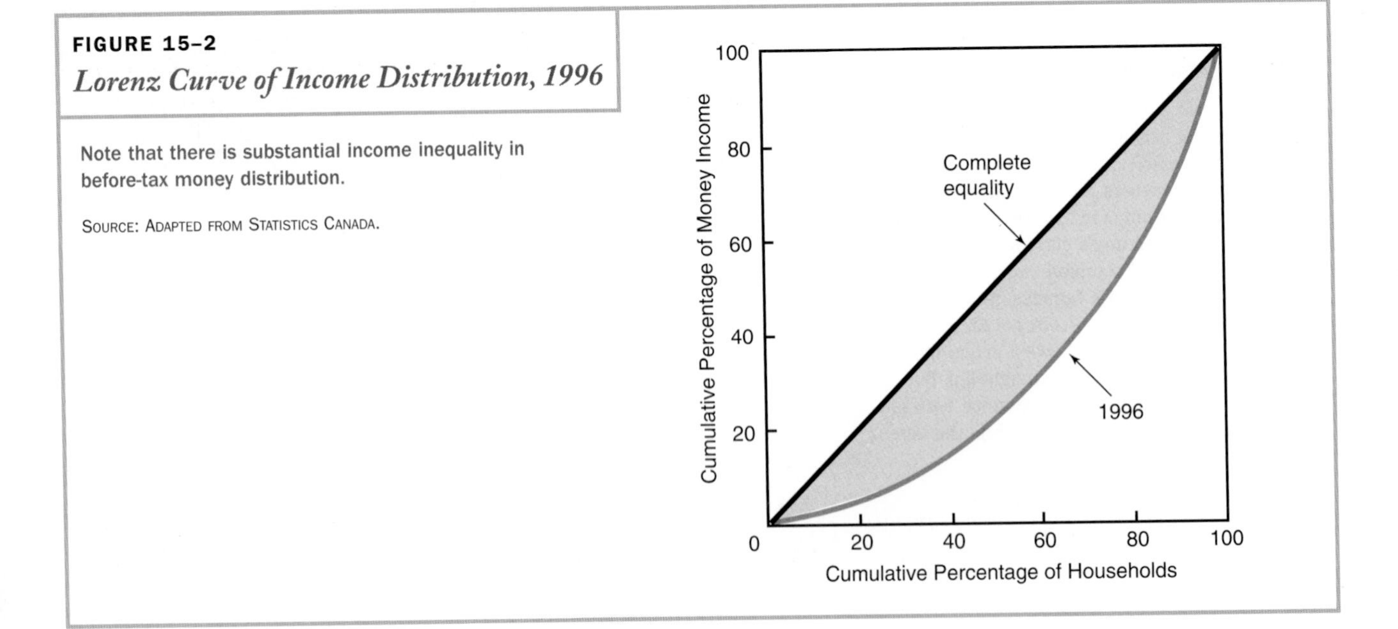

FIGURE 15–2
Lorenz Curve of Income Distribution, 1996

Note that there is substantial income inequality in before-tax money distribution.

SOURCE: ADAPTED FROM STATISTICS CANADA.

percentage share of income for households before direct taxes. The table groups households according to whether they are in the lowest 20 percent of the income distribution, the second-lowest 20 percent, and so on. We see that in 1994, the lowest 20 percent had a combined money income of 4.7 percent of the total money income of the entire population. This is a little more than the lowest 20 percent had 25 years ago. Accordingly, the conclusion has been drawn that there have been only slight changes in the distribution of money income. Indeed, considering that the definition of money income used by Statistics Canada includes only wage and salary income, income from self-employment, interest and dividends, and such government transfer payments as Old Age Security and Employment Insurance, we have to agree that the distribution of money income has not changed. *Money* income, however, understates *total* income for individuals who receive in-kind transfers from government in the form of medical care, government-provided schooling, and so on. See also how working spouses have changed income inequality in Example 15–1. In particular, since World War II, the share of total income—money income plus in-kind benefits—going to the bottom 20 percent of households has probably more than doubled. Take a look at Example 15–2 to see where Canada stands on a world basis.

TABLE 15-1

Percentage Share of Money Income for Households Before Direct Taxes

Income Group	1994	1984	1974
Lowest fifth	4.7	4.5	4.0
Second fifth	10.2	10.3	10.9
Third fifth	16.7	17.1	17.7
Fourth fifth	24.8	25.0	24.9
Highest fifth	43.6	43.0	42.5

SOURCE: ADAPTED FROM STATISTICS CANADA.

Note: Figures may not sum to 100 percent due to rounding.

EXAMPLE 15–1 Increasing Income Inequality and Working Spouses

The media have been having a field day pointing out that Canada has the fifth-greatest income inequality in the industrialized world. Underlying the statistics, though, is a little-known fact: Income inequality is measured with respect to households. No distinction is made between one- and two-earner households. If two $80 000-a-year lawyers marry, their household income is now $160 000, and they have moved into a higher income group. Not surprisingly, most single tax returns show smaller earnings than would joint returns of married couples. In 1972, some 22 percent of working-age married couples had two earners; today, that figure is 61 percent. Consequently, part of the reported increase in income inequality in Canada is simply due to an increase in the number of working spouses.

For critical analysis: Are households with two working spouses necessarily better off?

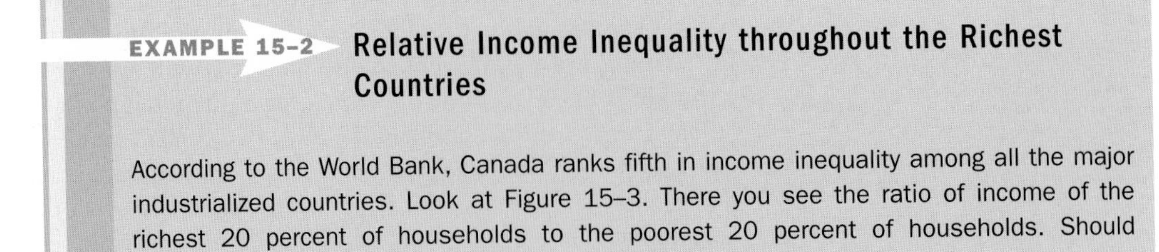

Relative Income Inequality throughout the Richest Countries

According to the World Bank, Canada ranks fifth in income inequality among all the major industrialized countries. Look at Figure 15–3. There you see the ratio of income of the richest 20 percent of households to the poorest 20 percent of households. Should something be done about such income inequality?

FIGURE 15–3

Relative Income Inequality in the World

According to the World Bank, Canada has the fifth-greatest income inequality of all the developed countries.

SOURCE: WORLD BANK.

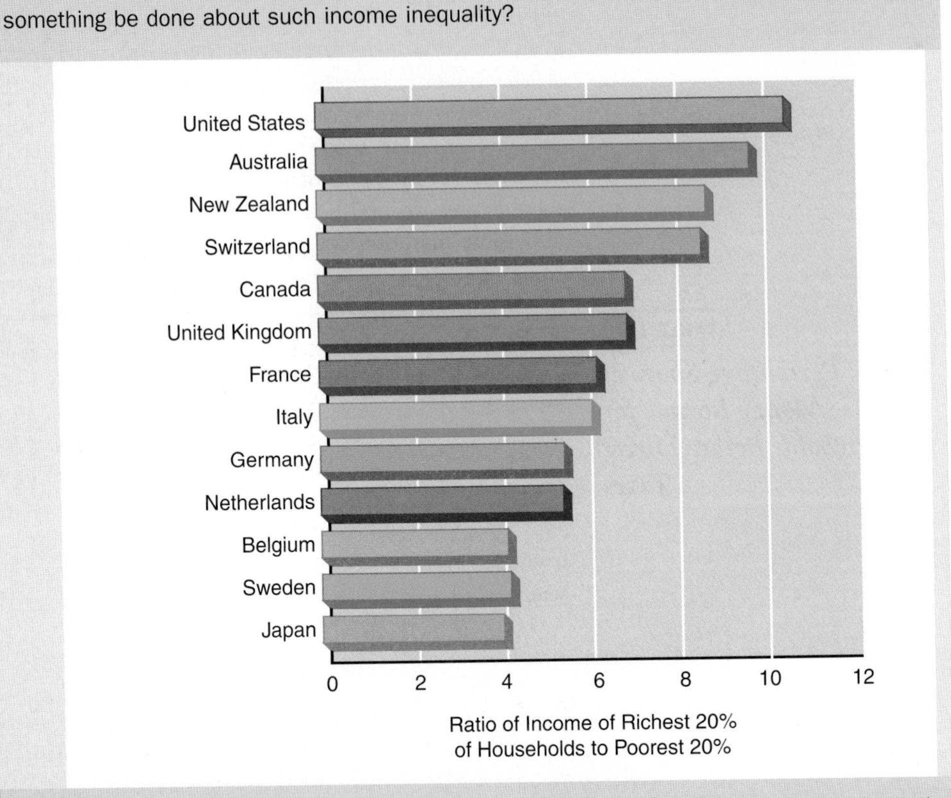

Public attitudes toward government's role in reducing income inequality differ dramatically from country to country. Whereas fewer than 30 percent of Americans believe that government should reduce income differentials, between 60 and 80 percent of Canadians, Britons, Germans, Italians, and Austrians believe it is government's job.

For critical analysis: Does it matter whether the same families stay in the lowest fifth of income earners over time? In other words, do we need to know anything about mobility across income groups?

The Distribution of Wealth

We have been referring to the distribution of income in Canada. We must realize that income (a flow) can be viewed as a return on wealth (both human and nonhuman), or as a capital stock. A discussion of the distribution of income in Canada is not the same thing as a discussion of the distribution of wealth. A complete concept of wealth would include tangible objects, such as buildings, machinery, land, cars, and houses—nonhuman wealth—as well as people who have skills, knowledge, initiative, talents, and so on—human wealth. The total of human and nonhuman wealth in Canada makes up our country's capital stock. (Note that the terms *wealth* and *capital* are often used only with reference to nonhuman wealth.) The capital stock consists of anything that can generate utility to individuals in the future. A fresh ripe tomato is not part of our capital stock. It has to be eaten before it turns rotten, and once it has been eaten, it can no longer generate satisfaction.

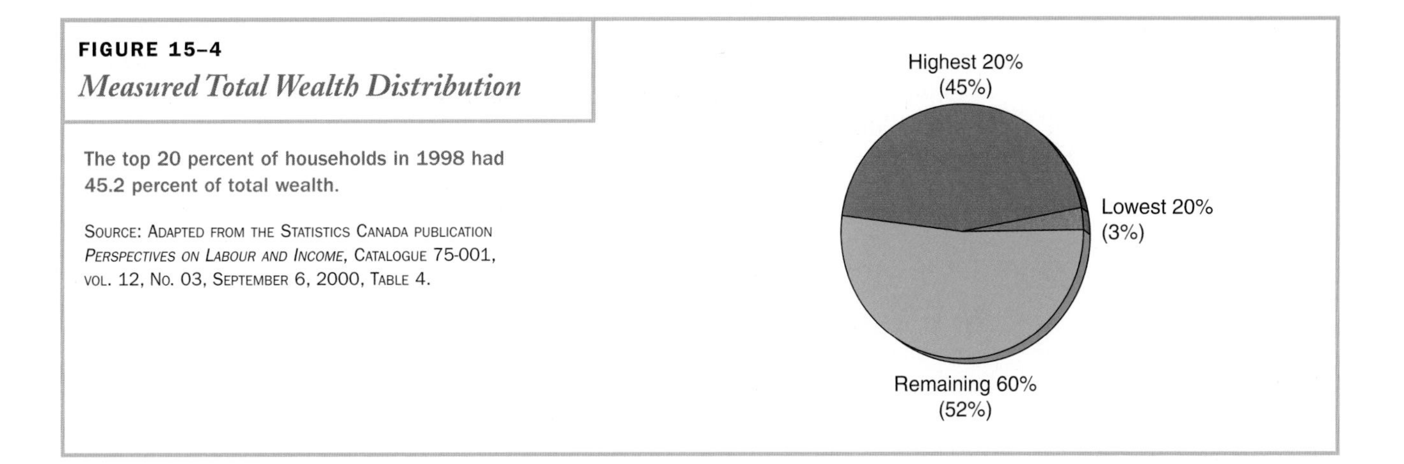

FIGURE 15–4
Measured Total Wealth Distribution

The top 20 percent of households in 1998 had 45.2 percent of total wealth.

SOURCE: ADAPTED FROM THE STATISTICS CANADA PUBLICATION *PERSPECTIVES ON LABOUR AND INCOME*, CATALOGUE 75-001, VOL. 12, NO. 03, SEPTEMBER 6, 2000, TABLE 4.

Figure 15–4 shows that the richest 20 percent of Canadian households hold about one-half of all wealth. The problem with those data is that they do not include many important assets. The first of these is workers' claims on private pension plans, contributions to which totalled $19.7 billion in 1995 alone. In addition, $23 billion was contributed to registered retirement savings plans that year. And public pension wealth is also left out. Contributions to the Canada Pension Plan (CPP) and the Quebec Pension Plan (QPP) totalled another $12.8 billion in 1995. Most of this additional wealth is "owned" by the middle class. How has this impacted our standard of living? Check out Example 15–3.

EXAMPLE 15–3 Are We Running to Stay in Place?

There are a lot of statistics to show that the typical working person in Canada has not experienced an increase in standard of living for the last 20 years. If we correct take-home wages for inflation, that is an accurate statement. Indeed, Statistics Canada has frequently shown that real wages have actually fallen since 1980. There are at least two problems with such statements, though. The first concerns total compensation. Compensation of workers does not consist solely of wages. Whereas in 1971, nonsalary benefits (Workers' Compensation, Employment Insurance, pension payments, and so on) amounted to 8.5 percent of wages, they now come to around 30 percent. Second, even if after-tax real wages have not increased, the typical Canadian household is at least 20 percent better off than in 1971. Why? Because more households have a second breadwinner. Furthermore, fewer babies are being born, and so expenses per household are lower.

One other piece of data is telling: Virtually every measure of consumption per capita is growing, year in and year out. Consequently, the majority of Canadians continue to experience increases in their standard of living as measured by their actual purchases of goods and services.

For critical analysis: Why might an individual be most concerned about total compensation?

CONCEPTS IN BRIEF

Learning Objective 15.1: Explain why the distribution of wealth is different from the distribution of income.

- The Lorenz curve graphically represents the distribution of income. If it is a straight line, there is complete equality of income. The more it is bowed, the more inequality of income exists.

- The distribution of wealth is not the same as the distribution of income. Wealth includes such assets as houses, shares, and bonds. Although the apparent distribution of wealth seems to be more concentrated at the top, the data used are not very accurate, and most summary statistics fail to take account of workers' claims on private and public pensions, which are substantial.

15.2 *Determinants of Income Differences*

We know that there are income differences—that is not in dispute. A more important question is why these differences in income occur, for if we know why they do, perhaps we can change public policy, particularly with respect to helping people in the lowest income classes climb the income ladder. What is more, if we know the reasons for income differences, we can ascertain whether any of these determinants have changed over time. We will look at four income difference determinants: age, marginal productivity, inheritance, and discrimination.

Age

Age turns out to be a determinant of income because with age comes, usually, more education, more training, and more experience. It is not surprising that within every class of income earners, there seem to be regular cycles of earning behaviour. Most individuals earn more when they are middle-aged than when they are younger or older. We call this the **age–earnings cycle**, the regular earnings profile of an individual throughout that person's lifetime.

Age–earnings cycle The regular earnings profile of an individual throughout that person's lifetime.

THE AGE–EARNINGS CYCLE. Every occupation has its own age–earnings cycle, and every individual will probably experience some variation from the average. Nonetheless, we can characterize the typical age–earnings cycle graphically in Figure 15–5. Here, we see that at age 18, income is relatively low. Income gradually rises until it peaks at about age 50. Then it falls until retirement, when it becomes zero (that is, currently earned income becomes zero, although retirement payments may then commence). The reason for such a regular cycle in earnings is fairly straightforward. When individuals start working at a young age, they typically have no work-related experience. Their ability to produce is less than that of more seasoned workers—that is, their productivity is lower. As they become older, they obtain more training and accumulate more experience. Their productivity rises, and they are therefore paid more. They also generally start to work longer hours. As the age of 50 approaches, the productivity of individual workers usually peaks. So, too, do the number of hours per week that are worked. After this peak in the age–earnings cycle, the detrimental effects of aging—decreases in stamina, strength,

FIGURE 15–5

Typical Age–Earnings Profile

Within every class of income earners there is usually a typical age–earnings profile. Earnings are lowest when starting work at age 18, reach their peak at around age 50, and then taper off until retirement around age 65, when they become zero for most people. The rise in earnings up to age 50 is usually due to increased experience, longer working hours, and better training and schooling. (We abstract from economywide productivity changes that would shift the entire curve upward.)

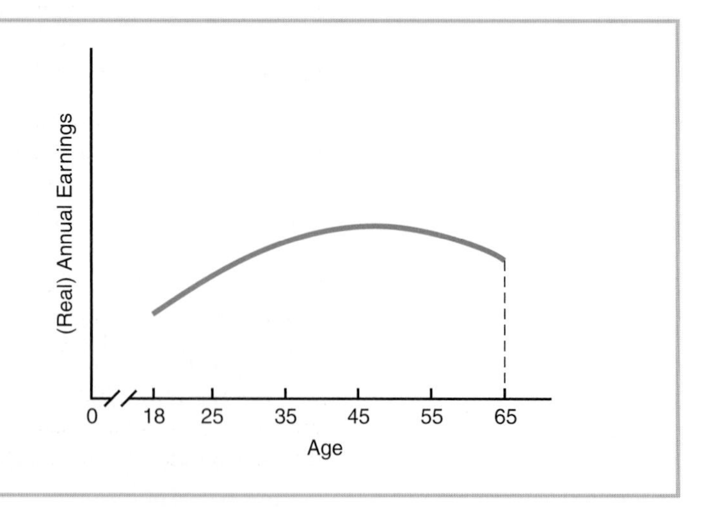

reaction time, and the like—usually outweigh any increases in training or experience. Also, hours worked usually start to fall for older people. Finally, as a person reaches retirement, both productivity and hours worked diminish rather drastically.

Note that general increases in overall productivity for the entire workforce will result in an upward shift in the typical age–earnings profile given in Figure 15–5. Thus, even at the end of the age–earnings cycle, when just about to retire, the worker would not receive a really low wage compared with the starting wage 45 years earlier. The wage would be higher due to factors that contribute to rising real wages for everyone, regardless of the stage in the age–earnings cycle.

Now we have some idea why specific individuals earn different incomes at different times in their lives, but we have yet to explain why different people are paid different amounts of money for their labour. One way to explain this is to recall the marginal productivity theory.

Marginal Productivity

When trying to determine how many workers a firm would hire, we had to construct a marginal revenue product curve. We found that as more workers were hired, the marginal revenue product fell due to diminishing marginal returns. If the forces of demand and supply established a certain wage rate, workers would be hired until their marginal physical product times marginal revenue was equal to the going wage rate. Then the hiring would stop. This analysis suggests what workers can expect to be paid in the labour market: They can each expect to be paid their marginal revenue product (assuming that there are low-cost information flows and that the labour and product markets are competitive).

In a competitive situation, with mobility of labour resources (at least on the margin), workers who are being paid less than their marginal revenue product will be bid away to better employment opportunities. Either they will seek better employment themselves, or other employers will offer them a slightly higher wage rate. This process will continue until each worker is being paid that individual's marginal revenue product.

You may balk at the suggestion that people are paid their marginal revenue product because you may personally know individuals whose MRP is more or less than what they are being paid. Such a situation may, in fact, exist because we do not live in a world of perfect information or in a world with perfectly competitive input and output markets. Employers cannot always seek out the most productive employees available. It takes resources to research the past records of potential employees, their training, their education, and their abilities. Nonetheless, competition creates a tendency toward equality of wages and MRP.

DETERMINANTS OF MARGINAL PRODUCTIVITY. If we accept marginal revenue product theory, we have a way of finding out how people can earn higher incomes. If they can increase the value of their marginal physical product, they can expect to be paid more. Some of the determinants of marginal physical product are talent, education, experience, and training. Most of these are means by which marginal physical product can be increased. Let us examine them in greater detail.

TALENT. This factor is the easiest to explain but difficult to acquire if you do not have it. Innate abilities and attributes can be very strong, if not overwhelming, determinants of a person's potential productivity. Strength, coordination, and mental alertness are facets of nonacquired human capital and thus have some bearing on the ability to earn income. Someone who is extremely tall has a better chance of being a basketball player than someone who is short. A person born with a superior talent for abstract thinking has a better chance of making a relatively higher income as a mathematician or a physicist than someone who is not born with that talent.

EXPERIENCE. Additional experience at particular tasks is another way of increasing productivity. Experience can be linked to the well-known *learning curve* that applies when the same task is done over and over. The worker repeating a task becomes more efficient:

The worker can do the same task in less time or in the same amount of time but better. Take an example of a person going to work on an automobile assembly line. At first, the individual is able to fasten only three bolts every two minutes. Then, the worker becomes more adept and can fasten four bolts in the same time plus insert a rubber guard on the bumper. After a few more weeks, another task can be added. Experience allows this individual to improve productivity. The more effectively people learn to do something, the more quickly they can do it and the more efficient they are. Hence, we would expect experience to lead to higher productivity. And we would expect people with more experience to be paid more than those with less experience. More experience, however, does not guarantee a higher wage rate. The *demand* for a person's services must also exist. Spending a long time to become a first-rate archer in modern society would probably add very little to a person's income. Experience has value only if the output is demanded by society. Look at Example 15–4 to see the impact of age on productivity.

EXAMPLE 15–4 Economics, Aging, and Productivity

Do the actions of professional economists fit the model that predicts a decrease in productivity after some workers peak at around age 50? Yes, according to economist Daniel Hamermesh. One measure of productivity of economics professors is the number of articles they publish in professional journals. The over-50 economists constitute 30 percent of the profession, but they contribute a mere 6 percent of the articles published in leading economics journals. Of economists between ages 36 and 50, 56 percent submit articles on a regular basis, while only 14 percent of economists over 50 do so.

For critical analysis: Why should we predict that an economist closer to retirement will submit fewer professional journal articles than a younger economist? (*Hint*: Normally, professors who have tenure cannot be fired.)

TRAINING. Training is similar to experience but is more formal. Much of a person's increased productivity is due to on-the-job training. Many companies have training programs for new workers. On-the-job training is perhaps responsible for as much of an increase in productivity as is formal education beyond high school.

INVESTMENT IN HUMAN CAPITAL. Investment in human capital is just like investment in any other thing. If you invest in yourself by going to college or university, rather than going to work after high school and earning more current income, you will presumably be rewarded in the future with a higher income or a more interesting job (or both). This is exactly the motivation that underlies the decision of many students to obtain a formal higher education. Undoubtedly there would be students going to school even if the rate of return on formal education were zero or negative. But we do expect that the higher the rate of return on investing in ourselves, the more such investment there will be. Statistics Canada data demonstrate conclusively that on average, high school graduates make more than elementary-school graduates and that university graduates make more than high-school graduates. The estimated annual income of a full-time worker with four years of university in the mid-1990s was about $50 000. That person's high school counterpart was estimated to earn only $30 000, which gives a "university premium" of about 67 percent. Generally, the rate of return on investment in human capital is on a par with the rate of return on investment in other areas.

To figure out the rate of return on an investment in a university education, we first have to figure out the marginal costs of going to school. The main cost is not what you have to pay for books, fees, and tuition, but rather the income you forgo. *The main cost of education is the income forgone—the opportunity cost of not working.* In addition, the direct expenses of going to university must be paid. Not all students forgo all income during their university years. Many work part-time. Taking account of those who work part-time and those who are supported by grants and other scholarships, the average rate of return on going to university is somewhere between 8 and 12 percent. This is not a bad rate. Of course, this type of computation does leave out all the consumption benefits you get from going to university. Also omitted from the calculations is the change in personality after going to university. You undoubtedly come out a different person. Most people who go through university feel that they have improved themselves both culturally and intellectually in addition to having increased their potential marginal revenue product so that they can make more income. How do we measure the benefit from expanding our horizons and our desire to experience different things in life? This is not easy to measure, and such non-money benefits from investing in human capital are not included in normal calculations.

Inheritance

It is not unusual to inherit cash, jewellery, shares, bonds, and homes or other real estate. Yet, only about 8 percent of income inequality in Canada can be traced to differences in wealth that was inherited. If, for some reason, government confiscated all property that had been inherited, there would be very little measured change in the distribution of income in Canada.

Discrimination

Economic discrimination occurs whenever workers with the same marginal revenue product receive unequal pay due to some noneconomic factor, such as their race, gender, or age. Alternatively, it occurs when there is unequal access to labour markets. It is possible—and, indeed, quite obvious—that discrimination affects the distribution of income. Certain groups in our society are not paid wages at rates comparable with those received by other groups, even when we correct for productivity and education. Differences in income remain between whites and nonwhites and between men and women. For example, the median wage for Aboriginal men is about 80 percent that of white men. The median wage rate of women is about 73 percent that of men. What we need to do is discover why differences in income between groups exist and then determine if factors other than discrimination in the labour market can explain them. Then the unexplained part of income differences can rightfully be considered the result of discrimination.

THE DOCTRINE OF COMPARABLE WORTH. Discrimination can occur because of barriers to entry in higher-paying occupations and because of discrimination in the acquisition of human capital. Consider the distribution of highest-paying and lowest-paying occupations. The lowest-paying jobs are dominated by females, both white and nonwhite. For example, the proportion of women in secretarial, clerical, janitorial, and food service jobs ranges from 60 percent (food and beverage service) to 80 percent (clerical). Proponents of the **comparable-worth doctrine**—the belief that women should receive the same wages as men if the levels of skill and responsibility in their jobs are equivalent—feel that female secretaries, janitors, and food service workers should be making salaries comparable to those of male truck drivers or construction workers, assuming that the levels of skill and responsibility in these jobs are comparable. These advocates also believe that a comparable-worth policy would benefit the economy overall. They contend that adjusting the wages of workers in female-dominated jobs upward would create a move toward more efficient and less discriminatory labour markets.

Comparable-worth doctrine The belief that women should receive the same wages as men if the levels of skill and responsibility in their jobs are equivalent.

Theories of Desired Income Distribution

We have talked about the factors affecting the distribution of income, but we have not yet mentioned the normative issue of how income *ought* to be distributed. This, of course, requires a value judgment. We are talking about the problem of economic justice. We can never completely resolve this problem because there are always going to be conflicting values. It is impossible to give all people what each thinks is just. Nonetheless, two particular normative standards for the distribution of income have been popular with economists. These are income distribution based on productivity and income distribution based on equality.

Productivity

The *productivity standard* for the distribution of income can be stated simply as "To each according to what he or she produces." This is also called the *contributive standard* because it is based on the principle of rewarding according to the contribution to society's total output. It is also sometimes referred to as the *merit standard* and is one of the oldest concepts of justice. People are rewarded according to merit, and merit is judged by one's ability to produce what is considered useful by society.

However, just as any standard is a value judgment, so is the productivity standard. It is rooted in the capitalist ethic and has been attacked vigorously by some economists and philosophers, including Karl Marx, who felt that people should be rewarded according to need and not according to productivity.

We measure a person's productive contribution in a capitalist system by the market value of that person's output. We have already referred to this as the marginal revenue product theory of wage determination.

Do not immediately jump to the conclusion that in a world of income distribution determined by productivity, society will necessarily allow the aged, the infirm, and the physically or mentally challenged to die of starvation because they are unproductive. In Canada today, the productivity standard is mixed with a standard based on people's "needs" so that the aged, the physically and mentally challenged, the involuntarily unemployed, the very young, and other unproductive (in the market sense of the word) members of the economy are provided for through private and public transfers.

Equality

The *egalitarian principle* of income distribution is simply "To each exactly the same." Everyone would have exactly the same amount of income. This criterion of income distribution has been debated as far back as biblical times. This system of income distribution has been considered equitable, meaning that presumably everybody is dealt with fairly and equally. There are problems, however, with an income distribution that is completely equal.

Some jobs are more unpleasant or more dangerous than others. Should the people undertaking these jobs be paid exactly the same as everyone else? Indeed, under an equal distribution of income, what incentive would there be for individuals to take risky, hazardous, or unpleasant jobs at all? What about overtime? Who would be willing to work overtime without additional pay? There is another problem: If everyone earned the same income, what incentive would there be for individuals to invest in their own human capital—a costly and time-consuming process?

Just consider the incentive structure within a corporation. Much of the pay differential between, say, the CEO and all of the vice-presidents is meant to create competition among the vice-presidents for the CEO's job. The result is higher productivity. If all incomes were the same, much of this competition would disappear, and productivity would fall.

There is some evidence that differences in income lead to higher rates of economic growth. Future generations are therefore made better off. Elimination of income differences may reduce the rate of economic growth and cause future generations to be poorer than they otherwise might have been.

CONCEPTS IN BRIEF

Learning Objective 15.2: Discuss the four main determinants of income differences and two ways that income should be distributed.

- Most people follow an age–earnings cycle in which they earn relatively small incomes when they first start working, increase their incomes until about age 50, and then slowly experience a decrease in their real incomes as they approach retirement.
- If we accept the marginal revenue product theory of wages, workers can expect to be paid their marginal revenue product. However, full adjustment is never obtained, and so some workers may be paid more or less than their MRP.
- Marginal physical productivity depends on talent, education, experience, and training.
- Going to school and receiving on-the-job training can be considered an investment in human capital. The main cost of education is the opportunity cost of not working.
- Proponents of the comparable-worth doctrine contend that disparate jobs can be compared by examining efforts, skill, and educational training and that wages should therefore be paid on the basis of this comparable worth.
- Two normative standards for income distribution are income distribution based on productivity and income distribution based on equality.

15.3 Poverty and Federal Income Support Programs

Throughout the history of the world, mass poverty has been accepted as inevitable. However, this country and others, particularly in the Western world, have sustained enough economic growth in the past several hundred years so that *mass* poverty can no longer be said to be a problem for these fortunate countries. As a matter of fact, the residual poverty in Canada strikes us as bizarre, an anomaly. How can there still be so much poverty in a country of such abundance? Having talked about the determinants of the distribution of income, we now have at least some ideas of why some people are destined to remain low-income earners throughout their lives.

There are methods of transferring income from the relatively well-to-do to the relatively poor, and as a country, we Canadians have been using them for a long time. Today, we have a vast array of income support programs set up for the purpose of redistributing income. However, we know that these programs have not been entirely successful. Are there alternatives to our current income support system? Is there a better method of helping the poor? Before we answer these questions, let us look at the concept of poverty in more detail and at the characteristics of the poor. See Example 15–5 to see if other countries are more successful.

EXAMPLE 15–5 **Poverty Rates in the European Union**

For years, politicians throughout much of the European Union have proclaimed their unwillingness to adopt the more *laissez-faire*, "let the chips fall where they may" economic model that prevails in the United States. They are convinced that the result is too much poverty. But they were shocked to discover in an article published in the newspaper *Le Monde* in 1997 that the poverty rate for the European Union was more than 17 percent—fully 57 million people out of a population of 330 million. Whereas the poverty rate in the United States

continued

has hovered between 13 and 15 percent of the population since the 1970s, the rate in Europe has increased over the same period from 10 percent to the current 17 percent. One-third of the officially poor in the European Union work, one-third are retired, and one-third are unemployed.

For critical analysis: What problems might there be in comparing poverty rates across nations? We see in Figure 15–6 that in Canada, the proportion of individuals classified as poor rose from 1980 to 1985 during the recession of the early 1980s. The percentage of poor then fell between 1985 and 1989, only to rise again during the recession of the early 1990s.

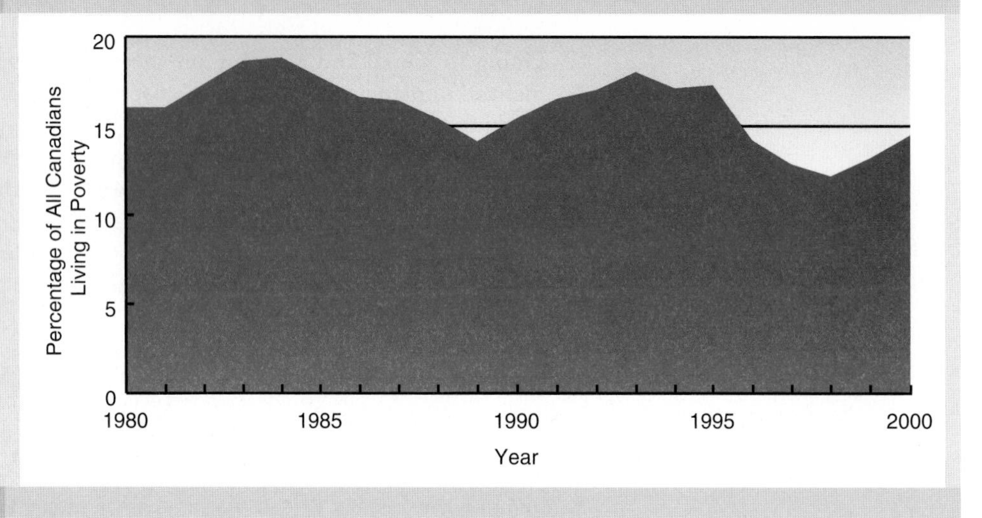

FIGURE 15–6

The Proportion of People Who Are Poor in Canada

The proportion of Canadians classified as poor rose in the early 1980s. It then fell between 1985 and 1989, then it rose again during the early 1990s. It dropped in 1998 and then began rising again.

SOURCE: ADAPTED FROM THE STATISTICS CANADA PUBLICATION *THE DAILY*, CATALOGUE 11-001, MONDAY, JUNE 12, 2000.

Defining Poverty

There is no official poverty line announced each year in Canada. However, Statistics Canada releases income thresholds, which it calls low-income cut-offs (LICOs), below which families and individuals are said to be living in "straitened circumstances." The LICO is widely used by both government and nongovernment agencies as a poverty line.

Statistics Canada first defined the LICO in 1959 as 70 percent of the average family income. It reasoned that the average family required one-half of its income to pay for necessities—food, shelter, and clothing. Thus, any family that needed 20 percent more than the average for necessities would have insufficient income left for transportation, health care, recreation, and so on. (The choice of 20 percent was arbitrary.) Over time, the LICO has changed as incomes have grown, from 70 percent of average family income in 1959 to 62 percent in 1962, 58.5 percent in 1980, and 56.2 percent in 1986 and is currently set at 54.7 percent of the average family income.

The LICO has also been expanded to apply to both families and single persons living in urban and rural areas. In 2001, the before-tax LICO for an individual living in a large city was $18 141, and for an urban family of seven it was $47 988. For rural areas, the LICO for a single person was $13 021 and $33 166 for a large family.

Transfer Payments as Income

The LICO is based on pretax income, including wages, net income from self-employment, government transfer payments—such as Employment Insurance and Canada Pension Plan benefits, scholarships, and alimony payments. Excluded from the income calculation are winnings from gambling, inheritances, and income in kind, such as food produced on the farm for domestic use. If we correct the LICO for government transfers, the percentage of the population that is below the poverty line drops dramatically. Some economists argue that the way the LICO is calculated makes no sense in a country that redistributed over $60 billion in cash and noncash transfers in 1996.

Furthermore, some of the people living below the poverty line partake in the informal, or underground, sectors of the economy without reporting their income from these sources. And some of the poor obtain benefits from owning their own homes.

Attacks on Poverty: Major Federal Income

SUPPORT PROGRAMS. There are a variety of federal income support programs designed to help the poor. We examine a few of them here.

OLD AGE SECURITY. The current Old Age Security Plan came into force in 1952. It provides for income supplements for seniors aged 65 and over, and has three components: old age security (OAS), guaranteed income supplement (GIS) and spouse's allowance (SPA).

The amount of the OAS component payment is dependent on the recipient's length of residence in Canada, with longer residence earning a higher payment. This payment comes out of the federal government's general revenue; it is indexed to the Consumer Price Index (CPI) and is raised four times each year. In 2000, over 3.7 million seniors were receiving cheques averaging $400 per month. If the recipient's total income exceeds $53 960, however, 15 cents of each OAS dollar is clawed back through income tax.

The GIS is paid to OAS recipients who have little or no additional income. This supplement is not taxable and its size is dependent on the marital status of the recipient. While the single rate exceeds the married rate, the combined married rate exceeds the single rate. The SPA is paid to the spouse of an OAS and GIS recipient when those pension payments constitute the only income for the family. This benefit is dependent on the spouse passing an income test.

CANADA PENSION PLAN. The Canada Pension Plan (CPP) and its counterpart Quebec Pension Plan (QPP) enroll virtually all employed and self-employed workers between the ages of 18 and 70 years. Both employees and employers must contribute a percentage of the employee's earnings to the plan, which provides insurance against retirement, disability, and death. (A self-employed person must contribute both shares.) No part of the pension payments comes from general government revenues; the CPP is a "pay-as-you-go" plan funded entirely by premiums and investment earnings.

The CPP came into force in 1966; it is fully indexed to the CPI and is adjusted each January. With the increase in the Canadian population, the contributory rates have risen; in 1986, employees and employers paid a combined 3.6 percent of eligible earnings into the plan; by 1997, they paid 5.85 percent. Beginning in 1998, in anticipation of the retirement of our "baby boomers" and the estimated 75 percent increase in the over-65 population, the premium rates were increased significantly to the year 2003, when they were capped at 9.9 percent. It is estimated that the CPP fund will grow to $100 billion, sufficient to pay out the necessary pensions.

Benefit payments from the CPP redistribute income to some degree. However, benefit payments are not based on recipient need. Participants' contributions give them the right to benefits even if they would be financially secure without them. Thus, the CPP is not an insurance program because people are not guaranteed that the benefits they receive will be in line with the contributions they have made. It is not a personal savings account either. The benefits are legislated by government. In the future, government may not be as sympathetic toward older people as it is today. It could (and probably will have to) legislate for lower real levels of benefits instead of higher ones.

EMPLOYMENT INSURANCE. Employment Insurance (EI) is designed to provide income for the unemployed while they are looking for work. Like the CPP, it is funded by compulsory employee and employer contributions. Unlike the CPP, however, the premiums and benefit payments are part of the federal government's general revenues and expenditures. In 1997, there was a substantial surplus in the EI account, which helped government achieve the budget surplus that year.

The EI program replaced the Unemployment Insurance (UI) plan in 1996. While UI was designed to provide income support to contributors who became unemployed, EI is designed to help the unemployed find work as well. Re-employment benefits, such as retraining funds, act as incentives for the unemployed to find jobs in other fields. Automated job market information and federally funded job search services assist recipients in their quest for work.

Budget 2000 also increased the parental leave from six months to a year. It has been found that parents are using up to 85% of the full year available. In 2003, men's participation in parental benefits increased by 26%.

CANADA CHILD TAX BENEFIT. The federal government's primary program for helping families with children is the Canada Child Tax Benefit (CCTB). The CCTB provides families with benefits of up to $100.66 per month for each child under 18 and an additional $7 per month for three or more children. The benefit is reduced if your family net income is more than $35 000. For example, a family living in Ontario with two children under 18 with a net family income of $60 000 would get a payment of about $118 per month.

No Apparent Reduction in Poverty Rates

In spite of the numerous programs in existence and the hundreds of millions of dollars transferred to the poor, the poverty rate in Canada has shown no long-run tendency to decline. It reached its low of around 14 percent in 1981, peaked at over 21 percent in 1995, and since then has been hovering at just above 19.5 percent. Is there a way that we can reform welfare to improve the situation? We attempt to shed some light on this question in the Issues and Applications section on child poverty at the end of this chapter.

CONCEPTS IN BRIEF

Learning Objective 15.3: Define poverty and the four major federal income support programs.

- If poverty is defined in absolute terms, economic growth eventually decreases the number of officially defined poor. If poverty is defined relatively, however, we will never eliminate it.
- Major attacks on poverty have been made by income support programs, such as Old Age Security, Canada Pension Plan, and Employment Insurance.
- Although the relative lot of the poor measured by household income seems to have worsened, the after-tax gap between the richest 20 percent and the poorest 20 percent of households has been narrowing.

ISSUES AND APPLICATIONS

Eradicating Child Poverty

Concepts Applied: Incentives, Marginal Tax Rate

Food banks provide essential nourishment for millions of children who live in poverty. In spite of a federal government resolution to eradicate child poverty by the year 2000, poverty rates are still on the rise.

In 1989, the House of Commons passed a resolution to "seek to achieve the goal of eliminating poverty among Canadian children by the year 2000." However, child poverty rates have only climbed since then, as Figure 15–8 shows. One of the reasons for continuing child poverty is that many of the programs designed to help low-income families apply only to those families on welfare. The working poor—those with low-paying jobs—do not qualify and so remain below the poverty line.

Work versus Welfare

In most provinces, families receiving social assistance also receive other benefits for their children. These include free health and dental care and optometric services. Thus, finding employment brings with it a penalty: not only does the family lose its welfare payments, it also loses the subsidized services. In 1993, the federal Working Income Supplement was created to address this problem by providing a maximum payment of $1000 per family to the working poor. Nevertheless, the working poor still lag behind families on social assistance in combined federal and provincial child benefits.

An Integrated Plan

The federal and provincial governments have been working on an integrated child benefit plan to assist all poor families, whether working or receiving social assistance. For its part, the federal government will provide a child tax credit, thereby

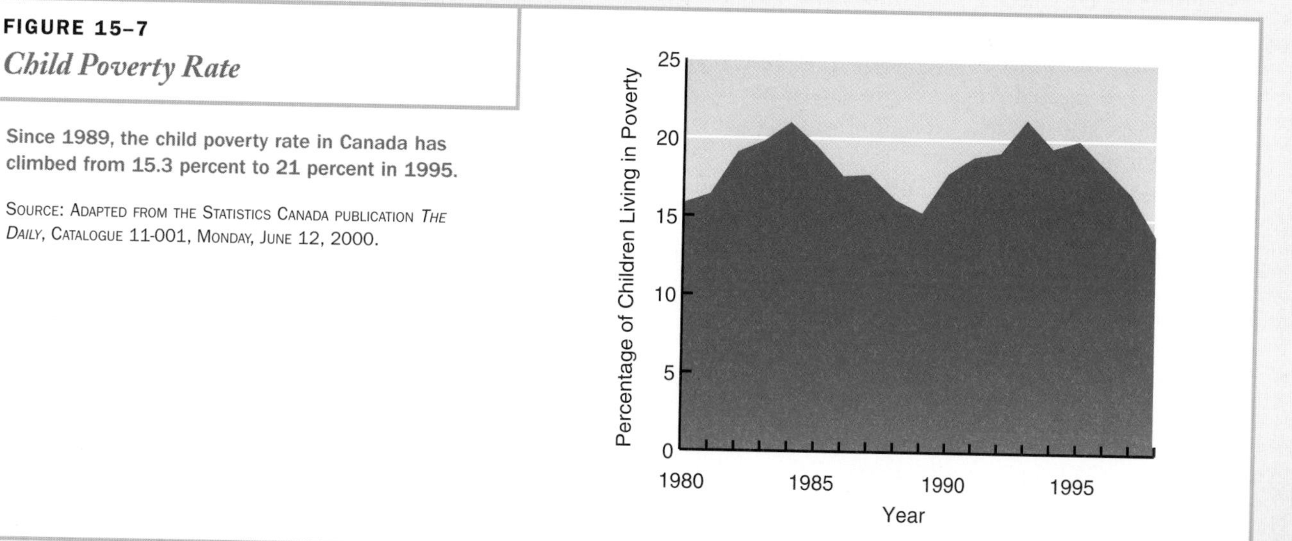

FIGURE 15–7
Child Poverty Rate

Since 1989, the child poverty rate in Canada has climbed from 15.3 percent to 21 percent in 1995.

SOURCE: ADAPTED FROM THE STATISTICS CANADA PUBLICATION *THE DAILY*, CATALOGUE 11-001, MONDAY, JUNE 12, 2000.

raising a family's after-tax income. To create an incentive for families on welfare to find employment, the provinces will cut welfare payments by a part of the additional disposable income. The working poor, however, will be able to keep all of the increase. A further condition of this proposal is that the provincial governments redirect the savings on welfare payments to other programs to aid poor children: school lunch programs and health and dental services, for example.

Several of the provinces have already reformed their welfare systems to dovetail with the proposed federal plan, and to create incentives for families on social assistance to find employment. In British Columbia, for example, the BC Family Bonus program provides benefits to both working and non-working families. A maximum bonus of $105 per month per child is paid to families with annual incomes of $18 000 or less. The bonus decreases as family income rises, finally disappearing at an annual income of $42 000 for a family with three children. Thus, the bonus acts to soften the effect of increasing marginal tax rates as the family works toward self-sufficiency. A recent study found that in BC the poverty gap for the working poor in general had been reduced by 19 percent and by 26 percent for single parents. (The poverty gap is that amount of income required to lift families below the poverty line out of poverty.)

Support Payments or Job Creation?

Critics of improved social assistance plans argue that the money put into supporting the poor would be better spent improving economic conditions, which would, in turn, lead to more jobs for the unemployed. They also suggest that falling welfare cheques act as a better incentive than child tax benefits to induce welfare families to look for work. And once the families are working, child poverty would be reduced.

For critical analysis:

1. Do you think that the new integrated child benefit plan will end child poverty in Canada? Why, or why not?
2. If the critics of improved social assistance plans succeeded in having money put into supporting the poor allocated instead to improving economic conditions, would this end child poverty?

SUMMARY DISCUSSION OF LEARNING OBJECTIVES

15.1 The Distribution of Wealth and Income. We can represent the distribution of income graphically with a Lorenz curve. The extent to which the line is bowed from a straight line shows how unequal the distribution of income is.

The distribution of pretax money income in Canada has remained fairly steady for the last 25 years. The lowest fifth of income earners still receive only about 5 percent of total pretax money income, while the top fifth of income earners receive over 40 percent.

The distribution of wealth is not the same as the distribution of income. Wealth includes such assets as houses, shares, and bonds. Though the apparent distribution of wealth seems to be more concentrated at the top, the data used are not very accurate, nor do most summary statistics take account of workers' claims on private and public pensions.

15.2 Determinants of Income Differences. Most individuals face a particular age–earnings cycle. Earnings are lowest when starting out to work at age 18 to 24. They gradually rise and peak at about age 50, then fall until retirement age. They go up usually because of increased experience, increased training, and longer working hours.

The marginal productivity theory of the distribution of income indicates that workers can expect to be paid their marginal revenue product. The marginal physical product is determined largely by talent, education, experience, and training.

Discrimination is usually defined as a situation in which a certain group is paid a lower wage than other groups for the same work.

One way to invest in your own human capital is to go to university or college. The investment usually pays off; the rate of return is somewhere between 8 and 12 percent.

15.3 Poverty and Federal Income Support Programs. A definition of poverty made in relative terms means that there will always be poor in our society because the distribution of income will never be exactly equal.

The major federal income support programs are Old Age Security (OAS), Canada Pension Plan (CPP), and Employment Insurance (EI).

PROBLEMS

(Answers to the odd-numbered problems appear at the back of the book.)

LO 15.1 Explain why the distribution of wealth is different from the distribution of income.

1. It is often observed that women, on average, earn less than men in Canada. What are some possible reasons for these differences?
2. The accompanying graph shows Lorenz curves for two countries.

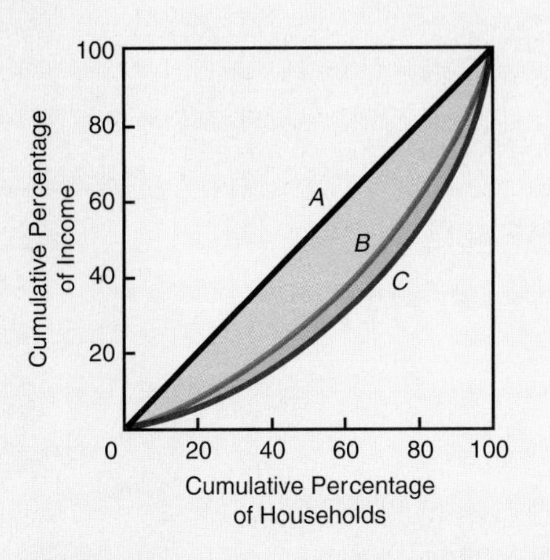

   a. Which line indicates complete equality of income?
   b. Which line indicates the most income inequality?
   c. One country's "income inequality" is described by line *B*. Suppose that this country's income is to be adjusted for age and other variables such that income on the *y*-axis reflects lifetime income instead of income in a given year. Would the new, adjusted Lorenz curve move inward toward *A* or outward toward *C*?
3. Example 15–1, "Increasing Income Inequality and Working Spouses," shows that income measures have flaws. What are some of the issues in the measurement of incomes?
4. Example 15–2, "Relative Income Inequality throughout the Richest Countries," shows income inequality in various countries. What are some problems with comparing incomes from different countries?

LO 15.2 Discuss the four main determinants of income differences and two ways that income should be distributed.

5. What are the four main determinants of income differences?
6. What are two ways that income ought to be distributed?

LO 15.3 Define poverty and the four major federal income support programs.

7. What are the four major income support programs?
8. There is no real standard measurement for poverty. Should Canada update its low-income cut-offs (LICOs)?

CHAPTER 16

Environmental Economics

Flooding, hurricanes, drought, and melting icecaps are all being pointed to as evidence of climate change. Global warming has become a "hot" environmental issue that will impact all countries of the world. So, economically, what is the impact of such things as climate change and pollution? This chapter deals with environmental issues and the costs associated with those issues.

LEARNING OBJECTIVES

After reading this chapter, you should be able to:

16.1 Explain the difference between private and social costs and how externalities can occur.

16.2 Discuss the marginal benefits and costs of pollution.

16.3 Describe how common property impacts the environment.

16.4 Explain how recycling is changing the way we look at our environment.

DID YOU KNOW THAT...

Plants pollute. That's right, plants generate toxins as nature's attempt at protecting them from being eaten. Many of these toxins are known carcinogens. There are, for example, more known carcinogens in that cup of coffee you drink than in all of the pesticide residue on food that you consume in one year. Brussels sprouts, broccoli, mushrooms, potatoes, parsnips, and pears all contain natural carcinogens. When you think of pollution, nonetheless, you are probably thinking of smelly, foul, ugly air emanating from smokestacks across the country, oil spills fouling pristine waters and killing wildlife, and other natural resources being ruined. Today, the Canadian public, in general, appears to be willing to pay more to keep the environment "in good shape." But what does that mean?

As you might expect after having read the previous chapters in this textbook, the economic way of thinking about the environment has a lot to do with costs. But of course your view of how to clean up the environment has a lot to do with costs also. Are you willing to give up driving your car in order to have a cleaner environment? Or would you pay $2 for a litre of gas to help clean up the environment? How much of your current standard of living are you willing to give up to help the environment? The economic way of looking at ecological issues is often viewed as anti-environmental. But this is not so. Economists want to help citizens and policy makers opt for informed policies that have the maximum possible *net* benefits (benefits minus costs). As you will see, every decision in favour of the environment involves a trade-off.

16.1 Private versus Social Costs

Human actions often give rise to unwanted side effects—the destruction of our environment is one. Human actions generate pollutants that go into the air and the water. The question that is often asked is, "Why can individuals and businesses continue to create pollution without necessarily paying directly for the negative consequences?"

Until now, we have been dealing with situations in which the costs of an individual's actions are borne directly by the individual. When a business has to pay wages to workers, it knows exactly what its labour costs are. When it has to buy materials or build a plant, it knows quite well what these will cost. An individual who has to pay for car repairs or a theatre ticket knows exactly what the cost will be. These costs are what we term *private costs.* **Private costs** are borne solely by the individuals who incur them. They are *internal* in the sense that the firm or household must explicitly take account of them.

Private costs Costs borne solely by the individuals who incur them; also called *internal costs*.

What about a situation in which a business dumps the waste products from its production process into a nearby river or one in which an individual litters a public park or beach? Obviously, a cost is involved in these actions. When the firm pollutes the water, people downstream suffer the consequences. They may not want to swim in or drink the polluted water. They may also be unable to catch as many fish as before because of the pollution. In the case of littering, the people who come along after our litterer has cluttered the park or the beach are the ones who bear the costs. The cost of these actions is borne by people other than those who commit the actions. The creator of the cost is not the sole bearer. The costs are not internalized by the individual or firm; they are external. When we add *external* costs to *internal,* or private, costs, we get **social costs**, the full costs borne by society whenever a resource use occurs. Pollution problems—indeed, all problems pertaining to the environment—may be viewed as situations in which social costs exceed private costs. Because some economic participants do not pay the full social costs of their actions but, rather, only the smaller private costs, their actions are socially unacceptable. In such situations, in which there is a divergence between social and private costs, we therefore see "too much" steel production, automobile driving, and beach littering, to pick only a few of the many possible examples.

Social costs The full costs borne by society whenever a resource use occurs.

The Costs of Polluted Air

Why is the air in cities so polluted from automobile exhaust fumes? When automobile drivers step into their cars, they bear only the private costs of driving. That is, they must pay for the gas, maintenance, depreciation, and insurance on their automobiles. However, they cause an additional cost, that of air pollution, which they are not forced to take account of when they make the decision to drive. Air pollution is a cost because it causes harm to individuals—burning eyes, respiratory ailments, and dirtier clothes, cars, and buildings. The air pollution created by automobile exhaust is a cost that individual operators of automobiles do not bear directly. The social cost of driving includes all the private costs plus at least the cost of air pollution, which society bears. Decisions made only on the basis of private costs lead to too much automobile driving or to too little money spent on the reduction of automobile pollution for a given amount of driving. Clean air is a scarce resource used by automobile drivers free of charge. They will use more of it than they would if they had to pay the full social costs.

Externalities

Externality A situation in which a private cost diverges from a social cost; a situation in which the costs of an action are not fully borne by the two parties engaged in exchange.

When a private cost differs from a social cost, we say that there is an *externality* because individual decision makers are not paying (internalizing) all the costs. **Externality** is a situation in which a private cost diverges from a social cost and the costs of an action are not fully borne by the two parties engaged in exchange. Some of these costs remain external to the decision-making process. Remember that the full cost of using a scarce resource is borne one way or another by all who live in the society. That is, society must pay the full opportunity cost of any activity that uses scarce resources. The individual decision maker is the firm or the customer, and external costs and benefits will not enter into that individual's or firm's decision-making processes.

We might want to view the problem as it is presented in Figure 16–1. Here, we have the market demand curve, *D*, for the product X and the supply curve, S_1, for product X. The supply curve, S_1, includes only internal, or private, costs. The intersection of the demand and supply curves as drawn will be at price P_1 and quantity Q_1 (at E_1). However, we will assume that the production of good X involves externalities that the private firms did not take into account. Those externalities could be air pollution, water pollution, scenery destruction, or anything of that nature.

We know that the social costs of producing product X exceed the private costs. We show this by drawing curve S_2. It is above the original supply curve S_1 because it includes the full social costs of producing the product. If firms could be made to bear these costs, the price would be P_2 and the quantity Q_2 (at E_2). The inclusion of external costs in the

FIGURE 16–1

Reckoning with Full Social Costs

The supply curve, S_1, is equal to the horizontal summation (Σ) of the individual marginal cost curves above the respective minimum average variable costs of all the firms producing good X. These individual marginal cost curves include only internal, or private, costs. If the external costs were included and added to the private costs, we would have social costs. The supply curve would shift upward to S_2. In the uncorrected situation, the equilibrium price would be P_1, and the equilibrium quantity would be Q_1. In the corrected situation, the equilibrium price would rise to P_2, and the equilibrium quantity would fall to Q_2.

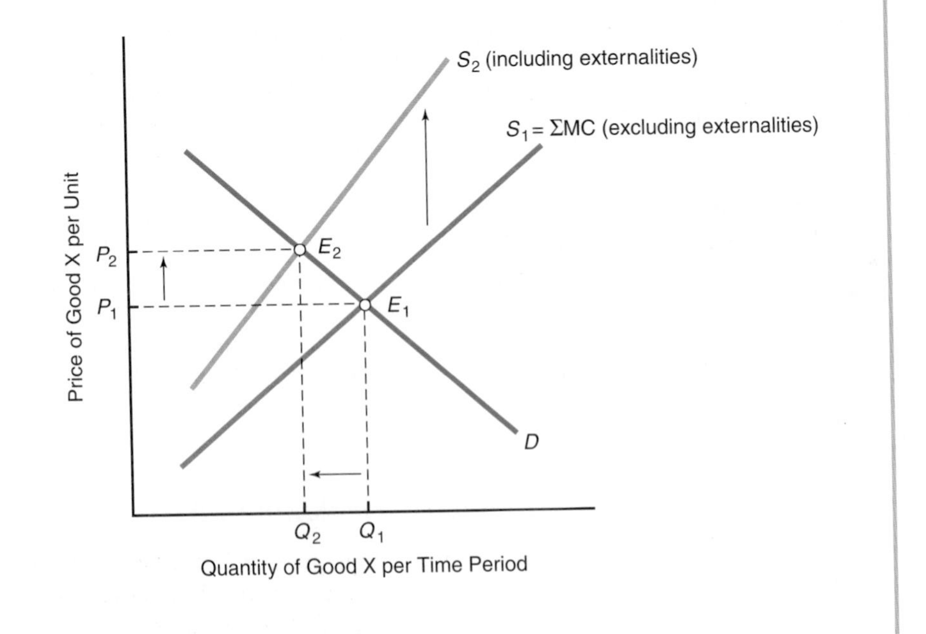

decision-making process leads to a higher-priced product and a decline in quantity produced. Thus, we see that when social costs are not being fully borne by the creators of those costs, the quantity produced is "excessive," because the price is too low.

Correcting for Externalities

We can see here an easy method for reducing pollution and environmental degradation. Somehow the signals in the economy must be changed so that decision makers will take into account *all* the costs of their actions. In the case of automobile pollution, we might want to devise some method by which motorists are taxed according to the amount of pollution they cause.

The Polluters' Choice

POLLUTION TAXES OR EFFLUENT FEES. If government were to impose a pollution tax or effluent fee on the firm according to the amount of pollution it creates, the firm might be induced to install pollution abatement equipment or otherwise change production techniques so as to reduce the amount of pollution. This can be very costly for the firm, and even extra taxes or fines might not be enough to induce the firm to change its ways.

REGULATION. If the government regulates the allowable rate of pollution, firms might be induced to reduce pollution-causing activity, or simply pay the price to pollute. One way that government has looked at regulating industries is through the use of tradable pollution permits. These permits allow the highest bidder to obtain certain pollution rights. If one firm does not use all of its allotment, and another firm exceeds its limit, the overall amount of pollution could still be reduced. One firm could sell or auction its excess allotment to the other firm, but overall the industry would have to stay within the allowable rate of pollution. Will regulation work in Example 16–1?

EXAMPLE 16–1 **The Black Sea Becomes the Dead Sea: The Results of Externalities**

The Black Sea is one of the dirtiest bodies of water in the world because for nearly 30 years, it has been the dumping ground for half of Europe—the repository of phosphorus, inorganic nitrogen, DDT, and mercury, all generated by the 165 million people living around it. Only five out of the 26 species of fish that lived in the sea in the 1960s remain. Because of pollution, the approximately 16 500 square kilometres of oyster and blue mussel fields now yield one-tenth of their previous output. Cholera outbreaks have occurred routinely because raw sewage enters the Black Sea virtually everywhere. Prior to the breakup of the Soviet Union, there was virtually no concern for the environmental degradation of the Black Sea. Currently, Russia, Georgia, Ukraine, Bulgaria, Romania, and Turkey have agreed to control maritime pollution. Because the cleanup will cost billions, it is not likely to occur very rapidly in these developing countries.

For critical analysis: If the Black Sea were surrounded by just one country, could its degradation be more easily controlled? Why, or why not?

Is a Uniform Tax Appropriate?

It may not be appropriate to levy a *uniform* tax according to physical quantities of pollution. After all, we are talking about social costs. Such costs are not necessarily the same everywhere in Canada for the same action.

Essentially, we must establish the amount of the *economic damages,* rather than the amount of the physical pollution. A polluting electrical plant in Toronto will cause much more damage than the same plant in Carstairs, Alberta. There are already innumerable demands on the air in Toronto, and so the pollution from smokestacks will not be cleansed naturally. Millions of people will breathe the polluted air and thereby incur such costs as sore throats, sickness, emphysema, and even early death. Buildings will become dirtier faster because of the pollution, as will cars and clothes. A given quantity of pollution will cause more harm in concentrated urban environments than it will in less dense rural environments. If we were to establish some form of taxation to align private costs with social costs and to force people to internalize externalities, we would somehow have to come up with a measure of *economic* costs instead of *physical* quantities. But the tax, in any event, would fall on the private sector and modify private-sector economic agents' behaviour. Therefore, because the economic cost for the same physical quantity of pollution would be different in different locations according to population density, the natural formation of mountains and rivers, and so forth, the so-called optimal taxes on pollution would vary from location to location. (Nonetheless, a uniform tax might make sense when administrative costs, particularly the cost of ascertaining the actual economic costs, are relatively high.)

CONCEPTS IN BRIEF

Learning Objective 16.1: Explain the difference between private and social costs and how externalities can occur.

- Private costs are costs that are borne directly by consumers and producers when they engage in any resource-using activity.
- Social costs are private costs plus any other costs that are external to the decision maker. For example, the social costs of driving include all the private costs plus any pollution and congestion caused.
- When private costs differ from social costs, externalities exist because individual decision makers are not internalizing all the costs that society is bearing.
- When social costs exceed private costs, we say that there are negative externalities.

16.2 Pollution

The term *pollution* is used quite loosely and can refer to a variety of by-products of any activity. Industrial pollution involves mainly air and water but can also include noise and such concepts as aesthetic pollution, as when a landscape is altered in a negative way. For the most part, we will be analyzing the most common forms, air and water pollution.

When asked how much pollution there should be in the economy, many people will respond, "None." But, again, if we ask those same people how much starvation or deprivation of consumer products should exist in the economy, many will say, "None at all." Growing and distributing food or producing consumer products creates pollution, however. In effect, therefore, there is no correct answer to how much pollution should be allowed in an economy because when we ask how much pollution there *should* be, we are entering the realm of normative economics. We are asking people to express values. There is no way to disprove somebody's value system scientifically. One way we can approach a discussion of the "correct" amount of pollution would be to set up the same type of marginal analysis we used in our discussion of a firm's employment and output decisions. That is to say, we should pursue measures to reduce pollution only up to the point at which the marginal benefit from further reduction equals the marginal cost of further reduction.

Look at Figure 16–2. On the horizontal axis, we show the degree of cleanliness of the air. A vertical line is drawn at 100 percent cleanliness—the air cannot become any cleaner. Consider the benefits of obtaining a greater degree of air cleanliness. These benefits are represented by the marginal benefit curve, which slopes downward because of the law of diminishing marginal utility. When the air is very dirty, the marginal benefit from air that is a little cleaner appears to be relatively high, as shown on the vertical axis. As the air

FIGURE 16–2

The Optimal Quantity of Air Pollution

As we attempt to get a greater degree of air cleanliness, the marginal cost rises until even the slightest attempt at increasing air cleanliness leads to a very high marginal cost, as can be seen at the upper right of the graph. Conversely, the marginal benefit curve slopes downward: The more pure air we have, the less we value an additional unit of pure air. Marginal cost and marginal benefit intersect at point E. The optimal degree of air cleanliness is something less than 100 percent at Q_0. The price that we should pay for the last unit of air cleanup is no greater than P_0, for that is where marginal cost equals marginal benefit.

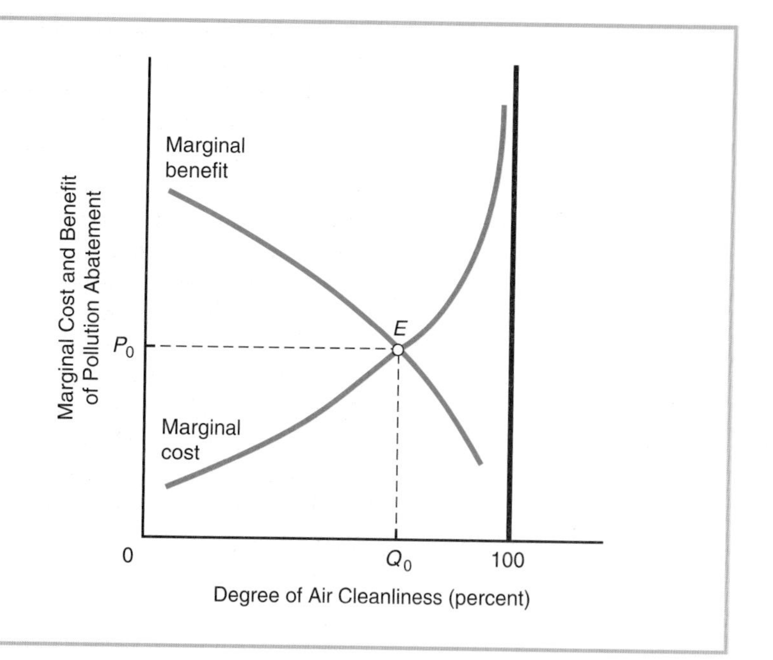

becomes cleaner and cleaner, however, the marginal benefit of a little bit more air cleanliness falls.

Consider the marginal cost of pollution abatement—that is, the marginal cost of obtaining cleaner air. In the 1960s, automobiles had no pollution abatement devices. Eliminating only 20 percent of the pollutants emitted by internal-combustion engines entailed a relatively small cost per unit of pollution removed. The cost of eliminating the next 20 percent rose, though. Finally, as we now get to the upper limits of removal of pollutants from the emissions of internal-combustion engines, we find that the elimination of one more percentage point of the amount of pollutants becomes astronomically expensive. To go from 97 percent cleanliness to 98 percent cleanliness involves a marginal cost that is many times greater than going from 10 percent cleanliness to 11 percent cleanliness.

It is realistic, therefore, to draw the marginal cost of pollution abatement as an upward-sloping curve, as shown in Figure 16–2. (The marginal cost curve slopes up because of the law of diminishing returns.)

The Optimal Quantity of Pollution

Optimal quantity of pollution The level of pollution at which the marginal benefit equals the marginal cost of obtaining clean air.

The **optimal quantity of pollution** is defined as the level of pollution at which the marginal benefit equals the marginal cost of obtaining clean air. This occurs at the intersection of the marginal benefit curve and the marginal cost curve in Figure 16–2, at point E, which is analytically exactly the same as for every other economic activity. If we increased pollution control by one more unit greater than Q_0, the marginal cost of that small increase in the degree of air cleanliness would be greater than the marginal benefit to society.

As is usually the case in economic analysis, the optimal quantity of just about anything occurs when marginal cost equals marginal benefit. That is, the optimal quantity of pollution occurs at the point at which the marginal cost of reducing (or abating) pollution is just equal to the marginal benefit of doing so. The marginal cost of pollution abatement rises as more and more abatement is achieved (as the environment becomes cleaner and cleaner, the *extra* cost of cleansing rises). The state of technology is such that early units of pollution abatement are easily achieved (at low cost), but attaining higher and higher levels of environmental quality becomes progressively more difficult (as the extra cost rises to prohibitive levels). At the same time, the marginal benefit of a cleaner and cleaner environment falls; the marginal benefit of pollution abatement declines as the concept of a cleaner and cleaner environment moves from human life-support requirements to recreation to beauty to a perfectly pure environment. The point at which the increasing marginal cost of pollution abatement equals the decreasing marginal benefit of pollution abatement defines the (theoretical) optimal quantity of pollution.

Recognizing that the optimal quantity of pollution is not zero becomes easier when we realize that it takes scarce resources to reduce pollution. It follows that a trade-off exists between producing a cleaner environment and producing other goods and services. In that sense, nature's ability to cleanse itself is a resource that can be analyzed like any other resource, and a cleaner environment must take its place with other societal wants.

CONCEPTS IN BRIEF

Learning Objective 16.2: Discuss the marginal benefits and costs of pollution.

- The marginal cost of cleaning up the environment rises as we get closer to 100 percent cleanliness. Indeed, it rises at an increasing rate.
- The marginal benefit of environmental cleanliness falls as we have more of it.
- The optimal quantity of pollution is the quantity at which the marginal cost of cleanup equals the marginal benefit of cleanup.
- Pollution abatement is a trade-off. We trade off goods and services for cleaner air and water, and vice versa.

16.3 Common Property

Private property rights Exclusive rights of ownership.

Common property Nonexclusive property that is owned by everyone and therefore by no one.

In most cases, you do not have **private property rights**—exclusive rights of ownership—to the air surrounding you, nor does anyone else. Air is a **common property**—nonexclusive property that is owned by everyone and therefore by no one—resource. Therein lies the crux of the problem. When no one owns a particular resource, no one has any incentive (conscience aside) to consider misuse of that resource. If one person decides not to pollute the air, there normally will be no significant effect on the total level of pollution. If one person decides not to pollute the ocean, there will still be approximately the same amount of ocean pollution—provided, of course, that the individual was previously responsible for only a small part of the total amount of ocean pollution. Try Example 16–2.

EXAMPLE 16–2 Wind as a Renewable Resource

Air is considered common property, owned by everyone. Some companies and governments are now starting to harness wind to create energy. The Nova Scotia power company has a green power choice that allows individuals to purchase green power, power generated from wind, for their homes. As prices for gas increase, companies are looking to produce electricity using renewable energy resources, such as wind.

For critical analysis: Why would people be willing to pay more for green energy, when air, or wind, is owned by everyone?

Basically, pollution occurs where we have poorly defined private property rights, as in the case of air and common bodies of water. We do not, for example, have a visual pollution problem when it comes to people's attics. That is their own property, which they choose to keep as clean as they want, given their preferences for cleanliness as weighed against the costs of keeping the attic neat and tidy.

Where private property rights exist, individuals have legal recourse to any damages sustained through the misuse of their property. When private property rights are well defined, the use of property—that is, the use of resources—will generally involve contracting between the owners of those resources. If you own land, you might contract with another person who wants to use your land for raising cows. The contract would most likely be written in the form of a lease agreement.

Voluntary Agreements and Transactions Costs

Is it possible for externalities to be internalized via voluntary agreement? Take a simple example. You live in a house with a nice view of a lake. The family living below you plants a tree. The tree grows so tall that it eventually starts to cut off your view. In most cities, no one has property rights to views; therefore, you cannot normally go to court to obtain relief. You do have the option of contracting with your neighbour, however.

VOLUNTARY AGREEMENTS: CONTRACTING. You have the option of paying your neighbours (contracting) to trim the tree. You could start out with an offer of a small amount and keep going up until your neighbours agree or until you reach your limit. Your limit will equal the value you place on having an unobstructed view of the lake. Your neighbours will be willing if the payment is at least equal to the reduction in the intrinsic value of their property due to a stunted tree. Your offering the payment makes your neighbours aware of the social cost of their actions. The social cost here is equal to the care of the tree plus the cost suffered by you due to an impeded view of the lake.

In essence, then, your offer of money income to your neighbours indicates to them that there is an opportunity cost to their actions. If they do not comply, they forfeit the money that you are offering them. The point here is that *opportunity cost always exists, whoever has property rights.* Therefore, we would expect under some circumstances that voluntary contracting will occur to internalize externalities.[1] The question is, "When will voluntary agreements occur?"

TRANSACTION COSTS. One major condition for the outcome just outlined above is that the **transaction costs**—all costs associated with making and enforcing agreements—must be low relative to the expected benefits of reaching an agreement. If we expand our example to a much larger one such as air pollution, the transaction costs of numerous homeowners trying to reach agreements with the individuals and companies that create the pollution are relatively high. Consequently, we do not expect voluntary contracting to be an effective way to internalize the externality of air pollution.

Transaction costs All costs associated with making and enforcing agreements.

Changing Property Rights

In considering the problem of property rights, we can approach it by assuming that initially, many property rights and many resources in a society are not defined. But this situation does not cause a problem so long as no one cares to use the resources for which there are no property rights, or so long as enough of these resources are available that people can have as much as they want at a zero price. Only when and if a use is found for a resource, or the supply of a resource is inadequate at a zero price, does a problem develop. The problem requires that something be done about deciding property rights. If not, the resource will be wasted and possibly even destroyed. Property rights can be assigned to individuals who will then assert control; or they may be assigned to government, which can maintain and preserve the resource, charge for its use, or implement some other rationing device. What we have seen with common property, such as air and water, is that governments have indeed attempted to take over the control of those resources so that they cannot be wasted or destroyed.

[1]This analysis is known as the *Coase theorem*, named after its originator, Ronald Coase, who demonstrated that negative or positive externalities do not necessarily require government intervention in situations in which property rights are defined and enforceable and transaction costs are relatively low.

Another way of viewing the pollution problem is to argue that property rights are "sacred" and that there are property rights in every resource that exists. We can then say that each individual does not have the right to act on anything that is not that person's property. Hence, no individual has the right to pollute because that amounts to using property that the individual does not specifically own.

Clearly, we must fill the gap between private costs and true social costs in situations in which we have to make up somehow for the fact that property rights are not well defined or assigned. There are three ways to fill this gap: taxation, subsidization, and regulation. Government is involved in all three. Unfortunately, government does not have perfect information and may not pick the appropriate tax, subsidy, or type of regulation. We also have to consider cases in which taxes are hard to enforce or subsidies are difficult to give out to "worthy" recipients. In such cases, outright prohibition of the polluting activity may be the optimal solution to a particular pollution problem. For example, if it is difficult to monitor the level of a particular type of pollution that even in small quantities can cause severe environmental damage, outright prohibition of such pollution may be the only alternative. Consider Example 16–3 and, later, Issues and Applications.

EXAMPLE 16–3 **Privatizing the Right to Pollute**

In late 1997, negotiators from 159 countries met in Kyoto, Japan, to work out an agreement to limit the emission of greenhouse gases, those gases produced from burning fossil fuels. In recent years, scientists have become convinced that the increase in greenhouse gases is leading to changes in weather patterns around the world—the devastating 1997 flood in Southern Manitoba is an example.

Following days of tough negotiations, the countries present finally reached an agreement. Overall, the 38 most developed countries will cut emissions by 5.2 percent. Canada, which accounts for 2 percent of world production of greenhouse gases, will cut its emissions by 6 percent by the year 2012. The European Union will cut its emissions by 8 percent, the United States, who has not signed the agreement, by 7 percent, and Japan by 6 percent. Interestingly, Australia can increase its emissions by 8 percent, and Iceland by 10 percent!

In spite of the apparent progress made at Kyoto, environmentalists are disappointed. For one thing, the Kyoto agreement creates private property rights in pollution. Each country will be given the right to produce an agreed level of greenhouse gases. Countries able to reduce emissions below the agreed level will be able to sell their unused property rights to countries that fail to meet their targets. The sale of "pollution permits" thus represents the monetization of a social cost and raises the cost of pollution in the offending countries.

In addition, on June 20, 1999, the World Bank established the Prototype Carbon Fund (PCF), which pools private and public capital and invests in climate-friendly projects in the developing countries. Returns on Canada's $15 million investment are in the form of carbon credits, which Canada, other investor countries, and companies may be able to use to help meet their Kyoto Protocol targets.

For critical analysis: How much do you think the rich countries of the world would be prepared to pay for excess pollution rights?

Are There Alternatives to Pollution-Causing Resource Use?

Some people cannot understand why, if pollution is bad, we still use pollution-causing resources, such as coal and oil, to generate any electricity at all. Why don't we forgo the use of such polluting resources and opt for one that apparently is pollution-free, such as solar energy? The plain fact is that in the short run, the cost of generating solar power in most circumstances is much higher than generating that same power through conventional means. We do not yet have the technology that allows us all the luxury of driving solar-powered cars—though such cars do exist. Moreover, with current technology, the solar parts necessary to generate the electricity for the average town would cover massive sections of the countryside, and the manufacturing of those solar parts would itself generate pollution.

Wild Species, Common Property, and Trade-Offs

One of the most distressing common property problems concerns endangered species, usually in the wild. No one is too concerned about the quantity of dogs, cats, cattle, sheep, and horses. The reason is that virtually all of those species are private property. Peregrine falcons, swift foxes, piping plovers, and the like are typically common property. No one has a vested interest in making sure that they perpetuate in good health.

The federal government's *Canadian Endangered Species Protection Act* was proclaimed into law on March 31, 2000, in an attempt to protect certain species from extinction. As well, most provincial governments have similar legislation to protect dwindling stocks of wildlife. In the mid-1990s in British Columbia, for example, logging was cut back in two forestry districts when only 30 pairs of nesting spotted owls could be located. Up to 100 jobs in forestry were lost, and the process of generating a plan to save the spotted owl cost taxpayers $1 000 000, or about $17 000 per bird. The issues are not straightforward. Today, the earth has only 0.02 percent of all of the species that have ever lived. Every year, 1000 to 3000 new species are discovered and classified. Estimates of how many species are actually dying out vary from a high of 50 000 a year to a low of one every four years. See Example 16–4.

EXAMPLE 16–4 Preventing Overfishing by Trading Quotas

Under the European Union's Common Fisheries Policy, countries are allocated quotas for the amounts of different kinds of fish that their fishermen can catch in various areas of the sea. In most European nations, governments control the allocation of fishing rights under these quotas. When a fisherman retires or dies, his quota goes into a pool to be reallocated. In the United Kingdom, however, fishermen can buy, sell, or lease their quotas. It turns out that this has had beneficial side effects for fish conservation.

The reason is that because many fishermen would like to catch more fish than their quotas permit them to catch, there is always a temptation to exceed quota limits. If a British fisherman thinks that he is more efficient at hauling in fish than another fisherman, he can buy or lease the other fisherman's quota. If he is right, he earns higher profits than he would by overfishing and trying to sell his excess catch (which the fishermen call "black fish") illegally in the black market.

Indeed, many British fishermen might be pleased if the European Union were to cut quotas in a further effort to repopulate stocks of fish. Their current incomes would fall, but the market value of their quotas would rise. The values of quotas are already relatively high. When a tragic accident recently led to the sinking of a fishing boat off the coast of Scotland, the deceased owner's quotas for herring, mackerel, and other fish sold for about $10 million.

For critical analysis: How does the existence of a market for quotas help keep the stocks of fish off the shores of Europe from dwindling?

CONCEPTS IN BRIEF

Learning Objective 16.3: Describe how common property impacts the environment.

- A common property resource is one that no one owns—or, otherwise stated, that everyone owns.

- Common property exists when property rights are indefinite or nonexistent.
- When no property rights exist, pollution occurs because no one individual or firm has a sufficient economic incentive to care for the common property in question, be it air, water, or scenery.
- Private costs will not equal social costs when common property is at issue unless only a few individuals are involved and they are able to contract among themselves.

16.4 Recycling

Recycling The reuse of raw materials derived from manufactured products.

As part of the overall ecology movement, there has been a major push to save scarce resources via recycling. **Recycling** involves the reuse of raw materials derived from manufactured products, such as paper products, plastics, glass, and metals, rather than putting them into solid waste dumps. Many cities have instituted curbside pickup recycling programs. See Example 16–5 for more discussion.

The benefits of recycling are straightforward. Fewer *natural* resources are used. But some economists argue that recycling does not necessarily save *total* resources.

EXAMPLE 16–5 Reducing Waste by Recycling

Recycling has come a long way from those first years where hardly anything could be recycled. Now cities are recycling everything from paper to computer products. In Toronto, residents can place organic materials into a green box, and in Edmonton, you can get rid of unwanted items at garbage fairs. Computers and their components are becoming a huge problem as more and more people are upgrading every one to two years, and the old computers have little or no resale value. A company in Toronto, Logic Box, hires artists to change old computer components into earrings and bracelets, and plans to sell these creations on eBay. Recycling has been proven to work as long as the people believe they are benefiting from it. Recently, Toronto exceeded its goal of reducing waste sent to Michigan by 30 percent and hopes to reduce it further to 60 percent by 2006.

For critical analysis: What are some of the benefits of recycling?

Recycling's Invisible Costs

The recycling of paper can also pollute. Used paper has ink on it that has to be removed during the recycling process. According to the National Wildlife Federation, the production of 98 tonnes of de-inked (bleached) fibre generates approximately 39 tonnes of sludge. This sludge has to be disposed of, usually in a landfill. A lot of recycled paper companies, however, are beginning to produce unbleached paper. In general, recycling does create waste that has to be disposed of.

There is also an issue involved in the use of resources. Recycling requires human effort. The labour resources involved in recycling are often many times more costly than the potential savings in scarce resources not used. That means that net resource use, counting all resources, may sometimes be greater with recycling than without it.

Landfills

One of the arguments in favour of recycling is to avoid a solid waste "crisis." Some people believe that we are running out of solid waste dump sites in Canada. This is perhaps true in and near major cities, and indeed, the most populated areas of the country might ultimately benefit from recycling programs. In the rest of the country, however, the data do not seem to indicate that we are running out of solid waste landfill sites.

Throughout urban Canada, the disposal price per tonne of city garbage is rising rapidly. Prices vary, of course, for the 20 million tonnes of garbage generated each year. Toronto plans to end its reliance on the Michigan landfill by 2010.

Currently, municipalities burn about 16 percent of their solid waste and recycle a few percentage points more. In all likelihood, partly because of increased recycling efforts, the amount of solid waste disposal will continue to drop as municipalities restrict the number of landfill sites in response to pressure from community groups that believe landfills are unsafe. If the number of landfill sites is being reduced, is it possible that we are running out of everything? See Example 16–6.

EXAMPLE 16–6 **We Are Running Out of Everything!**

It is going to be a world with no more oil, natural gas, copper, or zinc. At least that is the impression one gets these days from the media. In reality, as economists have discovered, the real (inflation-corrected) prices for most nonrenewable resources have fallen over the past 125 years. Real energy prices have dropped an average of 1.6 percent per year; major mineral prices have dropped 1.3 to 2.9 percent a year; even the price of land has dropped 0.8 percent per year. Unless supply and demand analysis is no longer valid, those numbers indicate that the supply of nonrenewable resources is increasing faster than the demand.

For critical analysis: Why would we not switch to using renewable resources?

Should We Save Scarce Resources?

Periodically, the call for recycling focuses on the necessity of saving scarce resources because "we are running out." There is little evidence to back up this claim because virtually every natural resource has fallen in price (corrected for inflation) over the past several decades. In 1980, economist Julian Simon made a $1000 bet with well-known environmentalist Paul Erlich. Simon bet $200 per resource that any five natural resources that Erlich picked would decline in price (corrected for inflation) by the end of the 1980s. Simon won. (When Simon asked Erlich to renew the bet for $20 000 for the 1990s, Erlich declined.) During the 1980s, the price of virtually every natural resource fell (corrected for inflation), and so did the price of every agricultural commodity. The same was true for every forest product. Though few people remember the dire predictions of the 1970s, many noneconomists throughout the world argued at that time that the world's oil reserves were vanishing. If this were true, the pretax, inflation-corrected price of gasoline would not be the same today as it was in the late 1940s (which it is).

In spite of predictions in the early 1980s by World Watch Institute president Lester Brown, real food prices did not rise. Indeed, the real price of food fell by more than 30 percent for the major agricultural commodities during the 1980s. A casual knowledge of supply and demand tells you that since demand for food did not decrease, supply must have increased faster than demand.

CONCEPTS IN BRIEF

Learning Objective 16.4: Explain how recycling is changing the way we look at our environment.

- Recycling involves reusing paper, glass, and other materials, rather than putting them into solid waste dumps. Recycling does have a cost both in the resources used for recycling and in the pollution created during recycling, such as the sludge from de-inking paper for reuse.
- Landfills are an alternative to recycling. Expansion of these solid waste disposal sites is outpacing demand increases.
- Resources may not be getting scarcer. The inflation-corrected price of most resources has been falling for decades.

ISSUES AND APPLICATIONS

Climate Change Impacts All Nations

Concepts Applied: Common Property, Trade-Offs, Externalities

Pollution is a concern of all nations.

Climate change is becoming a major concern in all nations, developed or not. Recently, Lord Oxburgh, chairman of Shell Transport and Trading Co. PLC, told newspapers that he was worried about the threat of climate change. He was quoted as saying "Sequestration is difficult, but if we don't have sequestration, I see very little hope for the world." Sequestration or "sinks" are forests and agricultural soils that remove and store carbon dioxide. This method of removing carbon dioxide is very expensive but the trade-off could be better management of forests and agricultural areas.

The World Bank is monitoring the reduction of carbon dioxide emissions of countries that have signed the Kyoto Protocol. Countries are able to buy and sell credits in three ways:

1. Clean Development: Countries can earn credits by investing in emission reduction projects or clean energy production in the developing countries.
2. Joint Implementation: Countries can earn credits by investing in emission reduction projects in the developed countries that have taken on a Kyoto target.
3. International Emissions Trading: The developed countries that have taken on a Kyoto target can buy and sell emission credits among themselves.

This allows countries who need more time to reduce their emissions the ability to buy credits from countries who have lowered their emissions. This gives incentives to countries that are developing to make sure that they use renewable resources for energy.

The Kyoto Protocol brings together more than 160 countries with the common goal of reducing greenhouse gases (GHGs). Some greenhouse gases are natural, but others are caused by our use of energy. So, even though air is a common property, we as individuals are being asked to help reduce the GHGs. Canada has a program called the "OneTonne Challenge" where each household is challenged to reduce GHG emissions at home by doing such things as not letting vehicles idle, composting more garbage, and lowering thermostats.

So, just ratifying the Kyoto Protocol means nothing unless individuals, companies, and governments from around the world are prepared to cooperate.

SOURCE: CANOE MONEY, http://money.canoe.ca/News/Sectors/Energy/2004/06/17/503298-ap.html

For critical analysis:

1. What renewable energy sources could be used to help reduce the GHGs?
2. Will companies just move their plants to other undeveloped countries in an attempt to comply with government regulations?

SUMMARY DISCUSSION OF LEARNING OBJECTIVES

16.1 **Private versus Social Costs.** In some situations, there are social costs that do not equal private costs—that is, there are costs to society that exceed the cost to the individual. These costs may include air and water pollution, for which private individuals do not have to pay. Society, however, does bear the costs of these externalities. Few individuals or firms voluntarily consider social costs.

16.2 **Pollution.** One way to analyze the problem of pollution is to look at it as an externality. Individual decision makers do not take into account the negative externalities they impose on the rest of society. In such a situation, they produce "too much" pollution and "too many" polluting goods.

It might be possible to ameliorate the situation by imposing a tax on polluters. The tax, however, should be dependent on the extent of the economic damages created, rather than on the physical quantity of pollution. This tax will therefore be different for the same level of physical pollution in different parts of the country because the economic damage differs, depending on location, population density, and other factors.

The optimal quantity of pollution is the quantity at which the marginal cost of cleanup equals the marginal benefit of cleanup. Pollution abatement is a trade-off. We trade off goods and services for cleaner air and water, and vice versa.

16.3 **Common Property.** Another way of looking at the externality problem is to realize that it involves the lack of definite property rights. No one owns common property resources, such as air and water, and therefore no one takes into account the long-run pernicious effects of excessive pollution.

There are alternatives to pollution-causing resource use—for example, solar energy. We do not use solar energy because it is too expensive relative to conventional alternatives and because the creation of solar parts would itself generate pollution.

16.4 **Recycling.** Recycling involves reusing paper, glass, and other materials, rather than putting them into solid waste dumps. Recycling does have a cost both in the resources used for recycling and in the pollution created during recycling. Landfills are an alternative to recycling. In rural Canada, these solid waste disposal sites are being expanded faster than the demand for them.

Resources may not be getting scarcer. The inflation-corrected price of most resources has been falling for decades.

PROBLEMS

(Answers to the odd-numbered problems appear at the back of the book.)

LO 16.1 Explain the difference between private and social costs and how externalities can occur.

1. Construct a typical supply-and-demand graph. Show the initial equilibrium price and quantity. Assume that the good causes negative externalities to third parties (persons not involved in the transactions). Revise the graph to compensate for that fact. How does the revised situation compare with the original?
2. Construct a second supply-and-demand graph for any product. Show the equilibrium price and quantity. Assuming that the good generates external benefits, modify the diagram to allow for them. Show the new equilibrium price and quantity. How does the revised situation compare with the original?
3. Why has the free market not developed contractual arrangements to eliminate excess air pollution in major Canadian cities?

LO 16.2 Discuss the marginal benefits and costs of pollution.

4. Examine the following marginal costs and marginal benefits associated with water cleanliness in a given locale.

Quantity of Clean Water (%)	Marginal Cost ($)	Marginal Benefit ($)
0	3 000	200 000
20	15 000	120 000
40	50 000	90 000
60	85 000	85 000
80	100 000	40 000
100	Infinite	0

a. What is the optimal degree of water cleanliness?
b. What is the optimal degree of water pollution?
c. Suppose that a company creates a food additive that offsets most of the harmful effects of drinking polluted water. As a result, the marginal benefit of water cleanliness declines by $40 000 at each degree of water cleanliness at or less than 80 percent. What is the optimal degree of water cleanliness after this change?

5. Examine the following marginal costs and marginal benefits associated with air cleanliness in a given locale:

Quantity of Clean Air (%)	Marginal (Cost) $	Marginal Benefit ($)
0	50 000	600 000
20	150 000	360 000
40	200 000	200 000
60	300 000	150 000
80	400 000	120 000
100	Infinite	0

a. What is the optimal degree of air cleanliness?
b. What is the optimal degree of air pollution?
c. Suppose that a state provides subsidies for a company to build plants that contribute to air pollution. Cleaning up this pollution causes the marginal cost of air cleanliness to rise by $210 000 at each degree of air cleanliness. What is the optimal degree of air cleanliness after this change?

6. The following table displays hypothetical annual total costs and total benefits of conserving wild tigers at several possible worldwide tiger population levels.

Population of Wild Tigers	Total Cost ($ million)	Total Benefit ($ million)
0	0	40
2 000	5	90
4 000	15	130
6 000	30	160
8 000	55	185
10 000	90	205
12 000	140	215

a. Calculate the marginal costs and benefits.
b. Given the data, what is the socially optimal world population of wild tigers?
c. Suppose that tiger farming is legalized and that this has the effect of reducing the marginal cost of tiger conservation by $15 million for each 2000-tiger population increment in the table. What is the new socially optimal population of wild tigers?

LO 16.3 Describe how common property impacts the environment.

7. What is the problem with common property resources?
8. Suppose that polluters are to be charged by government agencies for the privilege of polluting.
   a. How should the price be set?
   b. Which firms will treat waste, and which will pay to pollute?
   c. Is it possible that some firms will be forced to close down because they now have to pay to pollute? Why might this result be good?
   d. If producers are charged to pollute, they will pass this cost on to buyers in the form of higher prices. Why might this be good?

LO 16.4 Explain how recycling is changing the way we look at our environment.

9. In Example 16–2, "Wind as a Renewable Resource," companies are offering people the choice to use renewable resources. Why would companies be willing to switch technologies at a great cost to them?
10. In Example 16–5, "Reducing Waste by Recycling," recycling is now considered something that everyone should participate in. How can people who are not recycling be forced to participate without a huge cost to governments?

CHAPTER 17

The Public Sector

In Canada, over the course of a year, thousands of tax lawyers and accountants labour alone or with clients to help those clients reduce their tax liabilities and fill out their tax returns. Canadian taxpayers are each estimated to spend approximately 20 hours a year preparing their taxes. The opportunity cost exceeds $4 billion a year. And that is not the end of the story—many individuals spend a lot of valuable time figuring out ways to change their lifestyle so as to reduce the taxes they owe. Although there is never any way to avoid the cost of a tax system completely, there are ways to reduce compliance costs to society. One way is to switch to a more simplified tax system. To understand this issue, you need to know more about government and the public sector.

LEARNING OBJECTIVES

After reading this chapter, you should be able to:

17.1 Explain externalities and the four other economic functions of government.

17.2 Describe the two main political functions of government and how decision making differs depending on whether the individual is in the public or private sector.

17.3 Distinguish between average and marginal tax rates and explain the Canadian tax system.

curve as S. The equilibrium price is P_1, and the equilibrium quantity is Q_1. We assume, however, that flu shots generate external benefits to individuals who may not be vaccinated but will, nevertheless, benefit because epidemics will not break out. If such external benefits were taken into account, the demand curve would shift outward from D_1 to D_2. The new equilibrium quantity would be Q_2, and the new equilibrium price would be P_2. With no corrective action, this society is not devoting enough resources to flu shots.

When there are external costs, the market will tend to overallocate resources to the production of the good or service in question, for those goods or services will be deceptively low-priced. With the example of steel, too much will be produced because the steel mill owners and managers are not required to take account of the external cost that steel production is imposing on the rest of society. In essence, the full cost of production is unknown to the owners and managers, and so the price they charge the public for steel is lower than it would be otherwise. And, of course, the lower price means that buyers are willing and able to buy more. More steel is produced and consumed than is socially optimal.

When there are external benefits, the market underallocates resources to the production of that good or service because the good or service is relatively too expensive (due to relatively low demand). In a market system, too many of the goods that generate external costs are produced and too few of the goods that generate external benefits are produced.

How Government Corrects Negative Externalities

Government can, in theory, correct externality situations in a variety of ways in all cases that warrant such action. In the case of negative externalities, at least two avenues are open to government: special taxes and legislative regulation or prohibition.

SPECIAL TAXES. In our example of the steel mill, the externality problem originates from the fact that the air as a waste disposal area is costless to the firm but not to society. Government could make the steel mill pay a tax for dumping its pollutants into the air. Government could attempt to tax the steel mill commensurate with the cost to third parties from smoke in the air. This, in effect, would be a pollution tax, or an **effluent fee**. The ultimate effect would be to reduce the supply of steel and raise the price to consumers, ideally making the price equal to the full cost of production to society.

Effluent fee A pollution tax.

REGULATION. To correct a negative externality arising from steel production, government could specify a maximum allowable rate of pollution. This action would require that the steel mill install pollution abatement equipment within its facilities, that it reduce its rate of output, or some combination of the two. Note that government's job would not be that simple, for it still would have to determine the level of pollution and then actually measure its output from steel production in order to enforce such regulation.

How Government Corrects Positive Externalities

What can government do when the production of one good spills benefits over to third parties? It has several policy options: financing the production of the good or producing the good itself, subsidies (negative taxes), and regulation.

GOVERNMENT FINANCING AND PRODUCTION. If the positive externalities seem extremely large, government has the option of financing the desired additional production facilities so that the "right" amount of the good will be produced. Consider again vaccinations against communicable diseases. Government frequently finances campaigns to vaccinate the population. It even operates centres where such vaccinations are free.

SUBSIDIES. A subsidy is a negative tax; it is a payment made either to a business or to a consumer when the business produces, or the consumer buys, a good or a service. In the case of vaccinations against influenza, government could subsidize everyone who receives a flu shot by directly reimbursing those vaccinated or by making payments to doctors who provide the shots. If you are attending a university or college, taxpayers are helping pay the cost of providing your education; you are being subsidized by as much as 80 percent of the total cost. Subsidies reduce the net price to consumers, thereby causing a larger quantity to be demanded.

REGULATION. In some cases involving positive externalities, government can require by law that a certain action be undertaken by individuals in the society. For example, regulations require that all school-aged children be vaccinated before entering public and private schools. Some people believe that a basic school education itself generates positive externalities. Perhaps as a result of this belief, we have regulations—laws—that require all school-aged children to be enrolled in a public or private school.

Other Economic Functions of Government

Besides compensating for externalities, government performs many other functions that affect the way in which exchange is carried out in the economy.

Let us look at four more economic functions of government.

PROVIDING A LEGAL SYSTEM. The courts and the police may not at first seem like economic functions of government (although judges and police personnel must be paid). Their activities, nonetheless, have important consequences on the economic activities in any country. You and I enter into contracts constantly, whether they be oral or written, express or implied. When we believe that we have been wronged, we seek redress of our grievances within our legal institutions. Moreover, consider the legal system that is necessary for the smooth functioning of our society. Our society has defined quite explicitly the legal status of businesses, the rights of private ownership, and a method for the enforcement of contracts. All relationships among consumers and businesses are governed by the legal rules of the game. We might consider government in its judicial function and then as the referee when there are disputes in the economic arena.

Property rights The rights of an owner to use and to exchange that property.

Much of our legal system is involved with defining and protecting *property rights*. **Property rights** are the rights of an owner to use and to exchange that property. One might say that property rights are really the rules of our economic game. When property rights are well defined, owners of property have an incentive to use the property efficiently. Any mistakes in their decision about the use of property have negative consequences that the owners suffer. Furthermore, when property rights are well defined, owners of property have an incentive to maintain that property so that if those owners ever desire to sell it, it will fetch a better price.

Establishing and maintaining a well-functioning legal system is not a costless activity, as you can see in Policy Example 17–1.

POLICY EXAMPLE 17–1

Who Should Pay the High Cost of a Legal System?

When a huge multinational corporation gets into a lengthy and expensive "shouting match" with its detractors, the public ends up footing part of the legal bill. McDonald's operates worldwide, with annual sales of about $50 billion. It has property rights in the goodwill associated with its name. When two unemployed British social activists published a pamphlet with such chapter headings as "McDollar, McGreedy, McCancer, McMurder, McRipoff, McTorture, and McGarbage," McDonald's was not pleased. The pamphlet accused the American company of torturing animals, corrupting children, and exploiting the Third World. So, McDonald's went to court in London. When the case began, there were 26 preliminary hearings spread over a four-year time period, and when it went to trial, 180 witnesses were called. McDonald's itself will end up spending many millions of dollars, but British taxpayers will foot the entire bill for the use of the court system. According to the Lord Chancellor's Department, British taxpayers will pay at least £2.5 million (well over $5.5 million).

continued

Should taxpayers continue to pay for all of the court system? No, according to policy makers in Britain. They have a plan to make litigants pay the full cost of court services, specifically judges' salaries. Such a system that forces litigants to pay for the full opportunity cost of the legal system has yet to be instituted in Canada or elsewhere.

For critical analysis: What other costs, besides judges' salaries, do citizens implicitly pay for in their legal system?

Anticombines legislation Laws that make illegal certain economic activities that might restrain trade.

Monopoly A firm that has great control over the price of a good it sells.

PROMOTING COMPETITION. Many people believe that the only way to attain economic efficiency is through competition. One of the roles of government is to serve as the protector of a competitive economic system. The federal and provincial governments have passed **anticombines legislation**, which makes illegal certain (but not all) economic activities that might, in legal terms, restrain trade—that is, prevent free competition among actual and potential rival firms in the marketplace. The avowed aim of anticombines legislation is to reduce the power of **monopolies**—firms that have great control over the price of the goods they sell. A number of laws have been passed that prohibit specific anticompetitive business behaviour. The Competition Bureau, which is part of Industry Canada, attempts to enforce these anticombines laws. Various provincial judicial agencies also expend efforts at maintaining competition.

Private goods Goods that can be consumed by only one individual at a time.

Principle of rival consumption The principle that one person's consumption reduces the amount of private goods available for others to consume.

Public goods Goods that can be consumed jointly by many individuals simultaneously at no additional cost and with no reduction in quality or quantity.

PROVIDING PUBLIC GOODS. The goods used in our examples up to this point have been **private goods**—goods that can be consumed by only one individual at a time. When I eat a cheeseburger, you cannot eat the same one. So, you and I are rivals for that cheeseburger, just as much as rivals for the title of world champion are. When I use a CD player, you cannot use the same player. When I use the services of an auto mechanic, that person cannot work at the same time for you. That is the distinguishing feature of private goods—their use is exclusive to the people who purchase or rent them. The **principle of rival consumption** is that one person's consumption reduces the amount of private goods available for others to consume. Rival consumption is easy to understand. With private goods, either you use them or I use them.

There is an entire class of goods that are not private goods. These are called **public goods**—these can be consumed jointly by many individuals simultaneously at no additional cost and with no reduction in quality or quantity. Military defence, police protection, and the legal system, for example, are public goods. If you partake of them, you do not necessarily take away from anyone else's share of those goods.

CHARACTERISTICS OF PUBLIC GOODS. Several distinguishing characteristics of public goods set them apart from all other goods.[1]

1. *Public goods are often indivisible.* You cannot buy or sell $5 worth of the army's ability to protect you from foreign invasion. Public goods cannot usually be produced or sold very easily in small units.
2. *Public goods can be used by more and more people at no additional cost.* Once money has been spent on the armed forces, the defence protection you receive does not reduce the amount of protection bestowed on anyone else. The opportunity cost of your receiving military protection once it is in place is zero.
3. *Additional users of public goods do not deprive others of any of the services of the goods.* If you turn on your television set, your neighbours do not get weaker reception because of your action.
4. *It is difficult to design a collection system for a public good on the basis of how much individuals use it.* It is nearly impossible to determine how much any person uses or values

[1]Sometimes the distinction is made between pure public goods, which have all the characteristics we have described here, and quasi- or near-public goods, which do not. The major feature of near-public goods is that they are jointly consumed, even though nonpaying customers can be, and often are, excluded—for example, movies, football games, and concerts.

Exclusion principle The principle that no one can be denied the benefits of a public good for failing to pay for it.

defence. No one can be denied the benefits of military protection for failing to pay for that public good. This is often called the **exclusion principle**.

One of the problems of public goods is that the private sector has a difficult, if not impossible, time in providing them. There is little or no incentive for individuals in the private sector to offer public goods because it is so difficult to make a profit in so doing. Consequently, a true public good must necessarily be provided by government. Read Example 17–1 for further discussion.

EXAMPLE 17–1 Are Lighthouses a Public Good?

One of the most common examples of a public good is a lighthouse. Arguably, it satisfies all the criteria listed in points 1 through 4 on page 388. In one instance, however, a lighthouse was not a public good in that a collection system was devised and enforced on the basis of how much individuals used it. In the 13th century, in the city of Aigues-Mortes, a port in Southern France, a tower called the King's Tower was erected to assert the will and power of Louis IX (Saint Louis). The 32-metre-high tower served as a lighthouse for ships. More importantly, it served as a lookout so that ships sailing on the open sea, but in its view, did not escape paying for use of the lighthouse. Those payments were then used for the construction of the city walls.

For critical analysis: Explain how a lighthouse satisfies the characteristics of public goods described in points 1, 2, and 3.

Free-rider problem A situation in which some individuals take advantage of the fact that others will shoulder the burden of paying for public goods.

FREE RIDERS. The nature of public goods leads to the **free-rider problem**, a situation in which some individuals take advantage of the fact that others will shoulder the burden of paying for public goods, such as defence. Free riders will argue that they receive no value from such government services as defence and therefore really should not have to pay for them. Suppose that citizens were taxed directly in proportion to how much they told an interviewer that they valued military protection. Some people would probably say that they are unwilling to pay for it because they do not want any—it is of no value to them. Many of us may end up being free riders when we assume that others will pay for the desired public good. We may all want to be free riders if we believe that someone else will provide the commodity in question that we actually value.

The free-rider problem is a definite issue among nations with respect to the international burden of defence and how it should be shared. A country may choose to belong to a multilateral defence organization, such as the North Atlantic Treaty Organization (NATO) but then consistently attempt not to contribute funds to the organization. The nation knows it would be defended by others in NATO if it were attacked but would rather not pay for such defence. In short, it seeks a "free ride."

ENSURING ECONOMYWIDE STABILITY. Government attempts to stabilize the economy by smoothing out the ups and downs in overall business activity. Our economy sometimes faces the problems of unemployment and oscillating prices. Government, especially the federal government, has made an attempt to solve these problems by trying to stabilize the economy. The notion that the federal government should undertake actions to stabilize business activity is a relatively new idea in Canada, encouraged by high unemployment rates during the Great Depression of the 1930s and subsequent theories about possible ways by which government could reduce unemployment. In 1945, government formally assumed responsibility for economic performance. It established three goals for government accountability: full employment, price stability, and economic growth. These goals have provided the justification for many government economic programs during the post–World War II period.

CONCEPTS IN BRIEF

Learning Objective 17.1: Explain externalities and the four other economic functions of government.

- External costs lead to an overallocation of resources to the specific economic activity. Two possible ways of correcting these spillovers are taxation and regulation.
- External benefits result in an underallocation of resources to the specific activity. Three possible government corrections are financing the production of the activity, subsidizing private firms or consumers to engage in the activity, and regulation.
- The economic activities of government include (1) correcting for externalities, (2) providing a judicial system, (3) promoting competition, (4) producing public goods, and (5) ensuring economywide stability.
- Public goods can be consumed jointly. The principle of rival consumption does not apply as it does with private goods.
- Public goods have the following characteristics: (1) They are indivisible; (2) once they are produced, there is no opportunity cost when additional consumers use them; (3) your use of a public good does not deprive others of its simultaneous use; and (4) consumers cannot conveniently be charged on the basis of use.

17.2 The Political Functions of Government

At least two areas of government are in the realm of political—or normative—functions, rather than that of the economic ones discussed in the first part of this chapter. These two areas are (1) the regulation and/or provision of merit and demerit goods, and (2) income redistribution.

Merit and Demerit Goods

Merit good Any good that the political process has deemed socially desirable.

Certain goods are considered to have special merit. A **merit good** is defined as any good that the political process has deemed socially desirable. (Note that nothing inherent in any particular good makes it a merit good. It is a matter of who chooses it.) Some examples of merit goods in our society are museums, ballets, sports stadiums (see Policy Example 17–2), and concerts. In these areas, government's role is the provision of merit goods to the people in society who would not otherwise purchase them at market clearing prices or who would not purchase an amount of them judged to be sufficient. This provision may take the form of government production and distribution of merit goods. It can also take the form of reimbursement for payment on merit goods or subsidies to producers or consumers for part of the cost of merit goods. Governments do, indeed, subsidize such merit goods as concerts, ballets, and museums. In most cases, such merit goods would rarely be so numerous without subsidization.

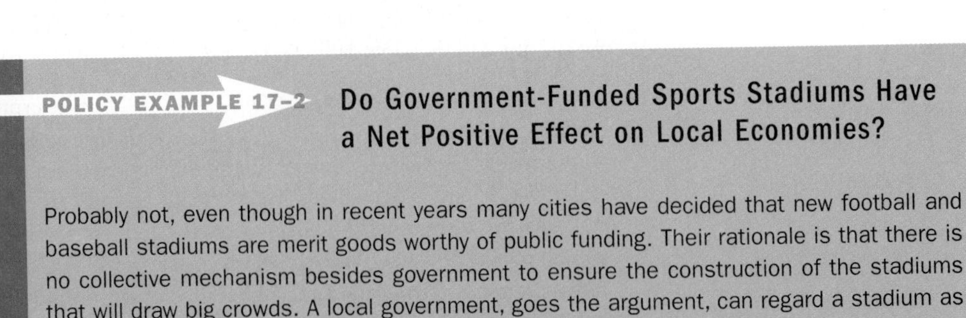

POLICY EXAMPLE 17–2 Do Government-Funded Sports Stadiums Have a Net Positive Effect on Local Economies?

Probably not, even though in recent years many cities have decided that new football and baseball stadiums are merit goods worthy of public funding. Their rationale is that there is no collective mechanism besides government to ensure the construction of the stadiums that will draw big crowds. A local government, goes the argument, can regard a stadium as an investment because the crowds it draws benefit the local economy. Spending by the crowds can also generate tax revenues that help government recoup its expenses. According to economist Andrew Zimbalist, however, "there has not been an independent

continued

study by an economist over the last 30 years that suggests you can anticipate a positive economic impact" from government investments in sports facilities.

For Critical Analysis: In theory, explain how a sports stadium might result in positive externalities for the local economy.

Source: Noll, Roger G. & Andrew Zimbalist, editors. *Sports, Jobs, and Taxes: The Economic Impact of Sports Teams and Stadiums.* Brookings Institution, 1997.

Demerit good Any good that the political process has deemed socially undesirable.

Demerit goods are the opposite of merit goods—they are goods that the political process has deemed socially undesirable. Cigarettes, gambling, and illegal drugs are examples. Government exercises its role in the area of demerit goods by taxing, regulating, or prohibiting their manufacture, sale, and use. Governments justify the relatively high taxes on alcohol and tobacco by declaring them demerit goods. The best-known example of governmental exercise of power in this area is the stance against certain psychoactive drugs. Most psychoactives (except nicotine, caffeine, and alcohol) are either expressly prohibited, as is the case for heroin, cocaine, and opium, or heavily regulated, as in the case of prescription psychoactives.

Income Redistribution

Transfer payments Payments made to individuals for which no services or goods are concurrently rendered in return.

Transfers in kind Payments that are in the form of actual goods and services for which no goods or services are rendered concurrently in return.

Another relatively recent political function of government has been the explicit redistribution of income. This redistribution uses two systems: the progressive income tax (described later in this chapter) and transfer payments. **Transfer payments** are payments made to individuals for which no services or goods are concurrently rendered in return. The three key money transfer payments in our system are welfare, old age security payments, and employment insurance benefits. Income redistribution also includes a large amount of income **transfers in kind**—payments that are in the form of actual goods and services for which no goods or services are rendered concurrently in return. Two income transfers in kind are health care and low-cost public housing.

Government has also engaged in other activities as a form of redistribution of income. For example, the provision of public education is, at least in part, an attempt to redistribute income by making sure that the very poor have access to education (see Example 17–2).

EXAMPLE 17–2 Education Transfer Payments

The federal government has recently increased its transfers in kind to postsecondary students. The federal budget contained a number of incentives to encourage more Canadians to continue their education following secondary school. For example, government is making available $285 million in Canada Study Grants of $3000 each for needy students with dependants. In addition, the education credit and child-care expense deductions for income tax are extended to part-time as well as full-time students.

The federal government is also providing annual Canada Education Savings Grants of 20 percent of the first $2000 in contributions to your registered education savings plan. You are also now able to make tax-free withdrawals from your RRSP of up to $10 000 per year to a maximum of $20 000 over four years. However, withdrawals must be paid back within 10 years.

Finally, government has made a number of improvements to the Canada Student Loan program. For example, interest on student loans is now tax deductible. And for students who have problems repaying their student loans, government provides up to 30 months of interest relief following graduation.

For critical analysis: Why might a tax deduction for postsecondary education expenses be more beneficial to society than an equivalent dollar tax deduction for home mortgage expenses?

Collective Decision Making: The Theory of Public Choice

The public sector has a vast influence on the Canadian economy. Yet, the economic model used until now has applied only to the behaviour of the private sector—firms and households. Such a model does not adequately explain the behaviour of the public sector. We shall attempt to do so now.

Governments consist of individuals. No government actually thinks and acts; rather, government actions are the result of decision making by individuals in their roles as elected representatives, appointed officials, and salaried bureaucrats. Therefore, to understand how government works, we must examine the incentives for the people in government as well as those who would like to be in government—avowed candidates or would-be candidates for elected or appointed positions—and special-interest lobbyists attempting to get government to do something. At issue is the analysis of *collective decision making*. **Collective decision making** involves how voters, politicians, and other interested parties act and how these actions influence nonmarket decisions. The analysis of collective decision making is usually called the **theory of public choice**. It has been given this name because it involves hypotheses about how choices are made in the public sector, as opposed to the private sector. The foundation of public-choice theory is the assumption that individuals will act within the political process to maximize their individual (not collective) well-being. In that sense, the theory is similar to our analysis of the market economy, in which we also assume that individuals are motivated by self-interest.

Collective decision making How voters, politicians, and other interested parties act and how these actions influence nonmarket decisions.

Theory of public choice The analysis of collective decision making.

To understand public-choice theory, it is necessary to point out other similarities between the private market sector and the public, or government, sector; then, we will look at the differences.

Similarities in Market and Public-Sector Decision Making

In addition to the similar assumption of self-interest being the motivating force in both sectors, there are other similarities.

SCARCITY. At any given moment, the amount of resources is fixed. This means that for the private and the public sectors combined, there is a scarcity constraint. Everything that is spent by all levels of government, plus everything that is spent by the private sector, must add up to the total income available at any point in time. Hence, every government action has an opportunity cost, just as in the market sector.

COMPETITION. Although we typically think of competition as a private market phenomenon, it is also present in collective action. Given the scarcity constraint government also faces, bureaucrats, appointed officials, and elected representatives will always be in competition for available government funds. Furthermore, the individuals within any government agency or institution will act as individuals do in the private sector: They will try to obtain higher wages, better working conditions, and higher job-level classifications. They will compete and act in their own, not society's, interests.

SIMILARITY OF INDIVIDUALS. Contrary to popular belief, there are not two types of workers, those who work in the private sector and those who work in the public sector; rather, individuals working in similar positions can be considered similar. The difference, as we shall see, is that the individuals in government face a different **incentive structure**, the system of rewards and punishments individuals face with respect to their own actions, from that in the private sector. For example, the costs and benefits of being efficient or inefficient differ when one goes from the private sector to the public sector.

Incentive structure The system of rewards and punishments individuals face with respect to their own actions.

One approach to predicting government bureaucratic behaviour is to ask what incentives bureaucrats face. Take Canada Post as an example. The bureaucrats running that Crown corporation are human beings with qualities similar to those possessed by workers in comparable positions at, say, Northern Telecom or Air Canada. Yet, the post office does not function like either of these companies. The difference can be explained, at least in part, in terms of the incentives provided for the managers in the two types of institutions. When the bureaucratic managers and workers at Northern Telecom make incorrect decisions, work slowly, produce shoddy products, and are generally "inefficient," the profitability of the company declines. The owners—millions of shareholders—express their displeasure by selling some of their shares of the company. The market value, as tracked on the stock exchange, falls. But what about Canada Post? If a manager, a worker, or a bureaucrat in the post office provides shoddy service, there is no straightforward mechanism by which the organization's owners—the taxpayers—can express their dissatisfaction. Despite the post office's status as a "government corporation," taxpayers as shareholders do not really own the organization's shares that they can sell.

The key, then, to understanding purported inefficiency in the government bureaucracy is not found in an examination of people and personalities but, rather, in an examination of incentives and institutional arrangements.

Differences between Market and Collective Decision Making

There are probably more dissimilarities between the market sector and the public sector than there are similarities.

Government, or political, goods Goods (and services) provided by the public sector; they can be either private or public goods.

GOVERNMENT GOODS AT ZERO PRICE. The majority of goods that governments produce are furnished to the ultimate consumers without direct money charge. **Government, or political, goods** (and services) are goods and services provided by the public sector; they can be either private or public goods. The fact that they are furnished to the ultimate consumer free of charge does not mean that the cost to society of those goods is zero, however; it only means that the price charged is zero. The full opportunity cost to society is the value of the resources used in the production of goods produced and provided by government.

For example, none of us pays directly for each unit of consumption of most highways nor for police protection. Rather, we pay for all these things indirectly through the taxes that support our governments—federal, provincial, and municipal. This special feature of government can be looked at in a different way. There is no longer a one-to-one relationship between the consumption of a government-provided good and the payment for that good. Consumers who pay taxes collectively pay for every political good, but the individual consumer may not be able to see the relationship between the taxes paid and the consumption of the good. Indeed, most taxpayers will find that their tax bill is the same whether or not they consume, or even like, government-provided goods.

USE OF FORCE. All governments are able to engage in the legal use of force in their regulation of economic affairs. For example, governments can exercise the use of expropriation, which means that if you refuse to pay your taxes, your bank account and other assets may be seized by the Canada Revenue Agency. In fact, you have no choice in the matter of paying taxes to governments. Collectively, we decide the total size of government through the political process, but individually we cannot determine how much service we pay for just for ourselves during any one year.

VOTING VERSUS SPENDING. In the private market sector, a dollar voting system is in effect. This dollar voting system is not equivalent to the voting system in the public sector. There are, at minimum, three differences:

Majority rule A collective decision-making system in which group decisions are made on the basis of 50.1 percent of the vote.

Proportional rule A decision-making system in which actions are based on the proportion of the "votes" cast and are in proportion to them.

1. In a political system, one person gets one vote, whereas in the market system, the dollars one spends count as votes.
2. The political system is run by **majority rule**, a collective decision-making system in which group decisions are made on the basis of 50.1 percent of the vote, whereas the market system is run by **proportional rule,** a decision-making system in which actions are based on the proportion of the "votes" cast and are in proportion to them.
3. The spending of dollars can indicate intensity of want, whereas because of the all-or-nothing nature of political voting, a vote cannot.

Ultimately, the main distinction between political votes and dollar votes here is that political outcomes may differ from economic outcomes. Remember that economic efficiency is a situation in which, given the prevailing distribution of income, consumers get the economic goods they want. There is no corresponding situation using political voting. Thus, we can never assume that a political voting process will lead to the same decisions that a dollar voting process will lead to in the marketplace.

Indeed, consider the dilemma every voter faces. Usually, a voter is not asked to decide on a single issue (although this happens); rather, a voter is asked to choose among candidates who present a large number of issues and state a position on each of them. Just consider the average Member of Parliament who has to vote on hundreds of different issues during a five-year term. When you vote for that representative, you are voting for a person who must make hundreds of decisions during the next five years.

The Role of Bureaucrats

Bureaucrats Nonelected government officials.

Bureaucracy An administrative system run by a large staff following rules and procedures set down by government.

Government programs require people to deliver them. This is manifested today in the form of well-established bureaucracies, in which **bureaucrats** (nonelected government officials) work. A **bureaucracy** is an administrative system run by a large staff following rules and procedures set down by government. Bureaucracies can exert great influence on matters concerning themselves—the amount of funding granted them and the activities in which they engage. In the political marketplace, well-organized bureaucracies can even influence the expression of public demand itself. In many cases, they organize the clientele (interest groups), coach that clientele on what is appropriate, and stick up for the "rights" of the clientele.

Gauging Bureaucratic Performance

It is tempting, but incorrect, to think of bureaucrats as mere "technocrats," executors of orders and channels of information, in this process. They have at least two incentives to make government programs larger and more resistant to attack than we might otherwise expect. First, society has decided that in general, government should not be run on a profit-making basis. Measures of performance other than bottom-line profits must be devised. In the private market, successful firms typically expand to serve more customers; although this growth is often incidental to the underlying profitability, the two frequently go hand in hand. In parallel, performance in government is often measured by the number of clients served, and rewards are distributed accordingly. As a result, bureaucrats have an incentive to expand the size of their clientele—not because it is more profitable (beneficial) to society but because that is how bureaucrats' rewards are structured.

In general, performance measures that are not based on long-run profitability are less effective at gauging true performance. This makes it potentially easier for the government bureaucrat to appear to perform well, collect rewards for measured performance, and then leave for greener pastures. To avoid this, a much larger proportion of the rewards given to bureaucrats are valuable only as long as they continue being bureaucrats—large staffs, expensive offices, generous pensions, and the like. Instead of getting large current salaries (which can be saved for a rainy day), they get rewards that disappear if their jobs disappear. Naturally, this increases the incentives of bureaucrats to make sure that their jobs do not disappear.

Rational Ignorance

At this point, you may well be wondering why this system still goes on. The answer lies in rational ignorance on the part of voters, ignorance that is carefully cultivated by the members of special interest groups.

On most issues, there is little incentive for the individual voter to expend resources to determine how to vote. Moreover, the ordinary course of living provides most of us with enough knowledge to decide whether we should invest in learning more about a given issue. For example, suppose that Canadian voters were asked to decide if the sign marking the entrance to an obscure national park should be enlarged. Most voters would decide that the potential costs and benefits of this decision are negligible: The new sign is unlikely to be the size of Prince Edward Island, and anybody who has even heard of the national park in question probably already has a pretty good idea of its location. Thus, most voters would choose to remain rationally ignorant about the exact costs and benefits of enlarging the sign, implying that (1) many will choose not to vote at all, and (2) those who do vote will simply flip a coin or cast their ballot on the basis of some other, perhaps ideological, grounds.

WHY BE RATIONALLY IGNORANT? For most political decisions, majority rule prevails. Only a coalition of voters representing slightly more than 50 percent of those who vote is needed. Whenever a vote is taken, the result is going to involve costs and benefits. Voters, then, must evaluate their share of the costs and benefits of any budgetary expenditure. Voters, however, are not perfectly informed. That is one of the crucial characteristics of the real world—information is a resource that is costly to obtain. Rational voters will, in fact, decide to remain at some level of ignorance about government programs because the benefits from obtaining more information may not be worth the cost, given each individual voter's extremely limited impact on the outcome of an election. For the same reason, voters will fail to inform themselves about taxes or other revenue sources to pay for proposed expenditures because they know that for any specific expenditure program, the cost to them individually will be small. At this point, it might be useful to contrast this situation with what exists in the nonpolitical private market sector of the economy. In the private market sector, the individual chooses a mix of purchases and bears fully the direct and indirect consequences of this selection (ignoring for the moment the problem of externalities).

CONCEPTS IN BRIEF

Learning Objective 17.2: Describe the two main political functions of government and how decision making differs depending on whether the individual is in the public or private sector.

- Political, or normative, activities of government include the provision and regulation of merit and demerit goods and income redistribution.
- Merit and demerit goods do not have any inherent characteristics that qualify them as such; rather, collectively, through the political process, we make judgments about which goods and services are "good" for society and which are "bad."
- Income redistribution can be carried out by a system of progressive taxation, coupled with transfer payments, which can be made in money or in kind, such as health care and public education. Collective decision making involves the actions of voters, politicians, political parties, bureaucrats, and interest groups.
- The similarities between market and public-sector decision making include assumption of self-interest as the motivating force, scarcity of resources, and competition for available funds and resources.
- The key differences between the market and public sector include government goods at zero price, use of force, and proportional rule versus majority rule.
- The theory of public choice implies a situation called rational ignorance where on most issues there is little incentive for the individual voter to expend resources to determine how to vote. This allows bureaucrats and special interest groups to have a significant effect on choices in the public sector.

17.3 Tax Rates and the Canadian Tax System

Jean-Baptiste Colbert, the 17th-century French finance minister, said the art of taxation was in "plucking the goose so as to obtain the largest amount of feathers with the least possible amount of hissing." In Canada, governments have designed a variety of methods of plucking the private-sector goose. To analyze any tax system, we must first understand the distinction between marginal tax rates and average tax rates.

Marginal and Average Tax Rates

Marginal tax rate The change in taxes due divided by the change in taxable income.

If somebody says, "I pay 28 percent in taxes," you cannot really tell what that person means unless you know whether the individual is referring to average taxes paid or the tax rate on the last dollar earned. The latter concept has to do with the **marginal tax rate.**[2]

The marginal tax rate is expressed as follows:

$$\text{Marginal tax rate} = \frac{\text{Change in taxes due}}{\text{Change in taxable income}}$$

Tax bracket A specified level of taxable income to which a specific and unique marginal tax rate is applied.

Average tax rate The total taxes due divided by total taxable income.

It is important to understand that the marginal tax rate applies only to the income in the highest tax bracket reached, where a **tax bracket** is defined as a specified level of taxable income to which a specific and unique marginal tax rate is applied.

The **average tax rate** is not the same thing as the marginal tax rate; it is defined as follows:

$$\text{Average tax rate} = \frac{\text{Total taxes due}}{\text{Total taxable income}}$$

Taxation Systems

No matter how governments raise revenues—from income taxes, sales taxes, or other taxes—all of those taxes can fit into one of three types of taxation systems—proportional, progressive, and regressive, expressing a relationship between the percentage tax, or tax rate, paid and income. To determine whether a tax system is proportional, progressive, or regressive, we simply ask the question: "What is the relationship between the average tax rate and the marginal tax rate?"

Proportional taxation A tax system in which regardless of an individual's income, the tax bill comprises exactly the same proportion. Also called a *flat-rate tax.*

PROPORTIONAL TAXATION. **Proportional taxation** means that regardless of an individual's income, the taxes comprise exactly the same proportion, also called a flat-rate tax. In terms of marginal versus average tax rates, in a proportional taxation system, the marginal tax rate is always equal to the average tax rate. If every dollar is taxed at 20 percent, then the average tax rate is 20 percent, as is the marginal tax rate.

As mentioned earlier, a proportional tax system is also called a flat-rate tax. Taxpayers at all income levels end up paying the same percentage of their income in taxes. If the proportional tax rate were 20 percent, an individual with an income of $10 000 would pay $2000 in taxes, while an individual making $100 000 would pay $20 000, the identical 20 percent rate being levied on both. See the Issues and Applications for a more in-depth look at the flat tax issue.

Progressive taxation As taxable income increases, the percentage of income paid in taxes also increases.

PROGRESSIVE TAXATION. Under **progressive taxation,** as a person's taxable income increases, the percentage of income paid in taxes also increases. In terms of marginal versus average tax rates, in a progressive system, the marginal tax rate is above the average tax rate. If you are taxed 5 percent on the first $10 000 you make, 10 percent on the next $10 000 you make, and 30 percent on the last $10 000 you make, you face a progressive income tax system. Your marginal tax rate is always above your average tax rate. See Policy Example 17–3 to see how Canada compares with other countries.

Regressive taxation A smaller percentage of taxable income is taken in taxes as taxable income increases.

REGRESSIVE TAXATION. With **regressive taxation,** a smaller percentage of taxable income is taken in taxes as taxable income increases. The marginal rate is below the average rate. As income increases, the marginal tax rate falls, and so does the average tax rate. The Goods and Services Tax (GST) is regressive. Someone earning $10 000 per year pays the same 7 percent sales tax on a tube of toothpaste as someone earning $100 000 per year. But the tube of toothpaste takes up a much larger proportion of the low-income earner's budget, and so the marginal tax rate for that person is higher. The federal government tries to address this inequity by giving GST rebates to low-income earners who apply for them on their income tax returns each year.

[2]The word *marginal* means "incremental" (or "decremental") here.

POLICY EXAMPLE 17–3 **Average and Marginal Tax Rates Around the World**

We Canadians frequently complain that we pay too much income tax, especially when compared with the United States. However, the average tax rate for the average production worker are not as different as one would think, when social security and income tax deductions are combined.

The Organisation for Economic Co-operation and Development (OECD) surveyed tax rates in the industrialized world. Table 17–1 shows average tax rates for an average production worker, and for workers in the highest income bracket. For a Canadian production worker making about $37 000 per year, the combined average tax rate—income taxes plus contributions to the Canada Pension Plan plus employment insurance premiums—is about 26 percent, just 2 percentage points above that in the United States.

TABLE 17–1
Average and Marginal Tax Rates in the Industrialized World, 2002, 2001

	Combined Average Tax Rate (%) for an Average Production Worker (2002)	Marginal Tax Rate (%) for Highest Income Bracket (2001)
Australia	24	48
Canada	26	43
France	27	48
Germany	41	51
Italy	28	46
Japan	16	50
New Zealand	20	39
United Kingdom	23	40
United States	24	48

SOURCE: ADAPTED FROM "TAXING WAGES" OECD. MAY 30, 2004. http://www.oecd.org/dataoecd. COPYRIGHT OECD (JUNE 2000).

Canada's personal income tax structure is also less progressive than many other countries'. For example, France, Germany, and Japan all have higher marginal tax rates for the highest income bracket.

For critical analysis: Theoretically, do you think one's average tax rate or marginal tax rate plays a bigger role in affecting one's incentive to work harder to earn additional income?

The Most Important Federal Taxes

The federal government imposes income taxes on both individuals and corporations, and collects sales taxes as well as a variety of other taxes.

The Federal Personal Income Tax

The most important tax in the Canadian economy is the federal personal income tax, which accounts for about 48 percent of all federal revenues. All Canadian citizens, resident aliens, and most others who earn income in Canada are required to pay federal income tax on all taxable income. The tax rates depend on the amount of taxable income earned, as can be seen in Table 17–2. Marginal income tax rates at the federal level have varied from as low as 4 percent after the passage of the *Income Tax Act* in 1917, to as high as 98 percent during World War II.

Advocates of a more progressive income tax system in Canada argue that such a system redistributes income from the rich to the poor, taxes people according to their ability to pay, and taxes people according to the benefits they receive from government. Although there is much controversy over the "redistributional" nature of our progressive

TABLE 17-2

Federal Tax Rates

16% on first $35 000
22% on next $35 000
26% on next $43 804
29% of taxable income over $113 804

SOURCE: CANADA REVENUE AGENCY.

tax system, there is no strong evidence that, in fact, the tax system has ever done much income redistribution in this country. Currently, about 80 percent of all Canadians, rich or poor, pay roughly the same proportion of their income in federal income tax.

The Treatment of Capital Gains

Capital gain The positive difference between the buying and selling prices of an asset.

Capital loss The negative difference between the purchase price and the sale price of an asset.

The positive difference between the buying and selling prices of an asset, such as a share of stock or a plot of land, is called a **capital gain**, and the negative difference between the purchase price and the sale price of an asset is called a **capital loss**. Capital gains are taxed at ordinary income marginal tax rates. The taxable part of a capital gain is 50 percent of the net amount of your capital gains minus 50 percent of your capital losses for the year.

Capital gains are not always real. In Canada, gains on principal are not taxed, but if in one year you pay $100 000 for a house you plan to rent and sell it at a 50 percent higher price 10 years later, your nominal capital gain is $50 000. But what if, during those 10 years, there had been such inflation that average prices had also gone up by 50 percent? Your real capital gain would be zero. But you still have to pay taxes on that $50 000. To counter this problem, many economists have argued that capital gains should be indexed to the rate of inflation.

The Corporate Income Tax

Corporate income taxes account for about 14 percent of all federal taxes collected, and 3.4 percent of all provincial taxes collected. Corporations are generally taxed at a flat rate of 28 percent on the difference between their total revenues (or receipts) and their expenses.

DOUBLE TAXATION. Because individual shareholders must pay taxes on the dividends they receive, paid out of after-tax profits by the corporation, corporate profits are taxed twice. If you receive $1000 in dividends, you have to declare it as income, and you must pay taxes at your marginal tax rate. Before the corporation was able to pay you those dividends, it had to pay taxes on all its profits, including any that it put back into the company or did not distribute in the form of dividends. Eventually, the new investment made possible by those **retained earnings**—profits not given out to shareholders—along with borrowed funds will be reflected in the increased value of the shares in that company. When you sell your shares in that company, you will have to pay taxes on the difference between what you paid for them and what you sold them for. In both cases, dividends and retained earnings (corporate profits) are taxed twice.

Retained earnings Profits not given out to shareholders.

WHO REALLY PAYS THE CORPORATE INCOME TAX? Corporations can exist only as long as employees make their goods, consumers buy their products, shareholders (owners) buy their shares, and bondholders buy their bonds. Corporations *per se* do not do anything. We must ask, then, who really pays the tax on corporate income. This is a question of **tax incidence**, the distribution of tax burdens among various groups in society. (The question of tax incidence applies to all taxes, including sales and payroll taxes.) There remains considerable debate about the incidence of corporate taxation. Some economists say that corporations pass their tax burdens on to consumers by charging higher prices. Other economists believe that it is the shareholders who bear most of the tax. Still others believe that employees pay at least part of the tax by receiving lower wages than they would otherwise. Because the debate is not yet settled, we will not hazard a guess here as to what the correct conclusion should be. Suffice it to say that you should be cautious

Tax incidence The distribution of tax burdens among various groups in society.

when you advocate increasing corporate income taxes. You may be the one who ends up paying the increase, at least in part, if you own shares in a corporation, buy its products, or work for it.

Unemployment and Pension Taxes

An increasing percentage of federal revenues is accounted for each year by taxes (other than income taxes) levied on payroll. These payroll taxes are for Canada Pension Plan (CPP) benefits and employment insurance (EI).

Employment insurance is a compulsory federal program that provides income assistance in the event of unemployment. EI premiums are paid by employees and matched by employers. (The employer's contribution is really paid, at least in part, in the form of a reduced wage paid to employees, as explained in Example 17–3.) Self-employed people must pay both shares. The maximum personal contribution to EI in 2004 was $772.20. EI premiums become part of government's general revenues; as of 1999, there was a large surplus in the EI account, which helped government balance the budget for the 1999–2000 fiscal year.

EXAMPLE 17–3 Employment Insurance

Countless articles have been written about the problem with the employment insurance (EI) system in Canada. They all make reference to the employer and employee "contributions" to the EI fund. One gets the impression that EI premiums paid by employees go into a special government account and that employees do not pay for their employers' "contribution" to this account. Both concepts are not only flawed but grossly misleading as well. EI premiums are mixed in with the rest of government taxes collected and spent every year. The "contributions" are not contributions at all; they are merely taxes paid to the federal government. The so-called employer contribution, which matches the employee payments, is not, in fact, paid for by employers but, rather, by employees because of the lower wages that they are paid. Anybody who quits a job and becomes self-employed finds this out when the time comes to pay one's self-employment taxes (employment insurance "contributions"), which effectively double the payments previously being made as an employee.

For critical analysis: Should EI premiums go into a special account?

In 2004, the Canada Pension Plan (CPP) premium payable on eligible earnings to $40 500 was 4.95 percent, with employers contributing an equal share on behalf of the employee. CPP premiums do not form part of government's general revenue but are managed separately from the government budget. The CPP is a system in which current workers subsidize already retired workers. With the coming retirement of the postwar "baby boomers," the number of retired people will grow much more rapidly than the number of current workers. In anticipation of increased outlays in pension plan benefits, the combined (employer–employee) premium has risen to 9.9 percent of eligible earnings.

The Goods and Services Tax

The Goods and Services Tax (GST) is a sales tax that makes up about 18 percent of federal government revenues. Consumers pay a 7 percent tax on virtually all goods and services they purchase in addition to any applicable provincial sales taxes. The GST is a regressive tax, since it taxes consumption at the same rate for both the rich and the poor. The federal government tries to mitigate this, however, by giving a rebate of up to $76 four times a year to low-income earners. While consumers must pay GST on imports, Canadian exports are exempt. Visitors to Canada may apply for a rebate of the GST they paid on their Canadian purchases when they leave the country.

Some economists argue that in spite of the regressive nature of sales taxes, such a tax as the GST is preferable to an income tax. Income taxes tax all income, whether it is spent or saved. Therefore, they argue, saving is discouraged. However, a sales tax taxes only income that is consumed, and so saving is encouraged. The Issues and Applications section at the end of this chapter revisits the pros and cons of this topic.

Spending, Government Size, and Tax Receipts

The size of the public sector can be measured in many different ways. One way is to count the number of public employees. Another is to look at government outlays. Government outlays include all of the government expenditures on goods and services as well as all transfer payments. Transfer payments include employment insurance benefits, welfare, and old age security. In Figure 17–2, you see that since 1961, total government outlays made by all levels of government in Canada peaked at 51 percent of the Canadian gross domestic product (size of the Canadian economy) in 1992. As a percentage of Canada's GDP, total government outlays have dropped from 51 percent in 1992 to 41 percent in 2002.

Government Receipts

The main revenue raiser for all levels of government is taxes. We show in the two pie diagrams in Figure 17–3 the percentage of receipts from various taxes obtained by the federal government and by the provincial and municipal governments.

THE FEDERAL GOVERNMENT. The largest source of receipts for the federal government is the individual income tax. During the 2002–03 fiscal year, it accounted for 62.9 percent of all federal revenues. Next come the GST revenues, employment insurance premiums, and a number of other items—taxes on imported goods and excise taxes on such things as gasoline and alcoholic beverages.

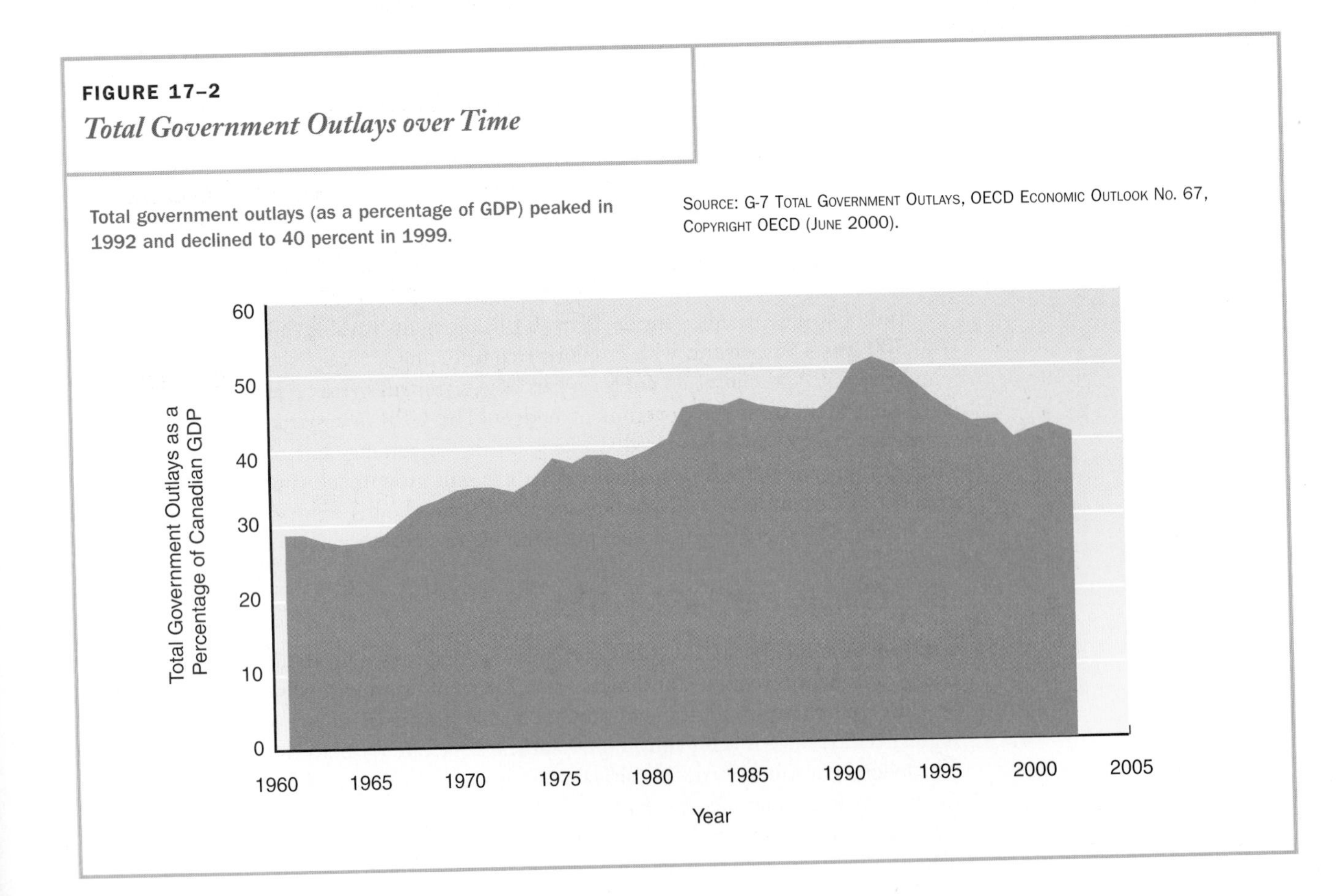

FIGURE 17–2
Total Government Outlays over Time

Total government outlays (as a percentage of GDP) peaked in 1992 and declined to 40 percent in 1999.

SOURCE: G-7 TOTAL GOVERNMENT OUTLAYS, OECD ECONOMIC OUTLOOK NO. 67, COPYRIGHT OECD (JUNE 2000).

PROVINCIAL AND MUNICIPAL GOVERNMENTS. As can be seen in Figure 17–3, there is quite a bit of difference between the origins of receipts for the provincial and municipal governments and for the federal government. Personal and corporate income taxes account for only 30.2 percent of total provincial and municipal revenues. The next largest source of receipts is from sales taxes (used by provincial governments), property taxes (used mainly by municipal governments), and transfers from the federal government.

COMPARING FEDERAL SPENDING WITH PROVINCIAL AND MUNICIPAL SPENDING. A typical federal government budget is given in Figure 17–4. The largest three categories are interest on the debt, social services, and transfers to the provinces, which together constitute over 80 percent of the total federal budget.

The makeup of provincial and municipal expenditures varies quite considerably. Education and health are the biggest categories, accounting for over 60 percent of all expenditures.

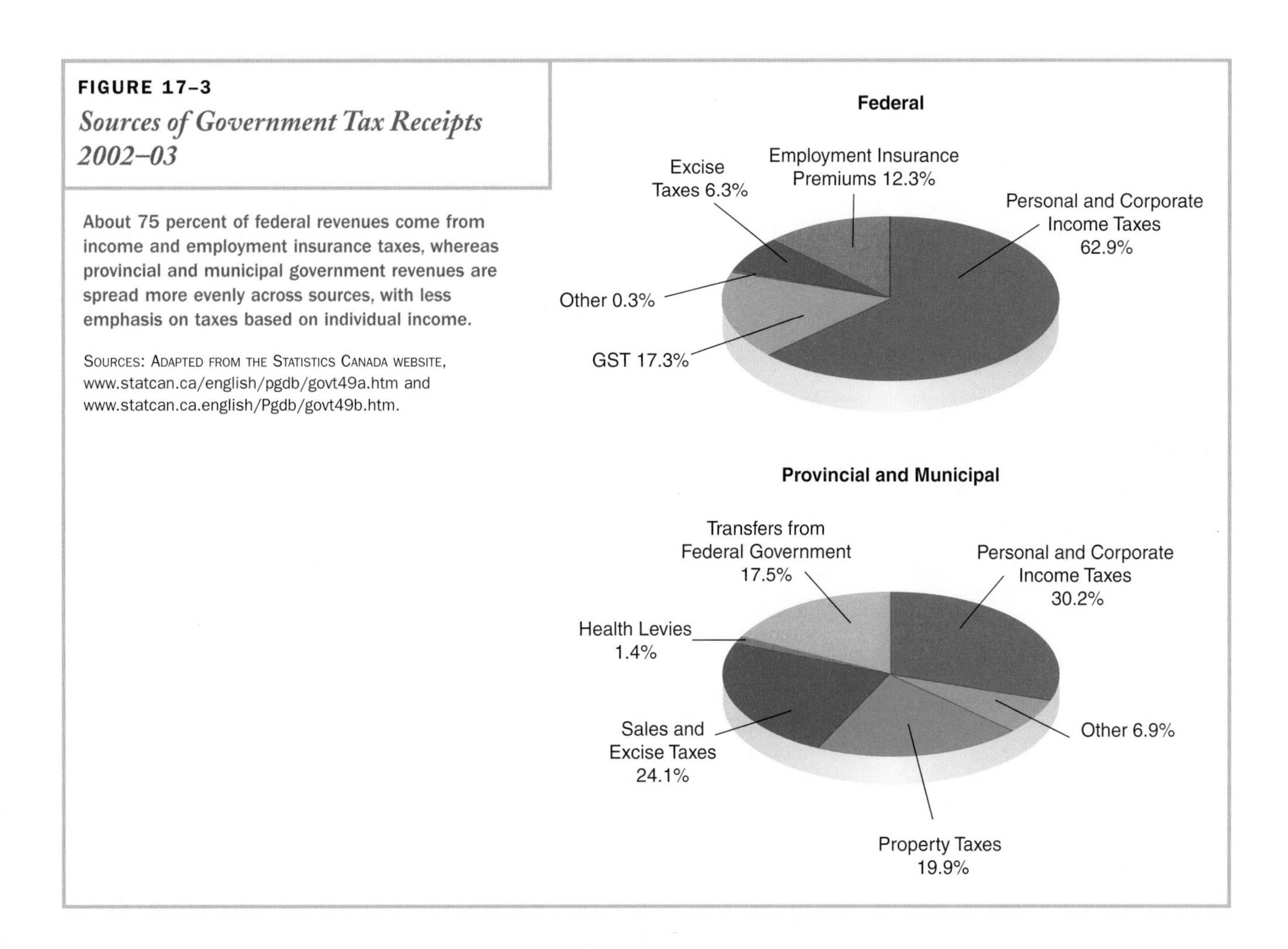

FIGURE 17–3

Sources of Government Tax Receipts 2002–03

About 75 percent of federal revenues come from income and employment insurance taxes, whereas provincial and municipal government revenues are spread more evenly across sources, with less emphasis on taxes based on individual income.

SOURCES: ADAPTED FROM THE STATISTICS CANADA WEBSITE, www.statcan.ca/english/pgdb/govt49a.htm and www.statcan.ca.english/Pgdb/govt49b.htm.

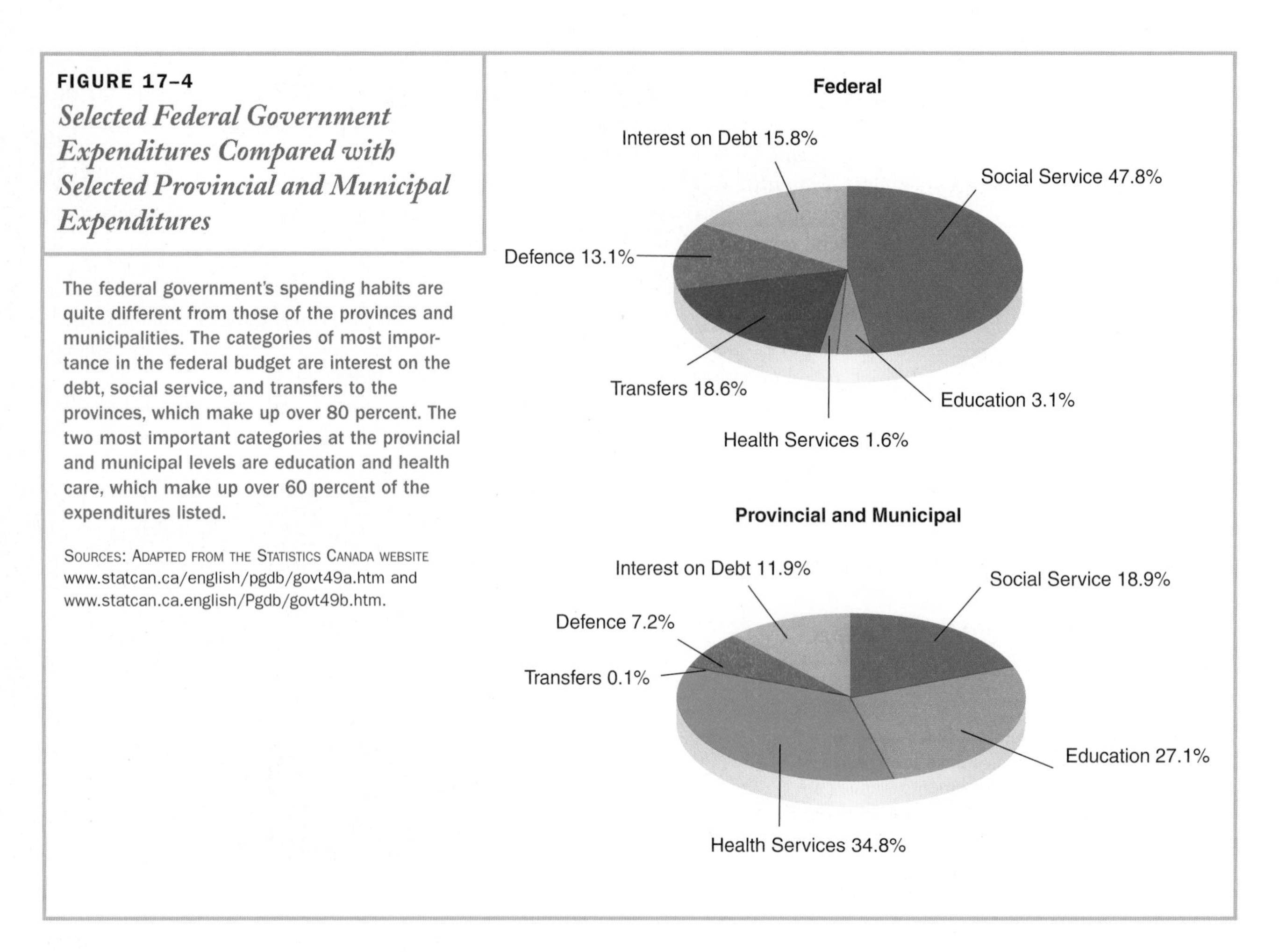

FIGURE 17–4

Selected Federal Government Expenditures Compared with Selected Provincial and Municipal Expenditures

The federal government's spending habits are quite different from those of the provinces and municipalities. The categories of most importance in the federal budget are interest on the debt, social service, and transfers to the provinces, which make up over 80 percent. The two most important categories at the provincial and municipal levels are education and health care, which make up over 60 percent of the expenditures listed.

SOURCES: ADAPTED FROM THE STATISTICS CANADA WEBSITE www.statcan.ca/english/pgdb/govt49a.htm and www.statcan.ca.english/Pgdb/govt49b.htm.

CONCEPTS IN BRIEF

Learning Objective 17.3: Distinguish between average and marginal tax rates and explain the Canadian tax system.

- Marginal tax rates are applied to marginal tax brackets, defined as spreads of income over which the tax rate is constant.
- Tax systems can be proportional, progressive, or regressive, depending on whether the marginal tax rate is the same as, greater than, or less than the average tax rate as income rises.
- Because corporations must first pay an income tax on most earnings, the personal income tax shareholders pay on dividends received (or realized capital gains) constitutes double taxation.
- The corporate income tax is paid by one or more of the following groups: shareholder-owners, consumers of corporate-produced products, and employees in corporations.
- In Canada, total government outlays as a percent of Canadian gross domestic product peaked in 1992 at 51 percent and declined to 40.6 percent in 2002.
- Government spending at the federal level is different from that at the provincial and municipal levels. At the federal level, interest on the debt, social services, and transfers to the provinces account for over 80 percent of the federal budget. At the provincial and municipal levels, education and health comprise over 60 percent of the expenditures graphed.

ISSUES AND APPLICATIONS

Should We Switch to a Flat Tax?

Concepts Applied: Average versus Marginal Tax Rates, Opportunity Cost, Progressive Income Tax System

Each year, Canadian taxpayers spend numerous hours preparing their taxes or hire accountants to do so for them. Switching to a national sales tax, one alternative to our current system, would lead to the downsizing of the Canada Revenue Agency and all of the expenses associated with that organization.

Since the enactment of the federal income tax, Canadians have faced a progressive system of taxation. The top marginal tax rate soared to 98 percent in 1943, dropped to 80 percent in 1948, dropped again to 60 percent in 1968, and settled at 47 percent starting in 1971. Government reduced the top marginal tax rate to 34 percent in 1983; today, it stands at 29 percent. The idea behind a progressive tax system is that the "rich" should pay more. In actuality, what happens is quite a different story. In Figure 17–5, you see that regardless of what the top tax rate is, the federal government obtains around 48 percent of its annual income as tax revenues.

Why? Because people respond to incentives. At high marginal tax rates, the following occurs: (1) Rich people hire more tax lawyers and accountants to help them figure out loopholes in the tax system to avoid high marginal tax rates; (2) some people change their investments to take advantage of loopholes that allow them to pay lower marginal tax rates; (3) some people drop out of the labour force, particularly secondary income earners, such as lower-paid working women; and (4) more people engage in off-the-books "underground" activities for cash on which no income taxes are paid.

An Alternative: The Flat Tax

For decades, many economists have argued in favour of scrapping our progressive income tax system and replacing it with a so-called flat tax. The idea behind a flat tax is simple. To calculate what you owe, simply subtract the appropriate exemption from your income and multiply the rest by the flat tax rate, say, 20 percent. For example, a family of four might be able to earn as much as $25 000 or $35 000 a year before it paid any income tax. The major benefits of such a system, according to its advocates, would be the following: (1) fewer resources devoted to figuring out one's taxes; (2) fewer tax lawyers and accountants, who could then be engaged in more productive activities; (3) higher savings and investment; and (4) more economic growth. Opponents of a flat tax argue that (1) federal revenues will fall and a federal budget deficit will occur; and (2) the rich will pay less tax.

Another Alternative: A National Sales Tax

Alternatively, we could apply some form of a value-added tax (VAT) in place of the current income tax. VAT is common throughout Europe. VAT is assessed on the value added by a firm at each stage of production. It is a tax on the value of products that a firm sells minus the value of the materials that it bought and used to produce the products. Such a tax is collected by all businesses and remitted directly to the federal government. One of the major benefits of VAT is that it would significantly downsize the Canada Revenue Agency and the expenses associated with that government department. A VAT of, say, 15 to 20 percent in lieu of a federal income tax would be quite similar to a consumption tax.

A Consumption Tax

With a consumption tax, taxpayers pay taxes only on what they consume (spend) out of their incomes, not on all of what they earn. One way to determine such consumption in any year is simply to subtract what is saved from what is earned. The difference is consumption, and that is the base to which a consumption tax would apply. (A consumption tax is actually equivalent to the GST on all goods and services purchased.) In essence, a consumption tax provides an

FIGURE 17–5

Changing Maximum Marginal Income Tax Rates and Revenues Collected

At the top of the diagram, you can see listed the top marginal tax rates from 1960 to 2000. On the side is the percentage of total annual income collected by the federal government from the income tax system. No matter how high the marginal income tax rate has been, government has collected about the same percentage of national income in taxes.

SOURCE: W. IRWIN GILLESPIE, *TAX, BORROW & SPEND: FINANCING FEDERAL SPENDING IN CANADA 1867–1990.*

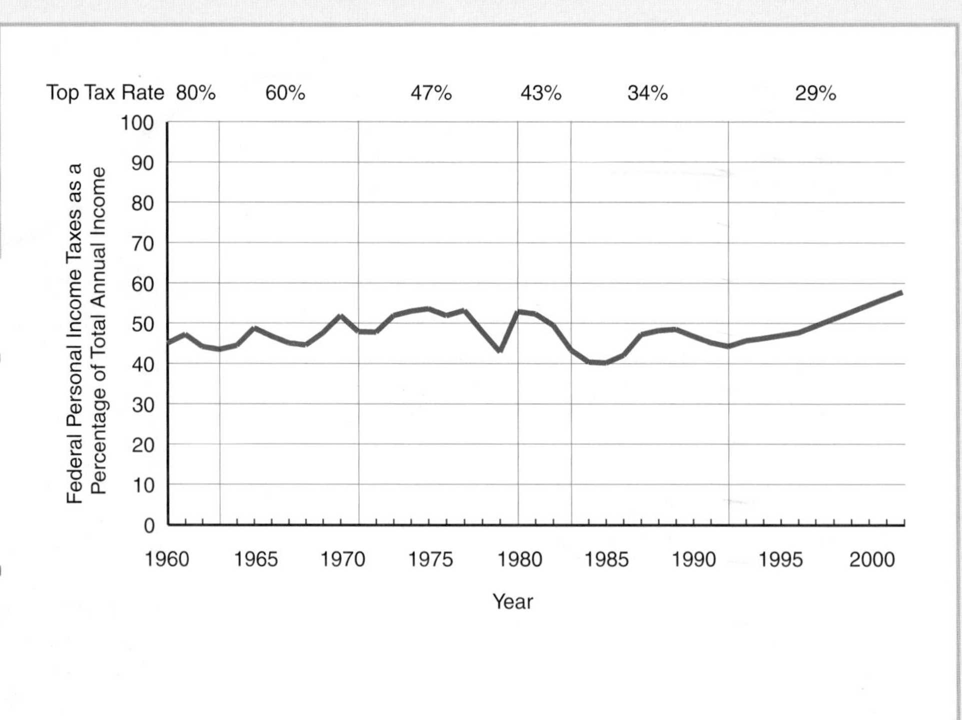

unlimited deduction for saving. As such, it encourages more saving. The less people choose to consume today, the faster the production possibilities curve will shift outward to the right, leading to more economic growth.

What about Fairness?

Every time a new tax system is discussed, the issue of fairness arises. Is it fair, as with a flat federal income tax, that everybody pays the same marginal tax rate, no matter how much each individual earns? Stephen Entin of the Institute for Research on the Economics of Taxation thinks it is: "It is hard to find a definition of 'fairness' more compelling than the idea that every citizen is treated equally." What about a consumption tax, which might be regressive because the poor spend a larger portion of their income than the rich? Is that a "fair" system? For most economists, these are difficult questions because they are in the realm of the normative, the value-laden. We can point out that an examination of the evidence shows what reality is. Simply stated, when marginal income tax rates are high, the rich do not, in fact, pay a higher average tax rate than when marginal tax rates are lower. It behooves the rich to find methods to reduce tax liabilities and to expend resources to influence politicians to insert an increasing number of loopholes in the *Income Tax Act* in order to reduce effective marginal tax rates on those who earn a lot.

For critical analysis:

1. Do you think employees at the Canada Revenue Agency would be for or against the flat-tax system? Explain your choice.
2. Why is a flat-tax system more efficient than a progressive income tax system?

SUMMARY DISCUSSION OF LEARNING OBJECTIVES

17.1 **Externalities and Other Economic Functions of Government.** Government can correct external costs through taxation, legislation, and prohibition. It can correct external benefits through financing or production of a good or service, subsidies, and regulation.

Government provides a legal system in which the rights of private ownership, the enforcement of contracts, and the legal status of businesses are provided. In other words, government sets the legal rules of the game and enforces them.

Public goods, once produced, can be consumed jointly by additional individuals at zero opportunity cost. If users of public goods know that they will be taxed on the basis of their expressed valuation of those public goods, their expressed valuation will be low. They expect to get a free ride.

17.2 **The Political Functions of Government.** Merit goods (chosen as such, collectively, through the political process) may not be purchased at all or not in sufficient quantities at market clearing prices. Therefore, government subsidizes or provides such merit goods at a subsidized or zero price to specified classes of consumers.

When it is collectively decided that something is a demerit good, government taxes, regulates, or prohibits the manufacture, sale, and use of that good.

The market sector and the public sector both face scarcity, feature competition, and contain similar individuals. They differ in that many government, or political, goods are provided at zero price, collective action may involve the use of force, and political voting can lead to different results from that of dollar voting.

Bureaucrats often exert great influence on the course of policy because they are in charge of the day-to-day operation of current policy and provide much of the information needed to formulate future policy. Bureaucracies often organize their clientele, coach clients on what is appropriate, and stick up for their rights.

17.3 **Tax Rates and the Canadian Tax System.** Marginal tax rates are those paid on the last dollar of income, whereas average tax rates are determined by the proportion of income paid in income taxes.

With a proportional income tax system, marginal rates are constant. With a regressive system, they go down as income rises, and with a progressive system, they go up as income rises.

Government spending at the federal level is different from that at the provincial and municipal levels. Interest on the debt, social services, and transfers to the provinces account for over 80 percent of the federal budget. Health care and education constitute over 60 percent of provincial government expenditures.

PROBLEMS

(Answers to the odd-numbered problems appear at the back of the book.)

LO 17.1 Explain externalities and the four other economic functions of government.

1. What is meant by the expression "market failure"?
2. TV signals have characteristics of public goods, yet TV stations and commercial networks are private businesses. Analyze this situation.
3. Assume that you live in a relatively small suburban neighbourhood called Parkwood. The Parkwood Homeowners' Association collects money from homeowners to pay for upkeep of the surrounding stone wall, lighting at the entrances to Parkwood, and mowing the lawn around the perimeter of the area. Each year you are asked to donate $50. No one forces you to do it. There are 100 homeowners in Parkwood.
   a. What percentage of the total yearly revenue of the homeowners' association will you account for?
   b. At what level of participation will the absence of your $50 contribution make a difference?
   c. If you do not contribute your $50, are you really receiving a totally free ride?
4. Assume that the only textile firm that exists has created a negative externality by polluting a nearby stream with the wastes from production. Assume further that government can measure the external costs to the community with accuracy and charges the firm for its pollution, on the basis of the social cost of pollution per unit of textile output. Show how such a charge will lead to a higher selling price for textiles and a reduction in the equilibrium quantity of textiles.
5. The existence of information and transactions costs has many implications in economics. What are some of these implications in the context of issues discussed in this chapter?

LO 17.2 Describe the two main political functions of government and how decision making differs depending on whether the individual is in the public or private sector.

6. A favourite political campaign theme in recent years has been to reduce the size, complexity, and bureaucratic nature of the federal government. Nonetheless, the size of the federal government, however measured, continues to increase. Use the theory of public choice to explain why.
7. Your small town would like to showcase all of the history of the town in a museum. What type of good would that be, and would government be likely to subsidize the museum or not? Why?
8. You find that you are having trouble paying back your student loan after you graduate. According to Example 17–2, "Education Transfer Payments," government will provide you with up to 30 months of interest relief. Why would government support such a program?

LO 17.3 Distinguish between average and marginal tax rates and explain the Canadian tax system.

9. Consider the following system of taxation, which has been labelled *degressive*. The first $5000 of income is not taxed. After that, all income is assessed at 20 percent (a proportional system). What is the marginal tax rate on $3000 of taxable income? $10 000? $100 000? What is the average tax rate on $3000? $10 000? $100 000? What is the maximum average tax rate?
10. You are offered two possible bonds to buy as part of your investing program. One is a corporate bond yielding 9 percent. The other is a tax-exempt municipal bond yielding only 6 percent. Assuming that you are certain you will be paid your interest and principal on these two bonds, what marginal tax bracket must you be in to decide in favour of the tax-exempt bond?
11. Consider the following tax structure:

Income Bracket	Marginal Tax Rate
$0–$1500	0%
$1501–$2000	14%
$2001–$3000	20%

Mr. Smith has an income of $2500 per annum. Calculate his tax bill for the year. What is his average tax rate? His highest marginal tax rate?

12. In 2004, Canada Pension Plan premiums on wages were 4.95 percent on wages up to $40 500. No further CPP premiums are paid on earnings above this figure. Calculate the average CPP tax rate for annual wages of (a) $4000, (b) $51 300, (c) $56 000, (d) $100 000. Is the CPP system a progressive, proportional, or regressive tax structure?
13. According to Figure 17–4, the federal government spends only about 3.1 percent of the listed expenses on education, while the provinces spend about 27.1 percent on education. Why does it appear that the federal government spends so little on education? Do transfer payments play any part in that equation?

ANSWERS TO ODD-NUMBERED PROBLEMS

Chapter 1: The Nature of Economics

1. a. Human capital
   b. Land
   c. Entrepreneurship
   d. Physical capital
   e. Labour
3. a. Macroeconomic, as the unemployment rate is national or economywide.
   b. Microeconomic, as wage increases of specific occupations, such as nurses and doctors, relate to specific parts of the economy.
   c. Microeconomic, as prices of a specific part of the economy—cigarettes—are being studied.
   d. Macroeconomic, as the inflation rate tracks the average price of all goods, which is an economywide measure.
   e. Macroeconomic, as the nation's total annual production is an economywide measure.
   f. Microeconomic, as an individual firm's situation, such as Eaton's bankruptcy, focuses on a specific part of the economy.
5. No, your cash withdrawals are not free as there is an opportunity cost equal to the interest sacrificed by not putting your $5000 in an account (or another investment) giving you a higher rate of interest.
7. The decision based on availability of funds is not a rational one. In order to allocate resources in a manner that maximizes the satisfaction of the city's wants, the mayor should compare the marginal (extra) benefit of constructing the city hall with the marginal (extra) cost, including alternatives sacrificed. If the extra benefit to the city of constructing the city hall is less than the value of some other alternative that has to be sacrificed, such as paving of city roads, the mayor's decision is not rational.
9. a. We should observe younger drivers to be more frequently involved in traffic accidents than older persons.
   b. Slower monetary expansion should be associated with less inflation.
   c. Professional basketball players receiving smaller salaries should be observed to have done less well in their high-school studies.
   d. Employees being promoted rapidly should have lower rates of absenteeism than those being promoted more slowly.
11. a. Positive, for it is a statement that can be tested by the facts.
    b. Normative, involving a value judgment about what should be.
    c. Normative, involving a value judgment about what should be.
    d. Positive, for it is a statement that can be tested by the facts.

Appendix A: Reading and Working with Graphs

A-1. a. Price is independent, number of notebooks is dependent.
     b. Work-study hours is independent, credit hours is dependent.
     c. Hours studied is independent, and grade is dependent.

A-3.

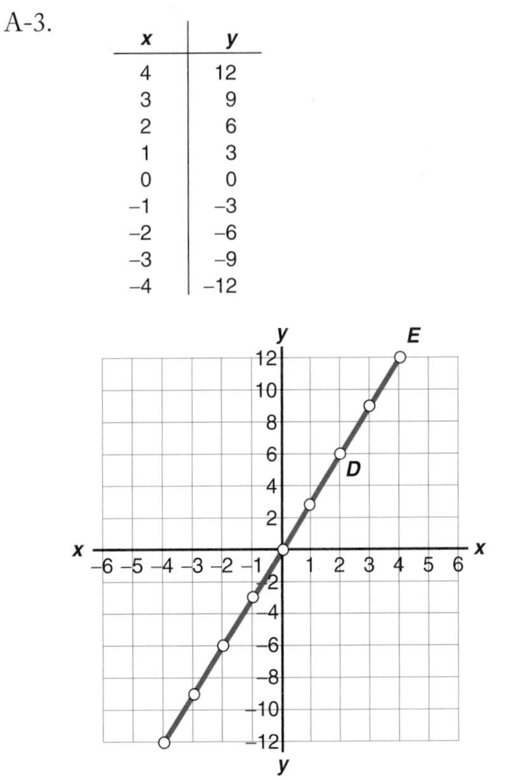

x	y
4	12
3	9
2	6
1	3
0	0
–1	–3
–2	–6
–3	–9
–4	–12

A-5. If you move along the line in Problem A-3 from point D to point E, the slope equals the change in the y-values divided by the change in the x-values, which is:

$$(12 - 6)/(4 - 2) = 6/2 = 3.$$

A-7. For the ordered pair (4, 16) the tangent line is upward sloping, slope is positive.

For the ordered pair (0, 0) the tangent line is horizontal, slope is zero.

For the ordered pair (−4, 16) the tangent line is downward sloping, slope is negative.

Chapter 2: Production Possibilities and Economic Systems

1. a. The maximum amount of factories will be 2000 as shown by the production possibilities curve.

   b. The maximum number of factories would be 5000, as shown by combination A.

   c. A fixed amount of resources and technology prevents Epica from being able to produce combination J in 2006.

   d. If Epica is at point I, this could conflict with the goals of productive efficiency and full employment.

   e. i. The opportunity cost of an additional factory when moving from point E to D would be 2 yachts.

   ii. The opportunity cost of an additional factory when moving from point C to B would be 4 yachts.

   f. i. The opportunity cost of an additional yacht when moving from point A to B would be 1/5 of a factory.

   ii. The opportunity cost of an additional yacht when moving from point E to F would be 1 factory.

   g. The Law of Increasing Relative Cost

   h. This situation conflicts with allocative efficiency.

   i. Economic growth will shift the production possibilities curve outward.

3. The plot of the product possibilities curve is displayed in the graph below.

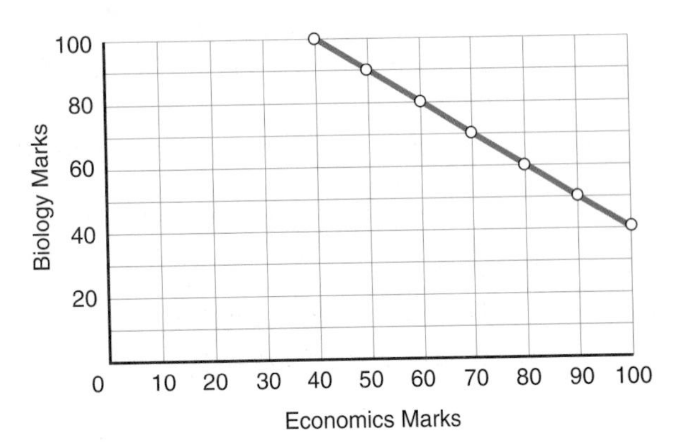

The PPC exhibits constant opportunity costs. That is, the cost of earning an additional mark in economics is always the same, in terms of additional biology marks sacrificed. In this case, the PPC is a straight line with the opportunity cost of earning an additional mark in economics always being 1 mark in biology.

5.

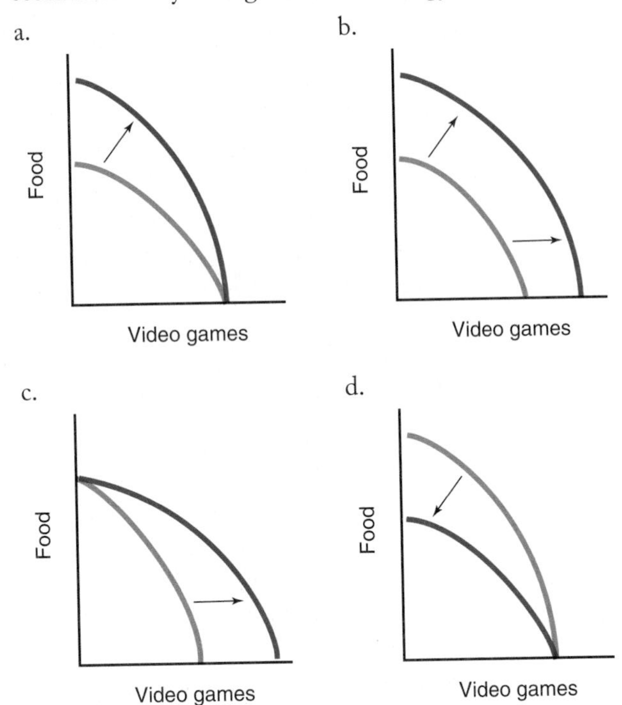

7. If we assume that a two-year college diploma consists of four 15-week semesters, this amounts to committing 60 weeks to college studies. The opportunity cost is: 60 wks × 35 h × $7 = $14 700. The incentive of incurring this cost is that, upon graduating, you will be earning an amount significantly in excess of $7 per hour. You are sacrificing current consumption to obtain a greater amount of future consumption.

9. Yes, you and your roommate should specialize. Since your opportunity cost of completing a basket of laundry (two meals) is lower than your roommate's (three meals) you should specialize in the laundry completion, while your roommate should specialize in the meal preparation. As an example, if you complete an extra basket of laundry, you give up only two meals. However, you free up an additional three hours of your roommate's time, which allows your roommate to produce an additional three meals. Overall, one extra meal is gained.

11. The invisible hand of self-interest and competition helps to ensure that firms serve the consumer, without the heavy hand of government.

13. a. In the market system, the techniques that yield the highest (positive) profits will be used.

    b. Profit equals total revenue minus total cost. Because revenue from 100 units is fixed (at $100), if the firm wishes to maximize profit, this is equivalent to minimizing costs. To find total costs, simply muliply the price of each input by the amount of the input that must be used for each technique.

Costs of A = (\$10)(6) + (\$8)(5) = \$100

Costs of B = (\$10)(5) + (\$8)(6) = \$98

Costs of C = (\$10)(4) + (\$8)(7) = \$96

Because technique C has the lowest costs, it also yields the highest profits (\$100 − \$96 = \$4)

c. Following the same methods yields these costs: A = \$98, B = \$100, and C = \$102. Technique A will be used because it is the most profitable.

d. The profits from using technique A to produce 100 units of X are \$100 − \$98 = \$2.

Appendix B: The Production Possibilities Curve and Comparative Advantage

B-1 a. The Richard family has the absolute advantage in each product, assuming that both families use the same amount of labour input, each day.

b. For the Martin family the opportunity cost of one litre of beer is one litre of wine. For the Richard family the opportunity cost of one litre of beer is three litres of wine.

c. The Martin family has the comparative advantage (lower opportunity cost) in beer and the Richard family has the comparative advantage in wine.

d. Total combined beer production increases from three litres to four litres per day, a gain of one litre. Total combined wine production increases from 17 litres to 18 litres per day, a gain of one litre.

e. For both families to share the gains, one litre of beer should trade for somewhere between one and three litres of wine (between each family's opportunity cost for beer).

Chapter 3: Demand and Supply

1. The absolute prices of heating oil and natural gas have both increased. The relative price of heating oil decreased as it went from \$1.00/\$0.80 = 1.25 to \$2.00/\$3.20 = 0.63. This implies that the relative price of natural gas increased. Yes, consumers will increase their purchases of heating oil relative to natural gas, as heating oil's relative price has declined. This assumes that the prices shown in the table are per constant-quality unit.

3. a. Since the price of a substitute decreases, there will be a decrease in demand for Canadian beef and the demand curve will shift leftward.

b. An increase in demand will occur, where the demand curve shifts rightward.

c. An increase in quantity demanded will occur, which can be described as a movement along (downward) the same demand curve.

d. A decrease in demand will occur, where the demand curve will shift leftward.

e. A decrease in quantity demanded will occur, which can be described as a movement along (upward) the same demand curve.

5. a. P_e = \$11 and Q_e = 80 million CDs.

b. At a price of \$13, there would be a surplus equal to (120 − 60) = 60 million CDs. The surplus will drive down the price.

c. At a price of \$10, there would be a shortage equal to (90 − 60) = 30 million CDs. The shortage will drive up the price.

7. The graph below illustrates a shift to the right in the demand curve, which indicates an *increase in demand*. The new equilibrium price and quantity are \$12 and 100 million CDs. A change in any factor other than the price of CDs will cause an increase in demand, such as an increase in income or an increase in the popularity of rock music.

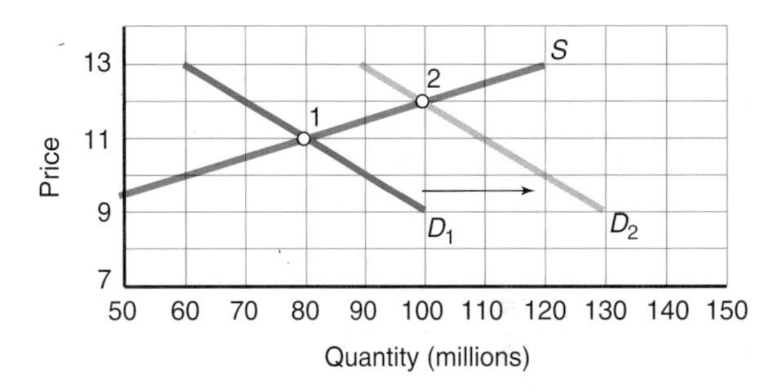

9. a. Increase in quantity demanded P_e ↓, Q_e ↑ as a result of an increase in supply.

b. Increase in demand P_e ↑, Q_e ↑

c. Increase in demand P_e ↑, Q_e ↑

d. Increase in demand P_e ↑, Q_e ↑

e. Decrease in demand P_e ↓, Q_e ↓

11. a. At a price of \$1.40, there would be a surplus equal to (5 − 3) or 2000 dozen eggs. This will drive down the price.

b. At a price of \$0.80, there would be a shortage equal to (6 − 2) or 4000 dozen eggs. This will drive up the price.

c. The equilibrium price and quantity is \$1.20 and 4000 dozen eggs.

d. i. Increase in demand, P_e ↑, Q_e ↑

ii. Decrease in supply, P_e ↑, Q_e ↓

iii. Decrease in demand, P_e ↓, Q_e ↓

iv. Increase in supply, P_e ↓, Q_e ↑

13. a. The equilibrium rent and quantity are $400 and 4000 units per month.
    b. There will be a shortage equal to (6 – 2) or 4000 units per month.
    c. In the short run, by keeping the price of a substitute (one-bedroom units) lower, there will be a decrease in demand for two-bedroom units, causing a decrease in equilibrium rent and quantity of two-bedroom units. In the longer run, due to the shortage of one-bedroom units, there will be an increase in demand for two-bedroom units causing equilibrium price and quantity to increase.
15. a. Increase in demand and increase in supply. While the equilibrium quantity will increase, the combined effect on equilibrium price is indeterminate.
    b. Decrease in supply and increase in demand. While the equilibrium price will increase, the combined effect on equilibrium quantity is indeterminate.
    c. Increase in supply and decrease in demand. While the equilibrium price will decrease, the combined effect on equilibrium quantity is indeterminate.

Chapter 4: Elasticity

1.

Quantity Demanded per Week (kilograms)	Price per Kilogram	Elasticity
1000	$ 5	
		$\frac{1}{3}$, or 0.33
800	10	
		$\frac{5}{7}$, or 0.714
600	15	
		$\frac{7}{5}$, or 1.4
400	20	
		$\frac{9}{3}$, or 3
200	25	

3. The problem is with the denominator, percentage change in P. Because the initial price was zero, any increase in price is of infinite percentage. However, if we take the average elasticity over a segment, there will be no problem. P will become the average of P_1 (= 0) and P_2 (= 10), or $(P_1 + P_2)/2 = 5$.
5. a. The price elasticity of demand for cars is elastic.
   b. The dealer's total revenue will increase.
7. a. Salt has few substitutes but is a very small portion of the total budget, and so it would be more inelastic.
   b. There are many suppliers of ski boats, and so you would probably shop around for the best deal, so it would be more elastic.
   c. A guitar pick takes up a very small portion of the total budget for a major rock band, and so it would be very inelastic.

Chapter 5: Extensions of Demand, Supply, and Elasticity

1. Ticket scalpers are middlemen who ensure that the scarce tickets get sold to those consumers who value the tickets the most. In other words, scalpers use the price system to ensure an efficient allocation of tickets.
3. a. The equilibrium price and quantity of $4 and 7 million would result.
   b. A shortage of (8 – 4) or 4 million crates would occur. This is an example of a price ceiling policy.
   c. The maximum black market price is that price associated with a quantity demanded of 4 million crates, which is $6 per crate.
   d. A surplus of (8 – 6) or 2 million crates would occur. This is an example of a price floor policy.
5. a. The equilibrium price and quantity of $1 and 40 million litres would result.
   b. At a maximum price of $0.80, a shortage of (50 – 30) or 20 million litres will result. This would be called a price ceiling policy.
   c. The black market price would be $1.20.
   d. At a minimum price of $1.40, a surplus of (60 – 20) or 40 million litres will result. This would be called a price floor policy.
7. a. Total revenue received is $4 per crate × 7 million crates = $28 million.
   b. A surplus of (8 – 6) or 2 million crates would occur. Total revenue received is $5 × 8 million crates = $40 million. The total taxpayer cost would be (Support price × Surplus) or ($5 × 2 million) or $10 million.
   c. At a restricted quantity of 6 million crates, the quantity demanded schedule indicates that consumers would pay a price of $5. With the marketing board, the total revenue would be ($5 × 6 million) or 30 million. When the price is increased from the equilibrium price of $4 to the marketing board price of $5, the total revenue increases from $28 million to $30 million. This implies that the demand is inelastic.
9. a. Total revenue received is $1 per litre × 40 million litres, or $40 million.
   b. An Offer to Purchase price policy of $1.20 would result in a surplus equal to (50 – 30) or 20 million litres. Total revenue received is $1.20 × 50 million litres or $60 million. The total taxpayer cost equals ($1.20 × 20 million) or $24 million.

c. If a marketing board restricts the quantity sold to 30 million litres, the price would be \$1.20. The total revenue would be \$1.20 × 30 = \$36 million. When the price is increased from \$1 to \$1.20 the total revenue decreases from \$40 million to \$36 million, indicating that demand is elastic—the marketing board policy does not support the farmer!

11. a. At the price of \$0.70 per litre, the gas suppliers will receive \$0.50 per litre in their pockets, after paying the \$0.20 per litre tax to the government. According to the before-tax supply table, if the firms receive \$0.50 per litre in their pockets, they will supply 60 million litres per day. Therefore, the after-tax market quantity supplied is 60 million litres when the price is \$0.70 per litre. The other market supplies (in millions of litres) starting with a price of \$0.60 per litre are: 50, 40, 30, 20, 10.

b. The after-tax equilibrium price and quantity is \$0.50 per litre and 40 million litres per day, respectively.

c. Since the equilibrium went up from \$0.40 per litre to \$0.50 per litre, the buyer's portion of the tax burden equals \$0.10 per litre, which is the price increase. The seller's portion of the tax burden is the tax minus the buyer's portion, which is \$0.20 – \$0.10 = \$0.10 per litre.

d. The total tax revenue equals the tax per unit multiplied by the after-tax equilibrium quantity, which equals \$0.20 per litre × 40 million litres = \$8 million per day.

e. The daily tax revenue will increase when demand becomes less elastic.

f. The tax will more effectively reduce gas consumption when the demand becomes more elastic.

13. a. The before-tax equilibrium price and quantity are \$0.60 per CD and 50 million CDs per month.

b. The excise tax equals \$0.20 per CD, which is the vertical distance between the S_1 and S_2 supply curves.

c. The after-tax equilibrium price and quantity are \$0.70 per CD and 40 million CDs.

d. The buyers' portion of the tax burden equals the increase in equilibrium price, which is \$0.10 per CD. The seller's portion is equal to the tax per CD minus the buyer's tax burden, which is \$0.20 – \$0.10 = \$0.10 per CD.

e. The total monthly tax revenue equals the after-tax equilibrium quantity multiplied by the per-unit tax, which equals 40 million CDs × \$0.20 per CD equals \$8 million.

f. The tax revenue will increase when supply becomes less elastic.

g. The excise tax will more effectively discourage the use of CDs when supply becomes more elastic.

Chapter 6: Consumer Choice

1. For you, the marginal utility of the fifth kilogram of oranges is equal to the marginal utility of the third ear of corn. Apparently, your friend's tastes differ from yours—for her, the marginal utilities are not equal. For her, corn's marginal utility is too low, while that of oranges is too high—that's why she wants you to get rid of some of the corn (raising its marginal utility). She would have you do this until marginal utilities, for her, were equal. If you follow her suggestions, you will end up with a market basket that maximizes her utility subject to the constraint of your income. Is it any wonder that shopping from someone else's list is a frustrating task?

3. Her marginal utility is 100 at \$1. It is 200 at 50 cents, and 50 at \$2. To calculate marginal utility per dollar, divide marginal utility by price per unit.

5. Optimum satisfaction is reached when marginal utilities per dollar of both goods are equal. This occurs at 102 units of A and 11 units of B. (Marginal utility per dollar is 1.77.)

7. Either your income or the relative price of eggs and bacon must have changed. Without more information, you can't make any judgments about whether you are better or worse off.

9. a. Purchase first cheeseburger at 10 units, leaving \$4.

b. Purchase first fries at 8 units, leaving \$3.

c. Purchase second cheeseburger at 8 units, leaving \$1.

d. Purchase second fries at 6 units, leaving \$0.

11. You can only eat so many potatoes, so why would you take more that you need? There is also no added value in taking more than you need and trying to sell the extra to someone else, as people can buy the potatoes directly from the farmers.

Chapter 7: Rents, Profits, and the Financial Environment of Business

1. a. Bob earns a high economic rent. With a specialized skill that is in great demand, his income is likely to be high and his opportunity cost relatively low.

b. Sally earns a high economic rent. As a supermodel her income likely to be high and, without any education, her opportunity cost relatively low.

c. If Tim were to leave teaching, not a relatively high-paying occupation, he could sell insurance full-time. Hence, his opportunity cost is high relative to his income and his economic rent is low.

3. The economic rents that Michael Jordan would enjoy as a basketball player relative to those he enjoyed as a baseball player surely played a large role in his decision to return to basketball. Hence, they help direct his talent (resources) into their most efficient use.

5. A sole proprietorship is a business entity owned by a single individual, whereas a partnership is a business entity owned by more than one individual. A corporation, in contrast, is a legal entity that is owned by shareholders, who own shares of the profits of the entity. Sole proprietorships and partnerships do not face double taxation as do corporations. The owners of corporations, however, enjoy limited liability, whereas the sole proprietor or partner does not.

7. Accounting profit is total revenue, $77 250 minus explicit costs, $37 000, for a total of $40 250. Economic profit is total revenue, $77 250, less explicit costs, $37 000, and implicit costs, $40 250, for a total equal to zero.

9. The real rate of interest in Japan is 2% – 0.5% = 1.5%. The real rate of interest in Canada is 4% – 3% = 1%. Japan, therefore, has the higher real rate of interest.

11. a. Common shares give you the right to vote; preferred shares do not allow you to vote.
    b. Expected wealth would be $100 lower.
    c. The expected value of stocks rises to $1320, so the choice of stocks has a higher expected value.
    d. Expected wealth would be $120 higher.

Chapter 8: The Firm: Cost and Output Determination

1.

Input of Labour	Total Output of DVD Drives	Average Physical Product
0	0	–
1	25	25
2	60	30
3	85	28.33
4	105	26.25
5	115	23
6	120	20

3. The long-run average costs represent the points that give the least unit cost of producing any given rate of output. The concept is important when one must decide which scale of operations to adopt. Such a decision usually takes the form of deciding what size plant to construct.

5. a.

Output	AVC
0	$ 0
5	20
10	18
20	11
40	8

b. The marginal cost is $40 when increasing output from 10 to 20 units and $100 when increasing from 20 to 40.

c.

Output	ATC
0	$ 0
5	60
10	38
20	21
40	13

7. a. Experiencing economies of scale, costs are still decreasing.
   b. Plant Size E.

9. In the short run, the cost of switching to solar power is more expensive, but in the long run, it is much cheaper.

Chapter 9: Perfect Competition

1. a. Since there is one firm that can affect the market price, this is not perfect competition.
   b. This is not perfect competition, as each firm's product is not identical (not homogeneous) due to the differences in quality.
   c. Since government restricts entry through licensing, the easy-entry feature of perfect competition is violated.

3. a.

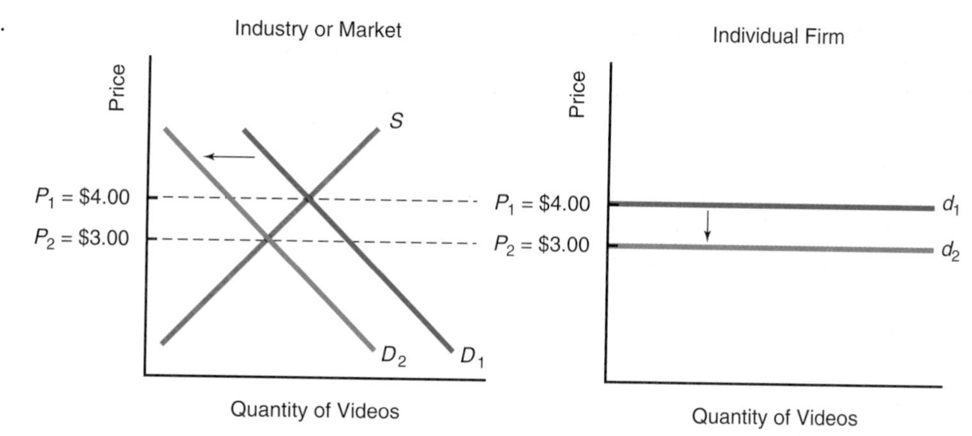

b. The industry's demand curve is typically downward sloping, while the firm's demand curve is perfectly elastic (horizontal). The firm's demand curve is perfectly elastic due to the assumption of having many firms supplying the identical product. If a firm were to raise its price just above the going price, it would lose all its sales.

5. In the table below, Total Profit is calculated by the formula: Total Revenue – Total Cost:

Hourly Quantity (# pizzas)	0	1	2	3	4	5	6	7	8	9	10
Total Profit (Price = \$10)	–3	1	9	18	26	32	36	38	37	33	26
Total Profit (Price = \$3)	–3	–6	–5	–3	–2	–3	–6	–11	19	–30	–44
Total Profit (Price = \$2)	–3	–7	–7	–6	–6	–8	–12	–18	–27	–39	–54

a. The profit at a price of \$10 is based on the total revenue formula: TR = $10 \times Q$. The profit-maximizing quantity is seven pizzas per hour with a total positive economic profit of \$38 per hour.

b. The profit at a price of \$3 is based on the total revenue formula: TR = $3 \times Q$. The loss-maximizing quantity is four pizzas per hour with a total negative economic profit (loss)of \$2 per hour. Note that by operating at four pizzas per hour, the firm minimizes its losses to be \$2. If it shuts down, its total losses would be its total fixed cost of \$3. The reason it should operate at four pizzas is that its total revenue of \$12 exceeds its total variable cost of \$11. By operating, it is able to contribute \$1 toward covering its total fixed costs.

c. The profit at a price of \$2 is based on the total revenue formula: TR = $2 \times Q$. The loss-maximizing quantity is zero pizzas per hour with a total negative economic profit (loss) of \$3 per hour, equal to total fixed cost. Since, at all quantities, total revenue is less than total variable cost, the firm should shut down.

7.

Output (units per hour)	Average Fixed Cost (AFC)	Average Variable Cost (AVC)	Average Total Cost (ATC)	Marginal Cost (MC)
1	\$102.00	\$40	\$142.00	
2	51.00	35	86.00	\$30
3	34.00	40	74.00	50
4	25.50	45	70.50	60
5	20.40	50	70.40	70
6	17.00	55	72.00	80
7	14.57	60	74.57	90

a. At a price of \$81, the profit-maximizing quantity is where marginal revenue (price) approximately equals marginal cost, at six units per day. The total profit equals (Price – ATC) × Quantity = $(81 - 72) \times 6$ = \$54 per hour.

b. At a price of \$61, the profit-maximizing quantity is where marginal revenue (price) approximately equals marginal cost, at four units per day. The total profit equals equals (Price – ATC) × Quantity = $(61 - 70.50) \times 4$ = –\$38 per hour (minimum loss). No, if the firm were to shut down, it would face a larger loss equal to its total fixed cost of $102 per hour.

c. At a price of $31, the price is below minimum average variable cost, which is approximately $35, and so the firm should shut down. Its minimum loss equals its total fixed cost of $102.

d. The short-run breakeven point occurs at minimum average total cost, which is approximately $70.40 per unit.

e. The short-run shutdown point occurs at minimum average variable cost, which is just below $35.

9. a. At the price of $50, firm J will sell 81 units, where price or marginal revenue equals marginal cost.

b. Total profit equals $(P - \text{ATC}) \times Q = (\$50 - \$43) \times 81 = \$567$.

c. Firm J will shut down when the price drops just below $20, which is minimum average variable cost.

d. Long-run price = $42 = minimum ATC

11.

Price per Unit	Individual Quantity Supplied	Industry Supply (1000 firms)	Industry Demand
$91	7	7000	5000
$81	6	6000	6000
$51	3	3000	8000
$31	0	0	9000

a. The short-run equilibrium price will be $81 per unit.

b. Short-run equilibrium is at six units, where marginal revenue (price) equals marginal cost. The total profit equals (Price – ATC) × Quantity = (81 – 72) × 6 = $54 per hour.

13. a. No, $81 will not be the long-run equilibrium price, as each firm is making a positive economic profit of $54 per hour. In the long run, new firms will enter the industry, attracted by the positive profits. As new firms enter, the industry price will fall below $81 and will keep falling until no more economic profit is being earned.

b. The long-run equilibrium price will just equal minimum long-run average total cost, which is approximately $70.40. At this price, each firm will earn zero economic profit so that there will be no incentive for new firms to continue to enter the industry.

15. a. Since per-unit costs increase, as the industry expands, this is an increasing-cost industry with an upward-sloping long-run supply curve.

b. Since per-unit costs decrease, as the industry expands, this is a decreasing-cost industry with a downward-sloping long-run supply curve.

17. a. Since this competitive industry is producing a product that entails external benefits, it will underallocate resources to its product.

b. Since this competitive industry is producing a product that entails external costs, it will overallocate resources to its product.

Chapter 10: Monopoly

1. a. Predatory behaviour

b. Legal restriction

c. Economies of scale

3. The perfectly competitive firm faces a perfectly elastic (horizontal) demand curve—it is a price-taker. This is because it competes with many firms in supplying the identical product. If the competitive firm were to increase its price just above the going price, it would lose all of its sales. The monopoly firm faces a downward-sloping demand curve, where the elasticity is neither perfectly elastic nor perfectly inelastic—it is a price-searcher. This is because the firm is the industry, and, as industry sales increase significantly, the price will decline.

5. a. The rectangle that shows total costs under ATC_1 is *0WCQ*. Total revenue is shown by *0XBQ*. This monopolist is in an economic profit situation. MC = MR is the output at which profit—the difference between total cost and total revenue—is maximized.

b. With ATC_2, the rectangle showing total costs is *0XBQ*. The same rectangle, *0XBQ*, gives total revenue. This monopolist is breaking even. MC = MR shows the only quantity that does not cause losses.

c. Under ATC_3, total costs are represented by rectangle *0YAQ*, total revenue by *0XBQ*. Here the monopolist is operating at an economic loss, which is minimized by producing where MC = MR.

7. a. The filled-in table should look as follows:

Price	Quantity Demanded	Total Revenue	Marginal Revenue	Average Total Cost	Marginal Cost
$20	0	$ 0	$ –	–	–
16	1	16	16	$ 8.00	$ 5.00
12	2	24	8	7.50	7.00
10	3	30	6	8.00	9.00
7	4	28	–2	9.25	13.00
4	5	20	–8	11.00	18.00
0	6	0	–20	13.16	24.00

b. The maximum profit output would be 2 units where marginal revenue is close to, but exceeds, marginal cost.

c. The profit-maximizing price would be $12.00.

d. The amount of maximum profit would be $(P - \text{ATC}) \times Q$ or $(12 - 7.5) \times 2$ or $9.00.

9. a. The profit-maximizing output is 200, where MR equals MC.

b. The profit-maximizing price is $14.00, derived from the demand curve.

c. The amount of maximum profit is equal to $(P - \text{ATC}) \times Q$ or $(14 - 12) \times 200$ or $400.00.

11. If the monopolist charges a single price for all suits cleaned, it will earn a maximum profit of $14 per day (where MR = MC). If the monopolist practises perfect price discrimination, it will clean eight suits per day (where P = MC) and earn a maximum profit of $23. Therefore, it will increase profits by $9 per day.

13. a. Under perfect price discrimination, the marginal revenue column would be the same as the price column.

b. The maximum profit output would be where price approximately equals marginal cost or at three units.

c. The maximum profit is calculated by taking total revenue minus total cost or (16 + 12 + 10) minus (3 × 8), which equals (38 – 24) = $14 profit.

15. a. The business people's demand for hotels would be more inelastic than the leisured people's demand for the same hotel. Therefore, the monopolist could enhance its profit by charging a higher price for those who use the hotel for business purposes. That is why you often see lower hotel rates offered on weekends than during the week.

b. Business people do not have time to shop around for their fast-food meal, while retired people do have the time. Also business people are likely to have a greater amount of income than retired people. These considerations would make the business people's demand for fast food more inelastic than the retired people's demand. The monopolist could increase profit by charging higher fast food prices to business people.

c. The cost of a movie for a family of four is a larger part of the family budget than for a couple only. The family's demand for movies will be more elastic than the couple's demand. The monopolist can increase profit by charging the family less, per person. This is often done by charging children a lower admission fee than adults.

17. a. A natural monopoly can promote productive efficiency. That is, because of economies of scale, one large monopoly firm could produce the product at a lower average total cost than a smaller competitive firm.

b. A perfectly discriminating monopoly can promote allocative efficiency to the extent that it produces at a quantity level where price (marginal benefit) just equals marginal cost.

19. The daily total revenue and marginal revenue are shown below.

Quantity	Price	TR	MR	ATC	MC
1	$500	$ 500	$ 500	$500	–
2	450	900	400	350	$200
3	395	1185	285	300	200
4	350	1400	215	275	200
5	300	1500	100	260	200
6	250	1500	0	250	200
7	200	1400	(100)	243	200

a. The maximum profit quantity (MR = MC) is 4 dishes per day, with a price of $350 and a daily profit of $300.00.

b. Under marginal cost pricing (P = MC), the daily quantity would be 7 dishes per day, with a price of $200 and a daily profit of –$301.

c. Under average cost pricing (P = ATC), the daily quantity would be 6 dishes per day, with a price of $250 and a daily profit of $0 or normal profit.

d. An unregulated monopolist tends to restrict output in order to drive up the price so as to make excess profits. Average cost pricing regulation provides a higher daily quantity at a lower price. The profit earned by the company is no more than a normal profit.

Appendix D: The Deadweight Loss Due to Monopoly

D-1 a. Use the table in part (a) of Figure 10–4 to compute the consumer surplus assuming that the monopoly firm maximizes profit and produces at nine units of output and charges $5.75 per unit. As shown in the table below, you can add up the surplus derived by the consumers for each of the nine units of output produced. The total consumer surplus is $9. (See Table D-1a.)

b. Use the table in part (a) of Figure 10–4 to compute the producer surplus assuming that the monopoly firm maximizes profit and produces at nine units of output and charges $5.75 per unit. As shown in the table below, you can add up the surplus derived by the producer for each of the nine units of output produced. The total producer surplus is $22.50. (See Table D-1b.)

Table D-1a

Quantity	1	2	3	4	5	6	7	8	9	Total Surplus
Maximum willing to pay (see price column)	$7.75	$7.50	$7.25	$7.00	$6.75	$6.50	$6.25	$6.00	$5.75	
Price actually paid	5.75	5.75	5.75	5.75	5.75	5.75	5.75	5.75	5.75	
Surplus	$2.00	$1.75	$1.50	$1.25	$1.00	$0.75	$0.50	$0.25	$0.00	$9.00

Table D-1b

Quantity	1	2	3	4	5	6	7	8	9	Total Surplus
Minimum prepared to accept (see marginal cost table)	$4.00	$3.50	$3.25	$3.05	$2.90	$2.80	$2.90	$3.15	$3.70	
Price actually received	5.75	5.75	5.75	5.75	5.75	5.75	5.75	5.75	5.75	
Surplus	$1.75	$2.25	$2.50	$2.70	$2.85	$2.95	$2.85	$2.60	$2.05	$22.50

c. No, the monopoly firm is not maximizing the sum of consumer and producer surpluses. Both surpluses would be maximized where price equals marginal cost (allocative efficiency level) at approximately 11 units of output, with price being close to $5.25.

C-3 a. Under perfect competition, the price and quantity would be $4 and 3000 bagels, respectively, where demand equals supply. The total consumer surplus would be the area under the demand curve and above the price line, which would be (1/2)($3 × 3000 bagels) = $4500. The total producer surplus would be the area under the price line and above the supply curve, which would be (1/2)($3 × 3000 bagels) = $4500. The sum of both surpluses would be $9000.

b. Under monopoly, the price and quantity would be $5 and 2000 bagels respectively. The loss due to allocative inefficiency would be the deadweight loss equal to: (1/2)($2 × 1000 bagels) =$1000.

Chapter 11: Monopolistic Competition and Oligopoly

1. Local night clubs would be classed as monopolistically competitive firms. This is because each night club sells a differentiated product in terms of the physical facilities and decor; the type of music played; the type of entertainment and food offered; and, finally, the type of clientele that regularly visits the establishment. Note that there are typically numerous night clubs competing with each other and that entry into this type of business is relatively easy.

3. It is not rational for a perfectly competitive firm to advertise, as it can sell all it wants at the given price (perfectly elastic demand).

5. a. The filled-in table should look as follows:

Quantity (# rooms)	Price (per room)	Total Revenue	Marginal Revenue	Marginal Cost	Average Total Cost
0	$95	$ 0			
4	90	360	$90	$36	$86
8	85	680	80	34	60
12	80	960	70	33	51
16	75	1200	60	34	46.75
20	70	1400	50	36	44.60
24	65	1560	40	39	43.67
28	60	1680	30	43	43.57
32	55	1760	20	48	44.13

b. The maximum profit output is 24 rooms per night.

c. The profit-maximizing price is $65 per room per night.

d. The total amount of maximum profit is $(P - \text{ATC}) \times Q$ or ($65 – $43.67) × 24 or $511.92.

e. No, due to easy entry the long-run profit will decline to zero economic profits.

f. Product differentiation may include: spa facilities, pool, good food, different style of rooms, free parking, computer facilities, good entertainment, in-room movies, continental breakfast.

7. a. This bookstore operates in monopolistic competition, as it competes with numerous rivals, it differentiates its product in terms of location and its coffee, it sells books that will differ from its competitors', and finally, it is relatively easy to enter this type of business.

b. The profit-maximizing quantity is at five books per hour, where the marginal revenue of $3.75 is approximately equal to the marginal cost of $3.70.

The profit-maximizing price is $4.75 and the total profit is ($4.75 – $3.16) × 5 = $7.95 per hour.

c. At a quantity of two books per hour, the long-run equilibrium price will be $3.75, which just equals average total cost so that zero economic profits are earned.

d. If this were a perfectly competitive firm, it would have its price just equal minimum average total cost, which is somewhere between $3.03 and $3.16. At this price, zero economic profits would be earned.

9. a. Homogeneous oligopoly
   b. Differentiated oligopoly
   c. Homogeneous oligopoly
   d. Differentiated oligopoly.
   e. Differentiated oligopoly

11. a. The payoff matrix is described below. Firm A's payoffs are in the shaded areas.

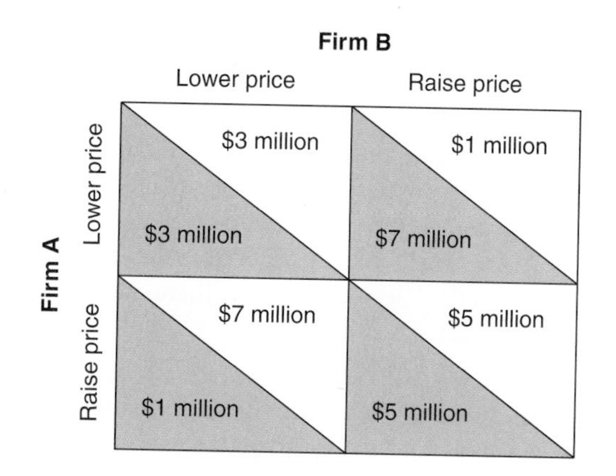

b. The dominant strategy is for each firm to lower the price.

c. Firm A's annual profit would be $5 million.

d. Firm A's annual profit would be $7 million.

e. Firm A's annual profit would be $1 million.

f. The most profitable long-run strategy would be for each firm to raise the price, where the long-run average annual profit would be $5 million.

13. a. Assuming the Kinked Demand Curve Model, the firm will produce 3000 units (at the kink).
    b. The price will be $8.00.
    c. Marginal cost can vary from $2.00 to $6.00 without changing the price.

15. a. Decrease
    b. Increase
    c. Decrease

17. When Pepsi quickly responds to Coke's ads, this can result in a positive-sum game for both firms in a number of ways. First, the heavy advertising can help both firms build significant barriers to entry and therefore prevent other firms from competing in a major way. Second, heavy advertising by both firms may cause the industry demand for their types of products (soft drinks, bottled water, and so on) to increase, thus benefiting all the firms in the industry.

Chapter 12: Regulation and Competition Policy

1. Under a natural monopoly situation, per-unit costs are lower with just one firm supplying the product or service compared with a competitive situation. To the extent that, through economic regulation, the government can force the monopolist to charge a price that reflects these lower costs, consumers will enjoy lower prices under the monopoly situation.

3. a. Under marginal cost pricing, the government would enforce a price of $75 at a quantity level of five units. Since at five units of output the price of $75 is less than the average total cost of $81.20, the firm would incur economic losses. If this situation persisted in the long term, the firm would go out of business.
   b. Under rate-of-return regulation, the price is set to equal average total cost. This would occur if the price were set at $85 at a quantity level of three units. The economic profit is zero.
   c. Critics argue that rate-of-return regulation will encourage the monopoly firm to overpurchase capital equipment, which inflates the average total cost of production. This breeds productive inefficiency.

5. The capture hypothesis best explains this situation. The American government is serving the interests of the American beef producers. The ban on Canadian beef significantly increased the price that American producers received for their beef. American beef producers benefit from this regulation, at the expense of American consumers.

7. In a natural monopoly, even under the conditions of free entry, only one company will survive in the industry due to economies of scale. This one surviving monopoly firm will likely earn positive economic profits under deregulation.

9. a Resale price maintenance
   b. Abuse of dominant position
   c. Tied selling
   d. Bait-and-switch selling
   e. Exclusive dealing

11. The three provisions that were examined were exclusive dealing, refusal to supply, and abuse of a dominant position. Exclusive dealing was not violated as competition was not substantially lessened due to the

agreement, as only one DVD set from one artist was excluded for a limited period of time. Refusal to supply was ruled out as HMV was not significantly negatively impacted by the agreement. Finally, there was no abuse of a dominant position situation, as no dominant firm seemed to exist.

Chapter 13: Labour Demand and Supply

1.

Total Quantity of Labour	Product per Week	MPP	MRP
1	250	250	$500
2	450	200	400
3	600	150	300
4	700	100	200
5	750	50	100
6	750	0	0

a. Demand schedule for labour:

Weekly Wage	Labourers Demanded per Week
$500	1
400	2
300	3
200	4
100	5

b. $100 each

c. Four

3. a. 15 million worker-hours per time period

b. 10 million per time period

c. Buyers can get all the labour they want at W_1; labourers can't sell all they want to sell at W_1.

d. Because a surplus of labour exists, the unemployed will offer to work for less, and industry wage rates will fall toward W_e.

5. Suppose that the demand for the output product is highly elastic. Even a relatively small increase in the price of the input factor, which correspondingly raises the price of the output product, will cause a large decrease in the quantity of output demanded and therefore in the employment of the input.

7. The MRP of labour is $40 per worker-day ($3040 less $3000, divided by a change in labour input of one worker-day). The maximum wage that would still make it worthwhile to hire this additional employee would be $39.99 per day. If the going market wage is above that figure, you will not expand output.

9. Imposing limitations such as these implicitly reduces the ability of employers to compete for your services. Thus you can expect to receive a lower wage and to work in a less desirable job.

Chapter 14: Unions and Labour Market Monopoly Power

1. In Canada, unions protect the option of the right to strike. Joint and unanimous agreements would be few and long in coming.

3. Three union goals are:
   - To employ all members in the union.
   - To maximize total income of workers.
   - To maximize wages.

5. The state of the economy can have an impact on wages and, therefore, the number of strikes.

7. No, you should not. The MRP when you employ 31 people is $89.50 ($99.50 in revenue from selling the twenty-first unit, less $10 forgone in selling the first 20 units for 50 cents less than originally). The MFC is $91 ($61 to attract the twenty-first employee to your firm, plus the additional $1 per day to each of the original 20 employees). Because MFC exceeds MRP, you should not expand output.

Chapter 15: Income and Poverty

1. Men might invest more in human capital; women might receive less and a lower-quality education and/or training; women in the workforce may take periods out of the workforce in order to raise children and thus accumulate less experience than men; discrimination may exist.

3. Some of the issues are what exactly should be included as income; self-employed individuals can claim expenses that reduce their income for income tax purposes. What about full-time employment versus part-time employment?

5. The four main determinants of income differences are: talent, experience, training, and investment.

7. The four income support programs are: Old Age Security, Canada Pension Plan, Employment Insurance, and Child Tax Benefit.

Chapter 16: Environmental Economics

1. When the external costs are added to the supply curve (which is itself the sum of marginal costs of the industry), the total (private plus public) marginal costs of production are above the private supply schedule. At quantity Q_1 in the graph, marginal costs to society are greater than the value attached to the marginal unit. The demand curve is below the social supply curve. To bring marginal cost and marginal benefit back into line, thus promoting an economically efficient allocation of resources, quantity would have to be reduced to Q_2 and price raised to P_2.

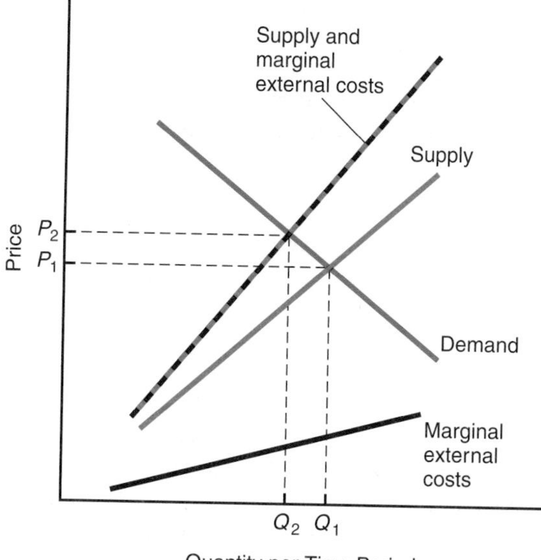

3. The free-market costs would increase, and therefore, their profits would decrease.
5. a. The optimal degree of air cleanliness is 40 percent.
   b. The optimal degree of air pollution is 40 percent.
   c. The optimal degree of air cleanliness now becomes 20 percent, taking into account that optimal occurs where the marginal cost equals the marginal benefit.
7. Everyone owns them and nobody owns them. Consequently, there is no incentive for any user to be concerned with the future value of the resource in question. This is perhaps most clearly observable in the behaviour of fishing boat owners. The goal of each boat owner is to harvest fish as long as marginal private cost is less than the going price of such fish. The opportunity cost of depleting the stock of fish does not affect the decisions of the proprietor. In light of the nonownership of the fish, any single boat operator would be foolish to behave otherwise.
9. Companies would be willing to switch technologies as long as they can persuade their customers to switch with them.

Chapter 17: The Public Sector

1. Market failure means that the unrestrained operation of a market leads to either too few or too many resources being used in that activity.
3. a. If you give and everyone else does also, you account for 1 percent. If you are the only one who gives, you account for 100 percent. If you give nothing, you account for 0 percent, regardless of what others give.
   b. In principle, your contribution matters whatever the level of participation. But as a practical matter, if participation is near 100 percent, the absence of your contribution may have little effect.
   c. There is no free ride. If you do not make your contribution, total contributions will be lower, and the quality of the services provided will be lower.
5. The existence of these costs implies the notion of rational ignorance so that individuals choose not to be informed about certain issues because the cost of being informed is high relative to any benefits forthcoming from the state of the issue. This also contributes to the growth of special-interest groups because individuals have no strong economic incentives to act against them.
7. This is a merit good. The government would subsidize the museum because, without the subsidy, merit goods would not be as numerous as deemed necessary for the public good.
9. The marginal tax rate on the first $3000 of taxable income is 0 percent because no taxes are imposed until $5000 is earned. The marginal rate on $10 000 is 20 percent, as it is on $100 000 and all other amounts above the $5000 level because for each additional dollar earned after $5000, 20 cents will be taxed away. The average tax rate, which is the tax amount divided by the pretax income, is 0 for $3000, 10 percent for $10 000, and 19 percent for $100 000. The average tax rate will approach a maximum of 20 percent as income increases. It cannot reach exactly 20 percent because of the untaxed $5000 at the beginning. Such is the nature of the degressive tax system.
11. Mr. Smith pays nothing on his first $1500 of income, 14 percent ($70) on the $500 of earnings between $1500 and $2000, and 20 percent ($100) on the $500 that he earns above $2000. Thus, Mr. Smith has a total tax bill of $170 on an income of $2500; his average tax rate is 6.8 percent, and his marginal tax rate is 20 percent.
13. Education is a provincial responsibility. Part of the transfer payments that provinces receive will be directed toward education.

ANSWERS TO "FOR CRITICAL ANALYSIS" QUESTIONS

Chapter 1: The Nature of Economics

Example 1–1: The Economics of Web Page Design

The web designer of a frequently visited web page, such as Yahoo!'s home page, has "unlimited wants" that include such goals as: provide maximum exposure to all of Yahoo!'s own products and services; maximize revenue from selling advertising space to other companies; present high-quality images and animations; and prevent the web page from becoming too cluttered. The "limited resources" include a limited screen space size (that one views without scrolling) and limited time to hold the web surfer's attention.

Example 1–2: The Opportunity Cost of Finding a Mate—Lower on the Internet?

There is a smaller selection of available people who match very specific characteristics. Therefore, the desire by persons to find people with very specific characteristics will involve higher search costs, in terms of the time spent dating, than would be the case with less picky requirements. In other words, the opportunity cost of dating in person is higher, which implies that people would be willing to pay more to avoid this by using the Internet alternative. This example shows how understanding opportunity cost can help the Internet firm decide on the appropriate price to charge for its different matching services.

Example 1–3: What Does a Year at College Really Cost?

Jane did not correctly determine the cost related to the decision to enroll in college full-time for eight months. She should only add the *extra* or *marginal* costs, which would be the tuition, books, college fees, and the income she sacrifices from not working full-time for eight months. This implies that the total costs of going to college would be $3057 + (8 months) × ($1600 per month) = $15 857 for the eight months spent at college. The other expenses, such as rent, food, transportation, personal care, and entertainment, can be viewed as unavoidable expenses she decided to incur before making any education decision that we would class as sunk costs. Sunk costs should not be included in computing the marginal or extra cost relating to her education decision. In order to make a rational decision, the marginal cost should be compared to the marginal benefit of enrolling in the business college program.

Policy Example 1–1: Chinese Smuggling

Any actions that reduce the benefits or increase the costs incurred from smuggling cigarettes and diesel fuel into China will reduce the incentives to smuggle. There are a number of policies that would reduce the benefits derived from smuggling. If the Chinese government lowered the domestic taxes on cigarettes manufactured in China, this would reduce the profit derived from exporting the cigarettes and then smuggling them back into China. Similarly, if the price of domestically produced diesel fuel were lowered, this would reduce the profit resulting from smuggling foreign-produced diesel fuel into the country. One way the government could increase the costs of smuggling is to significantly increase the criminal penalty attached to the act of smuggling goods into China.

Example 1–4: Giving Charity to Oneself?

The evidence that low-income households contribute a higher portion of their income to charity than those with higher incomes can be explained in terms of rational cost–benefit behaviour. When compared with a high-income household, the total extra (marginal) benefits that the low-income household derives over a lifetime is much more likely to exceed the extra costs incurred from contributing to these charities.

Example 1–5: Incentives Work for Pigeons and Rats, Too

The series of experiments with pigeons and rats illustrates how scientifically controlled experiments involve the application of the *ceteris paribus* concept. That is, in order to identify precise relationships between two variables, scientists must try to hold the effects of other related variables constant. In this case, the relationship between the "price" and "purchasing" behaviour is being precisely observed by holding constant the "income" or number of lever pushes per day. Therefore, the animals were responding to the "price" incentive factor when they changed their "purchasing" behaviour. The simple model one can formulate on the basis of this experiment is that when the price of a good is decreased, the animals will tend to increase their purchases of the good.

Issues and Applications: Decriminalizing Marijuana, An Economic Perspective

1. Since the application focuses on one product, the cannabis industry, it entails a microeconomic focus. A macroeconomic focus would relate to the level of production or consumption taking place in all Canadian industries.

2. The first and third goals are primarily normative in nature as they consist of value judgments, such as "what constitutes a serious crime to society" and "the level of punishment should fit the nature of the crime." The second goal is positive in nature as one should be able to gather real-world facts to test the statement "the strategy will decrease the number of people who abuse and experiment with illegal drugs."
3. In this Issues and Applications, we have used the economic way of thinking to present a rational economic model that attempts to explain the production behaviour of the marijuana grower. In this model, we assume that the grower makes production decisions based on maximizing his or her own self-interest. This implies that the grower will compare the marginal benefit with the marginal cost in deciding how much marijuana to produce. This is a simplification of reality because the economic model ignores such details as the criminal's personality or social background. As this Issues and Applications illustrates, the economic model can provide useful real-world predictions, such as "an increase in penalties related to growing marijuana will increase the costs of this action and therefore decrease the amount of marijuana produced." Of course, to be scientific, these predictions have to be verified by real-world facts.
4. The new drug policy can decrease the marginal benefit and increase the marginal cost to users of marijuana, respectively, by making them more aware of serious consequences of using marijuana and by resulting in higher rates of enforcement of cannabis offences through the issuance of tickets bearing fines.
5. In this Issue and Application, we have attempted to evaluate the new drug policy by relating the policy to its suggested goals. This is the process of policy analysis.

Chapter 2: Production Possibilities and Economic Systems

Example 2–1: Skipping Class without Skipping Lectures

1. The example notes that if you skip class, you give up the opportunity to ask questions during the lecture, as well as to interact with other class members. Other costs that you might incur include the cost of having to take the full responsibility of pacing yourself appropriately through all the course material in all of your courses. It becomes too easy to postpone the viewing of the online lectures so that you eventually get way behind in your course studies. By not getting to know your instructor, you might incur the cost of not being able to use your instructor as a reference for a future job opportunity.
2. Students who do attend class bear some of the opportunity cost of your absenteeism, as they have may not be able to complete the work that requires teamwork or group discussion.

Policy Example 2–1: The Multibillion Dollar Park

This example illustrates the potential trade-off between preserving a natural wilderness area and the exploration and production of natural resources. Activities needed in order to explore and produce oil and gas—such as the logging of land and the building of roads, pipelines, camps, and other structures—can disrupt the natural beauty and the ecosystems that support the wildilfe in the region.

The policy decision of opening up the M-KMA to oil and gas exploration will promote allocative efficiency if the marginal benefit of oil and gas production, estimated to be upward of $16 billion, exceeds the marginal cost, which would be the estimated loss of natural beauty and wildlife due to the oil and gas exploration and production. It is interesting to note that oil and gas are nonrenewable resources, while natural wilderness and wildlife are renewable resources.

Example 2–2: Making Death Illegal—At Least, Inside City Limits

The opportunity cost of additional land used for cemeteries will increase as the demand for land for use in other employments increases. As well, land that is increasingly more productive in other uses will have to be used for additional cemetery plots, causing a greater loss of output in other goods.

Example 2–3: Canadian Postsecondary Education Pays Off Big Time!

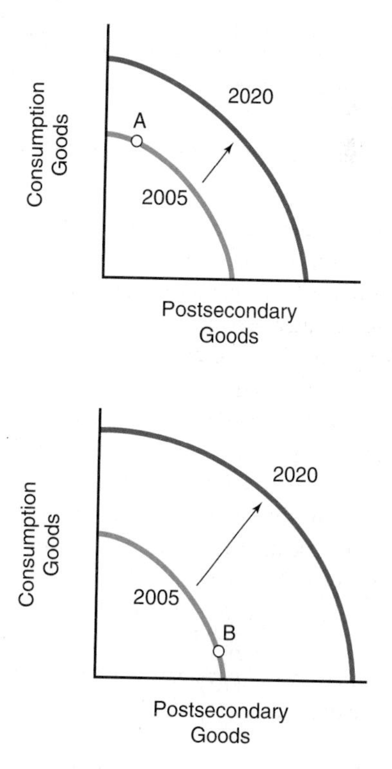

Example 2–4: Why Men Marry: Is It for Love or the Marriage Premium?

Unmarried men must divide their time between labour market goods from which they derive a paycheque and home production goods, which include food shopping, making meals, housecleaning, laundry, paying the bills, and possibly bringing up the children. Married men have greater opportunities to specialize in labour market goods (paid work) activity when their wives specialize in home production goods. The married man has the greatest opportunity to specialize in labour market activity when his wife devotes her time exclusively to home production and does not earn any income. In this example, we see that this leads to the greatest marriage premium.

Part of the gains from specialization can be explained in terms of comparative advantage to the extent that the stay-at-home wife can produce home goods at a lower opportunity cost than her husband and therefore the husband can produce labour market goods at a lower opportunity cost. As well, the gains from specialization can be due to the extra time that the husband can spend in accumulating human capital, since his wife looks after the home front.

Policy Example 2–2: The Edmonton Revolution in Public Education

1. The pure command economic system best relates to Edmonton Public before the revolution due to public ownership of resources (public schools) and centralized decision making.
2. A mixed economy best relates to the current Edmonton model as resources are publicly owned, like a command system, yet most education decisions are decentralized, similar to a capitalist system. Features of capitalism that are present in the current model include decentralized decision making, freedom of choice, consumer sovereignty, and competition.

Issues and Applications: Private or Public Auto Insurance: What Is Best for Canada?

1. Due to its no-fault feature, the pure command system does not have to employ the expensive legal and court-related resources to establish fault and the amount of damages experienced by injured parties. Since the government is the sole insurance provider in the province, it does not have to employ resources to market its services to the customer. Moreover, a government monopoly is able to avoid the duplication in administrative resources that typically occurs when numerous private car insurance companies compete with each other in the same province. Because the public system can offer the same insurance coverage with minimal use of resources, it is productively efficient.
2. By charging higher premiums for those individuals falling into high-risk classes, such as younger males, the private system helps to keep the riskier drivers off the road. Also, the fault system can provide an incentive to be more careful and avoid accidents. In a fault system, the injured party's right to sue for damages helps to ensure that the dollar value of the compensation resulting from an accident claim (marginal benefit) is sufficient to cover the full marginal cost related to the individual injuries and losses sustained from the accident. In this way, a fault system allocates the claim benefits (marginal benefits) in a way that matches the marginal accident costs of each individual, promoting allocative efficiency.
3. When a pure command system does not charge higher premiums based on age and gender, an equity trade-off may occur. On the one hand, equity is promoted when younger drivers with clean driving records pay lower premiums than older people who have accident histories. On the other hand, equity is compromised if the "no discrimination" practice increases collisions by encouraging riskier drivers to take to the road. In this case, older, female, safe drivers end up in more accidents caused by the riskier drivers and end up paying higher premiums.
4. With a rate freeze, the revenue from premiums stays the same but the expenses for paying out claims could increase with inflation, causing financial losses. In this situation, the private insurance companies may refuse to provide insurance in the province operating this type of mixed system. As a result, the only option would be for the government to provide the insurance.

Chapter 3: Demand and Supply

Policy Example 3–1: Price per Constant-Quality Unit and Teen Marijuana Use

Since the potency of a typical ounce of marijuana sold today has increased by more than 50 percent, compared with 1992, the price per constant-quality unit of marijuana has declined by an amount significantly greater than the 20 percent stated in this example.

The Canadian government can effectively increase the "price" of marijuana use by significantly increasing the level of criminal enforcement and the level of penalties, including the fines, associated with marijuana possession. Even if marijuana possession were to be legalized in the future, the government could levy heavy taxes on marijuana purchases, which would result in an increased price related to marijuana possession. For each of these policies, the law of demand implies that the higher marijuana price will reduce the amount of marijuana purchased.

Example 3–1: Is Dental Care Becoming an Inferior Good?

Cosmetic dentistry is more likely to be a normal good. That is, as aggregate Canadian income levels continue to increase, many more Canadians can now afford the luxury of making their teeth appear more beautiful. Therefore, more dentists are responding to the increased demand for this normal good by specializing in cosmetic dentistry.

Example 3–2: Getting Your Degree via the Internet

As this example notes, online learning resources are both substitutes for and complements of the services provided by professors. To the extent that these learning resources are used more as substitutes (and not as complements) this will likely reduce the demand for college and university professors in the next decade, thus shifting the demand curve for professors leftward. However, if in the next decade the online teaching resources strongly complement the services of professors, it is conceivable that the demand curve for professors could shift rightward, reflecting an increase in demand. Since effective online courses require substantial "up front" preparation, many instructors will be needed to develop and maintain high-quality online learning resources. Thus, one may find that some of the instructors who traditionally taught in the classroom will now switch to online course development and maintenance. Also, the convenience of online resources may well bring in additional consumer demand for college and university education, which again may increase the demand for professors.

Example 3–3: Garth Brooks, Used CDs, and the Law of Demand

According to this example, a used-CD market lowers the net price of a CD from $15 to $10, which would result in "an increase in quantity demanded" and a movement along the demand curve from point *A* to point *B*. At the same time, used CDs serve as a cheaper substitute for new music CDs. This second effect will decrease the demand for new music CDs and shift the demand curve to the left. If this decrease in demand exceeds the increase in quantity demanded, as shown in the accompanying diagram, Garth Brooks' fear of the used-CD market is justified.

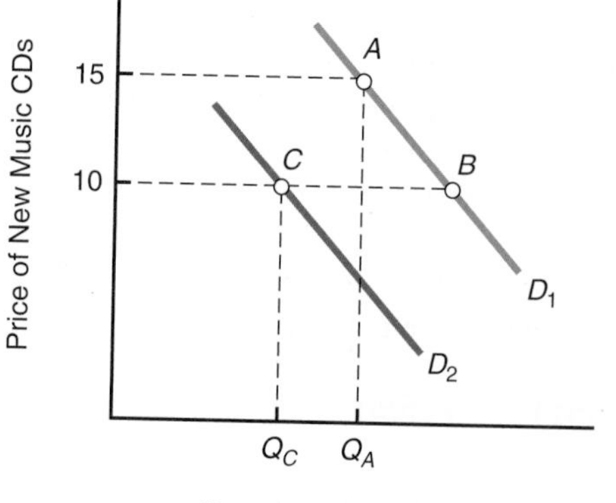

Example 3–4: Falling Costs of Fighting the War on Terror

There has been an increase in supply, which we describe as a rightward shift in the supply curve. According to this example, two nonprice determinants of supply have been responsible for this shift. Improved technology in the form of innovative new monitoring tools as well as technology in the form of new lower cost techniques in diagnosing exposure to toxins has increased supply. As well, new biochemical companies have entered this industry, causing a rightward shift in supply.

Policy Example 3–2: Assisted Human Reproduction Not for Sale in Canada?

Bill C-13 will decrease the supply of legal assisted human reproduction in Canada by reducing the number of available ova and sperm donors. Canadian couples will be faced with significantly higher prices, as they either go underground in Canada or they travel to the United States to purchase the desired assisted human reproduction. These higher prices place a much greater burden on lower-income infertile couples, resulting in an equity conflict.

Example 3–5: Air Canada Losses Are Flying High

Both the demand for and supply of the air travel services provided by international air carriers are declining due to the following factors: terrorist attacks, increased use of teleconferencing technologies, and increased competition from regional airlines. Increased fuel, labour, and security costs are factors decreasing the supply of international airline services. With both the demand and supply curves shifting to the left, we can predict that the equilibrium quantity of passengers using these airlines will significantly decrease. However, without additional information, the change in equilibrium air fares (price) is indeterminate. The significant decrease in quantity of passengers served has had a detrimental effect on international airlines such as Air Canada.

Issues and Applications: Is Canada the Prescription for Lower Drug Prices in the United States?

1. In this Issues and Applications, it was noted that the lower household income in Canada, compared with the United States, results in a decrease in demand for prescription drugs. This direct relation between household income and prescription drug demand implies a normal good situation.
2. Nonprice determinants mentioned in this Issues and Applications that have the effect of increasing the demand for prescription drugs sold by Canadian Internet pharmacies include Internet promotion of Canadian drug prices in the United States; the ease of purchasing Canadian drugs using Internet and fax technology; the storefront operations located in the

United States; the higher American drug prices (higher priced substitutes); the purchase of Canadian pharmaceuticals by American government drug insurance plans (more buyers), the legalization of reimportation (if it happens).

3. Nonprice determinants mentioned in this Issues and Applications that have the effect of decreasing the supply of prescription drugs sold by Canadian Internet pharmacies include reduction in the number of Canadian doctors willing to co-sign American prescriptions, and multinational drug manufacturers' efforts to reduce the distribution of prescription drugs to Canadian Internet pharmacies.
4. The first event will tend to increase demand for prescription drugs sold by Canadian Internet pharmacies. The second event will tend to decrease the supply of prescription drugs sold by Canadian Internet pharmacies. A simultaneous increase in demand and decrease in supply will significantly increase equilibrium drug prices in Canada. The overall effect on equilibrium quantity is indeterminate.

Chapter 4: Elasticity

Example 4–1: "If They Doubled the Price, We'd Still Drink Coffee"

As we have all experienced, when the price of gas rises, because there are few substitutes, we usually do not change the amount we drive. Some will perhaps take the bus or start to carpool, but most will go on as before.

Example 4–2: The Price Elasticity of Demand for World's Fair Tickets

If we had not used the average-values formula, we would not have taken into account the change over a range. It makes a difference where we start the analysis when we deal with a range.

Policy Example 4–1: To Cut Drug Abuse, Make the Price of a "High" Higher

If adult demand is inelastic an increase in the price would mean that adults are less likely to respond, while teens would be more likely to respond to the change by substituting other drugs.

Example 4–3: A Pricing Decision at Disneyland Paris

There are many things that could have impacted the attendance at Disneyland Paris, anything from the level of inflation to the weather.

Example 4–4: What Do Real-World Price Elasticities of Demand Look Like?

Food is a necessity, while a car can be thought to be a luxury by some people. Food also takes up a small portion of a person's total budget while a car is a major purchase.

Policy Example 4–2: Should Public Libraries Be Shut Down?

One of the major costs is in time spent searching. It may be more convenient and faster to search from home over the Internet. But, we have all had trouble finding information over the Internet. Also, with the price of books increasing, it is often much cheaper to get the book from the library than to purchase it online.

Example 4–5: Frequent Flyer Miles as Income

The demand for travel will decrease because people will not perceive the flights as "free" anymore.

Issues and Applications: To Combat Cigarette Consumption, Should the Government Raise Taxes on Beer?

1. Cigarette consumers pay the bulk of the taxes imposed on cigarettes.
2. Cigarette consumers would need a large price change before they changed their habits, while beer drinkers could substitute some other alcoholic beverage for beer, so the beer producers would be more likely to see a decrease in their total revenues.

Chapter 5: Extensions of Demand, Supply, and Elasticity

Example 5–1: Technology and the Death of Intermediaries

As intermediaries, independent of the airlines, travel agents can reduce the transaction costs of finding the lowest-cost carrier(s) for customers to reach and return from a given destination. Online services do, indeed, allow airline customers the advantage of making their own reservations for relatively uncomplicated flights to their destinations. The cost of time spent searching for the best deal for more complicated routes could be quite high for someone who only occasionally flies, and is thus unlikely to be familiar with the timetables, or for someone who has a high opportunity cost of time. Travel agents would be valuable to such persons.

Example 5–2: Should Shortages in the Ticket Market Be Solved by Scalpers?

If there are many unsold seats on the day of the event, this would imply a situation where the original ticket purchase price of $135 ends up being above the equilibrium ticket price for the Heritage Classic. Scalpers are now facing a surplus of tickets at the price of $135. Due to this surplus, scalpers would have to reduce the price they charged to a level below $135, which would result in a loss for the scalpers.

Policy Example 5–1: Rent Controls in Manitoba

By exempting newly constructed rental units, the Manitoba government is attempting to minimize the reduction in quantity supplied that results from rent controls. Moreover, if this exemption encourages the construction of new rental units, the proportion of property taxes paid by landlords could increase, relieving the property tax burden on homeowners. The exemption of more expensive rental units reminds us that the policy of rent controls is aimed at promoting equity by providing rent relief to low-income renters and not high-income renters. Exempting newly constructed rental units from the controls does nothing to encourage landlords to maintain the upkeep and quantity supplied of older rental properties.

Policy Example 5–2: Wheat Farmers and the Canadian Wheat Board

One advantage the Canadian Wheat Board has is that it controls the supply of Canadian wheat to the world market. If equilibrium prices are low, the Wheat Board can restrict the supply of all Canadian farmers so as to gain significant price increases. If half the farmers sold their products independently, then this would undermine the Wheat Board's ability to convince the other half of the farmers to continue to hold back some of what they produce. Instead of a crop restriction policy, which would drive up both the price and the total revenue (with demand inelastic), each farmer would drive down both the price and the total revenue through price competition.

Policy Example 5–3: Should the Legal Quantity of Cigarettes Supplied Be Set at Zero?

Psychoactive drugs, such as marijuana and cocaine, were all legal around the turn of the century. The illegal supply was zero. When these drugs were outlawed, that is, the legal supply was set at zero, illegal demand developed and the illegal supply increased. The price of these psychoactive drugs increased.

Policy Example 5–4: An Excise Tax on Music Piracy?

The more inelastic the demand for or supply of blank media and digital audio recorders, the greater are the proceeds collected from the private copying levies. These levies will be relatively effective in discouraging the copying of music, the more elastic the demand and/or supply. Consumers who use blank media, such as CDs, to back up noncopyrighted material unfairly pay the private copying levies. Similarly, consumers who pay a monthly fee to download music from the Internet unfairly pay these levies.

Issues and Applications: For-Profit Health Care in Canada?

1. Medicare's zero price ceiling policy for visits to the doctors and the hospitals prevents prices from efficiently allocating the limited health-care resources. Since the Canadian patient does not pay an additional charge for each additional hospital or doctor's visit, there is the danger that the limited health-care resources do not get allocated to the highest value uses. Inefficient nonprice forms of rationing health-care resources, such as queuing, result from this price ceiling policy.
2. a. Features of the American system, such as insurance co-payments (user fees) and experience ratings serve as allocatively efficient forms of price rationing. In other words, only the patients who value the medical visits the most will be willing to pay the additional user fees or experience rating premiums. These user fees will discourage frivolous use of the limited health-care resources.

   b. The private for-profit health maintenance organizations are faced with incentives to provide a given level of health care with minimal use of resources and thus promote productive efficiency. These incentives include the profit motive and competition from other private health corporations.
3. User fees paid by the patients will not promote allocative efficiency, as consumers (patients) do not possess the expertise necessary to judge the true value of a contemplated visit to the doctor or hospital due to a health problem. Also, in many cases, the doctors act on behalf of the patient in decisions relating to the additional consumption of health-care resources.
4. User fees will reduce the access that poorer consumers have to health-care resources. In addition, the chronically ill are the ones who will pay the most out of their pockets, with user fees. The chronically ill end up paying twice—once because they are ill and a second time when they pay the user fee.
5. In the United States, there are a number of private for-profit corporations (HMOs) providing health insurance and hospital services. As a result, a much larger portion of every dollar spent on health care in the United States is spent on activities not directly related to patient health care, such as administration, marketing, and earning corporate profits. In other words, it costs more for the United States to provide the same patient care, which is productively inefficient.

Chapter 6: Consumer Choice

Example 6–1: Newspaper Vending Machines versus Candy Vending Machines

There are certain events that would make people want more than one paper, such as disasters, sports (winning the Stanley Cup), major celebrations, and so on.

Example 6–2: The World of Water in Saudi Arabia

Some of the effects on human behaviour would be: fewer baths/showers, less waste of water, and the purchase of more perfume.

Issues and Applications: Contingent Valuation: Pricing the "Priceless"

1. Opinion polls ask people to value something they are not purchasing. It is easy for an individual to put a $500 value on the use of a park; it is unlikely that this same individual would pay $500 to use it. Demand curves show real willingness to pay for a quantity of a specific good or service.
2. Individuals normally express their perceived level of satisfaction by purchasing or not purchasing the good or service in question. If the individual values a product more than the price, that individual will purchase the product.

Chapter 7: Rents, Profits, and the Financial Environment of Business

Example 7–1: Do Entertainment Superstars Make Super Economic Rents?

Superstar entertainers rely on their fans to keep demanding that they perform. They can also determine how much they supply (number of concerts) of their talents to their fans.

Policy Example 7–1: Nonprofit Firms Join in the Quest for Profits

A normal rate of return is the amount that must be paid to an investor to induce investment in a business, and so nonprofit organizations still need some way to entice people to contribute to their organization.

Example 7–2: How to Read the Financial Press: Stock Prices

There does not have to be a relationship between the net change in a stock's price and shares sold; many other factors have to be considered.

Issues and Applications: Can Investors Profit from Publicly Available Stock Tips?

1. Clients do not always have the time to analyze specific stocks, and so they rely on someone else.
2. Brokerage houses want to attract new clients, and if they publicly announce a winning stock, people are more likely to trust their advice.

Chapter 8: The Firm: Cost and Output Determination

Example 8–1: Europeans Use More Capital

A firm decides to buy more machines when the benefits outweigh the costs.

Example 8–2: The Cost of Driving a Car

Variable costs are the per-kilometre costs, while the fixed costs are the annual costs. The average total costs are the $19.32 per day, and the marginal costs are dependent on the kilometres driven.

Example 8–3: Economies of Scale at Dell Computer Corporation

Dell's short-run average cost curves have decreased, making Dell more cost-efficient.

Issues and Applications: Technology and Costs

1. BC Hydro is aware that solar power, in time, will be more cost-efficient and by placing itself in the forefront of new sources of power, it is making sure that if people are going to switch to solar power, they will choose BC Hydro.
2. In the short run, the blackout scared people into using less power, but memories are short, and so in the long run, more power will be demanded.

Chapter 9: Perfect Competition

Example 9–1: The Global Coal Market

No, it does not. A coal buyer will not want the commodity called "coal" but will want a given grade of coal. Within that grade, all producers' coal will be homogeneous. Indeed, the establishment of grades helps ensure that competitors sell a uniform product. This practice of grading is seen in many other perfectly competitive markets, such as the global beef and wheat industries.

Policy Example 9–1 Quelling Fears of "Mad Cow Disease" in Asia

According to this example, the marginal revenue of selling an additional cow carcass to Europe is $200. On the basis of marginal analysis, beef producers would be willing to incur a marginal cost of up to $200 to test all animals destined for Asian consumption.

Example 9–2 High Sunk Costs Can Mean Deep Discounts

Moments before take-off, virtually all the costs related to filling an additional seat on the flight are fixed. These fixed costs would include the expenses related to the capital costs of the plane, airport landing fees, making the reservations and issuing tickets for this flight, hiring the flight's pilot and crew, and paying for the fuel for the flight. Since the marginal cost of filling an additional seat is very close to zero, the airline would be getting a contribution toward its fixed costs, as long as the standby fee were a positive amount (deep discount).

Example 9–3 How the Dot-Com Boom Went Bust

Owners of a new entrant will be basing their decision to enter the market on existing economic profits that they have observed (or hear about). Since we are assuming perfect competition, other entrepreneurs will make the same evaluation and enter the market, assuming that their entry will not have a noticeable impact on prices and profits. However, collectively, the entrance of many new firms will increase the industry supply and cause the price to decrease, thus decreasing the economic profits that can be earned in these dot-com industries. This example highlights the fact that firms compete very independently of each other in perfectly competitive markets.

Issues and Applications: Does Your Local Video Store Have a Future?

1. The new-release and best-seller home-video movie industry in Canada possesses a number of characteristics that conform to perfect competition. In a typical Canadian city, such as Toronto, there are a large number of buyers and sellers for the rental services relating to new-release and best-seller video movies. The large number of sellers include the many bricks-and-mortar stores renting videos in the same market area, as well as competition from close substitutes, including online video rentals, and purchases of videos from mass retailers. Each of the video rental firms competing with each other rents a homogeneous or identical service—the same new-release videos and best-sellers. There is easy entry in the video movie rental industry. That is evident from the fact that there are numerous small independent firms competing in this industry. As well, new close substitutes have entered the industry, such as renting videos online and buying DVDs supplied by mass retailers.
2. According to the theory covered in this chapter, the selling of a DVD at a price below average total cost could still contribute to fixed costs and possibly profit from other operations, as long as the price exceeds the average variable cost of selling the DVD—the shutdown price. If we assume that the average variable cost of each DVD is equal to the cost of goods sold of $25 per DVD, then, as long as the price exceeds $25, the DVD sale will contribute to fixed costs and possibly profit from the sale of other company products. Also, it was noted in this Issues and Applications that selling DVDs at low prices can attract additional customer traffic to the store. Once more customers enter the store, there is a greater chance that some of these customers will purchase other items, besides DVDs.
3. The typical firm renting new-release and best-seller video movies operates in an industry that new firms can easily enter. This being the case, new firms will continue to enter until zero economic profit, or a normal profit, will be earned.
4. The home-video movie industry's long-run supply curve will be downward sloping, as it is a decreasing-cost industry. As the home-video movie industry has expanded over time, new technology has lowered (and will continue to lower) the cost that the supplier will pay for video movies. The technological change to DVDs (versus VHS) has significantly lowered the cost of goods sold to the video retailer. In the future, when movies are typically downloaded over the Internet, the cost of distributing each DVD will be significantly lower (no shipping costs etc.).

Chapter 10: Monopoly

Example 10–1: Microsoft's Abuse of Monopoly

According to this example, Microsoft engaged in predatory behaviour in a number of ways. It significantly eliminated competition in the browser market by giving Internet Explorer away, by integrating Explorer into its operating system, and by entering into agreements with computer manufacturers and Internet providers that restricted the distribution of competing software, such as Netscape Navigator. Similarly, by closely bundling Microsoft Media Player with its Windows operating system, it puts its rivals, such as RealNetworks, at an unfair disadvantage.

Policy Example 10–1: Should Canada Post Remain a Monopoly—Or Does It Matter?

The price elasticity of demand for Canada Post's letter mail service has become more elastic due to the increased competition from faxes and e-mail. Similarly, the price elasticity of demand for Canada Post's parcel delivery service has become more elastic due to the increased competition from large private courier companies. Since the emerging e-commerce industries involve the delivering of goods to one's home by courier, Canada Post could increase its presence in e-commerce and the package courier service.

Policy Example 10–2: In Germany Watch Out—Your Price May Be Too Low!

The marginal or extra revenue received from continuing the illegal sale exceeds the amount of the fine (extra cost). Therefore, breaking the law adds to the company's profit.

Example 10–2: Fuji Film Price Discrimination

Price discrimination would have benefited Canadian consumers who would have been paying a lower price for film. Fuji would have been making higher profits so its shareholders and workers would also have benefited.

Policy Example 10–3: Swapping Songs on the Internet: Is it Really Free?

There are many individuals and companies that "pay" for the actions of those who freely download music files over the Internet. Because of the infringement of copyright, the music artists and recording companies suffer a loss of income due to the decline in legitimate music sales noted in the example. Other parties that lose out include the industries that distribute music legally, such as the manufacturers of music CDs, the companies that supply music downloads over the Internet for a fee, and the bricks-and-mortar music stores. Users who are successfully sued for their practice of freely downloading music files will also pay a price. Finally, we all lose out when copyright is infringed, to the extent that artists and recording companies lose the incentive to create high-quality musical productions that contribute to the enrichment and diversity of our culture and our freedom of expression.

Issues and Applications: Should a Company be Allowed to Monopolize Genetic Information?

1. GlaxoSmithKline's monopoly related to various genetic sequences is due to legal barriers to entry in the form of patents.
2. No, being a company that has a monopoly over its genetic information, we can expect that GlaxoSmithKline will attempt to maximize profits by equating marginal revenue and marginal cost. This means that it will restrict the distribution of its discoveries to the point where the price (or marginal benefit) relating to the last unit of information sold will exceed its marginal cost. It is conceivable that GlaxoSmithKline would be reluctant to release genetic information that resulted in the cure for various diseases to the extent that this would significantly reduce the profit it derives from the sale of its various pharmaceuticals.
3. We can expect that GlaxoSmithKline will earn positive economic profits on the sale or exploitation of its discoveries, as it can prevent other competing firms from using and exploiting its valuable genetic information.
4. We can justify granting monopolies for the discovery of valuable medical information or new drugs to the extent that this creates incentives to come up with additional discoveries and additional new drugs that benefit society.

Chapter 11: Monopolistic Competition and Oligopoly

Example 11–1 The Makeover of Bluenotes

The Canadian retail clothing industry would be classified as monopolistic competition. One of the key features of monopolistic competition is product differentiation. Bluenotes plans to use product differentiation to enhance its sales. Examples of Bluenotes' product differentiation strategies include focusing more on denim merchandise; adding new private labels and brand names; fostering an image that connects with younger teens and extreme-sports enthusiasts; using rock bands in live concerts, magazine advertisements, and in-store promotions and contests; and changing the store layout, music system, and fitting rooms. Also, different retail firms can offer different price ranges for similar items, which contrasts with the one standard price set in perfect competition. Finally, like perfect competition, there are numerous firms competing in this industry and entry can be relatively easy.

Example 11–2 The Prisoners' Dilemma

Yes. Assume that two firms, A and B, agree to share the market and charge a high monopoly profit-maximizing price. Assume that there are now four possibilities:

(1) Both stick to the price agreement and each makes \$100 in profits; (2) both ignore the agreement and charge lower prices, and each makes \$40 in profits; (3) A sticks to the agreement, while B ignores and lowers the price. A makes a profit of \$30 and B makes a profit of \$120; and (4) B sticks to the agreement, while A ignores and lowers the price. B makes a profit of \$30 and A makes a profit of \$120. The dominant strategy is for neither to stick to the agreement, if it cannot be enforced.

Policy Example 11–1 Taxpayers Get Snowed in Quebec

By agreeing, in advance, which company will submit the winning bid, the industry is acting like a monopoly. A \$1 million fine will not be an effective deterrent to this type of illegal behaviour if the marginal revenue is also \$1 million, as implied by the example. In other words, the expected marginal cost of engaging in this illegal behaviour (from the firm's view) will be less than \$1 million, as there is a chance of not getting caught. This being the case, the expected marginal revenue of engaging in this illegal behaviour exceeds the expected marginal cost.

Example 11–3 OPEC Continues to Rule the World Oil Market

Saudi Arabia, as the largest oil producer, can have the largest impact on oil production and prices. Since all OPEC members know this, they will be less likely to cheat when it is clear that Saudi Arabia will practise a tit-for-tat strategy and flood the market for oil if it finds one or more members of the cartel cheating.

Example 11–4 DeBeers Diamond Cartel: A Thing of the Past?

The increased competition due to the greater presence of Russia, Canada, and Australia and due to better quality artificial diamonds moves the industry away from cooperative pricing tactics, such as cartels.

Policy Example 11–2 Turbulence in the Canadian Airline Industry

According to this example, Air Canada is being charged with two entry-deterring strategies—excess capacity and pricing below "avoidable costs," which we would call variable costs. The excess capacity allows Air Canada to add flights to any route that is challenged by WestJet or CanJet. Even without the excess capacity, a strategy of pricing below average variable cost would deter entry by WestJet or CanJet.

Example 11–5 High Switching Costs in the Credit World

In the auto industry, such firms as General Motors offer customers GM credit cards that accumulate reward points toward a discount for the purchase of a new vehicle, if purchased from General Motors. Gas stations, such as Petro-Canada, offer cards (i.e., Petro Points) that accumulate gas discounts based on volume usage.

Example 11–6: Do Pet Products Have Nine Lives?

On the basis of this example, when Heinz lowers the price of its 9-Lives cat food, other firms match the price cut, and demand is inelastic. If, instead, Heinz raises the price, others do not match the increase, and so Heinz loses a lot of sales—demand becomes elastic. Thus, we can envision a "kinked demand curve" in the price ranges noted in this example.

Example 11–7 Can Advertising Lead to Efficiency?

According to this example, both can be true. "We are better because we are bigger" is really the theme of this example, in that advertising allows a firm to get bigger, and this, in turn, can make the firm more efficient. To the extent that the firm gets more efficient, it can get even bigger (as it steals market share from rivals), and so the phrase "We are bigger because we are better" can also hold true.

Issues and Applications: Game Theory: Opening up the Brewing Industry

1. This game is a negative-sum game. Although the microbrewery gains $15 million, Labatt and Molson together lose $16 million.
2. Labatt and Molson could use other entry-deterring strategies. They could substantially increase their already high annual advertising expenditures, as a barrier to entry. They could also reduce the price of their beer to average total cost. They would not earn economic profits, but the competing breweries would no longer have an incentive to enter the industry. Labatt and Molson could also introduce switching costs. For example, they could offer frequent flyer miles so that customers have a vested interest in staying with one company. In fact, Molson has offered Air Miles with the purchase of 15-can cases of its Canadian brand.

Chapter 12: Regulation and Competition Policy

Policy Example 12–1: Can the CRTC Effectively Regulate Cable TV?

The CRTC would have to be able to block transmission of the American channels if it were to enforce Canadian content regulations. Given the increasing effectiveness and decreasing cost of satellite dishes, it is unlikely the CRTC would be successful. The CRTC has established rules that are meant to apply to approved cable TV and satellite TV providers. These rules ensure that the "basic" cable and satellite packages consist of specified Canadian channels and that "optional" packages be designed to ensure that Canadians receive a majority of Canadian programming. There will always be some nonapproved satellite providers operating in Canada who do not abide by these Canadian content rules.

Example 12–1: The Effectiveness of Auto Safety Regulations

The purpose of the safety regulations was to make automobile accidents less dangerous and reduce the number of injuries and deaths by eliminating certain hazardous features and by the addition of safety devices to cars. The regulators did not consider that *ceteris paribus* conditions would not continue as a result of the regulations. The unintended effect of having safer cars has been an increase in reckless driving and more accidents, which has increased, or at least not reduced, the number of injuries. Regulation to achieve a certain goal does not take into account that people's likely response can have effects that were unforeseen and not intended.

Policy Example 12–2 Ontario's Feeble Attempt at Energy Deregulation

First of all, the Ontario government dragged its feet in implementing deregulation, with the Act being passed in 1998 and the actual implementation taking place in 2002. This created a lot of uncertainty, which hindered private-sector investment in new electricity capacity. Second, the price freeze will have the effect of reducing private-sector investment in additional electricity generating capacity. If the government had stayed out of the electricity market, the higher prices would have served as an incentive to increase the private-sector supply of electricity. As well, the higher prices would have encouraged energy conservation and thereby would have reduced the shortage situation. Finally, the fact that the Liberal government subsequently talked about the possibility of the government's investing public funds in new electricity capacity would likely have had the effect of stifling additional private sector investment in new electricity facilities.

Example 12-2: Cutting through the "Red Tape"

Government costs attached to reviewing and revising regulations are mainly the opportunity costs of labour. Civil servants must research the effects of the regulation and then devise improvements. This is a time-consuming task. In addition, every time regulations change, businesses must spend valuable time reviewing these changes so as to abide by the new regulations. In many cases, businesses will have to incur legal and accounting costs in order to keep abreast of, and abide by, changes in regulations.

Example 12-3: HMV Boycotts Rolling Stones Products

The example clearly illustrates that not all exclusive agreements contravene the *Competition Act*. For a violation to take place, competition must be substantially lessened at the industry level or one competitor must be significantly negatively impacted, if not precluded from carrying on its business.

Example 12-4: Suzy Shier Pays $1 Million to Settle Misleading Advertising Dispute

According to Canada's *Competition Act*, a representation pertaining to an article's regular (ordinary) price constitutes a reviewable matter when the article did not sell at this stated regular price in significant quantities over a reasonable period of time.

Issues and Applications: Media Concentration in Canada: A Public Concern?

1. The CRTC's approval of media acquisitions is an example of social regulation, not economic regulation. In economic regulation, the goal is typically to reduce the rates or prices that would be charged by the companies being regulated. In the media examples, the acquisitions being approved have the effect of increasing media concentration, which, if anything, will lead to an increase in the rates charged by the media providers. The CRTC has approved the media acquisitions on the basis of the social goal of fostering new Canadian television productions that contribute to our cultural identity.
2. Increased media concentration can operate to the detriment of the Canadian public in a number of ways. By lessening competition, it can result in higher rates being charged for the services being provided by the Canadian media companies. In addition, as more and more of the Canadian media are concentrated in fewer and fewer hands, there is a danger that editorial diversity will be reduced. In other words, the media companies will produce and distribute news that is biased to serve narrow corporate interests. This may include news that is biased toward governments and political parties that support the media corporations.

Chapter 13: Labour Demand and Supply

Policy Example 13-1: Should the Minimum Wage Be Raised to Help Young People?

Young workers are most affected by changes in the minimum wage because they are the most likely to be in positions where they are only earning the minimum wage. They are also the most likely to be laid off if the minimum wage increases.

Example 13-1: Does It Pay to Study?

Identical twins have exactly the same genetic make-up. Therefore, they have the same physical appearance and abilities. They will normally have the same childhood influences from family. They may also have the same (or nearly the same) IQ. Thus, any innate abilities and familial influences should be the same. The only real differences between them that would determine wage differences would be education, training, and experience, or all of those factors that determine human capital differences.

Example 13-2: Cost Minimization and the Substitution of Software for Labour

Yes, software could have an impact on doctors similar to the effect on lawyers and CGAs. Expert diagnostic programs could allow doctors' assistants or RNs to be able to diagnose many medical conditions. The demand for doctors would grow more slowly as a result.

Issues and Applications: Are Immigrants Pushing Down Canadian Wages?

1. When immigrants come to Canada, they become part of the consuming public. Their demand for goods and services, *ceteris paribus,* increases the domestic demand and prices rise. The rise in output prices increases the affected firms' marginal revenues, and hence their marginal revenue products. Through this mechanism, the demand for labour increases. The final effect on the wage is indeterminate, except that it will be higher than if there were no demand increase at all.
2. In the absence of immigration, Canada's labour force would shrink. With a smaller supply of labour, wages would rise, but the quantity of output would decline unless there were major productivity increases.

Chapter 14: Unions and Labour Market Monopoly Power

Example 14-1: Europe's Management–Labour Councils

Unions feel threatened by management attempts to improve quality at the cost of jobs.

Example 14-2: Strike Activity in Canada

A strike can help increase the wages of workers in the long run. Yes, an increase in profit sharing would make workers less likely to strike and lose those profits.

Example 14-3: Monopsony in College Sports

College athletics can increase the visibility of a college, thereby attracting more students in all fields.

Issues and Applications: Pro Sports Means Big Bucks

1. A monopoly is an output market with one producer. A monopsony is an input market with one employer. A bilateral monopoly is an input market with one employer and one employee association.
2. One argument to justify subsidizing professional sports would be the revenues that the sport brings to the city from sports fans coming to see games. Out-of-town fans would eat in restaurants, stay in hotels, and shop, in addition to seeing the games. Tax revenues from these purchases would repay over the long term the short-term subsidy provided during the building of the stadium or arena.

Chapter 15: Income and Poverty

Example 15-1: Increasing Income Inequality and Working Spouses

No, households with two incomes have other expenses that must be considered, such as child care, two vehicles needed, and so on.

Example 15-2: Relative Income Inequality Throughout the Richest Countries

It would be important to know if the same people are staying in the lowest rankings, as it would indicate whether the income support systems are working or not.

Example 15-3: Are We Running to Stay in Place?

The "perks" of a job can have an impact on an individual's living standard. For example, if you get a company car to drive, you do not need to purchase one of your own and gas is paid by the company, saving hundreds of dollars.

Example 15-4: Economics, Aging, and Productivity

An economist close to retirement has already made his name and is not fighting for a permanent position at a college. A lot of colleges require that their professors publish articles as a condition of employment.

Example 15-5: Poverty Rates in the European Union

Every nation collects income information differently, and so in order to have an equal basis for comparison, all countries would have to agree to collect the information in the same manner.

Issues and Applications: Eradicating Child Poverty

1. The new integrated child benefits plan will probably not end child poverty in Canada although it will likely improve the material conditions of many poor children. There are too few resources to be allocated to this plan to bring all children up to income equality. Since poverty is measured on a relative scale, some children will always be at the low end of the scale and will be classified as poor.
2. There are two main reasons implementing the critics' plan might be unsuccessful. First, putting money into improving economic conditions might not work. The money could be misplaced, it could provide a one-time improvement that doesn't continue over the long run, or it could be insufficient to make noticeable improvements in the economy. Second, people who are currently on social assistance may not necessarily get the jobs created by economic improvement. A physically challenged unemployed person may not qualify for the job. The jobs created may not be close to a centre of poverty, so that those who need the jobs would not be able to get to work.

Chapter 16: Environmental Economics

Example 16-1: The Black Sea Becomes the Dead Sea: The Results of Externalities

If only one country was responsible for the pollution of the Black Sea, there would be no doubt as to who should clean up the pollution.

Example 16-2: Wind as a Renewable Resource

In the short run, it might cost more to switch to alternative methods of using energy, but in the long run, the costs should be reduced.

Example 16-3: Privatizing the Right to Pollute

The rich countries would be willing to pay more so that they would not have to force people and companies to reduce the pollution, as long as it was cheaper to do this than to clean up the environment.

Example 16-4: Preventing Overfishing by Trading Quotas

The quotas themselves become valuable only if the fishermen do not exceed the quotas. If they exceed their quotas, then the value of having a quota decreases and the fishermen lose.

Example 16–5: Reducing Waste by Recycling

The benefits of recycling are less pollution and reuse of materials.

Example 16–6: We Are Running out of Everything!

Switching to using renewable resources is often more expensive than using nonrenewable resources.

Issues and Applications: Climate Change Impacts All Nations

1. Using wind and solar energy would help to reduce the GHGs.
2. Companies will use cost–benefit analysis to determine if moving their plants is feasible.

Chapter 17: The Public Sector

Policy Example 17–1: Who Should Pay the High Cost of a Legal System?

Some of the implicit costs that you could list would be time, buildings and their maintenance, court clerks, and public officers who must appear before the court.

Example 17–1: Are Lighthouses a Public Good?

In point 1, it would be difficult to sell a lighthouse to one individual. In point 2, the cost of the lighthouse does not increase if more people make use of its services, and in point 3, because one person makes use of the lighthouse, it does not mean that others cannot use it as well.

Policy Example 17–2: Do Government-Funded Sports Stadiums Have a Net Positive Effect on Local Economies?

A sports stadium will increase employment and spending within the economy. It is often seen that facilities built for the Olympics are then used by the cities for years after the event. This improves the image of the cities, as they can offer first-class facilities and attract other events, boosting their economies.

Example 17–2: Education Transfer Payments

The tax deduction allows students to complete their education, thereby becoming productive members of society who will then be more likely to be able to afford to purchase a house. The education expenses tend also to be lower than mortgage expenses.

Policy Example 17–3: Average and Marginal Tax Rates around the World

Most people are more aware of their average tax rate than their marginal tax rate. The trend lately has been to work overtime for days in lieu of pay. This indicates that the average taxpayer is well aware of the impact of moving into a higher tax bracket because of overtime.

Example 17–3: Employment Insurance

Canada Pension Plan payments are not part of government's general revenue, and it might be reassuring to workers to know that EI premiums are handled the same way. If there is a surplus in the account, government should not be able to use it to balance its budget.

Issues and Applications: Should We Switch to a Flat Tax?

1. Employees at the Canada Revenue Agency (CRA) might well be against a flat-tax system. Advocates of a flat tax claim that one of the benefits would be a significantly downsized CRA, implying that many CRA employees might lose their jobs. We know from Chapter 1 that the rationality assumption tells us that people usually do not make decisions that reduce their well-being. It is likely that CRA employees would want to keep their jobs to maintain their well-being and would thus oppose a flat-tax system.
2. A flat-tax system is more efficient than a progressive tax system because the method of calculation of tax owing is much simpler: There is only one calculation to make, rather than the many calculations required in a progressive system. There would be efficiencies realized by taxpayers who could complete their tax returns easily, and by CRA employees who could check the calculation equally simply. The opportunity cost of the yearly tax return would fall, leaving resources free to pursue more productive activities.

GLOSSARY

Absolute advantage The ability to perform a task using the fewest number of labour hours.

Accounting profit Total revenue minus total explicit costs.

Age–earnings cycle The regular earnings profile of an individual throughout that person's lifetime.

Aggregates Economy-wide measures.

Allocative efficiency Producing the mix of goods and services most valued by consumers.

Anticombines legislation Laws that make illegal certain economic activities that might restrain trade.

Average cost pricing Occurs when the monopoly firm is forced to set price equal to average total cost.

Average fixed costs Total fixed costs divided by the number of units produced.

Average physical product The total product divided by the number of workers expressed in output per hour.

Average tax rate The total taxes due divided by total taxable income.

Average total costs Total costs divided by the number of units produced; sometimes called per-unit total costs.

Average variable costs Total variable costs divided by the number of units produced.

Best response function The manner in which one oligopolist reacts to a change in price, output, or quality made by another competitor in the industry.

Bilateral monopoly A market structure in which a single buyer faces a single seller.

Black market A market in which the price-controlled good is sold at an illegally high price through various, under-the-table methods.

Bond A legal claim against a firm, entitling the owner of the bond to receive a fixed annual coupon payment, plus a lump-sum payment at the maturity date of the bond.

Breakeven The output that a firm must produce to reach the point where its profits are zero.

Budget constraint All of the possible combinations of goods that can be purchased (at fixed prices) with a specific budget.

Bureaucracy An administrative system run by a large staff following rules and procedures set down by government.

Bureaucrats Nonelected government officials.

Capital gain The positive difference between the buying and selling prices of an asset.

Capital loss The negative difference between the purchase price and the sale price of an asset.

Capture hypothesis A theory of regulatory behaviour that predicts that the regulators will eventually be captured by the special interests of the industry being regulated.

Cartel An association of suppliers in an industry that agree to set common prices and output quotas to prevent competition.

***Ceteris paribus* [KAY-ter-us PEAR-uh-bus] assumption** The assumption that nothing changes except the factor or factors being studied; "other things constant," or "other things equal."

Collective bargaining Bargaining between the management of a company, or a group of companies, and the management of a union, or a group of unions, for the purpose of setting a mutually agreeable contract on wages, fringe benefits, and working conditions for all employees in all the unions involved.

Collective decision making How voters, politicians, and other interested parties act and how these actions influence nonmarket decisions.

Common property Nonexclusive property that is owned by everyone and therefore by no one.

Comparable-worth doctrine The belief that women should receive the same wages as men if the levels of skill and responsibility in their jobs are equivalent.

Comparative advantage The ability to perform an activity at the lowest opportunity cost.

Comparative Advantage Principle states that the combined production of two producers can be enhanced if each producer specializes in the product in which it has the comparative advantage.

Complements Two goods are complements if both are used together for consumption or enjoyment.

Concentration ratio The percentage of total industry sales contributed by the four largest firms.

Conglomerate merger The joining of two firms from unrelated industries.

Constant-cost industry An industry that can increase its output in the long run, without affecting input prices..

Constant returns to scale No change in long-run average costs when output increases.

Consumer optimum Reached when the consumer has attained an optimum consumption set of goods and services.

Consumer surplus The difference between the maximum amount that consumers are willing to pay and the actual amount paid for all units of a product consumed.

Consumption The use of goods and services for direct personal satisfaction.

Cooperative game A game in which firms get together to collude or fix prices.

Corporation A legal entity that may conduct business in its own name just as an individual does.

Cost-of-service regulation Regulation that allows the regulated companies to charge prices that reflect the actual average cost of providing the services, with a normal profit included in the assessment of these costs.

Craft unions Labour unions composed of workers who engaged in a particular trade or skill, such as shoemaking, printing, or baking.

Creative response A response that conforms to the letter of the law but undermines its spirit.

Cross-elasticity of demand (*Exy*) The percentage change in the quantity demanded of one good (holding its price constant) divided by the percentage change in the price of a related good.

Deadweight loss The combined loss in producer and consumer surplus resulting from the reduction in quantity under monopoly.

Decreasing-cost industry A situation where input prices decrease as the industry expands in the long run.

Demand Refers to the quantities of a specific good or service that individuals are willing to purchase at various possible prices, other things being constant.

Demand curve A graphical representation of the law of demand.

Demerit good Any good that the political process has deemed socially undesirable.

Dependent variable A variable whose value changes according to changes in the value of one or more independent variables.

Deregulation The elimination of regulations on economic activity.

Derived demand Input factor demand derived from demand for the final product being produced.

Diminishing marginal utility The principle that as an individual consumes more of a particular commodity, the total level of utility, or satisfaction, derived from that consumption usually increases. Eventually, however, the rate at which it increases diminishes as more is consumed.

Direct relationship A relationship between two variables that is positive, meaning that an increase in one variable is associated with an increase in the other, and a decrease in one variable is associated with a decrease in the other.

Discounting The method by which the present value of a future sum or a future stream of sums is obtained.

Diseconomies of scale Increases in long-run average costs that occur as output increases.

Distribution of income The way income is allocated among the population.

Dividends Portion of a corporation's profits paid to its owners (shareholders).

Division of labour Occurs when individuals specialize in a subset of tasks related to a specific product.

Dominant strategies Whenever a firm's decision makers can come up with certain strategies that are generally successful no matter what actions competitors take.

Economic profits Total revenues minus total opportunity costs of all inputs used, or total revenues minus the total of all implicit and explicit costs.

Economic regulation Regulation that controls the prices that firms are allowed to change.

Economic rent A payment to the owner of a resource in excess of its opportunity cost.

Economic system The social arrangements or institutional means through which resources are used to satisfy human wants.

Economic way of thinking Assumes that the typical response to an economic problem of scarcity is rational behaviour.

Economics A social science that studies how people allocate their limited resources to satisfy their wants.

Economies of scale Decreases in long-run average costs resulting from increases in output.

Effluent fee A pollution tax.

Elastic demand A demand relationship in which a given percentage change in price will result in a larger percentage change in quantity demanded.

Empirical Using real-world data to test the usefulness of a model.

Entrepreneurship Human resources that perform the functions of risk taking, organizing, managing, and assembling other factors of production to make business ventures.

Entry deterrence strategy A strategy to raise the cost of entry by a new firm.

Equilibrium A point from which there tends to be no movement unless demand or supply changes.

Excess capacity A situation where the firm is operating at an output level below that required to achieve minimum average total cost.

Excise tax A tax imposed on a particular commodity or service.

Exclusion principle The principle that no one can be denied the benefits of a public good for failing to pay for it.

Explicit costs Expenses that business managers must take account of because they must actually be paid out by the firm.

External benefits A situation where the marginal social benefits from producing a product exceed the marginal private benefits.

External costs Situations where the marginal social costs of producing a product exceed the marginal private costs of production.

Externality A situation in which a private cost diverges from a social cost; a situation in which the costs of an action are not fully borne by the two parties engaged in exchange.

Featherbedding Unions' tendency to bargain for excessive use of workers.

Financial capital Funds used to purchase physical capital goods, such as buildings and equipment.

Firm An organization that brings together factors of production—labour, land, physical capital, human capital, and entrepreneurial skill—to produce a product or service that it hopes can be sold at a profit.

Fixed costs All costs that do not vary—that is, all costs that do not depend on the rate of production.

Free-rider problem A situation in which some individuals take advantage of the fact that others will shoulder the burden of paying for public goods.

Game theory The analytical framework in which two or more individuals, companies, or nations compete for certain payoffs that depend on the strategy that the others employ.

Goods The physical items that consumers are willing to pay for.

Government, or political, goods Goods (and services) provided by the public sector; they can be either private or public goods.

Horizontal merger The joining of firms that are producing or selling a similar product.

Human capital The education and training of workers.

Implicit costs Expenses that business managers do not have to pay out of pocket.

Import quota A supply restriction that prohibits the importation of more than a specified quantity of a particular good in a one-year period.

Incentive structure The system of rewards and punishments individuals face with respect to their own actions.

Incentive Inducement to take a particular action.

Income–consumption curve The set of optimum consumption points that would occur if income for a consumer were increased constantly, relative prices remaining constant.

Income elasticity of demand A horizontal shift in the demand curve in response to changes in income.

Income in kind Income received in the form of goods and services.

Increasing-cost industry A situation where input prices increase as the industry expands in the long run.

Independent variable A variable whose value is determined independently of, or outside, the equation under study.

Indifference curve A curve where every combination of the two goods in question yields the same level of satisfaction.

Industrial organization The study of how the industry environment affects the behaviour and performance of the firm.

Industrial unions Labour unions whose membership came from an entire industry, such as steel or automobile manufacturing.

Industry supply curve The locus of points showing the minimum prices at which given quantities will be forthcoming from the industry; also called the market supply curve.

Inelastic demand A demand relationship in which a given percentage change in price will result in a less than proportionate percentage change in the quantity demanded.

Inferior goods Goods for which demand falls as income rises.

Inside information Information that is not available to the general public about what is happening in a corporation.

Interest Income earned by capital; the payment for current rather than future command over resources; the payment for obtaining credit. Also, the return paid to owners of capital.

Inverse relationship A relationship between two variables that is negative, meaning that an increase in one variable is associated with a decrease in the other, and a decrease in one variable is associated with an increase in the other.

Labour Productive contributions made by individuals who work.

Labour market signalling The theory that even if higher education does not change productivity, it acts as an effective signal of greater individual abilities.

Labour unions Worker organizations that seek to secure economic improvements for their members.

Laissez-faire French term for "leave it alone"; the government should leave it (the economy) alone or "let it be."

Land Nonhuman gifts of nature.

Law of demand The observation that there is an inverse relationship between the price of any good and its quantity demanded, holding other factors equal.

Law of diminishing (marginal) returns The observation that after some point, successive equal-sized increases in a variable factor of production, such as labour, added to fixed factors of production, will result in smaller increases in output.

Law of increasing relative cost When society takes more resources and applies them to the production of any specific good, the opportunity cost increases for each additional unit produced.

Law of supply The observation that there is a direct relationship between the price of any good and its quantity supplied, holding other factors constant.

Limit-pricing model A model that hypothesizes that the existing firms will respond to new entrants by lowering the price below the one at which new firms can make a profit in order to maintain their market share.

Limited liability A legal concept where if the corporation incurs debts that it cannot pay, creditors have no recourse to the shareholders' personal property.

Long run The period of time in which all inputs can be varied.

Long-run average cost curve The locus of points representing the minimum unit cost of producing any given rate of output, given current technology and resource prices.

Long-run industry supply curve Amarket supply curve showing the relationship between quantities supplied by the entire industry and prices, after sufficient time has passed to allow firms to change plant sizes and enter or exit the industry.

Lorenz curve A geometric representation of the distribution of income.

Macroeconomics The study of the behaviour of the economy as a whole.

Majority rule A collective decision-making system in which group decisions are made on the basis of 50.1 percent of the vote.

Marginal benefit All the extra benefits that one receives in pursuing a course of action.

Marginal cost pricing A system where the price charged to the consumer is equal to the opportunity cost to society of producing the last unit of the good in question; occurs when the monopoly firm is forced to set price equal to marginal cost.

Marginal costs All the extra costs or sacrifices incurred; costs that result from a one-unit change in the production rate.

Marginal factor cost (MFC) The cost of using an additional unit of an input.

Marginal physical product (MPP) of labour The change in output resulting from the addition of one more worker.

Marginal revenue The change in total revenues attributable to changing production by one unit of the product in question.

Marginal revenue product (MRP) The marginal physical product (MPP) times marginal revenue.

Marginal tax rate The change in taxes due divided by the change in taxable income.

Marginal utility The change in total utility divided by the change in the number of units consumed.

Market All of the arrangements that individuals have for exchanging with one another.

Market clearing, or equilibrium, price The price at which quantity demanded equals quantity supplied.

Market demand Determined by adding the individual demand at each price for all the consumers in the market.

Market failure A situation in which perfect competition either overallocates or underallocates resources to a good or service; too few or too many resources going to a specific economic activity.

Marketing boards A policy that allows producers to band together to restrict total quantity supplied by using quotas.

Market structure Characteristics of an industry—such as the number of sellers, the ease of entry of new firms, each firm's ability to set the price, and the degree to which each firm's product differs from its competitor's.

Merit good Any good that the political process has deemed socially desirable.

Microeconomics The study of decision making undertaken by individuals and by firms in specific parts of the economy.

Minimum efficient scale (MES) The output rate when economies of scale end and constant economies of scale start.

Minimum wage The lowest hourly wage rate that firms may legally pay their workers.

Mixed economy An economic system in which decisions about how resources are used are made partly by the private sector and partly by the public sector.

Models or theories Simplified representations of the real world used to understand and predict economic phenomena.

Money price The actual price that you pay in dollars and cents for any good or service at any point in time.

Monopolist A single supplier of a good or service for which there are no close substitutes.

Monopolistic competition A market structure in which there is a relatively large number of firms offering similar but differentiated products.

Monopoly A firm that has great control over the price of a good it sells.

Monopsonist The single buyer of a factor of production.

Monopsonistic exploitation Monopsonistic exploitation is the difference between marginal revenue product and the wage rate.

Natural monopoly The firm that first takes advantage of economies of scale in order to establish a monopoly position.

Negative-sum game A game in which players as a group lose at the end of the game.

Nominal rate of interest The market rate of interest expressed in today's dollars.

Noncooperative game A game in which it is too costly for firms to negotiate collusive agreements and to enforce them.

Nonprice-rationing devices Methods used to ration scarce goods that are price controlled.

Normal goods Goods for which demand rises as income rises.

Normal rate of return The amount that must be paid to an investor to induce investment in a business.

Normative economics refers to analysis based on value judgments made about what ought tobe.

Number line A line that can be divided into segments of equal length, each associated with a number.

Offer-to-purchase policy A price floor policy reinforced by the purchase of surplus output by the government.

Oligopoly A market situation that consists of a small number of interdependent sellers.

Opportunistic behaviour Actions that focus solely on short-run gains and ignore the benefits of cooperation in the long run.

Opportunity cost The value of the best alternative that must be given up because a choice was made.

Opportunity cost of capital The amount of income, or yield, that could have been earned by investing in the next-best alternative.

Optimal quantity of pollution The level of pollution at which the marginal benefit equals the marginal cost of obtaining clean air.

Origin The intersection of the *y*-axis and the *x*-axis in a graph.

Partnership A business owned by two or more co-owners, or partners, who share the responsibilities of operating the firm and its profits, and they are each legally responsible for all of the debts incurred by the firm.

Payoff matrix A matrix of outcomes, or consequences, of the strategies available to the players in a game.

Perfect competition A market structure in which each firm is such a small part of the industry that it cannot affect the price of the product in question.

Perfectly elastic demand A demand that has the characteristic that even the slightest increase in price will lead to zero quantity demanded.

Perfectly elastic supply When the slightest reduction in price will cause quantity supplied to fall to zero.

Perfectly inelastic demand A demand that exhibits zero responsiveness to price changes.

Perfectly inelastic supply When, no matter what the price, the quantity supplied remains the same.

Physical capital Factories and equipment used in production.

Planning curve The curve that represents the various average costs attainable at the planning stage of the firm's decision making.

Planning horizon The long run, during which all inputs are variable.

Plant size The physical size of the factories that a firm owns and operates to produce its output.

Policies Action plans designed to achieve goals.

Positive economics refers to analysis that can be tested by observing the facts.

Positive-sum game A game in which players as a group end up better off.

Present value The value of a future amount expressed in today's dollars.

Price ceiling The maximum price that may be allowed in an exchange.

Price–consumption curve The curve that connects the tangency points of the budget constraints and indifference curves, thus showing the amounts of two goods that a consumer will buy when money income and the price of one commodity are held constant, while the price of the remaining good changes.

Price controls Government-mandated minimum or maximum prices that may be charged for goods and services.

Price discrimination The practice of charging different prices for units of the same product, not justified by cost differences.

Price elasticity of demand (*Ep*) The relative amount by which the quantity demanded will change in response to a change in the price of a particular good; a movement along the curve in response to price changes.

Price elasticity of supply (*Es*) The responsiveness of the quantity supplied of a commodity to a change in its price.

Price floor A minimum price below which a good or service may not be sold.

Price leadership A practice in many oligopolistic industries in which the largest firm publishes its price list ahead of its competitors, who then match those announced prices. Also called parallel pricing.

Price searcher A firm that must determine the price–output combination that maximizes profit because it faces a downward-sloping demand curve.

Price support policies Policies that aim to help the farmers by enhancing the prices they receive for the farm products they supply.

Price system An economic system in which relative prices are constantly changing to reflect changes in supply and demand for different commodities.

Price taker A competitive firm that takes price as a given, something determined outside the individual firm.

Price war A situation where competing firms respond to a rival's price cut with even larger price cuts.

Principle of rival consumption The principle that one person's consumption reduces the amount of private goods available for others to consume.

Prisoners' dilemma The strategic game in which two prisoners have a choice between confessing and not confessing to a crime.

Private costs Costs borne solely by the individuals who incur them; also called internal costs.

Private goods Goods that can be consumed by only one individual at a time.

Private property rights Exclusive rights of ownership.

Producer surplus The difference between the actual amount that producers receive for a product and the lowest amount that they would be prepared to accept for it.

Product differentiation The ways that the firm distinguishes its product, in a positive manner, from similar products or services offered by competitors.

Production Any activity that results in the conversion of resources into goods and services.

Production function The relationship between the amount of physical output the firm can produce and the quantity of capital and labour used to produce it.

Production possibilities curve (PPC) A curve that represents all possible production combinations of two goods that can be produced.

Productive efficiency Occurs when an economy is producing the maximum output with given technology and resources.

Productively inefficient point Any point below the production possibilities curve, assuming resources are fully employed.

Profit Income earned by the entrepreneur.

Profit-maximizing rate of production The rate of production that maximizes total profits, or the difference between total revenues and total costs; also, the rate of production at which marginal revenue equals marginal cost.

Progressive taxation As taxable income increases, the percentage of income paid in taxes also increases.

Property rights The rights of an owner to use and to exchange that property.

Proportional rule A decision-making system in which actions are based on the proportion of the "votes" cast and are in proportion to them.

Proportional taxation A tax system in which regardless of an individual's income, the tax bill comprises exactly the same proportion. Also called a flat-rate tax.

Public goods Goods that can be consumed jointly by many individuals simultaneously at no additional cost and with no reduction in quality or quantity.

Pure capitalist economy An economic system characterized by private ownership of all property resources.

Pure command economy An economic system characterized by public ownership of all property resources.

Random walk theory The theory that the best forecast of tomorrow's price is today's price.

Rate of discount The interest rate used to derive the present value.

Rate-of-return regulation Regulation that allows regulated companies to set prices that ensure a normal, or competitive, rate of return on the investment in the business.

Rationality assumption An individual makes decisions based on maximizing his or her own self-interest.

Real rate of interest The nominal rate of interest minus the anticipated rate of inflation.

Recycling The reuse of raw materials derived from manufactured products.

Regressive taxation A smaller percentage of taxable income is taken in taxes as taxable income increases.

Reinvestment When the firm uses some of its profits to purchase new capital equipment, rather than paying the profits out as dividends to shareholders.

Relative price Any commodity's price in terms of another commodity.

Rent Income earned by land.

Rent control The placement of a price ceiling or maximum price on rents.

Retained earnings Profits not given out to shareholders.

Scarcity The condition that arises because wants always exceed what can be produced with limited resources.

Securities Stocks and bonds.

Services The tasks performed by others that consumers are willing to pay for.

Share-the-gains, share-the-pains theory A theory of regulatory behaviour in which the regulators must take account of the demands of three groups: legislators, members of the regulated industry, and consumers of the regulated industry's products or services.

Share A legal claim to a share of a corporation's future profits.

Short run Any time period that is so short that there is at least one input that the firm cannot alter.

Short-run breakeven price The price at which a firm's total revenues equal its total costs.

Short-run shutdown price The price that just equals minimum average variable cost.

Shortage A situation in which the quantity demanded exceeds the quantity supplied at a price below the market clearing price.

Shutdown A short-run situation where the firm stays in business but temporarily produces at a zero quantity level.

Social costs The full costs borne by society whenever a resource use occurs.

Social regulation Regulation that reflects concern for public welfare across all industries.

Sole proprietorship A business owned by a single individual who makes the business decisions, receives all the profits, and is legally responsible for all the debts of the firm.

Specialization Involves working at a relatively well-defined, limited endeavour; individuals, regions, and nations produce a narrow range of products.

Strategic dependence A situation in which one firm's actions with respect to price, quality, advertising, and related changes may be strategically countered by the reactions of one or more other firms in the industry.

Strategy A rule used to make a choice.

Strikebreakers Temporary or permanent workers hired by a company to replace union members who are on strike.

Substitutes Two goods are substitutes when either one can be used to satisfy a similar want.

Sunk costs Irreversible costs incurred prior to your decision.

Supply Refers to the quantities of a specific good or service that firms are willing to sell at various possible prices, other things being constant.

Supply curve An upward-sloping curve that shows the direct relationship between price and quantity supplied.

Surplus A situation in which quantity supplied is greater than quantity demanded at a price above the market clearing price.

Tariffs Special taxes that are imposed on certain imported goods.

Tax bracket A specified level of taxable income to which a specific and unique marginal tax rate is applied.

Tax incidence The distribution of tax burdens among various groups in society; the division of the burden of a tax between the buyer and the seller.

Technology Society's pool of applied knowledge concerning how goods and services can be produced.

Terms of exchange The prices we pay for the desired items.

Terms of trade The amount of one product that must be traded in order to obtain an additional unit of another product.

Terms of Trade Principle Each producer will gain from specialization and trade if the terms of trade is between the producers' opportunity costs of production.

Theory of contestable markets A hypothesis that most of the outcomes predicted by the theory of perfect competition will occur in certain industries with relatively few firms, due to easy entry.

Theory of public choice The analysis of collective decision making.

Third parties Parties other than the buyer and seller of the product.

Three *P*s Private property, Profits, and Prices inherent in capitalism.

Tit-for-tat strategy A strategy in which a firm cheats in the current period if the rival firm cheated in the previous period but cooperates in the current period if the rival firm cooperated in the previous period.

Total costs The sum of all costs incurred.

Total revenues The quantity sold multiplied by the price.

Transaction costs All costs associated with making and enforcing agreements; the costs associated with finding out exactly what is being exchanged as well as the cost of enforcing contracts.

Transfer payments Payments made to individuals for which no services or goods are concurrently rendered in return.

Transfers in kind Payments that are in the form of actual goods and services for which no goods or services are rendered concurrently in return.

Unit elasticity of demand A demand relationship in which the quantity demanded changes exactly in proportion to the changes in price.

Unlimited liability A legal concept whereby the personal assets of the owner of a firm can be seized to pay off the firm's debts.

Util A representative unit by which utility is measured.

Utility The want-satisfying power of a good or service.

Utility analysis The analysis of consumer decision making based on utility maximization.

Variable costs Costs whose magnitude varies with the rate of production.

Vertical merger The joining of a firm with another to which it sells an output or from which it buys an input.

Voluntary exchange Acts of trading between individuals that make both parties to the trade subjectively better off.

Wages Income earned by labour.

***x*-axis** The horizontal axis in a graph.

***y*-axis** The vertical axis in a graph.

Zero-sum game A game in which one player's losses are offset by another player's gains; at any time, sum totals are zero.

INDEX

Note: Key terms and the pages on which they are defined are in boldface.

A

absolute advantage, 40
abuse of dominant position, 304
accounting profits, 165
  vs. economic profits, 167
  simplified view, 167*f*
accounting rate of return, 211
advertising, 284, 285
age, and income differences, 356–357
age–earnings cycle, 356–357, 356*f*
aggregates, 4
air, 374
Air Canada, 83–84, 104, 112, 279
air pollution
  costs of, 369–370
  optimal quantity, 373*f*
airline standby rates, 209
A.J. Heinz, 282
All-Canadian Congress of Labour (ACCL), 333
allocative efficiency, 32, 259
  graphic illustration, 220–221, 220*f*
  and monopoly, 246–247, 259–260
  and perfect competition, 220–221, 259, 259*f*
allocative inefficiency
  monopoly, 260*f*
  perfect competition, 221
alternative cost principle, 165
American Cancer Society, 166
American Congress of Industrial Organizations, 333
American Eagle Outfitters, 265
American Federation of Labour (AFL), 333
American Medical Association, 166
Anticombines Act of 1910, 303
anticombines legislation, 302–304, **388**
anticompetitive behaviour
  abuse of dominant position, 304
  anticompetitive conspiracies, 305
  bait and switch selling, 307
  deceptive marketing practices, 306
  exclusive dealing, 305
  mergers detrimental to the public interest, 304
  price discrimination, 305
  refusal to supply, 305
  resale price maintenance, 305
  tied selling, 306
anticompetitive conspiracies, 305
assisted human reproduction, sale of, 81
assumptions
  ceteris paribus assumption, 11–12
  described, 11
Atomic Energy Control Board (AECB), 295
auto insurance, private *vs.* public, 48–50
auto safety regulation, 297
average cost pricing, 251
average fixed costs, 186
average physical product, 181
average tax rate, 396, 397, 397*t*
average total costs, 186
average variable costs, 186

B

Bagwell, Kyle, 285
bait and switch selling, 307
barriers to entry
  adequate capital, necessity of, 231
  economies of scale, 231–270
  legal or governmental restrictions, 233, 270
  mergers, 270
  monopoly, 230–233
  oligopoly, 270
  predatory behaviour, 232
  resource ownership without close substitutes, 230
  tariffs, 233
Bell Canada Enterprises (BCE), 292, 295, 308
Bell Globemedia, 309
Bentham, Jeremy, 136
Best Buy, 305
best response function, 272
bilateral monopoly, 345, 347
Bill C-13, 81
Bill C-20, 303–304
Bill C-23, 304
Bill C-38, 16–17
Black, Conrad, 292, 308–309
black market, 116
Black Sea, 371
Bluenotes, 265–266
bond markets, 172
bonds, 171, **172**
breakeven, 191
brewing industry, 286–287
British North America Act, 303
Brooks, Garth, 69–70
budget, and price elasticity of demand, 100
budget constraint, 152, 153*f*
Budget Rent-a-Car, 104
bureaucracy, 394
  incentive structure, 392
  measurement of performance, 394
  prediction of behaviour, 393
  rational ignorance, 394–395
bureaucrats, 394

C

C&A Mode KG, 239
Canada
  health achievement levels, 131*t*
  income distribution, 352–353, 353*t*
  market-oriented health care model, 129–131
  media concentration in, 308–309
  medicare system, 113, 129, 130*f*, 130*t*
  mixed capitalist system, 44
  national income, composition of, 159
  poverty in, 361, 362*f*
  standard of living, 355
  strike activity in, 336
Canada Child Tax Benefit (CCTB), 364
Canada Gazette, 293
Canada Pension Plan (CPP), 363, 399
Canada Post Corporation, 393
Canadian Airlines International, 279
Canadian Automobile Association, 188
Canadian College of Physicians and Surgeons, 233
Canadian Endangered Species Protection Act, 377
Canadian Imperial Bank of Commerce, 280
Canadian Internet pharmacies, 68, 80, 85–87
Canadian labour movement, 333–334
Canadian National Railway (CNR), 299
Canadian Radio-television and Telecommunications Commission (CRTC), 233, 292, 295, 296
Canadian Recording Industry Association (CRIA), 248
Canadian Standard Travel Agent Registry (CSTAR), 112
Canadian Tire, 285
Canadian Wheat Board, 122–123
CanJet, 279

CanWest Global Corporation, 292, 308–309
capital
  European Union and, 180
  financial capital, 168
capital gains, 398
capital goods
  vs. consumption goods, 36–38
  and growth, 37*f*
  purpose of, 36
capital loss, 398
capitalism
  auto insurance and, 49–50
  competition, 45
  consumer sovereignty, 45
  features of, 44–45
  laissez-faire, 45
  limited government, 45
  markets, 45
  prices, 45
  private ownership of resources, 44
  pure capitalist economy, 43, 44
  and self-interest, 44–45
  and three economic questions, 45–46
  Three *P*s, 45
capture hypothesis, 298
cardinal utility analysis, 137*n*
cartel, 276, 277, 278
cellular phone ownership, 61
Central Selling Organization, 278
CEO compensation, 313
***ceteris paribus* assumption, 11**, 61, 213
Chamberlin, Edward, 263
change in demand, 68–69
change in quantity demanded, 68–69
change in quantity supplied, 75
change in supply, 75
charitable giving, 10
child poverty, 365–366, 365*f*
Chinese smuggling, 9
cigarettes
  consumption, 107, 111
  legal quantity of, 123
Circular Flow model, 13–14, 44*f*
climate change, 380
coal market, 201
collective bargaining, 333, 335–339
collective decision making, 392
  and competition, 392
  dissimilarities with market decision making, 393–394
  government goods at zero price, 393
  and incentive structure, 392
  individuals, similarity of, 392–393
  majority rule, 393
  and scarcity, 392
  similarities with market decision making, 392–393
  theory of public choice, 385
  use of force, 393
  voting *vs.* spending, 393–394
college sports, 341–342
Combines Investigation Act, 303
common property, 374
  see also pollution
  air as, 374
  changing property rights, 375–376
  contracting, 375
  endangered species, 377
  pollution-causing resource use, alternatives to, 376
  trade-offs, 377
  transaction costs, 375
  voluntary agreements, 375
  wind, as renewable resource, 374
common shares, 171
comparable-worth doctrine, 359
comparative advantage, 40
  after-specialization, after-trade possibilities, 56–57, 57*f*
  after-specialization, before-trade possibilities, 55–56
  before-specialization, before-trade production possibilities, 54, 55*f*
  described, 40
  and international trade, 41–42
  and production possibilities curve (PPC), 54–57
  Terms of Trade Principle, 56–57
Comparative Advantage Principle, 55–56
competition
  and capitalism, 45
  and collective decision making, 392
  in product market, 313
  promotion of, 388
Competition Act, 275, 303, 304
  see also competition policy
Competition Bureau, 279, 292, 305–306, 307
competition policy
  abuse of dominant position, 304
  anticombines legislation, 302–304
  anticompetitive conspiracies, 305
  bait and switch selling, 307
  benefits of, for consumers, 302–307
  deceptive marketing practices, 306, 307
  exclusive dealing, 305, 306
  mergers detrimental to public interest, 304
  price discrimination, 305
  prohibited anticompetitive behaviour, 304–307
  refusal to supply, 305
  resale price maintenance, 305
  reviewable matters, 303
  tied selling, 306
Competition Tribunal Act, 304
complements, 67
concentration ratios, 271, 271*t*
conglomerate merger, 270
conspiracies, 305
constant-cost industries, 218–219, 218*f*
constant-quality unit, 62
constant returns to scale, 193, 193*f*
consumer choice
  budget constraint, 152–154, 153*f*
  consumer optimum, 140–141, 142–143, 142*t*, 143*f*, 153–154, 153*f*
  demand curve, deriving, 155–156, 156*f*
  diminishing marginal utility, 139–144
  income–consumption curve, 154, 154*f*
  indifference, 148–150
  indifference map, 151
  marginal rate of substitution, 150–151
  monopolistic competition, 268
  optimizing consumption choices, 140–141, 142*t*
  price changes, 142–143, 143*f*
  price–consumption curve, 154–155, 155*f*
  utility theory, 136–139
consumer optimum, 140–141, 142–143, 142*t*, 143*f*, 153–154, 153*f*
consumer sovereignty, 45
consumer surplus, 257–258, 257*f*
consumption, 36
  choices, optimizing, 140–141, 142*t*
  foregoing current consumption, 36
  income-consumption curve, 154, 154*f*
  post-secondary education, rate of return for, 38
  price-consumption curve, 154–155, 155*f*
consumption goods, *vs.* capital goods, 36–38
consumption possibilities curve, 152
consumption tax, 403–404
contestable markets, 300–301
contingent valuation, 145–146
contracting, 375
contributive standard, 360
cooperative game, 272
cooperative price behaviour
  cartel, 276, 277, 278
  factors conducive to, 277–278
  price fixing, 275, 276

price leadership, 277
coordinate axes, 22*f*
copyright, 248
Copyright Board of Canada, 128
corporate financing methods
bonds, 172
efficient markets, theory of, 174
inside information, 174
markets for shares and bonds, 172
random walk theory, 174
reinvestment, 172
shares, 171
corporate income tax, 164, 398
corporation, 164
advantages of, 164
disadvantages, 164–165
dividends, 164
double taxation, 164
limited liability, 164
cost-benefit approach, 301, 302
cost curves
and diminishing marginal returns, 189–191
long-run average cost curve, 192, 192*f*, 193–196
long-run cost curves, 191–192, 193–196
marginal factor cost curve, 343–344, 343*f*
monopolistic competition, 266–267
short-run average cost curves, 186
cost minimization, 326, 327*f*
cost-of-service regulation, 293–294
costs
of air pollution, 369–370
alternative cost principle, 165
average fixed costs, 186
average total costs, 186
average variable costs, 186
of driving a car, 188
explicit costs, 165
external costs, 221–222
fixed costs, 184
implicit costs, 165
law of increasing relative cost, 34–34*f*
marginal cost, 7, 186–187
minimum cost points, 188
monopoly, 238*f*
and physical output, 190*f*
private costs, 369
production costs, 46*t*
of recycling, 378
short-run costs, 184–191
social costs, 369, 370*f*
sunk costs, 7
and technology, 196
total costs, 184
transaction costs, 111, 375
variable costs, 184
of war on terror, 75
coupons, 113, 172
craft unions, 333
creative response, 297
credit, and interest, 168
Criminal Code, 303
cross-elasticity of demand *(Exy)*, 102–103
CTV, 295

D

deadweight loss, 260
death, regulation of, 34–35
DeBeers diamond cartel, 278
deceptive marketing practices, 306, 307
decreasing-cost industry, 218*f*, **219**
Dell Computer Corporation, 194
demand, 61
see also supply-and-demand system
change in demand, 68–69
change in quantity demanded, 68–69
decrease in, 79, 82, 83
demand curve, 63–64
demand schedule, 62–63, 63*f*, 64*f*
determinants of demand, 66–68
elastic demand, 95, 98
increase in, 79, 81–82, 83
inelastic demand, 95, 98
for labour. *See* labour demand
law of demand, 61
market demand, 63–64
for non-union-made goods, 339
perfectly elastic demand, 96
perfectly inelastic demand, 96
shifts in, 65–68, 65*f*, 79–80
time dimension, 62–63
for union-made goods, 339
unit elasticity of demand, 95, 98
demand curve, 63
contingent valuation, 145–146
described, 63
and diminishing marginal utility, 143
indifference curve analysis, 155–156, 156*f*
individual demand curve, 63–64, 63*f*
kinked demand curve, 280–283, 281*f*
monopolistic competition, 266–267
monopolist's input demand curve, 323–324
movement along, 69*f*
perfect competitor, 202, 202*f*
shifts in, 65*f*
and utility maximization rule, 143
demand elasticities. *See* price elasticity of demand *(Ep)*
demand schedule, 62–63, 63*f*, 64*f*, 76–78
demerit goods, 391
dental care, and inferior goods, 66
dependent variable, 20
deregulation, 299
and contestable markets, 300–301
relatively costless entry and exit, 301
short-run *vs.* long-run effects, 299–301
unconstrained entry and exit, 301
derived demand, 316, 316*f*
desired income distribution theories, 359–360
determinants of demand
expectations, 68
income, 66
population, 68
preferences, 67
prices of related goods, 67
tastes, 67
determinants of price elasticity of demand, 99–101
determinants of supply, 74
diamond-water paradox, 143–144, 144*f*
diminishing marginal returns, 181–183, 189–191
diminishing marginal utility, 139
consumer optimum, 140–141, 142*t*
and demand curve, 143
diamond-water paradox, 143–144, 144*f*
price change, and consumer optimum, 142–143, 143*f*
utility maximization rule, 142
vending machines, 140
direct relationship, 20
discounting, 170
discounts, and high sunk costs, 209
discrimination, 359
diseconomies of scale, 193, 193*f*, 195
Disneyland Paris, 99
distance education, 67–68
distribution of income, 351
in Canada, 352–353, 353*t*
egalitarian principle, 360
Lorenz curve, 351–352, 351*f*, 352*f*
measurement of, 351–352
productivity standard, 360
theories of desired income distribution, 359–360
distribution of wealth, 354–355, 355*f*
dividends, 164, 171
division of labour, 42
dominant strategies, 272
donations, by household income, 10*f*
dot-com boom, 217

double taxation, 398
Dutch East India Company, 171

E

economic analysis
 economic policy and socioeconomic models, 14–15
 economic way of thinking, 5, 10
 normative analysis, 14
 positive analysis, 14
 power of, 5
 rational decision making, 5–10
 scientific method, 10–14
economic damages, 372
economic discrimination, 359
economic growth
 and capital goods, 37*f*
 and production possibilities curve (PPC), 35, 35*f*
 and scarcity, 35
economic model. *See* models
economic policy
 see also policy examples
 equitable distribution, as goal, 15
 goals, 15
 marijuana, decriminalization of, 16–17
 and socioeconomic models, 14–15
 and theory, 15
economic profits, 167
 vs. accounting profits, 167
 simplified view, 167*f*
 zero economic profit, 210–211
economic regulation, 293–295
economic rent, 159, 160*f*
 David Ricardo and, 159
 entertainment superstars, 161, 162*t*
 labour services and, 159–160
 in long run, 162
 and resource allocation, 160–161, 161*f*
 as short-run phenomenon, 162
 taxes and, 162
economic stability, 389–390
economic systems, 43
 capitalism, 44–47
 mixed economic systems, 44
 mixed economies, 50
 pure capitalist economy, 43, 44, 49–50
 pure command economy, 43, 49
 three economic questions, 43
economic way of thinking, 5, 10
economics, 3
 macroeconomics, 4
 microeconomics, 4
 normative economics, 14
 positive economics, 14
 of web page design, 4
economies of scale, 193, 193*f*
 barriers to entry in monopoly, 231–232
 at Dell Computer Corporation, 194
 dimensional factor, 194
 improved productive equipment, 194
 oligopoly, 270
 reasons for, 194
 and specialization, 194
Edmonton public education revolution, 46–47
education, cost of, 358–359
efficiency
 advertising, 285
 allocative efficiency, 32
 meaning of, 32
 monopoly, 246–247
 and perfect competition, 220–221
 and production possibilities curve (PPC), 32
 productive efficiency, 32
 productively inefficient point, 32
 and rent control, 116–117
efficient markets, theory of, 174
effluent fees, 371, **386**
egalitarian principle, 360
elastic demand, 95, 98
elasticity
 cross-elasticity of demand, 102–103
 and excise taxes, 124–128
 and government tax revenue, 127–128
 income elasticity of demand, 103–104, 104*t*
 and monopoly, 235–236
 price elasticity of demand. *See* price elasticity of demand *(Ep)*
 price elasticity of supply. *See* price elasticity of supply *(Es)*
 and resource allocation, 127
 and tax incidence, 126–127, 127*f*
empirical, 12
employment. *See* labour demand; labour supply
Employment Insurance (EI), 363–364, 399
endangered species, 377
Energy Competition Act, 300
entertainment superstars, and economic rent, 161, 162*t*
entrepreneurship, 3
entry deterrence strategies, 279
 Air Canada, 279
 increased entry costs, 279
 limit-pricing model, 280
 switching costs, increasing, 280
environmental economics
 air pollution, costs of, 369–370
 climate change, 380
 common property, 374–377
 contracting, 375
 correcting for externalities, 371
 effluent fees, 371
 externalities, 370–371
 government regulation, 371
 greenhouse gases, 380
 landfills, 378–379
 nonrenewable resources, 379
 pollution, 372–374
 pollution taxes, 371
 private costs, 369
 recycling, 378–379
 sequestration, 380
 social costs, 369, 370*f*
 transaction costs, 375
 uniform tax, appropriateness of, 371–372
 voluntary agreements, 375
equilibrium, 78
 changes in, 79–82
 and shifts in both demand and supply, 81–83
 and shifts in demand or supply, 79–80
 short-run. *See* short-run equilibrium
equilibrium point, 78
equilibrium price, 76, 112–113
equilibrium wage rate model, 320*f*
equity, and rent control, 117
European Union
 capital, use of, 180
 fishing rights, allocation of, 377
 management-labour councils, 334
 poverty rates, 361
excess capacity, 268
excise tax, 124
 and elasticity, 124–128
 music piracy, 128
 per-unit tax, effects on market supply, 124–125, 125*f*
 tax incidence, 125–126, 127
exclusion principle, 389
exclusive dealing, 305, 306
executive compensation, 313
expectations
 as determinant of demand, 68
 price expectations, 74
experience, and marginal productivity, 357–358
explicit costs, 165
external benefits, 222, 385*f*, 385–386
external costs, 221–222, 385, 385*f*
externalities, 370, 384
 see also environmental economics
 correcting for, 371, 384, 386–387
 effluent fees, 386

government financing and production, 386
negative, 221–222, 385, 385*f*, 386
positive, 222, 385*f*, 385–386, 387
regulation, 386, 387
spillover benefits, 222, 384
subsidies, 387
Exxon Valdez, 146

F

factors of production
classification of, 3
described, 2–3
see also resources
entrepreneurship, 3
human capital, 3
income earned by, 3
labour, 3
labour demand, impact on, 323–326
land, 3
physical capital, 3
fairness, 404
featherbedding, 340
federal government, 401, 402*f*
federal income support programs
Canada Child Tax Benefit (CCTB), 364
Canada Pension Plan (CPP), 363
Employment Insurance (EI), 363–364
Old Age Security (OAS), 363
Quebec Pension Plan (QPP), 363
federal personal income tax, 398
federal regulatory agencies, 296*t*
federal tax rates, 398*t*
feedback effects, 297
financial capital, 168
financial press, 173, 173*t*
firm, 179
average physical product, 181
breakeven analysis, 191
law of diminishing marginal returns, 181–183
long-run cost curves, 191–192, 193–196
marginal physical product, 181
number of firms. *See* number of firms
organization of. *See* legal organization of firms
organizational structure of typical firm, 179
output and input, relationship between, 180
production function, 181
profit. *See* profit
residual claimant, 179
short-run costs, 184–191
short-run equilibrium, in perfect competition, 215
short run *vs.* long run, 179–183
total costs, 184
first-come, first served, 113
fixed costs, 184
flat-rate tax, 396, 403–404
For whom question, 43, 46
Forbes magazine, 161
free-rider problem, 389
Freeman, Richard B., 340
Fuji Film, 244, 244*f*

G

game theory, 272
basic notions, 272
in brewing industry, 286–287
cooperative game, 272
dominant strategies, 272
negative-sum game, 272
noncooperative game, 272
and noncooperative price behaviour, 272–275
opportunistic behaviour, 274
payoff matrix, 273, 273*f*
positive-sum game, 272
and pricing strategies, 274*f*
prisoners' dilemma, 272–273, 273*f*
repeated games, 274–275
strategy, 272
tit-for-tat strategy, 275
zero-sum game, 272
general hiring rule, 315
genetic information, 252
global coal market, 201
Global Television Network, 309
Globe and Mail, 173, 173*t*, 308
goods, 2
capital goods, 36–38, 37*f*
complements, 67
consumption goods, 36–38
demerit goods, 391
government goods, 393
inferior goods, 66
merit goods, 390
non-union-made goods, 339
normal goods, 66
political goods, 393
private goods, 388
public goods, 388–390
related goods, prices of, 67
substitutes, 67
union-made goods, 339
Goods and Services Tax (GST), 399–400
government
see also bureaucracy
collective decision making. *See* collective decision making
comparison of expenditures, 401, 402*f*
competition, promotion of, 388
demerit goods, 391
economic stability, 389–390
exclusion principle, 389
externalities, correcting for, 386–387
federal government, 401, 402*f*
free-rider problem, 389
income redistribution, 391
legal system, provision of, 387
limited, and capitalism, 45
merit goods, 390
municipal government, 401, 402*f*
political functions, 390–395
provincial government, 401, 402*f*
public goods, 388–390
receipts, 400–401*f*
regulation. *See* government regulation
size of, 400
sports stadiums, funding of, 390–391
total outlays over time, 400*f*
transfer payments, 391, 400
transfers in kind, 391
use of force, 393
government goods, 393
government regulation
auto safety regulation, 297
as barrier to entry, 233
capture hypothesis, 298
competition policy. *See* competition policy
cost-benefit analysis, 301, 302
cost-of-service regulation, 293–294
creative response, 296–297
deregulation, 299, 301
economic regulation, 293–295
federal regulatory agencies, 296*t*
feedback effects, 297
monopoly, 233
negative externalities, correction for, 386
oligopoly, 270
of pollution, 371
and profit maximization, 294*f*
rate-of-return regulation, 294–295
rate regulation, 293
regulators' behaviour, 298–299
results of, 296–297
share-the-gains, share-the-pains theory, 298
social regulation, 295–296
types of, 293–297
graphs
construction of, 20–24
coordinate axes, 22*f*

dependent variable, 20
described, 20
direct relationship, 20
horizontal number line, 21, 21*f*
independent variable, 20
inverse relationships, 20
linear curve, 24–26
negative slope, 25*f*
nonlinear curves, 26, 26*f*
number line, 21
numbers in table, 22–24
ordered set of points, 21
positively sloped curve, 24*f*, 25*f*
slope of a line, 24–26
table, 20
vertical number line, 21, 22*f*
x-axis, 22
y-axis, 22
greenhouse gases, 380
Grokster, 248
Grossman, Michael, 95
growth. *See* economic growth

H

handling charges of loan, 168
HMV Canada, 305–306
Hollinger Inc., 292, 308–309
Home Depot, 285
homogeneous product, 201
horizontal merger, 270
horizontal number line, 21, 21*f*
How question, 43, 45–46
human capital, 3, 358–359

I

immigration, 312, 328
imperfect capital market argument, 231
implicit costs, 165
import quota, 124
incentive structure, 392
incentives, 8
pigeons and rats experiment, 12
response to, and rational decision making, 8–9
income
circular flow of income, 13–14
as determinant of demand, 66
distribution. *See* distribution of income
donations, by household income, 10*f*
equitable distribution, as goal, 15
family spending patterns, 136
frequent flyer miles as income, 104
inequality, 353, 354, 354*f*
lifetime income, inequality of, 352
redistribution, 391
transfer payments as, 362–363
income–consumption curve, 154, 154*f*
income differences
and age, 356–357
comparable worth doctrine, 359
and discrimination, 359
and inheritance, 359
and marginal productivity, 357–359
income distribution. *See* distribution of income
income elasticity of demand, 103–104, 104*t*
income in kind, 352
income support programs. *See* federal income support programs
income tax. *See* taxes
increased division of tasks or operations, 194
see also specialization
increasing-cost industry, 218*f*, **219**
independent variable, 20
indifference, 148–149
indifference curve, 149
curvature, 149–150
downward slope, 149
straight-line indifference curve, implications of, 150*f*
upward slope, impossibility of, 149*f*
indifference map, 151
individual demand curve, 63–64, 63*f*
individuals, similarity of, 392–393
industrial organization, 200
industrial unions, 333
industry
concentration, measurement of, 271
concentration ratios, 271, 271*t*
constant-cost industries, 218–219, 218*f*
decreasing-cost industry, 218*f*, 219
imperfect capital market argument, 231
increasing-cost industry, 218*f*, 219
monopolizing, effects of, 246*f*
short-run equilibrium, in perfect competition, 213–215, 214*f*, 214*t*
industry supply curve, 212
long-run, 218–219
short-run, 212–213, 212*f*, 213*f*
inelastic demand, 95, 98
inferior goods, 66
infringement of copyright, 248
inheritance, 359
innovation
and oligopoly, 285
and perfect competition, 222
inputs
costs of, 74
demand elasticity for inputs, determinants of, 318
monopolist's input demand curve, 323–324
and output, relationship between, 180
price elasticity of demand *(Ep)*, 318
inside information, 174
interdependence in oligopoly, 270
interest, 3, 168
allocative role of interest, 169
and credit, 168
nominal rate of interest, 169
personal rate of discount, 170
and present value, 169–170
rate of discount, 170
real rate of interest, 169
intermediaries
death of, and technology, 112
and price system, 111–112
international trade. *See* trade
Internet
Canadians and, 4
dating, opportunity cost of, 7
distance education, 67–68
dot-com boom, 217
music file sharing, 248–249
online airline ticket bookings, 112
pharmacies online, 68, 80, 85–87
interprovincial trade, 42
inverse relationships, 20
invisible hand, 45

J

job flexibility, 323
job sharing, 323

K

Kazaa, 248
kinked demand curve, 280–283, 281*f*
Knights of Labor, 333
Kodak, 244
Kyoto Protocol, 376, 380

L

Labatt Breweries, 286
labour, 3
and economic rent, 159–160
immigration, 312, 328
marginal physical product, 181
monopsonistic exploitation, 345
shifts in demand and supply, 319–323
software as substitute, 327
labour demand
competition in product market, 313
cost minimization, 326, 327*f*
demand elasticity for inputs, determinants of, 318
derived demand, 316, 316*f*
general hiring rule, 315
labour unions, effect of, 338–339

marginal physical product (MPP) of labour, 313–315
marginal revenue product (MRP), 314*f*, 315
marginal revenue product (MRP) curve, 315–316
monopoly, 324
monopsony, 344–345
other factors of production, impact of, 323–326
profit maximization, 326
under various market conditions, 346*f*

labour demand curve, 320–322

labour market
changes in demand for final product, 320
demand, 317–318, 317*f*
labour productivity, changes in, 320
price of related factors, changes in, 322
reasons for shifts in labour demand curve, 320–322
shifts in demand and supply, 320–322

labour market signalling, 322

labour relations. *See* labour unions

labour supply
described, 319*f*
determinants of, 322–323
labour unions, effect of, 338, 339*f*
monopsony, 344
under various market conditions, 346*f*
wage determination, 319

labour unions, 333
altering demand for union labour, 338–339
benefits of, 340–341
Canadian labour movement, 333–334
collective bargaining, 333
and collective bargaining contracts, 335–339
craft unions, 333
current status of, 334
demand for non-union-made goods, 339
demand for union-made goods, 339
employment of all members, 337
goals, 336–337
income, maximization of, 337–338
industrial unions, 333
labour productivity, effect on, 339, 340
limiting entry over time, 338, 339*f*
maximization decision, 338*f*
public-sector dominated industries, 335*f*
Rand formula, 333
rationing methods, 337, 337*f*
strategies, 337–338
strikes, 335–336, 336*f*
wage rates, maximization of, 338
wages, effect on, 339–340

laissez-faire, 45

land, 3

landfills, 378–379

law of demand, 61
ceteris paribus assumption, 61
demand curve, 63–64
demand schedule, 62–63, 63*f*, 64*f*
described, 61
Garth Brooks and used CDs, 69–70
market demand schedule, 65*f*
money price, 61–62
and price elasticity of demand, 92–93
prices per constant-quality unit, 62
and rational behaviour, 61
relative price, 61–62

law of diminishing (marginal) returns, 181
example of, 183
measurement of diminishing returns, 183
point of saturation, 183

law of diminishing marginal utility. *See* diminishing marginal utility

law of increasing relative cost, 34, 34*f*

law of supply, 70
market supply curve, 72
supply curve, 71
supply schedule, 71, 71*f*, 73*f*

Le Lavandou, France example, 34–35

learning curve, 357

least-cost combination of resources, 326

legal organization of firms
corporations, 164–165
partnerships, 163–164
sole proprietorships, 162–163

legal system, 387, 388

legislation. *See* government regulation

license, 233

lighthouses, 389

limit-pricing model, 280

limited liability, 164

linear curve, 24–26

loans, 168

Logic Box, 378

long run, 180

long-run average cost curve, 192
and constant returns to scale, 193, 193*f*
diseconomies of scale, 195
and diseconomies of scale, 193, 193*f*, 195
and economies of scale, 193–194, 193*f*
minimum efficient scale, 195–196
preferable plant size and, 192*f*
U-shaped, 193–196

long-run cost curves
long-run average cost curve, 192, 193–196
planning horizon, 191
preferable plant size and, 192*f*
technology and costs, 196

long-run equilibrium
adjustments to, 216–217
described, 216
monopolistic competition, 265*f*, 267–268
perfect competition, 216–218, 216*f*

long-run industry supply curve, 218
constant-cost industries, 218–219, 218*f*
decreasing-cost industry, 218*f*, 219
increasing-cost industry, 218*f*, 219
technological change, adjustments to, 219

long-run price elasticity of demand, 101, 101*f*

long-run price elasticity of supply, 106*f*

Lorenz, Max Otto, 351

Lorenz curve, 351–352, 351*f*, 352*f*

loss minimization, 207–209, 208*f*

lotteries, 113

low-income cut-offs (LICOs), 362

M

macroeconomics, 4
aggregates, 4
vs. microeconomics, 4

majority rule, 393

management-labour councils, 334

Manitoba, rent control in, 117–118

maps, 11

marginal analysis
profit-maximizing rate of production, 205
of utility, 137

marginal benefit, 7

marginal cost, 7, 186
and average costs, 187
of pollution abatement, 373
schedule, 187

marginal cost pricing, 220, 251

marginal factor cost, 342–344, 343*f*

marginal factor cost curve, 343–344, 344*f*

marginal physical product (MPP), 181

marginal physical product (MPP) of labour, 313–315

marginal productivity, 357–359

marginal rate of substitution, 150–151

marginal revenue, 205
monopoly, 234–235, 235*f*
perfect competition, 233–234
marginal revenue-marginal cost approach, 237
marginal revenue product (MRP), 314*f*, **315**
curve, 315–316
monopoly, 325*f*
marginal tax rate, 396, 397, 397*t*
marginal utility, 137, 138–139, 143–144
marijuana, decriminalization of, 16–17
market clearing price, 76
market demand, 63
market demand for labour, 317–318, 317*f*
market demand schedule, 65*f*
market failures, 221–222, **384**
market-oriented health care model, 129–131
market structure, 200
comparison of, 200*t*
monopolistic competition. *See* monopolistic competition
monopoly. *See* monopoly
oligopoly. *See* oligopoly
perfect competition. *See* perfect competition
types of, 200
market supply curve, 72, 73*f*
market supply schedule, 73*f*
market system. *See* price system
marketing boards, 121
described, 121, 122*f*
losers, in regulation of supply, 121–122
wheat farmers and Canadian Wheat Board, 122–123
winners in regulation of supply, 122
markets, 63
and capitalism, 45
quantity restrictions, 123–124
unfettered markets, 79
marriage premium, 41
media concentration in Canada, 308–309
medicare system, 113, 129, 130*f*, 130*t*
Medoff, James L., 340
mergers
conglomerate merger, 270
detrimental to public interest, 304
horizontal merger, 270
oligopoly, 270
vertical merger, 270
merit goods, 390
merit standard, 360
microeconomics, 4
vs. macroeconomics, 4
Microsoft Corporation, 232
Mills, Russell, 309
minimum cost points, 188
minimum efficient scale (MES), 195–196
minimum wage, 118–119, 118*f*, 321, 321*f*
mixed economies, 44, 50
models, 10
and alternative economic policies, 15
assumptions, 11–12
behaviour, *vs.* thought processes, 12
Circular Flow model, 13–14
and realism, 11
socioeconomic models, and economic policy, 14–15
testing models, 12
Molson Breweries, 286
money price, 61–62
monopolist, 230
monopolistic competition, 263
characteristics of, 263–268
consumer choice, 268
cost curve for individual firm, 266–267
demand curve for individual firm, 266–267
ease of entry, 264
excess capacity, 268
long-run equilibrium, 265*f*, 267–268
long-run profits, 267–268
number of firms, 263–264
output, 266–267
vs. perfect competition, in long run, 267–268, 268*f*
price, 266–267
product differentiation, 264
productive efficiency, 268
profit, 266–267
short-run equilibrium, 265*f*, 267
monopoly, 388
adequate capital, necessity of, 231
and allocative efficiency, 246–247, 259–260
and allocative inefficiency, 260*f*
anticombines legislation and, 388
barriers to entry, 230–233
bilateral monopoly, 345, 347
characteristics of, 230–236
copyright, 248
costs, 238*f*
and deadweight loss, 257–260
economies of scale, 231
effects of, on industry, 246*f*
and elasticity, 235–236
elimination of, 247–248
and genetic information, 252
input demand curve, 323–324
and intellectual property, 247–248
labour, 324
legal or governmental restrictions, 233
and long-run excess profit, 247
marginal revenue, 234–235, 235*f*
marginal revenue-marginal cost approach, 237
marginal revenue product, 325*f*
natural monopoly, 231, 249–251
output, determination of, 239
patent, 247
vs. perfect competition, 234*f*
predatory behaviour, 232
price, determination of, 236–241
price discrimination, 241–245
price searcher, 230
price under, 233–236
in product market, 323
and productive efficiency, 247
profit, determination of, 238*f*, 239–241, 241*f*
profit maximization, and regulation, 294*f*
resource ownership without close substitutes, 230
revenue, 237, 238*f*
revenue behaviour, 233–236
social evaluation of, 245–248
tariffs, 233
total revenues-total costs approach, 237
monopsonist, 341
monopsonistic exploitation, 345
monopsony
in college sports, 341–342
described, 341
employment under, 344–345
marginal factor cost, 342–344, 343*f*
marginal factor cost curve, 343–344, 344*f*
professional sports, 347, 348*f*
Morpheus, 248
Mukswa Kechika land use area, 33
municipal government, 401, 402*f*
music piracy, 128

N

Napster, 248
National Cancer Institute, 107
National Collegiate Athletic Association, 341–342
National Geographic Society, 166
National Geographic Ventures, Inc., 166
National Post, 308
natural monopoly, 231
average cost pricing, 251
marginal cost pricing, 250–251
output decision, 249

pricing decision, 249
regulation of, 249–251
natural resource, 3
negative slope, 25*f*
negative-sum game, 272
nominal rate of interest, 169
noncooperative game, 272
noncooperative price behaviour
kinked demand curve, 280–283, 281*f*
opportunistic behaviour, 274
payoff matrix, 273, 273*f*
prisoners' dilemma, 272–273, 273*f*
tit-for-tat strategy, 275
nonlinear curves, 26, 26*f*
nonprice determinants of supply, 74–75
nonprice-rationing devices, 116
nonprofit firms, 166
nonrenewable resources, 379
nonuse satisfaction, 145
normal goods, 66
normal profits, 211, 221
normal rate of return, 165
normative analysis, 14
normative economics, 14
North Atlantic Treaty Organization (NATO), 389
number line, 21
number of firms
in industry, 74
monopolistic competition, 263–264
oligopoly, 269
perfect competition, 263

O

offer-to-purchase policy, 120*f*, **121**
Old Age Security (OAS), 363
oligopoly, 269
barriers to entry, 270
best response function, 272
cartel, 276, 277, 278
characteristics of, 269–271
concentration ratios, 271, 271*t*
cooperative price behaviour, 275–278
dominant strategies, 272
economies of scale, 270
entry deterrence strategies, 278–280
game theory, 272, 274*f*
industry concentration, measurement of, 271
innovation, 285
interdependence, 270
kinked demand curve, 280–283, 281*f*
legal barriers, 270
mergers, 270
noncooperative price behaviour, 272–275
nonprice forms of competition, 283–285
number of firms, 269
opportunistic behaviour, 274
payoff matrix, 273, 273*f*
price behaviour, 272–283
price fixing, 275, 276
price leadership, 277
price rigidity, 281–282
price wars, 283
prisoners' dilemma, 272–273, 273*f*
product differentiation, 284
social evaluation, 285
strategic dependence, 269–270
strategy, 272
tit-for-tat strategy, 275
online degrees, 67–68
Ontario, energy deregulation in, 300
Ontario Hydro, 300
opinion data, 146
opportunistic behaviour, 274
opportunity cost, 6
of capital, 165–166
described, 6–7
education, 358–359
highest-ranked alternative, 6
Internet dating, 7
owner-provided labour and capital, 166
and production possibilities curve (PPC), 33–35
opportunity cost of capital, 165–166
optimal quantity of pollution, 373–374, 373*f*
optimizing consumption choices, 140–141, 142*t*
ordered set of points, 21
organization of firms. *See* legal organization of firms
Organization of Petroleum Exporting Countries (OPEC), 276–277
origin, 22
"other things equal," 11–12, 61
Ottawa Citizen, 309
output
and costs, 190*f*
effect, 322
and inputs, relationship between, 180
monopolistic competition, 266–267
in monopoly, 239
natural monopoly, 249
pricing of, 239
overfishing, 377

P

partnerships, 163
advantages, 163–164
disadvantages, 163–164
unlimited liability, 164
patent, 233, 247
payoff matrix, 273, 273*f*
pension taxes, 399
per-unit tax, 124–125, 125*f*
perfect competition, 200
and allocative efficiency, 220–221, 259, 259*f*
characteristics of, 200–203
constant-cost industries, 218–219, 218*f*
cost efficiency, 217
decreasing-cost industry, 218*f*, 219
demand curve, 202, 202*f*
easy entry and exit, 201
external benefits, 222
external costs, 221–222
global coal market, 201
and homogeneous product, 201
idealized definition, 201
increasing-cost industry, 218*f*, 219
and innovation, 222
and large numbers, 201
long-run equilibrium, 216–218, 216*f*
long-run industry supply curves, 218–219
loss minimization, 207–209, 208*f*
marginal cost pricing, 220
marginal revenue, 233–234
marginal revenue curve, 205
and market failure, 221–222
vs. monopolistic competition, in long run, 267–268, 268*f*
vs. monopoly, 234*f*
and normal profit, 221
number of firms, 263
output, in short-run, 203–211
perfect market information, 201
price takers, 200
and productive efficiency, 220
profit, in short-run, 203–211
profit maximization, 204*f*, 205–206
profit-maximizing rate of production, 203, 205
short-run break-even point, 210*f*
short-run break-even price, 209–210
short-run equilibrium, 213–215
short-run industry supply curve, 212–213, 212*f*, 213*f*
short-run profits, 203–211
short-run shutdown point, 210*f*
short-run shutdown price, 210
short-run supply, 211–213
shortcomings, 221–222
social evaluation of, 220–222
technological change, long-run adjustments to, 219

total costs, 203–204
total revenues, 203
zero economic profit, 210–211
perfect contestability, 301
perfectly elastic demand, 96
perfectly elastic supply, 105
perfectly inelastic demand, 96
perfectly inelastic supply, 105
personal rate of discount, 170
physical capital, 3
physical force, 113
planning curves, 192
see also long-run cost curves
planning horizon, 191
plant size, 179
point of saturation, 183
policy analysis, 5
policy examples
assisted human reproduction, sale of, 81
Canadian airline industry and entry deterrence strategies, 279
drug abuse, and price changes, 95
Edmonton public education revolution, 46–47
energy deregulation in Ontario, 300
excise tax on music piracy, 128
Germany, sale prices in, 239
legal quantity of cigarettes supplied, 123
minimum wage and teenage unemployment, 321, 321*f*
Mukswa Kechika land use area, 33
music file sharing on Internet, 248–249
nonprofit firms, and quest for profits, 166
price per constant-quality unit, and teen marijuana use, 62
public libraries, subsidies of, 103
regulation of cable television, 296
rent controls in Manitoba, 117–118
sports stadiums, government-funded, 390–391
tax rates, international comparisons of, 397, 397*t*
wheat farmers and Canadian Wheat Board, 122–123
political functions of government, 390–395
political goods, 393
political power, 113
pollution
see also common property
alternatives to pollution-causing resource use, 376
Kyoto Protocol, 376, 380
marginal cost of abatement, 373
meaning of, 372
optimal quantity of pollution, 373–374, 373*f*
poorly defined private property rights, 374–375
private *vs.* social costs, 376
privatization of right to pollute, 376
regulation of, 371
taxes, 371, 372
uniform tax, appropriateness of, 371–372
population, as determinant of demand, 68
positive analysis, 14
positive economics, 14
positive slope, 24*f*, 25*f*
positive-sum game, 272
post-secondary education, rate of return for, 38
poverty
in Canada, 361, 362*f*
child poverty, 365–366, 365*f*
definition of, 362
in European Union, 361–362
federal income support programs, 363–364
low-income cut-offs (LICOs), 362
mass poverty, 361
no apparent reduction in, 364
transfer payments as income, 362–363
poverty, *vs.* scarcity, 2
predatory pricing, 232
preferences, as determinant of demand, 67
preferred shares, 171
prescription drug sales, online, 68, 80, 85–87
present value, 169
discounting formula, 170
for distant periods, 170
of a future dollar, 171*t*
and interest rates, 169
rate of discount, 170
price
and capitalism, 45
equilibrium price, 76, 112–113
market clearing price, 76
money price, 61–62
monopolistic competition, 266–267
monopoly, 233–236, 241
in oligopoly, 272–283
per constant-quality unit, 62, 295
of the "priceless," 145–146
rationing function of, 112–113
of related factors, 322
of related goods, 67
relative price, 61–62
rigidity, 281–282
short-run break-even price, 209–210
short-run shutdown price, 210
price ceiling, 115
and black market, 116
non-price-rationing devices, 116
rent controls, 115–117, 118
price–consumption curve, 155, 155*f*
price controls, 115
price ceiling, 115, 117
price floor, 115, 118–119
rent controls, 115–117, 118
price discrimination, 242
additional profits from, 243*f*
under *Competition Act*, 305
different prices for different buyer groups, 242–244
different prices for different units of same product, 242
Fuji Film, 244, 244*f*
in monopoly, 242–245
necessary conditions for, 245
price elasticity of demand *(Ep)*, 92, 103
see also elasticity
always negative, 92–93
calculation of, 93–94
and cigarette consumption, 107
coffee bean prices in Brazil, 93
determinants of, 99–101
Disneyland Paris, 99
elastic demand, 95, 98
for Expo 2000 tickets, 94
extremes in, 96, 96*f*
inelastic demand, 95, 98
for inputs, 318
labelling elasticity, 98
long-run price elasticity of demand, 101, 101*f*
percentage changes in price, 92
perfectly elastic demand, 96
perfectly inelastic demand, 96
ranges of, 95
real-world, 101
relative quantities, 92
for selected goods, 102*t*
and share of budget, 100
short-run price elasticity of demand, 101, 101*f*
and substitutes, 100
time allowed for adjustment, 100–101
and total revenues, 96–98, 97*f*, 99*t*
unit elasticity of demand, 95, 98
price elasticity of supply *(Es)*, 105
see also elasticity
classification of supply elasticities, 105
long-run price elasticity of supply, 106*f*

perfectly elastic supply, 105
perfectly inelastic supply, 105
short-run price elasticity of supply, 106*f*
and time allowed for adjustment, 105–106
unit-elastic supply, 105
price expectations, as determinant of supply, 74
price fixing, 275, 276
price floor, 115, 118–119
price leadership, 277
price searcher, 230
price support policies, 120
marketing board policy, 121–122
offer-to-purchase policy, 120–121, 120*f*
price system, 111
intermediaries, role of, 111–112
and market failures, 384
rationing function of prices, 112–113
signaling aspect of, 111
terms of exchange, 111
transaction costs, 111
voluntary exchange, 111
price taker, 200
price wars, 283
pricing
average cost pricing, 251
marginal cost pricing, 250–251
natural monopoly, 249
of output, in monopoly, 239
predatory pricing, 232
under various market conditions, 346*f*
principle of rival consumption, 388
prisoners' dilemma, 272–**273**, 273*f*
private auto insurance, 48–50
private costs, 369
private goods, 388
private property rights, 374–375
producer surplus, 258–259, 258*f*
product
average physical product, 181
homogeneous product, 201
marginal physical product, 181
product differentiation, 264, 284
product market
competition in, 313
monopoly in, 323
production, 2, 180
costs, 46*t*
pocket calculator production, 182*f*
profit-maximizing rate of production, 203, 205
production function, 181
production possibilities curve (PPC), 29
after-specialization, after-trade possibilities, 56–57, 57*f*
after-specialization, before-trade possibilities, 55–56
applications of, 30–35
automobile/newsprint trade-off, 30*f*
before-specialization, before-trade production possibilities, 54, 55*f*
and comparative advantage, 54–57
Comparative Advantage Principle, 55–56
consumption goods *vs.* capital goods, 36–38
death, regulation of, 34–35
described, 29
and economic growth, 35, 35*f*
and efficiency, 32
example, 29–30
law of increasing relative cost, 34–34*f*
and opportunity cost, 33–35
scarcity and trade-offs, 30–31
Terms of Trade Principle, 56–57
and unemployment, 31–32
productive efficiency, 32
monopolistic competition, 267–268
and monopoly, 247
and perfection competition, 220
productively inefficient point, 32
productivity
and aging, 358
as determinant of supply, 74
and distribution of income, 360
labour productivity, changes in, 320
marginal productivity, 357–359
and specialization, 39–42
professional sports, 347
profit, 3
accounting profit, 165
economic profits, 167, 167*f*
monopolistic competition, 266–267, 268
monopoly, 238*f*, 239–241, 241*f*, 247
normal profits, 211, 221
normal rate of return, 165
opportunity cost of capital, 165–166
opportunity cost of owner-provided labour and capital, 166
perfect competition, in short run, 203–211
zero economic profit, 210–211
profit maximization, 167
and labour demand, 326
natural monopoly, 250*f*
in perfect competition, 204*f*, 205–206
and regulation, 294*f*
profit-maximization model, 203
profit-maximizing rate of production, 203, 205
progressive taxation, 396
property rights, 387
see also common property
proportional rule, 393
proportional taxation, 396, 403–404
Prototype Carbon Fund, 376
provincial government, 401, 402*f*
provincial minimum wage rates, 118*f*
public auto insurance, 48–50
public franchise, 233
public goods, 388–390
public sector. *See* bureaucracy; government
public sector decision making. *See* collective decision making
public stock recommendations, 175–176
pure capitalist economy, 44, 49–50
see also capitalism
pure command economy, 43, 49

Q

quantity restrictions, 123–124
Quebec Pension Plan (QPP), 363
Quebecor Inc., 292, 295, 309

R

Ramey, Garey, 285
random walk theory, 174
rate of discount, 170
rate of return
accounting rate of return, 211
normal rate of return, 165
rate-of-return regulation, 294–295
rate regulation, 293
rational decision making
college tuition, year of, 8
decisions at the margin, 7–8
described, 5–6
incentives, response to, 8–9
and law of demand, 61
opportunity cost, 6–7
rationality assumption, 6
and resource use decisions, 9–10
self-interest, defined, 9
rational ignorance, 394–395
rationality assumption, 6
rationing
coupons, 113
essential role of, 113
first-come, first-served, 113
function of prices, 112–113
labour unions and, 337, 337*f*
lotteries, 113
physical force, 113
political power, 113
by queues, 113
waiting, 113

real rate of interest, 169
realism, and models, 11
recycling, 378
 benefits of, 378
 invisible costs of, 378
 and nonrenewable resources, 379
refusal to supply, 305
regressive taxation, 396
regulation. *See* government regulation
regulators' behaviour
 capture hypothesis, 298
 share-the-gains, share-the-pains theory, 298
reinvestment, 172
related goods, prices of, 67
relative cost, law of increasing, 34–34*f*
relative price, 61–62
rent, 3
 economic rent. *See* economic rent
rent control, 115, 115*f*
 black market, 116
 and efficiency, 116–117
 and equity, 117
 evasion attempts, 117
 in Manitoba, 117–118
resale price maintenance, 305
Residential Rent Regulation Act, 117
residual claimant, 179
resource allocation
 and economic rent, 160–161, 161*f*
 and elasticity, 127
resources
 see also factors of production
 income earned by, 3
 least-cost combination, 326
 limited, relative to wants, 3
 nonrenewable resources, 379
 pollution-causing resource use, alternatives to, 376
 private ownership of, 44
 and production, 2
 and scarcity, 2–3
 use of, and rational decision making, 9–10
retained earnings, 398
revenue
 marginal revenue, 205
 monopoly, 233–236, 237, 238*f*
 total revenues, 203
  see also total revenues
reviewable matters, 303
Ricardo, David, 159
risk, of nonrepayment, 168
Robinson, Joan, 263
Rolling Stones, 305–306
Royal Bank, 280

S

Saudi Arabia, water in, 144
scalping, 114, 114*f*
scarcity, 2
 and collective decision making, 392
 and economic growth, 35
 marriage premium example, 41
 meaning of, 5
 vs. poverty, 2
 production possibilities curve and trade-offs, 30–31
 and resources, 2–3
 self-interest and specialization, 40–41
 three economic questions, 43
 and wants, 2
 and web site owners, 4
scientific approach, 5
scientific method
 assumptions, 11–12
 behaviour, *vs.* thought processes, 12
 circular flow of income, in economic model, 13–14
 empirical meaning, 12
 models and realism, 11
 positive *vs.* normative economics, 14, 15
 testing models, 12
 three key processes, 15
self-interest
 and capitalism, 44
 charitable giving, 10
 invisible hand of, 45
 marriage premium example, 41
 and rational decision making, 9
 scarcity and specialization, 40–41
September 11, impact of, 75, 83
sequestration, 380
services, 2
share-the-gains, share-the-pains theory, 298
shares, 171
 inside information, 174
 markets for, 172
 public stock recommendations, 175–176
 random walk theory, 174
Shell Transport and Trading Co. PLC, 380
shifts in demand
 change in demand, 68–69
 change in quantity demanded, 68–69
 described, 65–66, 65*f*
 and determinants of demand, 66–68
 equilibrium, effect on, 79–80, 81–83
 inferior goods, 66
 normal goods, 66
shifts in supply, 73–75, 79–80, 81–83
shock, 78
short run, 179
short-run average cost curves
 average fixed costs, 186
 average total costs, 186
 average variable costs, 186
 described, 186
short-run break-even point, 210*f*
short-run breakeven price, 209–210
short-run costs
 average costs, and marginal costs, 187
 breakeven analysis, 191
 fixed costs, 184
 marginal cost, 186–187
 minimum cost points, 188
 short-run average cost curves, 186
 technology and costs, 196
 total costs, 184
 variable costs, 184
short-run equilibrium
 for the firm, 215
 for the industry, 213–214, 214*f*, 214*t*
 monopolistic competition, 265*f*, 267
short-run industry supply curve, 212–213, 212*f*, 213*f*
short-run price elasticity of demand, 101, 101*f*
short-run price elasticity of supply, 106*f*
short-run shutdown point, 210*f*
short-run shutdown price, 210
short-run supply, 211–213
shortages, 78, 112, 114, 114*f*
shutdown, 207
slope
 of budget constraint, 152–153
 indifference curve, 149, 149*f*
 of a line, 24–26
 negative slope, 25*f*
 positive slope, 24*f*, 25*f*
Smith, Adam, 5, 42, 143
smuggling, in China, 9
snow removal price fixing, 275–276
social costs, 369, 370*f*
social evaluation
 monopoly, 245–248
 oligopoly, 285
 perfect competition, 220–222
social regulation, 295–296
social sciences, 3
socioeconomic models, and economic policy, 14–15
software, 327
sole proprietorship, 163
 advantages, 163
 disadvantages, 163
 opportunity cost of owner-provided labour and capital, 166
 unlimited liability, 163

Southam Inc., 308–309
specialization, 39
absolute advantage, 39–40
after-specialization, after-trade possibilities, 56–57, 57*f*
after-specialization, before-trade possibilities, 55–56
before-specialization, before-trade production possibilities, 54, 55*f*
comparative advantage, 40
division of labour, 42
and economies of scale, 194
gains from, 54–57, 57*t*
marriage premium example, 41
and productivity, 39–42
scarcity and self-interest, 40–41
and trade, 41–42
spillover benefits, 222, 384
sports stadiums, government-funded, 390–391
Statistics Canada, 00–355
Stigler, George, 298*n*
stock markets, 172, 175–176
stock prices, 173, 173*t*
stocks, 171
strategic dependence, 269–270
strategy, 272
StreamCast Networks, 248
strikes, 335–336, 336*f*
subsidies
as determinant of supply, 74
as negative tax, 386
positive externalities, correcting for, 386–387
substitutes, 67
marginal rate of substitution, 150–151
and price elasticity of demand, 100
substitution effect, 322
Sun Media, 295, 309
sunk costs, 7, 209
supply, 70
see also supply-and-demand system
ceteris paribus conditions of, 213
change in quantity supplied, 75
change in supply, 75
decrease in, 79, 82, 83
determinants of supply, 74
increase in, 79, 81–82, 83
of labour. *See* labour supply
law of supply, 70–72
per-unit tax, effects of, 124–125, 125*f*
perfect competition, in short run, 211–213
perfectly elastic supply, 105
perfectly inelastic supply, 105
shifts in supply, 73–75, 79–80
supply curve, 71
supply schedule, 71, 71*f*, 73*f*
unit-elastic supply, 105
supply-and-demand system
equilibrium, changes in, 79–82
industry trends, effects of, 83–84
putting together demand and supply, 77*f*
schedules combined, 76–78
shock, 78
shortages, 78
surplus, 78–79
supply curve, 71
extremes in, 105*f*
horizontal summation, 72*f*
industry supply curve, 212–213, 212*f*, 213*f*
long-run industry supply curves, 218–219
market supply curve, 72, 73*f*
supply elasticities. *See* price elasticity of supply *(Es)*
supply schedule, 71, 71*f*, 73*f*, 76–78
surplus, 78–79
consumer surplus, 257–258, 257*f*
effect of, 112
producer surplus, 258–259, 258*f*
Suzy Shier, 307
switching costs, 280

T

table
described, 20
numbers, graphing, 22–24
talent, and marginal productivity, 357
tariffs, 233
tastes, as determinant of demand, 67
Tauras, John, 95
tax bracket, 396
tax incidence, 125–127, 126*f*, 127*f*, **398**
taxation systems
fairness, 404
flat-rate tax, 396
progressive taxation, 396
proportional taxation, 396
regressive taxation, 396
taxes
average tax rate, 396, 397, 397*t*
capital gains, 398
consumption tax, 403–404
corporate income tax, 164, 398
as determinant of supply, 74
double taxation, 164, 398
and economic rent, 162
elasticity, and government tax revenue, 127–128
excise tax, and elasticity, 124–128
federal personal income tax, 398
federal tax rates, 398*t*
flat-rate tax, 403–404
Goods and Services Tax (GST), 399–400
marginal tax rate, 396, 397, 397*t*
negative externalities, correcting for, 386
pension taxes, 399
pollution taxes, 371, 372
proportional taxation, 403–404
and sole proprietors, 163
subsidy, as negative tax, 386
tax bracket, 396
tax rates, 395–396
time worked to pay, 384
unemployment taxes, 399
value-added tax (VAT), 403
technology, 29
and costs, 196
and death of intermediaries, 112
as determinant of supply, 74
long-run adjustments to technological change, 219
teen marijuana use, and price per constant-quality unit, 62
terms of exchange, 111
terms of trade, 56–57
Terms of Trade Principle, 56–57
TGA Entertainment Ltd., 305
theories, 10
theories of desired income distribution, 359–360
theory of contestable markets, 301
theory of efficient markets, 174
theory of public choice, 385
third parties, 384
three economic questions, 43, 45–46
Three *P*s of capitalism, 45
Thriftys, 265
ticket market, shortages in, 114, 114*f*
tied selling, 306
tit-for-tat strategy, 275
total costs, 184, 203–204
total fixed costs, 184
total revenues, 203
and elasticity, 96–97*f*, 98, 99*t*
monopoly, 237
in perfect competition, 203
total revenues- total costs approach, 237
total utility, 137, 143–144
trade
and comparative advantage, 41–42
gains from, 54–57, 57*t*
terms of trade, 56–57
trade-offs
automobile/newsprint example, 30*f*
consumption goods *vs.* capital goods, 36–38
scarcity and production possibilities curve, 30–31
skipping class example, 31

Trade Union Act, 333
Trades and Labour Congress (TLC), 333
training, and marginal productivity, 358
transaction costs, 111, 375
transfer payments, 362–363, **391**, 400
transfers in kind, 391
TVA, 295, 309

U

unconstrained entry and exit, 301
unemployment
  and production possibilities curve (PPC), 31–32
  taxes, 399
Unemployment Insurance (UI), 364
unfettered markets, 79
unions. *See* labour unions
unit-elastic supply, 105
unit elasticity of demand, 95, 98
United Airlines, 104
United States
  annual national health-care expenditures, 130*t*
  health achievement levels, 131*t*
unlimited liability, 163, 164
use of force, 393
used CDs, 69–70
utility, 136
  see also utility theory
utility analysis, 136
  cardinal utility analysis, 137*n*
  graphic analysis, 137
  marginal analysis, 137
utility maximization rule, 142, 143
utility theory
  contingent valuation, 145–146
  diamond-water paradox, 143–144, 144*f*
  diminishing marginal utility, 139–144
  graphic analysis, 137
  marginal analysis, 137
  marginal utility, 137, 138–139, 143–144
  total utility, 137, 143–144
  utility, and utils, 136–137
utils, 137

V

vaccinations, 386
value-added tax (VAT), 403
variable costs, 184
variables
  dependent variable, 20
  direct relationship, 20
  independent variable, 20
  inverse relationships, 20
vending machines, 140
vertical merger, 270
vertical number line, 21, 22*f*
video rental stores, 223–224
Videotron, 295, 309
Visa, 104
voluntary exchange, 111

W

wage determination, 319
wages, 3
  equilibrium wage rate model, 320*f*
  labour unions, effect of, 339–340
  maximization of, 338
  minimum wage, 118–119, 118*f*, 321, 321*f*
  provincial minimum wage rates, 118*f*
  real wages, 355
waiting, 113
wants, and scarcity, 2
war on terrorism, 75
wealth, distribution of, 354–355, 355*f*
Wealth of Nations (Smith), 5, 42
welfare, 365
WestJet, 279
What question, 43, 45
wheat farmers and Canadian Wheat Board, 122–123
wild species, 377
wind, 374
World Bank, 376, 380

X

***x*-axis, 22**

Y

***y*-axis, 22**

Z

Zellers, 285
zero economic profit, 210–211
zero-sum game, 272